# Situated Practices of Strategic Planning

All over the world societies are facing a number of major problems. New developments, challenges and opportunities cause these issues and yet cases tell us that traditional spatial planning responses and tools are often insufficient to tackle these problems and challenges.

*Situated Practices of Strategic Planning* draws together examples from across the globe – from France to Australia; from Nigeria to the United States – as it observes international comparisons of the strategic planning process. Many approaches and policies used today fail to capture the dynamics of urban/regional transformation and are more concerned with maintaining an existing social order than challenging and transforming it. Stewarded by a team of highly regarded and experienced researchers, this book gives a synthetic view of the process of change and frames future directions of development. It is unique for its combination of analysis of international case studies and reflection on critical nodes and features in strategic planning.

This volume will be of interest to students who study regional planning, academics, professional planners, and policy makers.

**Louis Albrechts** is Emeritus Professor of Strategic Spatial Planning at the University of Leuven, Belgium.

**Alessandro Balducci** is Full Professor of Planning and Urban Policies at the Politecnico di Milano, Italy.

**Jean Hillier** is Emeritus Professor of Sustainability and Urban Planning at RMIT University, Australia.

# Routledge Advances in Regional Economics, Science and Policy

# Situated Practices of Strategic Planning

An international perspective

**Edited by Louis Albrechts, Alessandro Balducci and Jean Hillier**

LONDON AND NEW YORK

First published 2017 by Routledge

2 Park Square, Milton Park, Abingdon, Oxfordshire OX14 4RN
52 Vanderbilt Avenue, New York, NY 10017

*Routledge is an imprint of the Taylor & Francis Group, an informa business*

First issued in paperback 2019

*British Library Cataloguing in Publication Data*
A catalogue record for this book is available from the British Library

*Library of Congress Cataloging in Publication Data*
Names: Albrechts, L., editor. | Balducci, A. (Alessandro), editor. | Hillier, Jean, editor.
Title: Situated practices of strategic planning : an international perspective / edited by Louis Albrechts, Alessandro Balducci and Jean Hillier.
Description: Abingdon, Oxon ; New York, NY : Routledge, 2016. | Includes index.
Identifiers: LCCN 2016006442| ISBN 9781138932562 (hardback) | ISBN 9781315679181 (ebook)
Subjects: LCSH: City planning. | Regional planning. | Land use–Planning. | Spatial behavior.
Classification: LCC HT166 .S5756 2016 | DDC 307.1/216–dc23
LC record available at http://lccn.loc.gov/2016006442

ISBN: 978-1-138-93256-2 (hbk)
ISBN: 978-0-367-87409-4 (pbk)

Typeset in Times New Roman
by Cenveo Publisher Services

# Contents

# Figures

# Tables

# Preface

At the World Planning School Congress in Perth, Australia (July 2011), Louis Albrechts and Alessandro Balducci organized a roundtable on the topic 'Is strategic planning really strategic?' with Raine Mäntysalo, Mee Kam Ng and Marc Stringa as contributors. The purpose of the roundtable was to investigate selected practices of strategic spatial planning and to discuss to what extent the (often self-proclaimed) strategic plans were really strategic. The participants of the roundtable were invited to concentrate upon what makes a spatial plan strategic: is it its (in)formal nature, its legal status, the type of process to be designed, its selectivity, its capacity to produce a long-term vision, the connection between vision and actions, the theoretical background used by the planners, or the involvement of stakeholders? The reactions were such that we were challenged to continue the discussion by email. Patsy Healey, Luigi Mazza, Jef Van den Broeck, Valeria Monno and Willem Salet commented on an earlier version of a paper Albrechts and Balducci presented in Perth. In addition, Patsy Healey, Luigi Mazza, Jef Van den Broeck, Valeria Monno, Klaus Kunzmann, Jean Hillier and Raine Mäntysalo were invited to write short papers on issues selected for them. This material was used for another roundtable entitled 'What makes planning strategic?' in Ankara (July 2012). At the ACSP-AESOP joint congress in Dublin (2013) three sessions and a roundtable were organized: challenges and pitfalls in/for strategic planning, tensions between strategic planning and statutory planning contextualized cases on strategic planning, strategic planning and the quest for certainty. An additional output was a special issue of the journal *DisP* (2013).

As all contributions until then came from Europe and Australia, we started thinking about enlarging the scope to incorporate worldwide practices. This volume has three Parts. In Part 1, for the first time, selected cases from all over the world are dealt with following a grid of questions provided by the editors. Critical debate is the subject of Part 2, with a focus on critical nodes and features in strategic planning. In Part 3 we search for new ideas and address a possible profile to reinforce an interpretation of strategic planning that avoids carefully stage-managed processes with clearly defined parameters and favours its open, transformative, selective, visionary, participatory and action-oriented dimensions.

The case studies we selected reflect three 'fields' or 'scales' of situated practices:

The first is the *trans-national* field or scale. The second field or scale is that of *national* experiences. We have selected international cases from around the globe to illustrate the diversity of strategic spatial planning practices. We asked contributors to illustrate how different forms of strategic planning have emerged in relation to their national planning systems. The third field or scale of observation has been the selection of specific *local* experiences that look particularly meaningful to illustrate the transition from traditional to strategic forms of planning. By no means, however, can this collection be truly comprehensive. Our aim is, therefore, to provide a strong overview about what is at stake in different places in the world.

As editors, we sought out contributors who were critical academics/practitioners and also those actively involved in specific practices. We have contributions from well-established academics, from practitioners and from young academics who are relatively new in their academic careers.

With the book we aim to challenge planners, practitioners, politicians and engaged citizens in different locations to assess whether the ideas expressed in the book have relevance to their places and the issues which they engage on an everyday basis. The approach in the book is descriptive, analytical, critical and normative. Descriptive and analytical in the sense that it relies on the analysis of selected strategic planning processes, critical in the sense that the editors are not blind to the critique formulated on strategic planning. These critiques focus on very different registers of the strategic spatial planning approach. And normative in the sense that the third part of the book provides critical features for the design and implementation of strategic planning processes that can produce significant outcomes. The normative character of the book will provoke reactions we hope. This suits another purpose of this book, namely to contribute to the discussion (academics and practitioners) on the merits and the pitfalls of strategic planning.

We are extremely grateful to the authors of the chapters and to all those who have participated in this long-lasting dialogue since the beginning of this project in Perth.

All chapters were double-refereed. Our special thanks go to the referees of the chapters: John Friedmann, Steve Hamnett, Andy Inch, Christian Lefèvre, Raine Mäntysalo, Jonathan Metzger, Nancy Oldendaal, Federico Savini, Walter Schönwandt, Bruce Stiftel, Wing Shing Tang, Han Verschure, Andreas Voigt, Vanessa Watson, Fulong Wu, Torsten Wulf, Wil Zonneveld. And last but not least thanks to Elanor Best, Robert Langham and Lisa Thomson at Routledge and to Zachary Mark Jones for the index.

# Contributors

**John Abbott** Planning consultant with John Abbott Planning, South East Queensland (SEQ), Australia. John did his doctoral research on regional strategic planning processes in SEQ and Vancouver, Canada.

**Mona Abdelwahab** Assistant Professor, Department of Architecture and Environmental Design, AASTMT, Cairo branch. Visiting Research Fellow, SAPL: School of Architecture Planning and Landscape, University of Newcastle, UK.

**Louis Albrechts** Emeritus Professor of Planning, KU Leuven, Belgium.

**Alessandro Balducci** Professor of Planning and Urban Policies, Politecnico di Milano, Italy.

**John M. Bryson** McKnight Presidential Professor of Planning and Public Affairs, Hubert H. Humphrey School of Public Affairs, University of Minnesota – Twin Cities, USA.

**Kang Cao** Associate Professor, Department of Urban and Regional Planning, Zhejiang University, China.

**Christina DeMarco** Planning consultant with Planning Solutions Network, Vancouver, Canada. Christina was formerly lead planner with Metro Vancouver on the preparation of the Metro Vancouver 2040 plan.

**Christophe Demazière** Professor in Urban and Regional Planning, Université François-Rabelais de Tours, Research unit 'Cités, territoires, environnement et sociétés', France.

**Lawrence Esho** Senior Lecturer in Spatial Planning, Technical University of Kenya, Nairobi.

**Valeria Fedeli** Associate Professor, Department of Architecture and Urban Studies, Politecnico di Milano, Italy.

**Robin Goodman** Professor, Deputy Dean, Sustainability and Urban Planning, School of Global, Urban and Social Studies, RMIT University Melbourne, Australia.

**Kristi Grišako** Aalto University, Department of Build Environment, Finland.

**Nicole Gurran** Professor, Urban Planning, Urban and Regional Planning, Faculty of Architecture, Design and Planning, The University of Sydney, Australia.

**Philip Harrison** Professor, School of Architecture and Planning, University of the Witwatersrand, Johannesburg, South Africa.

**Jean Hillier** Emeritus Professor of Sustainability and Urban Planning, RMIT University, Melbourne, Australia.

**Paul J. Maginn** Associate Professor, School of Earth and Environment, The University of Western Australia, Australia.

**Raine Mäntysalo** Professor, Aalto University, Department of Built Environment, Finland.

**Jonathan Metzger** Associate Professor, Division for Urban and Regional Studies, Department of Urban Planning and Environment, Royal Institute of Technology/Kungliga Tekniska Högskolan, Stockholm, Sweden.

**Robert Obudho** Professor of Urban and Regional Planning, University of Nairobi, Kenya.

**Kristian Olesen** Associate Professor in Strategic Spatial Planning, Department of Development and Planning, Aalborg University, Denmark.

**Kristian Ruming** Associate Professor, Department of Geography and Planning, Macquarie University, NSW, Australia.

**Willem G. M. Salet** Professor of Urban and Regional Planning, Department of Geography, Planning and International Development Studies, University of Amsterdam, Netherlands.

**Francesca S. Sartorio** Lecturer in Planning at the Cardiff School of Geography and Planning, Cardiff University, Managing Editor of *International Planning Studies*, member of the Civic Trust Cymru Policy Group and a former Director and Trustee of Planning Aid, Wales.

**Glen Searle** Adjunct Associate Professor in Planning at the University of Sydney and the University of Queensland. He was previously Chief Editor of *Urban Policy and Research* journal and Director of the Planning programs at the University of Technology, Sydney and the University of Queensland.

**Yehya Serag** Associate Professor of urban and regional planning, Urban Design and Planning Department, Faculty of Engineering, Ain Shams University, – Cairo, Egypt.

**José Serrano** Senior Lecturer in Urban and Regional Planning, Université François-Rabelais de Tours, Research unit 'Cités, territoires, environnement et sociétés', France.

**Loris Antonio Servillo** Department of Architecture, Planning & Development Research Group, KU Leuven, Belgium.

**Carissa Schively Slotterback** Associate Professor, Hubert H. Humphrey School of Public Affairs, University of Minnesota – Twin Cities, USA.

**Carlos Vainer** Full Professor, Institute of Urban and Regional Planning and Research, Federal University of Rio de Janeiro, Brazil.

**Jef Van den Broeck** Honorary Professor, KU Leuven, Honorary Lecturer, Artesis University College/Antwerp, Planner/Urbanist, former CEO 'Team Omgeving', Belgium.

**Jiang Xu** Associate Professor, Head, Graduate Division, Department of Geography and Resource Management, The Chinese University of Hong Kong, Hong Kong.

**Anthony G. O. Yeh** Chair Professor and Chan To-Haan Professor in Urban Planning and Design, Department of Urban Planning and Design The University of Hong Kong, Hong Kong.

**Li Zheng** Department of Planning and Geography, Cardiff University Wales Department of Management, Radboud University, Nijmegen, Netherlands.

# 1 Some ontological and epistemological challenges

*Louis Albrechts*

Our society is facing major developments and challenges: the growing complexity (rise of new technologies, changes in production processes, crisis of representative democracy, diversity, globalization of culture and the economy), increasing concern about the rapid and uneven course of development, the problems of fragmentation, the ageing of the population in some parts of the world and youngsters and woman entering the labour market in other parts, the growing concern and awareness (at all scales, from local to global) about environmental issues, the longstanding quest for better coordination (both horizontal and vertical), the re-emphasis on the need for long-term thinking and the aim to return to a more realistic and effective method. Cases all over the world (but predominantly in the Global North) tell us that traditional planning tools are often insufficient to tackle these problems and challenges and are even unfit to govern processes of urban/regional transformation. A lot of traditional planning is about maintaining the existing social order rather than challenging and transforming it, and it fails to capture the dynamics and tensions of relations coexisting in particular places (see Albrechts and Balducci, 2013). It becomes less focused on the visionary and imagining the 'impossible' and more concerned with pragmatic negotiations around the 'immediate' in a context of the seeming inevitability of market-based forms of political rationality (see Haughton *et al.*, 2013: 232). Its rhetorical commitment to inclusivity limits perceptions of diversity and causes deliberate exclusions (see Watson, 2007). In a phase of deep and rapid change, traditional planning instruments seem to be ineffective because they are designed for situations of stability (Schön, 1971), certainty and a reasonable clarity on the problems to be addressed (Christensen, 1985; Forester, 1993). All these traits are lacking in contemporary cities, urban regions and regions. In many places, public authorities looked for new interpretations, new descriptions, which could give a sense of what could be appropriate and necessary, to contrast the negative effects of change and to devise positive actions. There is a growing need to give a synthetic view of the process of change (Part 1 of the book) and frame future directions of development: a sense-making activity that is critical (the subject of Part 2) in order to frame the actions of citizens and governments with a role in the decisions about urban and territorial transformations (the search for new ideas in Parts 2 and 3). But, often, this cannot be translated into a 'plan' in the traditional sense. This may imply the abandonment of bureaucratic approaches and the involvement of skills and resources that are external to the traditional administrative apparatus.

The roll-out of neoliberal policy privileges urban and regional competitiveness mainly through the subordination of social policy to economic policy and new – more elitist – forms of partnerships and networks (see Jessop, 2000; Allmendinger and Haughton, 2009a: 618). City and regional governments are lured to adopt a more entrepreneurial style of planning in order to enhance city and regional competitiveness.

As a result, planning faces major ontological and epistemological challenges. These may imply the scope of planning, approaches, use of skills, resources, knowledge base, and involvement of a wider range of actors. This book therefore argues (see also Allmendinger and Haughton, 2010; Sager, 2013) that spatial planning is in desperate need of both critical debate that questions the political and economic processes, of which existing planning approaches are an integral part (see Sager, 2013: xviii), and a search for new ideas (Allmendinger and Haughton, 2010: 328). Planning needs instruments for legal certainty and legitimacy on the one hand and the means for spatial quality, sustainability and equity on the other hand. All this leads to a demand to expand the agenda and to induce a planning theory and practices that embrace incompleteness and uncertainty, multiple possible alternative futures, acknowledging that people's desires are likely to change and that many decisions need to be flexible, exploratory and experimental. Hence, in many countries the need was felt for a different type of planning, moving away from regulatory policy and instruments to an approach that aims to intervene more directly, more coherently and more selectively in social reality and development (see Albrechts, 1995, 1999, 2004; Healey *et al.*, 1997). In response, more strategic approaches, frameworks and perspectives for cities, city-regions and regions became fashionable. A growing literature (Healey, 1997a, 2000, 2006, 2007; Albrechts, 2004, 2013, 2015; Motte, 2006; Balducci *et al.*, 2011) and an increasing number of practices, all over the world, seem to suggest that strategic spatial planning may be looked upon as a possible approach able to cope with the challenges our society is facing and to embed structural changes that are needed. But at the same time critical comments and reactions are raised on the theory and the practices of strategic spatial planning. The book reflects on what can be done to revive strategic planning as a critical theory and praxis. Looking at the logics behind statutory planning and strategic planning, and the critiques on statutory planning and on strategic planning, helps to focus on their core/ specificity (in terms of their typical aspects/characteristics), the appreciation of which do change through the expectations of the different actors. In this way, the identification is done by focusing on the contradictions, on what they stand for or against.

## Statutory planning: history, logic, critique

### *History*

Physical planners, dreaming to develop sustainable cities and regions for the good society, and planning regulators, obsessed to avoid potential conflicts by setting clear and enforceable rules, have dominated planning for a long time. This type of planning was associated, by the business community and politicians, with constraints on their freedom of manoeuvre (Healey, 2006: 533). The emergence of statutory planning systems across the world has some common roots. In many states, the first planning legislation was produced in the early twentieth century as a response to increasing development pressure and the consequent problems that arose from dense and disorganized development. Cultural, institutional and legal differences, but also the specificity of the purposes for which formal spatial planning systems were originally introduced, produced a wide variety of planning systems and traditions. Many states, with the exception of those influenced by the British planning model, use detailed planning instruments (regulatory zoning instruments, building control instruments and implementation instruments) which play a determining role in guiding the location of development and physical infrastructure and the form and size development takes (see CEC, 1997). Statutory plans have a legal status and embody the right of use associated with a piece of land. Planning permissions are granted on the basis of these documents.

## Logic

Land-use regulation helps to steer developments in a certain direction. The statutory plans used for this purpose are static documents, which are used as a control tool for the actions of third parties, as a (legal) framework for spatial development and for the building rights of owners. The logic behind the use of government intervention in the use and development of land is to guide development to occur in a way so that development proposals that do not accord with certain planning objectives or design standards can be refused under law. It claims legal equal rights, for bureaucratic and political control and legal certainty for investors. An additional aim is also to avoid clientelism and corruption within the permit policy. Today the main rationale seems to be the pursuit of legal certainty as a basis for the permit policy. As a consequence, documents have to set out land uses and formal requirements very carefully and very accurately, while eliminating uncertainty as much as possible. Indeed, building permits are granted (or refused) if a project or development proposal is in line (or not) with the approved land-use plan and regulations. Planned residential subdivisions give land and property owners the certainty of investment returns. In this way, land-use planning and economic growth are intrinsically connected. Progress is equated with order, with buildings and with economic development. Land-use planning – even in a simplified zoning form – is considered a necessity: urban markets need it; there is no way of managing city growth without some form of grids and regulations.

## Critique

Traditional land-use planning, as more passive, pragmatic and localized planning, aims at controlling land use and through a zoning system it helps to steer developments in a certain direction. In this way, the land-use plan ensures that undesirable developments do not occur, but it is not able to ensure that desirable developments actually take place where and when they are needed. Traditional land-use plans remain too much of an administrative framework for development instead of an action plan aimed at the implementation of visions and concepts. It entails false assumptions of certainty and static context. Statutory planning, as an instituted tool/instrument, as the domain of expert knowledge/skills and the techno-managerial management of a presumably inevitable socio-spatial ordering, reflects the practices of established policies.

Most of the statutory plans were designed for situations of stability and predictability in which plans can serve as blueprints offering investors (including local residents) and developers the certainty they want. It is guided by what the planners normatively would like to see happen (see Friedmann and Douglas, 1998) rather than form a fine-grained analysis of what actually takes place. The interpretation of land-use plans in terms of form and content (comprehensive, detailed, etc.) is in effect a negation of change, dynamics, uncertainty, etc., meaning that they soon become outdated, are often utopian, are often not based upon sufficient and correct data, and do not take into account resources or the time factor or even the possibilities for their implementation. In short, they focus on legal certainty which makes the plans far more rigid and inflexible and less responsive to changing circumstances. In this way, they seem unsuited for dealing with the dynamics of society, changing issues, changing circumstances and a changing context. Moreover, they force planners and politicians to make choices before the time is right to do this, and the mainly comprehensive nature of land-use plans is at odds with increasingly limited resources.

The approach to planning via a single policy field (that is, spatial planning) met fierce opposition from other, and usually more powerful, policy fields. Although land-use plans had formal status and served as official guidelines for implementation, when it came down to the actual implementation, other policy fields, which, because of their budgetary and technical resources, were needed for the implementation, were easily able to sabotage the spatial plans if they wanted (Scharpf and Schnabel, 1978; Kreukels, 2000). It became increasingly clear that a number of planning concepts cannot be achieved solely through physical hard planning. Moreover, most land-use plans have a predominant focus on physical aspects, providing physical solutions to social or economic problems. In this way, they often abstract from real, historically determinate parameters of human activity and gratuitously assume the existence of transcendent operational norms.

## Strategic spatial planning: history, logic, critique

### *History*

At some time strategic planning became the new hope of the community of (mainly academic) planners to overcome the shortcomings of statutory planning at local and regional tiers of planning and decision-making. Strategic planning has a long tradition; it has been defined in many different ways and has been called many different things – the structural plans, the American business model, the popularized Barcelona model – and there have been applications of this in many parts of the world (urban development plans, concept plans, structure plans…). All these are characterized by a specific definition of strategic planning. The word 'strategy' has its roots within a military context (see Sun Tzu, 1994 [500BC]). The focus is on an accurate understanding of the real situation, realistic goals, and the focused orientation of available strength and persistence of the action. In the early 1980s, a rash of articles have called on state and local governments to use the strategic planning approach developed in the corporate world (see Kaufman and Jacobs, 1987 for references). Others (Bryson and Roering, 1988; Bryson, 1995) stress the need to gather the key (internal and external) stakeholders (preferably the key decision-makers), and the importance of external trends and forces, and the active involvement of senior-level managers, to construct a longer-term vision. Even if some of the objectives and arguments furnished by plans that develop this perspective may seem innovative, the approach, the method and the working hypotheses remain quite traditional (see Albrechts and Balducci, 2013). More recently, some authors (see Healey, 1997a, 2000; Albrechts, 2004; Motte, 2006; Balducci *et al.*, 2011) have gradually developed a definition that is clearly different from the military and the corporate stance. Strategic planning is defined as: a socio-spatial process through which a range of people in diverse institutional relations and positions come together to design plan-making processes and develop contents and strategies for the management of spatial change; an opportunity for constructing new ideas and processes that can carry them forward; collective efforts to re-imagine a city, urban region or region and to translate the outcome into priorities for area investment, conservation measures, strategic infrastructure investments and principles of land-use regulation (see Healey, 1997b, 2000). Defined in this way, strategic spatial planning is as much about process, institutional design and mobilization as it is about the development of substantive theories. Content relates to the (strategic) issues selected in the process. The motivations for using strategic spatial planning in practice vary, but the objectives have typically been: to construct a challenging, coherent and coordinated vision, to frame an integrated long-term spatial logic (for land-use regulation, for resource protection, for sustainable development, for spatial quality, sustainability, equity, etc.), to enhance action-orientation beyond the idea of planning as control, and to promote a more open multi-level type of governance. As a result of a reawakening of 'the political' based on equality (see Swyngedouw, 2014, in line with Rancière), a claim for transformative practices leads to a call for a more radical strategic planning (Mitlin, 2008; Roy, 2009; Watson, 2011; Albrechts, 2013, 2015). It is based on dealing with structural issues, co-production as a political strategy, and in this way it acts as a base for democratic engagement, working with conflicts and legitimacy.

*Logic*

A basic purpose of strategic spatial planning is to tackle problems, raise aware-ness, meet challenges, and broaden the scope of the possible (see Zizek, 1999: 199 about the art of the impossible), to encourage hopes and dreams, to appeal to values, to provide a frame for decisions and to challenge existing knowledge, conventional wisdom and practices. It provides direction without destination, movement without prediction. Strategic planning aims to bring to the fore a plurality of interests and demands. So as values, interests and views from actors are different, strategic planning needs to work in a context of conflicts and clashes between the different actors. For some, the object of strategic planning should not be on the production of plans themselves (not even strategic ones), but on the production of insights of prospective change and in encouraging public debates on them (Friedmann, 2004: 56). It is a way of probing the future in order to make more intelligent and informed decisions in the present (ibid.: 56). The strategic probing of future uncertainties frames the fixing of certainties in the present. For others, the end product may consist of a critical analysis of the main processes and structural constraints shaping our places, which amounts to realistic, dynamic, integrated, and indicative long-term visions (frames), plans for short-term and long-term actions, a budget, and flexible strategies for implementation. It constitutes a commitment or (partial) (dis)agreement between the key actors. The voluntary character of many strategic planning experiences seems, for some, to act as a structural antidote against marked standardization (see Sartorio, 2005; Balducci, 2008). For these, any effort to standardize and legalize strategic plan-ning would be extremely counterproductive. Indeed, by doing this, the flexible instrument would soon become as procrustean and inflexible as traditional over-regulated land-use planning (Kunzmann, 2013). As long as strategic planning is not defined as a legally-defined instrument – and for many it would not be a wise move to strengthen or legalize the approach – strategic planning is a tool, which can convey innovation and creative action into processes of urban and regional development (Kunzmann, 2013). But even where spatial strategies are grounded in principles of adaptability, the pressure to deliver implementation agendas (projects, actions) makes it difficult to shift the gaze of governments and planners sufficiently to deal with continuously emergent policy shifts and their implica-tions (see Wilkinson, 2011). In their logic, it is claimed that all the main actors desire certainty in relation to the built environment (and the natural environment as well) and that it is the task of government and hence planning practitioners to deliver that certainty. Certainty is here associated with detailed land-use zoning schemes and regulations, together with fixed targets for employment, housing, retail floor space provision and so on. The question that comes up is whether this is possible and desirable and how this relates to statutory planning?

New concepts used in strategic planning as encouraging, emergence and trajec-tories signify a sea-change – at least in theory – in the purpose and rationale of spatial planning away from a traditional, positivist approach that sought to ensure and achieve specified goals and end-states in a given plan time-line (see Healey,

2008: 8). For Kunzmann (2000), a strategic plan is a possible opportunity, depending on political will and on specific circumstances, a blank slate waiting for collective action, which considers possible convergences of opinion and compromises and the relations between the forces in play. In this way, it deploys one of its most interesting potentials, its capacity to produce action frameworks and interpretative images capable of mobilizing people into action and in some cases of constructing a new governance culture (Albrechts, Healey and Kunzmann, 2003).

## *Critique*

Despite a certain popularity of strategic spatial planning (see Metzger, 2012: 781), one cannot be blind to the critiques formulated on strategic planning. The critiques focus on very different registers of the strategic spatial planning approach. Some of the critiques are related to the ontology and epistemology of strategic planning. Critics argue that the results of strategic planning, in terms of improvement of the quality of places, have been modest. They also question the conditions under which visions would materialize, the lack of concern about the path dependency of the resources; a too sequential view of the relationships between visioning, action, structure, institutions and discourse. They blame the weakness in theoretical underpinnings or are concerned about the legitimating of strategic spatial planning processes, and consequently of the role of planners. Questions are raised on how (and to what extent) the shift from a Euclidian concept of stable entities towards a non-Euclidian concept of many space–time geographies (see Friedmann, 1993: 482; Graham and Healey, 1999) is reflected in strategic spatial planning. How are the different types of knowledge (tacit/experiential knowledge of local communities versus traditional scientific knowledge) relevant for a relational strategic planning, reflected in strategic plans and actions based on these plans? Economic-political ideological critiques draw a link between the rise of strategic spatial planning and the strengthened neoliberal political climate (see Cerreta *et al.*, 2010; Olesen, 2011; Olesen and Richardson, 2012). They fear that the ideal of strategic spatial planning could be easily used to favour the most aggressive neoliberal models of urban and regional development (Cerreta *et al.*, 2010: x; see also Olesen, 2011; Sager, 2013), and questions are raised whether strategic spatial planning practices are able to resist the hegemonic discourses of neoliberalism (see Olesen, 2011). Others attack the militaristic and corporate terminology of strategic planning. And finally, there are those who focus on the implementation of the theory in practice, asking whether actually existing practices of strategic spatial planning really follow in line with its normative grounding (see Newman, 2008; Allmendinger and Haughton, 2009b, 2010).

## Aims of the book

Against this background the book aims to act as an encounter between different ways of doing strategic planning and to challenge planners in different places to assess whether the ideas expressed in the book have relevance to their places and their problems. Learning from other traditions, if done with a critical imagination, is good for all of us (Healey, 2010: 19). The book explores the circulation of ideas and practices around strategic planning (Borja and Castells, 1997; UN-Habitat, 2009). These ideas, although often formed in response to very particular problems, challenges in specific contexts, have spread worldwide through networks created by academics, practitioners and politicians attracted by planning 'imagery' (see also Healey, 2010: 9; Healey and Upton, 2010: xix). The editors have sought out contributors, from all continents, who are critical academics or practitioners. The approach in the book is descriptive, analytical, critical and normative. It is descriptive and analytical in the sense that it relies on the analysis of carefully selected strategic planning processes. Indeed, every case needs some understanding of the context, some grasp of who the key actors are and what networks are in play, how this relates to social, economic and political dynamics (see also Healey, 2010: 14). In their diversity, the cases mirror various ways of thinking about and doing strategic planning. It is critical in the sense that the editors are not blind to the critique formulated on strategic planning. With the Rio chapter we provide an interesting counter-case. It is normative in the sense that the book provides critical features and ingredients for the design and implementation of strategic planning processes that can produce significant outcomes. The normative character of the book will provoke reactions. This suits another purpose of this book, namely to contribute to the discussion (by academics and practitioners) on the merits and the pitfalls of strategic planning.

The book has three parts. In Part 1, for the first time, selected cases from all over the world are dealt with following a grid of questions provided by the editors. The grid forces the authors to go beyond a mere description of the cases and challenges them to reflect on the intellectual roots of strategic planning, to draw a link with the institutional context and to be open to critical voices and innovative practices. A great deal can be learned from this about the potential and pitfalls of strategic planning. Critical debate is the subject of Part 2, with a focus on critical nodes and features in strategic planning. In Part 3 we search for new ideas and address a possible profile to reinforce an interpretation of strategic planning that avoids carefully stage-managed processes with clearly defined parameters and favours its open, transformative, selective, visionary, participatory and action-oriented dimensions.

# References

Albrechts, L. 1995. Bâtir le visage d'une région. *Dokumente und Informationen zur Schweizerischen Orts-, Regional- und Landesplanung*, 122: 29–34.

Albrechts, L. 1999. Planners as Catalysts and Initiators of Change: The New Structure Plan for Flanders. *European Planning Studies*, 7(5): 36–46.

Albrechts, L. 2004. Strategic (Spatial) Planning Reexamined. *Environment and Planning B: Planning and Design*, 31: 743–758.

Albrechts, L. 2013. Reframing Strategic Spatial Planning by Using a Coproduction Perspective. *Planning Theory*, 12(1): 46–63.

Albrechts, L. 2015. Ingredients for a More Radical Strategic Spatial Planning. *Environment and Planning B: Planning and Design*, 42(3): 510–525.

Albrechts, L., Healey, P. and Kunzmann, K. 2003. Strategic Spatial Planning and Regional governance. *JAPA*, 69(2): 113–129.

Albrechts, L. and Balducci, A. 2013. Practicing Strategic Planning: In Search for Critical Features to Explain the Strategic Character of Plans. *DisP*, 194(49.3): 16–27.

Allmendinger, P. and Haughton, G. 2009a. Soft Spaces, Fuzzy Boundaries, and Metagovernance: The New Spatial Planning in the Thames Gateway. *Environment and Planning A*, 41: 617–633.

Allmendinger, P. and Haughton, G. 2009b. Commentary. *Environment and Planning A*, 41: 2544–2549.

Allmendinger, P. and Haughton, G. 2010. The Future of Spatial Planning: Why Less May Be More. *Town & Country Planning*, July/August: 326–328.

Balducci, A. 2008. Constructing (Spatial) Strategies in Complex Environments. In Van den Broeck, J., Moulaert, F. and Oosterlynck, S. (Eds), *Empowering the Planning Fields: Ethics, Creativity and Action*. Acco, Leuven: 79–99.

Balducci, A., Fedeli, V. and Pasqui, G. (Eds) 2011. *Strategic Planning for Contemporary Urban Regions*. Ashgate, Farnham.

Borja, J. and Castells, M. 1997. *Local and Global*. Earthscan, London.

Bryson, J. M. 1995. *Strategic Planning for Public and Nonprofit Organizations*. Jossey-Bass, San Francisco, CA.

Bryson, J. M. and Roering, W. D. 1988. Initiation of Strategic Planning by Governments. *Public Administration Review*, 48: 995–1004.

CEC. 1997. *The EU Compendium of Spatial Planning Systems and Policies*. Commission of the European Communities, Luxembourg.

Cerreta, M., Concilio, G. and Monno, V. (Eds) 2010. *Making Strategies in Spatial Planning: Knowledge and Values*. Springer, Dordrecht.

Christensen, K. 1985. Coping with Uncertainty in Planning. *Journal of the American Planning Association*, 51: 63–73.

Forester, J. 1993. *Critical Theory, Public Policy, and Planning Practice*. State University of New York Press, Albany, NY.

Friedmann, J. 1993. Toward a Non-Euclidian Mode of Planning. *Journal of the American Planning Association*, 59(4): 482–485.

Friedmann, J. 2004. Strategic Spatial Planning and the Longer Range. *Planning Theory & Practice*, 5(1): 49–67.

Friedmann, J. and Douglas, M. 1998. Editor's Introduction. In Douglas, M. and Friedmann, J. (Eds), *Cities for Citizens*. Chichester, John Wiley & Sons.

Graham, S. and Healey, P. 1999. Relational Concepts of Space and Place: Issues for Planning Theory and Practice, *European Planning Studies*, 7(5): 623–646.

Haughton, G., Allmendinger, P. and Oosterlynck, S. 2013. Spaces of Neoliberal Experimentation: Soft Spaces, Postpolitics, and Neoliberal Governmentality. *Environment and Planning A*, 45: 217–234.

Healey, P. 1997a. The Revival of Strategic Spatial Planning in Europe. In Healey, P., Khakee, A., Motte, A. and Needham, B. (Eds), *Making Strategic Spatial Plans*. UCL Press, London: 3–19.

Healey, P. 1997b. *Collaborative Planning: Shaping Places in Fragmented Societies*. Palgrave Macmillan, Basingstoke.

Healey, P. 2000. Planning in Relational Time and Space: Responding to New Urban Realities. In Bridge G. and Wastoke, S. (Eds), *A Companion to the City*. Blackwell, Oxford: 517–530.

Healey, P. 2006. Relational Complexity and the Imaginative Power of Strategic Spatial Planning. *European Planning Studies*, 14(4): 525–546.

Healey, P. 2007. *Urban Complexity and Spatial Strategies: Towards a Relational Planning for Our Times*. Routledge, London.

Healey, P. 2008. Making Choices that Matter: The Practical Art of Situated Strategic Judgement in Spatial Strategy-making. In Van den Broeck, J., Moulaert, F. and Oosterlynck, S. (Eds), *Empowering the Planning Fields: Ethics, Creativity and Action*. Acco, Leuven: 23–41.

Healey, P. 2010. Introduction: The Transnational Flow of Knowledge and Expertise in the Planning Field. In Healey, P. and Upton, R., *Crossing Borders: International Exchange and Planning Practices*. Routledge, Abingdon: 1–25.

Healey, P., Khakee, A., Motte, A. and Needham, B. (Eds) 1997. *Making Strategic Spatial Plans*. UCL Press, London.

Healey, P. and Upton, R. 2010. Preface. In Healey, P. and Upton, R., *Crossing Borders: International Exchange and Planning Practices*. Routledge, Abingdon: xix–xxii.

Jessop, B. 2000. The Crisis of National Spatio-Temporal Fix and the Ecological Dominance of Globalizing. *International Journal of Urban and Regional Research*, 24: 323–360.

Kaufman, J. L. and Jacobs, H. 1987. A Public Planning Perspective on Strategic Spatial Planning. *Journal of the American Planning Association*, 53: 21–31.

Kreukels, A. 2000. An Institutional Analysis of Strategic Spatial Planning: The Case of Federal Urban Policies in Germany. In Salet, W. and Faludi, A. (Eds), *The Revival of Strategic Spatial Planning*. Royal Netherlands Academy of Arts and Sciences, Amsterdam: 53–65.

Kunzmann, K. 2000. Strategic Spatial Development through Information and Communication. In Salet, W. and Faludi, A. (Eds), *The Revival of Strategic Spatial Planning*. Royal Netherlands Academy of Arts and Sciences, Amsterdam: 259–265.

Kunzmann, K. 2013. Strategic Planning: A Chance for Spatial Innovation and Creativity. *DisP*, 194(49.3): 28–31.

Metzger, J. 2012. Placing the Stakes: The Enactment of Territorial Stakeholders in Planning Processes. *Environment and Planning A*, 45: 781–796.

Mitlin, D. 2008. With and beyond the State: Coproduction as a Route to Political Influence, Power and Transformation for Grassroots Organizations. *Environment and Urbanization*, 20(2): 339–360.

Motte, A. 2006. *La notion de planification stratégique spatialisée en Europe (1995–2005)*. Puca, Lyon.

Newman, P. 2008. Strategic Spatial Planning: Collective Action and Moments of Opportunity. *European Planning Studies*, 16(10): 1371–1383.

Olesen, K. 2011. Strategic Spatial Planning in Transition: Case Study of Denmark. PhD Thesis. Department of Development and Planning, Aalborg University.

Olesen, K. and Richardson, T. 2012. Strategic Spatial Planning in Transition: Contested Rationalities and Spatial Logics in 21st Century Danish Spatial Planning. *European Planning Studies*, 20(10): 1689–1706.

Roy, A. 2009. Civic Governmentality: The Politics of Inclusion in Beirut and Mumbai. *Antipode*, 41(1): 159–179.

Sager, T. 2013. *Reviving Critical Planning Theory*. Routledge, New York/London.

Sartorio, F. 2005. Strategic Spatial Planning: A Historical Review of Approaches, its Recent Revival, and an Overview of the State of the Art in Italy. *DisP*, 162: 26–40.

Scharpf, F. W. and Schnabel, F. 1978. Durchsetzungsprobleme der Raumordnung im Öffentlichen Sektor [Performance Problems of Spatial [Planning in the Public Sector]. *Informationen zur Raumentwicklung*, 1: 19–28.

Schön, D. 1971. *Beyond the Stable State*. Maurice Temple Smith, London.

Sun-Tzu. 1994 [500BC]. *Art of War*. Translated by Sawyer, R. Westview Press, Boulder, CO.

Swyngedouw, E. 2014. Where is the Political? Insurgent Mobilisations and the Incipient 'Return of the Political'. *Space and Polity*, 18(2): 122–136.

UN-Habitat. 2009. *Global Report on Human Settlements 2009: Planning Sustainable Cities*. Earthscan, London.

Watson, V. 2007. Revisiting the Role of Urban Planning. Concept Paper for the 2009 Global Report on Human Settlements. Cape Town, South Africa.

Watson, V. 2011. Planning and Conflict – Moving On. Paper. WPSC, Perth, Australia.

Wilkinson, C. 2011. Strategic Navigation: In Search of an Adaptable Mode of Strategic Spatial Planning Practice. *Town Planning Review*, 82(5): 595–613.

Zizek, S. 1999. *The Ticklish Subject*. Verso, London.

# Part 1

# Situated experiences of strategic planning worldwide

# 2    Introduction

*Louis Albrechts and Alessandro Balducci*

The first part of the book illustrates the emergence of strategic spatial planning in different forms in various parts of the world. As we clarified in the general introduction, at the end of the twentieth century urban and regional planning, with its 'doctrines' (Faludi and van der Valk, 1994), traditions and practices, born at the beginning of the same century, has been challenged everywhere for its inability to cope with the speed of change and to serve the new demands emerging in the urban sphere: from urban competition to urban sustainability, from regeneration to the support of big events, from managing urban shrinkage to managing rapid growth in developing countries (Albrechts, 2004). On the one hand, the accelerated pace of change and the growing complexity favoured the crisis of any rigid and static form of planning, while on the other hand it emphasized the need for new instruments to orientate choices in a turbulent environment.

It has been in this context that new forms of planning have been experimented with and that strategic planning became the new hope of the community of (mainly academic) planners in Europe and beyond. Strategic planning aims to check government and corporate power to guarantee the use of local knowledge, to ensure that planning processes are responsive and democratic (see Friedmann, 1992). As it aims at securing political influence, it is certainly confrontational and conflicting, it is directed at change by means of specific outputs (a probe into the future, strategies, plans, policies, projects) framed through spaces of deliberative opportunities. As a consequence, strategic planning may take place beyond the boundaries of the (traditional) planning profession and planning laws and regulations. Its outcomes must be well informed, just and fair. There is ample evidence that in many strategic plans the often more abstract discourse is turned into something more tangible and is redefined into a more familiar vocabulary of statutory planning (see also Olesen and Richardson, 2012: 1703).

The meaning which has been attributed to the term 'strategic' has often been unclear and sometimes even contradictory. As strategic planning will be influenced by the available and effective policy levers and by past patterns of spatial and institutional development, it is unlikely that it means the same thing when it has been translated into a different cultural setting, political system, policy context and planning tradition. The policy levers and development patterns create both capacities and preferences among relevant actors (Friedmann, 2010: 325).

Moreover, research in the field of policy research reveals that the theoretical basis underlying a policy concept in such diffusion is often inadequately conceptualized (Ganapati and Verma, 2010: 237).

The term 'strategic' was often used to indicate the detachment from traditional forms of planning and to overcome the shortcomings of statutory planning at local and regional tiers of planning and decision-making. More and more, it became a key word representing the need to practise a more interactive, proactive, selective and visionary form of planning.

From this perspective, this Part of the book produces, for the first time, an overview of situated experiences of strategic spatial planning worldwide. It is not an attempt to document all the forms of planning that have been labelled as strategic, but rather to look at different contexts in which we have observed the emergence of strategic spatial planning that has been explicitly conceived to deal with a problem of designing the future in an open and innovative way. Cases help us to find out how the approach imagined and produced in one context then becomes susceptible to processes of reimagination and reproduction that appropriate their originality but also facilitate their ability to travel to other contexts (see Vidyarthi, 2010). It is clear that strategic planning has not always had the impact that its different streams intended. This is partly due to the fact that the capacity of a strategic spatial planning system to deliver the desired outcomes is dependent not only on the legal-political system itself, but also on the conditions underlying it (see also Mintzberg, 1994). These conditions – including political, societal, cultural and professional attitudes towards spatial planning (in terms of planning content and process) and the political will on the part of the institutions involved in setting the process in motion (and, with even more difficulty, in keeping it going) – affect the ability of planning systems to implement the chosen approaches. The surrounding political regime enhances or inhibits the institutional change needed for strategic planning.

Strategic planning does not work on its own. It needs change agents, what Kingdon (2003) has described as 'policy entrepreneurs' – a champion, in the terminology of Bryson (1995), to take the approach and deploy it. This means that the influence is not direct, but works through multiple processes in which relevant actors can see an opportunity to use strategic planning to push forward a policy change (see Sorensen, 2010: 133). Actors interpret strategic planning differently and will adopt those aspects of the approach that best fit their own situation. This may be a choice of elements that promise to solve some problems and can be implemented or reinterpreted within the frameworks of existing planning tools (see Healey and Upton, 2010). So, for strategic planning to be successful, a key task is to explore who has a stake in an issue. The question concerning who is to be considered a stakeholder in a particular context or situation is not only an epistemological challenge, but also a fundamentally ontological issue (Metzger, 2012: 782). When all public agents and all citizens are viewed as decision-makers, 'laws and rules should not be seen as prescribing a specific course of action. Rather they are frames within which people make decisions' (Whitaker, 1980: 242; see also Forester, 2010). They serve as 'benchmarks against which to assess the wisdom of alternatives, but they do not determine behavior; neither do frames prescribe fixed outcomes' (Whitaker, 1980: 242).

For some (see Mazza, 2011, 2013; Mäntysalo, 2013), the possible detachment of strategic spatial planning from the statutory planning system into a parallel informal system would pose a serious legitimacy problem. For Mäntysalo (2013: 51), the main purpose of strategic planning is framing the statutory-strategic planning relationship. A frame in this context embodies a sensitivity to the complexity, plurality and indeterminacy of particular urban development dynamics as they emerge, and which generate sufficient energy to inspire and direct transformative actions within those dynamics with the aim of shaping what happens in a place (Healey, 2008: 35). Many challenges that societies are facing are structural: diversity (race, class, age, religion), equity (unequal development), inclusivity (inclusion, exclusion), sustainability, climate change. Hence the need for transformative change. Transformative change is about systemic change (deep change) in society that cannot be undone. It focuses on the structural problems in society, and it needs to construct images/visions of preferred outcomes and how to implement them. The transformative agenda is a modern term for structural change that has been discussed by many in the past (Etzioni, 1971; Schön, 1971; Friedmann, 1987) in the context of planning theory. It simply refuses to accept that the current way of doing things is necessarily the best way. It differs from the established or traditional way of thinking, in which there is hardly any choice and hardly an awareness of other possibilities. The construction of different futures, which lies at the very heart of transformative practices, requires creativity and original synthesis. Therefore, strategic planning must involve a creative effort to imagine futures that are structurally different, and to bring this creative imagination to bear on political decisions and the implementation of these decisions. To construct visions for the future, we need both the solidity of the analysis that seeks to discover a place that is – this includes the multiplicity of the webs of relations which transect a territory and the complex intersections and disjunctions which develop among them (Healey, 2006: 526) – and that might exist, and the creativity of the design of a place that would not otherwise be.

As it is impossible to do everything that needs to be done, much of the process lies in making the tough decisions about what is most important for the purpose of producing fair, structural responses to problems, challenges, aspirations and potentials. To create particular future states is an act of choice involving valuation, judgement and the making of decisions that relate to the selection of perceived appropriate means for going forward.

Strategic spatial planning focuses on a limited number of strategic key issues; it takes a 'collective' critical view of the environment in terms of determining strengths and weaknesses in the context of opportunities and threats. Strategic spatial planning focuses on place-specific qualities and assets (social, cultural and intellectual, including physical and social qualities of the urban/regional tissue) in a global context.

Conceptions of the future in statutory plans were often based on linear derivations from the present and tended to create the impression that there was something logically and factually inevitable in both the sequence and the final configuration of predicted events. This approach resulted in plans that are closed systems constructed to solve specific classes of problems in the light of given goals which had been conceived outside the plan's own system. In strategic planning, the future needs to transcend mere feasibility and must result from judgements and choices formed with reference, first, to the idea of what is desirable, and then to that of betterment. Such futures might (and perhaps, must) be imagined as differing radically from present reality: they must represent situations which are not mere temporal extensions of the here and now; they must be free of the weight of what we are able simply to predict. A particular future state becomes, in this way, an act of choice that involves valuations, judgements and decisions and, when these decisions are carried out, which will lead to a gradual shift in a desirable direction. 'Futures' must symbolize some good, some qualities and some virtues that the present lacks (diversity, sustainability, equity, spatial quality, inclusiveness, accountability). Speaking of sustainability, spatial quality, virtues and values is a way of describing the sorts of place we want to live in, or think we should live in.

We don't look upon strategic spatial planning as the ultimate model, nor as a new ideology preaching a new world order, nor as a panacea for all challenges. Strategic planning is not meant as a substitute but as a complement for other planning tools (statutory planning, urban design). For us, it is a method for creating and steering a (range of) better future(s) for a place. Its focus on 'becoming' produces quite a different picture from traditional planning.

The theoretical notions introduced above will be reflected on in the cases described in the various chapters. The editors have developed a grid as a conceptual framework for the chapter authors, enabling a more systematic and coherent treatment of the cases. The grid is used to fuse the cases into a framework and to draw interesting conclusions from them. On the one hand, the grid allows the creation of a common ground for this exploration and, on the other hand, it facilitates our efforts to profile a number of characteristics that can make strategic spatial planning really strategic.

The grid is as follows:

- Describe how and why strategic spatial planning has developed. What was the context? What created the momentum? Who were the actors who started the process and why were other forms of planning not used (if appropriate)?
- Describe the nature of strategic spatial planning, in terms of its intellectual roots, the model assumed, if any, to understand the propagation of ideas and the emergence of specific patterns.
- Describe in what sense the strategic spatial planning is 'strategic'. What meaning has been attributed to the term?
- Describe where the focus of the planning action is. Is it on longer-term visions of the future, or rather is it on pragmatic actions?

- Describe the underlying spatial and temporal logics.
- Describe what issues these processes cover and what kind of societal challenges are dealt with (for example, if and how they make reference to climate change, environmental issues, social exclusion, ageing, and equity, etc.). Describe whether these and other such problems are addressed in a comprehensive or a selective manner.
- Describe the relationship of strategic spatial planning with statutory planning and what is its legal status.
- Describe how uncertainty is conceptualized and dealt with in the specific case.
- Describe what the output of the strategic spatial planning process is. Is it a vision, a planning document, strategies, a number of projects, or something else?
- Describe how strategic spatial planning deals with multi-level governance issues, the changing boundaries of 'the urban', and the involvement of stakeholders and citizens.
- Describe what degrees of control/stability or flexibility are evident in the case and its planning processes. How has the need for adaptation been considered and experienced? What has been the capacity to deal with unintended effects?
- Offer a critical evaluation of the planning processes examined. What has been really new and innovative? What could be considered an effective way of dealing with emerging problems? What have been the major limitations of this approach to strategic spatial planning?
- Describe what lessons the case study might offer for strategic spatial planning practice elsewhere.

This grid also guides us in connecting the plurality of case-related experiences to the critical reflection of the second Part of the book. In their diversity, the different cases mirror the various ways of thinking about strategic planning to be found in planning literature and worldwide practices.

The selection of particular case studies reflects three 'fields' or 'scales' of situated practices.

The first is the *trans-national* field or scale. We present the use of strategic planning in situations of territorial development which cross the borders of different nations. The case examples here are the Pearl Delta River region in China, the quest for integration in East Africa, and the Øresund region between Denmark and Sweden. The second field or scale is that of *national* experiences. We have selected international cases from around the globe to illustrate the diversity of strategic spatial planning practices. We asked contributors to illustrate how different forms of strategic planning have emerged in relation to their national planning systems. Cases are drawn from the United States, China, Egypt, Europe

(France, Italy and Wales in the UK) and Australia. The third field or scale of observation has been the selection of specific *local* experiences that look particularly meaningful to illustrate the transition from traditional to strategic forms of planning. Here we present the cases of Johannesburg in South Africa, Antwerp in Belgium, Vancouver in Canada and Rio de Janeiro in Brazil. The Rio case is an example of the transformative use of strategic planning in a discriminatory and, in the end, wrong direction.

As editors, we sought out contributors who are critical academics/practitioners and also those who are actively involved in specific practices. We have contributions from senior academics and from those who are relatively new in their academic careers. The resultant range of cases is not meant to be comprehensive but serves to provide a strong overview about what is at stake in different places in the world.

As our cases clearly demonstrate, strategic spatial planning is not a monolithic block of axioms set in stone. It is not a single concept, procedure or tool. In fact, it is a set of concepts, procedures and tools that must be tailored carefully to the situation at hand if desirable outcomes are to be achieved. The context forms the setting of the planning process, but also takes form and undergoes changes in the process (see Dyrberg, 1997). Therefore, we are well aware that this set of cases cannot be reported as a comparative study as such, but rather as an exploration that allows readers to investigate the adoption of new forms of planning in a phase of transition.

## References

Albrechts, L. 2004. Strategic (Spatial) Planning Reexamined. *Environment and Planning B: Planning and Design*, 31: 743–758.

Bryson, J. M. 1995. *Strategic Planning for Public and Non-profit Organizations*. Jossey-Bass, San Francisco, CA.

Dyrberg, T. B. 1997. *The Circular Structure of Power*. Verso, London.

Etzioni, A. 1971. *The Active Society: A Theory of Societal and Political Processes*. Collier Macmillan, London.

Faludi A. and van der Valk, A. 1994. *Rule and Order: Dutch Planning Doctrine in the Twentieth Century*. Kluwer Academic, Dordrecht.

Forester, J. 2010. Foreword. In Cerreta, M., Concilio, G. and Monno, V. (Eds), *Making Strategies in Spatial Planning*. Springer, Dordrecht: v–vii.

Friedmann, J. 1987. *Planning in the Public Domain: From Knowledge to Action*. Princeton University Press, Princeton, NJ.

Friedmann, J. 1992. *Empowerment: The Politics of Alternative Development*. Blackwell, Oxford.

Friedmann, J. 2010. Crossing Borders: Do Planning Ideas Travel? In Healey, P. and Upton, R. (Eds), *Crossing Borders: International Exchange and Planning Practices*. Routledge, Abingdon: 313–328.

Ganapati, S. and Verma, N. 2010. Institutional Biases in the International Diffusion of Planning Concepts. In Healey, P. and Upton, R. (Eds), *Crossing Borders: International Exchange and Planning Practices*. Routledge, Abingdon: 237–264.

Healey, P. 2006. Relational Complexity and the Imaginative Power of Strategic Spatial Planning. *European Planning Studies*, 14(4): 525–546.

Healey, P. 2008. Making Choices that Matter: The Practical Art of Situated Strategic Judgement in Spatial Strategy-making. In Van den Broeck, J., Moulaert, F. and Oosterlynck, S. (Eds), *Empowering the Planning Fields: Ethics, Creativity and Action*. Acco, Leuven: 23–41.

Healey, P. and Upton, R. 2010. *Crossing Borders: International Exchange and Planning Practices*. Routledge, Abingdon: 1–25.

Kingdon, J. W. 2003. *Agendas, Alternatives and Public Policies*. Longman, New York.

Mäntysalo, R. 2013. Coping with the Paradox of Strategic Spatial Planning. *DisP*, 194(49.3): 51–52.

Mazza, L. 2011. Personal Communication by email, 24 August.

Mazza, L. 2013. If Strategic Planning is Everything Maybe it's Nothing. *DisP*, 194(49.3): 40–42.

Metzger, J. 2012. Placing the Stakes: The Enactment of Territorial Stakeholders in Planning Processes. *Environment and Planning A*, 45: 781–796.

Mintzberg, H. 1994. *The Rise and Fall of Strategic Planning*. The Free Press, New York.

Olesen, K. and Richardson, T. 2012. Strategic Spatial Planning in Transition: Contested Rationalities and Spatial Logics in 21st Century Danish Spatial Planning. *European Planning Studies*, 20(10): 1689–1706.

Schön, D. A. 1971. *Beyond the Stable State*. W. W. Norton & Co. New York/London.

Sorensen, A. 2010. Urban Sustainability and Compact Cities Ideas in Japan: The Diffusion, Transformation and Deployment of Planning Concepts. In Healey, P. and Upton, R. (Eds), *Crossing Borders: International Exchange and Planning Practices*. Routledge, Abingdon: 117–140.

Vidyarthi, S. 2010. Reimagining the American Neighbourhood Unit for India. In Healey, P. and Upton, R. (Eds), *Crossing Borders: International Exchange and Planning Practices*. Routledge, Abingdon: 73–9.3

Whitaker, G. 1980. Coproduction: Citizen Participation in Service Delivery. *Public Administration Review*, 40(3): 240–246.

# Cross-national and national experiences

# 3   Regional strategic planning for China's Pearl River Delta

*Jiang Xu and Anthony G.O. Yeh*

## How and why has strategic spatial planning developed in China?

Beginning with the economic reforms of the late 1970s, the last three decades have witnessed an extraordinary urban growth in China. Promoting urbanisation has become a central policy to sustain economic prosperity. While various projections anticipate an 'urban billion' era for China, other dynamics, such as globalisation and the development of vast mega-city regions, will reinforce the role of cities as centres of production and consumption as well as of social and political transformation.

The scale and speed of urbanisation have overwhelmed Chinese governments at all levels, leading to a range of urban problems, such as social exclusion, urban sprawl, misuse of land in all cities, but especially in those that are under the threat of rapid (and often uncontrolled) growth, inadequate and poorly maintained infrastructure, rapid industrialisation and escalating vehicle ownership. Equally paramount are problems of spatial regulation at both urban and regional scales. While individual cities are eager to implement entrepreneurial strategies to enhance their competitiveness, they pay little heed to intercity networking, thus failing to address the many urgent social and environmental issues at the regional scale.

Against this background, strategic planning is emerging rapidly under a range of umbrellas at different geographical scales. At the city scale, some municipalities have experimented with strategic plans to supplement the traditional master plans, which are statutory documents but become easily obsolete in the face of hyper-rapid local growth. Strategic planning, on the other hand, allows for considerable flexibility in guiding local developments.

At the regional scale, strategic plans are normally made by superior governments (individual provinces, groups of provinces, the State Council) to guide regional transformation. In some mega-city regions, such as the Pearl River Delta (PRD), many formerly rural areas have developed into active economic centres. This has resulted in a polycentric spatial form with profound impacts on the environment. Moreover, political fragmentation has weakened cities' governing capacity, thus creating an urgent need for regulating and constraining ongoing urbanisation processes. In response to this challenge, regional strategic planning has evolved as a key political strategy to reposition provinces in both the national and global economic sphere and to impose better regulation.

In recent years, central agents at the national scale have been using strategic planning to influence local economic governance for better top-down regulation. One example is the invention of the Primary Functional Zones (PFZ), which is a kind of large-scale zoning system officially initiated by the National Development and Reform Commission (NDRC) in the 12th Five-Year Plan (2011–2015). PFZ classifies China's territory into four functional zones, which are placed under four types of spatial regulation. For example, one functional zone is called 'development-prohibited zones', which are critical ecological areas that must be placed under the protection of enforceable laws. To ensure implementation of this zoning system, provinces and cities are required to categorise these 'four zones' in their respective territories, and thus impose a restrictive framework for urban and regional development.

Strategic planning at different geographical scales serves different purposes. This chapter will focus on strategic planning at the regional scale.

## Intellectual roots of, and societal challenges for, regional strategic planning

Although the term 'strategic planning' was not mentioned explicitly until the late 1990s in China, the idea of planning as a quest to define developmental strategies and make decisions on allocating resources to pursue a desired spatial outcome has been around for a lot longer.

The form of extant regional strategic planning is embedded in an institutional structure that was originally formed under state socialism. Horizontal relationships between different jurisdictions have not traditionally been considered important, even though hierarchical linkages more or less unintentionally create spatial formations on the ground. Prior to 1978, this tradition resulted in regions becoming dependent on the centre. Urban and regional services were sectorally organised.

During the first Five-Year Plan period (1953–1957), regional planning was imported from the Soviet Union, in an attempt to apply a unified approach in selecting sites for 694 industrial projects. This early planning effort was a practice that combined economic and physical planning. It introduced a territorially integrated approach in providing land use and infrastructure for a group of projects. This new way of addressing the location of development was in contrast with the then prevailing ministry-led spatial production. This approach was frequently used in the second and third Five-Year Plans as well. During the Great Leap Forward (1958–1962), regional planning in municipal areas was recommended by experts from Poland and the Soviet Union to achieve unrealistic targets for the expansion of large cities by allowing their development plans to link up with surrounding suburban or fringe areas. In general, regional planning under state socialism can be viewed as a political strategy either serving to consolidate power at the centre or fulfilling planning targets of its accumulation regime rather than achieving administrative efficiency or economic rationality.

Most tasks were undertaken by the central economic planning agency established in 1952 – the State Planning Commission (SPC).

Since the late 1970s, the introduction of a series of reform packages engendered a deep transformation towards an accumulation regime that identifies cities as strategic sites for capital creation and state regulation. This is fundamentally different from the preceding regime, where the central state was the primary agent for redistribution and governance. Thus, the 1980s saw an interest in establishing economic regions in order to explore the advantages of central cities and their networks with surrounding jurisdictions. More than 100 economic regions were created, in an attempt to strategically break out of the hierarchical system of production and planning and thus to achieve a territorially integrated growth. This effort, led by the State Council and governed by SPC, created new directions for strategic planning.

Localities were urged to make regional plans based on economic linkages rather than on purely administrative boundaries. Different kinds of regional planning led by diverse ministries began to emerge. First, economic priorities replaced socialist ideology to mainstream policy regime. This led to a massive use of resources, such as agricultural land, and gave rise to the dual concern of effective land use and farmland protection. Since 1981, SPC was required to make national territorial planning (*guotu guihua*) at central, trans-provincial, provincial, regional, and city levels following the experiences of Western Europe and Japan. This kind of planning attempted to provide strategic elements of spatial coordination between economic development on one hand and population, resources, and environment on the other (Hu, 2006). And to take this still further, the State Land Administration Bureau (SLAB) was required to make land-use plans at various levels primarily to address the issue of farmland protection.

Second, as urbanisation proceeded at break-neck speed, coordination of urban settlements became urgent. Urban planning departments under the Ministry of Construction (MOC) began to create an urban systems plan (*chengzhen tixi guihua*) that was intended to rationalise the functional, hierarchical, and spatial orders of infrastructure and urban areas. To complement this effort, a municipal regional plan (*shiyu guihua*) provided an additional attempt to coordinate development of the central city and the outlying counties and towns that were traditionally not covered by the master plan.

By the mid-1990s, with the rise of urban entrepreneurialism, a new mosaic of regional development and territorial competition began to crystallise, adding to the former concerns of growth, the maintenance of an efficient urban system, and farmland protection. Informal government organisations were set up for political negotiations on a variety of regional issues. These newly formed institutions are no longer being promoted only in response to internally-triggered demands or mandated from above, but are emerging as bottom-up initiatives and the interplay of internal and external forces in the unfolding processes of globalisation and market reform.

At the same time, political fragmentation is further exacerbated by the growing local discretion that has increasingly weakened the governing capacity of both the provincial and central state. This has given rise to an urgent need to recompose strategic interventions at the regional level. Strategic planning has thus become a key political strategy to reassert the functional importance of the state in regional growth. The outcome is a series of new efforts to rebuild state power since the 1990s. As early as 1992, SPC began to give more attention to trans-provincial development plans, attempting to rely on central resource allocations to achieve spatial coordination. Unfortunately, these plans failed largely because of an insufficient anticipation of market forces, which are beyond the control of the state planning system. In 1998, SLAB was upgraded to the Ministry of Land and Resource (MLR). SPC passed its national territorial planning functions to MLR, and concentrated on its traditional function: socioeconomic planning. SPC was renamed twice in 1998 and 2003 respectively to become the National Development and Reform Commission (NDRC). In more recent years, adding to its economic planning function (e.g. Five-Year Plan), NDRC revived its interest in making plans for mega-city regions to provide both strategic and spatial elements for regional growth.

The MOC and its local subordinates expanded the *urban system plan* to include more spatial coordination elements, such as regulatory policies (*kongjian guanzhi*), which are similar to zoning. They added strategic considerations to these plans to provide a comprehensive vision for territorial development. And complementing the urban system plan, *regional studies and plans* were made for polycentric city regions. In large municipal areas such as Guangzhou, Shanghai and Beijing, new types of regional studies, i.e. *spatial strategic plans* or *concept plans*, were undertaken as experiments to provide strategic guidance for important urban developments in a regional perspective. These strategic plans had imported overseas planning ideas, such as Guangzhou's 2000 Concept Plan, which made reference to Hong Kong's new town development, proposing a spatial structure that was intended to preserve various open spaces.

Over the past decade, discourses such as sustainability, livability, climate change, low carbon growth, and green transport, which originated from western strategic planning practice, have become buzzwords in many strategic plans made by different ministries for China's cities and regions. However, regional strategic planning in China has some characteristics which may not mirror overseas planning practice. First, it accentuates economic growth, industrial sectors, and spatial strategies. Climate change, energy saving, resource management, and ecological conservation are frequently cited, but the selection and legitimating of these discourses in strategic plans has been often associated with their benefits to economic growth. For instance, low carbon is not directly linked to any arguments relating to climate change, but is closely tied to the need of developing low-carbon sectors of production. Second, most regional strategic plans are customarily made to recommend general development directions and broadbrush aspirations. There are few quantified objectives and implementation details. For instance, developing green transport (e.g. public transit and slow transport) is a discursively strong strategy in many strategic plans, yet its implementation faces tremendous difficulties partly due to deficiency in translating policies into concrete actions. Third, strategic plans tend to highlight spatial expansion rather than optimising existing land uses until a recent call to reverse this trend. Finally, most strategic plans are not statutory in nature, leading to a large implementation deficit.

To sum up, one cannot deny that strategic plans in China are being made with good intention to shift territorial development trajectories and coordinate regional growth patterns. Even so, these plans may also appear to be part of a state-led project for continuing capital accumulation and growth.

## Who have been the actors for regional strategic planning?

From the aforementioned intellectual history, it is obvious that strategic planning is a function of the state in China. Nevertheless, such function is highly fragmented among different ministries, overlapping in both functional and territorial term.

NDRC is a central super-agent to draw up socioeconomic plans. These plans have been in operation since the pre-reform period, and recently have come to contain a strong spatial element. Socioeconomic plans are strategic and holistic in nature, are made to clarify the overall positioning of regions and major cities, provide blueprints for priority development areas, and give solutions to problems that are difficult for one city or one province to solve (Hu, 2006). NDRC is also entrusted to demarcate PFZ and make regional coordination plans to formulate key strategies for guiding regional growth. A recent example is the ongoing effort of the NDRC in making the strategic plan for the Beijing-Tianjin-Hebei Region. Taking this further, NDRC is in charge of mapping China's path and solutions for climate change. For historical reasons, NDRC is a central agency which ranks a half-level higher than other ministries. Therefore, the strategic plans of NDRC and its local subordinates have the capacity to guide and constrain the functionally specific spatial plans made by other ministries and their institutional representatives at a local level. NDRC's plans directly connect state resource allocation to urban and regional growth, and are thus being taken seriously by local governments.

MOC was renamed as the Ministry of Housing and Urban-Rural Development (MOHURD) in 2008. MOHURD and its local subordinates, such as construction commissions and municipal urban planning bureaus, are responsible for spatial planning at both the city and urban systems (polycentric) scale. They are commissioned to make regional studies and plans to furnish the necessary elements for spatial coordination, such as the functional relationships among cities, the distribution and location of regional infrastructure facilities, and other strategic contents and spatial elements (e.g. regional development strategies, industrial location, transportation hubs, wilderness, and conservation areas). The renaming of the 1989 City Planning Act, which became the 2008 City and Country Planning Act, in part reflects the new geographical scope of spatial planning.

The Ministry of Land and Resources (MLR) and local land bureaus are entitled to prepare land use plans at all levels. Primarily, however, they address issues of farmland protection. In recent years, new content has been added to these plans by incorporating strategic land use projections for major projects and demarcating different zones subject to specific regulation. MLR has extensively applied GIS technologies to monitor national land use changes, thus providing a cutting-edge solution for policy makers. Also, MLR has controlled the yearly land use quota for different provinces, which has become a critical resource for local economic growth under the strict land use policy. These policy interventions reinforce the role of MLR in urban and regional development.

Last but not least, other line ministries, such as the Ministry of Transportation, the former Ministry of Railway, and the Ministry of Environmental Protection, have their own regional plans to guide sectoral development.

The fragmented functions of regional strategic planning contribute to inter-ministerial conflicts. For instance, MOHURD dislikes the idea of two rival government entities competing for the strategic planning market, both claiming that their plans have spatial elements that legitimately belong to the upper echelon of spatial plans. More fundamentally, however, NDRC, MOHURD, and MLR have been assigned overlapping functions. While such a fragmented structure may weaken top-down regulatory power, it is this same structure that sets up a system of checks and balances to help ensure that no single ministry becomes too powerful. In the following sections, we turn to the regional strategic planning in the Pearl River Delta (PRD) as a case study.

## Pearl River Delta strategic planning: contents, output and uncertainty

### *Context and momentum*

The PRD covers a land area of 54,744 square-kilometres with a resident population of about 57.15 million in 2013. The PRD, divided into nine municipalities (Figure 3.1), arguably has one of the highest degrees of administrative fragmentation in China.

Three forces reinforce this trend. First, the proliferation of a *laissez-faire* economic culture has long established fragmentation in the delta since a majority of economic power was devolved to cities, towns, and villages. The second force is the decentralised land development in the PRD, because village collectives are permitted to trade rural construction land with developers directly. Third, a dispersed governance structure leads to even greater fragmentation. The PRD has a provincial capital, Guangzhou, and two special economic zones, Shenzhen and Zhuhai. Guangzhou and Shenzhen are two sub-provincial level cities, which are followed by seven prefecture-level cities. Below them are county-level divisions, which include county-level cities, counties, and urban districts. This is followed by more than 230 towns. Jurisdictions at these different levels have idiosyncratic status and enjoy specific power in development and planning.

The high-level of administrative fragmentation leads to tremendous difficulties to implement regional strategies. Since the late 1990s, inter-regional competition

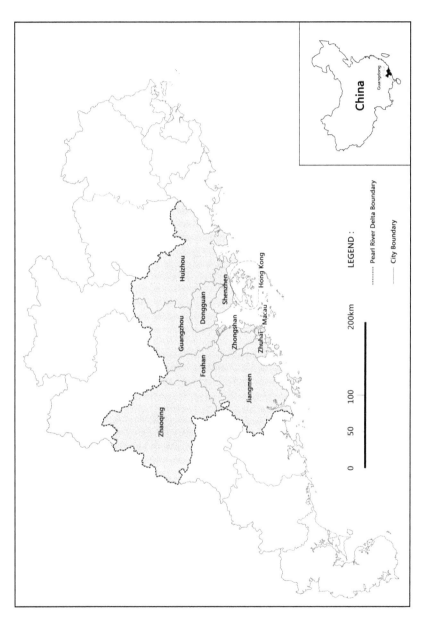

*Figure 3.1* Location of the Pearl River Delta

for central resource and policy support has intensified. The State Council approved the plans of the Tianjin Binhai New Area and Chengdu-Chongqing Region as free trade zones and experimental fields for further economic reform. Together with Pudong in Shanghai, they are counted as three new 'economic engines'. This trend works to the disadvantage of Guangdong Province, which wishes to keep the PRD as an important national economic hub. Regional strategic planning, the provincial government believes, can make the delta more competitive.

### *Who started the process?*

Since the late 1980s, seven regional strategic plans have been produced. They were formulated by the Guangdong government in collaboration with four different ministries: NDRC, MLR, the Ministry of Environmental Protection (MOEP), and MOC. NDRC made two regional (i.e. socioeconomic) plans in 1994 and 1998, in an attempt to coordinate growth in the delta through central state resource allocation. But these plans soon failed because they were overwhelmed by market forces that were beyond state control. MLR made a regional plan in 2005, primarily to address the issue of farmland protection, while MOEP's 2003 plan focused on environmental issues. MOC made two PRD plans in 1990 and 1994, respectively, to guide functional and spatial distribution of delta cities. But both plans failed because they were intended to manipulate spatial development such as city size, which is difficult to control even under a centrally planned system (Wu *et al.*, 2007). They offered no concrete measures that would link the planned spatiality with the resource allocation of economic planning, the enforcement of development control, or any tangible socioeconomic policies. In 2004, Guangdong, in collaboration with MOC, made another regional plan which is commonly called the PRD Urban Cluster Coordinated Development Plan (UCCDP). Providing a general framework for future development, UCCDP marks a significant change in the philosophy of Chinese regional planning. The blueprint concept that focuses on 'what should be done' has shifted to a more regulatory and strategic approach which stresses the policy basis, and further direction of the region.

The UCCDP plan-making process is a bureaucratic bargaining process involving different scales of governments and their respective institutional agents (Figure 3.2). Under the instruction of the Guangdong Party Committee, the provincial government collaborated with MOC to devise the plan. A joint planning team was formed to comprise both local planning institutes and CAUPD (China Academy of Urban Planning and Design) planners under MOC. When drafting the plan, several rounds of intensive bargaining were conducted to collect comments from all PRD cities and relevant government departments. These comments were carefully examined and compromises were negotiated. A draft plan was decided and then assessed by an expert group before being submitted to the provincial government for approval. The final endorsement from Guangdong People's Congress was essential to grant the plan legal status.

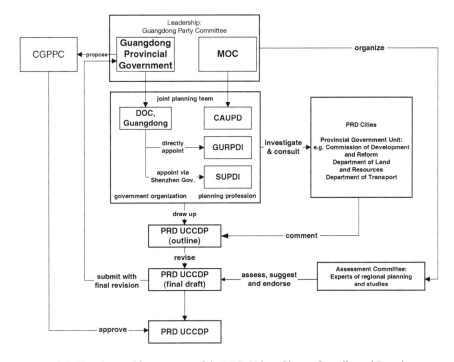

*Figure 3.2* The plan-making process of the PRD Urban Cluster Coordinated Development Planning (UCCDP) in 2004

Notes
CGPPC: Committee of Guangdong Provincial People's Congress
DOC: Department of Construction
CAUPD: China Academy of Urban Planning and Design
GURPDI: Guangdong Urban and Rural Planning and Design Institute
SUPDI: Shenzhen Urban Planning and Design Institute
UCCDP: Urban Cluster Coordinated Development Planning

### What issues does UCCDP cover?

The strategic elaboration and implementation are covered by ten chapters of UCCDP in a total of 106 articles. Table 3.1 summarises the strategies proposed by UCCDP to address the delta's challenges.

*Chapter one* defines the nature of the plan, the boundaries of the PRD and a planning horizon that is set to 2020. *Chapter two* outlines development objectives and targets for population growth and land use. The overarching objective is to promote the structural competitiveness of the PRD and develop the delta into a significant world manufacturing base and a vigorous global metropolitan region. Objectives are further broken down into six sub-components. *Chapter three* defines six spatial development strategies for the PRD's urban systems. A central feature is the enhancement of existing central cities and growth corridors and the

*Table 3.1* Strategies recommended in the PRD Urban Cluster Coordinated Development Plan (UCCDP) in 2004

**Development objectives and scale**
- Leader in global cooperation; National economic engine
- Cultural demonstration region
- Reform experimental region
- Pioneer in regional coordination
- Example in urban-rural integration
- Population: 60 million by 2050
- Land use: Control urban land use
- Eco-regions conservation

**Spatial development strategies**
- Enhance the role of central cities & develop growth spines
- Increase cooperation with inland provinces & waterfront development
- Promote growth in the west & improve development in the east
- Emphasize territorial balanced development
- Introduce eco-regions
- Improve living environment through completing infrastructure provision

**Spatial layout strategies**
- Identify and define functions for development corridors, nodes and spines
- Introduce a hierarchical system of central cities
- Define functional distribution of cities
- Identify and define different kinds of clusters and character areas
- Provide guidance for three major metropolitan areas

**Regional supporting system**

*Environment*
- Identify locations for eco-conservation
- Define conservation policies for each eco-region
- Protect critical habitats
- Invest in green infrastructure networks of open space
- Strictly control development in eco-regions
- Use greenbelts to control urban expansion
- Protect cultivated land
- Protect water resource
- Address water supply, drainage, point pollutants management
- Encourage effective energy use and reduce air pollution
- Encourage coordinative environmental infrastructure planning

*Identity*
- Preserve cultural landscape & heritage regions
- Improve community services
- Transportation
- Improve external connection
- Improve transportation efficiency
- Enhance intercity link
- Emphasize intermodal connections
- Complete transportation network
- Establish regional integration in transportation

**Policy zones and spatial regulation**
- Define nine policy zones
- Establish policy guidance for each policy zone
- Set up four levels of spatial regulations

*Table 3.1*   Strategies recommended in the PRD Urban Cluster Coordinated Development Plan (UCCDP) in 2004 (Continued)

**Spatial coordination planning**

- Conserve land in new projects
- Promote compact land use
- Develop affordable commodity housing and social housing program
- Consider environmental sustainability when locating new development areas
- Continue bio-diversity
- Address rural development
- Provide respective spatial coordination guidance for nine PRD cities

**Major action plan**

- Enhance external connection
- Develop bay areas
- Implement green-line policy to protect eco-conservation areas
- Promote heavy industry
- Materialize regional transportation integration
- Introduce waterfront development
- Address small towns management
- Establish a platform for data-sharing
- Set up a province office for coordinating planning issues
- Enact an ordinance to enforce plan implementation

Source: Adapted from China Academy of Urban Planning and Design (2004)

provision of a balanced portfolio of sites to incubate peripheral developments. These guidelines are to be achieved via the better integration of the delta's population, manufacturing industries and environmental conditions. Article 14 makes it clear that these spatial strategies would lead to 'a spatial structure with a high degree of adaptability and openness to [future uncertainties]'. Essentially, directing spatial expansion towards designated nodes/corridors is a key feature of UCCDP to deal with future growth.

To take this further, six spatial strategies outlined in *Chapter three* are translated into spatial distribution policies which are set forth in *Chapter four*. Spatial and functional distribution of central cities, major development axes, three sub-regions, and industrial clusters are defined in this chapter. A pattern of 'One Spine, Three Corridors, Five Axes' is formed to optimise regional spatial structure and offers linkages with distant regions (Figure 3.3). Advice in *Chapter five* focuses on inserting supporting systems in regional space. This chapter identifies ecological zones, sites for heritage conservation, and other areas having a special character. It also includes policies on integrated service provision and transportation. For example, the chapter provides guidance on how to provide an integrated and balanced transport system, stressing the need to maintain and improve transportation networks and to facilitate intercity transit systems.

To address uncertainties, a region-wide zoning system is designed in *Chapter six*. This system is considered the 'cutting edge' capacity of UCCDP. It sets up a hierarchical order of spatial control by dividing the PRD into nine policy zones which are under four different levels of spatial regulation (see Xu, 2008 for details). The central idea is to amplify the supervisory and regulatory functions

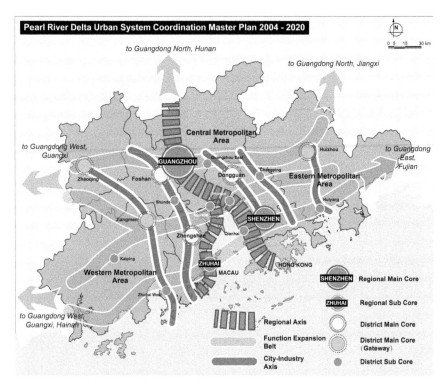

*Figure 3.3* The regional spatial pattern proposed in UCCDP

Source: Adapted from China Academy of Urban Planning and Design (2004)

of the provincial government through upward rescaling of land development and downgrading planning responsibilities of localities. For example, one policy zone is defined as 'regional open spaces and transport corridors'. This zone is subject to the strictest top-down control. Cities and towns are not allowed to make investment decisions for projects located within this zone as they had done before. Nor can they alter defined uses of land. Planning authorisation for similar areas has been rescaled upwards to the provincial government. Such an approach has the potential to divert development away from ecologically sensitive areas. To further reinforce the provincial government's capacity to address uncertainties arising from possible local discretion, *Chapter seven* continues to articulate in more detail the spatial principles to be used by individual cities to ensure that local growth accords with regional strategies.

In a sense, UCCDP is on both long-term visions of the future and pragmatic actions. It envisions a strategic direction and spatial strategies for over 15 years. Yet, it also includes short-term actions to be taken, such as those for tightening up top-down project authorisation. It is made to deal with uncertainties such as declining competitiveness and environmental quality of the PRD. But it is also made for regulatory purpose within the state regime.

### Planning action: implementation provisions

UCCDP is equipped with two key implementation provisions. The first is a phased approach. Within this approach, it specifies eight action plans for the immediate period (2004–2010), and spells out the responsibilities of relevant government units at provincial and municipal levels. To enhance top-down regulation and optimise regional resources, four action plans are proposed, including: (1) developing the waterfront of the Pearl River Estuary as a core for both new sectors and ecological conservation; (2) demarcating an ecological baseline for protecting natural properties; (3) taking advantage of the natural coastline to incubate a 'Sunshine Coast' as a tourist attraction; and (4) building a region-wide information-sharing platform to integrate data of a wide range of government units. Further, and to promote regional competitiveness, three action plans are defined. The first is to highlight the external linkages to distant provinces through expanding and integrating a regional transportation network. The second plan is to chart a path of 'heavy industrialisation' towards a world-class manufacturing base. And the third is to integrate the transport network so as to increase accessibility to major PRD cities. Finally, and to elevate the regional urbanisation level, a 'new towns' plan is proposed, designed to develop small towns in order to further a more compact settlement pattern while constraining urban sprawl.

The second implementation mechanism comprises two institutional reforms. One is to set up the PRD Urban Cluster Planning Administrative Office (PRD-UCPAO) under the Guangdong Construction Commission to undertake UCCDP-related works. The other is to promulgate the PRD Urban Cluster Planning Ordinance in order to legitimise the spatial policies of the plan. This Ordinance was endorsed by the Guangdong People's Congress in 2006 to become the first legal document to guide regional planning in China. The Ordinance requires the establishment of a provincial government-led joint conference of PRD cities that will serve as a platform for political negotiations regarding regional issues. Despite all these actions for plan implementation, there are no provisions with respect to how UCCDP is linked with the provincial budget.

### Capacity to deal with unintended effects

UCCDP provides a strategic and coherent framework for translating the central and provincial initiatives into regional agendas and urban policies. However, such planning efforts have undoubtedly bred tensions, particularly in the hyper-competitive environment that prevails in the delta.

Overall, the UCCDP is probably not a successful plan to deal with unintended effects. To be sure, some of its ideas are being realised. These include key transportation projects and development of local growth poles (e.g. Nansha in Guangzhou and Qianhai in Shenzhen). But most of its proposed ideas have not been taken up. This can be highlighted by three observations. First, rather than integrating regional growth and stitching together fragmented administrative entities, UCCDP has caused discontent among cities because the plan tends to divert large capital projects to a handful of important cities, including the provincial capital. Unsurprisingly, other cities see themselves peripheralised. Zhuhai, for instance, was being unfairly categorised as a sub-centre.

Second, the regional zoning system embedded in UCCDP is a failure as most cities did not follow its requirement to demarcate open space for conservation. Cities view zoning as an instrument to undermine local economic interests. In 2005, even senior officials of Guangdong government commented publicly that 'economic growth' should be prioritised over regional coordination because (at least in that year) the province had lagged behind the national average in key economic indicators (Zou, 2006). All this goes to show that the pressure for maximising growth makes it very difficult to implement hierarchical zoning policies.

## A critical evaluation of plan-making and implementation: the politics of scale perspective

The incapacity of UCCDP is closely related to politics of scale in strategic plan-making and implementation. To borrow the framework of Leitner *et al.* (2008), we concur that two dimensions are essential to understand the evolving nature of the politics of scale. The first relates to *inter-scalar politics*, which refers to the vertical relations that permeate the making and implementation of strategic plans. Previously, central state hegemony was accepted as the normal way of doing business. Nowadays, though unfunded, many state functions are being rearticulated downwards to local governments, establishing a new inter-scalar regime through which planning and investment decisions are negotiated, evaluated, and regulated between different tiers of government.

The second dimension, *intra-scale politics*, relates to the struggles among agents at a particular hierarchical scale. This is a vital factor to consider in strategic planning as it affects contested relations that connect agents horizontally. Since the administrative structure for central and provincial strategic planning is poorly coordinated and notoriously incoherent, it is bound to undermine the role of state strategic planning. Top-tiered disputes tend to be translated into and intersect at lower scales. At central level, inter-ministerial relation is a visible dimension of intra-scale politics. Central ministries are constitutionally of the same administrative level. One ministry cannot rule over another because they both hold the same rank. This feature often contributes to inter-ministerial rivalries in ways that make regional planning practices more complex. At municipal level, intercity relation reflects another dimension of intra-scale politics. It reveals the efforts of local state regimes to engage or disengage from particular regional planning obligations. Both *inter- and intra-scalar politics* are visible in the plan-making process and plan implementation of UCCDP.

*Inter-scalar politics*

The process of devising a vision for Nansha District in Guangzhou is perhaps a case in point to illustrate the inter-scalar politics in making UCCDP. When negotiating with planners from CAUPD, which was commissioned by the Guangdong provincial government to lead the joint planning team, Guangzhou insisted on its vision of developing Nansha into a heavy industrial zone, featuring a US$5 billion joint venture refinery. It was argued that this project was of overriding importance, that it would boost local GDP, etc. Others pointed out that the project would be detrimental to Nansha, an ecologically sensitive wetland in the heart of the PRD. Environmentalists, seeking to protect ecological properties, were outraged. Surrounding cities were uneasy. And investors were concerned about the project's uncertainty. Cognizant of these difficulties, CAUPD planners refused to incorporate the vision into their plan. At this point, the Mayor of Guangzhou, furious about this perceived insubordination, called upon the Party Secretary of Guangdong as well as the Minister of Construction to compel planners to embrace his developmental vision for Nansha. In the end, he was successful. The state at different scales was caught up in the web of tensions that ensued from this: ecological conservation versus economic imperative, the competing claims of different stakeholders, and the discursive struggles over the policy inclusion/exclusion of these claims.

Spatial strategies and associated action plans under UCCDP are meant to amplify top-down regulation and weaken local discretion. Yet, this intention was also vigorously resisted by local governments. Our interview notes recount the remark of a planning official in Jiangmen: 'PRD-UCPAO sent planning inspector to our city, requiring us to demarcate open space for conservation. But we did not respond because the open space proposal would be contrary to our core interest. Also, we were not happy that UCCDP treats Jiangmen as a third-tier city, paying little heed to our demand for a higher status and consequently a higher density of development.' The dissatisfactions of other cities are divergent. Guangzhou, for instance, was not pleased because the plan treats it as a regional centre in parallel with Shenzhen. In a similar vein, Shenzhen was dissatisfied because it had wanted to highlight the role of Hong Kong as the regional central city instead of Guangzhou, but this proposal was not accepted in the final plan. These discontents among cities led to outright refusals in some instances, which in substance exemplify their efforts to avoid being forced to accept top-down planning obligations. The hierarchical reordering of space for ecological conservation was not viewed kindly by mayors keen to advance their own economic interests.

These examples illustrate how the particular planning discourse of UCCDP is infused with inter-scalar politics and power relations in intricate ways. Its formation and implementation is a contested political act with material consequence for the choices made in planning practice. Such process takes place with forces that operate at a variety of interlocked and nested geographical scales of governance.

*Intra-scalar politics*

This is a critical factor in determining the result of plan implementation. It occurs at both central and local levels. At the central level, the inter-ministerial conflicts between MOC and NDRC are one major reason that led to the failure of UCCDP. In official central government documents, NDRC is a functionally holistic agent to coordinate development across the entire spectrum of economic sectors. It is also expected by the central government to draw up regional plans wherever appropriate. MOC (now named MOHURD), on the other hand, is a sectoral unit that has been granted the responsibility to make spatial plans at the city scale. Yet when the People's Congress in Guangdong endorsed the UCCDP, the State Council refused to approve the plan precisely because it was made by MOC rather than NDRC. The legal status of UCCDP was consequently put in question. The plan is supported by neither NDRC nor MLR, which control state resources (i.e. capital and land) for implementation. To overcome this hurdle, Guangdong invited NDRC to draft a new plan, which resulted in the 2008 PRD Reform and Development Outline Plan (PRD-RDOP) that was soon approved by the State Council. At the same time, PRD-RDOP was heavily criticised by the MOC spatial planners because it failed to provide what they considered to be adequate guidelines for developments in space. Still, the PRD-RDOP is the centrally authorised plan. It signals official central support for implementation in the PRD. To some extent, this recognition is more important than actual planning contents, because it links directly with central policy preferences and resource allocation, further marginalising the status of UCCDP. Clearly, the intra-scalar politics between MOC and NDRC has intersected at the local scale, exerting great influence over the development trajectory of the PRD region.

At the local level, intra-scalar politics can be best illustrated by conflicts between cities. When CAUPD planners collected views regarding regional development, all cities considered regional cooperation an important issue yet every city required other cities' collaboration to fulfil its own projects. Another contentious issue is how to adjust urban strategies to achieve a more sustainable regional growth path. Zhuhai, for example, a city in the western part of the PRD with a relatively good living environment, wanted to give up its efforts to attract clean industries because it claimed to be polluted by industrial expansion in neighbouring cities. Zhongshan, a city located to the north of Zhuhai, acknowledged that its air pollution affects Zhuhai but claimed itself to be a victim of water pollution from upstream Jiangmen. No city was willing to give up its local interests for regional benefit. This situation makes it very difficult, if not impossible, to implement UCCDP.

### Recent efforts to redefine inter-scalar politics

Given the failure of UCCDP and the inability of PRD-RDOP to guide spatial development, Guangdong has implemented a project-based approach to facilitate a more coordinated development. Two projects have been used as important policy tools for this purpose.

The first project is the Greenway System – a range of high-quality bicycle and pedestrian pathways linking the major natural properties in the delta, such as riversides, valleys, and ridges (see Xu and Yeh, 2012 for a map and details). The Greenway System is proposed as a means to address the pressing environmental problems. In the establishment of the greenways, the Guangdong provincial government employs a 'centralized planning regulation' that sets out technological standards for managing urban and rural areas, landscape features, natural ecology, and cultural resources. Cities are required to follow provincial guidelines to demarcate greenway boundaries, propose buffer zones for protection, and define parameters of auxiliary facilities. They are also obligated to finance greenway projects from the regular budget. City cadres are finally evaluated based on the performance and results of plan implementation. The Greenway System is a successful practice for integrating spatial planning at the regional scale. It has been used as a policy instrument to force local governments to conserve land for open space and reverse the long-term trend of urban sprawl.

The second regional project is the PRD Intercity Railways Network (PRD-ICRN). The project was initiated by Guangdong and the former Ministry of Railway (MOR) in 2003, with the intention to reduce spatial fragmentation by connecting nine delta cities with a single transit net. PRD-ICRN comprises 16 lines with a total length of 1,478 km, amounting to an investment of US$58 billion. In order to collect project funding, the province initiated a round of the 'scaling-up' process in developing land parcels in the vicinity of railway stations. A provincial document was released to forcibly require that a large percentage of the income from land development around railway stations flow into the provincial government's pocket. Thus, by scaling-up land development rights, the provincial government further extends and reinforces its intrusion in both local and regional governance. It is expected that this proposal will lead to intensive bargaining between the province and cities, as another instance of inter-scalar politics arising from plan implementation.

In 2014, a new initiative is underway to 'scale-up' land development rights and planning responsibilities still further. The Guangdong Party Secretary has proposed to make a 'PRD Whole-Territory Plan' (*quanyu guihua*). At the time of writing this chapter, this spatial plan is still under preparation. However, its purposes are clearly laid out. It aims at underscoring the functional role of the provincial government in regulating land uses to identify new spaces for economic growth, coordinating public utilities and services at a regional scale, and explore overseas markets, especially in Southeast Asia and Africa. The plan will certainly redefine the inter-scalar relations in regional development.

## Critical voices

There are critical voices regarding the right sort of planning and/or governance institutions for mega-city regions. Proponents of 'big government' and 'functional consolidation' argue for municipal annexations and mergers to cope with pressures that incumbent local officials are unable to handle (Leng, 2004). This approach has been adopted in some places (see Zhang and Wu, 2006 for details), including the PRD. For instance, between 2000 and 2014, Guangzhou changed all of its county-level cities into urban districts. In these cases, the abolition of county-level cities is directly linked to spatial reorganisation through top-down political consolidation.

Other scholars suggest a 'neoliberal approach' geared to the 'survival of the fittest'. They tend to encourage political fragmentation for economic efficiency (Zhao, 2002). Strategic interventions should be minimised, they say. This discourse validates 'urban entrepreneurialism' and encourages the practices of place-branding in recent years.

Between these two extremes is the 'governance approach' that argues for 'learning from the West' and stresses the importance of participatory processes for regional governance and planning. But the difficulty with this argument is that it raises the question of a fundamental reform of government in a country where organised civil society can scarcely be said to exist. Although many economists both inside and outside China advocate a 'retreat of the state' in the current transition from a non-market to a market society, the state remains an essential actor in urban and regional development. We argue that the role of the state is critical for China's transitional society at least for now, since it is essential for the creation of market institutions.

## Lessons and conclusion

This chapter has reviewed the changes of regional strategic planning in China. Regional planning was once a political strategy, either serving to consolidate communist power or to achieve central planning targets. By examining the strategic plan in the PRD UCCDP and the more recent initiatives, we have illustrated the emerging functions of regional strategic planning – it serves more than a mechanism for strategically controlling land use and directing development; it also becomes a means for the central and provincial states to reassert their functional importance in the local and regional governance. This alternative agenda generates a politics of scale in the preparation and implementation for these plans.

With such an assessment, we have developed a two-dimensional analytical framework to look at the intra- and inter-scalar politics in regional planning practice. First, as the primacy of the central and provincial states decreases due to the delegation of power to localities, both the central and provincial states are losing responsibilities and power. On the other hand, they also gain new scope and dimensions for intervention. Regional strategic planning is a key political tool for such endeavour, which enables the central and provincial levels to continue to be strategically important sites in regional growth.

To complicate this state of affairs, the socialist principles that guide regional planning state that 'local interests should obey national or regional interests'. Cities may be asked to sacrifice their own interests for fulfilling regional agendas. This can lead to strong local resistance. Our study suggests that localities are not passive agents in inter-scalar politics. They have their own institutional interests to protect and are not merely weaker or diluted segments of the state apparatus. Cities are *de facto* owners of local land resources that are not accessible at other scales (e.g. provinces and the centre). This gives them substantial bargaining power. Also, materialising a plan is a complex undertaking of 'social engineering'. It involves tough issues such as land acquisition and household resettlement, which require local state participation. Thus, local governments, localised capital sources, locally specified land assets, and the geographical attachments of these forces are increasingly becoming active in shaping regional development pattern. Our study shows that cities also use regional strategic planning to better position themselves in the politics of scale.

Intra-scalar politics is also a key factor in determining the outcome of plan implementation. The conflicts between MOC and NDRC and the clashes between different cities have become evident at the regional level. Rather than shifting territorial development trajectories and coordinating regional growth patterns, regional strategic planning may appear to be little more than a cosmetic make-over that hides the intensifying competition within major city regions in China. It is this distinctive combination of 'path-dependent' politics and new regional initiatives that demands further research.

## Acknowledgements

The work described in this chapter was partially supported by a grant from the Research Grants Council of the Hong Kong Special Administrative Region, China (Project No. CUHK455712). A particularly massive thank you is due to John Friedmann for meticulously reading the manuscript and carefully navigating the way through a final round of revisions. We assume full responsibility for any limitations in the final text.

## References

Guangdong People's Government (2012), *On the Improvement of Land Comprehensive Development Mechanism along Intercity Railways*. Guangzhou: unpublished government document, 2012, No. 16.

Guangdong Rural and Urban Planning and Design Institute (2014), *Pearl River Delta Whole Territory Planning*. Unpublished Planning Document.

China Academy of Urban Planning and Design (2004), *Pearl River Delta Urban Cluster Coordinated Development Plan*. Unpublished Government Document.

Hu, X. W. (2006), 'Evaluation and prospect of China's regional planning', *City Planning Review*, 30: 8–12, 50.

Leitner, H., Sheppard, E. and Sziarto, K. M. (2008), 'The spatialities of contentious politics', *Transactions of the Institute of British Geographers*, 33: 157–172.

Leng, Guan (2004), 'City consolidation: A convenient strategy for modernization in middle and western region in China', *Shanghai Economic Research*, 6: 48–53.

Wu, F., Xu, J. and Yeh, A. G. O. (2007), *Urban Development in Post-Reform China: State, Market, and Space*. Abingdon, Oxon: Routledge.

Xu, J. (2008), 'Governing city regions in China: Theoretical discourses and perspectives for regional strategic planning', *Town Planning Review*, 79(2–3): 157–185.

Xu, J. and Yeh, A. G. O. (2012), 'Re-building regulation and re-inventing governance in the Pearl River Delta, China', *Urban Policy and Research*, 30(4): 385–401.

Zhang, J. X. and Wu, F. (2006), 'China's changing economic governance: Administrative annexation and the reorganization of local governments in the Yangtze River Delta', *Regional Studies*, 40: 3–21.

Zhao, Y. J. (2002), 'From urban administration towards urban management', *City Planning Review*, 26: 11, 7–15.

Zou, B. (2006), 'Dilemmas and trends of implementing urban cluster plan in China', *City Planning Review*, 30(1): 47–54.

# 4 Space as an integrating frame

## Manifestations of and prospects for strategic spatial thinking in East Africa's quest for integration

*Lawrence Esho and Robert Obudho*

## Introduction

Arguably, the African Renaissance has commenced. This is evident in East Africa, where constitutional reforms in a number of nations, together with accelerated democratization processes, have ushered in an era of renewed hope for real and meaningful change in the circumstances of the region's almost quarter-billion population. Recent finds in oil and gas and discoveries of significant deposits of high-value minerals have added to this new wave of optimism. Regional economies, long-battered by decades of bad governance and unaccustomed austerity programmes, have recorded impressive growth rates in the last decade. Many credit such growth to a targeted refocusing and aggressive pursuit of the geopolitical interests of individual countries and the region as a collective. This awakening has led to restructuring of key growth sectors, assisted by heavy governmental investment in requisite infrastructures (EAC Secretariat, 2012).

Such impressive growth may also derive from factors external to each individual country's internal processes and dynamics. It is no secret that the region has seen significant capital infusions from global financial markets, with investment by non-traditional trade partners (China, India, Brazil and Russia, among others) surpassing that of Europe and North America. Closer to home, decades-long consultative processes saw the revival of the defunct East African Economic Bloc (EAC), an intergovernmental organization that incorporates five countries in East Africa, namely Kenya, Uganda, Tanzania, Rwanda and Burundi, with ongoing discussions for the inclusion of South Sudan and perhaps Ethiopia. This means that hitherto aggressive pursuits of individual countries are increasingly being subjugated to an overarching territorial growth ideology and development agenda. The expectation is that localized growth trends will coalesce into a regional growth maelstrom, or that accruing regional synergies will infuse a much needed impetus to local development processes.

Whatever the case, none of this growth would have been possible without some form of framing or referencing device, be it a vision, growth strategy or development programme, springboards from which states, as individuals or collectives, launch and pursue their growth aspirations. Indeed, almost all of the region's nations have forged new visions outlining respective futures. These visions are further clarified through a variety of contrivances that are operational-ized at cascading spatial-political scales and dealing with key national sectors. These include development policies, plans, strategies and programmes, and projects (see Table 4.1). Regionally, the quest for integration in East Africa is framed by a Treaty for the Establishment of the East African Community, which has been in force since July 2000. The Treaty is operationalized through targeted medium-term (four-year) development strategies (EAC Secretariat, 2011a). These strategies outline the EAC's approach towards cross-cutting issues and shape programme formulation and the design of projects in key sectors.

It is important to note here that although deliberations related to East Africa's quest for greater territorial integration often lack explicit spatial referencing (in the sense that there is a spatial plan, or any other official document, that communi-cates the spatiality of such intentions at the level of the regional bloc), the adopted strategies and associated programmatic interventions betray an underpinning ideology of space. The critical question to be asked, however, is the extent to which these enlist a strategic planning philosophy? The question may best be answered by critically examining existing development blueprints – be they for individual countries or those of the regional conglomerate of states – especially as they espouse and seek to actuallize the vision of Regional Integration. In the following sections, we shall explore the subject in light of its contextual specificity within the Eastern African Community, and uncover traces of strategic thinking in past and ongoing inter-territorial integration initiatives. The scope of the analysis extends beyond the five EAC partner states to include South Sudan and Ethiopia, countries which, despite not being members, have expressed interest to join the bloc and frequently collaborate on matters of regional importance.

## The genesis and anatomy of EAC integration

### The setting

The East African Community (EAC) is a regional intergovernmental organization established under Article 2 of a renegotiated Treaty for the Establishment of the East African Community (EAC Secretariat, 1999) that entered into force in July 2000. The organization oversees activities of a large regional bloc encompassing five contiguous Republics: Kenya, Uganda, Tanzania, Rwanda and Burundi. The countries share close historical, commercial, industrial, cultural and infrastruc-tural links, among other ties. Membership into the bloc is not closed, as evidenced with the inclusion of Rwanda and Burundi in 2007, and ongoing discussions for the inclusion of South Sudan and perhaps Ethiopia (Hansohm, 2014).

The bloc covers an area of 1,817,700 square kilometres with a combined projected (2012) population of about 141.1 million (EAC Secretariat, 2013). This accounts for about 22% of the continental landmass and 26% of Africa's popula-tion.The possible inclusion of South Sudan and Ethiopia will push this figure to 3.57 million square kilometres and a population of 255 million people, with the two countries accounting for about 0.6 and 1.1 million square kilometres,

*Figure 4.1* The EAC within Africa

Source: Author (2015)

*Table 4.1* East Africa: key facts and figures

| Country | Size (km²) | Population (millions) | Real GDP (billion US$) | HDI |
|---|---|---|---|---|
| Kenya | 580,367 | 38.6 | 17.3 | 0.535 |
| Uganda | 241,038 | 32.9 | 8.8 | 0.484 |
| Tanzania | 947,300 | 44.5 | 11.4 | 0.488 |
| Burundi | 27,830 | 8.7 | 1.2 | 0.389 |
| Rwanda | 26,338 | 10.7 | 4.2 | 0.506 |
| *Ethiopia | 1,104,300 | 74 | 51.9 | 0.435 |
| *South Sudan | 644,329 | 8 | 11.4 | - |
| Total/**Mean | 3,571,502 | 217.4 | 106.2 | **0.473 |

Sources: EAC Publications (www.eac.int)
*Source 2008-National Population Census Council (South Sudan); 2007-Population and Housing Census Commission (Ethiopia)

respectively (see Table 4.1). The combined Gross Domestic Product (GDP) of the five countries is US$74.5 billion and an average GDP per capita of $558 (2010 figures).This accounts for about 16% of the combined continental GDP in 2009 prices (African Development Bank, 2011). The sheer vastness of this aggregation of contiguous territories, the enormity of its population, and accruing economies of scale not only auspicates a renewed and reinvigorated East African Community, but is of great strategic import to the wider continental setting.

### The history

The quest for regional integration in Africa is not new and predates the transition to independence by the region's states in the 1960s. It is possible to trace the development of such pursuits through three phases of the continent's decade-long existence in the modern era. The first phase stretches from the late nineteenth century to the postwar period (1980s–1950s), where convergence of economic and geopolitical interests of a number of European powers ensued in the partition of the continent into regional blocs administered by respective colonial powers (Mackenzie, 1983; Pakenham, 1992; Khapoya, 1998). These blocs were to play an important strategic role in the rapidly globalizing economy (Mockler, 1984; Förster *et al.*, 1989; Henderson, 1993; Oliver and Atmore, 2005).

The declaration of independence by many African territories brought an abrupt end to European imperialism. Independence motivated a powerful Pan-Africanist sentiment that promoted inter-territorial cooperation as an ideology and strategy to evolve a continental identity and coherence (Fouroutan, 1993), and boost regional integration and economic development (Hartzenberg, 2011). The Pan-Africanist debate, though largely political, was also underpinned by the need by new African administrations to effectively exploit the continent's immense wealth and economic potential for the overall benefit of its peoples. Hitherto, continental fragmentation created small domestic markets that negated scale economies in the production and distribution of goods and services (Kamanga, 2013). The debate culminated in the proliferation of separate regional integration arrangements or Regional Economic Communities (RECs) across the continent (see Figure 4.2 and Table 4.2).

In East Africa, a Treaty for Cooperation was signed in 1967, paving the way for the establishment of the East African Community in 1967 (EAC 1). The EAC was to serve as a joint organization to re-orient pre-independence structures and administer matters of common interest within the region. In particular, it focused on harmonizing economic policies of member states, common institutions and a common market (Mohiddin, 2005). It equally emphasized strengthening and regulating the industrial, commercial and other relations of the member states in a way that promotes accelerated harmonious and balanced development and equitable distribution of benefits. Unlike the more better-known federations COMESA, SADC and ECOWAS, EAC has enshrined political union in its founding treaty.

These initial REC arrangements, for the most part, have recorded little progress towards set goals (Lyakurwa *et al.*, 1997; Geda and Kibret, 2002). Although

*Figure 4.2* Map of regional blocs in Africa

Source: Adaptation from www.targetmap.com

countries regularly engage under the auspices of the African Union, the absence of a strong and sustained political commitment precludes any meaningful achievements on the economic front (Geda and Kibret, 2002). This means that the continent, as a global bloc, is yet to capitalize on the sizeable investment opportunity presented by its near 1 billion people and a GDP of approximately US$1.7 trillion. Intra-regional trade accounts for a meagre 10%, compared to almost 40% in North America and 60% in Western Europe. Economic output at the country-level is less impressive, with the majority of countries suffering from a lack of economic diversification and stagnation of existing sectors (Lyakurwa *et al.*, 1997).

East Africa had its share of false starts, with the colonial EAC treaty becoming obsolete with the onset of independence. On its part, the 1967 (EAC II) collapsing in 1977, in part due to ideological differences, mistrust, lack of political will, and structural problems that impinged upon the management of common services (EAC Secretariat, 1999; Kamala, 2006). Notwithstanding the failure of EAC II, the leaders of Eastern Africa have kept alive the vision for a United East Africa, and have taken decisive steps towards attaining it. Renewed efforts saw the

*Table 4.2* Structure of African regional groupings

| 1960s | 1980s | 1990s |
|---|---|---|
| **West Africa** | | |
| | ECOWAS 1975 Economic Community of West African States | 1993 revised ECOWAS Treaty |
| UDEAO 1966 Customs Union of West African States | CEAO 1973 Economic Community of West Africa; UMOA West African Monetary Union | WAEMU 1994 West African Economic and Monetary Union |
| **Central Africa** | | |
| | ECCAS (CEEAC) 1983 Economic Community of Central African States | |
| UDEAC 1964 Economic and Customs Union of Central Africa; BEAC 1961 Bank of the Central African States | | CEMAC 1994 Economic and Monetary Union of Central Africa |
| **Southern and Eastern Africa** | | |
| | PTA 1981 Preferential Trade Area | COMESA 1993 Common Market for Eastern and Southern Africa; CBI 1993 Cross Border Initiative |
| SACU (originally 1889, 1969) Southern African Customs Union; CMA Common Monetary Area | | |
| | SADCC 1980 Southern African Development Coordination Conference | SADC 1992 Southern African Development Community |
| East African Community (EAC I) 1967 | | EAC 1999 East African Community II |
| | IGADD 1986 Intergovernmental Authority on Drought and Development | IGAD 1996 Intergovernmental Authority on Development |

Source: Matthews (2003)

establishment of the East African Cooperation in 1999 (EAC III). Membership was initially restricted to Uganda, Kenya and Tanzania. Two new members, Rwanda and Burundi, joined the Community in 2007. In spite of not being members, South Sudan and Ethiopia have actively participated in the region's activities.

Owing to the lull that followed the EAC II collapse, EAC III followed a more cautious path and strategic approach towards achieving its goals, choosing a phased operationalization of the new Treaty. Consequently, the period 1997–2000 focused on confidence-building initiatives towards the EAC's re-launch.

The period 2001–2005 mainly focused on the establishment of the EAC Customs Union and laying the groundwork for the Common Market. The period 2006–2010 prioritized the establishment of the EAC Common Market, and the period 2011–2016 mainly focuses on the establishment of the EAC Monetary Union and laying the foundation for the attainment of a Political Federation. Throughout the four periods, cross-cutting projects and programmes of mutual benefit were launched and implemented in sectors such as legal and judicial, infrastructure, energy, social development and institutional development (EAC Secretariat, 2011a).

Since the Community's re-establishment in 1999, EAC III has made significant progress in all of these areas. It succeeded in establishing the organs of the Community, as stated in the EAC Treaty, and established a Customs Union in 2005 (Kamala, 2006). The cooperation is now at the stage of a Common Market, having successfully negotiated and concluded two successive Protocols. The harmonization of monetary and fiscal policies is giving impetus to efforts to create a Monetary Union. And although the ultimate goal of a Political Federation of the East African States is beyond the horizon, the EAC's three main organs – the Secretariat, the Legislative Assembly (EALA) and the Court of Justice (EACJ) – are already established and hosted in the organization's headquarters in Arusha, Tanzania. Respective national parliaments have domesticated the EAC Treaty by enacting requisite statutes, thus laying a sound legal basis for the implementation and enforcement of EAC law. Strong political will among the leadership of the bloc has seen the intergovernmental initiative survive its eleventh year. Expansion in its membership to include Burundi and Rwanda, and expressed interests by South Sudan and Ethiopia, attests to confidence in the EAC enterprise on the part of neighbouring states (Kamanga, 2013).

In addition to consolidating long-standing political, economic, social and cultural ties, the EAC III has also made progress towards its other stated goals. The bloc is jointly implementing several regional initiatives, including the sustainable development of Lake Victoria Basin – this, in line with the goal to promote sustainable utilization of the natural resource base in the region (EAC Secretariat, 2006). Significant investments have been directed towards the improvement of a number of framing structures and enabling sectors. These include large-scale investments in inter-regional infrastructure, particularly transport and communications systems, as laid out in the East Africa Infrastructure Master Plan (EAC Secretariat, 2007) and the East Africa Power Master Plan (EAC Secretariat, 2011b). Other initiatives include the Lake Victoria Transport Project, Joint Concessioning of Railroads, East Africa Submarine System, and joint tourism marketing and standardization of hotels (African Development Bank, 2011). Under the auspices of the Intergovernmental Authority on Development (IGAD), the EAC has launched several initiatives to improve peace and stability in the region (notably in Somalia and Sudan) with a view to increasing economic development prospects (Healy, 2009).

In complete contrast with the previous experience, the last decade has seen greater participation of the private sector in the achievement of EAC's economic objectives, with greater mobility of private capital across economic sectors of partner states, access to an expanding market, and increased competition between suppliers (Karega, 2009). To date, the integration remains an important avenue of capital formation and collective self-reliance for a significant number of East Africans (Jonyo and Misaro, 2013). And although intra-Africa trade has remained consistently low compared with its intercontinental trade (United Nations Economic Commission for Africa, 2010), intra-REC exports have been growing in value across most RECs in recent years (Hartzenberg, 2011) (see Table 4.3). It is instructive that East Africa has demonstrated strong growth performance over the decade and a half since the launching of EAC III, with regional real GDP growth averaging 6.6% annually (African Development Bank, 2011). Internally, key microeconomic indications point to the fact that EAC states are on the path to poverty reduction.

Notwithstanding its catalogue of achievements, the EAC's third attempt at integration is beset by contextual challenges and structural deficiencies that leave it with a lot of ground to cover. Insecurity in and around EAC countries and poor linkage between development strategies and democratization continue to dampen the region's attractiveness to foreign direct investment. Low endowments of pertinent infrastructure systems continues to stiffle intra-regional trade. This, together with weak national currencies and financial systems, and over-reliance on donor funding, inhibit competitiveness at the global level. The organization's secretariat has limited institutional capacity to oversee the harmonization of regional and national policies, laws and regulations, prioritization of community initiatives above those of the individual countries, and instigation of the necessary reforms. Likewise, marked differences in the economies of partner states, and skewed distribution of skilled manpower and technology, account for uneven levels of enterprise competitiveness and productivity in some countries, and further dampen policy-level appetite for greater regional integration in the short term (Kamanga, 2013).

In spite of these challenges, the political backing for the EAC is very strong and we expect progress to continue, bringing with it an increasing number of benefits to organizations established within the EAC.

*Table 4.3* Intra-REC exports, 2000-2009 (US$ millions)

| RECs | 2000 | 2001 | 2002 | 2003 | 2004 | 2005 | 2006 | 2007 | 2008 | 2009 | *Average 2000-09* |
|---|---|---|---|---|---|---|---|---|---|---|---|
| **COMESA** | 1,443 | 1,626 | 1,739 | 2,004 | 2,293 | 2,695 | 2,918 | 4,021 | 6,676 | 6,114 | 3,153 |
| **EAC** | 689 | 753 | 804 | 879 | 1,006 | 1,075 | 1,062 | 1,385 | 1,797 | 1,572 | 1,102 |
| **ECCAS** | 182 | 193 | 186 | 183 | 219 | 255 | 313 | 385 | 449 | 378 | 274 |
| **ECOWAS** | 2,715 | 2,242 | 3,136 | 3,037 | 4,366 | 5,498 | 5,902 | 6,717 | 9,355 | 7,312 | 5,028 |
| **SADC** | 4,461 | 4,048 | 4,597 | 5,650 | 6,636 | 7,770 | 8,598 | 11,874 | 15,896 | 11,599 | 8,113 |

Source: Hartzenberg (2011), quoting IMF Direction of Trade Statistics, February 2011

# The strategic import of the EAC's quest for integration

## *The lens: a spatial frame, a strategic philosophy*

In our exploration, we set out to respond to two related questions, namely: (1) the extent to which East Africa's quest for greater territorial integration, which is explicitly a strategy to position itself within continental and global economies, is underpinned by an overarching ideology of space?; and (2) the extent to which it enlists a strategic planning philosophy? The first question stems from an appreciation of the central *role of space* as a coherent basis for integrating all socioeconomic courses of action of governments and, by extension, attendant developmental processes. According to Healey (2004), the term 'space' or 'spatial' brings into focus the 'where' of things, whether static or dynamic; the interrelationships between different activities and networks in an area; and significant intersections and nodes that are physically co-located in an area. Consequently, the interrogation as to the spatial nature of regional integration initiatives would, of necessity, seek to address itself, primarily, to the spatial relationships engendered by the federation of territories that constitute the EAC. It asks how the underpinning framework, whether explicitly or implicitly spatial, has served as a basis for integrating different agendas (economic, environmental, cultural and social), and the extent to which it facilitates the efficient realization of the bloc's policy aspirations and programmatic interventions.

In their debate about the strategic nature of strategic plans, Albrechts and Balducci (2013) explore critical factors that might explain the strategic character of plans. Subsequently, they highlight four relevant dimensions that may constitute the building blocks of a strategic planning endeavour. In our interpretation, such may include: (1) the limited-in-scope and almost always action-project-oriented content of plans; (2) the continuously evolving and never-quite-settled form of the planning process; (3) its relational flair and conjunctive prosecution of sought-after process outputs; and (4) the ahierarchical and inherently indeterminate nature of framing institutional structures.

In the following sections, we shall critically revisit the EAC's key building blocks and deploy both Healey's, and Albrechts and Balducci's lenses with a view to respond to the queries highlighted above. We shall apply these at the territorial scale of the supra-region, where we begin by revisiting the contextual rationale for inter-territorial cooperation and integration efforts. Here, we limit ourselves to the matter of the spatiality of East African integration pursuits. Next, and in a bid to uncover traces of strategic thinking in past and present EAC activities, we consider the primary focuses that serve as overarching framing references for EAC integration efforts. Here, we also map out the scope of the organization's activities as presently constituted, both in terms of territorial coverage and issues that constitute the objects of integration. Subsequently, we consider what instruments the Community has deployed to firm up and secure its vision and development agenda. Likewise, we evaluate the EAC's key processes, and particularly consider the manner in which they have addressed the question of citizen participation and treated uncertainties and bottlenecks that often accompany quest for integration. Finally, we reflect on the various process outputs, be they strategies, projects or plans, which will be considered with a view to ascertain the possibilities they offer relative to the Community's vision and development agenda. Most importantly, we evaluate the extent to which these have enlisted strategic spatial planning as a framing ideology. The exploration may inform further deliberations on what ought to be constitutive elements of a durable regional integration strategy.

### The strategy: space as an integrating frame

In this first section, we traced the evolution of the EAC through three distinct periods straddling roughly over a century. It is important to note that statehood, or that bounded territorial entity under jurisdiction of a sovereign state, is a phenomenon that only came into existence in Africa a little more than a century ago, when the entire continent fell prey to the exploits of European imperial powers. Hitherto, the region that we now know as East Africa constituted a patchwork of disparate spatial geographies that lent themselves to the then occupational pursuits of mostly pastoral native tribal groupings. And while it is possible that one group or the other, by virtue of an arrogated inhabitancy, might have laid claim to a specific swathe of territory, its jurisdiction over the area was never the subject and/or object of rigid delimitation in the fashion of present-day country boundaries. Besides, existing delimitations were often blurred by intersecting migratory paths and overlapping dispersal domains, and reciprocal engagements across conterminous cultural landscapes.

Such was the backdrop to European conquest, annexation and colonization of Africa. This was, however, to change following the global strategic interests of imperial powers. Initially, the aspiration to control maritime trade would negate the initial tendency towards the greater parcellation of acquired territories (Mackenzie, 1983; Pakenham, 1992). The British, for instance, desired to control the flow of traffic through the Suez Canal. Its wishes were granted following the German handing over of Tanganyika to the British immediately after the First World War. Subsequently, the British now controlled territory stretching from Egypt in the North to South Africa. In colonial East Africa, it was the British government that provided strategic impulses for integration. Economic factors motivated regional integration initiatives between the then Kenya Colony, the Uganda Protectorate and the Tanganyika Territory. Initially, this saw the three colonial enclaves enter common agreements to regulate customs, currency, income tax, and common services.

Motivations were slightly different during the post-independence era, where the establishment of Regional Economic Communities (RECs) across the continent had the primary strategic objective of positioning such entities to take advantage of existing economies of agglomeration. In her exploration of the subject in relation to the EU, Briggid (1992) reinforced the idea that small economies would find it difficult to compete with large economies and cooperation would enhance their bargaining power. The same pertains to Africa's case. By building a strong and sustainable continental economy, it was intimated that African nations might subsequently be able to collectively insulate themselves against the potential marginalizing impacts of globalization (World Bank, 2000; Nyin'guro, 2005). Within the EAC, the aspiration to reclaim the once boundless, shared territory had a number of other critical imperatives. Of the five existing and two aspiring East African members, only Kenya and Tanzania have direct access to global markets through maritime channels that straddle the adjoining Indian Ocean. The other countries, Uganda, Rwanda, Burundi, South Sudan and Ethiopia, are land-locked. Their membership in the EAC would subsequently accord them the same opportunity to access large global markets.

The EAC, both then and as presently constituted, has the added internally-focused and strategic objective to promote, through enhanced industrial, commercial and other relations of the member states, a harmonious and balanced development and equitable distribution of benefits across regional territory (EAC Secretariat, 1999). The need to reduce regional growth disparities by influencing the geographical structure of the economic activity across the territories of the East African states is a goal that has subsisted since the formative years of the regional integration effort. Such efforts, however, are hampered by an acute lack of capital for infrastructure development and, as a result, the economic growth dynamic tends to gravitate towards already developed economic centres. Notwithstanding, the aspiration betrays an implicit desire to predicate EAC's development agenda on a spatial structuring strategy.

The presence of an overarching spatial reference becomes even more apparent in the EAC III's adopted fusion strategy and associated programmatic pursuits. The community has already launched a number of grandiose projects aimed at enhancing connection and facilitating gainful interaction between member states. This includes the construction of a standard gauge railway (SGR) connecting Kenya, Uganda and Rwanda, as well as a similar initiative across the expansive territory of Tanzania. The connection between Kenya, South Sudan and Ethiopia is to be significantly enhanced upon conclusion of ongoing road projects and oil pipeline (see Figure 4.3).

Finally, it is necessary to view the seemingly unyielding commitment by leaders of the five countries to progressively realize a stated goal of political unification as evidence that these countries have made significant progress in overcoming traditional suspicions that led to the failure of past integration attempts. This, in spite of substantial disparities persisting in terms of countries' access to the benefits of integration. The fact that non-state actors, particularly industry players, are increasingly diffusing their activities and services across Regional territory, taking advantage of the accruing economies of agglomeration, is testament to their faith in the East African integration enterprise. In turn, this may auspicate the emergence of a broad-based African spatial consciousness.

### *The focus: a limited set of convergent aims*

It may be inaccurate to credit the EAC's earlier 'false starts' to inherent unsoundness or contextual impertinence of the operative ideology of integration. Rather,

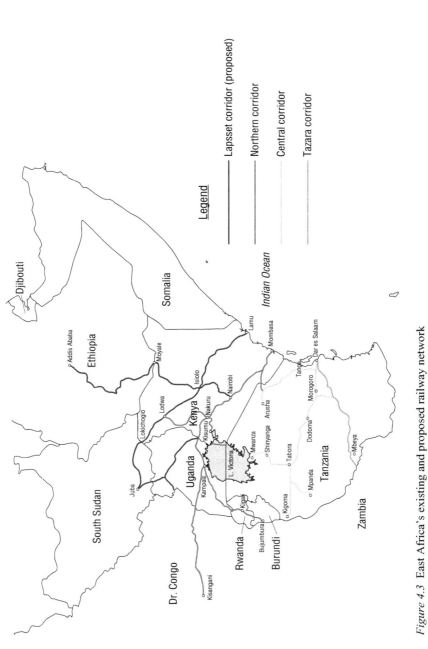

*Figure 4.3* East Africa's existing and proposed railway network

Source: Adaptation from the EAC Railways Master Plan (CPCS Transcom, 2009)

one may say that both the first and second inter-territorial engagements were aborted courtesy of factors external to, and far beyond the control of, any of the three East African states. It is, for instance, difficult to see how cooperative arrangements, appropriately structured and well-intentioned as they may have been, could have survived in an environment where the legitimacy of the colonial authority that propelled it was in contestation. Neither can it be fathomed that it would be possible to sustain the same in a post-colonial context pervaded by a global ideological split between capitalism and socialism, diametric systems which EAC states, particularly Kenya and Tanzania, espoused and aligned them-selves to, respectively. Likewise, co-existence of nascent democracies of Kenya and Tanzania with a fledgling authoritarian regime in neighbouring Uganda would prove to be the Achilles' heel that eventually ground down the EAC II after a decade-long post-independence existence.

Notwithstanding these birthing difficulties, it is evident that the East Africa's project of integration recorded significant successes to compel its repeated revival by successive regimes. In turn, such success may derive in the very specific manner in which the Community's agenda is framed. Albrechts and Balducci (2013) point to the selective scope of the content of Strategic Planning. They argue that whereas Strategic Planning values the potential advantages of working with the multiple – and often conflicting – viewpoints and behaviour of actors, it looks for convergence (compromises, trading zones, collective spatial agreements). Therefore, despite the fact that the entire framework and associated processes are inevitably inspired by an overarching referencing device, such as a broad, long-term vision, what constitutes the core of the planning activity is a limited set of objectives that are within the purview of attainment in the short term.

It is instructive that throughout its history, the EAC has repeatedly restricted its pursuits to a handful of objectives, a limited set of focuses to which the Community's efforts are directed. EAC I initially restricted inter-territorial activi-ties to framing overseas revenue functions of the British Crown, and later expanded it to include line infrastructures and services (post and telecommunica-tions). EAC II concentrated on implementing three pillars of integration, namely: establishing a Customs Union, a Common Market, and laying the foundation for establishing a Monetary Union and a Political Federation. The EAC III main-tained the same agenda, with an added emphasis on harmonization of economic policies and the strengthening and regulation of industrial, commercial and other relations of the member states (EAC Secretariat, 2006). The EAC's present agenda traverses nine key areas of mutual interest, including: (1) Trade, invest-ment and industrial development; (2) Monetary and fiscal affairs; (3) Infrastructure and services; (4) Human resources, science and technology; (5) Agriculture and food security; (6) Environment and natural resources management; (7) Tourism and wildlife management; (8) Health, social and cultural activities; and (9) Cooperation in political matters, including defence, security, foreign affairs, legal and judicial affairs. As overarching focuses, these are considered to be regional growth drivers, areas whereby further cooperation and integration is thought to assist the Community's pursuit of its stated strategic objective of attaining a harmonious and balanced development, and equitable distribution of benefits across and between member states, and eventual vision of forging *a prosperous, competitive, secure and politically united East Africa* (EAC Secretariat, 1999).

In their execution, the EAC further pursues a selective implementation policy and strategy. As was the case in its infancy, the Community's drive to attain its goals is presently suppressed by an acute shortage of infrastructural endowments to facilitate effective linkages between and across the territories of member states and support production, manufacturing, cross-border trade and commerce. It is therefore no surprise that respective infrastructures form the focal point for inter-governmental investment in the short and medium term. Again, current activity is restricted to a limited set of flagship infrastructural investments, such as reha-bilitating dilapidated road and rail arteries, and terminal structures that serve to anchor and connect the region to regional and global markets. Other areas include legislative and institutional reforms, to allow for greater participation and the contribution of private actors in the Community's pursuits. This eschewal of the all-encompassing, and the commitment to a select catalogue of unifying goals and actions, we argue, is a critical explanatory feature for the EAC's past and present success, and attests to the strategic character of the integration effort.

### *The process: pitfalls of a politically driven process*

It is often said that the lack of a meaningful participation by the private sector and general public and incorporation of the civil society were major contributory factors for the collapse of EAC II (EAC Secretariat, 1999). According to Albrechts and Balducci (2013), Strategic Planning starts not with an abstract idea of planning and governance, but rather with the concrete activities of citizens, politicians and planners. Based on this criterion, it may be said that none of the three phases of EA integration (I, II and III) created an enabling environment for meaningful broad-based participation of citizens. It is clear that the various activities of the EAC ride on, and thrive upon, governmental bureaucracies that still rely on top-down decision processes and comprehensive planning practices. This is understandable given the legacy of colonial spatial planning values, prin-ciples and practices that sought to create and institute hierarchical institutional structures and centralize decision-making in the hands of the top leadership. EAC I was largely dependent on the activities of the Council of Governors for traction, while EAC II and III thrived on the goodwill and discretion of the Community's leadership at the top. Today, the supreme organ of the Community, known as the Summit of Heads of State, equally exercises immense power over all decision-making in the EAC.

Albrechts and Balducci highlight the presence of strong political will as being important in setting the process in motion, keeping it going, and in guaranteeing the implementation of chosen strategies. However, the experience of the EAC II, which collapsed in 1977, demonstrates what can happen with an overly political process. The lack of convergence of ideological views and leadership styles of the Community's leadership at the time effectively stalled a promising integration effort. Perhaps in cognizance of such pitfalls, Article 7.1a of the EAC III Treaty explicitly specifies the peoples of East Africa as the ultimate beneficiaries of integration. Unlike EAC I and EAC II, EAC III is designed as a pro-people and market-driven process. The Treaty that established EAC III embraces the principle of subsidiarity, with an emphasis on multi-level participation and the involvement of a wide range of stakeholders in the process of integration. The principle is to be actualized through a number of institutionalized decision-making frameworks. Article 9 of the EAC Treaty (2002) establishes the organs of the EAC. The main organs of the EAC are: (1) the Summit of Heads of State; (2) the Council of Ministers; (3) the Coordination Committee; (4) the Sectoral Committee; (5) the Secretariat; (6) the East African Court of Justice; and (7) the East African Legislative Assembly. The first five share executive powers, while the latter two execute the Community's judicial and legislative functions, respectively (Kamala, 2006).

By all standards, the above framework is still top-heavy. It is implied that the East African Legislative Assembly (EALA) should allow for a broad-based participation of the citizens of member states through their elected representatives. Currently, the Assembly has 45 elected members, with each partner state represented by nine members. There are another seven ex-officio members, totalling a membership of 52 (East African Legislative Assembly, 2014). Article 50(1) of the EAC Treaty provides for electing members through national parliaments of each partner state (Nyin'guro, 2005). Political parties have a significant say in electing members. This is unlike in the European Union, where the people directly participate in electing representatives of the EU parliament through political parties. Consequently, the so-called representational process is much the subject of the whims of the top-down decision-making frameworks. A case in point is the situation in Kenya, where the Head of State wanted to change the rules, through the national parliament, in order to strengthen his hand in the process of identifying Kenyan MPs to the Assembly (Jonyo and Misaro, 2013).

In view of the foregoing, it is apparent that the EAC is yet to institutionalize *broad-based, open* and *inclusive planning processes* that enlists the active, effective and meaningful participation of diverse stakeholder interests in vision-building, strategy, and programme formulation and implementation processes. It is doubtful that processes that fail to expand the space for private sector organizations, non-governmental organizations (NGOs), trade unions, and Community-based organizations to more directly influence decision-making within the bloc will be successful in achieving desired outcomes. In particular, the EAC must, of necessity, enhance cooperation with business organizations towards the co-production of organizational aspirations and agendas. There are, however, signs that this situation is beginning to change as, more recently, private sector groupings such as the East African Business Council (EABC) have been accorded observer status in the Community, thereby allowing them to advocate for a conducive environment for private sector development (Mwangi, 2001). The initiative is already paying off as some of the Community's biggest industry players are increasingly expanding their businesses ventures beyond their traditional host countries. This not only attests to their growing confidence in the prospects of greater integration within the EAC, but may also indicate their willingness to partner in the process of achieving the organization's goals.

There is also evidence that a wide range of stakeholders and actors representing governmental institutions and agencies, civil society organizations and the private sector in the partner states and development partners are involved in a number of cross-border initiatives of mutual interest. A case in point is the formulation of a shared vision and strategy framework for the management and development of Lake Victoria Basin. The process was completed in 2003 (EAC Secretariat, 2007). Likewise, a number of professional, civil society, local government associations and youth organizations have formed alliances across borders and meet regularly. Indigenously owned SMEs, particularly in the transport sector, have either resumed or initiated business in East Africa.

Still, the possibility for greater involvement of citizens' grassroots organizations (especially weak groups) in the EAC integration processes is crucial to attaining some degree of empowerment, ownership and acceptance of such processes, thereby giving them the kind of broad-based legitimacy that is evident in the European Union integration processes. This is particularly significant now that each of the EAC countries has instituted reforms that seek to replace traditional centralized governance structures with devolved and semi-autonomous territorial units. It is hard to see how hierarchical structures can continue to persist at the supra-regional level of the EAC, while individual countries are moving towards adopting ahierarchical governance and development coordination structures.

### The instruments: a process sustained by a common vision

According to Mintzberg (1994), a strategic planning process is launched with three types of objective in mind: 'thinking about the future', 'integrating decision-making' and 'improving coordination mechanisms'. In a sense, the East African integration process meets each of these criteria. Under the EAC Treaty, the partner states forged a Long-Term Strategic Vision that conveys their aspiration to have a prosperous, competitive, secure and politically united East Africa. This vision derives from, and is propelled by, what Albrechts and Balducci (2013) refer to as 'a shared stock of values, knowledge, information, sensitivities and mutual understanding'. Particularly, it responds to the very unique circumstance of the EAC, both as a historical-cultural and emergent geographical-political-economic entity that aspires to positively position itself as a dominant player at the global stage, and is determined to profit from benefits accruing.

The global vision of the EAC, which is more of a statement than a detailed catalogue of aspirations, serves as an overarching reference to frame developmental agendas at the supra-national scale. Subsequently, it is stepped down in more elaborate visions formulated at the localized level of member states, for instance: the *Kenya Vision 2030* (Government of Kenya, 2008), the *Uganda Vision 2040* (Government of Uganda, 2007), the *Tanzania Development Vision 2020*

(Government of Tanzania, 1999), the *Rwanda Vision 2040* (Government of Rwanda, 2000) and the *Burundi Vision 2023* (Government of Burundi, 2011). Even aspiring candidates, Sudan and Ethiopia, have their respective *South Sudan Vision 2040* (Government of South Sudan, 2010) and *Ethiopia Vision 2025* (Government of Ethiopia, 2011) (see Table 4.4). These localized Visions, even while responding to specific issues, needs and challenges that are unique to each country, nevertheless reflect a significant degree of convergence in interpreting the collective aspirations of the EAC as an inter-territorial entity. The Visions are further concretized through strategy frameworks that are formulated both at the level of the EAC and within member states. Consequently, these frameworks act as tools for planning. They lay the groundwork for commencement of actual implementation processes, which in turn deploy a variety of instruments that include policies, detailed actionable plans, laws and regulations.

Since its inception in 1999, the EAC has formulated a total of four Development Strategies to assist in implementing its Vision. It has also formulated a number of plans, largely sectoral in scope, proffering policies, strategies and programmes to address a variety of thematic sectors, such as industry, commerce, trade, roads and infrastructure, transport and communications, environment and natural

*Table 4.4* EAC partner states' strategic visions

| Partner State | Time Frame | Strategic Vision | Priority Areas |
|---|---|---|---|
| Kenya | Vision 2030 | Globally competitive and prosperous Kenya with a high quality of life. | To achieve sectoral objectives, including meeting regional and global commitments. |
| Uganda | Vision 2040 | Transform Ugandan society from peasant to a modern prosperous country. | Prominence being given to a knowledge-based economy. |
| Tanzania | Vision 2020 | High quality of life anchored on peace, stability, unity, and good governance, rule of law, resilient economy and competitiveness. | Inculcate hard work, investment and savings culture, a knowledge-based economy, infrastructure development and private sector development. |
| Rwanda | Vision 2040 | Become a middle income country by 2020. | Reconstruction, HR development and integration to regional and global economy. |
| Burundi | Vision 2023 | Sustainable peace and stability and achievement of global development commitments in line with MDGS. | Poverty reduction, reconstruction and institutional development. |
| EAC | Treaty | Attain a prosperous, competitive, secure and politically united East Africa. | To widen and deepen economic, political, social and cultural integration at regional and global levels. |

Source: EAC Secretariat (2011a)

resources, tourism, regional safety and security, gender affairs, and poverty reduction, among others. Each of these countries has prepared National Development Plans to deal with macro-economic issues at the national level. There is, however, a need to ensure that such national policies, strategies and plans are subjected to regional standards, a requirement upon which compliance is currently not evident in the EAC.

Prior to the EAC III, Spatial Plans were conspicuously lacking, both at the national level of the EAC partner states and at the supra-national level of the bloc. This is, however, set to change as both Kenya and Uganda are in the process of finalizing their National Spatial Plans (Kenya, Ministry of Lands, 2010; Government of Uganda, 2007). Each of the countries has a form of policy that communicates its spatial development perspective, a legislative framework, instruments and institutional structures to realize it (see Table 4.5). The absence of an overarching spatial referencing device at the supranational level does not, however, suggest that the EAC is completely oblivious of the role of territorial spaces and places in assisting the organization's goals. As we saw earlier, the EAC leadership is very much awake to the challenges and inhibitions of unbalanced development and growth, and indeed production processes are afflicted by the skewed distribution of infrastructure and across the Region. Consequently, a number of initiatives entailing the preparation of sector plans and strategies, most of which exhibit an explicitly spatial flair, have been launched with a view to remedy the situation. They include: the East Africa Railways Master Plan (CPCS Transcom, 2009), the East African Power Supply Master Plan (EAC Secretariat, 2011b), and the Strategic Action Plan for the Lake Victoria Basin (EAC Secretariat, 2007). There is, however, a need to further anchor the EAC's development agenda through a variety of sub-territorial plans at cascading spatial scales. Critical areas include cross-country resource regions (river basins, arid and semi-arid lands, fosil fuel basins, wildlife habitats, etc.) and political-administrative jurisdictions such as Counties, Metropolitan, City and Municipal areas. The challenge, however, will be on how to integrate plans formulated at the supranational level, and which are informed by a strategic planning philosophy, and those at the national and sub-regional levels that still rely on top-down decision-making processes and comprehensive planning practices.

The EAC's various plans are further operationalized through legislative, regulatory and enforcement frameworks that are made possible by two organs of the EAC, the East African Legislative Assembly (EALA) and the East African Court of Justice (EACJ). The EALA is mandated to exercise both legislative and oversight functions on all matters within the purview of the EAC and has, to date, enacted ten regional laws. The EACJ is charged with ensuring 'the adherence to law in the interpretation and application of and compliance with the Treaty' (EAC Secretariat, 2011a). Both these organizations face immense difficulties as weak institutional infrastructure and inadequate enforcement capacity prevents them from discharging their mandates. Likewise, inadequate institutional frameworks between the regional and national parliaments have hampered the requisite domestication of the EAC's laws. Notwithstanding these challenges, there are signs that the partner states are

*Table 4.5* Spatial development frameworks in EAC partner states

| Country | National Policy Guiding Development | Legislative Framework | National Instrument Guiding Spatial Planning | Institutional Mandates over Spatial Planning |
|---|---|---|---|---|
| Kenya | Kenya Vision 2030 | Physical Planning Act | National Spatial Plan | Directorate of Physical Planning |
| | | County Governments Act | Regional Physical Development Plans | Regional Development Authorities |
| | | Urban Areas and Cities Act | County Spatial Plans | County Governments |
| Tanzania | Tanzania Development Vision 2020 | The Town and Country Planning Act cap 335 | | |
| | | The Urban Planning Act 2007 | | |
| Uganda | Uganda Vision 2040 | Physical Planning Act | National Spatial Plan | National Planning Authority |
| | | | National Development Plan | |
| | | | Sector Strategies and Master Plans | |
| Rwanda | Rwanda Vision 2040 | Land Use Planning Law | | |
| | | Organic Land Law 2005 | | |
| Burundi | Burundi Vision 2023 | | | |
| South Sudan | South Sudan Vision 2040 | The Land Act 2009 | | South Sudan Strategic Planning Council |
| | | The Local Government Act 2009 | | |
| Ethiopia | Ethiopia Vision 2025 | Urban Planning Proclamation No. 574/2008 | National Regional Self-Government | Federal Urban Planning Institute |

Source: Authors' compilation

serious in improving the operational efficiency and effectiveness of these organs within the bloc.

## Conclusion

In this chapter, we have established that a significant degree of strategic thinking informed the formation of the EAC and its steerage into a viable sub-continental body. Likewise, we have demonstrated that the pursuit of EAC integration is very much informed by and subscribes to the key tenets of Strategic Planning, in content, form of process and scope of outputs. We have also established that the initiative, in spite of lacking an all-encompassing spatial reference, in the fashion of the European Spatial Development Perspective, premises its joint programmes and projects on an appreciation of the possibilities that space offers both as a framing and integrating device, both at the supra-regional scale and the national scale of partner states. Such appreciation certainly will assist the EAC to deal with its present-day challenge of skewed development across the territory. This notwithstanding, we have observed significant differences between the EAC integration processes and those of other global regions, particularly the European Union. The uniqueness of the former derives in the fact that the momentum for integration is almost entirely dependent on the political will of the leaders of the respective partner states, and lacks the kind of broad-based participation of non-governmental entities witnessed in the latter. Nonetheless, there are indications that the idea of integration is gaining widespread appeal, especially within the business community, further underscoring the faith of the bloc's citizens in the integration enterprise. Overall, however, a more deliberate and explicit enlisting of a spatial ideology in the region's strategic planning efforts is critical to its future success.

## References

African Development Bank (AfDB) Regional Departments – East I & East II (Orea/Oreb) (2011). *Eastern Africa Regional Integration Strategy Paper (RISP) 2011–2015*. AfDB, Tunis.

Albrechts, L. and Balducci, A. (2013). Practicing Strategic Planning: In Search of Critical Features to Explain the Strategic Character of Plans, *The Planning Review*, 49(3).

Briggid, L. (1992). *Integration and Cooperation in Europe*. Routlege, London.

CPCS Transcom (2009). *East African Railways Master Plan Study, Final Report*. Bridgetown.

EAC Secretariat (1999). *Treaty for the Establishment of the East African Community*. EAC Secretariat, Arusha.

EAC Secretariat (2006). *Deepening and Accelerating Integration*. EAC Development Strategy 2006–2010. EAC Secretariat, Arusha.

EAC Secretariat (2007). *Strategic Action Plan for the Lake Victoria Basin*. EAC Secretariat, Arusha.

EAC Secretariat (2011a). *Deepening and Accelerating Integration: One People, One Destiny*. EAC Development Strategy (2011/12–2015/16). EAC Secretariat, Arusha.

EAC Secretariat (2011b). *The East African Power Systems Master Plan and Grid Code Guide*. EAC Secretariat, Arusha.

EAC Secretariat (2012). *The Second EAC Heads of State Retreat on Infrastructure Development and Financing: Deepening EAC Integration Process through the Development of Efficient Infrastructure Systems to Support Trade and Industrialization*. Priority Projects up to 2020 in Railways, Ports and Energy Sectors, 29 November 2012, Nairobi, Kenya.

EAC Secretariat (2013). *East African Community Facts and Figures (2013)*. EAC Secretariat, Arusha.

East African Community (2014). EAC Facts and Figures 2010. Accessed at: http://eac.int/ statistics/index.php?option= com_docman&Itemid=153 (accessed 30 September 2014).

East African Legislative Assembly (EALA) (2014). Members of the Third EALA. Accessed at: http://eala.org/new/index.php/members/3rd-assembly-2012-2017 (accessed 10 September 2014).

Förster, S., Mommsen, W. J. and Robinson R. E. (1989). *Bismarck, Europe, and Africa: The Berlin Africa Conference 1884–1885 and the Onset of Partition*. Oxford University Press, Oxford.

Fouroutan, F. (1993). Regional Integration in Sub-Saharan Africa: Past Experience and Future Prospects. In de Melo, J. and Panagariya, A. (eds.), *New Dimensions in Regional Integration*. Cambridge, Cambridge University Press.

Geda, A. and Kibret, H. (2002). Regional Economic Integration in Africa: A Review of Problems and Prospects with a Case Study of COMESA. Working Papers 125. Department of Economics, SOAS, London.

Government of Burundi (2011). *Burundi Vision 2023*. Government of Burundi, Bujumbura.

Government of Ethiopia (2011). *Ethiopia Vision 2025*. Government of Ethiopia, Addis Ababa.

Government of Kenya (2008). *Kenya Vision 2030*. Government of Kenya, Nairobi.

Government of Rwanda (2000). *Rwanda Vision 2040*. Government of Rwanda, Kigali.

Government of South Sudan (2010). *South Sudan Vision 2040*. Government of South Sudan, Juba.

Government of Tanzania (1999). *Tanzania Development Vision 2020*. Government of Tanzania, Dar-es-salaam.

Government of Uganda (2007). *Uganda Vision 2040*. Government of Uganda, Kampala.

Hansohm, D. (2014). Sudan and South Sudan in the East African Community: An Option? In Grawert, E. (ed.), *Forging Two Nations Insights on Sudan and South Sudan*. African Books Collective, Oxford.

Hartzenberg, T. (2011). Regional Trade Integration in Africa. WTO Staff Working Paper ERSD-2011-14. World Trade Organization, Economic Research and Statistics Division, Geneva.

Healey, P. (2004). The Treatment of Space and Place in the New Strategic Spatial Planning in Europe, *International Journal of Urban and Regional Research*, 28: 45–67.

Healey, S. (2009). Peacemaking in the Midst of War: An Assessment of Igad's Contribution to Regional Security. *Working Paper No. 59: Regional and Global Axes of Conflict*. Royal Institute of International Affairs, London, November 2009.

Henderson, W. O. (1993). *The German Colonial Empire, 1884–1919*. Frank Cass, London.

Jonyo, F. and Misaro, J. (2013). Perspectives of Regional Integration in the East African Community, *Research Journal in Organizational Psychology and Educational Studies (RJOPES)*, 2(4), July 2013.

Kamala, D. B. (2006). The Achievements and Challenges of the New East African Community Co-operation. *Research Memorandum No. 58* (June), The Business School, University of Hull, UK.

Kamanga, Khoti (2013). EAC Integration: Progress Achieved, Challenges and Opportunities, *The Guardian on Sunday*, 3 November.

Karega, Regina G. M. (2009). *Benefits Experienced by Ordinary Citizens from East African Regional Integration, Final Report*. EAC Secretariat/GTZ, Arusha.

Kenya, Ministry of Lands (2010). *National Spatial Plan: Concept Paper*. Ministry of Lands, Nairobi.

Khapoya, V. B. (1998). *The African Experience: An Introduction*. Prentice-Hall, Upper Saddle River, NJ.

Lyakurwa, W., McKay, Andres, Ng'eno, Nehemiah and Kennes, Walter (1997). Regional Integration in Sub-Saharan Africa: A Review of Experiences and Issues. In Oyejide, Ademola, Elbadawi, Ibrahim and Collier, Paul (eds.), *Regional Integration and Trade Liberalization in Sub-Saharan Africa. Vol. I: Framework, Issues and Methodological Perspectives*. Macmillan, London.

Mackenzie, J. M. (1983). *The Partition of Africa, 1880–1900, and European Imperialism in the Nineteenth Century*. Methuen, London.

Matthews, A. (2003). Regional Integration and Food Security in Developing Countries. *Training Materials for Agricultural Planning 45*. Food and Agriculture Organization of the United Nations, Rome.

Mintzberg, H. (1994). *The Rise and Fall of Strategic Planning*. The Free Press, New York.

Mockler, A. (1984). *Haile Selassie's War: The Italian–Ethiopian Campaign, 1935–1941*. Random House, New York.

Mohiddin, A. (ed.) (2005). *Deepening Regional Integration of the East African Community*. Development Policy Management Forum, Addis Ababa.

Mwangi, W. (2001). *Civil Society Participation in Regional Integration: Lessons for East Africa from European Commission*. Steven and Sons, London.

National Population Census Council (2008); 5th Sudan Population and Housing Census, Khartoum.

Nyin'guro, P. (2005). The East African Community's Prospects on Global stage. In Rok Ajulu (ed.), *The Making of a Region: The Revival of the East African Community*. Institute for Global Dialogue, Midrand, South Africa.

Oliver, Roland and Atmore, Anthony (2005). Africa South of the Equator. In *Africa since 1800*. Cambridge University Press, Cambridge, UK: pp. 24–25.

Pakenham, T. (1992). *The Scramble for Africa*. Avon Books, London.

Population and Housing Census Commission (2007) *Population and Housing Census Ethiopia, Addis Ababa*.

United Nations Economic Commission for Africa (UNECA) (2010). *Assessing Regional Integration in Africa IV: Enhancing Intra-African Trade*. UNECA, Addis Ababa. Available online at: http://www.uneca.org/aria4/index.htm as (accessed 10 September 2014).

World Bank (2000). *Can Africa Claim the 21st Century?* The World Bank, Washington, DC.

# 5 The region is dead, long live the region

## The Øresund Region 15 years after the bridge

*Kristian Olesen and Jonathan Metzger*

The Øresund Region already exists – but then it does not really – yet.
(Danish and Swedish Government 1999, p.10)

Developing the Øresund Region into a growth engine for entire Scandinavia and creating an Øresund identity cannot be done in a short time – it takes a long haul.
(Öresundskomiteen 2013, p.2)

The opening of a bridge between the two countries in 2000 gave a strong boost to the integration process, which was years in the making. More than ten years after the symbolic bridge opening, the integration process of the Oresund is losing steam, having reached its peak of integration just before the crisis.
(Nauwelaers, Maguire and Ajmone Marsan 2013, p.7)

## Introduction

If it today is commonly accepted that regions are 'constructs', then who or what construct them, for what reasons, and by which means? How are they made manifest and durable as both mental geographies and mundane everyday realities (cf. Metzger, 2013)? Paasi (2010, p.2298) suggests that regions become actualized through 'a plethora of practices, discourses, relations, and connections that can have wider origins in space and time but are assembled and connected in historically contingent ways in cultural, economic, and political contexts and struggles'. Furthermore, he suggests that regions are 'performed and made meaningful' through 'material and discursive practices and networks that cross borders and scales, often simultaneously giving expression or shape to such borders and scales' (Paasi, 2010, p.2298). In this chapter we will investigate the spatiotemporally distributed heterogeneous practices that have led to the formation and more recently encroaching dissipation of a well-known European region: Öresund. In this endeavour we will make an effort to be sensitive to how Öresund as a spatial entity interrelates with, depends upon or partially challenges/is challenged by other geographical entities, boundaries and imaginations. We will be paying specific attention to the role played (or not) by strategic spatial planning practices in contributing to making the Öresund Region a manifest, seemingly self-evident reality.

In European discourses on regionalization, the Öresund Region[1] – located around the Öresund Strait, which separates Denmark from Sweden and the North Sea (Kattegatt) from the Baltic Sea (see Figure 5.1) – often figures as a school book example of successful cross-border regionalization and integration processes (Perkmann, 2003; Hospers, 2006). However, compared to other cross-border regions in central Europe, the Øresund Region is still young. Only up until a little more than a century ago, it was traversed by one of the most hostile national borders in Europe. As a wider transnational metropolitan region, it currently tallies at a population count of around 3.7 million inhabitants (Andersson, Andersson and Wichmann Matthiessen, 2013). The imposing and impressive Øresund Bridge, which physically ties together the city of Malmö in Sweden with Denmark's capital city, Copenhagen, and, on a wider scale, the Scandinavian Peninsula with the rest of continental Europe, constitutes the grand centrepiece of the region since its opening in 2000.

The opening of the Øresund Bridge marked the physical manifestation of a cross-border region that had been on the drawing board for decades (Ek, 2003; Metzger, 2013). For many, the Øresund Region became 'real' with the opening of the Øresund Bridge – thus shifting the status of the region from the realm of existence as a mere project or potential into instead taking the form of a manifest reality. As is noted in a recent research report on the state of the Öresund Region, the bridge in itself can reasonably be labelled as a success, both financially and

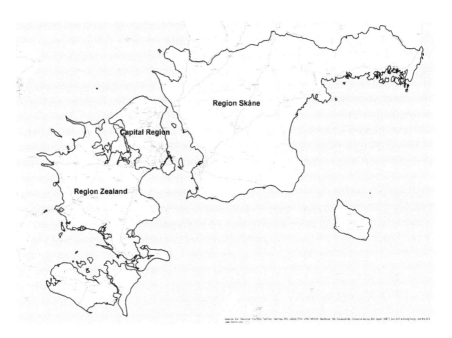

*Figure 5.1* The Øresund Region

Source: Illustration by Jan Kloster Staunstrup

technically (Cars *et al.*, 2013, p.7). For instance, the traffic across the bridge has widely surpassed projections. Since the opening of the bridge, the total number of crossings by cars is over 70 million and over 300,000 vehicles are registered in the frequent customers' scheme (Hasselgren and Lundgren, 2014, p.3). In 2012, 18,500 vehicles crossed the bridge daily, 41% of these were commuters (Hasselgren and Lundgren, 2014, p.10). Railway traffic hit a record in 2012, with on average 30,000 passengers crossing the bridge per day, a total of 11 million for the year. Sixty per cent of these were regular commuters (Hasselgren and Lundgren, 2014, p.14).

Nevertheless, disappointment and frustration ferments among some leading political stakeholders and civil servants in the region. According to them, regional cooperation should have developed further by now. The potential of the region is not being fulfilled at present. The region is simply not all that it could be. To make things even worse, the level of regional integration has been declining since 2008 (Öresundskomiteen, 2015b). In the light of these developments, this chapter revisits the Øresund Region 15 years after the opening of the bridge, with the aim of examining the evolution of strategic planning in one of the most praised cross-border regions in Europe. We take the temperature on the Øresund Region and ask the question: is the region (still) alive? And if so, in which ways, and through the care of whom?

The chapter is structured as follows. First, we outline the context and discuss how the momentum for strategic planning at the scale of the Øresund Region emerged in the Danish and Swedish context, respectively. Second, we discuss the European dimension of the Øresund Region and illustrate how European discourses and funding have influenced strategy-making in the Øresund Region. Third, we outline the governance arrangements in the Øresund Region and discuss the role of the Øresund Committee in spearheading strategic planning initiatives. Then we analyse two areas of strategic intervention: the building of regional identity (in section five) and strategic plans and projects (in section six). In section seven, we outline the relationship between strategic planning at the scale of the Øresund Region and statutory planning in Denmark and Sweden. In section eight, we discuss the impact of strategic planning in the region and some of the critiques of the Øresund project. In the final section, we conclude and offer some perspectives on how strategic planning in the Øresund Region might evolve in the future.

## The Danish and Swedish context

It is said that the idea of the Øresund Region was conceived at a lunch meeting between a Danish and Swedish professor in urban planning in the summer of 1959, where the first sketch of a coherent city around the Øresund Strait was outlined on a piece of sandwich paper (Gaardmand, 1991; Ek, 2003).[2] Despite some momentum behind the idea of the Øresund City in the 1960s, the idea of a cross-border city remained largely a utopian dream among planning academics and professionals. The economic stagnation of the 1970s and the following decade of deindustrialization and rising unemployment rates weakened the national interest for the planning project on both sides of the strait.

Towards the end of the 1980s, the old utopian dream of the Øresund Region was resurrected as a proposed cure to the ails of both cities. In Denmark, the Øresund Region was largely perceived as a means to reinvigorate Copenhagen's competitiveness and position on the European map. By the end of the 1980s, Copenhagen was on the edge of bankruptcy. The Danish Government had for more than a decade prioritized investments elsewhere in the country with the aim of securing equal development across its territory. At the same time, the City of Copenhagen had primarily focused its activities on providing welfare services and developing public housing, which had put considerable constraints on the city budget (Bisgaard, 2010). At this point in time, a coalition was created between the social democratic lord mayor of Copenhagen and the conservative prime minister, with the aim of reinvigorating Copenhagen. Building a fixed link across the Øresund Strait was, along with other infrastructure and urban development projects, perceived as a stepping-stone towards strengthening Copenhagen's position as an international city.

Just like Copenhagen, the city of Malmö and the surrounding region of Skåne on the Swedish side were suffering from the economic crisis in the 1970s and 1980s. The closing of the shipyards in Landskrona and Malmö, and the subsequent failure of the Swedish Government's reindustrialization project, the Scania-Saab assembly plant, which closed in 1991, put the region into economic crisis and contributed to a national peripheralization of the region (Wichmann Matthiessen and Andersson, 1993). For Skåne, the idea of the Öresund Region represented a timely opportunity for developing an independent regional development strategy, rather than relying on the not always receptive central powers in Stockholm, which were often regarded with suspicion in Skåne (Ek, 2003). At the same time, the Öresund Region would transform Skåne's peripheral location in Sweden into a central location in Europe, by offering an opportunity to better link up to the European mainland and consumer markets in Western Europe, while at the same time reducing the locational disadvantages compared to Denmark (Hospers, 2006).

## The European dimension

The Øresund Region is not only a Danish–Swedish enterprise, but also a European project reflecting EU policies of integration, regionalization and friction-less mobility – and has consequently also been described as a 'full-scale laboratory experiment in the construction of a region' in an EU-context (Persson, 2003, p.256). Two European discourses, with related plans and policy programmes, have been central to this experiment: a *Europe of the Regions* (with ESDP and INTERREG) and a *Europe of Flows* (with TEN-T).

The discourse of a 'Europe of the Regions' gained prominence in Denmark and Sweden, as it merged with local ambitions of revitalizing Copenhagen and Malmö. Even though Sweden was not a member of the EU until 1995, the support of regionalization was strong in Skåne for geopolitical reasons (Jerneck, 2000). The European policies of integration and regionalization materialized in political ambitions of preparing the European Spatial Development Perspective (ESDP) (Faludi and Waterhout, 2002). One of the central objectives of the ESDP was to promote economic and social cohesion across the European territory (European Commission, 1999). Here cooperation between member states in cross-border regions became an important element in the application of the ESDP, in particular in terms of transnational cooperation in macro-regions, which was linked to INTERREG funding.[3] However, smaller cross-border regions, such as the Øresund Region, also received significant attention and funding from the EU. In 1994, the Øresund Region became the first cross-border region separated by water eligible for INTERREG II funding (Jerneck, 2000). INTERREG funding has from thereon played a crucial role in mobilizing cross-border collaboration, and has therefore been described as a critical 'lubricant' of transnational coopera-tion in the region (Persson, 2003). INTERREG funds have been the central source of co-financing for most of the flagship transnational cooperation projects in the region, as well as innumerable other projects, including the formulation of a number of strategic plans of various inclinations and foci (see further below). Box 5.1 demonstrates how the Øresund Region's INTERREG funding has significantly increased since the region became eligible for INTERREG funding in the mid-1990s.

The other main European discourse influencing the Øresund Region was the idea of a 'Europe of flows'. This discourse was linked to European policies of developing the Trans-European Transport Network (TEN-T), a projected fine-meshed transport network tying European space together. With a point of depar-ture in the policy of promoting fast and friction-less travel, the TEN-T identified 'bottlenecks' and 'missing links' throughout Europe (Jensen and Richardson, 2004). The fixed link across the Øresund Strait was highlighted as one of the missing links in developing an integrated transport network and promoting friction-less travel through Europe.

---

**Box 5.1 Overview of INTERREG funding allocated to the Øresund Region**

- INTERREG IIA (1996–2001): EUR 13.5 million
- INTERREG IIIA (2000–2006): EUR 30.8 million
- INTERREG IVA (2007–2013): EUR 121 million
- INTERREG VA (2014–2020): EUR 136 million

INTERREG IIA and IIIA funding were targeted the Øresund Region specifically, while INTERREG IVA and VA funding have been targeted towards the larger Øresund/Kattegat/Skagerak Region.

European discourses like 'Europe of the Regions' and 'Europe of Flows' must be understood as deliberate attempts to redraw the map of Europe. Within these discourses the Øresund connection was not only perceived as the solution to a mobility problem, a missing link in the TEN-T policy. The fixed link across the Øresund Strait was also understood as the foundation for regional integration and economic growth, and thereby the very foundation for the Øresund Region (Ek, 2003; Jensen and Richardson, 2004).

## Governance in the Øresund Region

The overall governance arrangements in the Øresund Region can be characterized as 'very fuzzy' (Berg and Löfgren, 2000, p.12), and practically amount to a non-arrangement. Similarly, in 2003, the OECD described the governance model in the Øresund Region as 'governance without government' (OECD, 2003, p.16) with reference to the rather generic governance approach in the region. The decision by the Swedish and Danish government to build the bridge in 1991 generated a veritable boom in the formation of transnational cooperation initiatives and organizations in Öresund. The region building process has been characterized as an 'open house' (Tangkjær, 2000), which unites a broad range of actors who have agreed to work under the umbrella of the Øresund Region. One observer has noted that over 500 organizations were active in various projects, programmes, events and activities that could be ascribed to the regionalization process from the mid-1980s up until the opening of the bridge in 2000 (Berg, 2000). Partially due to the heavy reliance on INTERREG co-funding, and the consequent temporary project character of a lot of cooperation initiatives, much of the recent and ongoing transnational regionalization process has been characterized by criss-crossing cross-scalar and cross-sectoral connections across Danish and Swedish society, with a particular focus on various regional and local actors in the public sector, business and civil society (Persson, 2003, p.260).

Perhaps the most important governance body on a transnational regional level is the Öresund Committee, *Öresundskomiteen*. This formal political cooperation goes back to the foundation of the Øresund Council in 1964, a predecessor to the Øresund Committee which was in turn founded in 1993 and today constitutes the political steering committee in the cross-border region. The committee has 12 membership entities: nine local municipalities (five Danish and four Swedish) and three regional bodies (two Danish and one Swedish). Its decision-making assembly consists of 32 indirectly elected politicians from these bodies, divided 50/50 between Swedes and Danes. An Executive Committee consists of six Swedish and six Danish representatives, and the day-to-day business is run by a permanent secretariat of professionals. The primary source of financing for the organization is through membership dues, which in 2013 amounted to 2.82 DKK per inhabitant, or a total of EUR 1.4 million. A smaller contribution, amounting to 10% of the running costs, is also granted by the Nordic Council of Ministers (Öresundskomiteen, 2015a).

During the early years of the regionalization process, the committee played an important role in the integration efforts, for instance through political lobbying towards the national governments and the EU, and the dissemination of information to the general public. Today the committee primarily functions as a 'clearing house' with 'the mandate to identify issues and funnel them towards the decision makers' (Hasselgren and Lundgren, 2014, p.26). In this sense the committee is perhaps best understood as a network organization for public authorities on both sides of the Øresund. Still, there is some dissatisfaction with the efficiency of the committee in its current guise. Cars *et al.* (2013, p.20) note that demands for a thorough revision of the role and function of the committee are rising, due to frustration with the current (lack of) progress of further cross-border integration. The Øresund Committee's annual reporting on the integration process, the so-called 'integration index', documents that the integration in the region has steadily declined since 2008 (Öresundskomiteen, 2015b).[4]

Compared to the national governments, the Øresund Committee remains a fairly weak political body. Many of the serious barriers to further integration – such as labour legislation, social security entitlements, institutional mismatches in the education and tax systems, etc. – appear to be solvable only on the national level (Cars *et al.*, 2013). Nevertheless, it appears as if the central governments have a shared distinct lack of interest in any sustained efforts towards facilitating or contributing to further integration. This has been identified as a serious barrier towards further transnational regional integration in the region (Cars *et al.*, 2013; Hasselgren and Lundgren, 2014).

## Building regional identity

The project of the Øresund Region aims not only at merging the Danish and Swedish side of the Øresund Strait physically, but also mentally by building a regional identity. In the Øresund Region, branding and marketing strategies became an important aspect of building a cross-border identity. While the Øresund Bridge probably is the strongest symbol of the Øresund Region, attempts have been made to introduce softer symbols and brands. In general, the branding and marketing work has focused on the production of predominantly economic storylines about the potential of the Øresund Region, what Berg and Löfgren (2000, p.12) refer to as 'Ørespeak'.

The Øresund Committee's most prestigious branding projects within research and innovation have been the 'Medicon Valley Alliance' (MVA) and the 'Öresund University' (ÖU) (Hall, 2008). The MVA was based on an identified potential for the region to develop a world leading transnational life sciences cluster, a Nordic life science equivalent of the Californian IT hub. The organizational idea was based on transnational 'triple-helix' cooperation through a formal partnership with a mutual goal frame and common policy making for actors in government, business and academia on both sides of the strait. Nevertheless, due to increasingly stiff international competition in the area, as well as a waning interest among the academic actors, the cooperation is presently in the doldrums (Cars *et al.*, 2013, p.41). The ÖU, founded in 1997, functioned as a cooperation and coordination body for higher education in the region, and was initially heralded as a success – praised by both the OECD and the EU (recipient of the StarRegion-prize in 2008). But behind the scenes, opposition from leading circles among the top universities in the region emerged as the organization assumed a very fixed and hierarchical structure. This resulted in an authority clash, which eventually brought on the demise and official discontinuation of the organization in 2012 (Cars *et al.*, 2013, p.46).

Overall, the main branding and marketing strategies have been very focused on placing the Øresund Region in a European competitive landscape, and therefore also primarily targeting an audience of European (and to some degree national) political and business elites, rather than a local transnational public. The brand of Medicon Valley is a very explicit example of this. Here the ambition has been to attract businesses and knowledge workers to Øresund to arm the region in the (supposed) competitive race with other European metropolitan regions. In a perverse way, this has led to the situation where the Öresund Region might be a more concrete and taken-for-granted reality for policy makers in Brussels and other European regions than for local residents (Hospers, 2006; Löfgren, 2008).

Nevertheless, there have also been some efforts to communicate the Öresund identity to local citizens, particularly through cultural events such as the Øresund Day and Öresund festival – efforts which in general have been described as bearing the mark of more or less monumental failures (cf. Cars *et al.*, 2013, p.39), lacking any degree of 'resonance' with the general public (Righolt, quoted in Cars *et al.*, 2013, p.88). It has also been argued that a truly transnational regional identity can only be achieved through intense everyday interactions and interpersonal relations (Cars *et al.*, 2013, p.9). At present, the preconditions for such developments nevertheless seem to be deteriorating rather than improving, partially due to transnational labour market integration decreasing in the region since 2008, the housing market integration – i.e. transnational settlement – not increasing, and the possibilities for cultural exchange being weakened through increased institutional barriers against student mobility (see Cars *et al.*, 2013, p.50), and add to that, sinking levels of language comprehension skills in Danish for Swedes, and vice versa.[5]

## Strategic planning in the Øresund Region

In many ways the strategic planning work in the Øresund Region mirrors the region's fuzzy governance arrangements. Strategy-making in the Øresund Region is continuously performed by a range of different actors and organizations in a seemingly rather uncoordinated way, through partially overlapping and mutually enforcing, and partially conflicting, visions and suggestions. As such there is not one overarching *Plan* (capital 'P') for the region, but there have been – and are – innumerable *plans* (small 'p'), and a lot of *planning* going on according to more or less a 'live and let live' principle. From 1991 to 2000, over 150 strategy documents concerning the Öresund Region were produced, including vision statements and strategic plans, in addition to a number of regional policy documents sponsored by various national and regional authorities in both countries. In this context, it is interesting to reflect on to what extent any strategic *spatial* planning is going on at the scale of the Øresund Region.

The Øresund Committee has generally had a project-oriented approach to strategic planning, reflecting the availability of INTERREG and other types of project funding. As a consequence, there has been a limited focus on preparing an integrated and holistic spatial vision. It could be argued that ÖU and MVA – as well as the more successful project of merging the harbour operations of Malmö and Copenhagen – have been important strategic projects of regionalization. Nevertheless, it is dubious whether they could be considered strategic *spatial* projects, since they have considered the spatial impacts, or planned for the spatial development, of the wider region only to a limited degree (cf. Albrechts, 2006; Oosterlynck *et al.*, 2011). But even if the most high-profile cooperation projects have not been of that character, in recent years, a number of strategic planning endeavours have been initiated that have had a more distinct spatial perspective, particularly focusing on transport infrastructure – which again appears to be becoming the central focus of attention in the Öresund Region. Two initiatives that warrant closer attention are the work in the *ÖRIB/IBU*-process as well as the *ÖRUS*-strategy.

The ÖRIB project (the Øresund Region's Infrastructure and Urban Development) was a two-staged project initiated in 2005 with the support of INTERREG funding. The project was led by the three regional administrative bodies in the Øresund Region with the involvement of municipalities and the national transport agencies on both sides of the strait. The project aimed at developing scenarios (*fremtidsbilder*) for future needs in terms of transport infrastructure and urban development. The scenarios pointed to, among other things, the need for an additional link across the Øresund Strait, linking Helsingør and Helsingborg, the so-called 'HH link' (Region Skåne, 2008). Its successor, the IBU-project (Infrastructure and Urban Development), was initiated in 2008 with a budget of EUR 3.8 million (half funded by the INTERREG IVA programme). As its predecessor, the project sought to promote integration and cross-border collaboration in terms of transport infrastructure and urban development.

In 2010 the Øresund Committee adopted its first political development strategy, the ÖRUS (Öresundskomiteen, 2012). The strategy presents the Øresund Committee's visions and strategic actions within its key focus areas: *knowledge and innovation, culture and experiences, coherent and varied labour market,* and *accessibility and mobility.* Mirroring much of the Øresund Committee's work, the ÖRUS is remarkably non-spatial in character. The strategy contains very few considerations on the future spatial development of the region. The only spatial considerations in this regard are related to future transport infrastructures, which, as in the projects discussed above, remain a core focus area for the committee. Nevertheless, the ÖRUS does aspire to constitute the crossbar to the plethora of strategic work being doing at the auspices of the Øresund Region.

The ÖRIB/IBU and ÖRUS-projects both contain grand visions of the future Öresund Region, where the former is clearly more spatially focused than the latter. Whereas the IBU-report has been lauded by academic commentators as working 'from a regional development perspective, where the possibilities for future growth and international competitiveness based on assets of the whole Öresund region are highlighted' (Hasselgren and Lundgren, 2014, p.16), the ÖRUS has instead been criticized as a document that sets unrealistically high expectations that can be very difficult to live up to in practical action (Cars *et al.*, 2013, p.11). In addition, the ÖRUS clearly lacks the spatial perspective that was included in the ÖRIB and IBU projects. In this sense, there is no sign that the committee's work is becoming more spatially anchored.

## The link to statutory planning

The Øresund Committee's policies are to a large extent a bricolage of its members' policies. On the one hand, a strong link between the ÖRUS and regional and municipal statutory planning can be expected. On the other hand, the ÖRUS – although signed by the committee and its members – is not a legally binding document for statutory planning in either Denmark or Sweden. The relationship between the ÖRUS and statutory planning therefore remains rather ambiguous, especially due to the weak spatial perspective of the strategy. Nevertheless, the link between the ÖRUS and the three regional bodies is particularly important, since they are some of the most ardent supporters of the regionalization idea. However, the regional bodies in Denmark and Sweden are weak and have fairly limited spatial planning power. The existence of parallel planning/territorial policy systems in both Sweden and Denmark and a very rigid planning framework for the Greater Copenhagen Area weaken the links to statutory planning further.

In Denmark, the Capital Region and Region Zealand prepare regional spatial development plans aimed at promoting regional economic development.[6] While these plans to some extent reflect policy issues discussed at the scale of the Øresund Region, there is no direct link between the regional spatial development plans and land use planning. In the Greater Copenhagen Area, land use is regulated by the Finger Plan, which is prepared by the Ministry of the Environment. The Finger Plan constitutes a very rigid planning framework, which leaves little room for manoeuvre for the municipalities in the Greater Copenhagen Area. As issues regarding the Øresund Region are mainly a regional affair, the link between national spatial planning and strategy-making at the scale of the Øresund region is fairly weak. The Finger Plan 2013, for example, does not once refer to the Øresund Region! (Miljøministeriet, 2013).

In Region Skåne's new regional development strategy, adopted in 2014, the Öresund Region figures prominently (Region Skåne, 2014). The analysis in the strategy firmly places Skåne as a sub-region within a wider transnational Öresund Region, establishing that Skåne is the Swedish 'link to the continent', but also stating that regional integration in Öresund has 'lost momentum' (Region Skåne, 2014, p.12) – highlighting as particularly troublesome that transnational commuting is decreasing and that Danish residents in Skåne are moving back to Denmark in increasing numbers, primarily due to the down-turn in the property market in

Copenhagen in recent years, making housing more affordable in the capital region. The strategy's goal frame for 2030 includes the vision that Skåne should become completely functionally integrated with Copenhagen and Zealand in a common labour market.

At the city level, Copenhagen and Malmö are much more explicit about their relationship with the Øresund Region. In the municipal plan for Copenhagen from 2011, a chapter is dedicated to the Øresund Region (Københavns Kommune, 2011). However, here the Øresund Region is primarily discussed in terms of the synergies and cooperation between the *cities* of Copenhagen and Malmö. A similar trend is apparent in Malmö's latest comprehensive plan (Malmö Stad, 2014). In the plan, a whole section is dedicated to the development of spatial linkages between Copenhagen and Malmö. Between the lines – and also in the included maps – it becomes obvious that 'the Öresund Region' in this context is understood as being synonymous with Copenhagen–Malmö (sometimes also enacted as including Lund on the Swedish side). The strategically more narrow focus of the plan is further clarified and also defended by the city in the so-called Remittance Reply related to the plan, in which the city responds to criticism from other organizations and public bodies of an earlier draft of the plan, in accordance with Swedish public administration praxis. Here the City clearly states that: 'It is correct that the whole Öresund Region needs to be taken into consideration. At the same time, the broader perspective must not become so dominating that focus on the major cities and engines of the region is lost' (Malmö Stad, 2013, p.29).

The institutional arrangements and planning legislation in Denmark and Sweden prevent clear linkages between strategy-making at the scale of the Øresund Region and statutory planning. While Øresund policies to some extent are reflected in regional strategies, these remain rather non-spatial, due to the regional bodies' limited planning powers. Instead, there seems to be a strategic move from the local level to rearticulate the Øresund Region as primarily made up by Copenhagen and Malmö. More recently, the regions and municipalities on the Danish side of the strait have created yet another network organization, Greater Copenhagen. The region and municipalities in Skåne have also expressed an interest in joining this network. These new interpretations seem to be at odds with the branding of the Øresund Region as an integrated unity. One consequence might be that the label of the Øresund Region will not last for long. In an interview in the British newspaper *The Guardian*, the mayor of Copenhagen has already reflected on the need to rebrand the Øresund Region as Greater Copenhagen, as the Øresund Region is not a strong enough brand (*The Guardian*, 2015).

## The impact of the Øresund Region and critical voices

Given the complex ecologies of action surrounding the project of building the Öresund Region, it is difficult to say exactly which impact or effects strategic planning initiatives have had. Yes, there has been a lot of strategic planning going on – especially leading up to the opening of the bridge. As highlighted in the introduction to this chapter, the opening of the bridge has had a significant impact on the traffic flows across the Øresund. Even if the opening of the Öresund Bridge in 2000 manifested the coming to fruition of the region-building project into a simple, taken-for-granted reality, 'a simple, commonplace and non-dramatic phenomenon — well-integrated into the rhythms of everyday life' (Metzger, 2013, p.22), it might not be quite as well integrated for quite as many as has sometimes been thought. As already discussed, transnational integration indicators for the region have been steadily declining since 2008. The commuter flows across the border are extremely unidirectional. According to some reports, nine out of ten people commuting to work across the strait live in Sweden, where the housing market is more affordable, and work in the better paid labour market in Copenhagen (Cars *et al.*, 2013, p.65).

Critique has in recent years also mounted in the region, particularly among engaged public officials that turn against the view that 'integration will happen by itself, given the existence of the Öresund Bridge' (Cars *et al.*, 2013, p.12). Consequently, a new push for further regional integration is presently gaining some momentum among local and regional policy makers. But at the same time, it is important to caution that this new enthusiasm is hardly evenly distributed in the region, but is rather quite variegated and asymmetric according to a number of fault-lines. The clearest indication of this is perhaps the different levels of general enthusiasm for the Öresund idea between Swedish and Danish actors. Even though Copenhagen *as a city* seems quite interested in linking up with Malmö *as a city*, and the Danish Capital Region and Region Zealand with their Swedish counterparts, these interests seem to a large extent to be somewhat instrumental – as pragmatic and convenient vehicles or tools to accomplish *other* goals, and work towards *other* ends – compared to the more lofty and idealist proclamations of allegiance to the transnational regional idea that are often heard from Swedish regional and local actors, to whom integration more often appears to be a goal in itself. The recent attempt to rebrand the region as Greater Copenhagen from Danish actors underlines this phenomenon.

In light of the slow progress in amending institutional barriers and mismatches between Sweden and Denmark on issues such as taxation and labour regulation, increased focus is being placed on transport infrastructure development as a possible route forward to strengthen regional cooperation. However, it is problematic that many of the proposed infrastructure projects build upon very *local* interests, which are only dressed up in a regional and, to some degree, national rhetoric (cf. Hasselgren and Lundgren, 2014, p.36). One of these projects is the proposed new Copenhagen Metro-extension to Malmö, which is pushed by city councils on both sides (Cars *et al.*, 2013, p.19). An identified weakness in the argumentation for these investments is that they all take as their bottom line a projected lack of capacity on the current Bridge – an assumption which according to academic observers is highly questionable (Hasselgren and Lundgren, 2014, p.27).

The above recounted critical voices are those that question the pace or focus of further regionalization efforts in Öresund. But there also exists a different strain of criticism which in one way is much more fundamental and which rather questions the rationale of the whole region-building project. Ek (2003) has argued that the Øresund Region to a large extent remains an elitist project, the success of which is measured through the number of commuters daily crossing the bridge. This suggests that the 'ideal' Øresund citizen is one who lives on one side of the strait and works on the other. As a consequence, it is the (imagined) needs and desires of these commuter pioneers which are placed in the centre of strategy-making in the region. Such 'imagined mobile subjects' (Jensen and Richardson, 2007) also contribute to the construction of cross-border governmentalities, which promote certain rationalities and logics in the process of building a quite narrowly-framed regional identity which resonates very little with the experiences of most ordinary citizens in the Øresund Region. Such governmentalities are furthermore institutionalized in the monitoring of customized indexes and indicators intended to inform policy making. Despite extensive campaigns of branding and building regional identity, the inhabitants still, first and foremost, identify themselves as Danes or Swedes.

## Conclusions and future perspectives

The Øresund Region is often highlighted as a textbook example of successful cross-border regionalization and integration processes. The cross-border region has definitely come a long way since the old utopian dream of the Øresund Region gained momentum in the end of the 1980s, as an answer to national concerns in a context of economic restructuring and emerging European agendas of integration, regionalization and mobility. The opening of the Øresund Bridge in 2000 represented not only the manifest materialization of the Øresund Region. It also positioned Denmark and southwest Sweden more centrally on the European map, transport-network wise as well as discursively/symbolically in the European regional discourse. In many ways, the Øresund Region represents a classic example of how European spatial policies and funding opportunities influence spatial policy making in (trans)national contexts.

This context has implications for the strategic planning work carried out at the scale of the Øresund Region. In particular, the region seems to be struggling with finding an appropriate format for strategic spatial planning. While the Öresund Committee politically represents regional and municipal bodies on both sides of the Øresund Strait, strategic planning is probably best characterized as taking place through governance networks constituted by a range of public, semi-public and private organizations. This means that strategic planning is done on an *ad hoc* basis, organized around possibilities for acquiring EU funding. The ÖRUS represents the Öresund Committee's most elaborate attempt to prepare a holistic strategic framework for the Øresund Region. The ÖRUS is probably best understood as a catalogue of strategic initiatives and objectives within the Öresund Committee's strategic focus areas. However, the strategy remains remarkably non-spatial in character, which leads one to question to what extent any strategic *spatial* planning work is going on. This reflection of course opens up onto a wider conceptual discussion concerning what meaning we give to the term 'spatial'. Does a spatial approach only entail planning processes that proceed from a very specific territorial, topographical understanding of space, or should this concept also be expanded to include planning that is perhaps not so cartographically inclined, but nevertheless aims at generating a new spatial sensibility or strengthening the 'staying power' of a specific regionalization or spatial entity (cf. Metzger and Schmitt, 2012, on the EUSBSR)? In the case of Øresund, we argue that the absence of the former also seems to have had a negative impact on the possibility of the latter.

Since the opening of the bridge a keen political interest in lobbying for new transport infrastructures has emerged. This interest has been supported by various strategic analyses advocating for the need for future investments in transport infrastructure in conjunction with urban development perspectives, most noticeably another link across the Øresund. Perhaps this focus can be understood as a yearning for concrete, tangible results that can function as material beacons of future transnational regional integration, just as the Öresund Bridge did in the recent past. In this sense, the actors in the Øresund Region are much more concerned with strategic (spatial) projects and strategic planning than preparing a strategic spatial plan *per se* (Friedmann, 2004; Oosterlynck *et al.*, 2011).

But perhaps this is also one of the reasons why there exists a dissatisfied sense of missed opportunities and unfulfilled potentials among – primarily Swedish – public officials in the region. These 'Öresund nerds' see the existing level of transnational integration as something of a 'reality failure' (cf. Law, 2010), according to which – in the present – the region is not 'all it could be', thus demanding an adjustment of reality to approach the ideal of what virtually could be, the imagined unfulfilled potential of a truly integrated transnational region. Lurking in the shadows of these discussions are two reluctant key players, to some degree holding the fate of the future of the region in their hands: the national governments of Sweden and Denmark. For beyond all the regionalist jargon, both Sweden and Denmark are still today highly centralized unitary states, whose national administrations function as obligatory passage points for any new major infrastructure investments. They hold the key to any attempts at a lowering of institutional barriers that could contribute to furthering regional integration in Öresund.

At present there are probably few, if any, who believe that Öresund as a geographical entity will supersede or replace other existing geographies in the wider area. The question is rather to what degree relevant actors see it as an important complement, and what future relevance this geography will have as an additional, 'layered' spatial entity – and the potential level of competition from other 'soft' regional spaces in the wider area (Haughton *et al.*, 2010). The recent framings of the 'Copenhagen Malmö Region' and 'Greater Copenhagen' seem to represent competing spatial mentalities to the Øresund Region, calling into question the relevance of the Øresund Region as a brand. To what degree and in what aspects these somewhat different geographical imaginaries will come to compete and conflict, or whether they will be able to co-habit according to a 'live and let live' motto – or even might synergize somehow – remains to be seen. Alongside the construction of new geographical imaginaries always comes a potential for reinvigorating and reinventing strategic spatial planning anew. What we are witnessing at the moment might be another momentum for strategic spatial planning in the Øresund Region, under a different brand.

## Postscript

While we were putting the finishing touches to this chapter news broke that the Øresund Region had finally been declared officially dead as a concept. Following a transnational high-level meeting between regional representatives from Skåne and Zealand on 22 June 2015, it was declared that on 1 January 2016 the present Öresund Committee was to be merged with the Danish place-marketing organ 'Greater Copenhagen' and would from now on be formally known as the 'Greater Copenhagen and Skåne Committee', but publicly referred to simply as *Greater Copenhagen*. All 79 municipalities in Skåne and Zealand would be invited to join the new organization. The main areas of cooperation are to be place marketing, labour market, economic growth and cross-border integration. The central argument given for this change was that the brand 'Øresund' had been inefficient in attracting investments, visitors and new residents.

## Notes

1 In this chapter the Danish and Swedish spelling of Øresund/Öresund will be used interchangeably, as it is done in many strategic documents for the Øresund Region.
2 Ek (2003) traces the first ideas of a fixed link between Denmark and Sweden back to the end of the nineteenth century as part of grand plans to develop a European rail network. Also, fixed connections across the Öresund were included in the comprehensive plan of Malmö already in the early 1950s (Malmö Stad, n.a., p.22).
3 INTERREG is a financing instrument of European regional development designed to support cooperation across (internal and external) borders in the European Union. INTERREG provides funding for 50% of the project costs, leaving initiators to invest 50% themselves.
4 The Øresund Committee publishes an annual report monitoring the integration of the Øresund Region. The 'integration index' is a measure for the aggregate integration in the region based on five themed indexes monitoring the labour market, transport and communication, the housing market, business development, and culture, respectively (Öresundskomiteen, 2015b). For further statistics on the Øresund Region, please visit www.orestat.se.
5 The culture index is the only index that has steadily declined since the integration index was introduced in 2000 (Öresundskomiteen, 2015b).
6 The outline for the regional spatial development plans in Denmark was changed in 2014. In its most recent incarnation the Danish regions are to prepare regional growth and development strategies.

## References

Albrechts, L., 2006. Bridge the gap: From spatial planning to strategic projects. *European Planning Studies*, 14(10), pp.1487–1500.
Andersson, Å. E., Andersson, D. and Wichmann Matthiessen, C., 2013. *Öresundsregionen: Den Dynamiska Metropolen*. Stockholm: Dialogos.

Berg, O. B. and Löfgren, O., 2000. Studying the birth of a transnational region. In Berg, P. O., Linde-Laursen, A. and Löfgren, O. (eds.), *Invoking a Transnational Metropolis: The Making of the Oresund Region*. Copenhagen: Copenhagen Business School Press, pp.7–26.

Berg, P. O., 2000. Dreaming up a region? Strategic management as invocation. In Berg, P. O, Linde-Laursen, A. and Löfgren, O. (eds.), *Invoking a Transnational Metropolis: The Making of the Oresund Region*. Copenhagen: Copenhagen Business School Press, pp.55–94.

Bisgaard, H., 2010. *Københavns Genrejsning*. Copenhagen: Bogværket.

Cars, G., Hasselgren, B., Hansen, M. and Rostvik, M., 2013. *Vision och verklighet i Öresundssamarbetet: Forskningsrapport om samarbete och utvecklingspotentialer i Örsundsregionen*. Stockholm: KTH Royal Institute of Technology, Department of Urban Planning and Environment.

Danish and Swedish Government, 1999. *Øresund – en region bliver til*. Report by the Danish and Swedish Government, May 1999.

Ek, R., 2003. *Öresundsregion – bli till! De geografiska visionernas diskursiva rytm*. PhD thesis. Lund: Lund University.

European Commission, 1999. *ESDP European Spatial Development Perspective: Towards Balance and Sustainable Development of the Territory of the European Union*. Luxembourg: Office for Official Publications of the European Communities.

Faludi, A. and Waterhout, B., 2002. *The Making of the European Spatial Development Perspective: No Masterplan*. London: Routledge.

Friedmann, J., 2004. Hong Kong, Vancouver and beyond: Strategic spatial planning and the longer range. *Planning Theory & Practice*, 5(1), pp.50–56.

Gaardmand, A., 1991. *Bro til Drømmeland*. Copenhagen: Forlaget Urania.

Hall, P., 2008. Opportunities for democracy in cross-border regions? Lessons from the Øresund region. *Regional Studies*, 42(3), pp.423–435.

Hasselgren, B. and Lundgren, A., 2014. *TransGovernance Öresund: Experiences and Future Development in Transport Infrastructure Development and Governance in the Öresund Region*. Stockholm: KTH Royal Institute of Technology, Department of Urban Planning and Environment.

Haughton, G., Allmendinger, P., Counsell, D. and Vigar, G., 2010. *The New Spatial Planning: Territorial Management with Soft Spaces and Fuzzy Boundaries*. Abingdon: Routledge.

Hospers, G. J., 2006. Borders, bridges and branding: The transformation of the Øresund region into an imagined space. *European Planning Studies*, 14(8), pp.1015–1033.

Jensen, A. and Richardson, T., 2007. New region, new story: Imagined mobile subjects in transnational space. *Space and Polity*, 11(2), pp.137–150.

Jensen, O. B. and Richardson, T., 2004. *Making European Space: Mobility, Power and Territorial Identity*. London: Routledge.

Jerneck, M., 2000. East meets west. Cross-border co-operation in the Öresund – a successful case of transnational region-building? In Gidlund, J. and Jerneck, M. (eds.), *Local and Regional Governance in Europe: Evidence from Nordic Regions*. Cheltenham: Edward Elgar, pp.197–230.

Københavns Kommune, 2011. *Kommuneplan 2011*. Copenhagen: Københavns Kommune.

Law, J., 2010. *Reality Failures*. Department of Sociology, Open University. Available at: www.heterogeneities.net (accessed 3 October 2014).

Löfgren, O., 2008. Regionauts: The transformation of cross-border regions in Scandinavia. *European Urban and Regional Studies*, 15(3), pp.195–209.

Malmö Stad., n.a. *Malmös General- och Översiktsplaner 1950–2000.* Malmö: Stadsbyggnadskontoret.

Malmö Stad, 2013. *Översiktsplan för Malmö ÖP2012: Samrådsredogörelse.* Malmö: Stadsbyggnadskontoret.

Malmö Stad, 2014. *Översiktsplan för Malmö: Planstrategi.* Malmö: Malmö Stad.

Metzger, J., 2013. Raising the regional leviathan: A relational-materialist conceptualization of regions-in-becoming as publics-in-stabilization. *International Journal of Urban and Regional Research*, 37(4), pp.1368–1395.

Metzger, J. and Schmitt, P., 2012. When soft spaces harden: The EU strategy for the Baltic Sea Region. *Environment and Planning A*, 44(2), pp.263–280.

Miljøministeriet, 2013. *Fingerplan 2013: Landsplandirektiv for Hovedstadsområdets Planlægning.* Copenhagen: Miljøministeriet.

Nauwelaers, C., Maguire, K. and Ajmone Marsan, G., 2013. The case of Oresund (Denmark–Sweden) – Regions and innovation: Collaborating across borders. *OECD Regional Development Working Papers* 2013/21. Paris: OECD Publishing. http://dx.doi.org/10.1787/5k3xv0lk8knn-en.

OECD, 2003. *OECD Territorial Reviews Öresund, Denmark/Sweden.* Paris: OECD Publishing.

Oosterlynck, S., Van den Brock, J., Albrechts, L., Moulaert, F. and Verhetsel, A. (eds.), 2011. *Strategic Spatial Projects: Catalysts for Change.* London: Routledge.

Öresundskomiteen, 2012. *ØRUS: Øresund Regional Development Strategy.* Copenhagen: Öresundskomiteen.

Öresundskomiteen, 2013. *Flerårig strategi for implementering af ÖRUS og handlingsplan 2013.* Copenhagen: Öresundskomiteen.

Öresundskomiteen, 2015a. *Om Öresundskomiteen.* [online] Available at www.oresund-skomiteen.org/om-oss (accessed 24 November 2015).

Öresundskomiteen, 2015b. *Öresundskomiteens Integrationsindeks.* June 2015. Copenhagen: Öresundskomiteen.

Paasi, A., 2010. Regions are social constructs, but who or what 'constructs' them? Agency in question. *Environment and Planning A*, 42(10), pp.2296–2301.

Perkmann, M., 2003. Cross-border regions in Europe: Significance and drivers of regional cross-border co-operation. *European Urban and Regional Studies*, 10(2), pp.153–171.

Persson, C., 2003. Öresundsregionen: ett experiment i europeiskt regionbygge. In Arvidsson, H. and Persson, H.Å. (eds.), *Europeiska Brytpunkter.* Lund: Studentlitteratur.

Region Skåne, 2008. *Øresundsregionen 2025: Scenarier for trafik- og byudvikling.* Kristianstad: Region Skåne.

Region Skåne, 2014. *Det öppna Skåne 2030: Skånes regionala utvecklingsstrategi.* Kristianstad: Region Skåne.

Tangkjær, C., 2000. Øresund as an open house strategy by invitation. In Berg, P. O., Linde-Laursen, A. and Löfgren, O. (eds.), *Invoking a Transnational Metropolis: The Making of the Oresund Region.* Copenhagen: Copenhagen Business School Press, pp.165–190.

*The Guardian*, 2015. Denmark wants to rebrand part of Sweden as 'Greater Copenhagen'. [online] Available at: www.theguardian.com/world/2015/mar/05/denmark-wants-to-rebrand-part-of-sweden-as-greater-copenhagen (accessed 5 March 2015).

Wichmann Matthiessen, C. and Andersson, Å. E., 1993. *Øresundsregionen: Kreativitet, Integration, Vækst.* Copenhagen: Munksgaard.

# 6 Urban strategic spatial planning in China

## A two-round development since the late 1990s

*Kang Cao and Li Zheng*

The term *strategy* originates from a military context (Albrechts, 2004; Yang, 2006) and is literally understood as an overall plan or decision aimed to pursue survival and long-term development. Apart from the military sense, this term has been widely used in political and economic fields as well. Strategic thinking has been adopted since the twentieth century as guidance for urban and regional development. As a response, the term *strategic planning* (SP) has emerged. The world has witnessed a revival and buoyant development of strategic (spatial) planning in recent years because of various driving factors, such as globalization, sustainable development, marketization, and decentralization. In China, rapid urbanization plays a particularly important role in facilitating the rise of SP studies and practices, and a two-round development of SP has emerged in the last decade or so.

This chapter aims to shed light on urban strategic spatial planning in China through conceptualizing the idea and practices; depicting the development trajectories; and analyzing the characteristics, modes, theories, and methods commonly used in it.

## Conceptualization

In China, concepts such as *concept plan*, *structure plan*, *strategic spatial plan* and *spatial plan* are associated with SP. These concepts are understood and used equally in some literature but are differentiated in other literature. SP in China can be interpreted in both a broad sense and a narrow sense. In the broad sense, SP generally refers to plans with strategic thinking. Thus, generalized SP can be found in different geographic scales and administrative levels. At the national level, spatial development strategic plans are prepared by central ministries (mainly the National Development and Reform Commission and the Ministry of Land and Resources) to guide the socioeconomic development, spatial development, and land use nationwide. At the regional level, metropolitan area plans, urban agglomeration plans, and provincial urban system plans are prepared to guide the enhancement of regional competitiveness. At the local or city level, strategic plans are made to improve the city. Observably, there is a strong administration orientation in the SP preparation in China.

SP in the narrow sense solely refers to strategic planning for cities (particularly the metropolises in China) covering a long period, such as 25 or 30 years. In fact, in the previous decades when China experienced rapid urban development, the SP practices and the relevant theoretical studies were mainly concentrated on the metropolitan level. Thus, SP in China is pervasively perceived as the 'SP for cities', which is also the focus of this chapter. In the opinion of Yang (2006), Chinese SP emerges as a response to the dynamic and challenging urban context in the globalization era. It is an overall and comprehensive plan or decision made by the city government to pursue self-survival and long-term development. Thus when preparing SP, the strategic guidelines to tackle potential important issues, development opportunities, or challenges should be clarified (Wu and Wu, 2012), and special attention should be given to the overall urban development strategy and land use policy guidelines (Lu, et al., 2010). The names for Chinese SP vary from case to case. 'Development strategic plan' is used popularly among cities; some also borrow the name 'concept plan' from Singapore; some further add the word 'study' after 'plan' to highlight the nature of SP as a study (Zou, 2003). Hence, diverse names such as 'urban strategic plan', 'urban development strategic plan', 'urban development strategic study' and 'urban spatial development strategic study' have emerged. Such inconsistency on names reflects the freshness, diversity and variability of SP in China.

## The origin of urban strategic spatial planning in China

SP has different origins and evolving processes in countries or regions. In China, two rounds of SP development can be identified, but only for a short period of ten-odd years since the late 1990s. In the 1990s, China continued with its significant economic and administrative reform, which, together with major changes in the external environment, consequently facilitated a rapid urbanization process. Meanwhile, with more autonomy through a range of reforms, the enterprising local governments also desired to develop cities and enhance urban competitiveness. Confronted with economic and administrative challenges against such a backdrop, the discussion on a new type of planning that is independent from traditional ones was brought into agendas both by practitioners and academics. Several seminars were held by these people in cities like Guangzhou, Nanjing and Ningbo to explore the logic and model of the emerging planning type. All of these factors lead to the birth of SP in China.

To sum up, SP has emerged in China due to the following reasons (Wang, 2002; Zhang, 2002; Zou, 2003; Yang, 2006; Chen, et al., 2011; Wang, et al., 2011; Xu, et al., 2012):

- *External influence.* Globalization has brought cities and regions into the global economy web. The previous stable urban system based on the domestic administrative system is broken. Instead, a global urban system is being established. As a result, the dominant statuses of some cities are challenged by their neighbors, while a few other metropolitan areas start to become global strategic nodes. To meet the challenges and to perform internationally, these two types of area act as forerunners in practising SP.

- *The new urban development trend in China.* China has witnessed rapid urban development since its reform and opening-up policy, and multiple urbanization patterns have emerged during the process (Wang, 2006). The diversity of city development patterns has prompted a heterogeneous regional development, which then requires cities to take strategic action to improve their competence.

- *Institutional reform.* (1) Institutional reform is embodied in the establishment and improvement of the socialist market economy, and also in the increasing decentralization. Since the tax allocation reform in 1994, the interrelationship between the central government and local governments has experienced subtle changes, and the latter have started to become the main body in marketization (Jiang, 2009). The housing system was reformed in 1998 as a response to the Asian financial crisis, which further catalyzed local governments to participate in the market. The huge demand in the domestic real-estate market has offered local governments an opportunity to actively participate in land development to promote urban prosperity. From the tenth five-year plan[1] (2001–2005) on, the transformation of government-planned mandatory targets into market-oriented targets, the reform of the national investment system, and the market diversification have created more opportunities for local governments to make decisions concerning city development. These changes have also facilitated decentralization, where more autonomy has been distributed to the local level. (2) A limitation exists in the five-year planning and in traditional city planning. The five-year planning could no longer meet the requirement for a long-term urban development because of its short time span and lack of concerns on spatial issues. Additionally, the traditional city master plan still carries the legacy from the planned economy. The lack in political, economic and environmental considerations, rigidity of planning methods, and incapability to solve problems in a flexible way all prevent the city master plan from being an efficient tool to facilitate the local development. (3) Adjustment of administrative regions. Adjustment of administrative regions occurs in a way that central cities annex their surrounding counties and turn them into urban districts. The annexation requires cities to adopt a new development pattern. Additionally, the enlargement of city jurisdiction areas has promoted urban regionalization and regional urbanization. Both of them require a joint city-regional development, but contradictions have become increasingly prominent under the market economic condition, whereas collaborative mechanism is yet to be built.

Both external influences and internal reforms lead to the emergence of the first urban SP in China. At Professor Wu Liangyong's initiative, Guangzhou municipal government prepared the 'Strategic concept planning guideline for overall urban development in Guangzhou' in 2000. Thus, Guangzhou became the first city in China with a strategic plan[2] (Lu, et al., 2010; Wang, et al., 2011; Xu, et al., 2012). Subsequently, approximately 200 large or middle-sized cities copied the experience of Guangzhou and started to prepare strategic plans as well (Chen, et al., 2013). This wide application of SP opened a new era for SP development (Lu, et al., 2010), which marked the beginning of the first wave of SP practices in China (Chen, et al., 2011; Wang and Luo, 2011).

The first wave implies that decision makers and planners were exploring the right strategies and effective policies for city development, and were rethinking and innovating the traditional planning preparation methods (Wang and Zhao, 2013). The core value orientation in the first round of SP was to enhance city competitiveness (Xu, et al., 2012). Shen (2007) also regarded SP at that time as a demand- and marketing-oriented planning, which apparently mirrors the influence of globalized neoliberalism on China. This value orientation further promoted the study of urban competitiveness in China, which led to the introduction of relevant overseas classic theories to China, such as Porter's 'Diamond Theory'.

The main task of the first round of SP is to explore a new planning form to meet the above-mentioned economic and administrative challenges. The differences between SP and traditional master planning are as follows: (1) The traditional master planning, characterized as a linear and comprehensive process, is goal-oriented, where the optimal alternative is decided based on wide data collection and analysis. By contrast, SP is problem-oriented, which differentiates it substantively from traditional master planning. Based on the analysis of the urban development background and the diagnosis of primary problems, SP aims to provide an overall and long-term strategy for spatial arrangement, industry optimization, important infrastructure constructions, and eco-environmental protection and so on, while offering suggestions for government administration and city management (Lu, et al., 2010). For example, Shenyang city highlighted the diagnosis of existing problems when formulating its strategic development plan, based on which framework for city development and assessment mechanism of plan implementation were established (Wu, et al., 2003). (2) Because SP is more selective than traditional master planning, it mainly focuses on 'the prospective (concerning time), regional (concerning space), strategic (concerning content), and organizational (concerning form) issues that are most influential on future sustainable urban development' (Chen, et al., 2011); and avoids the pervasive mode of master planning, where nearly all problems are covered (Jiang, 2009). For instance, as a harbour city, Ningbo underlined the port-city relations in its first round of SP, while Hangzhou, as a tourism city, paid the primary attention to analyzing how tourism could promote city development when preparing its first SP. Mainly, there are two types of SP in the first round. One is comprehensive SP,[3] which focuses on economic development, resolves issues such as social development, environmental protection, population growth, land demand, transportation, spatial development direction, spatial arrangement and so on, and gives suggestions on the spatial structure along with optimal allocation of resources. The other type is specific SP, which usually deals with one particular issue or aspect concerning urban development, such as strategies for transportation, environment, ecology, urban characteristics, urban images, etc.

Three different understandings currently exist with regard to the role of SP. Some consider SP as a preliminary study that serves master planning (see for example, Li, 2003; Zou, 2003); some argue that SP is a new direction for the future development of city master planning, and that the current master planning should be simplified (Zhang, 2001); others regard SP as different from master planning (in a sense similar to regional planning), and insist that a coordination between SP and master planning should be established (Wang, et al., 2011). In 2005, five years after the beginning of the first round of SP, the Ministry of Housing and Urban–Rural Development of China announced the 'Notice about City Master Planning Preparation and Approval' (Building Code [2005] No. 2), and clarified that 'Before preparing the city master plan, a proactive strategic study should be organized to work on the strategic issues like the city positioning and spatial structure'. This statement established the legal status of SP as the 'preliminary study for master planning', which was the biggest achievement in the first round.

However, a problematic implementation of SP was noticeable in the first round. Given that all SP practices were performed in a somehow bottom-up and informal manner by the governments themselves, these practices were sometimes inconsistent with the corresponding statutory master plan formulated in a top-down manner, which then made a smooth implementation of SP difficult. Additionally, there were disputes concerning the nature of SP. Whether SP is a new planning form or just a transitional short-term product which will be substituted sooner or later remained unclear (Zhang, 2007). Moreover, given that the dominant tone of SP in this round was 'competing', the primary goal for cities was always set as enhancement of competitiveness, which thus placed cities in an adversarial or confrontational relationship with each other. However, this situation has changed significantly in the second round.

## Second round of strategic planning

With the promulgation and enforcement of the new 'Measures for Formulating Urban Planning' in 2006, and the 'Urban and Rural Planning Act' in 2008, the development of SP faces new opportunities. This new 'Measures' stipulates that 'before preparing city master plan, the responsible governments should […] carry out the proactive study on issues like city positioning, development objectives, urban functions, and spatial arrangement and so on according to the national urban system plan and provincial urban system plan, and taking regional integration and urban–rural integration into consideration'. This clause confirms the content of 'Building Code [2005] No. 2' and sets a status for SP as a preliminary study prior to preparing the city master plan, which initiates a new wave of SP formulation in China.

Compared with the first round, the context in this round has changed substantially. From a rapid development period into a transformation one, China has begun to make major adjustments in its national development strategy, especially the economic development. 'Maintaining growth, facilitating transformation, and adjusting structure' has become the tenet of economic policies in China, and the economic development pattern has been evolving from an 'exogenous' type to an 'endogenous' one. The following reasons have led to the second round of SP (Chen, et al., 2011; Xu, et al., 2012): (1) The changed external environment. With the outbreak of the global financial crisis in 2008, China has faced huge challenges with its export-led economic mode. Promoting a competitive advantage based on 'innovation' becomes the key during this new period. (2) Emphasis on regional issues. Through central government macro-control, the 'National Major Function Regionalization' scheme is implemented and regional planning has received unprecedented attention. Therefore, SP in this round focuses on implementing national strategy at regional level in order to acquire policy support from the central government. (3) China is in a new urbanization stage. Since 2011, the urbanization rate in China has exceeded 50%, which indicates that China has genuinely entered the urbanized age. As a response, the twelfth five-year economic plan for the first time highlights urbanization quality and changes the national guideline from emphasizing urban development alone into enhancing urban–rural integration.

In contrast with the first round of SP, the most significant change in the new round is that SP is no longer a competing means against city master planning, but incrementally becomes a tool that coordinates with master planning and provides a wide input for master planning preparation. Hence, a mutual supportive and coordinated relationship between the two planning types is developed (Wang, et al., 2011). For instance, in the new urban–rural planning preparation system of Guangzhou, a synergetic mechanism that involves 'development study (strategic plan) – statutory plans (master plan, regulatory detailed construction plan) – action plans (short-term construction plan, annual action plan)' has been established, which marks the emergence of a new planning system that combines statutory planning (master plan and regulatory detailed construction plan) and non-statutory planning (SP).[4] Non-statutory plans are considered to be complementary to statutory plans. Specifically, on the one hand, SP elaborates on issues like city positioning, city development goals, overall development strategy, spatial development strategy, and strategies for specific projects, which serves as inputs to master planning. On the other hand, SP offers guidance on spatial arrangements of particular projects and district development, which thus connects itself with regulatory detailed construction planning (Lu, et al., 2010).

Additionally, the second round of SP differs from the first round in terms of the objective, value orientation, perspective, content, method, organization, time span, and name (Chen, et al., 2011; Wang and Luo, 2011; Xu, et al., 2012; Chen, et al., 2013).

First, the objective of SP in the second round is to improve city sustainability rather than enhance city competitiveness. For instance, the overall objective of Guangzhou 2020 is changed from 'Expansion' to 'Optimization and Improvement', which could be articulated as spatial integration, industrial structure optimization, ecological and historical protection, and regional integration. The positive sum game among cities has replaced the previous zero-sum game, which means, apart from competitions, intercity or interregional cooperation is also highlighted in urban development.

Additionally, economic development is no longer the only target of the current SP because a coordinated development among the economy, society, population, and natural environment is also emphasized (Yang, 2007). For example, the key word of 'Changsha City Development Strategy' is spatial equilibrium, which is embodied in aspects like the jobs–housing relationship, allocation of public resources, ecological issues, and civil rights (Zhao, 2010).

In terms of value orientation, given that the first round of SP is characterized as 'a planning in a rapid development period', SP at that time thus focuses more on quantitative growth. By contrast, the second round focuses more on qualitative growth against the background of national (economic) transformation that is mentioned at the beginning of this section. For instance, Ningbo 2030 proposes that city development should be transformed from 'expansion in quantity' into 'enhancement in quality'. Similarly, SP of Guangzhou city advocates the changes from 'expansion' to 'improvement'. Moreover, SP in this round is more policy-oriented because of the influence of the national strategy on regions. For example, influenced by the new national policies concerning development of coastal areas, Tianjin, as a seaside city, sets the goals of 'developing into a national growth pole, establishing national scientific development model regions, and constructing international economic nodes'.

Regarding perspective, the new SP adopts a combination of long-term and short-term views in making strategies instead of a simple macroscopic and long-term view. This increases the possibility of SP being implemented. In addition, the new SP in particular pays attention to the formulation of action plans. Taking Shenzhen as an example, seven action plans have been finalized to support the effectuation of Shenzhen 2040. They include the 'internationalization plan, income doubling plan, stock management plan, international harbor development plan, conurbation development plan, smart city development plan, and urban fiber development plan'.

Regarding content, the first round of SP focuses more on specific thematic issues, whereas comprehensiveness has improved in the second round, which means an increasing number of urban-related issues and the interrelationship among these issues are incorporated into the framework of the strategic thinking. Hence, SP develops into a tool that gives suggestions for urban development in all aspects (Wang and Luo, 2011; Xu, et al., 2012).

With regard to technical methods, interdisciplinary techniques are used in the second round in addition to the methods employed in the first round, which turns SP into a dynamic one with uncertainty thinking (Wang and Luo, 2011). The second round employs methods such as scenario planning,[5] cross-impact analysis, and so on (Qian, et al., 2009), indicating cities' emphasis on the uncertainty of the external environment and the unpredictability of the future. For instance, the scenario planning method proposed by scholars from Tsinghua University is used in the new round SP of Nanjing, and ten possible developing scenarios are built for shaping further strategies and spatial plans (Wang and Luo, 2011). Methods such as resource capability carrying analysis and environment capability assessment are also introduced in this round, showing that cities start to consider constraint conditions such as environment and resource limitations (Chen, et al., 2011).

In terms of organization, the second round strengthens public participation in the planning process. For example, when formulating Guangzhou 2020, different channels are available for the general public to get involved in the planning process. Local citizens can either write to Guangzhou municipal government, or take part in the community consultation meetings organized by the government, or upload opinions at the government website (Lu, et al., 2010). As for Changsha city, in 2008 it introduced SP to the communities, which has effectively increased the citizens' role throughout the planning process and significantly promoted public awareness towards SP (Zhao, 2010). Similarly, Ningbo municipal government reinforces the participation of the public when preparing Ningbo 2030. The final plan is decided after collection of public opinion (Xu, et al., 2012).

The time span of the SP in the second round is extended to 20 or 30 years. Through such middle- to long-term SP (see Table 6.1), a comprehensive and proactive study concerned with the future of cities becomes available.

The names for SP have changed as well. SP with the name format of 'city name + time range' is preferred in big cities (see Table 6.1), which actually reveals the influence from overseas SP practices, such as New York 2030, Sydney 2030, Melbourne 2030, Chicago 2040, and Frankfurt 2030.

The second round of SP is a product of active adjustment to the changed urban development context. The second round does not only inherit the strategic thinking from the first round to strategically manage city resources, but also further overcomes the weaknesses of the first round in terms of comprehensiveness, implementation, and spatiality so as to present SP as a dynamic planning tool. Nevertheless, despite the clearer methods and modes to prepare SP, a legal status has yet to be attached to this planning tool. Even though the new 'Measures' confirms the status of SP as the proactive study of strategic issues concerning the performance of urban development prior to preparing master planning, the 'Urban–Rural Planning Act' does not include SP into the statutory planning

*Table 6.1* A brief description of the strategic planning of some cities in the second round

| Cities | Name of strategic spatial planning | Time span |
| --- | --- | --- |
| Beijing | Beijing 2049 Spatial Development Strategy Study | 2012–2049 |
| Guangzhou | Guangzhou 2020: Urban Comprehensive Development Strategy Planning | 2010–2020 |
| Shenzhen | Shenzhen 2040 Urban Development Strategy | 2010–2040 |
| Wuhan | Wuhan 2049 Long-term Development Strategy | 2013–2049 |
| Ningbo | Ningbo Urban Development Strategy 2030 | 2010–2030 |

Source: The authors' own statistics.

system.[6] Hence, the Chinese SP can be characterized as 'inside the planning system but outside the legal system'. This feature implies that SP remains a non-statutory planning tool, although this tool is often prepared by official planning authorities, such as the 'Urban Planning & Design Institute'. SP actually serves the 'local mayor' rather than the general public (Liu, et al., 2013). Nonetheless, the non-statutory characteristic of SP is argued to actually contribute to the flexibility and openness that statutory planning lacks. It loses those important features once it is institutionalized and legalized (Wang, et al., 2011).

## Characteristics

Despite the division of the Chinese SP development into two rounds, some general characteristics can be found throughout the development process, which are summarized as follows (Zou, 2003; Yang, 2006; Jiang, 2009; Lu, et al., 2010):

- *Overall, integrative or comprehensive.* SP targets at the overall situation of a city and is formulated according to the overall city development. While city master planning solely focuses on issues at the city level, SP adopts a regional perspective. Additionally, SP puts emphasis on shaping the future vision of the city. Particular attention is given to relocating the city itself in an interrelationship with other cities.
- *Long-term.* The formulation of SP should start by analyzing the external and internal contexts. SP directs both the current action and future development.
- *Competitive.* SP provides alternatives for a city to compete against other cities so as to stand out in the regional, national, and even global arena. Moreover, SP is also an action programme to cope with the shocks, pressures, threats, and difficulties from all sides, and to meet the challenges in urban development.
- *Guideline.* The basic course of action, major measures, and essential steps of SP are often principled. SP is normally targeted at some pivotal issues, such as the industrial structure, core regional development, and infrastructure improvement. These issues are most urgent and can most likely generate propulsive effects.
- *Flexible.* The process and form of SP formulation are flexible and research-oriented. Diverse methods and tools from the enterprise strategy are incorporated into SP preparation, such as SWOT analysis, scenario analysis, and competitiveness analysis, to enhance the capability of planning in response to the complex and ever-changing context.
- *Spatial-concerned.* The concept of space and the expression of city images are highlighted in SP.

Overall, SP in China can be characterized as integrative, predictable, long-term, and spatial-concerned. However, it is noteworthy that the capacity of Chinese SP to consider territory or regional collaboration and cooperation is lacking. Whether in the first round or the second one, Chinese SP is primarily regarded as a means for a city to compete against other cities.

## Theories and methods

### Theories

There is no theory of innovation in Chinese SP. Instead of proposing a 'theory of planning', cities in China only employ 'theory in planning' to prepare SP, namely introducing theories of relevant disciplines. Global city system theory, urban competiveness theory, spatial economics theory, urban governance theory, and regional coordination theory are commonly used as references (Yang, 2006).

### Methods

Numerous methods and tools, including those for enterprises, are applied to prepare Chinese SP to improve the resilience of cities in a period of uncertainty (Jiang, 2009). After a review of the relevant literature (Zhang, 2001; Li, 2004; Yang 2006; Chen, et al., 2011), the main methods that have been employed to make SP in China can be summarized as follows:

- *SWOT analysis from business management.* Confronted with the increasing external and internal uncertainty of development brought about by globalization and localization, many cities have paid their primary attention to figuring out external and internal potential factors for development prior to formulating SP. This method was once applied into the preparation of Ningbo 2030. It was recognized that the strength of Ningbo city was its world-renowned harbour; the weaknesses were its marginalized location, a problematic industrial structure, administrative fragmentation, etc.; the opportunity was the growing marketization and redevelopment of heavy industry in China; and the threat came from its neighbour cities with growing competitiveness (Xu, et al., 2012).
- *Systematic analysis method.* This method emerged in the 1940s with the rise of system theory. It requires people to observe things with an overall, integrated, and dynamic perspective. Compared with other methods, this method is the most comprehensive one and was once applied in the formulation of Shenzhen 2030. In particular, when preparing Shenzhen 2030, a variety of issues were analyzed in a systematic way, including planning situations, objectives, alternatives, implementation measures, evaluation tools and so on.
- *Regional analysis.* Urban issues are understood and addressed from a regional perspective though this method. Based on analyses at different scales, e.g., global scale, national scale, regional scale, and local scale, urban problems are unveiled precisely and the future is rationally positioned. Generally, Chinese cities located at metropolitan areas such as Beijing–Tian–Hebei Metropolitan Region, Pearl River Delta and Yangtze River Delta will take a regional perspective when formulating their SPs.

- *Structural analysis method based on urban structure theory*. This method includes analyses such as industry structure, city scale, spatial structure, landscape ecological net rack system, and transport network. For example, when making the most recent SP of Nanjing city, the industrial and spatial structures were given a special attention. The SP points out that Nanjing used to have a simple production structure where heavy industry absolutely dominated and other industries, like education and innovation technology, took a small share in the market. Simultaneously, The SP proposes that the spatial structure of Nanjing should be transformed from 'decentralization' into 'centralization' (Wang, 2002).

- *Dynamic mechanism analysis*. This method focuses on analyzing the dynamic mechanism of urban development. It helps understand the inherent law of urban spatial evolvement and avoids a superficial phenomenal perception of city development. For instance, when preparing Jiangyin SP, it was first recognized that industrial development alone could not facilitate urban development. To add impetus to Jiangyin's development and build Jiangyin into a competitive city, improving service facilities was pivotal. Thus, the development strategy of Jiangyin was decided as: Maintaining the growth of industrialization, promoting urbanization through the development of the service sector, and further facilitating modernization by providing high-quality cultural and commercial infrastructures.

- *Historical analysis*. By employing this method, city history is perceived to be important in future urban development and in shaping urban morphology. It is believed that the analysis of city history can provide inspiration for making SP. Taking Wuhan city as an example, the planners have spent a significant amount of time investigating the historical development path of Wuhan since the eighteenth century. It is concluded that geographical location has been an advantage for Wuhan for hundreds of years and Wuhan should further make use of this by improving its role as a traffic hub in inland China.

- *Goal-path analysis*. This analysis denotes that planners provide planning alternatives for decision-makers based on the proposed planning goals. In other words, goals are settled first, followed by the paths and means to reach them. It is noteworthy that through this approach, the planning goals are proposed by planners instead of clients (normally the governments), which differentiates SP from the traditional master planning in China.

- *Comparative study*. This method believes that through synchronic and diachronic comparative studies among similar cities or regions, experiences can be identified and the future direction can be clarified.

- *Institutional analysis*. When using this method, it is believed that the determinants for adopting a strategic alternative include not only the economic cost but also the institutional cost. A strategic plan would be more practical and operable if the plan is considered in an institutional environment.

- *Alternatives analysis*. This approach is commonly employed in Chinese SP preparation. After comparing each alternative, decision-makers can make more reasonable choices. It was applied in formulating the first SP of Guangzhou. At that time, considering the uncertainty of the external environment (such as the policy environment and economic environment), two alternatives for Guangzhou SP were proposed. One was to develop steadily and the other was to grow rapidly. The ultimate scenario was chosen according to the actual external environment of the time (Zhang, 2001).

Noticeably, three main bodies exist in urban SP preparation in China. One is planning institutes, among which the China Academy of Urban Planning and Design (CAUPD) is the forerunner. The other two are foreign consultant companies and planning academics. The theories and methods adopted by these three bodies are different. The knowledge system of the planning institutes is based on physical planning. Hence, the popular theories and methods for them are regional economics, urbanization theory, location theory, SWOT analysis, and so on, when formulating strategies for cities. By contrast, given that the SP knowledge of foreign consultant companies is from management disciplines, these companies often analyze the economic development of one region based on globalization theory, transnational corporation theory, and corporatization operational strategy theory. When preparing SP for Chinese cities, they usually refer to the spatial arrangement and spatial morphology of foreign cities such as London, New York, Paris, Tokyo and Portland, believing that the societal development in the West stands for the highest level, and western urban development experiences, especially those of the metropolises, can be copied to China (Liu, et al., 2013). Planning academics in universities and research institutes borrow theories and methods from related disciplines, such as economy, geography and management, which are more abstract than the other two.

## Modes

No uniform mode concerning SP preparation currently exists because of the diversity of the planning bodies that undertake the job of formulating SP, plus the lack of legal or uniform 'preparation methods'[7] at the national level.

### *Planning bodies*

As mentioned above, SP formulation bodies in China fall into three camps: (1) Chinese planning institutes headed by CAUPD. They are the professional planning groups in China who monopolize and act as the main supplier in the SP formulation market (Liu, et al., 2013). Owing to the rich experiences of these institutes on planning practices, a large proportion of innovations in SP preparation originates from them. (2) Foreign planning consultant companies. These companies approach the planning market of China after the country joined the World Trade Organization (WTO) and subsequently opened up overseas service procurement. By participating in the various strategic/concept planning competitions, these companies start to play a role in SP preparation (Liu, et al., 2013).

(3) Planning academics in universities and research institutes. By getting involved in planning institutes linked to colleges and universities, academics make SP with a strong research feature.

### Technical process

Four main types of technical processes can be identified in the Chinese SP practices (Sheng and Gu, 2005). (1) *Problem-deductive type*. This type follows the process of 'problems → strategies', which means looking for solutions (strategies) is performed following a clarification of urban development problems. (2) *Goal-oriented type*. Following the logic of 'goals → strategies', this type emphasizes goal setting for the city future, from which the development strategies are derived. The most recent SP of Tianjin city is such a type. When formulating the plan, the objective of building Tianjin into an 'International Port City', a 'North Economy Centre', and an 'Ecology City' were first confirmed, followed by detailed strategies in how to achieve those goals (Liu and Cao, 2014). (3) *Problem–goal-interacting type*. This type is guided by the process of 'problems + goals → strategies', where strategies are made based on both problem diagnosis and on urban development goal selection. For instance, when Shenzhen 2030 was formulated, both the existing problems hindering city development and the proposed development goal 'building Shenzhen into a globally pioneering sustainable city' were taken into account (Chen, et al., 2013). (4) *Conditions-inductive type*. The logic for this type is 'conditions → strategies', where strategies are developed according to the analysis of local conditions. For example, based on an analysis of Ningbo's competence as a harbour city, Ningbo 2030 suggests the harbour function should be further enhanced (Xu, et al., 2012).

Among these types, the 'problem–goal-interacting' technical process is dominant (Yang, 2006) because of the problem-oriented characteristic of Chinese SP (Lu, et al., 2010). After the incorporation of system theory, this type of technical process further evolves into 'identify the problems → set the goals → decide the alternative → establish supporting measures → evaluate and demonstrate alternative → decide the strategy' (Li, 2004).

It should be highlighted that in the first round, the experimental period of SP, different planning bodies have diversified types of technical process. Usually, the client (local municipal government) invites several planning institutes/agencies to attend a competition, which makes the SP 'market' competitive.

## Conclusion

In conclusion, the emergence of SP in China reflects both the urgent needs of local governments in a competitive era and the need of practitioners to explore new planning forms. In terms of practical applications, the first round of SP in China is an innovation of the traditional city master planning. By regarding SP as a preliminary study to master planning in the new Measures, a kind of 'legal status' is attached to SP. In the second round, Chinese SP begins to coordinate with other statutory planning types rather than compete with them. However, in terms of research, Chinese SP is still under exploration, which is characterized by a huge diversity in strategic thinking. This diversity is mainly embodied in the unconsolidated perception of SP and the lack of a united formulation mode, although they are acceptable against the background of increasing decentralization and when confronted with the diversity of different Chinese cities. Moreover, Albrechts (2006, p.1150) has also argued that 'there is no "one best or one single way" to carry out strategic spatial planning. The most appropriate approach depends to a large extent on the challenges faced, the particular (substantive and institutional) context of a place and the values and attitudes of the main actors in the process.' However, we hold the point that the confusing understanding of SP at the theoretical level should at least be avoided. Only when a clear theoretical framework is established can SP practices be guided in a more efficient and effective way.

The immaturity of Chinese SP is also reflected in its ambiguous position in the whole planning system. In other words, SP is not well integrated with the other types of planning into one system. Currently, various planning forms coexist in the planning pool of China. Different departments and sections make plans of different levels, scales, and styles that compete directly with SP.[8] Planning fragmentation (Huo, 2007) is becoming an increasingly hard-to-heal disease in China. Given its comprehensiveness, SP should have functioned as a coordinating tool in the fragmented planning system. However, drawbacks such as the lack of a stable legal status prevent SP from performing this function, and the connection between SP and other planning types is not well developed. Wang et al. (2011) even argue that SP is only perceived as a policy advice to city master planning. In addition, it is simply a tool that serves decision-makers (for example, the mayor), and only 'brings about a new situation for urban studies' (Zhang, 2007).

Additionally, all existing SP studies and practices in China focus mainly on the city level. A lack of SP that concerns the cross-border or transregional development is evident. China, a nation with such a big territory and population, is now confronted with a serious regional development imbalance. SP at the transregional level should be considered as an effective means to mitigate regional disparity.

In summary, compared with the strategic spatial planning in northwestern Europe, SP in China possesses strong 'Chinese characteristics', and is still in the early exploratory stage: (1) SP is mainly regarded as a physical tool to manage resources more than a public policy (Yang, 2006). Specifically, SP remains as a 'government-led' process, which emphasizes planning techniques rather than spatial governance. Particularly in the first round, SP in China seldom focuses on public policy study and rarely involves the general public into the decision-making process. However, the situation has improved in the second round. A growing public participation can be identified in the planning process in some cities. But it should be noted that the participation only occurs in the planning formulation stage and the role of the public is rather limited. (2) Chinese SP concentrates more on drawing a blueprint for the future rather than probing into the implementation measures (Yang, 2006). Since the new Measures explicitly stipulates that SP should be prepared as a proactive study prior to city master planning, SP has been commonly understood as a tool that serves city master planning. Based on careful comparison, the content of a strategic plan is actually an extension of the guideline of the corresponding city master plan. Hyslop (2007, p.59) even holds the viewpoint that 'in China, the city master plan is the king, and strategic approaches are not greatly in evidence'. Overall, China has a low awareness of the independence of SP from other planning types and the importance of well implementing SP. Notably, the content of the 'action plan' of SP is extended in the second round. In some cities, such as Ningbo and Guangzhou, implementation measures and actions are explicitly proposed in the planning documents. However, the implementation effects remain to be examined. (3) Chinese SP pays more attention to enhancing the economic competitiveness than to social equity and environmental quality. Although the focus of the second round has shifted from 'quantity' to 'quality', economic elements still occupy an absolutely bigger share in this 'urban quality'. In contrast with the developed northwestern European nations, the social and environmental concerns in China are yet to increase.

Despite the fact that the understanding and implementation of SP need improving, the achievements so far in the SP practices in China should not be overlooked. Particularly, various methods and different types of technical process concerning SP preparation have been established, which provides a wide range of choices for Chinese policy-makers and planners. They might also be used as references in the SP practices in the West when technical issues are concerned.

## Funding

This article is sponsored by the Australian Studies Competitive Projects Funding, Youth Fund of the Natural Science Foundation of China (51308491), the Chinese Ministry of Education of Humanities and Social Sciences Fund (13YJC770002), and the Philosophy and Social Sciences Planning Project of Zhejiang Province (13ZJQN018YB).

## Notes

1 The five-year plan in China is a long-term plan that maps the direction of economic and social development at different levels. This plan is reviewed every five years and each review will set new targets for economic and social development.
2 There is another opinion that argues that the first strategic planning in Mainland China should be the development strategy study called 'Shanghai: Towards 21st century' organized by the Shanghai municipal government in 1994.
3 It should be noticed that the comprehensive SP is different for the traditional comprehensive planning. Here 'comprehensive' means that more than one thematic issue is studied strategically.
4 Except Shenzhen 2030, SP in other Chinese cities are all non-statutory plans. Shenzhen 2030 includes 'statutory documents' and is approved by Standing Committee of Shenzhen NPC (National People's Congress). However, Shenzhen 2030 in nature is a preliminary study of Shenzhen city master planning.

5 Based on the analysis of the uncertainties and possibilities in urban development, scenario planning provides the possible scenarios for urban development considering all the elements. Scenario planning simulates different scenarios, makes comparative studies among these scenarios, and decides the final regulatory (or guiding) strategies for urban development. In scenario planning, the most appropriate alternatives are selected by identifying development opportunities. Thus, scenario planning makes it possible to adjust the development alternatives of cities in a changing development environment.

6 Notably, the new 'Urban–Rural Planning Act' in 2008 added provincial urban system planning as statutory planning. As mentioned, this chapter considers this planning as strategic planning in a broad sense, which somehow provides a statutory status to SP. However, SP in a narrow sense, particularly SP for a city, still remains non-statutory.

7 In China, all types of statutory planning are equipped with respective planning preparation methods.

8 For example, the National Development and Reform Commission in China also prepares regional planning and land use planning (generally called territorial planning). With the increasing power of these ministries and commissions, a decreasing role of city planning prepared by local governments becomes more evident (Yang, 2010).

## References

Albrechts, L., 2004. Strategic (Spatial) Planning Revisited. *Environment and Planning B: Planning & Design*, 31(5), 743–758.

Albrechts, L., 2006. Shifts in Strategic Spatial Planning? Some Evidence from Europe and Australia. *Environment and Planning A*, 38(6), 1149–1170.

Chen, D. R., Jiang, L. and Cheng, M. J., 2011. New Study on Urban Strategic Development in Transitional Period. *Nanjing Planning Studies*, 35(s1), 148–151 (in Chinese).

Chen, K. S., Yang, R., and Qian, Y., 2013. A Study on the Chinese Urban Mid-long Term Development and Strategic Planning: Based on the Comparison of Shen Zhen 2030, Hong Kong 2030, New York 2030, and Sydney 2030. *Urban Development Studies*, 20(11), 32–40 (in Chinese).

Huo, B., 2007. Revival and Innovation of Strategic Spatial Planning of China. *City Planning Review*, 31(8), 19–29 (in Chinese).

Hyslop, J., 2007. Comment 2. See Friedmann, J., 2007. Strategic Spatial Planning and the Longer Range. *Planning Theory & Practice*, 5(1), 49–67.

Jiang, T., 2009. Future Direction of Chinese Strategic Spatial Planning: An Internationally Comparative Perspective. *City Planning Review*, 33(8), 80–86 (in Chinese).

Li, X. J., 2003. Some Considerations on Urban Spatial Strategic Studies. *City Planning Review,* 27(2), pp.28-34 (in Chinese).

Li, X., 2004. City Spatial Strategy by Systematic Methodology. *City Planning Review*, 28(10), 44–48 (in Chinese).

Liu, C. Y., Lin, D. F. and Pan, T., 2013. Comparing Strategic Planning across the Taiwan Straits. *Urban Planning International*, 28(4), 37–42 (in Chinese).

Liu, Z. and Cao, K., 2014. On the Differentiation of Strategic Spatial Planning Making Mechanisms in New Era: Between Melbourne and Tianjin. *International Journal of Social, Education, Economics and Management Engineering*, 8(4), 969–974.

Lu, C. T., Wu, C. and Huang D. X., 2010. From Concept Planning to Structural Planning: Review and Innovation of Strategic Plan of Guangzhou. *City Planning Review*, 34(3), 17–24 (in Chinese).

Qian, X., Wang, D. and Sun, Y., 2009. The Application of Cross-impact Analysis in Strategic Planning Research: A Case Study on the TM Program in Nanjing Strategy Planning. *Urban Planning Forum*, 2, 69–74 (in Chinese).

Shen, T. Y., 2007. Speech. See Li, X. J. and Yang, B. J., 2007. Strategic Planning. *City Planning Review*, 31(1), 44–56 (in Chinese).

Sheng, M. and Gu, C. L., 2005. On Technical Process of Strategic Planning in China. *City Planning Review*, 29(2), 46–51 (in Chinese).

Wang, K., 2002. From Guangzhou to Hangzhou: The Arising Strategic Planning. *City Planning Review*, 26(6), 58–62 (in Chinese).

Wang, K., 2006. The Four Major Changes of Urban Spatial Structure in China in the Past 50 Years. *City Planning Review*, 30(12), 9–14, 86 (in Chinese).

Wang, L., Ma, C. Y. and Hu, J. Y., 2011. The Review and Study of Strategic Planning. *Urban Studies*, 18(6), 7–12 (in Chinese).

Wang, W. and Zhao, J. H., 2013. Strategic Hotspots and Transformation Revelation on Development Strategy of Global Cities in New Century: Based on 15 Urban Development Strategy Reports Analysis. *Urban Studies*, 20(1), 1–8 (in Chinese).

Wang, X. and Luo, Z. D., 2011. Strategic Planning Evolution within China's Transformation Context. *Planners*, 27(7), 84–88 (in Chinese).

Wu, L. Y. and Wu, W. J., 2012. *Beijing 2049 Spatial Development Strategies Study*. Beijing: Qinghua University Press (in Chinese).

Wu, Z. Q., Yu, H. and Jiang, N., 2003. An Integrated Methodology of Urban Strategic Planning: With Shenyang as the Case. *City Planning Review*, 27(1), 38–42 (in Chinese).

Xu, Z., Zhang, Y. F. and Xu, Y., 2012. Review and Prospect of Ten-Year Strategic Planning: A Case Study on Ningbo Urban Development Strategy 2030. *City Planning Review*, 36(8), 73–79, 86 (in Chinese).

Yang, B. J., 2006. *Some Thoughts on Strategic Planning*. Beijing: China Architecture & Building Press (in Chinese).

Yang, B. J., 2007. Speech. See Li, X. J. and Yang, B. J., 2007. Strategic Planning. *City Planning Review*, 31(1), 44–56 (in Chinese).

Yang, B. J., 2010. Urban Planning 30 Years: Reviews and Prospects. *Urban Planning Forum*, 1, 14–23 (in Chinese).

Zhang, B., 2001. A Preliminary Study on the Methodology of Concept Planning: A Case of Concept Planning for Guangzhou City Development. *City Planning Review*, 25(3), 53–58 (in Chinese).

Zhang, B., 2002. A Critical Review of the Strategic Planning Practice in Contemporary China with Guangzhou, Nanjing and Jiangyin as the Cases. *City Planning Review*, 26(6), 63–68 (in Chinese).

Zhang, B., 2007. Speech. See Li, X. J. and Yang, B. J., 2007. Strategic Planning. *City Planning Review*, 31(1), 44–56 (in Chinese).

Zhao, X. B., 2010. The Research of Changsha City Development Strategy Based on Spatial Equilibrium. *Urban Studies*, 17(11), 34–40 (in Chinese).

Zou, D. C., 2003. Some consideration on strategic planning. *City Planning Review*, 27(1), 17–18 (in Chinese).

# 7 The role of strategic spatial planning in territorial sustainability

## The case of France

*Christophe Demazière and José Serrano*

## Introduction

In the 1990s and noughties, strategic spatial planning was theorised by researchers who analysed a number of initiatives at work in some European regions (see *inter alia* Healey, 1997, 2007; Salet and Faludi, 2000; Albrechts, Healey and Kunzmann, 2003). This type of planning stands distinctly apart from the practices of past decades. There is now a wide consensus on the fact that the collaborative approach is the predominant paradigm in planning theory (Douay, 2010). To draw up and then implement planning requires setting up numerous exchange systems to promote interactions between actors, in order to create standards and visions of shared actions. The construction of strategies and networks of actors are thus closely entwined through legal standards.

However, in the context of France, we would like to qualify the enthusiasm that sometimes exists around the renewal of approaches to planning. The law *Solidarité et Renouvellement Urbains* (Urban Solidarity and Renewal), passed in 2000, certainly put strategic spatial planning on the agenda of local authorities. It also set spatial planning as a means to materialise the principles of sustainable development. However, since then the pace of artificialisation of natural and agricultural land has increased. There seems to be a gap between the legislator's 'good intentions' and the planning dynamics on the ground. A variety of practices can be observed due to the fact that spatial planning comes under the jurisdiction of municipal authorities and of newly created collaborative groupings of municipalities. This chapter will demonstrate that French urban development planning has difficulties in limiting urban sprawl, particularly when economic development and business sites are involved. Spatial planning has become more strategic in France, but its effectiveness depends primarily on the level of cooperation within and between the collaborative groupings of municipalities which have appeared since the 1990s.

## Fragmented local Government: is progress being made?

France is a unitary state. It is divided into 26 administrative regions, of which 22 are on the mainland and four are overseas. The regions are further subdivided into 100 departments and 36,682 municipalities. During the last decades, the autonomy of local authorities has increased. In the early 1980s, the Decentralization Acts created regions, transferred jurisdiction to sub-central levels and introduced the principle of free administration. The Constitutional reform in 2003 and the ensuing legislation represented a further step in terms of sharing revenue-raising powers between state and local governments. Nowadays, the region has compe-tence in economic development (management of direct and indirect subsidies to businesses), transport (management of the railroad network, development of seaports and airports), education (construction, maintenance and operation of secondary schools), and vocational training. The main responsibilities of depart-ments are social services, education (construction, maintenance and equipment of primary schools), and transport (extension and maintenance of all roads that are not part of the national public domain).

Municipalities were created by law in 1790. Nowadays, there are more than 36,000 municipalities over a territory of 550,000 km$^2$ and a population of 64 million. In comparison, Germany has 12,000 municipalities for an area of 360,000 km$^2$ and a population of 82 million, and Italy has 8,000 municipalities for an area of 300,000 km$^2$ and a population of 59 million. Since the Municipal Act in 1884, French municipalities have had their own administrative organisa-tion, regardless of their size. Since the 1980s their main competencies are plan-ning, economic development, housing, healthcare and the social sector, education and culture.

The expenditure of French local authorities represents 21% of general govern-ment expenditure, which is far less than in federal countries, like Belgium (42%) or in Northern state countries – e.g. the figure is 45% in Sweden (Ismeri Applica, 2010). On the other hand, France is a case of high financial autonomy: around 50% of the local revenue of subnational government is generated by local taxes (Dexia Research Department, 2008). To levy taxes, many French municipalities (as well as the departments and the regions) have promoted the setting up of companies, job creation and housing development. However, within a single conurbation, territorial competition to attract or to retain firms has proved to be sterile. It has even been costly when similar public investments (e.g. large congress centres, business parks, etc.) have been made in neighbouring munici-palities so as to stimulate economic development further.

Unlike most of its European neighbours, France has failed to merge its munici-palities. This has led to extreme polarisation: in 2008, more than three munici-palities out of four had less than 1,000 inhabitants, whereas 2.5% had more than 10,000 inhabitants and hosted half of the total population. The average population of a municipality is 1,600 in France, much less than in any of its neighbouring countries: 17,900 in Belgium, 6,700 in Germany, 7,000 in Italy, 5,500 in Spain and 137,000 in the UK (Baldersheim and Lawrence, 2010).

Since the 1960s, against this background, the French state has fostered the creation of collaborative groupings of municipalities through which resources, skills and tools are shared. This policy is based on the voluntarism of municipali-ties to unite, although the state subsidises these groupings and has enabled them to levy their own taxes. In some regions the cooperation has increased while in others it has lacked momentum, leaving municipalities at the centre of city-regions with the burden of financing services like welfare or culture, while neighbouring municipalities have developed as employment centres or as residential suburbs.

The Chevènement Act of 1999 tried to simplify and to reinforce the inter-municipality system, by defining three possible forms of cooperation. Urban communities (*'communauté urbaine'*) for conurbations over 500,000 inhabitants, and conurbation communities (*'communauté d'agglomération'*) of between 50,000 and 500,000 inhabitants, are in charge of major policies, such as urban regeneration, social balance of housing, environmental protection, and economic development. These strategic domains for the future of medium-sized or large cities have been transferred from the *communes*. The financial incentives provided by the state explain why many municipalities have been keen to participate in such collaborative groupings of municipalities, even in places which until then had had no clear interest in drawing up common policies (Baraize and Négrier, 2001). However, the officials of the collaborative grouping are not directly elected and are nominated to the inter-municipal council by each municipal council.

On the quantitative level, the Chevènement law was a success. At the beginning of 2012, 90% of the French population and 96% of municipalities were grouped together into *communautés*, while ten years before, both proportions were around 50%. With their single tax regime, the 202 conurbation communities and the 12 urban communities are home to half of the French population, but they cover only 3,600 municipalities. Inter-municipal cooperation has helped to unify public action in large cities and their suburban rings, but only to a certain extent. On average, the collaborative groupings of municipalities that lay at the heart of a city-region host 70% of the population of the city-region on 30% of its surface. The third form of cooperation proposed in the Chevènement Act, the community of municipalities (*'communauté de communes'*), was intended for the rural municipalities. However, it has also been used by suburban municipalities in a defensive way, to avoid being integrated into a cooperative structure where the urbanised municipalities would have the power. The Chevènement Act has given major sectoral responsibilities to *communautés*, but from a sustainability perspective, the protection and promotion of the natural assets of a territory (landscape, biodiversity, farm land, etc.) can only be achieved through the cooperation of these actors at the scale of a city-region. Communities of municipalities represent more than 40% of the total population in France and 80% of the total number of municipalities, so there is a risk that they can develop their own development strategy. Thus to ensure the coherence of overall actions, there is a need for dialogue between the communities of municipalities and the more densely populated *communautés urbaines* or *communautés d'agglomération*.

The Chevènement law aimed to regulate the competition between municipalities to attract companies and to levy business tax. However, in most cases it has exacerbated the competition by creating more powerful players, the collaborative groupings of municipalities. On the one hand, the local tax paid by businesses is the only tax which is levied directly by these new organisations, which need resources in order to develop policies and to prove their utility. Municipalities continue to collect the taxes paid by households. On the other hand, the suburban villages and small towns which previously had few resources can now pool them and develop an inter-municipal local economic development policy jointly with others. Within a city-region, new competition between collaborative groupings of municipalities has risen around greenfield sites. This was most probably a major cause of increased urban sprawl in France during the last decade (Petitet and Caubel, 2010).

## The revival of spatial planning in France: promoting territorial cohesion

In parallel to the devolution process and to the reorganisation of local government, there has been a renewal of spatial planning for large urban areas. After the end of the Second World War and until the 1990s, the main aim of spatial planning in France was to organise urban development and the location of economic activity. Within a context of steady economic growth, and also of a rural–urban shift, the Gaullist State multiplied its spatial interventions. Notable examples are the new towns policy, or the incentives given to industrial companies to leave the Paris region and to settle in the provinces. To keep full control of management operations that were launched around fast-growing cities or medium-sized towns, the state reinforced the spatial planning system at the end of the 1960s, with the *Loi d'orientation foncière*. The law introduced the Master Plan for Urban Planning and Development (*schéma directeur d'aménagement et d'urbanisme*, later *schéma directeur*) so as to create documents that fixed the main direction for growth at the scale of the urban areas as a whole. The *schéma directeur* was supposed to define the inter-scale broad zoning and the planning of major community facilities, while the local plan, at the level of the *commune*, controlled land use and the density for development. In the French system, a local plan has statutory power: it embodies the rights of use associated with a piece of land that are confirmed through the granting of planning permission to build in compliance with building regulations.

The *schéma directeur* was developed by the state representatives in each large city, at the inter-municipal level. Its objectives had to be fully integrated in the municipal land-use plan which was also defined by civil servants. For the state, a major objective was to reduce the quantitative shortage of available land for urban and industrial development at the local level by limiting speculative trends in land ownership. To achieve this, it imposed its will on the municipalities. However, the *schéma directeur* proved to have several shortcomings. First, it was not a strategic document with a prospective dimension but a legal framework for planning for growth. The forecasts of economic growth on which it was based faltered in the oil crisis of 1973 and the plans were discredited because of the supposed high rates of growth which were not achieved (Booth, Nelson and Paris, 2007). Furthermore, such a plan did not provide an adequate framework for strategic thinking at the metropolitan level (Motte, 1995). It was too narrow and rigidly focused on land use, and not aimed enough at implementation to be effective. Its orientations could not be applied directly to individual development decisions and had to be mediated by the municipal plans to take effect.

Since the 1980s, planning has been decentralised to municipalities. Therefore, the principle of local autonomy left the choice to the local authorities as to whether or not they would establish a plan. For several reasons, most municipalities focused on the local plan and, in contrast, the *schéma directeur* quickly fell into disuse. First, the level of inter-municipal cooperation was still low, with the exception of the largest conurbations of Bordeaux, Lille, Lyons, and Strasbourg, where in the late 1960s the state had forced the municipalities to create powerful organisations of cooperation. Second, many mayors had reservations about planning since plans for urban areas had hitherto been made (and imposed) by the state. At that time, only a minority of local decision-makers saw the interest of developing a prospective vision for their area. In general, they conducted this outside the planning system, like Raymond Barre, then mayor of Lyon and head of a collaborative grouping of 55 municipalities and 1.2 million inhabitants, with the forward-looking programme *Millénaire 3* (Verhage, Baker and Boino, 2007).

Furthermore, due to the economic crisis, large-scale planning documents were no longer able to fulfil their function of forecasting. Faced with the gradual calling into question of planning as expressed in land-use maps, the notion of the 'urban project', which was launched in various forms both in France and abroad, became appealing (Hebbert, 2006). Planning and the *schéma directeur*, in the French context, were thus seen as instruments which limited the capacity for collective action, whereas the urban project would make it possible to conduct urban change more effectively, by closely associating public- and private-sector players (Douay, 2010). Even though the French government was led by a socialist coalition throughout most of the 1980s, one could witness the influence of neoliberalism on urban policy, like in many other parts of the western world. This was illustrated by the joint efforts made by the French state and mayors of large cities to attract private investment into flagship projects like Disneyland Paris, *Euralille* or *Euroméditerranée* (respectively to the east of Paris, in Lille and in Marseilles). More generally, instead of regulating urban development, local authorities increasingly aimed at stimulating such development. In so doing, the question of ensuring coherence between the policies of individual *communes* at the level of the urban area as a whole was only partially addressed through sectoral planning documents.

In the late 1990s, a new initiative by the state, the *Solidarité et renouvellement urbains* law (SRU – solidarity and urban renewal), triggered a revival of urban development planning and rendered it more strategic. The underlying rationale for the reform of the planning system was fourfold: to ensure that the development of urban areas would be treated as a whole and not only through municipal plans; to improve the coherence of strategic and operational policy and to create direct linkages between land-use planning, transport and housing; to promote social balance within urban areas; and to foster local responsibility in the development of planning policy (Booth *et al.*, 2007).

When the bill was presented to the French Parliament, Jean-Claude Gayssot, the Minister of Planning, Transport and Housing, proposed to 'replace the *schéma directeur*, which was too rigid and inflexible, and therefore quickly ineffective, with an urban development plan (*'schéma de cohérence territoriale'*) combining flexibility and efficiency'.[1] The development plan was dressed up with the qualities attributed to the urban project approach: 'its aim is to express the conurbation's overall strategy and to state the main choices made in the area of housing, balance between natural and urban areas, infrastructure and commercial town planning'. The relevant scale put forward by the state is the city-region: the new plan created 'a single framework for negotiating strategies between urban and suburban or even rural areas that are part [...] of a given living space'.[2] The urban development plan operates at an inter-municipal level which is for the local authorities to define, but is fairly broad where possible. Based on a precise and shared diagnosis, such a plan is supposed to outline a development and sustainability strategy for the long term (15–20 years), and to define the conditions for its implementation. At the municipal or inter-municipal level, the local plan must be compatible with the urban development plan. It sets the land-use rules at the local level and is used for issuing spatial planning permits, whereas the urban development plan develops more a vision of the territory and its future.

In short, the urban development plan is supposed to be both strategic, including a prospective exercise on the tendencies of future development and their spatial dimensions, and effective, by having a legal status. Currently, 400 urban development plans have been approved or are in the process of being approved, which corresponds to most of urban France, even though only 55% of the national territory is covered. The SRU law is an attempt by the French state to relaunch strategic planning in a situation where the municipalities and their cooperative structures are now the key actors. The new planning system seeks to overcome the French municipal fragmentation, which leads to inconsistencies in the local choices that are made. While respecting the autonomy of local governments, the state sets out incentives for the development of plans, making them almost an obligation. The urban development plan creates a unique playing-field for negotiation between urban, suburban, and rural parts of the same city-region. The public institution in charge of the plan is perennial and many arenas are open to discussion. In terms of scale, the plan involves one or several collaborative municipal groupings. Thus, municipalities are involved through an intermediary body which is supposed to bear their interests.

While the Chevènement law led municipalities to reorganise the local government system, through the creation of collaborative groupings, the SRU law introduced the urban development plan so that such groupings could think through and organise spatial development in a more coherent way. This search for coherence goes beyond the sole aspect of land-use planning: it requires sector-based policies to be coordinated and the complementarity of urban and suburban areas to be strengthened. It requires scores of mayors and hundreds of local councillors in a given city-region to assess and to define collectively a spatial project at a scale that is far beyond any municipal perimeter, and, moreover, at a time horizon of

10–15 years, which exceeds by far the duration of a municipal electoral mandate (six years).

All this can make it difficult for local public actors to develop a plan with a real strategic content. The first question is how willing and able are collaborative groupings of municipalities to share their own development strategy (if they have one!) with other groupings? As the SRU law was passed (2000) only a year after the Chevènement law (1999), most collaborative groupings had only existed for a short time and, in addition, they had to deal with new major responsibilities, such as housing, transport or economic development. Thus, priority was often given to mutual learning between municipalities of the same grouping rather than to sharing views with other groupings which, in effect, could be seen as rivals for attracting jobs and people, and hence for levying taxes. This can be illustrated by the narrow perimeters of most urban development plans compared to city-regions (Desjardins and Leroux, 2007). The perimeter of an urban development plan can be limited to the scope of a single collaborative grouping of municipalities, whereas the scale of the problems it is supposed to deal with (socio-spatial segregation, land consumption, dependence on cars) goes beyond that scope. This is the case in Marseille-Aix, a polycentric city-region of 1.7 million inhabitants (the third largest city in France in terms of population). The city of Marseille does not occupy a dominant position in the city-region because, for a long time, it pursued its own development while ignoring its hinterland. After the Chevènement law, the 90 municipalities within the functional urban region created seven collaborative groupings and the fierce competition between them led to the development of seven urban development plans, each corresponding to one grouping (Demazière, 2012). More generally, A. Motte (2006: 19–20) considers that the city-region 'would constitute the ideal relevant scale for understanding the key territorial dynamics and public action. Today, this is considered "obvious" for central governments, researchers and technicians, but is often much less "obvious" for local authorities'.

Within city-regions, collaborative groupings demonstrate quite diverse experiences of inter-territorial cooperation (Vanier, 2010) because municipalities themselves can have a limited (or recent) experience of inter-municipal cooperation (Baraize and Négrier, 2001). Therefore, their abilities to get involved in strategic spatial planning are not equal. This is confirmed by the observation that the collaborative groupings of municipalities deal differently with urban planning, depending on the cases considered (Table 7.1). Conurbation communities or communities of municipalities may choose to complete an inter-municipal local plan. However, in most cases, the local plan remains a municipal privilege.[3] This raises doubts as to the real will of many municipalities to cooperate in the field of planning.

## Urban development plans and sustainable development

In their study of the changes in planning practice in the UK during the 1990s, Vigar *et al.* (2000) argue that the process of policy change 'is not just about the

*Table 7.1* Levels of cooperation in spatial planning: ideal-types

|  | *Weak or new* | *Strong and rooted* |
|---|---|---|
| Inter-municipal cooperation | Ex nihilo created *communauté d'agglomération/ urbaine* Local plan made at the municipal level | Transformation of an existing collaborative grouping of municipalities levying taxes (e.g. *district*) into a *communauté d'agglomération/urbaine* Local plan made at the level of the grouping of municipalities |
| Inter-territorial cooperation | Several urban development plans within the city-region, each made by a single collaborative grouping of municipalities | An urban development plan on most of the area of the city-region, drawn up by several collaborative groupings of municipalities The plan can be carried out by a public organisation which has other competencies than spatial planning |

Source: Authors

formal design of regulatory legislation and resource allocation: it also involves changing the discourse in all arenas which are significant for policy to have an effect' (Vigar *et al.*, 2000: 50–51). In the case of France, this can raise the question of the capacity of urban development plans to deal with sustainability issues, and primarily to limit urban sprawl. The concept of sustainable development was introduced for the first time into French planning law with the SRU law. However, according to Vigar *et al.* (2000), the rhetoric of sustainable development at the national level and the importance of the environment in decision-making need to be expressed in ideas and arguments that have salience for stakeholders at the local level, otherwise, the habits and traditions of action may resist change or channel change in particular directions, or reinterpret change using familiar terms.

France is a country where the density of urban population decreased from 600 to 400 inhabitants per square kilometre between 1960 and 2011. Through the 1990s and early 2000s, France used an average of 60,000 hectares per year of natural and agricultural land for building. This rate of land use is almost three times greater than the population growth rate and even seems to have increased over the last few years (2006–2010), to more than 80,000 hectares per year (Petitet and Caubel, 2010). The consequences of urban sprawl are harmful, making it harder to set up new farms, and also increasing energy consumption and greenhouse emissions (including longer car journeys between home and work). Urban sprawl and the artificialisation of natural and agricultural space are a major concern for the state. Increasingly, throughout the 2000s, the policy agenda for spatial planning acknowledged the undesirable social and environmental consequences of urban sprawl. In 2010, the law *Engagement National pour l'Environnement* (National Commitment to the Environment) promoted the urban development plan as the key instrument for addressing sustainable development at the local level. Since then, when devising a plan, it is necessary to analyse the change in land use during the previous ten years, particularly regarding natural, agricultural and forestry areas. This analysis is meant to justify the targets of future land-use change set by the plan guidelines. Any urban development plan must also determine the natural, agricultural and forestry areas which should be protected from future urbanisation. However, following Vigar *et al.* (2000), we may wonder how the orientation set by the state can be implemented locally. For instance, when carrying out an urban development plan, is the link between economic growth and the reduction in the amount of farmland recognised locally? Do areas marked by biodiversity or natural hazards constitute for the actors a clear limit to urban sprawl or to the spatial expansion of manufacturing?

## Contrasting planning processes and their results in two city-regions

In France, a city-region is made up of a set of collaborative groupings of municipalities whose common point is that their first mandatory function is the organisation of their space and economic development.[4] Undertaking an urban development plan therefore sets the question of how to coordinate strategies between territories that are institutionally distinct but interdependent in functional terms.

As our goal was to study how planners combine economic development priorities with environmental challenges into guidelines regarding new business sites, we focused on the most dynamic city-regions in France, where the tensions between economic growth and preservation of the environment would be exacerbated (Demazière, 2012). Using simple demographic and economic criteria (population growth, job growth and levels of unemployment), we selected Rennes and Tours among the most dynamic city-regions.[5] Table 7.2 shows that they have contrasting histories of inter-municipal cooperation.

For both territories, the first task was to characterise the context in terms of geography (growth of the urban area, progression in land artificialisation and spatial development) and economics (areas of growth or decline and trends in location of major activities). Regarding the planning process, the sources used combine data analysis and a review of the literature, and also interviews with the planners in charge of issuing the planning documents and with key decision-makers within groupings of municipalities. The semi-structured interviews focused on the strategies, institutional arrangements and coalitions, and on the relationship established between local economic development and the other areas of local public action (planning, environment, transport, etc.).

The two selected areas stand out through the variety of their inter-municipal cooperation. In Rennes, which is the major city of Brittany, the urban structure is of the monocentric type and the dichotomy between Rennes and its suburban hinterland is strong. The city-region forms an archipelago with the rural centres scattered along the main roads. The creation of a collaborative grouping of

*Table 7.2* Geographical and institutional context of the case studies

| City-region | Rennes | Tours |
|---|---|---|
| Population (2009) | 663,214 | 475,600 |
| Population change (1990–2006) | +26.5 % | +13.0 % |
| Total jobs market (2009) | 306,289 | 202,545 |
| Job variation, compared to the national average (1999–2009) | +24 % | +2.3 % |
| Surface area (2010) | 3,781 km² | 3,199 km² |
| Number of municipalities in the city-region (2010) | 189 | 144 |
| Number of collaborative groupings of municipalities in the city-region (2010) | 20 | 14 |
| Main collaborative grouping of municipalities | *Rennes Métropole* (43 municipalities and 420,707 inhabitants in 2012) | *Tours Plus* (19 municipalities and 286,260 inhabitants in 2012) |
| Number of urban development plans in the urban area (approved by 31/12/2012) | 8(6) | 5(3) |
| Inter-municipal cooperation history | 1970 District 1992 single local business tax rate 2000 Agglomeration community | 1959 District 1999 Agglomeration community |
| Quality of inter-municipal cooperation | Well established | New |

Source: Authors

municipalities goes back to 1970. Rennes' city councillors realised how scarce land was within the municipal boundaries. Gradually, the cooperation strategy within the grouping made it possible to conduct an affirmative and collective policy to orient development. As a result, urban sprawl was controlled.

The urban shape of the city-region of Tours is also of the monocentric type. Inter-municipal cooperation remained virtually non-existent until 1999, when the Chevènement law convinced the municipalities to create collaborative groupings. The suburban municipalities that did not wish to share resources and tools with Tours were able to create their own collaborative groupings with the aim of attracting people and jobs. In such a defensive context, establishing an urban development plan was not an easy task.

In the last 15 years, the artificialisation of land was stronger in Rennes than in Tours, due to greater economic and demographic pressure. The artificialised area increased at an annual rate of 0.8% and 0.3% for housing, and 1.8% and 1.5% for business sites in Rennes and Tours respectively (Demazière, 2012). Tours stands out through the extent of its economic sprawl, which is five times greater than its demographic sprawl, although the Tours city-region is significantly less dynamic than Rennes in terms of the number of jobs created (see Table 7.2).

### *Economic action of the groupings of municipalities marked by competition*

The collaborative groupings of municipalities in the centre of each city-region, *Rennes Métropole* and *Tours Plus*, conduct an economic development strategy that is based on diversifying economic activities. In general, regarding the recycling of wasteland for economic use, the size effect plays a role: the greater the concentration of population, jobs and functions, the more effectively the corresponding collaborative grouping of municipalities is able to carry through complex economic development projects within the urban fabric (Demazière, 2012). Rennes and Tours both have projects to reconvert economic and military wastelands. Presented as being part of a quest for a 'compact city', these projects do, however, require external triggering events, such as the realisation of a High-Speed Train link connecting the city to Paris (effective in 1991 in Tours and in 2017 in Rennes).

In addition to conducting economic projects in the existing urban fabric, the central collaborative groupings of municipalities also seek to welcome new companies by opening greenfield business parks, thus contributing to the economic sprawl. The technicians we met acknowledged that business parks hosted only a minority of jobs (around 30%), but in spite of this they believed that more business parks were necessary. In Rennes, the plan argues that the demand by some companies for land outside the conurbation (and close to motorways) has been identified and it is considered to be legitimate. In Tours, there is clearly a fear of businesses fleeing to neighbouring groupings of municipalities.

The relationships between collaborative groupings of municipalities are decisive concerning the content of economic development policies. For each city-region, the strategy of three collaborative groupings of municipalities was studied. In each case, the property and local job market is dominated by the central urban hub which brings together as much as two-thirds of the population and three-quarters of the jobs in the urban area. This implies that the development strategies of suburban groupings are defined with respect to what *Rennes Métropole* or *Tours Plus* decides. A suburban grouping can have an 'opportunity-based' action, merely opening business parks in its own area, hoping to catch the 'overflow' of business setups. Another strategy is to look for a differentiation from the action of the main grouping. In this case the idea is to attract economic activities in specific or 'innovative' markets, such as the 'green economy'. In the first case, the central and suburban groupings compete to attract the same types of firm, whereas in the second their strategies are complementary.

We can observe that, whatever their size, all the collaborative groupings of municipalities conduct an economic development strategy. Such economic strategies need to be coordinated when drawing up the urban development plan. The groupings are the major actors in the urban development plan. Subsequently, they are tasked with implementing the plan's orientations through their sectorial policies (housing, economic development, etc.). Hence the content of an urban development plan and also its outcomes in terms of urban projects are to a large extent in their hands.

*Table 7.3* Review of the main orientations and coordination between economic and environmental issues in the urban development plans of Rennes and Tours[1]

|  | *Rennes* | *Tours* |
| --- | --- | --- |
| Year of approval | 2007 | 2013 |
| Quantitative approach to economic development | Quantified estimation of land needs (short and medium term) | Limited information |
| Reluctance to control economic land | Weak | Strong |
| Concrete definition of economic aims | Strong Quantitative objectives | Weak Each collaborative grouping of municipalities decides |
| Control of economic sprawl | Strong Identification and mapping of strategic sites | Weak General aims formulated |
| Landscape protection | Strong Multifunctional areas | Weak Formulated only |
| Brownfield reclamation | Quantitative targets | Formulated only |

Source: Authors

[1]In each case, our results are based on analysis of the documents from the urban development plan as well as those which were produced during the elaboration process. The data were complemented by interviews with key players involved in each urban development plan.

### *Strategic spatial planning: how to curb territorial competition*

As we saw earlier, on paper the urban development plan is the preferred instrument for sustainable development at the city-region level. In particular, it deals with the location of current and future economic activities, notably with the help of cartographic data. The process of drawing up the plan therefore provides the opportunity for discussion, arbitration and settling conflicts between issues of economic development and environmental preservation. It also enables the economic development strategies of the groupings to be regulated.

The reduction in land artificialisation, particularly to favour the preservation of natural areas and farmland, appears to be a goal at the heart of both urban development plans (Table 7.3). However, in the case of Tours, a doubt remains concerning the real will to limit economic sprawl. The urban development plan, approved in 2013, includes an approach to reduce economic sprawl which is not really complete. Its orientations are not explicitly materialised in the form of quantified targets. The assessment highlights that Tours has experienced significant urban sprawl owing to residential expansion towards 'rurban' areas. On paper, the plan expresses the will of decision-makers to implement an improved organisation and spatial distribution of activities and residential areas. However, regarding this spatial distribution there is no clear notion of obligation. In the urban development plan the economic development policy is referred back to the collaborative groupings of municipalities. The wording clearly states that the collaborative groupings of municipalities can freely exercise their competence in the area of economic development: 'In terms of economic development, each area has its own specific needs. In this sense, the project recognises the role of the collaborative groupings of municipalities in the development, measured extension or redevelopment of activity sites or zones that are acknowledged to be of interest to the municipality or community. The deployment of local economic activities, whether this is in the existing central areas or on dedicated sites, is therefore organised at their level' (SMAT, 2011: 18). In order to reconcile the different interests of all the stakeholders, the plan only adds the economic development strategies and, particularly, their related land resources. According to this logic, the collaborative groupings of municipalities will continue to conduct their economic development actions in the same way as before the plan was adopted. Drawing up the urban development plan can be seen as a missed opportunity.

For Rennes, the plan comprises a map detailing and quantifying the land reserves that will be allocated to economic activities in the city-region for the next 10 years. This shows the prescriptive nature of the urban development plan regarding economic sprawl. The development of the plan has led the decision-makers to seek a more systematic spatialisation, by identifying strategic development sites that are named and quantified. These zones are reserved for economic development, but they must meet requirements in terms of landscape integration and fit in with the overall strategy to develop public transport. The places reserved and fixed by the plan provide a more precise framework for limiting economic sprawl, all the more so as these land reserves have been determined and positioned with respect to ecological corridors. The urban development plan of Rennes highlights the polycentric organisation of the urban fabric and defines the ecological corridors to counterbalance this. Moreover, the agricultural fields to be preserved from any urbanisation are delimited. A green belt aims at preventing the junction between built spaces.

The process of drawing up the urban development plan highlights the intensity of inter-municipal cooperation, which was, however, not an easy task. In economic and demographic terms, there is a strong dichotomy between Rennes and the other municipalities of the city-region, so that the latter are continually afraid of being absorbed. This is why the state's attempt to create an urban community in 1969 failed. Instead, a form of downward cooperation was created, but a strong inter-municipal cooperation process gradually gained momentum. In 1992, the collaborative grouping of the municipalities of Rennes voluntarily adopted a single business tax, being the first in France to do so. In 1994, on completion of the *schéma directeur*, the proposal from the city of Rennes to create a green belt reduced the fears of surrounding municipalities. Due to the lack of land for its development, the city of Rennes proposed developing suburban poles. The suburban municipalities were guaranteed to retain their identity and to have their share of economic development. For the city of Rennes, this was possible as the tax revenue generated by economic development is pooled into the collaborative grouping of municipalities. The creation of a green belt and the sharing of fiscal resources do not really correspond to a virtuous approach, but reflect a deal between the elected representatives of the central city and those of the rural areas.

Within the urban development plan approved in 2007, the definition of 'urban fields' gives credibility to the green belt conceptualised 10 years earlier rendering it operational. This is an important innovation in planning, a paradigm shift: agricultural areas are no longer land reserves for future urbanisation; they provide space for food production and make it possible to manage the urban form. Outside the planning sphere, we note that private developers highlight a place where 'life is good', the singularity of a highly urbanised city-centre that has a preserved green belt. Spatial planning has given rise to a resource which helps to improve the attractiveness of the whole city-region.

## Conclusion

In the last 15 years, strategic spatial planning has developed in France with the state as initiator. However, in a country where local government is based on the belief that local areas should be managed and developed according to local interests, planning practice relies on the will and resources of local actors. Local government has experienced a quasi-revolution with the creation of collaborative groupings of municipalities which are in charge of most local policies. These groupings are the key actors in the design and implementation of urban development plans. In principle, the urban development plan provides the arena for local councillors and technicians to agree collectively on a diagnosis, and define together medium-term orientations. The plan may facilitate an integrated approach to the economic, social and environmental challenges. In the case of Rennes, the plan expresses with creativity the agreement of local actors on balancing economic growth and the protection of agricultural land and natural areas. However, the most frequent case is closer to the situation of Tours, where the plan follows the development strategies of the collaborative groupings of municipalities, in relation to municipal interests.

The priorities put forward by the state when reforming the planning system (social balance, fight against urban sprawl and the loss of biodiversity, etc.) are to a large extent filtered by the local context. From one place to another, municipalities and their collaborative groupings have quite diverse (decades-long or recent, dense or modest) experience of sharing views, resources and policies. Therefore their capacities to get involved in an urban development plan with other groupings of the same city-region are different. The maturity of inter-municipal cooperation seems to be crucial in order for an urban development plan, on the one hand, to develop an economic strategy that can meet sustainability principles and, on the other hand, to define tools that will enable it to be realised at the scale of local projects.

French urban development plans are comprehensive plans with a prospective dimension; in this sense they might be considered as strategic. However, this is not the case if developing a strategic plan means setting up numerous exchange systems with stakeholders outside the planning sphere in order to create standards and visions of shared actions, as argued by many scholars (Albrechts, 2004; Healey, 2007). The mobilisation of public and private stakeholders is limited in the French context. The national planning system does not encourage that direction and it should be remembered that urban development plans are legally binding.

Strategic spatial planning is about the possibility for public- and private-sector actors to experiment with new forms of collective thought. In France, the urban development plan encourages a renewal of local planning methods. However, Motte (2006: 29–30) rightly considers that 'land use planning by zoning and controlling construction densities constitutes a baseline that impregnates all of the actors' representations [...] and undoubtedly corresponds to the most developed, and also the most humdrum, practices [...]. There is a problem of change of baseline in a certain number of countries, of adapting to new urban development requirements and political practices.' The effectiveness of planning practices cannot be disconnected from the capacity of the territory's actors to work together, in particular in the case of France around the inter-municipal and inter-territorial aspects of policy-making.

## Notes

1 Speech made by Jean-Claude Gayssot, Minister of Planning, Transport and Housing to present the 'Urban Solidarity and Renewal' bill to the French parliament at the session held on 8 March 2000, pp. 1629–1630 of the proceedings of parliamentary debates.
2 Idem.
3 By law, all urban communities have a local plan. But only a third of *Communautés d'agglomération* and 12% of *Communautés de communes* made the choice to have a local plan for their whole territory.
4 Following Motte (2006), we have adopted the travel-to-work area (*'aire urbaine'*) to approximate the city-region in the context of France.
5 Two other dynamic city-regions, Marseille-Aix and Nantes, were also studied. The results are presented in Douay, Nadou and Demazière (2014).

## References

Albrechts, L., 2004. Strategic (spatial) planning re-examined. *Environment and Planning B*, 31(5), 743–758.
Albrechts, L., Healey, P. and Kunzmann, K., 2003. Strategic spatial planning and regional governance in Europe. *Journal of the American Planning Association*, 69(2), 135–147.
Baldersheim, H. and Lawrence, E., 2010. *Territorial Choice: The Politics of Boundaries and Borders*. New York: Palgrave Macmillan.
Baraize, F. and Négrier, E. (Eds), 2001. *L'invention politique de l'agglomération*. Paris: L'Harmattan.
Booth, P., Nelson, S. and Paris, D., 2007. Actors and instruments in the planning system. In P. Booth, M. Breuillard, C. Fraser and D. Paris (Eds), *Spatial Planning Systems of Britain and France: A Comparative Analysis*. London: Routledge, pp. 67–82.
Demazière, C. (ed.), 2012. Viabilité de l'économie productive des régions urbaines: Investigation à partir de la planification stratégique. Une comparaison entre la France et l'Angleterre. Research report for Plan Urbanisme Construction architecture. Tours: University of Tours.

Desjardins, X. and Leroux, B., 2007. Les Schémas de cohérence territoriale: Des recettes du développement durable au bricolage territorial. *Flux*, 69, 6–20.

Dexia Research Department, 2008. *Sub-national Governments in the European Union.* Versailles: Dexia Editions.

Douay, N., 2010. Collaborative planning and the challenge of urbanization: Issues, actors and strategies in Marseilles and Montreal metropolitan areas. *Canadian Journal of Urban Research*, 19(1), 50–69.

Douay, N., Nadou, F. and Demazière, C., 2014. Entre défi stratégique et contraintes institutionnelles pour la planification spatiale: Le dialogue économie-environnement à Marseille et Nantes. In J. Dubois (ed.), *La construction métropolitaine face au développement durable*. La Tour d'Aigues: L'Aube, pp. 236–261.

Healey, P., 1997. *Collaborative Planning, Shaping Places in Fragmented Societies.* Vancouver: University of British Columbia Press.

Healey, P., 2007. *Urban Complexity and Spatial Strategies: Towards a Relational Planning for Our Times*. London: Routledge.

Hebbert, M., 2006. Town planning versus *Urbanismo*. *Planning Perspectives*, 21(2), 233–252.

Ismeri Europa and Applica, 2010. *Distribution of Competences in Relation to Regional Development Policies in the Member States of the European Union, Final Report*. Brussels: DG Regio.

Motte, A. (ed.), 1995. *Schéma directeur et projet d'agglomération*. Paris: Juris-Service.

Motte, A., 2006. *La notion de planification stratégique spatialisée en Europe (1995–2005)*. Paris: PUCA.

Petitet, S. and Caubel, D., 2010. Quel rôle pour les activités économiques dans la maîtrise de l'étalement urbain? *Etudes foncières*, 148–149, 6–12.

Salet, W. and Faludi, A. (Eds), 2000. *The Revival of Strategic Planning*. Amsterdam: Royal Netherlands Academy of Arts and Sciences.

SMAT (Syndicat Mixte de l'Agglomération Tourangelle), 2011. *Engager une stratégie commune de développement de l'activité et de l'emploi*. Tours: Syndicat Mixte de l'Agglomération Tourangelle.

Vanier, M. 2010. *Le pouvoir des territoires : Essai sur l'interterritorialité*. Paris: Economica.

Verhage, R., Baker, M. and Boino P., 2007. Strategic spatial planning at the metropolitan level: The cases of Manchester and Lyon. In P. Booth, M. Breuillard, C. Fraser and D. Paris (Eds), *Spatial Planning Systems of Britain and France: A Comparative Analysis*. London: Routledge, pp. 83–98.

Vigar, G., Healey, P., Hull, A. and Davoudi S., 2000. *Planning, Governance and Spatial Strategy in Britain*. London: Macmillan.

# 8  Strategic spatial planning in the USA

*John M. Bryson and Carissa Schively Slotterback*

## Introduction

The USA is obviously a very big place with about 320 million people and a land mass of 9.85 milllion km². It is the third largest country by population after China and India (but is smaller than the European Union) and is the fourth largest by area after Russia, Canada and China (though again smaller than the EU).

The US is also a very decentralized place with 50 states and the District of Columbia and approximately 89,000 units of local government, including counties, municipalities, townships, special districts, and school districts (US Census Bureau, 2012). The US is a federal republic in which dual sovereignty – federal and state – is exercised over localities. States have a separate constitutional status and rights reserved to them by the US Constitution (in part because states preceded the Constitution). Legally, local governments are creatures of the states, not of the national government (O'Toole, 2007). While there are federal laws applicable to all places, planning law is mostly a matter of state jurisdiction. However, the federal government often provides significant funding for particular activities and projects (e.g., national highways, transit, water and sewer provision, some kinds of housing, environmental protection, defense-related projects in localities, etc.) In practice this means that the federal government is generally a weak partner when it comes to state and local planning, except when it concerns federally authorized and funded activities and projects, and except when it involves the approximately 30 percent of US land owned by the federal government (mostly in the western states and Alaska). In this chapter, therefore, we will concentrate mostly on state – and especially community – planning efforts.

Given the size of the country and its complex governmental and intergovernmental structure, it is very difficult to make generalizations about planning in the US and about strategic spatial planning in particular. We begin by offering our own definition of strategic planning and then briefly discuss its intellectual history. We next discuss the relationship between strategic planning, strategic spatial planning, and statutorily mandated spatial planning. There are ways in which these three diverge, but the more recent history of spatial planning in the US shows more of a convergence both in theory and practice. We then present several examples of strategic spatial planning, including *The Partnership for*

*Sustainable Communities* initiative at the federal level, *Virginia Performs* at the state level, and some examples at the community and regional levels. These examples highlight trends that include a greater emphasis on: approaching planning holistically and integratively, including an emphasis on sustainability; public participation; and cross-sector collaboration and co-production. Spatial strategic planning is also responding to trends involving technology shifts; adjustments to changing demographics; and a conservative political shift emphasizing individual rights, including property rights, limited government, and no increases in taxes or regulations. The impacts of this rightward shift have been felt unevenly nationally and in the states and many localities. Given the US governmental and intergovernmental structure, what has in recent years often been national political paralysis has meant that while there are some important national initiatives, the most important innovations in planning are typically occurring at state and local levels. Finally, we offer some conclusions about strategic spatial planning in the US.

## Strategic planning

We define strategic planning as "a deliberative, disciplined effort to produce decisions and actions that shape and guide what an organization or other entity [such as a community or region] is, what it does, and why it does it" (Bryson, 2011, pp. 7–8). The definition helps clarify that strategic planning (at least in the US) is not any one *thing*, but instead consists of a *set* or *family* of concepts, procedures, and tools meant to help decision makers and other stakeholders address what is truly important for their organizations and places. The definition also means that there are a variety of *approaches* to strategic planning. What matters most is not the particular approach, but instead the extent to which the approach helps its users engage in strategic thinking, acting and learning. Said differently, the purpose of strategic planning is not necessarily to produce a plan, although plans may help, but instead to cause or catalyze consequential decisions and actions.

Strategic planning as a label in the US context has mainly been associated with business, government, and nonprofit organizational planning, and not explicitly with planning for places. In contrast, planning in general for places has typically been called simply planning, even when it has a distinctly strategic focus. Community-scale planning, which is sometimes statutorily mandated in some US states and regions, is more commonly called comprehensive planning, master planning, or general planning (Kelly, 2010). Planning may also be conducted at other scales such as neighborhoods, corridors, and areas, or for specific issues such as transportation, housing, hazard mitigation, and climate change. In part this labeling disjunction has to do with the fact that in the US the public administration and urban and regional planning literatures have generally developed separately with little cross-over, and public administrators and urban planners have generally not been educated in the same departments and schools. In spite of labeling incongruities, however, the need for strategic thinking, acting, and learning is a part of both streams of literature, especially more recently.

The history of strategic planning for organizations has been well documented by others (e.g., Mintzberg, Ahlstrand, and Lampel; Freedman, 2013). Historically, strategic planning for public organizations in the US got a highly influential prompt in 1942 from political scientist, public servant, and political activist John Vieg, who argued at the end of the Great Depression and the beginning of the Second World War that the country had seen enough of *negative planning* [italics in original] – by which he meant "deliberately refraining from public control over more than a few fields of social action in the confident belief that all would then go well in the vast areas left 'free'."[1] He believed that the American people were "prepared to move toward *positive planning* [italics in original]," by which he meant "the foreshaping of things to come" and "the experiment of a conscious design of living that, at least in the essentials of existence, will leave less to the play of chance" (Vieg, 1942, p. 63). Vieg saw planning as an executive function related to advising decision makers and intended "to protect and promote the public interest and the general welfare" (ibid., p. 65). In order to give decision makers a broader view, he thought planning should be more concerned with synthesis than analysis. In his strategic view, planning was needed at all levels. At the national level, the recent experience of the Great Depression and the New Deal convinced policy makers of the necessity for economic and social planning. Moreover, the need for massive war planning was painfully obvious and pressing. Vieg clearly recognized the limits of national planning and saw strong arguments for sub-national planning at regional and state levels. He also saw a crying need for broader and more effective municipal-level planning and planning for rural areas. Drawing on arguments in Robert Walker's (1941) influential book, *The Planning Function in Urban Government*, Vieg asserted that US municipal planning needed to embrace *all* of the functions of city governments, not just the physical functions of transportation, water, sewer, public facilities and parks.

Unfortunately, more strategic municipal planning of the sort Vieg wished to see did not take hold until the 1980s, although earlier in the century there had been some gains in particular substantive areas, such as public health, housing, and social planning, along with occasional reversals (Hall, 2014). In general, until the 1980s municipal planning primarily involved capital budgeting and so-called "comprehensive city planning" – which was not comprehensive at all, but limited to physical functions (Hall, 2002). Strategic planning instead had become a primarily private-sector phenomenon (Bryson and Einsweiler, 1988) and did not show up on the US public-sector screen until Olsen and Eadie's (1982) and Sorkin, Ferrris, and Hudak's (1984) path-breaking books. Mayors and city managers realized strategic planning could help them gain intellectual and practical control over their cities in a way that their city planners could not or would not. In contrast to then-comprehensive planning, strategic planning did consider the full range of city functions and stakeholders; the array of city strengths, weakness, opportunities, and threats; strategic issues and what might be done about them; and was very action oriented. At a time of resource shortages and rising citizen activism, strategic planning helped senior managers make substantively, procedurally, politically, and administratively rational decisions (Kaufman and

Jacobs, 1987; Bryson and Einsweiler, 1988). Vieg summarizes his predictions for the future by saying "planning will be far more firmly established in government than it is today" (Vieg, 1942, p. 86). He clearly was prophetic – though in general many decades premature.

Vieg also asserted that the "planners" should vary by organizational level: "At the top, where planning means choosing among ends, the planners are political leaders and philosophers; below this level planning is concerned with choices among means, and there is a place and need for persons who make public planning a profession – for specialists who prefer to specialize in generality" (ibid., p. 67). Because of his belief in representative government and democratic accountability, Vieg clearly thought professional planning should always be advisory, but just as clearly he thought the advice needed to be imaginative, thoughtful, practical and linked to decision making. The practice of strategic planning has evolved differently than Vieg imagined. Clearly, the "planners" at the top are political decision makers and managers and the rise of strategic planning in the last 35 years may be explained in part by its usefulness to them (Bryson and Einsweiler, 1988; Wheeland, 2004; Bryson, Crosby, and Bryson, 2009). But strategic planning's increasingly direct links to decision making and implementation sound less advisory than intimately entwined with ongoing organizational leadership and management, a trend also seen in Europe (Albrechts, 2013; Albrechts and Balducci, 2013).

Successes of strategic planning at the municipal level, as well as the desire to appear more "business-like," helped trigger use of strategic planning by nonprofit organizations, states and the Federal government. Osborne and Gaebler's best-selling 1992 book *Reinventing Government* was also an important catalyst. The Government Performance and Results Act of 1993 and the Government Performance and Results Modernization Act of 2010 require strategic planning by all federal agencies and many states have similar laws. At present, there are thus many possible explanations for why strategic planning is so widespread, including coercion (many governments are required to do it; many nonprofits are also required to do it by funders), normative pressures (strategic planning is seen as a sign of good professional practice and necessary to create legitimacy), and mimesis (meaning faddishness or copying what everyone else is doing) (DiMaggio and Powell, 1983). We find more persuasive, however, the argument that strategic planning, whether explicitly called strategic or not, is popular because in many circumstances it seems "to work" – in the sense of helping decision makers figure out what their organizations should be doing, how, and why. A growing number of studies indicate it works – and often strikingly well – in a variety of contexts (e.g., Borins, 1998, 2014; Boyne and Gould-Williams, 2003; Burby, 2003; Hendrick, 2003; Wheeland, 2004; Brody and Highfield, 2005; Bryson *et al.*, 2009; Andrews *et al.*, 2012; Ferlie and Ongaro, 2015). That said, plan implementation remains a particular challenge (e.g., Brody and Highfield, 2005; Margerum, 2005; Tang *et al.*, 2010; Sandfort and Moulton, 2015).

In sum, strategic planning has now become a conventional feature of most governments and nonprofit organizations. A growing body of evidence indicates that in general, across substantial populations of organizations, both public and nonprofit, strategic planning does produce positive benefits on a modest scale, and in some instances produces quite outstanding positive results. Strategic planning use and effectiveness have also increased in multi-organizational and cross-sector collaborations and in spatial planning applications. Mandated, as well as voluntary, spatial planning by governments is now very often undertaken within a broader strategic framework. The process is not necessarily or even usually called strategic planning, but in effect that is what it is, given the necessary focus on: carefully attending to context, and using deliberative and reasonably disciplined processes for figuring out purposes, attending to stakeholder needs and expectations, finding practical strategies, and producing public value often via co-production processes (e.g., Innes, 1996; Van Herzele, 2004; Huxham and Vangen, 2005; Agranoff, 2007; Evans-Cowley and Hollander, 2010; Innes and Booher, 2010). In other words, whatever the name, planning for organizations and for places are very often in effect converging and increasingly are expected to embody a strategic approach.

## Strategic spatial planning

In the US the following features characterize spatial planning that is *strategic* (e.g., Kaufman and Jacobs, 1987; Christensen, 1999; Poister and Streib, 1999; Conroy and Berke, 2004; Chakraborty *et al.*, 2011; Albrechts and Balducci, 2013):

- Close attention to context and to thinking strategically about how to tailor the strategic spatial planning approach to the context, even as a purpose of the planning is typically to change the context in some important ways.
- Careful thinking about purposes and goals, including attention to situational requirements (e.g., political, legal, administrative, ethical, and environmental requirements).
- An initial focus on a broad agenda and later moving to a more selective action focus.
- An emphasis on systems thinking; that is, working to understand the dynamics of the overall system being planned for as it functions – or ideally should function – across space and time, including the interrelationships among constituent subsystems.
- Intense attention to stakeholders, in effect making strategic spatial planning an approach to practical politics; typically, multiple levels of government and multiple sectors are involved in the process of strategy formulation and implementation.
- A focus on strengths, weaknesses, opportunities and threats; and a focus on competitive and collaborative advantages.
- A focus on thinking about potential futures and then making decisions now in light of their future consequences; in other words, joining temporal with spatial systemic thinking.

- Careful attention to implementation, i.e., strategy that cannot be operational-ized effectively is hardly strategic.
- A clear realization that strategies are both deliberately set in advance and emergent in practice.
- In short, there is a desire to stabilize what should be stabilized, e.g., overall directions, core infrastructure, tax bases, sensitive environmental areas, etc., via goals, policies, plans, funding, and management approaches, while maintaining appropriate flexibility in terms of goals, policies, and processes to manage complexity, take advantage of important opportuni-ties and advance resilience and sustainability in the face of an uncertain future.

## The connections to spatial planning

Strategic planning for organizations and places is not synonymous with what is often called comprehensive planning for communities in the US, even though there have been convergences in recent years. Given the structure of US govern-ment, comprehensive planning for communities is mostly governed by state law. This kind of spatial planning is mandated only in some states and regions, though it is widely practiced in other locations as well. There may be little difference between strategic planning and comprehensive planning if the agency or cross-organizational group doing the comprehensive planning has strong ties to govern-ment and other important decision makers. Indeed, the best comprehensive planning has probably always been strategic; however, in practice there may be significant differences.

When plans are mandated, the plans are often prepared to meet legal require-ments and must be formulated according to a legally prescribed process with legally prescribed content. As legal instruments, these plans have an important influence. On the other hand, the plans' typical rigidity can conflict with the political process with which public officials and planners must cope. Strategic plans can therefore provide a bridge from legally required and relatively rigid policy statements to actual decisions and operations.

Second, comprehensive plans are usually limited to a shorter list of topics than a government's full agenda of roles and responsibilities. They focus instead on issues that can be addressed directly or indirectly by urban planners and municipal planning departments. For that reason, comprehensive plans may be less relevant to municipal decision makers working community-wide or outside the planning department than strategic planning, which can embrace all of a government's actual and potential roles before deciding why, how, where, and when to act.

Third, strategic community-scale planning is often more action-oriented, more broadly participatory, more emphatic about the need to understand the commu-nity's strengths and weaknesses as well as the opportunities and threats it faces, and more attentive to inter-community competitive behavior. Strategic planning thus typically addresses a broader set of issues than comprehensive planning, while at the same time producing a more limited action focus oriented to strategic priorities.

Notwithstanding the above caveats, the theory and practice of spatial planning in the US have become increasingly strategic in the senses outlined above, and as the examples below will show. Strategic thinking, acting, and learning are now fairly well engrained in both planning theory and practice at both organizational and community scales. That said, and as noted, the label strategic planning is not typically associated with spatial planning in the US; instead, it is more frequently identified with organizational planning by businesses, governments, and nonprofit organizations.

In the subsequent three sections, we present three brief examples of spatial strategic planning, one each at the federal, state, and local levels. Focusing on any one or two levels would be quite misleading. While we cannot present each case in depth, we do think it is important to give a sense of the range of applications across governmental levels, offering at least a snapshot of the geographic and jurisdictional variation that exists.

## The partnership for sustainable communities: providing a federal framework for regional-scale strategic spatial planning

While most of the activity around spatial planning in the US occurs at the local and regional scales, the *Partnership for Sustainable Communities* has established a framework for sub-national planning that aligns clearly with the characteristics of strategic spatial planning. This interagency partnership established in 2009 across US federal agencies, including the Department of Housing and Urban Development, Department of Transportation, and Environmental Protection Agency, has facilitated the joint consideration of housing, transportation, and environmental issues at the community and regional scale (Partnership for Sustainable Communities, 2013; http://www.sustainablecommunities.gov/ mission/about-us). This program clearly aligns with a systems approach and has facilitated systems-scale planning at the regional level through Sustainable Communities Regional Planning Grants to regional governments and organizations to conduct sustainability-focused planning. Consistent with strategic planning, one of the reason that regional planning is pursued is "because it is the best or possibly only strategy for seeking commonly held goals" (Seltzer and Carbonell, 2011, p. 11).

Federal agency collaboration and the follow-on grants for planning and other activities (e.g., infrastructure, technical assistance, research) are guided by a set of mutually agreed upon Livability Principles (see Box 8.1). The organization of planning principles around the cross-cutting concept of livability clearly indicates a systemic understanding of the connections across housing, transportation, and environment at the community scale. In addition, the principles set a high-level strategic framework that can be tailored to the local and regional context.

---

**Box 8.1   Partnership for sustainability communities livability principles**

*Provide more transportation choices.* Develop safe, reliable, and econom- ical transportation choices to decrease household transportation costs, reduce our nation's dependence on foreign oil, improve air quality, reduce greenhouse gas emissions, and promote public health.

*Promote equitable, affordable housing.* Expand location- and energy- efficient housing choices for people of all ages, incomes, races, and ethnic- ities to increase mobility and lower the combined cost of housing and transportation.

*Enhance economic competitiveness.* Improve economic competitive- ness through reliable and timely access to employment centers, educational opportunities, services and other basic needs of workers, as well as expanded business access to markets.

*Support existing communities.* Target federal funding toward existing communities – through strategies like transit-oriented, mixed-use develop- ment and land recycling – to increase community revitalization and effi- ciency of public works investments and safeguard rural landscapes.

*Coordinate and leverage federal policies and investment.* Align federal policies and funding to remove barriers to collaboration, leverage funding, and increase the accountability and effectiveness of all levels of govern- ment to plan for future growth, including making smart energy choices such as locally generated renewable energy.

*Value communities and neighborhoods.* Enhance the unique character- istics of all communities by investing in healthy, safe, and walkable neigh- borhoods – rural, urban and suburban.

---

One example of regional planning conducted with funding from the Partnership and guided by these Livability Principles is the *Building a Resilient Region* plan prepared by the Region 5 Regional Development Commission in north-central Minnesota. The regional body covers five rural counties and advances planning, economic development, and community vitality through technical assistance services to local units of government in the region. The plan's organization goes well beyond the typical plan structure seen in many community-scale comprehen- sive plans (Kelly, 2010) by taking an integrative approach that makes connec- tions across topical areas. While typical plans are often organized around standard planning topics, each represented in separate elements or chapters (e.g., land use, transportation, demographics, natural systems) (Kelly, 2010), the Region 5 plan is organized around 11 themes:

- Infrastructure – Housing
- Infrastructure – Connectivity

- Infrastructure – Energy
- Natural Resources and Development Patterns
- Education and Workforce Development
- Infrastructure – Transportation
- Economic Engines
- Valuing Interdependent Communities and Neighborhoods – Health Care
- Valuing Interdependent Communities and Neighborhoods – Changing Population
- Valuing Interdependent Communities and Neighborhoods – Efficiency and Effectiveness
- Valuing Interdependent Communities and Neighborhoods – Affordable Housing

The plan notes that this integrative approach is akin to a spider web – "when you pull on one part of the spider's web it affects all other parts" (Region 5 Regional Development Commission, 2012). The plan's organization signals an understanding of the systemic nature of regions and regional planning, an approach that clearly aligns with the characteristics of strategic spatial planning. Note, however, that because school districts in the US are separate from general purpose governments (unlike many other parts of the world), they are not specifically targeted in the plan.

The planning effort also included significant emphasis on stakeholder engagement, consistent with the characteristics of strategic planning that call for engagement of multiple levels of government and multiple sectors in developing strategies and accomplishing implementation. As a regional planning effort, the *Resilient Region* plan necessarily engaged across multiple local units of government, including counties and cities, and with the Region 5 regional body. Many of these units of government, as well as additional stakeholders, were represented on an advisory board for the planning effort. Broader public and stakeholder engagement techniques were diverse and intended to accomplish meaningful engagement opportunities that fostered interaction and community-building. Using both in-person and online tools, the planning effort achieved a broad base of participation.

## Virginia performs: advancing strategic spatial planning at the state level

*Virginia Performs* provides a prominent state-level example of strategic spatially oriented planning (Council on Virginia's Future, *The Virginia Report, 2013*, 2013; http://vaperforms.virginia.gov/index.php).[2] Virginia Performs is a system initiated by the Council on Virginia's Future, which is chaired by the governor and includes state, business, and community leaders. The Council was established by the 2003 General Assembly to advise Virginia's leaders on development and implementation of what its authors call a "road map" for the state's future as a place, economy, and society. (The metaphor is inapt in the sense that the map is really more of a navigation device.) The roadmap includes: a long-term focus on high-priority issues; creating an environment for improved policy and budget decision making; increasing government performance, accountability, and transparency; and engaging citizens in dialogue about Virginia's future.

The Council helps establish the vision and goals for the state and makes assessments of progress. The State's executive branch is responsible for performance, efficiency, and effectiveness. The vision and high-level goals established by the Council and championed by the Governor are meant to serve as guides for state government decisions and actions, but are also intended to influence the thinking and actions of other actors in the state, including local governments. Achievement of the goals thus becomes in part a co-production process (Albrechts, 2013). *Virginia Performs* fits Albrechts and Balducci's (2013, p. 18) definition of strategic spatial planning in that it is meant to be "a transformative and integrative public sector-led co-productive socio-spatial process through which visions or frames of reference, justification for coherent actions, and means for implementation are produced that shape, frame and reframe what a place is and what it might become."

The Council's *Vision for Virginia* includes:

• Responsible economic growth
• Enviable quality of life
• Educated citizens prepared for a successful life
• The best-managed state government
• Informed and engaged citizens helping to shape the commonwealth's future

The Council's long-term goals for the state include:

• Be a national leader in the preservation and enhancement of our economy.
• Elevate the levels of educational preparedness and attainment of our citizens.
• Inspire and support Virginians toward healthy lives and strong and resilient families.
• Protect, conserve and wisely develop our natural, cultural and historic resources.
• Protect the public's safety and security, ensure a fair and effective system of justice, and provide a prepared response to emergencies and disasters of all kinds.
• Ensure Virginia has a transportation system that is safe, allows the easy movement of people and goods, enhances the economy, and improves our quality of life.
• Be recognized as the best-managed state in the nation.

Progress toward accomplishing the vision and long-term goals is measured by a set of approximately fifty overall indicators broken down into seven goal areas. State agencies are expected by the Governor and legislature to plan and budget in light of the long-term goals and indicators and related and relevant indicators specifically connected to the agency's work. Agency performance measures are organized into four categories: key measures tied to the long-term goals and mission, service area effectiveness measures, administrative measures meant to assess management quality and effectiveness, and productivity measures indicating efficiency levels. The Virginia Performs website provides a useful and visually appealing compendium of performance for the state as a whole, by goal area, and by agency (http://vaperforms.virginia.gov/). The attempted linkage of state agency goals, plans, and budgets to the state's long-term goals is the tightest part of the system. The success of the state's system depends on continued broad-based, bipartisan political support.

Cities, counties, communities, and others throughout the state are also encouraged to do their part by making use of the state-level goals and indicators to develop their own indicators linked to the state goals and indicators. Hampton Roads, Virginia, provides a well-known example of a municipal management system that is compatible with the Virginia Performs system and in fact is hot-linked to the Virginia Performs website (http://hamptonroadsperforms.org/). The desire to make progress against individual indicators or sets of indicators provides the basis for collaborative efforts throughout the state involving public, private, and nonprofit sectors. The whole approach links strategic planning for organizations with strategic planning for places.

## Advancing strategic spatial planning at the community scale

As noted earlier, planning at the community scale is becoming increasingly strategic. Several trends are apparent. First, community-scale land use planning has moved beyond the presumably purely technical/rational approach to planning outlined in earlier texts for planning students and practitioners. For example, the most current 2006 edition of the seminal *Urban Land Use Planning* text has a much more explicit focus on the planning process, values and stakeholder engagement than the previous 1995 text (Kaiser, Godschalk, and Chapin, 1995; Berke *et al.*, 2006). In addition, the approach has become more holistic, nesting urban land use planning within a more holistic framework of sustainability and livability that connects more fully to the agenda of government which often includes broader considerations across ecology, economy, and equity (Berke *et al.*, 2006). This is consistent with Campbell's (1996) earlier call for the planning discipline to be oriented more to sustainability and Godschalk's (2004) integration of livability as a core consideration within sustainability. *Urban Land Use Planning* now situates land use as a system among others (e.g., environmental systems, transportation and infrastructure systems) to be addressed in a community-scale comprehensive, general, or master plan – names variously used in different parts of the US. In addition, the book adds an expanded focus on context through its articulation of the content and process aspects of preparing a State of the Community Report. To produce such a report, planners must aggregate data related to the systems to provide "strategic intelligence" that can be combined with community-based information and involvement to build consensus for plan making (Berke *et al.*, 2006, p. 266). The text also calls for the use of stakeholder analysis, participation techniques such as charrettes and focus groups, and participatory scenario planning, with the intent of achieving a collaborative process to reach consensus (Berke *et al.*, 2006).

Additional comprehensive planning guides and the broader practice of planning places an increasing emphasis on participation (Quick and Feldman, 2011; Bryson *et al.*, 2013). Participation is clearly recognized as enhancing the quality of planning outcomes. As highlighted by Crewe (2001), participatory planning processes are more likely to produce outcomes that are aligned with interests and contexts. In addition, participants may have valid and relevant contextual or local knowledge that is complementary to expert knowledge generated by planners (Van Herzele, 2004; Innes and Booher, 2010). Finally, it is clearly recognized that participation can help support implementation activities (Burby, 2003; Deyle and Slotterback, 2009).

Portland, Oregon's *2035 Comprehensive Plan* (2015), which is currently under review and is expected to be adopted by the City Council in the spring of 2016, reflects both the systemic and participatory nature of contemporary planning practice and the integration of strategic planning approaches. First, in terms of its content, the plan is guided by five guiding principles that cut across the topic areas in the plan: (1) economic prosperity, (2) human health, (3) environmental health, (4) equity, and (5) resilience. These principles align with land use planning, but go further in envisioning land use as a component of the community's broader aspirations and the full agenda of government. For example, rather than focusing on infrastructure in isolation, the plan calls for using an equity lens when making infrastructure decisions, and considering the connection between infrastructure and gentrification. While the plan still includes specific topical chapters focused on the standard planning subjects of housing, economic development, transportation, and others, there are explicit connections made across systems. For example, in the housing chapter, housing is clearly connected to transportation, health, and equity.

Portland's planning process is also notable for its focus on process and participation, consistent with the characteristics of strategic planning. The planning effort has included an extensive focus on engagement, identifying strategic opportunities for participation during the planning process, key audiences, and potential participation tools. The planning process also engaged newly formed Policy Expert Groups to address key cross-cutting issues such as Education and Youth Success, Neighborhood Centers, and Infrastructure Equity. In order to develop the new plan, the city developed a Community Involvement Plan. In addition to engagement during the process, the draft plan also includes a chapter focused on Community Involvement, that sets forth goals and policies for ongoing engagement, including:

- Community involvement as a partnership
- Social justice and equity

- Value community wisdom and participation
- Transparency and accountability
- Meaningful participation
- Accessible and effective participation
- Strong civic infrastructure

## Critiques of spatial strategic planning

Spatial strategic planning, of course, is not without its critics. For example, the critiques that Albrechts and Baluducci (2013) highlight about European strategic spatial planning are relevant in a US context as well. First, there are concerns that government, business, and nonprofit elites can capture the process, thereby diminishing the extent to which it represents citizens' interests, as well as the legitimacy of the process and any resulting plans. Jacobs (2014), for example, believes that one should not underestimate the extent of dissensus in the US, the disproportionate influence of affluent citizens and organized interests, and the extent to which governing structures favor inaction and drift. The emphasis in US spatial strategic planning on public engagement and dialogue and deliberation may be seen as a counter to the weaknesses in the US polity that Jacobs high-lights, but Dahl and Soss (2014) argue that dialogue and deliberation in a system that favors elites and is stacked against ordinary citizens actually might turn out to be anti-democratic. The concerns these authors highlight are certainly apt at the national level, but the situation is much more mixed at state and local levels. Clearly, organized interests can have a disproportionate influence on local plans, including spatial strategic plans (e.g., Beatley, Brower, and Lucy, 1994; Burby, 2003), which means the real question concerns whether the resulting plans are democratic and legitimate *enough* to pass ethical and procedural justice muster in the US democracy, flawed though it is. Overall, the results would appear to be mixed, though planners' concerted efforts to build broad-based, and in some cases very inclusive, participation into spatial strategic planning processes in specific locations certainly can help support democratically defensible processes, plans, and implementation efforts (Quick and Feldman, 2011).

Second, and relatedly, spatial strategic planning processes and plans that are developed informally, or are not subject to review and adoption by publicly elected governing bodies, do not necessarily fit easily with typical norms of democratic accountability. All of the processes and plans discussed in this chap-ter were in fact subject to review, and typically adoption, by democratically elected governing bodies. Beyond that, however, there is the observation that legitimacy comes primarily from the efforts to have an open and reasonably representative dialogue about the future of a place, as well as from the formal decisions that flow from the process for which the strategic plan can serve as a guiding vision or framework (Innes and Booher, 2010; Albrechts and Balducci, 2013). The American Institute of Certified Planners' *Code of Ethics and Professional Conduct* (2009) explicitly prioritizes serving the public interest, requiring that planners offer the public meaningful opportunities to influence plans. However, plans may or may not be prepared by those certified and educated with these principles in mind.

Last, strategic spatial plans may be perceived as static documents, which are not updated to reflect changing conditions, including emerging opportunities and threats, as well as evolving public priorities and values. In contrast, strategic planning typically emphasizes the importance of flexibility and the iterative nature of plans and planning processes (e.g., Bryson, 2011). The focus on plan implementation may lead to more efforts to track plan performance and inform plan updates (Laurian *et al.*, 2004). Indeed, the federal Government Performance and Results Modernization Act of 2010 requires regular meetings of key personnel within agencies and across agencies to discuss performance, what is working, and what needs to be changed (Moynihan, 2013; Moynihan and Kroll, 2015). We might expect to see similar requirements across government levels as strategic spatial planning is increasingly required.

## Conclusions

Three conclusions may be offered based on this quick review of spatial strategic planning in the US. First, US planning has always been responsive to changing material and ideological conditions, although not necessarily as rapidly as might have been hoped. John Vieg's (1942) vision of public planning as being (1) concerned with the full agenda of government, (2) strategic, and (3) appropriate for a democracy is nearer to realization than ever, at least at the state and local level. This advance is driven by the demands by decision makers and planners themselves to have planning take a more systemic view, respond to issues that go well beyond traditional physical planning, be more participatory and engaged with diverse stakeholders, and be far more attentive to issues of implementation. We expect those demands to continue and grow in the future – and hope they do. However, given the size and governmental structure of the US and the great variety of the country on numerous dimensions, progress has clearly been uneven and likely will continue to be. This is to be expected, and also helps encourage continuous experimentation and learning across jurisdictions.

Second, the best planning in the US, regardless of what it is called, has always been strategic; and the best planners have always been strategic planners, regardless of their job titles. That said, more obviously strategic approaches are becoming more common (and possibly may even be the norm). In short, the emerging planning approaches – that cut across government jurisdictions, sectors, and physical and social systems – exemplify a strategic approach to spatial planning practice. We hope this trend continues.

Third, whether there has been a conscious integration or not of strategic planning for organizations, spatial strategic planning, and comprehensive planning for communities in the US, planning now generally appears to be practiced in a manner that aligns reasonably well with the characteristics of strategic planning noted above. Unfortunately, we are unaware of any studies that buttress that assertion. There clearly are well-known examples of strategic spatial planning and a few have been noted here, but they only offer a small sample of current planning practice. In US-focused planning theory, however, there is a clear move toward more strategic approaches. In other words, approaches and tools advanced in the urban and regional planning literature are now more closely aligned to approaches to, and tools for, strategic planning for organizations that have emerged in the public administration literature over the last several decades. In short, the future for both the theory and practice of spatial strategic planning in the US would appear to be very bright.

## Notes

1 This paragraph and the next three draw on Bryson (2010, pp. S257–S258).
2 The Virginia Performs example draws on Bryson (2011, pp. 337–341).

## References

Agranoff, R. (2007). *Managing within Networks: Adding Value to Public Organizations*. Washington, DC: Georgetown University Press.

Albrechts, L. (2013). Reframing strategic planning by using a coproduction perspective. *Planning Theory*, 12, 46–63.

Albrechts, L. and A. Balducci. (2013). Practicing strategic planning: In search of critical features to explain the strategic character of plans, *DisP – The Planning Review*, 49(3), 16–27.

American Institute of Certified Planners. (2009). *AICP Code of Ethics and Professional Conduct*. Accessed November 15, 2015 at https://www.planning.org/ethics/ethicscode.htm.

Andrews, R., G. A. Boyne, J. Law, and Richard M. Walker. (2012). *Strategic Management and Public Service Performance*. New York: Palgrave Macmillan.

Beatley, T., D. J. Brower, and W. H. Lucy. (1994). Representation in the comprehensive planning: An analysis of the Austinplan process. *Journal of the American Planning Association*, 60(2), 185–196.

Berke, P. R., D. R. Godschalk, E. J. Kaisier, and D. Rodriguez. (2006). *Urban Land Use Planning* (5th edn). Urbana, IL: University of Illinois Press.

Borins, S. (1998). *Innovating with Integrity: How Local Heroes are Transforming American Government*. Washington, DC: Georgetown University Press.

Borins, S. (2014). *The Persistence of Innovation in Government*. Washington, DC: Brookings.

Boyne, G. A. and J. S. Gould-Williams. (2003). Planning and performance in public organizations: An empirical analysis. *Public Management Review*, 5(1), 115–132.

Brody, S. D. and W. E. Highfield. (2005). Does planning work? Testing the implementation of local environmental planning in Florida. *Journal of the American Planning Association*, 71(2), 159–175.

Bryson, J. M. (2010). The future of public and nonprofit strategic planning. *Public Administration Review*, 70(Supplement), S255–S267.

Bryson, J. M. (2011). *Strategic Planning for Public and Nonprofit Organizations* (4th edn). San Francisco, CA: Jossey-Bass.

Bryson, J. M. and R. C. Einsweiler. (1988). *Strategic Planning: Threats and Opportunities for Planners*. Chicago, IL: Planners Press.

Bryson, J. M., B. C. Crosby, and J. K. Bryson. (2009). Understanding strategic planning and the formulation and implementation of strategic plans as a way of knowing: The contributions of actor-network theory. *International Public Management Journal*, 12(2), 172–207.

Bryson, J. M., K. S. Quick, C. S. Slotterback, and B. Crosby. (2013). Designing public participation processes. *Public Administration Review*, 73(1), 23–34.

Burby, R. J. (2003). Making plans that matter: Citizen involvement and government action. *Journal of the American Planning Association*, 69(1), 33–49.

Campbell, S. (1996). Green cities, growing cities, just cities? Urban planning and the contradictions of sustainable development. *Journal of the American Planning Association*, 62(3), 296–312.

Chakraborty, A., N. Kaza, G. Knaap, and B. Deal. (2011). Robust plans and contingent plans. *Journal of the American Planning Association*, 77(3), 251–266.

Christensen, K. S. (1999). *Cities and Complexity*. Thousand Oaks, CA: Sage.

City of Hampton Roads (VA). (n.d.). Accessed November 15, 2014 at http://hamptonroadsperforms.org/.

City of Portland. (2015). *2035 Comprehensive Plan Update*. Accessed October 4, 2015 at https://www.portlandoregon.gov/bps/article/545554.

Conroy, M. M. and P. R. Berke. (2004). What makes a good sustainable development plan? An analysis of factors that influence principles of sustainable development. *Environment and Planning A*, 36(8), 1381–1396.

Council on Virginia's Future. (2013). *The Virginia Report, 2013*. Accessed November 15, 2014 at http://vaperforms.virginia.gov/index.php.

Crewe, K. (2001). The quality of participatory design: The effects of citizen input on the design of the Boston Southwest Corridor. *Journal of the American Planning Association*, 67(4), 437–455.

Dahl, A. and J. Soss. (2014). Neoliberalism for the common good? Public value governance and the downsizing of democracy, *Public Administration Review*, 74(4), 496–504.

Deyle, R. E. and C. S. Slotterback. (2009). Group learning in participatory planning processes: An exploratory quasiexperimental analysis of local mitigation planning in Florida. *Journal of Planning Education and Research*, 29(1), 23–38.

DiMaggio, P. J. and W. W. Powell. (April, 1983). The iron cage revisited: Institutional isomorphism and collective rationality. *American Sociological Review*, 48, 147–160.

Evans-Cowley, J. and J. Hollander. (2010). The new generation of public participation: Internet-based participation tools. *Planning Practice and Research*, 25(3), 397–408.

Ferlie, E. and E. Ongaro. (2015). *Strategic Management in Public Service Organizations: Concepts, Schools, and Contemporary Issues*. New York: Routledge.

Freedman, L. (2013). *Strategy: A History*. New York: Oxford University Press.

Godschalk, D. R. (2004). Land use planning challenges: Coping with conflicts in visions of sustainable development and livable communities. *Journal of the American Planning Association*, 70(1), 5–13.

Hall, P. G. (2002). *Cities of Tomorrow: An Intellectual History of Urban Planning and Design in the Twentieth Century* (3rd edn). New York: Wiley-Blackwell.

Hall, P. G. (2014). *Cities of Tomorrow: An Intellectual History of Urban Planning and Design since 1880* (4th edn). New York: Wiley-Blackwell.

Hendrick, R. (2003). Strategic planning environment, process, and performance in public agencies: A comparative study of departments in Milwaukee. *Journal of Public Administration Research and Theory*, 13, 491–519.

Huxham, C. and S. Vangen. (2005). *Managing to Collaborate*. New York: Routledge.

Innes, J. E. (1996). Planning through consensus building: A new view of the comprehensive planning ideal. *Journal of the American Planning Association*, 62(4), 460–472.

Innes, J. E. and D. E. Booher. (2010). *Planning with Complexity: An Introduction to Collaborative Rationality for Public Policy*. New York: Routledge.

Jacobs, L. (2014). The contested politics of public value. *Public Administration Review*, 74(4), 480–494.

Kaiser, E. J., D. R. Godschalk, and F. S. Chapin. (1995). *Urban Land Use Planning* (4th edn). Urbana, IL: University of Illinois Press.

Kaufman, J. and H. Jacobs. (1987). A public planning perspective on strategic planning. *Journal of the American Planning Association*, 53(1), 21–31.

Kelly, E. D. (2010). *Community Planning: An Introduction to the Comprehensive Plan* (2nd edn). Washington, DC: Island Press.

Laurian, L., M. Day, P. Berke, N. Ericksen, M. Backhurst, J. Crawford, and J. Dixon. (2004). Evaluating plan implementation: A conformance-based methodology. *Journal of the American Planning Association*, 70(4), 471–480.

Margerum, R. D. (2005). Collaborative growth management in metropolitan Denver: "Fig leaf or valiant effort?" *Land Use Policy*, 22(4), 373–386.

Moynihan, D. (2015). *The New Federal Performance System: Implementing the GPRA Moderninzation Act*. Washington, DC: IBM Center for the Business of Government.

Moynihan, D. and A. Kroll. (2015). Performance management routines that work? An early assessment of the GPRA Modernization Act. *Public Administration Review, Public Administration Review*. Early view available at DOI: 10.1111/puar.12434.

Olsen, J. B. and D. C. Eadie. (1982). *The Game Plan: Governance with Foresight*. Washington, DC: Council of State Planning Agencies.

Osborne, D. and T. Gaebler. (1992). *Reinventing Government: How the Entrepreneurial Spirit is Transforming the Public Sector*. New York: Plume Books.

O'Toole, L. (ed.). (2007). *American Intergovernmental Relations*. Washington, DC: CQ Press.

Poister, T. and G. Streib. (1999). Performance measurement in municipal government: Assessing the state of the practice. *Public Administration Review*, 59(4), 325–335.

Quick, K. S. and M. S. Feldman. (2011). Distinguishing participation and inclusion. *Journal of Planning Education and Research*, 31(3), 272–290.

Region 5 Regional Development Commission. (2012). *Building a Resilient Region*. Accessed November 15, 2015 at http://www.resilientregion.org/region-plan/index.html.

Sandfort, J. and S. Moulton (2015). *Effective Implementation in Practice: Integrating Public Policy and Management*. Hoboken, NJ: John Wiley.

Seltzer, E. and A. Carbonell. (2011). Planning regions. In E. Seltzer and A. Carbonell (Eds), *Regional Planning in America: Practice and Prospect*. Cambridge, MA: Lincoln Institute of Land Policy.

Sorkin, D. L., N. B. Ferris, and J. Hudak. (1984). *Strategies for Cities and Counties: A Strategic Planning Guide*. Washington, DC: Public Technology.

Tang, Z., S. D. Brody, C. Quinn, L. Chiang, and T. Wei. (2010). Moving from agenda to action: Evaluating local climate change action plans. *Journal of Environmental Planning and Management*, 53(1), 41–62.

US Census Bureau. (2012). Census Bureau Reports There Are 89,004 Local Governments in the United States. Press release, August 30.

Van Herzele, A. (2004). Local knowledge in in action: Valuing nonprofessional reasoning in the planning process. *Journal of Planning Education and Research*, 24(2), 197–212.

Vieg, J. A. (1942). Developments in governmental planning. In L. D. White (ed.), *The Future of Government in the United States* (pp. 63–87). Chicago, IL: University of Chicago.

Walker, R. (1941). *The Planning Function in Urban Government*. Chicago, IL: University of Chicago Press.

Wheeland, C. (2004). *Empowering the Vision: Community-wide Strategic Planning in Rock Hill, SC*. Lanham, MD: University Press of America.

# 9 What's so strategic about Australian metropolitan plans and planning reform?

## The case of Melbourne, Perth and Sydney

*Paul J. Maginn, Robin Goodman,*
*Nicole Gurran and Kristian Ruming*

## Introduction

The two primary facets of state-based planning systems – strategic planning (e.g. strategic metropolitan plans or state planning strategies) and statutory planning (e.g. town planning or local planning schemes and development assessment policies) – are in a constant state of evolution within Australia (Gleeson and Low, 2000; Hamnett and Freestone, 2000). This is of course, also true of national, regional or local planning systems in other jurisdictions (Albrechts, 2004, 2006; Allmendinger and Tewdwr-Jones, 2009; Lord and Hincks, 2010; Servillo and Van Den Broeck, 2012). Ultimately, it is still arguably the case that most *formal* changes to the institutional structure, policy framework and procedural processes in planning systems are incrementalist in nature (Lindblom, 1959, 1979).

Structural changes to strategic and statutory planning tend to occur in the wake of a real crisis such as a natural hazard or disaster (Berke and Campanella, 2006; Blakely, 2011), or when there is a 'perceived/predicted crisis' such as the threat of climate change (Davoudi *et al.*, 2009; Rissik and Reis, 2013). Change also often occurs when there is a change of government (Allmendinger and Tewdwr-Jones, 2000; Ruming *et al.*, 2012; Tewdwr-Jones, 2012). The latter has been a key factor in the political and policy attention devoted to strategic spatial planning and reforms to the statutory planning processes across Australia during the last decade or so. The recent wave of planning system reforms and new metropolitan strategies in Western Australia (WA)/Perth, Victoria/Melbourne, New South Wales (NSW)/Sydney and Queensland/Brisbane, have mainly come about following state election victories by neo-liberalist/neo-conservative parties in WA (2008 and 2013), Victoria (2010), NSW (2011) and Queensland (2012). A change of government is not a prerequisite for the initiation of planning reforms or the development of a new metropolitan plan. This has been the case in South Australia, for example, where the Australian Labor Party (ALP), who have been in power since 2002, released their metropolitan strategy, *The 30 Year Plan for Metropolitan Adelaide*, in 2010 (Government of South Australia, 2010) and instigated a major review of the planning system in early 2013 (Expert Panel on

Planning Reform, 2013, 2014). The change of government in Victoria in late 2014 did not provoke calls for major changes to the planning system, however the metropolitan strategic plan, released earlier in 2014, is being 'refreshed'.

This chapter has two primary objectives. First, it explores the nature of two key facets of contemporary planning practice in Australia: (1) metropolitan planning strategies and (2) planning system reforms. Second, the policy connectivity, or lack thereof, between these two facets of planning is explored. This is done through an analysis of three case study cities – Perth (WA), Melbourne (Victoria) and Sydney (NSW). The chapter is in four major parts. First, an overview of what is meant by the term 'strategic planning', as used in research and policy circles, is outlined to provide a conceptual and analytical basis. Second, the broad evolution of metropolitan planning in the three case studies is discussed with particular emphasis given to the current metropolitan strategies. Third, the aims and objectives of planning reform agendas being rolled out in WA, Victoria and NSW, and the drivers underpinning these agendas are highlighted. Finally, some brief concluding comments on the policy complementarity between current metropolitan strategies and planning reforms are presented.

## The need for strategic planning

There are a multitude of imperatives to which city planning must respond in an increasingly urbanised and globalised world. These challenges are not new but have been exacerbated in recent years particularly since the onset of the global financial crisis in 2008. Many cities in both the global north and south have been faced with a myriad of pressures relating to population growth (and contraction), transport and infrastructure requirements, environmental risk, and increasing socio-spatial inequality. It is in the face of these various 'wicked problems' (Rittel and Webber, 1973) that planners have been tasked with the responsibility of devising strategic plans designed to manage and contain these problems. The goals for strategic planning have never been larger and the expectations on planning to deliver have never seemed so immense.

The Australian experience provides a useful demonstration of this pressured agenda. A plethora of metropolitan strategies for the nation's eight state and territorial capital cities have been published over the last decade, all with similar central objectives of promoting economic prosperity, containing urban growth, protecting environmental sustainability and providing direction for future development in the face of rapid population increases and globalisation. Simultaneously, however, there are concerns within government and across the development industry, that Australian planning systems impose artificial spatial constraints plus costly and inefficient regulatory burdens which stifle economic investment and exacerbate housing unaffordability (Productivity Commission, 2011; COAG Reform Council, 2012). Consequently, Australian state governments have embarked upon ambitious planning reforms, under often competing mantras of 'cutting red tape' to streamline decision-making processes, while also promising increased community participation and improved environmental outcomes

(Piracha, 2010; Searle and Bunker, 2010a, 2010b; Gurran, 2011; Ruming, 2011a, 2011b; Ruming *et al.*, 2012). At the same time, local residents are increasingly organised in their resistance to the large-scale urban changes needed to accommodate a greater share of the city's new housing development within established areas – a central platform of Australia's metropolitan strategies. This tension has positioned Australian planning ever more precariously between private development interests, property owners, and wider public good agendas.

In this context, questions abound in relation to the ability of contemporary metropolitan plans to be implemented and realise their stated objectives. This reflects two key factors. First, Australia's metropolitan planning strategies lack statutory authority and depend on loose arrangements for adoption within local (often land-use zoning) instruments. In appearance they are more like glossy place promotion brochures, rich in visual imagery and aspirational text, but there is little evidence that metropolitan strategies have had direct or tangible effects on development outcomes (Goodman *et al.*, 2010). Second, while the planning reform agendas being rolled out across Australian metropolitan regions also constitute a form of strategic planning in the sense that reforms are underpinned by an overarching policy rationale to *improve* the planning system, their focus appears to be exclusively on statutory planning processes. Although reforms often canvas major structural changes to planning systems and the instruments of implementation, sometimes even redrafting the content of spatial regulations, planning reforms have given relatively little, if any, direct attention to metropolitan strategic planning and plans. In short, there appears to be a policy disconnect between two of the main facets of the Australian planning system, thereby undermining that the overall strategic capacity of planning. So what is meant by strategic planning?

### *What is strategic planning?*

As Albrechts (2004, p. 746) notes, '[t]he word "strategy" originated within a military context'. The *Collins Concise Dictionary* defines strategy as 'the *art* and *science* of the planning and conduct of a war' (emphasis added) and 'a particular long-term plan for success, [especially] in politics, business, etc.'. It is easy to see how the militaristic underpinning of the term *strategy* resonates with the aims and objectives of planning. Our cities have been under *assault* since the industrial revolution – initially from the pressures of population growth, poor public health standards and an inadequate supply and quality of housing. These issues were seen as a major threat not only to social well-being but also to economic productivity and political stability. Hence, they provoked policymakers to take decisive action in the mid-nineteenth century. The course of action taken – new public health legislation and building controls – might be described as 'proto-strategic' planning. This was then followed by the first attempts at more comprehensive plans, such as Ebenezer Howard's garden city concept and Burnham's Plan of Chicago, which appeared in the late 1800s/early 1900s (Cullingworth and Nadin, 2006; Levy, 2012).

The emergence of urban planning in Australia was premised on much of the same challenges faced by cities in the UK and the USA during the 1800s. The major difference of course was that planning in the UK was responding to the pressures of industrialisation whereas early Australian planning was premised on the colonial development of what was considered 'terra nullius'. The orderly and coordinated planning of Australia's capital cities faced an uphill struggle during the early phases of settlement due to complex governance arrangements which in themselves were a catalyst for the emergence of a more strategic approach to planning. As Freestone (2010, pp. 12–13) notes:

> From the later nineteenth century, emerging problems of sanitation, subdivision, transport, water and sewerage provision, gas supply, housing and harbour facilities in the big cities called forth the need for a larger scale of thinking and the need for some measure of coordination. This realization helped lay the ground for more imaginative conceptions of town planning. [...] What also emerged during the rapid urbanization experienced from the 1880s was a view that orderly, efficient and healthful development of cities and towns could only be secured with some overall vision plus collaboration between the established professional fields of architecture, surveying and engineering.

It was not until the postwar period of the late 1940s that the first Australian metropolitan strategies were published and the idea of strategic planning, as used in contemporary planning discourses, began to take root. Although the term *strategic planning* is often used by planning scholars and practitioners, it remains something of a slippery and elusive term. As Albrechts (2006, p. 1150) highlights: 'There is no one type or form of strategic planning or universally accepted definitions for strategy and strategic spatial planning.' This sentiment is echoed by Healey (2006, p. 180), who identifies four different *meanings* of strategy in planning practice. In essence, these different meanings reflect the major evolutionary stages of strategic planning and strategic plans since the 1940s:

- a 'physical structure [premised on] morphological analysis' whereby strategic plans use 'maps and designs' to articulate policy aims and objectives – 1940s/1950s;
- a goal-oriented activity that uses 'socio-spatial analysis to identify threats to goals' and to develop 'policy statements about programmes of action to achieve goals' – 1960s/1970s;
- 'a framework of principles [that utilises] systematic technical and interactive search procedures to reduce certainty' that results in 'framing concepts, projects and programmes' – 1980s/1990s; and
- 'an inspirational vision [created via] interactive processes that produce imagined futures [so as to] mobilise attention [through the use of] metaphors, storylines and manifestos – 2000s.

Despite this lack of clarity, Albrechts (2010, p. 119) has posited a normative definition of strategic planning:

a transformative and integrative public-sector-led socio-spatial process through which the visions or frames of reference, the justification for coherent actions, and the means of implementation are produced that shape and frame what a place is and what it might become.

Moreover, Albrechts outlines that strategic spatial planning comprises a core set of ingredients. Of course, as a normative model, these ingredients can be relatively easily located, assembled and put into action. But as Newman (2008, p. 1373) cautions, theory is one thing and reality is another, such that 'the evidence for coherent strategic spatial planning is weak'. Although this observation is also acknowledged by Albrechts (2004) and Healey (2004), they both uphold a strong belief in the *potential* of and for strategic planning. The plethora of metropolitan strategies produced in Australia since the 1940s would seem to echo this belief too.

## Australian metropolitan strategic planning: an overview

Strategic planning commenced in Australia when the first comprehensive regional land-use and zoning plans – 'Mark One master plans' (Hamnett and Freestone, 2000, p. 6) – were developed for Sydney (Cumberland County Council, 1949),[1] Melbourne (Melbourne Metropolitan Board of Works, 1954) and Perth (Government of Western Australia, 1955) – see Table 9.1. The *1955 Plan for Perth and Fremantle*, commonly referred to as the Stephenson-Hepburn Plan after its two lead 'architects', who were both British, is arguably one the best examples of a 'statutory metropolitan blueprint' plan (Gregory, 2012). This initial style of strategic planning was essentially imported from Britain, as were some of the key planners charged with developing and implementing them, and represent an early form of international policy transfer (McCann, 2011).

The overall vision of these plans centred on 'improv[ing] the living conditions of city-dwellers' via the inclusion of 'green belts' or a networked hierarchy of public open spaces (local-district-regional) so as to afford people the opportunity to recreate and a 'lung' for the city to ensure that it and its people remained healthy (Bunker, 2009, p. 235). Moreover, these early strategic plans all anticipated significant population growth and, as such, considerable amounts of land were zoned for suburban residential development. Despite this, however, the overall rate of population growth in Sydney, Melbourne and to a lesser extent Perth far exceeded what had been projected. The impact of greater levels of international migrants from diverse cultural backgrounds throughout the 1950s–1980s did not feature as part of the strategic thinking underpinning these metropolitan plans. Part of the reason for this lies in the fact that no amount of strategic planning could actually predict future events that might provoke immigration. In addition, immigration policy was, and remains, the preserve of Australia's federal government and forms part of what might be considered 'supra-strategic policy planning' – a policy domain that the states have had relatively little influence over since federation in 1901.

*Table 9.1* Early Australian metropolitan plans

'This is a planning scheme for a vital and prosperous region, for the second white city of the British Empire, for the other towns of the regions and broad acres between them. Primarily, however, it is a plan for two million people. [...] Sydney, in common with most unplanned cities of the Industrial Revolution, grew too quickly, so that ugliness, inconvenience and discomfort grew in proportion and spread their influence over the surrounding countryside.'

(Cumberland County Council, 1949, p. 1)

'The purpose of this planning scheme is to find out what is efficient and what is not, to show how faults can be remedied and the city made more pleasant, more convenient and more efficient, a better place in which to live, work and play. [...] The scheme only points the way and preserves existing opportunities for civic improvement. In this way it will ensure that future community needs can be fulfilled at the lowest practicable cost. But the scheme itself does not provide any of the requisites of the city. These can be achieved only by positive action in the form of a continuous and co-ordinated programme of public works.'

(Melbourne Metropolitan Board of Works, 1954, p. 3)

'The need for an overall Plan for the Metropolitan Region of Perth and Fremantle has been apparent to most thinking people for many years. These two cities [...] have grown at a surprising rate since the first settlement took place, and it seems clear that expansion will go forward. [...] I do not think anyone will quarrel with the principles of town planning. It is, after all, very logical when carrying out any work, be it building a house or a boat or a city or running a business, to look ahead, assess the difficulties, and promote the work in accordance with a design or plan.'

(Government of Western Australia, 1955, p. iii)

Source: NSW Department of Planning and Environment, Department of Environment Land, Water and Planning (Victoria) and Western Australian Planning Commission

Hamnett and Freestone (2000, p. 5) highlight that while strategic planning has persisted in Australia, its significance ebbed and flowed between the 1950s and 1990s:

- *1950s*: 'statutory metropolitan blueprints in the British town and country planning tradition';
- *1960s*: 'new-look strategic "structure" plans to best facilitate long-term growth';
- *1970s*: 'the mythology of planning as politically neutral, land use arrangement exercise in the "the public interest" is exposed' resulting in strategic planning taking a backseat as 'new forms of planning come forward – environmental, social, advocacy, heritage, cultural and participatory planning';
- *1980s*: a 'revival of strategic planning' underpinned by principles of urban management and ecological sustainability and the emergence of urban consolidation as a key policy objective; and
- *1990s*: 'emergence of yet another round of strategic plans underpinned by renewed aspirations for coordinated planning' caught in a policy and ideological nexus – competitive cities versus ecological cities – during an era defined by the 'triumph' of neo-liberalism over sustainability and the ascendancy of globalisation.

### *Renewed interest in strategic planning*

Lennon (2000, p. 149) has noted that Australian metropolitan planning was 'in the doldrums' during the 1980s, and while various capital cities had plans, they were effectively out-of-date as their visions and aims were predicated on 'a continuation of car-based suburbanisation'. Lennon's (supposed) contention that there was a revival of strategic planning in the early 1990s is challenged by Bunker (2009). A closer reading shows that while Lennon (2000, p. 149) does indeed state that there was a 'revival of metropolitan planning in the late 1980s and early 1990s, his analysis of the state of strategic planning reveals a more nuanced and conservative evaluation:

> In summary, the years around 1990 saw a renewed interest in a form of strategic planning through which state governments and bureaucracies began to embrace the benefits of a systematic approach to coordination underpinning a long-term and integrated vision of metropolitan development. The aspirations of the proponents of this new style of planning have only been realised to a limited extent, however, in the face of an ideology [i.e. neo-liberalism] which is fundamentally antithetical to public sector planning and leadership. (Lennon, 2000, p. 167)

Worldwide, the neo-liberalist policy agenda during the 1980s resulted in urban planning being more about promoting economic development and less about regulating land (Fainstein, 1991). This focus on economic development resulted in a 'project- and area-based' approach to planning with the creation of enterprise zones and development corporations. In the UK, for example, the Thatcher government (1979–1991) channelled policy resources and funding into discrete, yet significant, flagship developments in key post-industrial locations, such as London Docklands, Cardiff, and Belfast Docks (Brownill, 1990; Imrie and Thomas, 1999). This might be viewed as 'site-specific strategic planning'. Again, this policy approach was imported to Australia, manifesting as the Building Better Cities Program which ran from 1991 to 1996.

The Building Better Cities Program (BBCP) was an interesting policy initiative in a number of ways. First, it marked the first time since the 1970s, following the dismantling of the Department of Urban and Regional Development (1973–1975), that the Federal government was directly involved in urban policy (Ruming *et al.*, 2009). Second, the BBCP advocated a partnership approach to urban renewal with Federal and state governments collaborating with one another; the former set the overall policy aims/objectives and provided financial support to state governments which had strategic responsibility for specific programs on the ground. In a number of instances, 'local development authorities' made up of state, local government and private sector representatives were created. These local development authorities proved particularly popular planning vehicles in Western Australia with four being set up across the metropolitan region: Subiaco, East Perth, Midland and Armadale.

While the BBCP might not strictly be considered to be strategic planning given its discrete area-based approach, it was underpinned by a strategic planning philosophy, aspirations and governance arrangements. As Neilsen (2008, p. 83) indicates, the purpose of the BBCP was:

> to promote improvements in the efficiency, equity and sustainability of Australian cities and to increase their capacity to meet the following objectives: economic growth and micro-economic reform; improved social justice; institutional reform; ecologically sustainable development; and improved urban environments and more liveable cities.

Given the geographical specifities and the intergovernmental relations underpinning the BBCP, it might be perceived as a particular mode of strategic planning – '*micro-strategic planning*'. Moreover, if Neilson's (2008) general assessment of the character and success of the BBCP is accepted, then this type/style of strategic planning would seem to be a rare, if socio-spatially limited, example that contains key elements of Albrechts (2010) idealised model of strategic planning.

### *The revival of the metropolitan strategy*

The 'revival' of strategic planning in Australia during the early 2000s is evident by the flurry of new strategic metropolitan plans produced by recently elected and/or re-elected Labor state governments:

- *Melbourne 2030: Planning for Sustainable Growth* (Department of Sustainability and Environment, 2002);
- *Network City: Community Planning Strategy for Perth and Peel* (Department of Planning and Infrastructure, 2004);
- *City of Cities: A Plan for Sydney's Future* (New South Wales Department of Planning, 2005);
- *South East Queensland Regional Plan 2005–2026* (Queensland Government, 2005); and
- *Planning Strategy for Metropolitan Adelaide* (Planning South Australia, 2006).

This revival was stimulated, among other things, by a renewed political interest and desire to reform and reinvigorate state planning systems and a need to react to the 'public outcry among the public and developers (in particular) about the lack of purpose and certainty in the direction of metropolitan growth and change' (Searle and Bunker, 2010b, p. 166). In addition to the development of metropolitan plans, some state governments during this period (2000–2008) also introduced state strategic plans and/or infrastructure strategies, thus signalling the emergence of what might be termed *integrated multi-scalar strategic planning*. For Bunker (2012), the major discursive themes emergent in metropolitan plans during the first decade of the 2000s included:

- *Multiplicity of planning documents* – the fact that important planning instruments lay outside the metropolitan plan;
- *Centralisation* – the process by which the state removed authority from local government;
- *Sustainability* – planning was committed to addressing the growing environmental crisis;
- *Promoting economic development and enhancing competitiveness* – a longing for 'global city' status;
- *Infrastructure provision* – a means of not only shaping the structure of the city but increasing its efficiency and competitiveness; and
- *The compact city* – pursuit of an idealised urban structure to counter suburban sprawl.

All of the Australian capital city regions, except Hobart (Tasmania) and Darwin (Northern Territory) currently have metropolitan-wide planning strategies – both Darwin City Council and Hobart City Council have generic strategic plans prepared by the councils. Metropolitan strategies for the other capital cities are prepared by the state/territory government which have 'constitutional responsibility for metropolitan planning' via their respective department of planning (Searle and Bunker, 2010b, p. 165) (see Table 9.2). The metropolitan strategies, along with a whole host of other associated state and/or metropolitan plans and planning policies, operate as a highly complex and hierarchical meta-strategic planning framework which local government town planning schemes (statutory planning and zoning) and/or local planning strategies must adhere to (Gleeson *et al.*, 2004; Bunker and Searle, 2009; Gurran, 2011).

The urban visions painted in metropolitan strategies tend to appear at the start of these policy documents and are often repeated through summaries and introductions offered by the relevant government minister. The policy utterings embedded in the visions, principles, aims and objectives contained within metropolitan planning strategies (and other associated planning policy documents) represent a grand narrative on the potential of planning in creating a brighter and better urban future (McCallum and Hopkins, 2011). Adopting a cynical view, Sandercock and Friedmann (2000, p. 530) argue that metropolitan strategies are 'first and foremost … *political [documents]*, rather than… planning document[s]'.

In the Australian context, recent metropolitan strategic planning documents and planning reforms have a distinct political hue. Since the election of various Liberal Party-led state governments since 2008 the policy emphasis of new metropolitan strategies and planning reforms have assumed a distinctly neoliberal character, giving both discursive and substantive policy emphasis to economic growth, competitiveness, globalisation and deregulation. Simultaneously, in an effort to demonstrate a commitment to planning being a democratically-informed practice, draft strategies and planning reform discussion papers have been released for stakeholder and public comment in WA (Western Australian Planning Commission, 2009, 2010, 2011 2013); Victoria (Victorian Planning System Ministerial Advisory Committee, 2011; Department of Planning

*Table 9.2* Contemporary Australian metropolitan planning strategies

| State/ Territory | Metropolitan plan | Nature/purpose of plan/strategy |
| --- | --- | --- |
| ACT | *The Canberra Spatial Plan (2004)* | *The Canberra Spatial Plan* outlines a strategic direction that will help manage change and provide for growth to achieve the social, environmental and economic sustainability of Canberra. Under the umbrella of *The Canberra Plan*, it forms part of a comprehensive, integrated strategic plan for Canberra's future. *The Canberra Spatial Plan* reflects the community's aspirations for the future of the city and its setting. |
| NSW | *A Plan for Growing Sydney (2014)* | *A Plan for Growing Sydney* is the government's plan to achieve these things. It's an action plan focused on bringing all stakeholders together with a common purpose – to develop a competitive economy with world-class services and transport; to deliver greater housing choice to meet our changing needs and lifestyles; to create communities that have a strong sense of wellbeing; and to safeguard our natural environment. |
| NT | *Evolving Darwin Towards 2020 Strategic Plan (n.d.)* | The *Evolving Darwin Towards 2020 Strategic Plan* is an accountability document that identifies the directions we need to take to improve the quality of life for the people of Darwin. The key element of this Strategic Plan is the medium to long-term vision for Darwin. This vision was developed in consultation with residents, special interest groups and businesses from across the Darwin community and represents a shared understanding of our future direction. |
| QLD | *South East Queensland Regional Plan 2009–2031 (2009)* | The purpose of the *South East Queensland Regional Plan 2009–2031* is to manage regional growth and change in the most sustainable way to protect and enhance quality of life in the region. [...] |
| SA | *The 30 Year Plan for Greater Adelaide (2010)* | *The 30-Year Plan for Greater Adelaide* (the Plan) sets out the land-use policies to manage the growth and change that is forecast to occur in the region. It builds on Light's vision and the 1962 *Report on the Metropolitan Area of Adelaide*, and positions South Australia to take advantage of our opportunities and be fully prepared for future challenges. |
| TAS | *Hobart 2025 Strategic Framework (2007)* | The *Hobart 2025 Strategic Framework* identifies the directions needed to continue to improve the quality of life of Tasmania's capital city. The key element of the strategic framework is a long-term vision for the city, developed in consultation with residents, business, interest groups, key city stakeholders, young people and students from across the city. |

*Table 9.2* Contemporary Australian metropolitan planning strategies (continued)

| State/ Territory | Metropolitan plan | Nature/purpose of plan/strategy |
|---|---|---|
| VIC | *Plan Melbourne: Metropolitan Planning Strategy (2013)* | *Plan Melbourne* is the vision for Melbourne. It is an evidence-based plan designed to guide Melbourne's housing, commercial and industrial development through to 2050. It seeks to integrate long-term land-use, infrastructure and transport planning to meet the population, housing and employment needs of the future. |
| WA | *Directions 2031 and Beyond (2010)* | *Directions 2031* is a high-level spatial framework and strategic plan that establishes a vision for future growth of the metropolitan Perth and Peel region; and it provides a framework to guide the detailed planning and delivery of housing, infrastructure and services necessary to accommodate a range of growth scenarios. *Directions 2031* builds on many of the aspirational themes of previous metropolitan plans which sought to guide the future structure and form of the city. |

and Community Development, 2012; Reformed Zones Ministerial Advisory Committee, 2012; Department of Transport, Planning and Local Infrastructure, 2013) and NSW (New South Wales Government, 2011, 2012, 2013; Stein 2012). Consultation exercises undertaken in NSW and Victoria were significantly more comprehensive than in WA. In NSW and Victoria expert advisory bodies were set up and charged with consulting institutional stakeholders and the wider public. Both expert panels held an extensive number of public meetings across their respective states (over 100 in the case of NSW). Ultimately, however, the consultation process in NSW failed to build community support for the new reform agenda, which came to a halt. In WA, the consultation process was more traditional in the sense that institutional stakeholders/local community were simply invited to respond in writing, by a certain date, to the draft metropolitan strategy and the various planning reform documents published by the WAPC. This approach has been 'successful' in that the government has secured many of the reforms it set out to introduce (WA Government, 2014).

Although the detailed nature – legal, institutional and procedural – of the planning systems in WA, NSW and Victoria are somewhat different, they share the same basic institutional and policy characteristics. Australia's six states and two territories have overall responsibility for land-use planning and exercise these responsibilities through overarching legislation within which local governments must prepare planning schemes (zoning and development controls) and assess local development proposals. While there has always been a degree of policy sharing and influence between Australia's states and territories, over the past decade policy thinking and approaches to metropolitan strategic planning have increasingly converged across Sydney, Perth and Melbourne, as have the stated goals and rhetoric of planning reform agendas in each respective state (Ruming *et al.*, 2012, 2013). This is reflected in the *policy aesthetics and discourses* of metropolitan planning strategies as well as planning reform agendas (see Table 9.3). In many respects this apparent convergence reflects the shared political and ideological dispositions of the state governments in WA, Victoria and NSW.[2] Notably, despite being the responsibility of state governments, in recent years the Federal government has sought to directly and indirectly colour the policy emphasis of metropolitan planning strategies with infrastructure funding linked to the quality of capital city plans (Ruming *et al.*, 2014). Furthermore, reforms and deregulation of statutory planning processes have been strongly influenced by calls from the Council of Australian Governments (COAG Reform Council, 2011; Local Government and Planning Ministers' Council, 2011), which provides for cooperation across all three tiers of Australian government, and the Development Assessment Forum (DAF), 'an independent think tank and advisory forum of government, industry, and the professions'.[3]

Despite this apparent convergence in the direction, visions and aims of the strategic planning frameworks in WA, Victoria and NSW (and elsewhere), there appears to be a meta-strategic policy disconnect between statutory planning systems and metropolitan planning strategies. The various reforms to the different state statutory planning systems – new legislation, the creation of 'independent' development assessment panels (DAPs), approved development for certain residential proposals, and the centralisation of decision-making – all form part of a *rolling back* of planning regulations via the streamlining of operational statutory planning structures and processes (Thornley, 1999; Peck and Tickell, 2002). While this rolling back of the 'regulatory burden' in statutory planning systems *may* increase the efficiency of decision-making and reduce costs for developers, it simultaneously undermines the strategic authority of planners to guide and manage the visions of Australian capital cities as outlined in metropolitan strategies.

In his review of metropolitan strategies, Bunker (2012) suggests that the similarities observed between metropolitan plans of the early 2000s were the product of a uniform political landscape at the state level. As seen in Table 9.3, there is a broadly shared vision across the metropolitan strategies for Perth, Melbourne and Sydney. The similarities in the appearance and content of contemporary Australian metropolitan strategies suggest a convergence of policy thinking and understanding of cities. While key urban problems afflicting cities throughout the world are in a sense generalisable, Australian metropolitan planning has underplayed the complex and dynamic socio-spatial, historical, economic, political and physical specificities defining capital city regions, and how, where and why different problems manifest and unfold across space and time. This policy groupthink at the state government level is also evident at the national level:

> This National Urban Policy sets a vision for our cities to deliver future prosperity and wellbeing for our communities and reinforces the Council of Australian Governments' (COAG) national objective to *ensure Australian cities are globally competitive, productive, sustainable, liveable, socially*

*Table 9.3* Capital city metropolitan plans: visions and key objectives

| Strategy | Vision | Key Principles/Directions/Objectives |
| --- | --- | --- |
|  | *By 2031, Perth and Peel people will have created a world class liveable city: green, vibrant, more compact and accessible with a unique sense of place.* | 1. A liveable city. 2. A prosperous city. 3. An accessible city. 4. A sustainable city. 5. A responsible city. |
|  | *Melbourne will be a global city of opportunity and choice.* | 1. Protecting the suburbs. 2. Developing in defined areas near services and infrastructure. 3. Creating a clearer and simpler planning system with improved decision-making. 4. Rebalancing growth between Melbourne and regional Victoria. 5. Identifying an investment and infrastructure pipeline. |
|  | *The government's vision for Sydney is: a strong global city, a great place to live.* | 1. A competitive economy with world-class services and transport. 2. A city of housing choice with homes that meet our needs and lifestyles. 3 A great place to live with communities that are strong, healthy and well connected. 4. A sustainable and resilient city that protects the natural environment and has a balanced approach to the use of land and resources. |

Source: Western Australian Planning Commission, Department of Environment Land, Water and Planning (Victoria) and NSW Department of Planning and Environment

*inclusive and well placed to meet future challenges and growth.* (Department of Infrastructure and Transport, 2011, p. 3)

### *Strategic planning and political strategising*

The 2007 election victory of then leader of the ALP, Kevin Rudd, marked the beginning of a 'new era' in Federal government interest *and* intervention in Australia's cities. The Federal government's previous forays into this policy domain have been few and far between, relatively short-lived and area-based

*Table 9.4* National reviews of planning systems and performance

| Agency | Report(s) | Year |
| --- | --- | --- |
| Productivity Commission | *Performance Benchmarking of Australian Business Regulation: Planning, Zoning and Development Assessments* | 2011 |
| COAG Reform Council | *Review of Capital City Strategic Planning Systems; Report to the Council of Australian Government* | 2011 |
| Local Government and Planning Ministers' Council: COAG Business Regulation and Competition Working Group | *First National Report on Development Assessment Performance 2008/09* | 2011 |

(Bunker and Ruming, 2010). The Rudd/Gillard governments' involvement (2007–2013) in urban policy could be described as an attempt to reframe and claim the 'metropolitan problem' as a *national* policy concern beyond the responsibilities and interests of the states. This has been achieved to an extent by the Federal government providing co-funding for major state-based infrastructure projects; the release of various *State of Australian Cities* reports (Major Cities Unit, 2010, 2011, 2012, 2013); the development of a non-statutory *National Urban Policy* (Department of Infrastructure and Transport, 2011); and benchmarking the health and wellbeing of state planning systems via national reviews of state planning systems (see Table 9.4) (COAG Reform Council, 2012).

## Planning reform: aims, objectives and political strategy

A common narrative and key objective of the reform of statutory planning processes in Australia has focused on 'cutting red tape' (Ruming *et al.*, 2012). This is symbolically (and literally) reflected, for example, on the front covers of the Government of Western Australia's (2009) and Government of Victoria's (2006) consultation papers on planning reform (see Figure 9.1). The emphasis on eliminating bureaucratic inefficiencies in planning reform documents implies that statutory planning systems are more concerned with *procedural* and *administrative* policy issues rather than strategic planning issues. The recent planning reform agendas presented by state governments in WA, Victoria and NSW are emblematic discursive containers of political ideology and aims.

### *Australian planning reform*

The past decade has seen significant reforms to the legislative and regulatory frameworks surrounding planning and development across Australia (Table 9.5). The content of these reforms are summarised in Table 9.6. As shown in the table, these include: (1) new timeframes for plan making and development assessments; (2) templates to prepare local plans; (3) standardised land-use zones

*Figure 9.1* (a) Government of Western Australia (2009); (b) Government of Victoria (2006)

Source: Western Australian Planning Commission and Department of Environment Land, Water and Planning (Victoria)

*Table 9.5* Australian planning reform, 2005-2014

| Jurisdiction | Key Reform Documents | Date |
|---|---|---|
| ACT | Introduction to Planning System Reform | 2008 |
| | Planning and Development Act | 2007 |
| NSW | A New Planning System for NSW: White Paper | 2013 |
| | A New Planning System for NSW: Green Paper | 2012 |
| | Environmental Planning and Assessment Amendment Bill | 2008 |
| | Improving the NSW Planning System | 2007 |
| NT | Planning Act | 2007 |
| QLD | Sustainable Planning Act | 2009 |
| | Planning for a Prosperous Queensland | 2007 |
| SA | Better Planning, Better Future | 2008 |
| TAS | Review of the Planning System of Tasmania Final Steering | 2009 |
| | Committee Report | 2012 |
| | Reformed Zones for Victoria: A Discussion Paper on Reforming Victoria's Planning Zones | |
| VIC | Planning & Environment Act 1987 Review Discussion Paper | 2009 |
| | Making Local Policy Stronger | 2007 |
| | Cutting Red Tape in Planning | 2006 |
| WA | Planning Makes it Happen Phase Two | 2014 |
| | Building a Better Planning System / Planning Makes It Happen | 2009 |
| | Planning and Development Act | 2005 |

Source: adapted from Gurran (2011)

(4) codification (i.e., automatic permission for compliant projects), and (5) the 'depoliticisation' of decision-making through DAPs. Despite different legislative foundations and histories, the process of planning reform across the states has also been characterised by a significant level of consistency in terms of the objectives and structures of reform. In broad terms, reforms have sought to address perceived complexity, unnecessary bureaucracy, and time delays in planning processes (Gurran *et al.*, 2009). Searle and Bunker (2010a) claim that recent reforms to the development control systems across Australia have sought to (1) generate/promote economic development and (2) reduce the scope for local opposition to urban consolidation. This is echoed by other commentators who highlight that reforms represent a response to a growing neo-liberalisation of the planning process as the planning system is repositioned as a *facilitator* of private enterprise which is now the sector with increased responsibility for delivering much of the urban spatial vision promoted by metropolitan strategies (Gleeson and Low, 2000; Gurran, 2011; Steele and Ruming, 2012).

There can be no guarantee that the goals of greater efficiency and certainty within the planning system can be achieved through planning reforms. Even where planning systems are demonstrably inefficient, procedural change itself can have unpredictable effects. The creation of 'new' leaner, more streamlined decision-making processes may in fact result in the development of more complex and inefficient processes as a result in the loss of staff and thus institutional knowledge (Ruming, 2009; Steele and Ruming, 2012). Furthermore, the political emphasis on

Table 9.6 Key planning reform directions, selected Australian states, 2006–2013

| State | Title | Red tape removal | Faster plan making | Faster assessment | Plan templates | Zone reform | Codification | Panels |
|---|---|---|---|---|---|---|---|---|
| **NSW** | A New Planning System for NSW Planning Green Paper 2012 | ✓ | ✓ | ✓ | ✓ | ✓ | ✓ | ✓ |
| **QLD** | Planning for Prosperous Queensland 2007 | ✓ | ✓ | ✓ | ✓ | ✓ | ✓ | |
| **SA** | Better Planning, Better Future 2008 | ✓ | | ✓ | ✓ | ✓ | ✓ | ✓ |
| **Victoria** | Cutting Red Tape in Planning 2006 | ✓ | | | ✓ | ✓ | ✓ | |
| | Reformed Zones for Victoria 2012 | ✓ | | ✓ | | ✓ | | |
| **WA** | Planning Makes it Happen; a Blueprint for Planning Reform 2009 | ✓ | ✓ | ✓ | ✓ | ✓ | | ✓ |
| | Planning Makes it Happen: Phase 2, 2013 | ✓ | ✓ | ✓ | ✓ | | | ✓ |

increasing speed and efficiency via a reduction of regulations and processes that are designed to offer environmental protection, manage risk, or ensure coordinated land use, infrastructure, and transport arrangements are paradoxically at odds with the visionary ambitions outlined in metropolitan planning strategies. So while the aspirations for Australia's metropolitan city regions are growing, the longstanding statutory planning instruments designed to realise these aims are being eroded and contributing to an implementation deficit.

## Conclusions

Australian strategic metropolitan planning began in the late 1940s when the first wave of metropolitan plans emerged. They were the product of international policy transfer, informed by planning ideas imported largely from the UK and overseen by British planners. These early metropolitan strategies may be characterised as comprehensive physical land-use blueprint plans with a 30–50-year vision. Since these early plans, strategic planning has waxed and waned but, ultimately, persisted. A revival in strategic planning emerged in the 1990s and since that time state governments have demonstrated an ongoing commitment to strategic metropolitan plans. Contemporary metropolitan strategies, however, are much less about physical land-use planning and more about offering blue-sky visions for the future of metropolitan Australia. Moreover, today's metropolitan plans lack any statutory authority. Hence, the potential to realise the visions outlined in metropolitan strategies is brought into question.

Australian state governments, over the last decade or so, have also shown a commitment to reforming their statutory planning systems. While there are always grounds for improving planning systems, not least because the issues planners seek to solve are constantly moving and evolving 'wicked problems' (Rittel and Webber, 1973), enacting reforms which are primarily designed to speed up decision-making are not going to solve the complex spatial problems facing Australian cities in the twenty-first century. Nor are they likely to help realise the visions and objectives outlined in metropolitan strategies. Reforms to state statutory planning systems across Australia are more the product of *strategic politics* than *strategic policy-making* and more fixated on streamlining bureaucratic decision-making processes. In fact, there appears to be a lack of policy complementarity between strategic planning and statutory planning across Australia. This, ultimately, brings into question the nature and substance of strategic planning and the purpose and potential of metropolitan planning strategies in realising their visions and tackling the myriad of issues – e.g., population growth, infrastructure provision, environmental protection, housing affordability and sustainable economic growth – facing metropolitan Australia.

## Notes

1 Sydney (1949) relates to the Cumberland County Plan. Cumberland County is an old name used to describe the administrative area for what is now the Sydney Metro region.

2 The Liberal Party lost the 2014 state government in Victoria to the Australian Labor Party.
3 http://www.pc.gov.au/inquiries/completed/regulation-benchmarking-planning/submissions/sub058.pdf.

# References

Albrechts, L. (2004) 'Strategic (spatial) planning re-examined'. *Environment and Planning B*, 33, 743–758.

Albrechts, L. (2006) 'Shifts in strategic spatial planning? Some evidence from Europe and Australia'. *Environmental and Planning A*, 38, 1149–1170.

Albrechts, L. (2010) 'More of the same is not enough! How could strategic spatial planning be instrumental in dealing with the challenges ahead?' *Environment and Planning B*, 37, 1115–1127.

Allmendinger, P. and Tewdwr-Jones, M. (2000) 'Spatial dimensions and institutional uncertainties of planning and the new regionalism'. *Environment and Planning C*, 18(6), 711–726.

Allmendinger, P. and Tewdwr-Jones, M. (2009) 'Embracing change and difference in planning reform: New Labour's role for planning in complex times'. *Planning Practice and Research*, 24, 71–81.

Australian Capital Territory (2004) *The Canberra Spatial Plan*. Canberra: ACT. Available from: http://apps.actpla.act.gov.au/plandev/sp-pdf/spatialplan.pdf (last accessed 17/03/16).

Berke, P. R. and Campanella, T. J. (2006) 'Planning for post-disaster resiliency'. *The ANNALS of the American Academy of Political and Social Science*, 604(1), 192–207.

Blakely, E. J. (2011) *My Storm: Managing the Recovery of New Orleans in the Wake of Katrina*. Philadelphia, PA: University of Pennsylvania Press.

Brownhill, S. (1990) *Developing London's Docklands: Another Great Planning Disaster?* London: Sage.

Bunker, R. (2009) 'Situating Australian metropolitan planning'. *International Planning Studies*, 14(3), 233–252.

Bunker, R. (2012) 'Reviewing the path dependency in Australian metropolitan planning'. *Urban Policy and Research*, 30(4), 443–452.

Bunker, R. and Searle, G. (2009) 'Theory and practice in metropolitan strategy: Situating recent Australian Planning'. *Urban Policy and Research*, 27, 101–116.

Bunker, R. and Ruming, K. J. (2010) 'How national planning might enrich metropolitan planning an Australia'. *Urban Policy and Research*, 28, 327–334.

City of Darwin (2012) *Evolving Darwin towards 2020 Strategic Plan*. Darwin: City of Darwin (Northern Territory). Available from: http://www.darwin.nt.gov.au/sites/default/files/City_Darwin_Strategic%20Plan%202012_web.pdf (last accessed 17/03/16).

COAG Reform Council (2011) *The COAG Deregulation and Competition Agenda*. Canberra: COAG Reform Council.

COAG Reform Council (2012) *Review of Capital City Strategic Planning Systems*. Sydney: COAG Reform Council.

Cullingworth, B. and Nadin, V. (2006) *Town and Country Planning in the UK*. Oxford: Routledge.

Cumberland County Council (1949) *The Planning Scheme for the County of Cumberland*. Sydney: Cumberland County Council (NSW).

Davoudi, S., Crawford, J. and Mehmood, A. (2009) *Planning for Climate Change: Strategies for Mitigation and Adaptation for Spatial Planners*. London: Earthscan.

Department of Infrastructure and Transport (2011) *Our Cities, Our Future: A National Urban Policy for a Productive, Sustainable and Liveable Future*. Canberra: Commonwealth of Australia.

Department of Planning and Community Development (2012a) *Reformed Zones for Victoria: A Discussion Paper on Reforming Victoria's Planning Zones*. Melbourne: State of Victoria.

Department of Planning and Infrastructure (2004) *Network City: Community Planning Strategy for Perth and Peel*. Perth: Western Australian Planning Commission.

Department of Planning, Transport and Infrastructure (2010) *The 30 Year Plan for Greater Adelaide*. Adelaide: SA Government. Available from: http://www.dpti.sa.gov.au/__ data/assets/pdf_file/0006/132828/The_30-Year_Plan_for_Greater_Adelaide_ compressed.pdf (last accessed 17/03/16).

Department of Sustainability and Environment (2002) *Melbourne 2030: Planning for Sustainable Growth*. Melbourne: State of Victoria.

Department of Transport, Planning and Local Infrastructure (2013) *Plan Melbourne, Metropolitan Planning Strategy*. Melbourne: Government of Victoria.

Expert Panel on Planning Reform (2013) *What We Have Heard*. South Australia's Expert Panel on Planning Reform, Adelaide, South Australia,

Expert Panel on Planning Reform (2014) *Our Ideas for Reform*. South Australia's Expert Panel on Planning Reform, Adelaide, South Australia.

Fainstein, S. S. (1991) 'Promoting economic development urban planning in the United States and Great Britain'. *Journal of the American Planning Association*, 57(1), 22–33.

Freestone, R. (2010) *Urban Nation: Australia's Planning Heritage*. Melbourne: CSIRO Publishing.

Gleeson, B. and Low, N. (2000) *Australian Urban Planning: New Challenges, New Agendas*. Sydney: Allen and Unwin.

Gleeson, B., Darbas, T. and Lawson, S. (2004) 'Governance, sustainability and recent Australian metropolitan strategies: A socio-theoretic analysis'. *Urban Policy and Research*, 22, 345–366.

Goodman, R., Buxton, M., Chhetri, P., Taylor, E. and Wood, G. (2010) 'Planning and the characteristics of housing supply in Melbourne'. *AHURI Final Report No. 157*. Australian Housing and Urban Research Institute, Melbourne, Victoria.

Government of South Australia (2008) *Better Planning, Better Future*. Adelaide: Government of South Australia. Available from: http://www.dplg.sa.gov.au/html/files/ Guide_Residential_Code.pdf (last accessed 17/03/16).

Government of South Australia (2010) *The 30 Year Plan for Greater Adelaide*. Adelaide: Department of Planning and Local Government.

Government of Victoria (2006) *Cutting Red Tape in Planning*. Department of Sustainability and Environment, Melbourne, Victoria.

Government of Western Australia (1955) *Plan for the Metropolitan Region Perth and Fremantle*. Perth: Government Printing Office.

Government of Western Australia (2009) *Building a Better Planning System*. Consultation Paper. Perth: Government of Western Australia.

Gregory, J. (2012) 'Stephenson and metropolitan planning in Perth'. *Town Planning Review*, 83, 297–318.

Gurran, N. (2011) *Australian Urban Land Use Planning Principles, Systems and Practice.* Sydney: Sydney University Press.

Gurran, N., Ruming, K., Randolph, B. and Quintal, D. (2009) *Counting the Costs: Planning Requirements, Infrastructure Contributions and Residential Development in Australia: Final Report.* Melbourne: AHURI.

Hamnett, S. and Freestone, R. (2000) *The Australian Metropolis: A Planning History.* St Leonards, NSW: Allen and Unwin.

Healey, P. (2004) 'The treatment of space and place in the new strategic spatial planning in Europe'. *International Journal of Urban and Regional Research*, 28, 45–67.

Healey, P. (2006) 'Transforming governance'. *European Planning Studies*, 14(3), 299–320.

Hobart City Council (2007) *Hobart 2025 Strategic Framework.* Hobart: Hobart City Council (Tasmania). Available from: http://www.hobartcity.com.au/files/0d5ddf2c-204f-4520-b327-9d2500919d6f/hobart-2025-a-strategic-framework.pdf (last accessed 17/03/16).

Imrie, R. and Thomas, H. (eds) (1999) *British Urban Policy: An Evaluation of the Urban Development Corporations.* London: Sage.

Lennon, M. (2000) 'The revival of metropolitan planning'. In S. Hamnett and R. Freestone (eds), *The Australian Metropolis: A Planning History* (pp. 149–167). Sydney: Allen and Unwin.

Levy, J. M. (2012) *Contemporary Urban Planning* (10th edn). New York: Routledge.

Lindblom, C. E. (1959) 'The science of "muddling through"'. *Public Administration Review*, 19, 79–88.

Lindblom, C. E. (1979) 'Still muddling, not yet through'. *Public Administration Review*, 39, 517–526.

Local Government and Planning Ministers' Council (2011) *First National Report on Development Assessment Performance 2008/09.* Adelaide: COAG Business Regulation and Competition Working Group.

Lord, A. and Hincks, S. (2010) 'Making plans: The role of evidence in England's reformed spatial planning system'. *Planning Practice and Research*, 25, 477–496.

Major Cities Unit (2010) *State of Australian Cities 2010.* Canberra: Commonwealth of Australia.

Major Cities Unit (2011) *State of Australian Cities 2011.* Canberra: Commonwealth of Australia.

Major Cities Unit (2012) *State of Australian Cities 2012.* Canberra: Commonwealth of Australia.

Major Cities Unit (2013) *State of Australian Cities 2013.* Canberra: Commonwealth of Australia.

McCallum, D. and Hopkins, D. (2011) 'The changing discourse of city plans: Rationalities of planning in Perth, 1955–2010'. *Planning Theory and Practice*, 12, 485–510.

McCann, E. (2011) 'Urban policy mobilities and global circuits of knowledge: Toward a research agenda'. *Annals of the Association of American Geographers*, 101(1), 107–130.

Melbourne Metropolitan Board of Works (1954) *Melbourne Metropolitan Planning Scheme Report.* Melbourne: MMBW.

Neilson, L. (2008) 'The "Building Better Cities" program 1991–96: A nation-building initiative of the Commonwealth government'. In J. Butcher (ed.), *Australia under Construction: Nation-building: Past, Present and Future.* Canberra: ANU EPress.

New South Wales Department of Planning (2005) *Metropolitan Strategy – City of Cities: A Plan for Sydney's Future*. Sydney: New South Wales Department of Planning.

New South Wales Department of Planning (2007) *Improving the NSW Planning System: Community Guide*. Sydney: New South Wales Department of Planning.

New South Wales Government (2011) *100 Day Action Plan*. Sydney: New South Wales Government.

New South Wales Government (2012) *A New Planning System for NSW: Green Paper*. Sydney: New South Wales Department of Planning and Infrastructure.

New South Wales Government (2013) *A New Planning System for NSW: White Paper*. Sydney: New South Wales Government.

New South Wales Government (2014) *A Plan for Growing Sydney*. Sydney: New South Wales Government. Available from: http://www.planning.nsw.gov.au/~/media/Files/DPE/Plans-and-policies/a-plan-for-growing-sydney-2014-12.ashx (last accessed 17/03/16).

Newman, P. (2008) 'Strategic spatial planning: Collective action and moments of opportunity'. *European Planning Studies*, 16, 1371–1383.

Peck, J. and Tickell, A. (2002) 'Neoliberalizing space'. *Antipode*, 34, 380–404.

Piracha, A. (2010) 'The NSW (Australia) planning reforms and their implications for planning education and natural and built environment'. *Local Economy*, 25, 240–250.

Planning South Australia (2006) *Planning Strategy for the Development of Metropolitan Adelaide*. Adelaide: Government of South Australia.

Productivity Commission (2011) *Performance Benchmarking of Australian Business Regulation: Planning, Zoning and Development Assessments*. Canberra: Productivity Commission.

Queensland Government (2005) *South East Queensland Regional Plan 2009–2031*. Brisbane: Queensland Government.

Queensland Government (2007) *Planning for a Prosperous Queensland*. Brisbane: Queensland Government. Available from: http://www.dilgp.qld.gov.au/resources/plan/planning-reform/part-1-reform-agenda-full.pdf (last accessed 17/03/16).

Reformed Zones Ministerial Advisory Committee (2012) *Residential Zones Progress Report: Reformed Zones Ministerial Advisory Committee*. Melbourne: State of Victoria.

Rissik, D. and Reis, N. (2013) *City of Melbourne Climate Change Adaptation Strategy and Action Plan*. Canberra: *Commonwealth of Australia (Department of Industry, Innovation, Climate Change, Science, Research and Tertiary Education)*.

Rittel, H. and Webber, M. (1973) 'Dilemmas in a general theory of planning'. *Policy Sciences*, 4, 155–169.

Ruming, K. J. (2009) 'Developer typologies in urban renewal in Sydney: Recognising the role of informal associations between developers and local government'. *Urban Policy and Research*, 28, 23–42.

Ruming, K. J. (2011a) 'Creating Australia's best planning system? Private sector responses to NSW planning change'. *Australian Planner*, 48, 257–269.

Ruming, K. J. (2011b) 'Cutting red tape or cutting local capacity? Responses by local government planners to NSW planning changes'. *Australian Planner*, 48, 43–54.

Ruming, K. J., James, P., Tice, A. and Freestone, R. (2009) 'Establishing a federal presence in Australian cities: Reflections on the role of the Department of Urban and Regional Development in urban regeneration in the 1970s. Paper presented at State of Australian Cities Conference, 24–27 November, Perth. Available at: http://www.be.unsw.edu.au/sites/default/files/upload/research/centres/cf/CFpresentations/SOAC09Ruming_James_Tice_Freestone.pdf (last accessed 17/03/16).

Ruming, K. J., Maginn, P. J. and Gurran, N. (2012) 'Converging visions? The case of contemporary Australian metropolitan planning'. *Proceedings of the 10th International Urban Planning and Environment Association Symposium*, 24–27 July, Sydney, NSW.

Ruming, K. J., Maginn, P. J. and Gurran, N. (2013) 'Old wine in new bottles? New wine in old bottles? Convergence/divergence in Australian metropolitan planning'. *Proceedings of the Planning Institute of Australia's 2013 National Congress*, 24–27 March, Canberra.

Ruming, K. J., Gurran, N., Maginn, P. J. and Goodman, R. (2014) 'A national planning agenda? Unpacking the influence of federal urban policy on state planning reform'. *Australian Planner*, 51, 108–121.

Sandercock, L. and Friedmann, J. (2000) 'Strategising the metropolis in a global era'. *Urban Policy and Research*, 18(4), 529–533.

Searle, G. and Bunker, R. (2010a) 'New century Australian spatial planning: Recentralization under Labor'. *Planning Practice and Research*, 25, 517–529.

Searle, G. and Bunker, R. (2010b) 'Metropolitan strategic planning: An Australian paradigm?' *Planning Theory*, 9, 163–180.

Servillo, L. A. and Van Den Broeck, P. (2012) 'The social construction of planning systems: A strategic-relational institutionalist approach'. *Planning Practice and Research*, 27(1), 41–61.

State Government Victoria (2012) *Reformed Zones for Victoria: A Discussion Paper on Reforming Victoria's Planning Zones*. Melbourne: State Government Victoria. Available from: http://www.dtpli.vic.gov.au/__data/assets/pdf_file/0015/230433/Reformed-Zones-for-Victoria-Discussion-Paper.pdf (last accessed 17/03/16).

Steele, W. and Ruming, K. J. (2012) 'Flexibility versus certainty: Unsettling the land-use planning shibboleth in Australia'. *Planning Practice and Research*, 27(2), 155–176.

Stein, L. (2012) *A Review of International Best Practice in Planning Law for the New South Wales Department of Planning*. New York: Centre for Environmental Legal Studies, Pace University School of Law.

Tewdwr-Jones, M. (2012) *Spatial Planning and Governance: Understanding UK Planning*. Basingstoke: Palgrave Macmillan.

Thornley, A. (1999) 'Is Thatcherism dead? The impact of political ideology on British Planning'. *Journal of Planning Education and Research*, 19(2), 183–191.

Victorian Planning System Ministerial Advisory Committee (2011) *Victorian Planning System Ministerial Advisory Committee Initial Report*. Melbourne: Department of Planning and Community Development.

WA Government (2014) *Planning Makes It Happen Phase 2: Blueprint for Planning Reform*. Perth: WAPC/DOP. Available from: http://www.planning.wa.gov.au/dop_pub_pdf/planning_reform_blueprint.pdf (last accessed 17/03/16).

Western Australian Planning Commission (2009) *Planning Makes It Happen: A Blueprint for Planning Reform*. Perth: Western Australian Planning Commission.

Western Australian Planning Commission (2010) *Directions 2031 and Beyond: Metropolitan Planning Beyond the Horizon*. Perth: Western Australian Planning Commission.

Western Australian Planning Commission (2011) *Capital City Planning Framework: A Vision for Central Perth*. Perth: Western Australian Planning Commission.

Western Australian Planning Commission (2013) *Planning Makes It Happen: Phase Two*. Perth: Western Australian Planning Commission.

# 10 The blessings of 'non-planning' in Egypt

*Mona Abdelwahab and Yehya Serag*

## Introduction

Strategic planning is intrinsically concerned with the 'becoming' of the city. It recognizes the complexities of reality, and emphasizes the state of 'uncertainty' that challenges planners and the planning systems. In Egypt, the planning process is confronted with a particular type of 'uncertainty', where the country struggles through day-to-day affairs dealing with the various issues as they arise rather than through a defined process. Many scholars have thus struggled to investigate and understand the planning process in Egypt. They described the Egyptian planning system as operating solely through 'parental blessings'. The latter is an Egyptian saying that refers to mystical or ambiguous ways that cannot be otherwise described. Simultaneously, this is dependent on the personal preferences of the actors involved in the decision-making, who are identified through the government and other municipality personnel who follow a top-down and central hierarchy. This state of ambiguity and uncertainty was further deepened by the recent political turmoil, which added another layer of instability and recurrent changes. In this context, the planning process in Egypt appears to require a degree of flexibility and adaptability, which is not dealt with in traditional planning. The country first embraced the ideas of strategic planning in the first half of the 2000s through cooperation with international development agencies such as UN-HABITAT and UNDP. This shift towards strategic process was perceived as successful, particularly in the early phases that were closely monitored by these international agencies. However, the transfer to national authorities was rather problematic. The Egyptian institutional and bureaucratic aspects confronted the planning process, and helped the development of a contextualized –'Egyptianized'- version of strategic planning. Not only was this version deemed less successful in comparison with the early phases, it was inserted in a vicious loop. The top-down institution of decision-making continued to perceive planning as a well-defined rational system to apply, and new projects continued to go back to the early 'un-contextualized' version of strategic planning. Furthermore, the role of citizen participation is rather challenging: on the one hand, it conflicts with the top-down institution and, on the other hand, the citizens overemphasized their personal interests in the spatial transformation of the land use and boundaries and disregarded other dimensions that reflected the common good of society.

In this chapter, we aim to re-explore the development of the 'Egyptianized' version of strategic planning. We thus draw on the deconstruction concepts of '*différance*' and 'trace', which helps to identify the structure, the inconsistencies, and the weak and missing points within the content of 'strategic planning in Egypt'. This argument is developed through three sections. The first section approaches the deconstruction of the binary strategic/traditional planning. This discussion is developed in the second section through the contextual reading of strategic planning in Egypt. The third part thus elaborates on the case study of the strategic plan-making of Meet Ghamr city in the Egyptian Delta. Finally, we end with the conclusion.

## Traditional and/or/nor strategic planning

> Strategic planning has become the new hope … as a means to overcome the shortcomings of traditional land use planning at the local and regional levels of planning and decision- making. (Kunzmann, 2014: 28)

Strategic planning is often perceived in opposition to the traditional comprehensive model (Mäntysalo, 2014). This discussion further questions the variances between the two theories: 'To what extent … [strategic planning is] … different from traditional planning?' (Albrechts and Balducci, 2013: 16). The definition and boundaries of what is strategic planning and 'what is not' are thus expected to be clear and well-defined through the provision of a checklist of both models. This perception brings about the western metaphysics of binary oppositions, which divides concepts and ideas into a pair of binary terms, e.g. masculine/feminine, strategic/traditional (Abdelwahab, 2010, 2013). These binary pairs are dependent on each other for meaning through 'difference': a fixed 'either/or' relation (McQuillan, 2001; Collins et al., 2005). However, these binary pairs are not opposites in reality; they are not equal – the first term is usually 'privileged', which is traditionally associated with masculinity (McQuillan, 2001). Simultaneously, Mäntysalo (2014) questions the independency of strategic and traditional planning defined through the 'either/or' relation. He acknowledges the interdependency between the two theories in practice, the blurriness of the boundaries that defines them. He thus suggests a shift towards a 'both/and' relation, and continues to question 'how to' bring both in practice. Significantly, it is evident that neither strategic nor traditional planning has a clear definition. They both hold different versions and practices based on their contexts (Albrechts and Balducci, 2013). This is particularly evident in the Egyptian context, which challenges not only the demarcation between strategic and traditional planning, but their realization and becoming within the embedded complexities, uncertainties and ambiguities.

Accordingly, we follow the argument developed by Mäntysalo that identifies the binary strategic/traditional planning as co-dependent rather than mutually exclusive. We further draw on the Derridean deconstruction project, which is basically concerned with the metaphysics of binary opposition (McQuillan, 2001;

Abdelwahab, 2010, 2013). Principally, deconstruction is not a method, or a set of rules, applied to content, of a theory or a case study, to interpret (Lucy, 2004). Deconstruction is totally dependent on the nature of this content, author/reader, and context. This dependency thus acknowledges the multiplicities of meaning and truth in this content. Consequently, our argument – a deconstruction reading – works from within planning, content (strategic/traditional), author/reader (involved actors, planner, citizen, government, etc.), and contextual reality embedded in time.

Similar to Mäntysalo's (2014) argument, deconstruction displaces the stable 'either/or' relation between the binary: strategic/comprehensive drawing on the concepts of *'différance'* and 'trace'. Through the concept of trace every term holds a trace of its reality, representation, and what is beyond. It is the factor of blurriness that refuses to draw a boundary line. Each term holds a trace of the other, as well as all the other terms. The later statement sustains that the actors and the context are inscribed in the content – of planning, and vice versa. The content becomes a part of the actors and contextual reality, consequently shaping and re-arranging (McQuillan, 2001; Abdelwahab, 2010). Furthermore, *'différance'* constitutes a dynamic oscillation between 'neither/nor' and 'both/and' relations. This oscillation destabilizes the notion of 'fixed' meaning and creates a potential for alternative interpretations (Alvesson and Skoldberg, 2000). The concept of *'différance'* thus deconstructs the hierarchy between the binary through the simultaneous presence of two conflicting ideas: neither/nor and both/and. In summary, the deconstruction of this binary – strategic/traditional – involves two steps. The first involves reversing the binary, e.g. feminine/masculine, and feminine becomes the privileged term. The other step continues to displace the binary oppositions so as not to 'involve binary logic at all' (McQuillan, 2001: 13, 19). Traditional/strategic planning thus becomes a third genre that constitutes both/and yet belongs to neither/nor. It emphasizes the blurring process between the boundaries of the content binary and represents 'trace'(s) of the involved actors and context.

> In contrast to traditional land use planning, strategic planning (this is the trust) is visionary, process-oriented, and transcends limited administrative boundaries. (Kunzmann, 2014: 28)

Furthermore, the binary presentation of strategic/traditional planning introduced another set of binaries, a two-part checklist to define the boundaries between the two theories (see Albrechts and Balducci, 2013; Kunzmann, 2014; Mäntysalo, 2014). Albrechts and Balduccci (2013: 14–20) discussed these sets in more detail that draws on 'the content, the form of the process, its relational [container] nature, and the institutional implication' of spatial planning. They question if strategic planning is thus defined by: 'its informal nature, its legal status, the type of process to be designed, its selectivity, its capacity to produce a long-term vision, the connection between vision and actions, the involvement of stakeholders?' Drawing on these lists, and for the purpose of our study in this chapter, we thus identify traditional/strategic binary through a three-part set that questions:

the epistemology of space, the design process, and Governance. The first part, epistemology, thus discusses the conceptions of container versus relational spaces; their complementary perception of the certainty versus uncertainty of the planning context; and their implication on 'essentialist zoning' in statutory planning. The second part continues to investigate the development of the design process that opens up a 'spectrum of possibilities' beyond the certainties of land-use master plans. The third part explores the governance relationship between the citizen and government in a rigid versus flexible institutional framework. We shall therefore discuss this three-part binary set in details.

## Epistemology

> [Strategic planning involves] … a departure from the traditional conceptu-alisation of space as territorial entity – a container which is given different functions (social, cultural, economic, administrative) – towards an under-standing of [relational] space as a social, cultural, economic, political and ecological construction. (Van den Broeck *et al.*, 2013: 324)

The shift towards strategic planning responds to 'a growing need for cities and regions to reposition themselves in [the complex network of] global competition' (Albrechts and Balducci, 2013: 17). This shift altered our understanding of space, and the unpredictable 'becoming' of the city in a state of uncertainty, which further implicated the planning process. On the one hand, traditional planning framed space as a 'real' container that 'holds objects inside…' with distinctive physical boundaries and edges (Van den Broeck *et al.*, 2013: 324). Accordingly, traditional planning was concerned with 'essentialist' zoning of urban containers of homogeneous characteristics, image, style and activities; and the city comprised a number of these containers (Hubbard *et al.*, 2004; Davoudi and Strange, 2009). On the other hand, strategic planning holds 'a relational view which stresses connections/relations between diverse meanings, identities, actions, places, and so on' (Healey, 2004: 324). However, this is not to say that space is a 'neutral backdrop of social actions and relations', but is a relational 'experience' between the physical and the social as well as other spatial values. Strategic relational planning is thus concerned with the 'experience' of 'both physical and social qualities of space … identified by perceiving, thinking, feel-ing … [and] dependent on the nature of the experienced objects, cultural, class, racial and gendered identities and spatial competences of experiencing subjects, as well as subjective elements' (Van den Broeck *et al.*, 2013: 325–327). Drawing on Deleuze and Gauttari (1987), Hillier (2014: 333) further emphasizes the rela-tional space in strategic planning as 'the lines rather than the points'. Complementary, the deconstruction reading of space perceives 'a relational space, continuously moving between two types of oscillation: neither/nor and both/and…'. Relational space is thus perceived as an intermediate dynamic space that helps the continuous construction of meaning, experience and events (Abdelwahab, 2010: 340–345).

**Design-process**

> In strategic planning, becoming is looked upon as a social process that
> stimulates the ability to view problems, situations and challenges in new and
> different ways and to invent and develop original, imaginative futures in
> response to these problems, situations and challenges. (Albrechts and
> Balducci, 2013: 21)

Planning is intrinsically an attempt to envision a presence in time and space yet
to come in the future, a future that can only be speculated on (Martin, 2014: 79).
The debate on the 'becoming' of the city is thus embedded in the dynamics of
relational space, rather than the certainty of fixed points in time and space. This
presence in space and time is the 'event' which is yet to come (Derrida, 1994).
This event is 'resistance to a future' dominated by a perception of a traditional,
past presence (Lucy, 2004; Abdelwahab, 2010). The event happens unexpectedly
and is 'absolutely different' from what is expected (Derrida, 1994). The event of
planning which comes about sets off an interruption of 'conventionally dominated acts and contexts' (Derrida, 1993). The future is continuously changing
along multiple trajectories of time from the present to the future(s) (Concilio,
2010). In this way, the unpredictability of planning practices is a reflection not
only to the changing future, but also the multiple trajectories of the continuous
status of oscillation.

In reflection to this debate, the question simplified and raised is: how to plan a
future that we cannot project? Martin (2014: 80) discusses the planner's need in
general to control the future, to reach a 'comfort zone' that enables the decision-
making process. 'The natural reaction is to make the challenge less daunting by
turning it into a problem that can be solved … [through] preparing a comprehensive [master] plan.' This method aims to eliminate 'uncertainty', which contradicts the nature of planning. Planners have to approach decision-making outside
the comfort zone of certainty. Consequently, the only seemingly possible
response to our question is: not based on the traditional land-use plan. However,
a counter-question is instantly raised: Is it even possible to plan a city without
statutory practices? This argument has become a significant attribute of the planning debate in both theory and practice. This debate called for embracing uncertainty, the complexity of city planning, and hence allowing for flexibility,
adaptability, and emergence of innovative practices (see Innes and Booher, 1999;
Hillier, 2003, 2010; Friedmann, 2004; Van den Broeck et al., 2013). 'The objective [of strategic planning] is not to eliminate risk but to increase the odds of
success' (Martin, 2014: 80). The method does not involve a pre-prepared comprehensive plan, but a 'process of thinking'. Strategic planning does not aim to
produce 'a strategy', but a strategic process to cope with uncertainty. The realization of the inability of planners to predict the 'becoming' of the city, put aside
any attempt to 'control' (Grosz, 2001), has thus helped to change the focus of
planning from product-oriented to process-oriented, to involve institutional
planning.

Visions and concrete actions that accept the full complexity of a place while focusing on local assets and networks in a global context, social justice, spatial quality, and a fair distribution of the joys and burdens. (Albrechts and Balducci, 2013: 22)

Consequently, the strategic/traditional binary has highlighted the process/product and co-produced the binary: strategic vision/master plan. The strategic vision helps the planning practice to relate to the context, place, time, and actors, 'the basic processes that shape places' (Albrechts and Balducci, 2013: 21). It extends beyond the 'technical knowledge' of planning content that focuses on a presence in space and time (Balducci, 2010; Van den Broeck et al., 2013: 323). In this way, the vision brings about the planning content/context binary. Simultaneously, the strategic vision aims to understand and construct the relations between them. Drawing on the concept of the 'trace', we recognize 'the inscription of the … context inside the content', and vice versa (McQuillan, 2001: 38; Abdelwahab, 2010). This inscription helps to blur the boundaries between the content and context of planning. Furthermore, the content – strategic/traditional – not only holds a trace of reality and representation of planning practices, but also traces the social, political and economic structures, frameworks, and institutions that induced the spatial changes and planning. As follows, the strategic vision is also inscribed in the master plan. The purpose is to realize, rather than construct, the relations between content and context. This brings about new possibilities and opportunities to re-approach the master plan as a strategic tool that incorporates the relational space, as opposed to the physical container.

### *Governance*

Whose vision is created remains a basic question to be asked? (Albrechts and Balducci, 2013: 18, 21)

A significant attribute of strategic planning is the shift towards 'co-productive form of governance' (Albrechts and Balducci, 2013: 22), which entails new institutional processes both flexible and inclusive. These processes recognize the multiple trajectories of decision-making, possibilities, 'power struggles and missed opportunities' (Van den Broeck *et al.*, 2013: 326). Co-productive governance both involves and *empowers* the citizen in the process; it basically constitutes the citizen, government, and the power-relations between them. However, drawing on Foucault's relational understanding of power, these are not seen as three independent elements, but rather as co-dependent relations that contribute to their identity construction. 'Power is not something that's acquired, seized or shared…' (Foucault, 1981: 94). Accordingly, co-productive govern-ance does not transfer the government power to the citizen. Power is recognized as a relational value that shapes the institutional practices and processes, and is simultaneously shaped by the perception of the citizen's role in the institution. Furthermore, the citizen is not identified as an independent point in the city; they are being constructed in space and time: 'certain bodies, certain gestures, certain discourses and certain desires [in the city] come to be constituted as ... [citizens]' (Foucault, 1980: 98). And the government is not a 'political institution' but the processes and practices – the relations – to the citizen; how the institution perceives and instantaneously shapes the governed, citizen, and city (Townley, 1993). Accordingly, co-productive governance also echoes Foucault's displaced question 'how?'. How these practices work? How they empower the institution? How are these power-relations perceived? Rather than who has the power?

> Traditional spatial plans are judged in terms of conformance; strategic plans in terms of performance. (Mastop and Faludi, 1997, in Albrechts, 2006: 1165)

The preliminary binary citizen/government is thus displaced by citizen–government relations (involved actors); and two binaries are introduced, actor/content and actor/context. The boundaries of these binaries are instantly blurred through the concept of the trace that recognizes the inscription of each term in all others, as discussed in the previous section. Simultaneously, it recognizes 'the fragmentation and multiplicities of the actors' (Albrechts and Balducci, 2013: 17). Strategic planning recognized the complexities within these relations. It thus instituted 'multi-level governance' that allows the inclusion of the various actors, planning frameworks and structures, embedded in context (social, political...). It also embraced 'the conditions of power, inequality and diversity' (Albrechts and Balducci, 2013: 21). Furthermore, the displacement of the 'who has the power?' by a 'how?' emphasized another binary of dominant/marginal power-relation. How are these powers manifested or withheld in the production, design, and representation of the planning content? And how is this embedded and reflected in context?

## The certainty of the 'uncertain': the Egyptianized strategic planning

The roots of modern city planning in Egypt track back to the construction of the Suez Canal in the nineteenth century. Simultaneously, the planning of downtown Cairo as a modern capital was ordered by Khedive Ismail in the second half of the 1860s. Inspired by Paris's Haussmannian plan, the Ismaili Cairo project involved a comprehensive plan for the development of the city, which projected the city's 'dream of westernisation'; 'street has primacy, grid urban geometry ... as well as new western architecture model...' (Abu-Lughod, 1971; Raymond, 2007: 309; Abdelwahab, 2013: 31).

The projection of a western image on the city planning continued. Four new cities were planned and constructed along the banks of the Suez Canal in the next half-century: for example, Port Fouad, which was designed by the Ecole des Beaux-arts in Paris in 1926, and the planning of the new district of Heliopolis in 1905, which was a direct investment by the Belgian Baron Empan, with many contributions from European planners and architects. Abdel Nasser's socialist system in the 1950s and 1960s pronounced the western model as unsuitable for city planning, and the city searched for a traditionalist and/or regionalist model to replace it. Egyptian planners developed most of these interventions, and were thus influenced by Abdel Nasser's nationalist, while seeking a modernist, approach (Adham, 2004; Mourad, 2014). Then the postwar policies of the Sadat presidency promoted an open market economy and the western model came back into favour (Salheen, 2001). 'Both cities – the nationalised and westernised/ globalised – and their problems continued to grow and to co-exist' (Abdelwahab, 2013: 32).

City planning in twentieth-century Egypt started to gain an official status in the mid-1960s. In 1965 the Higher Committee for Planning Greater Cairo was formed and was only responsible for the making of the structural plan for the Greater Cairo Region until 1973. This body evolved to form the General Organization for Physical Planning (GOPP) an affiliated agency to the Ministry of Housing that became responsible for the urban and regional planning in Egypt (GOPP, 2015).

During the second half of the 1970s and the 1980s the first generation of the New Cities was realized. The planning of many of these cities was inspired by European theories and practices, and in most cases were co-planned by joint Egyptian and European firms. For example, Sadat city, planned in 1975, was designed by an American firm, and the 10th of Ramadan city, planned in 1977, was designed by a joint Egyptian–Swedish team (INTI, 2015). However, planning of the second generation of new cities was mostly done by Egyptian planners, as was the case for most cities of the third generation. Subsequently, Egyptian scholars educated in Europe and the United States introduced strategic planning approach in the 1990s, but these were only confined within the academic circles.

Strategic planning was officially recognized and spread between 2006 and 2008. This can be tracked through two main projects introduced and led by UNDP and the UNHABITAT, respectively. Accordingly, we shall explore the development of the contextualized strategic planning (SP) in Egypt through these two projects drawing on the three-binary-set introduced in the previous section: epistemology, design process, and governance.

### *Epistemology*

in Ismaíl's urban projects of creating two cities side by side intensified ... the dividing line separated a traditional sector from a modern one, ... [and developed over time into] a boundary between different nationalities, a harsher and more intolerable division... (Raymond, 2007: 333)

The development of city planning in Egypt comprised 'multiple layers of inherited history'. Significantly, these layers did not replace each other; they 'appeared to grow independently, within defined boundaries, although they intrinsically overlap and interact'. This phenomenon was further reinforced through the emergence of New Cairo 'gated' communities. Simultaneously, these layers were projected not only through the spatial fabric, but also through the socio-cultural context. It could be said that 'the inner polarisation of city [planning] between [the binaries] the modern and the traditional...', eastern/western, has resulted in the development of 'spatial containers' (Abdelwahab, 2010: 143–144). And the epistemological approach to planning container space continued through contemporary practice and is 'manifested in the separation between the different social classes, culturally, institutionally, economically, and spatially' inside these physical containers (Abdelwahab, 2013: 45).

### Design process

Until roughly 2003, most of the planning projects in Egypt were based on the rational comprehensive model for planning. Planners were thus considered as merely technocrats and the government officials the decision-makers. And the produced master plan was binding to the whole city in terms of its building regulations and permits. Starting from 2003, strategic planning started to gradually take over, initiated and funded by international development agencies such as the UNDP and the UNHABITAT (Serag, 2008).

The UNDP, in cooperation with the Ministry of Local Development, introduced the Municipal Initiative for Strategic Recovery (MISR) project conducted in the period 2006–2008. The project aimed to produce development and investment plans on both governorate and district levels, drawing on strategic planning methodology. The project aimed first to formulate the investment development plans for all the 27 governorates of Egypt at that time. This was followed by a formulation of strategic development plans for several districts within these governorates (UNDP, 2006).

The planning process was composed of five steps. The initial preparatory step included data collection, as well as identifying the involvement of stakeholders and official bodies. The second step thus proceeded to analyse the present status, identifying the main problems and potentials of the study area. A SWOT analysis is intrinsically an integral part of this step. The third step comprised the development of future 'vision and goals'. The strategic plan was prepared in the fourth step, setting a development strategy, and then identifying the main strategic projects that would realize such a strategy. The last step thus involved acquiring the necessary approvals for the strategic plan, followed by a frequent process of monitoring and evaluation of achieving the set goals and future vision, hence making further modifications if needed to maintain the flexibility of the plan (UNDP, 2006).

GOPP launched another project in 2006, to prepare the strategic plans for the Egyptian villages. Hence, the UNHABITAT branch in Egypt presented the 'Strategic Urban Planning for Small Cities in Egypt' project, to support the GOPP in preparing strategic urban plans for 50 small cities (UNHABITAT, 2014). The project adopted a decentralized and integrated approach to address urban development and land management issues as well as identifying other

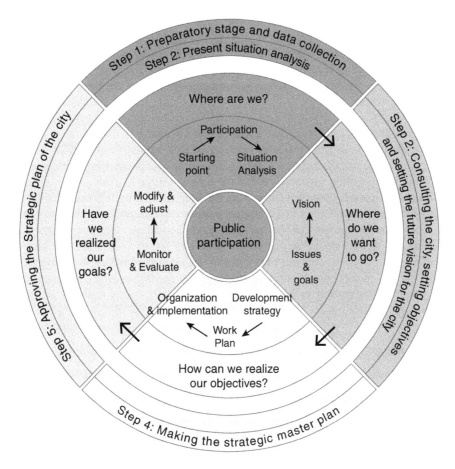

*Figure 10.1* Steps for developing a strategic plan for the UNDP project (MISR)

development-related concerns. It comprised two main components: developing a strategic plan and enhancing urban and land management.

In 2007, GOPP further adopted the methodology introduced by the UNHABITAT in Egypt. It is worth noting that this methodology is similar to that introduced by the UNDP. The Terms of References (TOR) for the strategic planning projects were built on this methodology, and constituted:

- A strategic vision for the future of the city or village composed of a justified statement that reflects the aspirations of the stakeholders.
- A package of selected strategic projects.

- A mapped strategic plan illustrating the relationships between the different plan components and outlining the areas for future urban development as well as the proposed areas for internal city upgrading.
- A comprehensive report illustrating the present situation analysis, the vision, the strategic projects and the strategic plan, and reflecting on the physical planning dimension, socio-economic studies as well as the basic infrastructure sectors.

The introduction of SP could be explained as a reaction to the failure of many traditional land-use plans that were made in the 1990s and the early 2000s. It thus highlights the binary traditional/strategic planning within the Egyptian context. Traditional planning was perceived at the time as failing to achieve their objectives, and master plans served only as binding documents to obtain building permits. Several violations to the original plans were made and considerable parts of them were never realized. On the other hand, the strategic plan is considered a binding legal document that is approved by the city, the province and the Ministry of Housing. Once the strategic plan is approved, a phase of making detailed plans for the city is carried out, while maintaining the guidelines set by the strategic plans. Building permits in the city are then issued based on the finalized detailed plans.

### Governance

For decades, the dominance of comprehensive planning in Egypt had held several implications to the planning institutions and involved actors. These actors could be identified as the GOPP, the government personnel, planners, international bodies, and the citizens or stakeholders. The General Organization for Physical Planning (GOPP) is considered the main actor, represented through several regional offices across the country. It is worth noting that the epistemological perspective of this body is embedded in the name 'physical planning', which highlights their emphasis on the production of physical containers within the city zones. Furthermore, GOPP held a customary practice to assign external consultants to do the planning work rather than depend on their cadres. Consequently, the role of planners who were assigned by the GOPP in most cases, was confined as technocrats, i.e. the GOPP gave away the power of their involvement in the decision-making process, which was made by the government personnel. And the city governor held the power to make the final decision to accept or reject the plan (Serag, 2006). Simultaneously, the citizens' perspective was marginalized in this process. They held a low profile of participation, which varied from one project to the other, and their opinion was not held binding in the decision-making process. The plan hearing session in many cases was done merely for tokenistic reasons according to the ladder of citizen participation (Arnestien, 1969).

The involvement of international bodies is a significant milestone in the Egyptian planning institution. The master plan for the Greater Cairo Region was developed in 1982, through a collaboration between the GOPP and the 'l'Institut d'aménagement et d'urbanisme de la Région d'Île-de-France' (IUARIF) (GOPP, 1983). It is also evident that the planning practices held by Egyptians in the second half of the twentieth century had substantial influences from the European and to some extent North American practice. Furthermore, strategic planning was introduced to Egypt through the UNDP and UNHABITAT, as discussed. Several city and village strategic planning projects were (and are) carried out across Egypt, e.g. the Meet Ghamr strategic planning project discussed in the next section. These projects recognized the multi-levels within the planning governance, in accordance to the SP methodology introduced by the international agencies.

Simultaneously, the introduction of SP promoted the involvement of a participatory process with local and national stakeholders, where they identify priority issues and actions (UNHABITAT, 2014). This participatory process thus developed an atmosphere of satisfaction and ambition among citizens, as they started to see their hopes and contributions for a better future taken into consideration in both the strategic vision and plan. The UNDP initiative, MISR, was abruptly stopped in 2008 and the strategic plans that were developed at that time never made it for approval. However, the project helped to initiate and spread the know-how among planners and other actors involved.

> [In post-revolution Egypt], the long marginalised multiplicities and complexities inherited in the city urban space have re-surfaced, highlighted at the centre, reflecting the changes in the 'existing relations and patterns of power'. (Abdelwahab, 2013: 48)

At the same time, strategic planning witnessed different challenges before and after the 2011–2013 revolution periods. The involved actors and consultants adhered to the TOR provided by the GOPP. However, the intrinsic dependency of strategic planning on institutional practices and processes instigated variations between the two periods. Furthermore, Abdelwahab (2013: 48) reflects on the consequent exposition of another binary within the Egyptian institution, 'a conflict on the authority and ownership of the people [citizen] versus the government', as well as 'the emerging culture of intolerance', i.e. in post-revolution planning projects the significance of strategic versus traditional planning in Egypt, and the intrinsic value and conflict, in involving the citizen in the process. Subsequently, the following section discusses the case of strategic planning of Meet Ghamr, a medium-sized Egyptian city in the Delta. The project period spanned over the pre- and post-January 2011 revolution. This case study thus helps us to reflect on the many changes in the process that followed, particularly the power struggle manifested in the citizen participation.

## SP re-contextualized: Meet Ghamr (2008–2013)

Meet Ghamr (MG) is a medium-sized city overlooking the Nile. The city is known for its aluminium industries and being a service centre for the neighbouring rural settlements. The main challenge facing MG, among other Egyptian cities, is the urban expansion on agricultural lands (GOPP, 2009a). This challenge is embedded in the land value of both agricultural and buildable lands. On one hand, it is illegal to build on agriculture land; on the other hand, the value of buildable land is ten times higher. The borders of urban expansion are hence perceived as the physical container of buildable land. Accordingly, the identification of these borders became an essential part of the planning process. These borders identify the zones of urban services and housing, and limit the city's further expansion on agriculture lands. This further implicated the involvement of stakeholders who owned lands adjacent to the urban mass, and brought about a conflict between personal and public interests. This conflict draws directly on the citizen/governance binary.

The project started in summer 2008, with the initial aim to have the plan ready in a period of ten months. The main objectives for the strategic planning project in this case were to:

- set a proper future development vision for the city;
- define and limit the urban expansion on agricultural lands;
- ensure proper service provision in the different areas of the city;
- ensure sufficient housing provision to meet future needs.

The project thus followed SP methodology and the process started within the GOPP terms of reference for the strategic planning of cities (GOPP, 2008). Accordingly, it involved a series of participatory workshops, implemented through the different project phases, between the consultancy team and the various stakeholders, including the government personnel. The first phase of the project included the analysis of the existing situation; the identification of the problems, potentials and development limitations in the city; and the introduction of the main stakeholders who would be involved in the project. The latter included representatives of the Local Citizens' Council (LCC) as well as city officials, non-governmental organizations (NGOs), the so-called natural leaders, as well as women's representatives. The second phase of the project considered the development of a future vision for the city, which stated 'MG: an industrial castle and a center for trade and services', as well as identifying the key strategic projects (GOPP, 2009b). It is worth noting that in most of the process the city governor did not intervene in any of the activities or decisions. The upper hand was clearly among the LCC. The third phase of the project was concerned with making the final strategic plan, and accordingly realizes the vision within the city new urban borders. This was the longest phase in the process. It started in summer 2009 and extended until 2013.

### Citizen participation and conflict in interest

Again, such steps were supposed to be made within a large-scale workshop. However, after the involvement of the Head of the Citizens' Council, it became clear that he had the upper hand and most of the remaining workshops in that period were made with him and few other stakeholders. The consultancy team was to make a plan-hearing session to inform the stakeholders and discuss the plan. In this session, it was clear that the Head of the Citizens' Council had the decisive voice and managed to get a full approval from the council on the plan in hand in November 2009. However, the GOPP did not approve the plan owing to reversible changes that it had made in the TOR, which stopped the plan from being approved.

However, already at this point the consultancy team had noticed the inconsistency from the stakeholders' representatives. This means that the persons attending the workshops differed almost every time, which later led to major disputes in the plan-making phase.

Several clashes took part between the consultancy team and some of the stakeholders, due to two main issues. The first one was the inconsistency of the individuals who attended the meetings and workshops and represented different social bodies. The team would reach specific agreements and understandings with the attendees of a specific workshop and apply these to the work in hand, only to find in the next session that what was agreed was still being discussed owing to the fact that new faces were attending.

The second issue was the personal interests of the involved stakeholders who were pushing for their lands to be included within the city border. The consultancy team rejected any attempts to include any agricultural lands within the new borders if there were no imminent needs. To do so, the team referred to the GOPP, whose representatives were in the workshops and would always act as referees, since at the end the plan had to be approved by them and according to their TOR. In some cases the city governor intervened as well, although not in a firm way. At this point, the planning process turned into a struggle to set the new urban expansion borders rather than making a good SP.

The tensions within the planning process continued until the Head of the LCC became fully involved in the process. During this period in 2009, the National Democratic Party (NDP) was the ruling party of Egypt before it was dissolved after the 2011 revolution. The head of the NDP branch in the city was also the head of the LCC. This double role gave him a stronger position when working closely with the planning team. However, he was keen to produce a proper plan. At a certain point; his power overrode most of the voices within the Citizens' Council.

The strategic planning process that was conducted at that period faced several obstacles. Despite the fact that the process started well, once it entered the stage of defining the urban expansion border most of the stakeholders focused on achieving personal gains in terms of their own agricultural lands, which they wanted to be included within the new expansion border. As such, the collective good of the city and achieving its future vision became secondary and maybe even a third priority of the project, thus diverting it from the main aim of the SP project. The power-relations at that period are illustrated in Table 10.1.

Table 10.1 Power analysis and the personal interests of the stakeholders (NDP, Local Citizens' Council, City administration) versus the aims of the planning process – pre-2011

| Stakeholder | Power status | | | | | |
|---|---|---|---|---|---|---|
| | Planning team | Governor of the city | City officials | GOPP representatives | Local Citizens' Council | Head of the Council and local NDP |
| Planning team | - | The governor was neutral in most of the process and intervened only to solve crucial disputes between the planning team and the stakeholders. | During the pre-revolutions period, the city officials assisted the planning team in the data collection and analysis. They did not have a strong say in the plan-making phase. | Acted mainly as a neutral referee, in case of disputes. | Had a strong power and impact during the planning process. The plan could not get approval without their satisfaction. | Powerful control over his Council, which resulted in some cases in conflicts with the planning team. |
| Governor of the city | * | - | The governor had the final say over his officials. He only directed them to help the planning team. | Only gave advice to the governor. | No control by the governor of the LCC. He could only try to influence them. | Similar level of powers. In some cases the Head of the Council had the final say, owing to the support of the Council. |
| City officials | * | * | - | Assistance in the technical and administrative issues. | * | No influence could be made by the city officials on the Head of the Council. |
| GOPP representatives | * | * | * | - | Acted mainly as a neutral referee, in case of disputes, and stopped any illegal intentions. * | - |
| Local Citizens' Council | * | * | * | * | - | The Council was strongly dominated by its Head. |
| Head of the Local Citizens' Council and local NDP | * | * | * | * | * | - |

Note: (*) this means the comment was stated earlier.

### Planning after 2011

In January 2011, the first Egyptian revolution in the Third Millennium took place. The revolution aimed to topple the reign of the president and overthrow the government. It also aimed to eradicate cooperation within the government. The belief at that time was that the NDP had dominated the political scene in a corrupt way. It had the larger share of representatives in the parliament and the LCCs, with claims of forged elections. Egypt witnessed the most unstable period in its recent history in terms of political instability and a lack of safety and security. This situation resulted in repeated delays in the project.

- *Dismissing Citizen Councils.* One of the actions that was taken by the interim government that followed the revolution was to dismiss the parliament and the LCCs until new elections are held. The dismissal decree was issued in June 2011 (ECESR, 2011).
- *Fear of the local government from the citizens.* In the aftermath of the revolution, many fragments of society started to adopt the concept of protests to manifest against governmental actions or decisions that might not be in their favour. In many cases, local government buildings were surrounded by protesters, making the local officials reluctant to take any actions, in fear of such demonstrations. This was reflected in the planning process.
- *More modifications in the plan.* Although the plan was approved in a public hearing before the revolution, the GOPP did not approve it, as mentioned above. Furthermore, because of a legal flaw in announcing the plan-hearing session,[1] it was considered illegal, hence the approval obtained in 2009 became worthless.

Following the dismissal of the Local Citizens' Council, several meetings were held with the local officials and the Heads of the local planning administration in the city. The modifications became more focused on the projects and where these projects were situated in the plan. The local officials did not want to have confrontational discussions with the citizens, especially when it came to service projects. The locations of some of these projects were made on privately owned land, and most citizens did not want to contribute parts of their lands in such a project unless they were profit-based. Hence, many projects were either relocated or cancelled.

At this point there was no citizen participation; all the discussions took place with the local government officials. In the original plan, there were several strategic projects to realize the city vision, but many of these were cancelled. Despite the attempts that were made by the planning team to keep the essence of the plan, the end product was not satisfactory at all.

A few examples can be given: among the proposed strategic projects was an institute for the advanced training for industrial workers, which seemed in line with the intended nature of the activities in the city and was allocated to a large area of land, but this was cancelled and substituted with residential areas. Another proposed project was to construct a conference complex for business development, which was approved in the first version of the plan together with supporting hotels, but yet again these were cancelled in the second revision. Table 10.2 shows the power-relations post-2011.

In conclusion, there was a strong derailing in the final version of the plan that was approved in a public-hearing session by early 2013. It should be mentioned that despite a limited citizens' participation at this stage, the local government officials were very sensitive in dealing with the planning team, to avoid any possibility of causing public anger. This paid off well in the plan-hearing session as there were only minor modifications. However, this of course came at the expense of the strategic vision and the strategic projects.

The planning team found it was much easier to work with the City Council directly as this saved much time in approving the suggested plans, rather than long negotiations, as was the case before the revolution. However, they considered that a very strong and important component in the strategic plan-making process was missing: citizen participation in the realization of a collaborative decision-making. The SP represented the vision of the planners and the city officials; it didn't represent the hopes and vision of the citizens, even if some of them only had personal interests to achieve.

## Strategic planning de-constructed/de-contextualized in Egypt

Strategic planning is concerned with the 'becoming' of the city, *in context*. Accordingly, there are different versions of strategic – as well as traditional planning – based on their context, the event of planning in space and time. At the same time, SP is introduced, in this chapter, in opposition to the traditional practice, through the three-part binary set that questioned the epistemology, design process, and governance. This argument was discussed in the Egyptian context, drawing on the case study of Meet Ghamr.

The SP process in Egypt started slightly more than a decade ago, in what seemed at the beginning to be an enthusiastic attempt to apply the SP process in place of the traditional comprehensive planning. However, this ended up in a blurry process that touches to some extent on SP and to another extent on the traditional comprehensive planning. It should be taken into consideration that planning in Egypt is challenged with different paradigms of uncertainty and fuzziness – parental blessing – which are adopted as rigid frameworks to apply to practice. This statement highlights the need and readiness to integrate SP within the Egyptian context, although it also anticipates the contradiction in this integration. As discussed in this chapter, the planning practice in Egypt is embedded in the epistemology of container space, which simultaneously focuses on the physical production of master and statutory plans, the identification of land use, and territory. This continued through the integration process with SP, which comprised an intrinsic conflict: SP retracted back from a process-oriented project to a product-oriented project. This was more than welcomed by local government officials, as it gave no space for manoeuvring or adjustment if needed in the

Table 10.2 Power analysis and the personal interests of the stakeholders (NDP, Local Citizens' Council, City administration) versus the aims of the planning process – post-2011

| Stakeholder | Power status | | | | | |
|---|---|---|---|---|---|---|
| | *Planning team* | *Governor of the city* | *City officials* | *GOPP representatives* | *Local Citizens' Council* | *Head of the Council and local NDP* |
| *Planning team* | - | The Governor had marginal powers. The change in the Heads of local governments was very frequent so that almost four governors were swapped following the revolution. | The city officials became the main player in finalizing the strategic plan. They became aware and afraid of the pressure laid down by the citizens to achieve certain interests. This fear caused further modification and delay in the plan. | Acted mainly as a neutral referee, in case of disputes. | Suspended | |
| *Governor of the city* | Very limited involvement in the planning process. Considered an honorary position by the planning team. | - | No involvement by the Governor, only in related administrative issues. | Only gave advice to the Governor. | | |
| *City officials* | * | * | - | The GOPP officials acted mainly as a neutral referee, in case of disputes. | | |
| *GOPP representatives* *Local Citizens' Council* *Head of the Local Citizens' Council and local NDP* | * | * | Suspended | - | | |

Note: (*) this means the comment was stated earlier.

future, perhaps because the local government officials related to city planning are not familiar or trained to deal with the outcome of SP. Furthermore, this rigid practice and governance continued to question the role of citizens rather than facilitate their involvement. The SP process is built on 'co-production' and collaboration between the different actors. In Egypt, this could still be valid but not in the essence of reaching a flexible strategic plan at the end; rather, to have a plan that takes into consideration the citizens' interests in terms of land values and definite land use, especially when it comes to private property.

It is perhaps that the country has gone through a phase of political instability in the inter-revolutions years, only a few years after the SP process had been introduced in Egypt, that a derailing from the essence of the SP, as discussed earlier, took place. Based on the flow of the events that took place from 2011, the level of local government involvement in the plan-making process has increased drastically post-2011, at the expense of citizen participation, which was stressed upon in pre-2011 years. However, despite this involvement, the concern from public citizens' reactions has since been conceived by the local government officials, hence making the whole process of plan-making blurry, with 'traces' of both SP and comprehensive planning. When it comes to SP in Egypt, and especially when applied in the Nile Valley and the Nile Delta cities, a tangible deviation is felt. The case study has shown how an SP process that started by having a vision for a willed future resulted in a product that was stripped of many of the components that would have realized that vision. This is mainly because of urban expansion challenges and limitations that were reflected in the stakeholders' behaviours in the different phases of the project, which aimed for some sort of 'blessing' to push things forward in the most convenient way to their perception.

Within the planning domain in Egypt, many practitioners embraced the SP approach and the decision to apply it in the city planning projects with great expectations. Normally the projects' durations were supposed to be ten months; however, the grim reality saw the projects span for over eight years. This caused a general feeling of frustration in the planning society, especially when the SP process turned into a method to realize the citizens' interests regardless of their appropriateness. Many planners believe that the produced SPs are not fulfilling their intended goals of realizing a willed future to the city; they rather became a tool to regularize the granting of building permits by the city officials, whom the planners believe did not understand the essence and the objectives of making a SP.

Some planners related the failure of the SP process in Egypt, to: the inconstancy of the decisions taken by the different bodies involved, e.g. Ministry of Housing and GOPP; the vague roles of the different stakeholders; and the lack of local capacity with the local governments' officials as well as unclear rules connecting the planning with implementation (Yousry, 2013). Because of such an outcome of the SP process in many projects, and because of the hurdles mentioned earlier, some planners went as far as claiming that the SP could be announced as 'out of context' and 'dead'. Others consider that the best place to practise a proper SP process in Egypt would be in its desert cities where city expansion space was and will never be the question, hence the true will to work for a better willed future of the city through a proper strategic planning process.

## Note

1 According to regulations, the local government should announce the date of the plan-hearing session to the public in a daily newspaper two weeks in advance. At the same time, the map for the proposed strategic plan of the city should be put on display to the public at the city hall. These two actions were not carried out by the local officials, hence the plan-hearing session was considered illegal.

## References

Abdelwahab, M. 2010. Cairo, Khōra and deconstruction: Towards a reflexive reading of place. Unpublished PhD thesis, School of Architecture, Planning and Landscape, Newcastle University, Newcastle-Upon-Tyne.

Abdelwahab, M. 2013. Cairo: A deconstruction reading of space. In P. Kellett and J. Hérnandez-Garcia (eds), *Researching the Contemporary City: Identity, Environment and Social Inclusion in Developing Urban Areas* (pp. 27–50). CEJA (Pontificia Universidad Javeriana), Bogota.

Abu-Lughod, J. 1971. *Cairo: 1001 Years of the City Victorious*. Princeton, NJ: Princeton University Press.

Adham, K. 2004. Cairo's urban déja vu: Globalization and urban fantasies. In Y. Elsheshtawy (ed.), *Planning Middle Eastern Cities: An Urban Kaleidoscope in a Globalizing World* (pp. 134–167). London: Routledge.

Albrechts L. 2006. Shifts in strategic spatial planning? Some evidence from Europe and Australia. *Environmental and Planning A*, 38, 1149–1170.

Albrechts, L. and Balducci, A. 2013. Practicing strategic planning: In search of critical features to explain the strategic character of plans. *DisP – The Planning Review*, 49(3), 16–27.

Alvesson, M. and Skoldberg, K. 2000. *Reflexive Methodology: New Vistas for Qualitative Research*. London: Sage.

Arnestien, S. 1969. A ladder of citizen participation. *JAIP*, 35(4), July, 216–224.

Balducci, A. 2010. Strategic planning as a field of practices. In M. Cerreta, G. Concilio and V. Monno (eds), *Making Strategies in Spatial Planning Knowledge and Values: Urban and Landscape Perspectives* (pp. 47–65). Amsterdam: Springer.

Concilio, G. 2010. Bricolaging knowledge and practices in spatial strategy-making. In M. Cerreta, G. Concilio and V. Monno (eds), *Making Strategies in Spatial Planning Knowledge and Values: Urban and Landscape Perspectives* (pp. 281–301). Amsterdam: Springer.

Davoudi, S. and Strange, I. 2009. Space and place in twentieth-century planning: An analytical framework and an historical view. In S. Davoudi and I. Strange (eds), *Conceptions of Space and Place in Strategic Spatial Planning* (pp. 7–43). The RTPI Library Series edition. Abingdon: Routledge.

Deleuze, G. and Guattari, F. 1987 [1980]. *A Thousand Plateaus: Capitalism and Schizophrenia*. Trans. B. Massumi. London: Athlone Press.

Derrida, J. 1993. *Aporias*. Trans. T. Dutoit. Stanford, CA: Stanford University Press.

Derrida, J. 1994. The deconstruction of actuality: An interview with Jacques Derrida. In J. Culler (ed.), *Deconstruction Critical Concepts in Literary and Cultural Studies* (Vol. 4, pp. 245–273). London: Routledge.

ECESR. 2011. The full details for the dismissal of the local councils. [online] Available at http://ecesr.org/?p=4051 [accessed in August 2014].

Foucault, M. 1980. *Power/Knowledge: Selected Interviews and Other Writings by Michel Foucault, 1972–77*. Ed. C. Gordon. Brighton: Harvester.

Foucault, M. 1981. *The History of Sexuality. Vol. 1: The Will to Knowledge*. London: Penguin.

Friedmann, J. 2004. Strategic spatial planning and the longer range. *Planning Theory and Practice*, 5(1), 49–56.

GOPP, 1983. *Master Plan for Greater Cairo Region*. Cairo: General Organization for Physical Planning.

GOPP, 2008. *Terms of Reference for the Project of Preparing the Strategic and Detailed Urban Planning Projects for the Egyptian Cities*. Cairo: General Organization for Physical Planning.

GOPP, 2009a. *The Strategic Urban Planning Project for Meet Ghamer City – Phase One Report: Present Situation Analysis*. Cairo: General Organization for Physical Planning.

GOPP, 2009b. *The Strategic Urban Planning Project for Meet Ghamer city – Phase Two Report: Setting the Future Development Vision for the City*. Cairo: General Organization for Physical Planning.

GOPP, 2015. General Organization for Physical Planning website. Available at http://gopp.gov.eg/about/ [accessed in November 2015].

Grosz, E. 2001. *Architecture from the Outside*. Cambridge, MA: MIT Press.

Healey, P. 2004. The treatment of space and place in the new strategic spatial planning in Europe. *International Journal of Urban and Regional Research*, 28(1), 45–67.

Hillier, J. 2003. Agonising over consensus: Why Habermasian ideals cannot be 'real'. *Planning Theory*, 2(1), 37–59.

Hillier, J. 2010. Post-structural complexity: Strategic navigation in an ocean of theory and practice. In M. Cerreta, G. Concilio and V. Monno (eds), *Making Strategies in Spatial Planning Knowledge and Values: Urban and Landscape Perspectives* (pp. 87–97). Amsterdam: Springer.

Hillier, J. 2014. On relationality and uncertainity. *DisP – The Planning Review*, 49(3), 32–39.

Hubbard, P., Kitchin, R. and Valentine, G. 2004. *Key Thinkers on Space and Place*. London: Sage.

Innes, J. and Booher, D. 1999. Consensus-building as role-playing and bricolage. *Journal of the American Planning Association*, 65(1), 9–26.

INTI, 2015. International New Towns Institute website. Available at http://www.newtowninstitute.org/newtowndata/index.php?countryId=17 [accessed in November 2015].

Kunzmann, K. R. 2014. 'Strategic planning: A chance for spatial innovation and creativity. *DisP – The Planning Review*, 49(3), 28–31.

Lucy, N. 2004. *A Derrida Dictionary*. Oxford: Blackwell.

Mäntysalo R. 2014. Coping with the paradox of strategic spatial planning. *DisP – The Planning Review*, 49(3), 51–52.

Martin, R. 2014. The big lie of strategic planning. *Harvard Business Review* Press, January–February, 79–85.

Mastop, H. and Faludi, A. 1997. Evaluation of strategic plans: The performance principle. *Environmental and Planning B: Planning and Design*, 24, 815–832.

McQuillan, M. 2001. *Deconstruction: A Reader*. New York: Routledge.

Mourad, M. 2014. Urban space and politics of transition in contemporary Cairo. *IUSD Journal*, 2. Ain Shams University, Cairo.

Raymond, A. 2007. *Cairo: City of History*. Trans. W. Wood. Cairo: The American University in Cairo Press.

Salheen, M. A. 2001. A comprehensive analysis of pedestrian environments: The case of Cairo city centre. Unpublished PhD thesis, Heriot-Watt University, Edinburgh College of Art.

Serag, Y. 2006. Regional planning in Egypt: Between myth and reality. In *The Proceedings of the ARUP International Conference*, Ain Shams University, Cairo.

Serag, Y. 2008. Networking and networks as tools for regional spatial development and planning: Human settlements' development potentialities in the western part of Egypt. Unpublished PhD thesis, KULeuven, Belgium.

Townley, B. 1993. Foucault, Power/Knowledge, and its relevance for human resource management. *Academy of Management Review*, 18(3), 518–545.

UNHABITAT. 2014. *Strategic Urban Planning for Small Cities in Egypt*. [online] Available at: http://mirror.unhabitat.org/content.asp?cid=7119&catid=192&typeid=13 [accessed in August 2014].

UNDP. 2006. *Municipal Initiative for Strategic Recovery (MISR): Setting the Investment Plan for Development of Aswan Governorate*. Cairo: UNDP.

Van den Broeck, P., Abdelwahab, M. *et al.* 2013. On analysing space from a strategic-relational institutionalist perspective: The Cultural Park for Children in Cairo. *International Planning Studies: Special Issue. Epistemology of Space: Exploring Relational Perspectives in Planning, Urbanism and Architecture*, 18(3–4), 321–341.

Yousry, S. 2013. Revolutionizing the planning process in Egypt: Decentralizing powers and actions. In *Democratic Transition and Sustainable Communities*. Conference proceeding of the SB13, Cairo.

# 11 15 years of strategic planning in Italian cities

## Premises, outcomes and further expectations

*Valeria Fedeli*

## Introduction

Strategic planning is not a form of statutory planning in the Italian context. Nevertheless, a consistent number of cities have promoted processes of strategic planning in the last 15 years. When the first experiences of strategic planning started, between the end of the 1990s and the start of the new century, the idea of strategic planning was, *per se*, perceived in contraposition to the limits and pitfalls of traditional statutory planning in Italy. During the last decade, indeed, this contraposition seems somehow to have weakened: apparently, strategic planning has been able to find its way and interact with traditional spatial planning. At the same time, in its heterogeneous forms and local interpretations, it has not been exempt from contradictions and problematic results – in particular due to its non-binding and voluntary character. Because of that, some authors have suggested that it has failed its promises of innovation; as such, it should be abandoned, rather than saved. However, in the most recent years, a new interest in strategic planning has emerged: a number of new processes of strategic planning are, in fact, flourishing in small- and medium-sized cities in Italy, while the new Local Institutions Reform Act,[1] implementing metropolitan government forms in large urban areas, refers to strategic planning as a possible task of the new metropolitan bodies. At the end of the day, suspended between mainstreaming, local innovations, critiques and new inputs, strategic planning in Italy remains a fairly unidentified object, while most of the limits of statutory planning are still unsolved. This chapter aims at illustrating the history of strategic planning in Italy, proposing a critical reconstruction of its role, interpretation and effects in the field of spatial planning and urban policies.

In order to do that, the first section will describe the first, original season of strategic planning in Italy (2000–2005), characterized by a strong voluntary, innovative and experimental character. The second will present the results of a phase of mainstreaming, characterized by an unexpected attempt to include strategic planning within urban policies and a general revision of statutory planning (2005–2010). The third section will focus on its unexpected resurgence in the most recent years (2010–2015), despite the significant criticisms levelled at it at the end of the 2000s. Finally, some general conclusions will be proposed about the future of strategic planning in Italy.

Three common research questions will lead this reconstruction: what are the reasons why strategic planning processes have been promoted and implemented, and under which political, economic and social context? What kind of interpretation of the idea of strategic planning has been enhanced, and with what objectives and scope? What kinds of evaluations of those experiences have been given by the protagonists of these different seasons of strategic planning? Travelling through the different communities of practices, planning cultures, rationales and rhetoric involved in these three seasons, the author will try to provide a tentative interpretation of the 'parabola' of strategic planning in Italy. In fact, this interpretation cannot be an overall and complete portrait. Due to its situated nature (Albrechts, 2004), strategic planning cannot be discussed out of the specific local conditions under which it has taken place. In fact, in order to assess their role, legitimacy and efficacy, strategic planning processes must be described and commented on the basis of an in-depth analysis and evaluation of the local context in which they have been implemented. What is more, in order to provide a thorough evaluation of their outcomes, *time also matters*: many strategic planning effects can only be evaluated in a long-term perspective. In this respect, when the author provides a critical evaluation of the general impact of a strategic approach on spatial planning and urban policies in Italy, this will be proposed as a temporary evaluation of the currently open interplay between local practices, expectations, results and general considerations.

## 1999–2005. Discovering strategic planning: a new local leadership looking for ways to deal with uncertainty

Between the end of the 1990s and the early 2000s, a number of strategic planning processes were activated in some important Italian cities (Turin, Florence, Pesaro, Genoa, Piacenza, La Spezia, Trento, Venice), as well as in medium-sized cities in large urban regions (Piano Strategico Nord Milano, Piano Strategico Dalmine Zingonia) or rich economic districts (Comuni del Copparese). Looking back at those experiences, 15 years on, we can identify some common features which basically have to deal, on the one hand, with nature and scope, and, on the other, with the impact and perceived outcomes of this first season of strategic planning processes (Balducci and Fedeli, 2014a).[2]

### Nature and scope

Voluntarism and innovation are the main features of this first season of experimentations: in fact, nothing like strategic planning was available in the national spatial planning system at that time in Italy. On the contrary, in those years, experts and practitioners were already engaged in a longstanding debate on the necessity of a reform of the Spatial Planning Act, issued in 1942 and essentially based upon the urgency of addressing the problems of urban growth. Already in the late 1970s, it was clear that the main spatial planning tool at municipal level[3] had become unable to deal with urban contexts, which were affected by strong decentralization processes and the emergence of new functions and social needs, as well as the crisis of public action, the complexification of urban arenas and processes of regional urbanization (Balducci, 2004).

The 1990s were particularly stressing years for Italian cities: uncertainty became one of the emergent characteristics, together with the necessity to experiment with new policy tools and modes of action. On the one hand, many important cities experienced a consistent change in their economic basis. Uncertainty about the economic future was patent: no more a threat, but a matter of fact. How to react was much more complicated. In this perspective, one first general reason to promote strategic planning was linked to the necessity for local contexts to deal with a consistent phase of economic restructuring.

At the same time, the Italian political system entered an even stronger condition of uncertainty. By the middle of the 1990s, the crisis of twentieth-century political parties was almost complete. After the discovery of a thick network of corruption in almost all national political parties, the political landscape lacked legitimacy and accountability. Not only did new political parties enter the scene, but a series of institutional reforms also tried to address the problem of political corruption and to re-establish the legitimacy of institutions, at both the local and national level – for example, by introducing the direct election of mayors.[4] Because of that, between 1993 and 1997, a new generation of directly elected mayors, supported by civil servants with new management responsibilities, started looking for innovative policy and leadership styles. This significant change in the political landscape represented the second most important element of this first season of strategic planning (Balducci, 2004; Formez, 2006; Armondi, Fedeli and Pasqui, 2010).[5]

Dealing with the uncertainty of the new political landscape and the shifting economical context was for these new mayors a common necessity: on the one hand, a new political leadership was required in order to find a renewed democratic dialogue with all those citizens who felt betrayed. On the other hand, imaginative scenario-making capacities had to be developed, in order to address the uncertainties of a missing economic basis and a new demand for public action. Mayors, concerned by the growing fragmentation of local societies and looking for new collective narratives, engaged with citizens, private actors and organizations of interests, promoting new forms and occasions for dialogue and interaction. All strategic planning processes launched in those years were (1) characterized by an unprecedented determination in promoting a large public discussion about the future of the city, and (2) based upon a new researched capacity for listening and interaction, through (3) the involvement of relevant stakeholders, (4) the production of scenarios in which the city was represented and thought of as a 'collective actor', and (5) the identification of pilot projects and strategic issues designed to be part of a shared agenda, in a long-term horizon. What was missing and researched, in other words, was a vision of the future, which had become less and less clear and path-dependent; a coalition of actors interested in sharing and feeding this vision; finally, projects that could make this future possible (Armondi, Fedeli and Pasqui, 2010).

As a consequence of this new approach, the rhetoric of those years was characterized by a strong emphasis on the idea of the city as a 'collective actor' (Bagnasco and Le Galès, 2000; Fedeli, 2006) and of the strategic plan, not as the plan of the municipality, but as the plan of the 'city'. The focus on cities was stronger than ever and most innovations happened in cities: the general climate of competition between cities, typical of those years and fed by the ideology of global cities, together with the debate on the hollowing out of the state, fed this new rhetoric.

A fourth significant ingredient of this season was the strong attention to the reform of public action in the urban sphere. In particular, strategic planning was perceived as an innovative space for political leaders to overcome the limits of traditional planning tools, seen as not able to address the above-described new challenges. Statutory spatial planning, as defined by Law 142/1992, was not based on an open and structured dialogue with society and a new leadership and governance model. Nor was it based on scenario-making that was able to address the economic crisis, being essentially linked with land-use planning. Nor was it able to deal with the growing complexity, uncertainty and dynamicity that affect the urban arenas. For all these reasons, new policy tools and governance models had to be experimented with.

But, what kind of strategic planning was required? If we keep in mind these four main characteristics as reflecting the main reasons for activating a strategic planning process (dealing with economic restructuring and uncertainty; addressing fragmentation and producing new collective frameworks for action; supporting new political elites; enhancing new public policies styles, as in Mintzberg, 1994), not only can we interpret and explain those first experiences in detail, we can also highlight some general consideration in terms of the impact produced on the very nature and scope of spatial planning.

The first family of strategic planning processes focused, in particular, on the renovation of the urban economic basis of the city and on the necessity to produce a network of actors able to support it (see, for example, the case of Turin, La Spezia and Piacenza, but also the first inter-municipal strategic plan in the Milan metropolitan area). This first family was characterized by a stronger presence of socio-economists among the consultants involved in the processes: strategic plans were in this case a mix of strategies and actions for local development. The second family was more oriented to innovation towards the limits of traditional spatial planning; in particular, in terms of its capacity to open a public dialogue on the future of the city and to produce a shared vision able to address urban challenges, like spatial integration, mobility, liveability. A mix of urban planners, urban scholars and sociologists were involved in this second family (see the case of Florence, or that of Trento), and the strategic plans were more oriented to spatial change. The third family was interested in producing change in public action and innovation in policy styles, promoting reorganization of public administration. Consultants with this kind of attitude came in particular from policy analysis and sociology of public administration, or were urban scholars (see, for example, the case of Nord Milano and Pesaro). Of course, these three families are just ideal clusters, each one based on a different expertise and understanding of strategic planning; actually, a mix of the three characterized most of the processes. All in all, these strategic planning processes seemed to have a different take on the nature of an established disciplinary field (Mazza, 1996, 2004; Perulli, 2004; Donolo, 2006; Balducci, Fedeli and Pasqui, 2011; Balducci, 2013), which was becoming more and more clearly a field of interaction between different disciplinary fields and types of expertise and skills. In every case, a new genera-tion of academic experts gained the field, characterized by a non-traditional, transdisciplinary interpretation of spatial planning. It was quite evident, at the end of the century, that spatial planning was confronted with challenges that deserved new reflective practitioners and new approaches to planning (Friedmann, 1993).

### Impact and evaluation

It is, in general, difficult to provide an evaluation of the results and impacts of strategic planning processes. Every evaluation needs to be produced on the basis of a careful reformulation of the traditional assessment model, grounded on an idea of efficacy as the capacity to fulfil objectives (Dente, 2007). In fact, evalua-tion becomes complicated when the family of practices is so heterogeneous, so full of different expectations and approaches, as the one we have described: what exactly are the objectives? In this case, we are more inside a 'trading zone' (Balducci, 2013) than a clearly defined and bounded space and model of action. The analysis of recent experiences, promoted by medium-sized cities belonging to the network of cities that have adopted a strategic plan (ReCS: Rete delle Città Strategiche), has shown some important results (Armondi, Fedeli and Pasqui, 2010).

Civil servants and public actors involved in similar experiences, when inter-viewed, perceive strategic planning mainly as a *tool for innovation in the sphere of public action*, in particular as a way to address the fragmentation of decision-making processes and to cope with the ineffectiveness of ordinary urban govern-ment tools. Strategic plans have been occasions to establish innovative processes of knowledge production, based on a new interaction between expert knowledge and diffuse, tacit, local knowledge. They have been regarded as spaces for *the production of generative images*, i.e. visions of the future. Not generic images of a possible future produced by technical interpretation and expert evaluation, but the temporary outcome of a dialogue of interests and identities; a political space for the exploration of the future. In this sense, strategic planning has been used both as a tool for *dealing with uncertainty and managing the present, and as a framework to imagine the future* and deal with a changing understanding of the present, past and future time. In this perspective, it *has not been conceived to replace other planning tools or public policies*. In many cases, it has been inter-preted as a framework for action and coordination between statutory planning tools and new problems and policy issues that are difficult to be addressed with traditional planning tools. Strategic planning has provided space for *innovative policy design*, shaking up in particular the relationship between planning and implementation. The spatial dimension has remained central, and was almost never left behind: in this respect, strategic planning in Italy has kept a very strong focus on the spatiality of economic and social processes. Despite this, *there has been a limited stabilization of results through institution-building and design.*

In terms of *expectations towards the production of new leadership and consensus building*, the perceptions of civil servants and public actors were not so univocal and positive. In many cases, the interactive process has involved and mobilized the most important stakeholders (industry associations, trade unions, the Chamber of Commerce, the universities, etc.). Just in a limited number of situations, it was able to involve, in a stable way, citizens and their grassroots local associations. In most cases, the tools used to promote and manage the interaction remained, in fact, quite traditional, and the approach of social actors and those interested in the process was often 'formal', based on the reproduction of traditional roles and positions. Only in a few cases, did it develop into new forms of local democracy and participation. In order to consider the city as a collective actor, where consensus among stakeholders is a precondition, the attitude has remained diffuse and contradictory: only in a few cases were strategic plans able to build and/or consolidate a strong local coalition. This condition has caused problems of legitimacy and continuity. After a first phase of strong interaction between the actors involved, often based on *a strong political leadership*, processes have become rhetorical exercises and networks have remained passive, unable to deal with conflicts and to promote cooperation between different actors.

From the point of view of *reducing fragmentation and dealing with uncertainty,* in particular, many strategic planning processes were apparently effective in supporting vertical cooperation: they have opened new windows of opportunities, activating a new dialogue at the regional, national and European level. Also in terms of horizontal cooperation, in many cases strategic planning processes were able to promote and support new agreements between municipalities. Even when they were not able to define a clear and successful strategy of institution building, these experiences of inter-institutional cooperation were an important outcome of the process, promoting new institutional capabilities and generating new resources for the cities and their territories. In this sense, strategic planning is perceived as a way to reduce fragmentation and deal with uncertainty related to the complexity of decision-making in thick policy arenas. More nuanced, in this respect, is the assessment of the real capacity of *innovating the economic base of the city*. On the one hand, it is generally quite difficult to show direct effects, also because of the necessity of a long-term perspective, in terms of economic change and development path. On the other hand, it should be mentioned that in the case of small- and medium-sized cities, the economic crisis was less evident than in large cities and less central in terms of expectations. Nevertheless, some strong critiques have been formulated, in particular on this issue, since just a few cases have produced a monitoring tool or activity able to show the efficacy and consistency of their strategies and projects.

The lookout provided by the implementation of strategic planning in small- and medium-sized cities can be complemented by some evaluations provided in a less systematic way by large cities involved in similar processes. In particular, while the cases of Turin and Genoa can be considered central in terms of their capacity of producing a real shift in the economic profile of the city, the cases of Venice and Turin, and later of Milan, have shown the relevance of strategic planning in raising the issue of metropolitan governance. In both cases, contrary to what can be observed in small- and medium-sized cities, the problems of governing in metropolitan areas were central, and both cases provided interesting elements to try to address this issue, which nevertheless remained central and open.

More generally, many scholars, from other lookouts and perspectives, have lamented the failures and risks of many of these experimentations: in several cases, they seem to have reproduced, rather than overcome, some of the behaviours that the strategic approach should have contributed to abandon. Many strategic plans have turned into a *renewed comprehensive and holistic approach to planning* (long lists of actions, strategies, and projects, covering the whole set of policies), being *unable to select issues and produce consensus and coalitions of actors* (thus also facing problems of legitimacy). They have remained *isolated paths inside more traditionally sectoral policies, powerless in fostering wider public confrontation on the city's future* and in assuring efficacy and efficiency, as well as in promoting innovation and permanent consensus and interest. Moreover, at the end of the last decade, the political, social, cultural and territorial context seemed again to be changing, as were the conditions for planning. In a few years, the interest in strategic planning seemed to be partially diminished, also due to these sometimes-limited outcomes. In some cases, strategic planning officially entered the consolidated praxis of planning, more like a routine premise to 'real' spatial planning. In this sense, the first round of the diffusion of strategic planning in Italy somehow paved the way for the transfer of innovation, as well as to the mainstreaming of strategic planning, which, by 2010, seemed to be in a deep quandary.

## 2006–2010. Mainstreaming of strategic planning

At the end of 2007, five Italian provinces, 13 large Italian cities or metropolitan areas, ten municipal aggregations with more than 100,000 inhabitants, another nine with less than 100,000 inhabitants, ten single municipalities with more than 100,000 inhabitants and another 27 above this threshold, had promoted or adopted forms of strategic planning (894 municipalities were involved, out of a total of more than 8,100, with more than 20 million people concerned) (RUR-CENSIS, 2007). All this despite (or because of) the fact that strategic planning in Italy had remained a voluntary form of planning, not regulated by any law at the local, regional or national level. In fact, two parallel processes, at both the national and regional level, produced this impressive and counterintuitive trend. The first was a process of experimentation fostered by the Ministry of Infrastructure and Transport and started in 2005,[6] in the regions of southern Italy, where major cities were invited to start processes of 'strategic planning' in order to obtain resources in the general programming regional framework of the new

EU programming season. Approximately 50 out of these 74 experiences in 2007 resulted from this specific policy input by the central government. The second had to do with a debate, started at the end of the 1990s, on the necessity of reforming statutory planning. A sort of *vexata questio* fed this general debate: whether or not – and if so, how – strategic planning could substitute, integrate or complement statutory planning. Seen together, these two elements have shaped what we could define as a sort of 'mainstreaming of strategic planning', providing more general elements of reflection on the impact of this decade of experimentations and on the policy transferability of its results.

### Nature and scope

The first front of mainstreaming was promoted in 2004 by two deliberative acts of CIPE, the Comitato Interministeriale per la Programmazione Economica (*tr.* the Inter-ministerial Committee for Economic Programming), according to which a specific amount of public funding had to be destined to promoting strategic planning in cities and metropolitan areas in the southern Italian regions. The basic idea was that strategic planning, experimented successfully in the previous years in several local contexts in northern and central Italy, could support southern cities in dealing with the new objectives and rationales of the EU 2007/2013 programming season, and in consolidating the potential of innovation accumulated in the previous season (in particular, through the Urban programme).

The Guidelines drawn up in 2004 by DICOTER (the Land Development Coordination Division, Ministry of Infrastructure and Transport) in order to support this objective, related the strategic plan 'of a city' to the political capacity to design a sustainable future in the medium to long term (ten years), in coexistence with statutory planning. According to the Guidelines, strategic plans were to be promoted by the administration of the leading municipality, which should be able to develop strategic guidelines and overcome the boundaries between urban and rural contexts and deal with a new regional perspective. They were to be built upon a process of 'communication' that was able to involve the local society in all its active components. In particular, strategic plans were to address a multi-governance dimension, involving not only the regional level, but also the national and European ones.[7] This large framework was the field of diverse interpretations by regional authorities, the central actors in the relationship between the local, national and EU authorities. In fact, regional authorities assumed different orientations, in some cases with a more proactive and guiding role: Puglia, Campania and Calabria played a guiding role in promoting strategic planning processes oriented towards certain targeted areas and policy issues (Vinci, 2010). In others, like Sicily and Sardinia, regional authorities provided large space to voluntary actions at the local level (Vinci, 2010). The result was a sum of different experiences and interpretations, while producing a sort of mainstreaming and a disordered Babel of interpretations.

The second front of mainstreaming is given by the Italian debate on the reform of statutory planning over the last 20 years.

Strategic planning started to be practised by Italian cities as a way of questioning the limits of statutory planning just a few years after the proposal made by INU, the Istituto Nazionale di Urbanistica, to introduce a reform of the National Planning Act of 1942. This was basically based on a single planning tool, at the municipal level, the so-called *piano regolatore generale*: a holistic tool for managing spatial challenges. The original idea of the INU reform proposal was based on an urban plan made of two different tools. The *structure plan* (the so-called '*piano strutturale*') was to contain relevant general choices on the structure of the city, with a non-conformative role and a ten-year length; the *operative plan* (the so-called '*piano operativo*') was to implement the decisions relating to the '*piano strutturale*' in a time-defined perspective, producing building rights and promoting feasible projects. An additional tool, the '*regolamento urbanistico*', or 'urban building code', was destined to deal with the regulation of existing cities and the built environment. This threefold structure was designed to deal with the growing uncertainty, complexity and articulation of urban change and urban arenas, where the issues of flexibility, efficacy, legitimacy, certainty and rapidity of decision-making had become more and more problematic (Mazza, 1996). The reform text stated the necessity to reform the main planning tool in order to make it respond to the new rhythms and actors of urban change. At the same time, it stated the necessity to look at spatial planning as merely a part of the complex activity of territorial government ('Governo del Territorio' in Italian), and that every reform should be completed by a fiscal reform and a federal organization of the State, in order to allow municipalities to act in an efficient and legitimate way. Under this perspective, the law tried to include spatial planning inside a process of general reorganization of public action and administration; limited attention was given to the challenges of public participation, consensus building or to the inputs related to local development strategies and economic change.

Strategic planning, however, was not conceived as the answer to the limitations of planning, and the reform proposal did not explicitly take advantage of the lessons learnt with the strategic planning experiences of those years. In fact, these were seen by some of the more traditional urban planners as being in contraposition to spatial planning, being abstract and far from the real problems of urban planning. From another perspective, strategic planning was seen as an aspect to be included or absorbed within structure planning: 'every plan should necessarily and clearly express the objectives and choices (whether strategic or otherwise) of the administrations. If a plan is strategic when it chooses its own objectives, then all plans should be strategic' (*author's tr.*, Avarello, 2010: 106). Under both perspectives, strategic planning was not central in the debate on the reform of spatial planning in Italy.

During the last national electoral campaign in 2012, the INU asked all the political parties' candidates to reflect again upon the necessity for a deep renewal in the field of spatial planning, moving beyond the reform model proposed – and never thoroughly implemented – in 1995 (INU, 1995). The new plan was to be 'programmatic and not produce building rights, granting the vision necessary for urban and territorial organization, but also acting as a framework for evaluating urban transformations and urban policies' (*author's tr.*, Oliva, 2012). The plan was to be 'more structural than ever, abandoning definitely its traditional regulative dimension, and concentrating on the management tools related to the existing city: a plan that would grant the necessary vision for the future of urban and territorial organization, but that would also be able to evaluate urban transformations and to structure urban policies'.[8] Even more recently, taking part in the public consultation on the legislative proposal issued in 2014,[9] the INU not only supported a reform of the plan as a non-conformative tool, but also mentioned the necessity to produce strategic documents so as to fix objectives and priorities, and proposed including strategic planning in the structural/operative planning tools. In particular, the INU proposed moving towards a 'real structure plan', far beyond zoning, able to represent the territorial organization and to support policies (strategic planning); not based on an improbable future scenario, therefore, but on an explicit strategy of urban regeneration. This plan was to be developed in tight coherence with the operative plan, so as to pursue the strategic objectives of the first, supporting them with operative mechanism and operations. In this respect, one could conclude that the national debate on spatial planning has partially concentrated on absorbing and trying to mainstream strategic planning, though limiting its symbolic role in terms of innovation.

### *Impact and evaluation*

Mainstreaming strategic planning actually produced contradictory results. On the one hand, if one considers the light mainstreaming framework provided by the national debate on the reform of statutory planning, one could argue that a small step was produced in terms of innovation in spatial planning. The INU reform proposal never passed at national level: around about the same time, the regions were attributed with the necessary competence and legislative power in the field of spatial planning. Since then, a number of regions have produced their own laws, introducing new planning tools mainly inspired by the principles of the INU proposal (INU, 1995). More than 15 years later, Federico Oliva, then president of the INU, commented (INU, 2010) that the new regional laws had not been able to innovate the field of practices or to address three key problems: first, *the efficacy of planning tools in addressing contemporary urban challenges* (such as the lack of financial resources, the necessity of public-private partnerships, the impact in terms of production of the public realm); second, in terms of their *ability to address the transcalar dimension of transformation processes* (and inter-institutional cooperation, both on the horizontal and vertical dimension, in particular in terms of land consumption and environmental challenges); third, the *communicative dimension and the legitimacy of planning*, which remained quite weak both in terms of public understanding and in the political debate (see INU, 2010; Oliva, 2012: viii). In this sense, statutory planning has not yet been able to reflect and learn from the innovations introduced by strategic planning.

On the other hand, the input from the national government produced quite a different kind of experience from the first season of strategic planning, the most consistent differences being the mix of voluntarism and top-down support offered by central and regional government. The availability of specific resources and the normative incentives provided by the central government produced a sort of 'forced' activism, not always based on strong coalitions or leadership. In this sense, the strategic plan became an objective *per se*, with several implications (Pasqui, 2010). Where responsibility was not really at play and was locally rooted and shared, the strategic character was often lost: the plan became a long list of impossible desires. Where coalitions were taken as pre-conditions and actors were involved merely in order to gain access to public resources, the strategic plan was not, *per se*, able to produce new, effective, thick networks or to generate new resources. Where a number of procedures regulated its development and implementation, its capacity for local and situated innovation was reduced: strategic plans became stylized and standardized. Moreover, there was the consistent risk of remaining abstract and distant from the context, generated by a new technical expertise that was scarcely able to speak to local civil servants and to feed innovation in public action. In addition to that, the strategic plans promoted in the second half of the decade took place at a time of reduced political 'momentum'. They were steered by local leaders who were less popular and who succeeded the previous generation, who in those years had moved on to the national political arena.

To a certain extent, the upscaling process promoted by the central government seemed to try to reproduce what had been successful at the local level in very different contexts, transferring a policy (McCann and Ward, 2011) while ignoring the specifics of the success factors. This produced more contradictions than achievements (Palermo, 2001, 2009; Pasqui, 2010). Despite the good intentions, many of the processes promoted inside this framework were not able to fulfil the central government's expectations. There are several reasons for this failure, and in particular: the absence of local politics; the market was in a critical economic situation; and a stressed or fragile local society, affected, if not defeated, by decades of illegality and corruption. These, along with other elements, seem to have produced an opportunistic rather than a strategic approach (Cremaschi, 2010). In other words, on the one hand, strategic planning was not able to display its potential in those cities because they were (and still are) lacking *the preconditions* for strategic planning, which cannot be taken for granted. At the same time, probably the central government initiative was not able to problematize strategic planning as a way to build these preconditions.

We could conclude that strategic planning cannot be imposed or should not be proposed top-down or institutionalized (Albrechts, 2004; Mazza, 2004; Camagni, 2010; Balducci, Fedeli and Pasqui, 2011), if this results in mainstreaming processes that reduce all the potential for innovation. In this perspective, strategic planning processes seem to be destined to remain non-statutory forms of planning in order not to lose this potential. Moreover, in this perspective, the challenge of making strategic planning become a part of a governance culture remains unsolved. While the first season of strategic planning revealed a number of limitations in terms of remaining out of ordinary practices – one being particularly related to its volatility and political frailty – the second season, related to mainstreaming, was unable to address the complex relationship between strategic planning innovation and consolidation into ordinary public action.

## A new phase for strategic planning in Italy: inputs from the debate on the new urban agenda and the metropolitan reform

The years 2013 and 2014 saw a renewed interest in strategic planning, which has been identified by the EU as a promising approach and will be reinforced in the next programming period (2014–2020): as such, it will become a key tool of the new European Cohesion Policy since it provides local players with a 'method' to innovate and progress in the field of urban/territorial development. On the basis of this new light cast by the European Commission upon strategic planning, new attention has been paid, at the national level, to a concept that seemed destined to fade away without any consistent ability to generate stable governance change. In this regard, an inter-parliamentary working group has been set up to draw up a *new urban agenda* at the national level, able to interact with the EU and at the same time to refocus on the role of Italian cities towards cohesion policies. In order to support this effort, a document has been published that attempts to highlight the main issues at stake for Italian cities, promoted under the then Ministry Fabrizio Barca. The process is still open and far from being implemented, but the premises are consistent with our reflection.

The document 'Metodi e obiettivi per un uso efficace dei Fondi comunitari 2014–2020' ('Methods and Objectives for an Efficient Use of Community Resources 2014–2020', *tr.*, DICOTER, 2012) issued by the Ministry identifies two main challenges, towards which strategic planning is seen as a resource.

First, the necessity to overcome the inconsistency of traditional administrative boundaries, and the problems to be addressed, namely institutional boundaries that do not match with design territories or with the space of everyday social practices. The document highlights how a new perspective has emerged over the last few decades: we have moved from the idea of a supra-local government defined by law to the shared idea that such a new form of government must be designed bottom-up and on the basis of shared problems, within 'a strategic vision'.

Second, the report comments upon the outcomes of a season of urban growth, which, on top of producing the explosion of the polycentric urban system into a diffuse city, has also resulted in a number of spatial and social problems. In this light, the report stigmatizes the inability of traditional urban planning tools to 'provide answers to the necessity to modernize the city and to keep in step with socio-economic changes and the changing practices of urban space due to a new relationship between politics and culture'.

Given this problematic condition, the report proposes not opting for producing a new reform law in the field of planning, but rather introducing 'a model of planning founded upon multilevel coalitions and partnerships, able to favour the co-presence and integration of local development policies with policies related to the organization of space, urban policies, environmental policies, infrastructural policies, public works, etc.'.[10]

A second reason for the renewed attention to strategic planning is provided by the recent reform on metropolitan governance. Almost 25 years after the first introduction of a form of metropolitan government in Italy in 1990 (L142/90), the approval of the new L56/2014 should represent the final step in the implementation of this new territorial level in a number of relevant urban contexts, such as Turin, Milan, Venice, Genoa, Bologna, Florence, Naples, Bari, Reggio Calabria and Rome, the capital city, which will have a specific status. This is the result of a large parliamentary debate,[11] during which stakeholders, cities and political actors have tried to support a more legitimate and efficient model of metropolitan government, as well as of negotiations supported by different perspectives and expectations.[12] According to the law, the 'città metropolitana' will have a number of new competences. In particular, it will be in charge of a three-year strategic plan (no more clearly described), which will be its main guiding act. The law does not provide specific hints, nor does it seem to introduce this issue with specific attention. It seems to leave space for local interpretation, but there is a large debate on the nature and scope of this strategic planning task (Urban@it, 2015).

At the end of the day, at the beginning of the current decade new expectations towards strategic planning seem to be rising: a coordination group has been instituted among the main metropolitan cities in order to discuss and experiment with the potential for innovation related to an innovative and non-mainstreaming interpretation of strategic planning.

What could we expect and what can we suggest to those initiating a new phase of strategic planning? After evaluating the contradictory results of the first 15 years of strategic planning, we cannot but conclude with some warnings.

Strategic planning is contextual and situated. This means that no blueprint can be proposed on how to develop it (Balducci, Fedeli and Pasqui, 2011). Especially under the current conditions of fragmentation and uncertainty, it should be *based upon an idea of planning as 'probing'* (Lindblom, 1990; Friedmann 1993, 2004). And *consist of an 'exploration'*, a 'strategic investigation of the future' (Hillier, 2007, 2008a, 2008b), aiming not at defining long-term detailed programmes but at 'raising questions of potential agency and of socio-economic-political conditions of change' (Wildawsky, 1973). At the same time, *strategic planning should be built upon the concept of 'agencement'* (Jullien, 2006: 37–39), alluding to strategy as the capacity to find favourable elements in a situation and draw advantages from it, and should look at action as 'transformation' (within a process perspective). It *should be able to shake up the relationship between intention and action, between planning and implementation* (Majone and Wildawsky, 1979), according to which the implementation process is to be seen as a process of 'evolution' since it consists of a continuous reformulation of the original policies. Consequently, the effectiveness must be measured in the transactional dimension of the process.

Finally, Strategic planning should develop an *idea of planning as 'sensemaking and reframing'* (Rein and Schön, 1994; Weick, 1995). Such a planning should be able to propose the strategic definitions of a situation or of a problem (Albrechts, 2004), which are strategic because they make it possible to address it. This is even more interesting today when the fragmentation, complexity and the plurality of interests and identities seem, more than at other times, to require opportunities to 'make sense' (Weick, 1995) for the cities in which we live.

For it to be able to produce effective changes in the planning and governance landscape and avoid simplifying mainstreaming processes, strategic planning should remain an open field of experimentation, providing space for the intelligence of society (Lindblom, 1990) and its capacity to organize, and offering society stimulation and space for projects as opportunities for action and empowerment. This quick overview of the Italian case seem to provide relevant elements to support this thesis and to highlight the necessity of a constitutive experimental approach to it.

## Notes

1  Law 56/2014, see the last paragraph for details.
2  For detailed accounts of this first season, see: Balducci (2003); Pugliese and Spaziante (2003); Curti and Gibelli (1996); Fedeli and Gastaldi (2004); Perulli (2004); Mazza (2004); Martinelli (2005).
3  The so-called *'piano regolatore generale'*.
4  The introduction of directly elected mayors in all Italian municipalities was established by Law 81/1993; the reform of the Municipal Councils and Executive Boards, directly appointed by mayors, and the introduction of city managers, was introduced by Lgs. D. 267/2000.
5  If we track back the origins of the first strategic planning processes, we cannot but notice that most of them were promoted by this new generation of directly elected mayors during their second mandate, supported by a new class of powerful civil servants. Valentino Castellani for Turin (1993–2001), Leonardo Domenici for Florence (1999–2009), Giuseppe Pericu (1997–2007), Oriano Giovannelli (1993–2004) are just some examples of a new generation of mayors, pivoted by a new political class, looking for new legitimation and accountability, but also for a new efficacy of public action, after decades of political stasis.
6  Ministero delle Infrastrutture e dei Trasporti (MIT), Dipartimento per il Coordinamento dello Sviluppo del territorio, il personale e i servizi generali, 'Il piano strategico delle città come strumento per ottimizzare le condizioni di sviluppo della competitività e della coesione- Linee Guida', 2005.
7  In terms of contents, priority went to infrastructures, proximity facilities, social security and urban welfare, physical and social degradation, sustainability and competitiveness. The Guidelines, in particular, suggested: displaying actions related to social inclusion and human capital production; enforcing the territorial structure; breaking apart peripheral conditions and social dualization; and building social cohesion, innovation and sustainable development. One of the central aims was that of improving the capacity of local administrations so as to promote public participation processes and the construction of actor coalitions.
8  'Per un rilancio del governo del territorio', il documento INU 08/02/2013.
9  Public Consultation on the Draft Law: 'Principi in materia di politiche pubbliche territoriali e trasformazione urbana Partecipante alla consultazione: Istituto Nazionale

di Urbanistica Contributo inviato da Silvia Viviani Presidente nazionale INU. Motivazioni del contributo proposto: Riflessioni sulla materia e indicazioni sul testo di legge proposto', http://www.inu.it/wp-content/uploads/Contributo_INU_DdL_principi_GdT_2014.pdf

10 Comitato Interministeriale Per Le Politiche Urbane, Metodi e Contenuti sulle Priorità in tema di Agenda Urbana, Ministro per la Coesione territoriale, Roma, 20.3.2013, http://www.coesioneterritoriale.gov.it/wp-content/uploads/2013/04/Politica-nazionale-per-le-citt%C3%A01.pdf.

11 The law was initiated by the government led by President Monti as part of the spending review and as such aimed at reducing public expenditure in Italy. It has been opposed by the Provinces, which are due to be abolished according to the same law; for this reason, it has been referred to as non-constitutional, due to the fact that the abolishment of the Provinces, the second tier level in Italy, was operated by ordinary law, rather than by constitutional law. After this consistent interruption, the newly elected parliament decided to keep supporting the initiative and re-approved the law with some major challenges in order to overcome problems of constitutionality. This year, the rationale and rhetoric of the law has experienced some changes, becoming oriented to a more general idea of promoting the reform of public administration in Italy; the new government, led by President Renzi, is pushing for its implementation as part of a general re-design of the institutions and public administrations – including the reform of parliament based on a two-chamber system. The new law, however, is not exempt from contradictions and limitations, both from the general and the local perspective.

12 Despite this, it still presents some basic problems, which are indeed typical ones in the field of metropolitan government, linked with the complex nexus territory–sovereignty–citizenship: the definition of the boundaries of the new metropolitan government, the nature of the institutions (elected or otherwise), the scope and competences. At the end of the day, it does not introduce innovative approaches to deal with the problematic issue of the boundaries of the new institutions, which are essentially designed on the boundaries of the pre-existing provinces. Amendments can be introduced, but clearly no experimentation and critical support is provided on this issue. Nor does it introduce an innovative solution to the problem of democracy in metropolitan governments. The new institution is indirectly elected: just in a few cases, it will be possible to introduce directly elected presidents and assemblies. Finally, from the point of view of competences, the *città metropolitane* will mainly inherit the competences and roles of the provinces, related to coordination of the actions of municipalities, but will also be in charge of new functions and will be reinforced in their *strategic role*.

## References

Albrechts, L. (2004). Strategic (Spatial) Planning Re-examined. *Environment and Planning B*, 31(5), 743–758.

Albrechts, L. (2006). Dynamic Visioning: A Catalyst for Change? Paper presented at the World Planning Schools Congress, Mexico City, July 12–16.

Armondi, S., Fedeli, V. and Pasqui, G. (2010). I piani strategici alla prova. In R. Florio (Ed.), *10 anni di Pianificazione strategica in Italia, Ragioni, esiti e criticità* (pp. 9–115). ReCS, Quaderni.

Avarello, P. (2010). Strategie o retoriche? In I. Vinci (Ed.), *Pianificazione strategica in contesti fragili* (pp. 103–109). Firenze: ALINEA.

Bagnasco, A. and Le Galès, P. (2000). *Cities in Contemporary Europe*. Cambridge, UK: Cambridge University Press.

Balducci, A. (2003). Policies, Plans and Projects Governing the City-Region of Milan. *DisP*, 152, 59–70.

Balducci, A. (2004). Pianificazione strategica e questioni di area vasta: alle origini del tema e attualità nel contesto italiano. In V. Fedeli and F. Gastaldi (Eds.), *Pratiche strategiche di pianificazione. Riflessioni a partire da nuovi spazi urbani in costruzione* (pp. 247–265). Milano: FrancoAngeli.

Balducci, A. (2013). 'Trading Zone': A Useful Concept for Some Planning Dilemmas. In A. Balducci and R. Mantysalo (Eds.), *Urban Planning as a Trading Zone* (pp. 23–35). Dordrecht, Heidelberg, New York and London: Springer.

Balducci, A. and Fedeli, V. (2014a). Strategic Planning in Italy: First Steps Inside an Open Field of Experimentation. In K. Kunzmann, W. Fang and P. Potz (Eds.), *Special Issue of Urban Planning International* (pp. 25–53). Beijing, China.

Balducci, A. and Fedeli, V. (2014b). The Strategic Project Città di Città: Interacting with Problematic Context Conditions. In K. Kunzmann, W. Fang and P. Potz (Eds.), *Special Issue of Urban Planning International* (pp. 97–114). Beijing, China.

Balducci, A., Fedeli, V. and Pasqui, G. (2011). *Planning for Contemporary Urban Regions*. Aldershot, UK: Ashgate.

Camagni, R. (2010). I piani strategici nel Mezzogiorno: questioni aperte e lezioni per il futuro. In I. Vinci (Ed.), *Pianificazione strategica in contesti fragili* (pp. 95–101). Firenze: ALINEA.

Cremaschi, M. (2010). Strumenti fragili, strategie incapaci: per un ripensamento. In I. Vinci (Ed.), *Pianificazione strategica in contesti fragili* (pp. 125–132). Firenze: ALINEA.

Curti, F. and Gibelli M. C. (Eds.) (1996). *Pianificazione strategica e gestione dello sviluppo urbano*. Firenze: ALINEA.

Dente, B. (2007). Valutare il piano strategico o valutare il governo urbano? In T. Pugliese (Ed.), *Monitoraggio e valutazione dei piani strategici* (pp. 5–11). ReCS, Quaderno 1.

DICOTER (2012). Metodi e obiettivi per un uso efficace dei fondi comunitari 2014-2020, Ministro per la Coesione Territoriale, d'intesa con i Ministri del Lavoro e delle Politiche Sociali e delle Politiche Agricole, Alimentari e Forestali, http://recs.it/userfiles/ file/CIPU/Doc%2014-20%20Master_27%20dic%202012.pdf (accessed 15 November 2015).

Donolo, C. (Ed.) (2006). *Il futuro delle politiche pubbliche*. Milano: Bruno Mondadori.

Fedeli, V. (2006). Pianificazione strategica: le città e la trappola dell'attore collettivo? In C. Donolo (Ed.), *Il futuro delle politiche pubbliche* (pp. 109–140). Milano: Mondadori.

Fedeli, V. and Gastaldi, F. (Eds.) (2004). *Pratiche strategiche di pianificazione: riflessioni a partire da nuovi spazi urbani in costruzione*. Milano: FrancoAngeli.

Formez (2006). *La pianificazione strategica partecipata in Italia*. Roma: Centro competenza Diffusione dell'innovazione e del benchmarking, Ufficio stampa ed editoria.

Friedmann, J. (1993). Toward a Non-Euclidean Mode of Planning. *Journal of the American Planning* Association, 59(4), 482–485.

Friedmann, J. (2004). Strategic Spatial Planning and the Longer Range. *Planning Theory and Practice*, 5(1), 49–67.

Hillier, J. (2007). *Stretching Beyond the Horizon: A Multiplanar Theory of Spatial Planning and Governance*. Aldershot, UK: Ashgate.

Hillier, J. (2008a). Plan(e) Speaking: A Multiplanar Theory of Spatial Planning. *Planning Theory*, 7, 24–50.

Hillier, J. (2008b). Interplanary Practice: Towards a Deleuzan-inspired Methodology for Creative Experimentation in Strategic Spatial Planning. In J. Van den Broeck, F. Moulaert and S. Oosterlynck (Eds.), *Empowering the Planning Fields: Ethics, Creativity, Action* (pp. 43–77). Leuven: ACCO.

INU (1995). *Le riforme possibili: le proposte dell'INU per la legislazione urbanistica a partire dalla formazione della legge del 1942* Ed. L. Falco. Roma: Quaderni di Urbanistica, Inu Edizioni.

INU (2010). *Rapporto da territorio*. Roma: Inu Edizioni.

Jullien, F. (1998). *Trattato dell'efficacia*. Torino: Einaudi.

Jullien, F. (2006). *Pensare l'efficacia in Cina e in Occidente*. Roma-Bari: Laterza.

Lindblom, Ch. E. (1990). *Inquiry and Change: The Troubled Attempt to Understand and Shape Society*. New Haven, CT: Yale University Press.

Majone, G. and Wildavsky, A. (1979). Implementation as Evolution. In J. Pressmann and A. Wildavsky (Eds.), *Implementation* (2nd edition, pp. 163–180). Berkeley, CA: University of California Press.

Martinelli, F. (2005). *La pianificazione strategica in Italia e in Europa. Metodologie ed esiti a confronto*. Milano: FrancoAngeli.

Mazza, L. (1996). Difficoltà della pianificazione strategica. *Territorio*, 27, 100–120.

Mazza, L. (2004). *Piano, progetti, strategie*. Milano: FrancoAngeli.

Mazza, L. (2009). Pianificazione e prospettiva repubblicana. *Territorio*, 48, 124–132.

McCann, E. and Ward, K. (Eds.) (2011). *Mobile Urbanism: City Policymaking in the Global Age*. Minneapolis, MN: University of Minnesota Press.

Mintzberg, H. (1994). *Rise and Fall of Strategic Planning*. London: Free Press.

Oliva, F. (2012). Semplificare la pianificazione, cambiare il piano. *Urbanistica*, 149, 89–99.

Palermo, P. C. (2001). *Prove di innovazione*. Milano: FrancoAngeli.

Palermo, P. C. (2009). *I limiti del possibile*. Roma: Donzelli.

Pasqui, G. (2010). Un ciclo politico al tramonto: perché l'innovazione delle politiche urbane in Italia ha fallito. Paper presented at XXIV CONVEGNO SISP, Venezia, 16–18 September 2010, Session: *Amministrazione e Politiche Pubbliche*, Panel: *Politiche urbane in Italia e governo della città*.

Perulli, P. (2004). *Piani strategici. Governare le città europee*. Milano: FrancoAngeli.

Perulli, P. (2007). Una griglia metodologica per l'inquadramento dei piani strategici. In T. Pugliese (Ed.), *Monitoraggio e valutazione dei piani strategici*. ReCS, Quaderno 1, pp. 27–41.

Pugliese, T. (Ed.) (2007). *Monitoraggio e valutazione dei piani strategici*. ReCS, Quaderno 1.

Pugliese, T. and Spaziante, A. (Eds.) (2003). *Pianificazione strategica per le città: riflessioni dalle pratiche*. Milano: FrancoAngeli.

Rein, M. and Schön, D. (1994). *Frame Reflection toward the Resolution of Intractable Policy Controversies*. New York: Basic Books.

RUR-CENSIS (2007). *Strategie per il territorio. Nuova cultura della programmazione o retorica del piano?* Milano: FrancoAngeli.

Urban@it (2015). Rapporto sulle città 2015, Metropoli attraverso la crisi. Bologna: Il Mulino.

Vinci, I. (Ed.) (2010). *Pianificazione strategica in contesti fragili*. Firenze: ALINEA.

Weick, K. E. (1995). *Sensemaking in Organizations*. Thousand Oaks, CA: Sage.

Wildawsky, A. (1973). If planning is everything, maybe it's nothing. *Policy Science*, 4(2), 127–153.

# 12 Strategy at work

## A decade of strategic planning in Wales

*Francesca S. Sartorio*

## Introduction

In the past two decades international literature has engaged widely with the concept of strategic planning. Healey describes strategic planning as 'a social process through which a range of people in diverse institutional relations and positions come together to design plan-making processes and develop contents and strategies for the management of spatial change' (Healey, 1997: 5). She also sees strategic planning as able to integrate and make sense of the multifaceted issues affecting specific localities drawing on various forms of knowledge and interventions (Healey, 2009). 'Strategic work' goes for Healey beyond mere institutionalised planning practices, involving the possibility to open up new avenues for action and contributing to the evolution of local governance in space (Healey, 2007).

Salet, Faludi and others (Salet and Faludi, 2000a, 2000b) define the general challenge for strategic planning as the need to 'reconcile the collective spatial goals [...] with the totality of social forces in which the actual development takes place' (Salet and Faludi, 2000a: 7). Salet and Faludi's view of the potential for strategic spatial planning is somewhat cautious by comparison with Healey's:

> Spatial planners often find themselves in a position where they must react to spatial initiatives and anticipate the future directions social actors or other policy areas will take. Although they can strongly encourage or discourage certain decisions, most initiatives remain in the hands of other actors. Spatial planning is by its very nature context-bound and reactive, and it is only through links with other actors that development perspectives could have a chance for success. (Salet and Faludi, 2000a: 4)

They also acknowledge that strategic perspectives 'substantively and institutionally change[s] over time'; that contextual power structures are very important in determining the potential of strategic planning initiatives (a point delved into also by Needham, 2000) and that strategic planning has limited scope for implementation on its own (Salet and Faludi, 2000a: 3).

Albrechts, Balducci and others (see Albrechts, 2004, 2010, 2012, 2015; Albrechts and Balducci, 2013; Balducci, 2008; Balducci, Boelens *et al.*, 2011) have been developing a much more positive normative perspective on what strategic (spatial) planning could be. Albrechts (2004) sees the essence of strategic planning in its ability to link negotiated long-term frames of reference for stakeholders with specific short-term actions by various actors: it is 'a democratic, open, selective, and dynamic process' capable of producing 'a vision to frame problems, challenges, and short-term actions within a revised democratic tradition' (Albrechts, 2004: 754). Albrechts and Balducci (2013: 24) define strategic planning as a 'set of concepts, procedures and tools that must be tailored carefully to whatever situation is at hand' in order

> to construct challenging, coherent and coordinated visions, to frame an integrated long-term spatial logic (for land-use regulation, resource protection, sustainable development and spatial quality), to enhance action orientation beyond the idea of planning as control, and to promote a more open multi-level type of governance. (Albrechts and Balducci, 2013: 24)

In an attempt to distil the nature of strategy in strategic planning, they suggest that – in terms of content – it is selective and long-term (rather than comprehensive) and action-oriented; in terms of forms it supports 'action, movement, emergence, relationship and creative experimentation' (2013: 21) and works with uncertainty; it is relational in nature and focuses on coproduction, framing and seizing momentum; it is able to cope with multi-level governance, changing boundaries and evolving cultures by making new ideas and concepts 'portable' (2013: 23). The eminently political nature of strategy, and of many of its features, is evident in this definition. Critiques of this specific normative view of strategic planning focus mainly on two aspects: legitimisation and accountability. Mäntysalo suggests that statutory planning and an informal system of strategic planning can only exist in interdependence and that the management of this interdependence is at the very core of what strategic spatial planning becomes (Mäntysalo, 2013: 51). Mazza calls for a more pragmatic look to the reality and boundness of planning as a societal activity and on how processes of spatial change actually tend to happen: he questions the appropriateness and desirability of visioning and strategising beyond what is strictly needed for land-use planning goals and suggests that in most situations 'plan-making is dependent on political decision-making' (Mazza, 2013: 41). Both Mazza (2013) and Kunzmann (2013) cite Wildawsky ('if planning is everything, maybe it is nothing') while referring to strategic planning, underlying the need for a more intensive operational definition of the term. Kunzmann, however, is more positive than Mazza on its prospects and its creative potential, provided it is not seen as a panacea and it is carefully developed to work in conjunction with existing tools, processes and stakeholders.

Friedmann (2004) provocatively questions the ability of any plan, and particularly of strategic plans, to address the long-range and the uncertain. Hillier (2011) directly addresses this latter point by focusing on the potential of post-structural planning. She advocates strategic planning as 'strategic navigation' and experiment (Hillier, 2011; Balducci, Boelens *et al.*, 2011) and celebrates its speculative nature, as opposed to a pretend-ability to erase uncertainty, by defining it as

> the investigation of 'virtualities' unseen in the present; the speculation about what may yet happen; the temporary inquiry into what at a given time and place we might yet think or do and how this might influence socially and environmentally just spatial form. (Hillier, 2007: 225, as in Balducci, 2011: 487)

Balducci (2011: 538), drawing on Lindblom, advocates the potential of plurality of actors, powers and interests – and of 'taking choices to interact[ion] and even to conflict' – in planning practice as the source of positive exploration and 'social probing' (Lindblom, 1990, as in Balducci, 2011:538). His reflection on practice acknowledges the limitations to purely open exploratory approaches brought about by politics and suggests developing a middle way 'that could balance exploration and certainty (Balducci, 2011:545). Balducci, Fedeli and Pasqui (2011) suggest that three ingredients are crucial for innovative practices to be adopted: motivated individuals, contexts open to change and strategies supporting new ways of thinking.

More markedly than elsewhere, in the UK theory and practice of strategic planning have merged with the concept of spatial planning since the outset (Tewdwr-Jones and Williams, 2001; Harris and Hooper, 2004). Tewdwr-Jones (2012: 53; see also Tewdwr-Jones *et al.*, 2010) sees the theoretical and political origins of strategic spatial planning in three areas: re-territorialisation and rescaling (following Brenner, 2004); Europeanisation; and integration of sub-national policy-making. Many tensions are generated as a result, relating to scale and multi-level governance as well as with multiple definitions of space (e.g. 'spaces of flow' versus 'spaces of places', as in Richardson and Jensen, 2003: 11, but also Tewdwr-Jones and Williams, 2001). Harris and Hooper – following Healey (2001) – suggest that in the UK strategic spatial planning has been pursuing 'forms of practice that are less sectoral and centralized than in the past' as well as aspiring to a horizontally integrated and 'joined-up' approach to policy-making (Harris and Hooper, 2004: 150). The Royal Town Planning Institute embraced this view by redefining planning 'as a strategic co-ordinating mechanism rather than strictly as a statutory land use activity' (Tewdwr-Jones *et al.*, 2000: 666, as in Harris and Hooper, 2004: 151). In a more comprehensive vein, Haughton *et al.* (2010: 5) summarise four defining characteristics for British spatial planning: 'an emphasis on long term strategic thinking' coagulating into 'agreed spatial strategies', a tool 'bringing coherence to increasingly fragmented systems of governance', 'a belief that planning has a central role in moving society towards sustainable development' and a tension towards 'inclusivity' and the opening up towards more sectors and actors in society.

Haughton *et al.* (2010: 2) suggest that 'some of the most innovative spatial planning practices are now being found outside the mainstream regulatory functions of planning'. He goes further by seeing 'spatial planning as the continuous remaking of planning and the spaces of planning' (Haughton *et al.*, 2010: 53).

Strategic spatial planning has taken different forms in the four nations of the United Kingdom, in what has been defined a 'differential experimentation' (Morphet, 2011). These different ways of developing and engendering strategy have their roots in the very diverse contexts for planning and governance that have been forming in England, Wales, Scotland and Northern Ireland since devolution has started to take momentum. Although rarely discussed in-depth in the international arena, devolution and the relational forms that narratives of sustainable development, democracy and institutional design have developed in the devolved nations are – according to many (e.g. Allmendinger and Tewdwr-Jones, 2006; Keating, 2006; Goodwin *et al.*, 2006; Haughton *et al.*, 2010; Tewdwr-Jones, 2012) – key to understanding and interpreting the emerging varied landscape for planning in the UK. Supporting the idea that context is important in strategic planning, Allmendinger and Tewdwr-Jones (2006) suggest that understandings of territory, identity and spatial planning go hand in hand with the (re)definition(s) of local spatial governance in the British regions.

Rather than presenting a summary of British approaches to strategic spatial planning, this chapter focuses specifically and in depth on the one decade-long Welsh experience with strategic spatial planning. It presents the evolution of strategic planning in Wales by highlighting similarities and differences with practices taking place elsewhere in the British Isles. As a thorough spatial analysis of the Wales Spatial Plan is available in Harris and Thomas (2009), this chapter will deliberately focus on an analysis of what 'strategic' means in the context of planning in Wales. The section below will introduce the context within which the Wales Spatial Plan (WSP) was first devised in 2004 and revised in 2008, as well as the Wales Infrastructure Plan (WIP), before discussing the most recent developments in the first completely devolved Welsh Planning Act 2015 (National Assembly for Wales, 2015). Drawing on the literature referred to above, the section will look closely at how the concept and understanding of strategic spatial planning has shifted in the – now three – definitions of strategy in the Welsh context and how this relates to specific phases of devolution, and policy-making, in Wales. The final section will draw conclusions from the Welsh case to link with the overall framing of strategic planning adopted in the book.

## The Welsh context: making sense of a devolved country and its diverse territory

Wales is the smallest nation of the United Kingdom, with a population of around 3 million – mostly concentrated in the former industrial south and in the northeast of the country – and vast portions of the country are designated as national parks and are still based on mostly rural and tourism-related economies. Within the UK, it has long been considered a region, and it is in fact comparable in size to some of the smallest English regions. Wales is not a rich country, with little natural resources apart from the potential for sustainable energy production, and its infrastructure network is limited and dated, leaving big sections of the population virtually cut off from linking up to the global economy. Deep differences between the conurbations and the countryside, between the affluent urban south and the areas still scarred by the industrial past, or those struggling to achieve sustainable development, characterise Wales; yet, alongside the language, it is its landscape and the distinct territories of the country that underpin its identity as a nation. The many contradictions linked to its territories (developed versus underdeveloped, densely urbanised versus unspoiled nature, etc.) are consistently used by assembly members and Welsh members of parliament as metaphors to justify policies, and particularly to highlight the distinctiveness of Welsh policy-making, in the ongoing process of devolution.

Devolution has affected the nations of the UK at a different pace. Officially initiated in 1997 by the Labour government, it has so far impacted mostly on Scotland – traditionally already substantially different in its legal and administrative systems from England – with Wales following suit at increased speed and Northern Ireland pacing behind, slowly due to political circumstances but steadily since recent progress of the peace process.

Before the introduction of the Welsh Assembly (WA) in 1999, the Welsh Development Agency (WDA) had been in charge for supporting regional development and the Welsh Office (WO) for policy-making. In WO times government seemed distant from Wales and policies developed by the Conservative government were met with discontent among the Labour-voting Welsh population (Morgan and Rees, 2000). Owing to its industrial past, since its inception, WA politics, as those of most Local Authorities (LAs), have been traditionally dominated by the Labour Party. A marker of Welsh politics' difference from English politics and constituencies, and possibly of the different character (e.g. their strong emphasis on sustainability) and more open nature of its policies, the predominance of the Labour Party has brought about uncomfortable and unhealthy situations too, where the lack of opposition has at times produced condescending, if not outright corrupted, networks and arenas (e.g. the so-called 'Taffia', see Morgan, 2006). The first three terms of government in Wales saw a Labour/LibDem coalition, a full Labour government and a Labour/Plaid Cymru coalition. WA priorities pursued so far remained broadly unaltered: economic development, sustainability and equality and social justice (Welsh Assembly Government, 2003 and 2007). There is also a distinct focus on joined-up thinking and an integrated approach – across government levels and statutory boundaries as well as with various actors in partnerships – to policy-making and service delivery. The WA even developed a 'policy integration tool' that assesses any policy produced against the Assembly's core objectives (Haughton *et al.*, 2010: 138).

Within an accepted and shared view of government as an enabler for the market and fostering the economy, the dialectic relationship developed between Welsh government and Westminster in the 14 years during which Labour led the UK government has developed into a more sustained exchange on the role of the public sector in democratic life and service delivery. Since the first Blair term as

Prime Minister, the public sector in Britain has started a process of modernisation of public administration aiming towards transparency, efficient use of resources and effective service delivery inspired by New Public Management theories. Administrative reforms have resulted in substantial changes that have affected Wales too, albeit with some delay in comparison with England. As a consequence, requirements on planners and civil servants generally have materialised into specific targets to complete specific procedures, both in development planning and development control, and pressures on individuals and divisions have considerably increased following the global economic crisis which resulted in substantial cuts to resources available in the public sector.

The first Minister in charge of planning in Wales was a former planning academic, very well embedded in Labour networks and the cabinet. According to Harris and Thomas (2009), her personal history and role have been crucial for the peculiar concept of strategic planning initially developed and pursued in Wales, and for its strong rooting in professional circles and academic debates. Flanking the Minister was an enthusiastic planner with extensive experience in the public sector, particularly at unitary authority level, acting as the first Chief Planning Officer.

The construction of the nation aligned with the development of an approach to strategic spatial planning (see Harris and Thomas, 2009, for an accurate interpretation of this process) as a response to specific regional goals: 'part of the process involves claims to policy innovation to meet distinctive Welsh needs' (Harris and Thomas, 2009: 50). In respect to city and regional planning, in 1999 the WA took on the policy-making, subordinate legislative and decision-making powers formerly in the hands of the WO (Powell, 2001: 215). The WO used to be responsible for the production of Planning Guidance (Wales) Planning Policy and of a series of Technical Advice Notes (TANs), both of which had few distinctively 'Welsh' features and mostly replicated English approaches to planning. One of the first things the newly founded WA initiated was a 'Welsh Planning Research Programme' with the view that

> Devolution does not mean separation; it does not mean inventing differences where they do not exist. But it does involve responding to needs and circumstances from the perspective of the new institution with direct democratic accountability to the people of Wales. (Powell, 2001: 217, which echoes also in Welsh Assembly Government, 2004: 4)

The WA swiftly embarked in a process of 'radical' policy review (Powell, 2001: 218) that fed into Planning Policy Wales (PPW) while the first WA's Corporate Plan (2000) stated the intent to form a 'Spatial Planning Framework' complementary to policy within three years. This latter had to be in line with the European Spatial Development Perspective (ESDP) and to provide a background for unitary development plans and decision-making (Powell, 2001: 218). The spatial framework was considered a crucial link between the principles of the WA's Corporate Plan (e.g. sustainable development) and development planning in Wales as well as a fundamental cornerstone to build consensus on the overall pattern of development and priorities, reconciling aspirations for economic development with the needs of people and the environment in the context of the search for development which is truly sustainable. (Powell, 2001: 219)

Until recently, the WA produced secondary legislation; following a step change in the devolution process only in July 2015, the first Welsh Planning Bill entirely developed in Wales has achieved royal assent.

The only other level of government providing planning services in Wales is constituted by the 25 LAs (22 unitary authorities and three national parks); these are in charge for the development of land-use plans and for local planning services delivery. The WA is largely dependent on LAs for the delivery of plans and policies. This constitutes a double-edged sword as, while being the level of government nearer to the people, there is widespread acknowledgement that Wales is characterised by 'individual identities and fierce local rivalries' (Harris and Thomas, 2009: 47) and the strong individualism displayed by some LAs acts as a barrier for effective cross-boundary work.

## The three lives of strategic spatial planning in Wales: innovation, normalisation and alignment

### *The 2004 Wales Spatial Plan*

The first Wales Spatial Plan (WSP) was produced in 2004 – almost at the same time as the Planning and Compulsory Purchase Order Act (re)introducing regional planning in the whole of the UK – and, by 'aim(ing) to co-ordinate different policies and their impacts across a territory' (Harris and Hooper, 2004: 149), it was the first tool ever to describe, analyse, make sense and interpret Wales *per se*, independently from England:

> This first Wales Spatial Plan is about reflecting honestly and clearly the way a whole range of activity and investment occurs across our particular geographic space and using our knowledge to shape the future. It aims to ensure the Welsh Assembly Government's policies and programmes come together effectively with the workings of local government, business and other partners across Wales, to enable a truly sustainable future – one that works for all the different parts of Wales. It sets a strategic, integrating agenda for the next 20 years. (Welsh Assembly Government, 2004: 3)

The WSP 'politicised' space, highlighting its double nature of physical container and political arena – and presenting Wales as a political, not just administrative, region (Harris and Hooper, 2006: 141). The 2004 WSP contained a vision and six aims for the whole of Wales. In addition, the plan introduced six regions in Wales, and described them in terms of functions and local characteristics; these six regions should provide the basis for improved inter-authority cooperation and shared delivery of public services, and for each of them a vision and a strategy to support collaborative work, as well as a set of actions to be undertaken at local and central level, were introduced. These were limited and for some (e.g. Glasson and Marshall, 2007) there is more description than vision in the WSP. A widespread criticism referred to the difficulty in pinning down character for the more rural areas of Wales. All sub-areas lacked prescribed boundaries. The boundaries and future directions for the regions would be self-defined through a process of exchange and the local endogenous development of narratives. This approach implied an innovative definition of space, much discussed in academic literature, but poorly understood on the ground and among practitioners (Haughton *et al.*, 2010; Welsh Assembly Government, 2012). Also, the way the plan was to be linked to policies was seen as open and developing with the plan's implementation: 'the linkages between the plan and different fields are to be negotiated rather than prescribed' (Harris and Hooper, 2006: 147). The WSP's peculiar way of dealing with uncertainty was to provide a platform for negotiation among various stakeholders and a 'direction of travel' (Harris and Thomas, 2009), in so doing relinquishing a strong directive role and creating 'useful uncertainty' (Haughton *et al.*, 2010: 159). This lack of certainty on crucial land allocation, though, was seen negatively by economic stakeholders (particularly developers) who feared that their efforts to maximise returns would be scattered on multiple consultation tables in LAs rather than concentrated on one, national, table. The lack of direction also seemed to fail to effectively guide choices of national interest, for example the budgeting and allocation of infrastructure. In a country that had mostly focused on foreign inward investment, 'The plan in its present form [was] considered to be insufficiently detailed or connected to funding programmes for it to act' as a framework for investment (Harris and Hooper, 2006: 143).

In terms of contents, the WSP appeared similar to other spatial strategies produced in the UK, such as in Ireland and Scotland, but 'of limited depth and complexity in comparison' (Harris and Thomas, 2009: 50). There seemed to be a clear choice in not introducing targets in the WSP and leaving it as high-level strategy in order to avoid the pitfalls experienced in Scotland and Northern Ireland, hence '[t]he approach adopted in Wales to spatial planning lies somewhere between the political and the technical' (Harris and Hooper, 2006: 140). Among the very first data used to develop the strategy were maps of multiple deprivation and Objective 1 support areas as well as maps depicting communication networks and topography. In fact, the main preoccupation of the WSP focused on reducing inequalities in space (Harris and Hooper, 2004; Harris, 2006), to a certain extent following central narratives in the ESDP (Kunzmann, 1998) and a longstanding issue of extreme socioeconomic differences between the urban cores and the rural peripheries in Wales (Alden, 2006), known as the 'prosperity gap' (Welsh Assembly Government, 2002). Inequalities had been on the agenda as a priority for a long time in Wales, with a widespread cross-parties political view that restructuring needed to be facilitated by public 'policy interventions – including planning interventions' (Harris and Thomas, 2009: 45, also Rees and Lambert, 1981, as in Harris and Thomas, 2009). Local culture and identity, also an issue at the heart of Welsh policy-making, was openly addressed by the WSP too, suggesting support for traditions. Remarkably, though, the WSP said very little in respect to these issues specifically, and particularly to the Welsh language.

The process developed to produce the WSP was seen as equally important to – if not more than – the product itself (cf. Powell, 2001: 219; Alden, 2006: 217; Harris, 2006: 101–102; Haughton *et al.*, 2010: 140–141) and it included research, seminars and discussions in international and academic circles, between WA and Planning Officers in all LAs, and various other stakeholders, both within Welsh Government Offices and via outreach. In order to maintain a two-ways line of communication, six spatial plan areas were formed with a National Steering Group chaired by the Minister overseeing progress of their work (Alden, 2006: 218; Harris, 2006: 102; Harris and Thomas, 2009: 52–53). According to Haughton *et al.*, 'The intention for those leading the process was that open consultation and deliberation would allow a distinctively Welsh approach to spatial planning to develop, rather than necessarily replicating the models adopted elsewhere' (Haughton *et al.*, 2010: 140). Also, following a consultation exercise covering not just the contents but also the process and nature of the plan, the character of it changed considerably, moving from a planning document of strategic nature to the basic corporate document for policy coordination (Harris and Thomas, 2009):

> the potential of the plan is evident in the increased political and professional profile that the plan has enjoyed in the past three years. The fact that a spatial plan can become one of the most important corporate policy documents of a government administration is a very positive lesson to be drawn from the Welsh experience. (Harris, 2006: 103; also Harris and Hooper, 2006: 142)

As a consequence of this, the Minister required all WA policies to consider the 'spatial implications of spending programs across Wales' (Alden, 2006: 217) to enhance effectiveness for planning activities. Spatial policy became crucial for 'securing coherence in policy delivery' (Harris and Thomas, 2009: 65). The Beecham Review (Welsh Assembly Government, 2006) on local services delivery, for example, relates to the WSP, and specifically to the six regions, as platforms for cooperation and partnership work. Strategic planning quickly developed, in the Welsh context, into the spatialisation of the Assembly's corporate project (Haughton *et al.*, 2010: 143).

The WSP did not have a statutory character requiring local plans to conform to it, although local plans had as a statutory requirement to have regard to it; and this 'regard' constituted part of the plans' test of soundness. The WSP was voluntary and, in absence of a statutory dimension, strong political will and consensus were needed for meaningful implementation (cf. Harris and Hooper, 2006; and Harris and Thomas, 2009). The WSP 2004 was backed by all Welsh Ministers and hence had a strong position in policy-making. This was crucial as it was to be applied rather than directly implemented: 'the Plan's essential function is the setting out of a common agenda for further application or elaboration (Harris and Thomas, 2009: 57). The WSP supported joined up thinking at a time of potential policy-making hyperactivity (Harris and Hooper, 2006) and in so doing it became a requirement for governments to abide. Notably, the non-statutory status sped up the process of preparing and approving it since it did not have to be consulted upon as extensively as statutory documents have. This aspect was criticised by some on principle, although, given the nature of the 2004 WSP, and its emphasis on building shared visions, this was not considered particularly worrisome by most actors at the time.

Observers interpreted the WSP in different ways. Some saw it in continuity with a strong tradition of regional planning for economic development and in conjunction with a renewed interest in it supported by devolution and the reintro-duction of statutory regional planning via the 2004 Planning and Compulsory Purchase Act, at national level, and by the ESDP, at European level (Alden, 2006: 221). The WSP was a 'strategic framework' first and foremost as it was under-lined by the strong commitment given to it by the Welsh First Minister and all eight cabinet ministers: 'Planning is no longer regarded as just a regulatory and bureaucratic process: it has galvanized people to change places, and has become a core activity of government' (Alden, 2006: 217). The document was seen also as a way to fill the gap in strategic capacity due to the fragmentation of the Welsh territory into the 25 LAs (Harris, 2006: 99). Haughton *et al.* (2010: 133) suggest the Welsh approach is peculiar and in many ways unique due to 'the combination of fuzzy boundaries with high-level policy and a lack of strong direction on issues such as housing', considered very important in the UK for any nation-wide docu-ment of strategic relevance. Critics also hinted at the fact that the WSP was too Wales-focused, presenting little in the way of context maps or an interpretation of supra-ordinate policy for Wales.

The 2004 WSP was in many ways strategic. It looked at the long range and aimed to develop frames of reference for a multitude of actors in a shared manner. Co-production extended well beyond service delivery, up to the definition of the regions' boundaries, and the process was very open. More than anything else, the process – and the document itself, produced outside the boundaries of traditional statutory planning – was creative and supported experimentation, working with uncertainty in a dynamic manner, addressing fuzzy boundaries, collaborating across levels of government and between LAs, and straddling between institu-tionalised and developing legitimation modes. The WSP owed its character and scope to the small team of committed individuals in charge for its production and provided the basis for innovative ways to look at the territory of Wales and its future.

All in all, the form, nature and process of the WSP were shaped to serve the nature and stage of devolution Wales was undergoing: 'the establishment of the Assembly, and the wider project of political devolution, have been important factors in setting the preconditions for the introduction of a national spatial plan-ning framework' (Harris and Hooper, 2006: 139). Also important were the time coincidence of the academic debates on spatial planning and the biographies and personal history of the actors leading the process. The context in which the document was developed was a substantial element in shaping its contents and process, but also in defining the extent and duration of its use.

### The 2008 Wales Spatial Plan update

In 2007 the WA issued an interim statement on the WSP implementation, duly followed in 2008 by a WSP update, which also acted as a regional strategy for Wales following the 2004 Planning and Compulsory Purchase Act requirements. The 2008 WSP developed from the critiques moved towards the previous spatial plan, but the broad 20 years period for the plan and its cross-cutting national spatial priorities remained broadly unchanged (Welsh Assembly Government, 2008: 3). The WSP 2008 update aimed at producing evidence to inform policy; shaping policies sensitive to place; providing a framework within which all sectors could work together; and informing plans and aligning investments to spatial priorities. It presented Area strategies for each of the six regions, developed in the previous years by the area groups. Delivery was going to be linked to annual reports, with indicators to monitor progress. The 2008 update also brought 'the Wales Spatial Plan into line with *One Wales*' (Welsh Assembly Government, 2008: 3), the WA's guiding document on sustainability policy. However, while the 2004 WSP had all Ministers endorsing it, the only minister signing the 2008 update was the one responsible for its preparation, the Minister for finance and public service delivery (taking regular reports from the Spatial planning Minister). Similarly to the 2004 WSP, the 2008 update remained part of the test of soundness for the Local Development Plans (LDPs) but was not part of the statutory development plan framework (so LDPs did not have to conform to it).

According to Haughton *et al.* (2010), the 2008 update of the WSP was spatially stronger, having absorbed some concept from the ESDP (2010: 141) and developed these through the work of the sub-regions (2010: 145). The 2008 WSP continued to be regarded as main vehicle for policy integration (2010: 140), an aspect which remained 'in many senses both stronger and more distinctive than the WSP's spatial dimension' (2010: 141).

The elements of strategy present in the 2004 WSP broadly remained in the 2008 update, although the refined Area strategies, and the efforts to monitor progress, evidently tried to address some of the intractable elements linked to uncertainty characterising the previous spatial plan and steered the exercise towards action.

The 2008 WSP update, however, addressed uncertainty by providing a basis for discussions in each of the regions and by offering a weakly defined direction for the whole of Wales, in so doing partially reproducing the uncertainties the previous spatial plan failed to address. By this time the plan was appreciated outside the planning arena in sectors of public service delivery where 'the process of building a strong policy community where spatial issues can be debated at different scales is no mean achievement' (Haughton *et al.*, 2010: 158). Within planning the effort to build consensus was seen positively but the lack of implementation on the ground and – generally – the unwillingness to treat crucial themes and pass them on to LAs tainted the view most actors in both the public and private sectors held of the plan (Haughton *et al.*, 2010: 143). It probably does not come as a surprise that the test of soundness for LDPs never proved contentious due to the level of generality of the indications in the 2008 update too.

In March 2012, the Minister for local government and communities and Minister of environment and sustainable development announced that responsibility for the spatial plan would move from the one ministry to the other and 'that the regional Ministerial and officials' structures relating to the Wales Spatial Plan will be discontinued, representing a significant simplification of the regional partnership landscape'. They acknowledged, however, the successes achieved by the WSP in the past eight years in integrating service delivery and working across boundaries.

### The Wales Infrastructure Plan

This change of direction, despite the evident progress in certain areas, did not come as a surprise as, since the previous year – mainly to ensure transparency on how capital spending is allocated across Wales but also as a way to align spatial policies to mainstream discourses of delivery and effectiveness and to provide a closer link with the budget (Welsh Assembly Government, 2012) – the WA had introduced the Wales Infrastructure Plan (WIP). The WIP was also prepared in order to cater for those actors in search of more certainty to justify their investments: 'a useful planning tool for the private sector' (Welsh Assembly Government, 2012: 19).

Certainty is provided indirectly to the private sector through the WIP by presenting a (binding on government actors) vision for public spending, both in terms of sector and location. The WIP gave details of how public funding in economic and social infrastructure would be allocated to specific sectors (i.e. education, health, transport, broadband, housing and flood defence) and presented simple maps with indicative (given the scale) location of investment, which was detailed in subsequent tables. Although the WIP shows little spatial awareness, nor any in-depth consideration of spatial consequences of investments, it gives a nod to the 2008 Wales Spatial Plan, suggesting that spatial planning remains important:

> A key purpose of spatial planning is to integrate across Ministerial portfolios and to recognise that policies and their delivery should reflect economic, social and geographical differences across Wales – one size does not fit all. We will ensure that this ethos of spatial planning is integrated into the Plan from the outset when developing the knowledge required to inform nationally strategic infrastructure investment decisions. (Welsh Assembly Government, 2012: 108)

The overall vision for the plan focused on boosting growth and jobs. The vision unravelled in seven highest-level priorities: improved transport links, particularly east–west; improved telecommunication and broadband; support to the development of the energy industry; investment in housing; delivery of more efficient and economical public services; improvement of the quality of education estates; and development of enterprise zones. The WIP saw delivery as central to its effectiveness and focused on schemes of national significance, supporting collaboration and cooperation within the public sector, and developing new routes for innovative financing of infrastructure. It makes also reference to *One Wales* (Welsh Assembly Government, 2007) and to the Sustainable Development Bill soon to be introduced.

The WIP can be considered a strategic document too, but in a very different way from the WSP. It was negotiated among stakeholders, mainly in the public sector, but not widely and democratically co-produced. The WIP addressed multi-level governance by providing a centrally-produced guiding document for investment. It was selective and long-term, and it was the first document of its kind in Wales, but its approach to dealing with uncertainty is very traditional and focused on reducing it rather than finding new ways to work with it. By leveraging on traditional top-down mechanisms of implementation, it also did not substantially foster transformative practice.

### The Planning (Wales) Act 2015

By mid-2014 the WA announced that the WIP has contributed to taking £3 billion of new capital investment into Wales since its launch in early 2012. Following the success of an approach able to provide some degree of certainty to investors, the first Planning Bill (National Assembly for Wales, 2015) developed in Wales for Wales introduced the National Development Framework for Wales (NDFW) (also called a 'national land use plan' in media releases): a statutory plan setting out priorities for the development and use of land in the whole of Wales. The NDFW must take into account the Wales Transport Strategy and all other statutory plans in Wales will have to comply with the framework. The framework needs to be appraised for sustainability, including the impact it would have on the Welsh language. The Planning (Wales) Bill 2015 defines no specified period for NDFW as each needs to indicate its duration until decay but – given their role and function – the frameworks can be revised at any time and are likely to be documents pitched on the longer term. Following an emphasis on delivery, the NDFW identifies Developments of National Significance (DNS) for which land would be subject to compulsory purchase and Welsh Ministers – not LAs, as had been the case until the new bill – have power of decision. DNS have been criticised for taking decision-making on crucial infrastructure – possibly the most controversial – out of localities and out of the hands of councils' elected members. The 12 weeks' consultation of the NDFW is making little amends against the perceived limitation in democratic accountability introduced in Wales for the first time with this provision.

Another statutory document introduced by the recent Planning (Wales) Bill 2015 that presents some strategic features is the Strategic Development Plan

(SDP). Following submission of proposals (invited or not) by a responsible LA, Strategic planning areas, comprising all of the area of one LA and all or some of the area of other LAs, can be set up to 'tackle issues that transcend LAs' boundaries, such as housing and areas for economic growth'. Strategic planning panels, holding the power to adopt plans, can be established by Welsh Ministers who are in charge for the approval of SDPs. Strategic planning areas need to produce SDPs in conformity with the NDFW and any existing adjoining SDP. Each SDP's duration is defined in the plan. LDPs needs to be in general conformity to both NDFW and SDPs and those in place at the time of approval of either need to be reviewed by the responsible authority to conform. Strategic planning panels comprise LAs' members as well as other nominated members (up to one-third of the total members of the panel). Costs associated to the set up and work of each panel will be covered by the Strategic planning areas' constituent LAs.

The provisions of the Planning (Wales) Act 2015 address certainty in a way that is radically different and much more traditional in comparison to the WSP, the central assumption being that a hierarchy of three statutory plans with binding character on both public and private actors would be more suited to effectively address uncertainty for stakeholders and investors alike. Consequently, the strategic features of both the NDFW and the SDPs are substantially different from those present in the WSP. The NDFW works on the long term with the SDPs possibly on the long to medium term. Both plans are openly selective, focusing only on those features that need to be treated at, respectively, national or regional scale to provide a meaningful solution. While the NDFW represents an eminently top-down approach, the SDPs should be the result of co-production among both public and private stakeholders. However, the treatment of multi-level and cross-boundary governance is addressed in very traditional ways, resorting to a rigid hierarchy embedded in the institutionalised legal system of planning, substantially limiting the creative potential of the documents and reverting to a codified and static type of legitimation.

## Taking stock of strategic planning in Wales

Definitions of strategy in planning in Wales have changed and evolved considerably in the past decade, and so have the documents, processes, goals and outputs of it. A first phase – defined by the development and refinement of the WSP – was very creative, embraced relational thinking and suggested a great openness towards change and the creative shaping of strategic planning, making processes suited to the newly devolved nation. The form, content and process of the WSP all thrive on institutional and political contexts yet to settle, and on a strong political will to search for innovative solutions to Welsh problems 'fitting' Wales, its people and its political structures. As evidence that strategic planning was straddling across policy areas, particularly interesting is the fact that actors involved in service delivery outside planning recognised the value and role of the WSP in supporting and shaping joint work and cross-boundary provisions – more than planners and developers ever did. It seems, however, that in subsequent years, with devolution settling in, and administrative reforms and financial restructuring taking the toll, the space for creativity shrank as the need for more effective policies and private investment to supply for the limited public finances increased. The second phase in strategy documents hinges on the WIP, a very pragmatic and dry document compared to the WSP, aiming almost only to leverage investments coming into Wales, working solely within given boundaries. The phase of experiments and strategic navigation ends abruptly with the provisions in the 2015 Planning (Wales) Bill, re-conducting strategic planning decisively within the realm of statutory planning and back to resorting to traditional rationales in respect to addressing uncertainties.

On the basis of the Welsh experience, it is evident that context is crucial in defining the space for strategic planning experiences; more openness seems to pertain to times of flux, while when arrangements settle spaces for creativity seem to close. Politics seems fundamental to define the boundaries for experimentation and the general goals of strategic planning. Individuals and their biographies seem to count too, not just to initiate new ways to look at problems and to support the emergence of innovative approaches, but also to ensure (or not) their absorption into more ordinary and fixed institutional arrangements. In a way, we can suggest here that strategic planning in Wales has been truly creative only when allowed – or called – to do so by the powers that be.

## References

Albrechts, L. (2004), 'Strategic (spatial) planning re-examined', *Environment and Planning B: Planning and Design*, 31, 743–758.

Albrechts, L. (2010), 'More of the same is not enough! How could strategic spatial planning be instrumental in dealing with the challenges ahead?', *Environment and Planning B: Planning and Design*, 37(6), 1115–1127.

Albrechts, L. (2012), 'Reframing strategic spatial planning by using a coproduction perspective', *Planning Theory*, 12(1), 46–63.

Albrechts, L. (2015), 'Ingredients for a more radical strategic spatial planning', *Environment and Planning B: Planning and Design*, 42, 510–525.

Albrechts, L. and Balducci, S. (2013), 'Practicing strategic planning: In search of critical features to explain the strategic character of plans', *DisP – The Planning Review*, 49(3), 16–27.

Alden, J. (2006), 'Regional planning: An idea whose time has come?', *International Planning Studies*, 11(3–4), 209–223.

Almendinger, P. and Tewdwr-Jones, M. (2006), 'Territory, identity and spatial planning', in Allmendinger, P. and Tewdwr-Jones, M. (Eds), *Territory, Identity and Spatial Planning: Spatial Governance in a Fragmented Nation*. Abingdon: Routledge.

Balducci, A. (2008), 'Constructing (spatial) strategies in complex environments', in Van Den Broek, J., Moulaert, F. and Oosterlynk, S. (Eds), *Empowering the Planning Fields: Ethics, Creativity and Action*. Leuven: Acco, pp. 79–99.

Balducci, A. (2011), 'Strategic planning as exploration', *Town Planning Review*, 82(5), 529–546.

Balducci, A., Boelens, L., Hillier, J., Nyseth T. and Wilkinson, C. (2011), 'Strategic spatial planning in uncertainty: Theory and exploratory practice', *Town Planning Review*, 82(5), 481–501.

Balducci, A., Fedeli, V. and Pasqui, G. (2011), *Strategic Planning for Contemporary Urban Regions*. Farnham: Ashgate.

Brenner, N. (2004), *New State Spaces: Urban Governance and the Rescaling of Statehood*. Oxford: Oxford University Press.

Friedmann, J. (2004), 'Strategic spatial planning and the longer range', *Planning Theory and Practice*, 5, 50–56.

Glasson, J. and Marshall, T. (2007), *Regional Planning*. London and New York: Routledge.

Goodwin, M., Jones, M. and Jones, R. A. (2006), 'The theoretical challenge of devolution and constitutional change in the United Kingdom', in Allmendinger, P. and Tewdwr-Jones, M. (Eds), *Territory, Identity and Spatial Planning: Spatial Governance in a Fragmented Nation*. Abingdon: Routledge.

Harris, N. (2006), 'Increasing and spreading prosperity: Regional development, spatial planning and the enduring "prosperity gap" in Wales', in Adams, A., Alden, J. and Harris, N. (Eds), *Regional Development and Spatial Planning in an Enlarged European Union*. Aldershot: Ashgate, pp. 87–106.

Harris, N. and Hooper, A. (2004), 'Rediscovering the "spatial" in public policy and planning: An examination of the spatial content of sectoral policy documents', *Planning Theory & Practice*, 5(2), 147–169.

Harris, N. and Hooper, A. (2006), 'Redefining "the space that is Wales": Place, planning and the Wales Spatial Plan', in Allmendinger, P. and Tewdwr-Jones, M. (Eds), *Territory, Identity and Spatial Planning: Spatial Governance in a Fragmented Nation*. Abingdon: Routledge, pp. 139–152.

Harris, N. and Thomas, H. (2009), 'Making Wales: Spatial strategy making in a devolved context', in Davoudi, S. and Strange, I. (Eds), *Conceptions of Space and Place in Strategic Spatial Planning*. Abingdon: Routledge.

Haughton, G., Allmendinger, P., Counsell, D. and Vigar G. (2010), *The New Spatial Planning: Territorial Management with Soft Spaces and Fuzzy Boundaries*. Abingdon: Routledge.

Healey, P. (1997), 'The revival of strategic spatial planning in Europe', in Healey, P., Khakee, A., Motte, A. and Needham, B. (Eds), *Making Strategic Spatial Plans*. London: UCL Press, pp. 3–19.

Healey, P. (2001), 'Towards a more place-focused planning system in Britain', in Madanipour, A., Hull, A. and Healey, P. (Eds), *The Governance of Place: Space and Planning Processes*. Aldershot: Ashgate, pp. 265–286.

Healey, P. (2007), *Urban Complexity and Spatial Strategies: Towards a Relational Planning for Our Times*. London: Routledge.

Healey, P. (2009), 'In search of the "strategic" in strategic spatial planning', *Planning Theory and Practice*, 10(4), 439–457.

Hillier, J. (2007), *Stretching beyond the Horizon: A Multiplanar Theory of Spatial Planning and Governance*. Aldershot: Ashgate.

Hillier, J. (2011), 'Strategic navigation across multiple planes: Towards a Deleuzian-inspired methodology for strategic spatial planning', *Town Planning Review*, 82(5), 503–527.

Keating, M. (2006), 'Nationality, devolution and policy development in the United Kingdom', in Allmendinger, P. and Tewdwr-Jones, M. (Eds), *Territory, Identity and Spatial Planning: Spatial Governance in a Fragmented Nation*. Abingdon: Routledge.

Kunzmann, K. (1998), 'Planning for spatial equity in Europe', *International Planning Studies*, 3(1), 101–120.

Kunzmann, K. (2013), 'Strategic planning: A chance for spatial innovation and creativity', *DisP – The Planning Review*, 49(3), 28–31.

Mäntysalo, R. (2013), 'Copying with the paradox of strategic spatial planning', *DisP – The Planning Review*, 49(3), 51–52.

Mazza, L. (2013), 'If strategic "planning is everything, maybe it's nothing"', *DisP – The Planning Review*, 49(3), 40–42.

Morgan, K. (2006), 'Re-scaling the capital: Cardiff as a city-region', in Hooper, A. and Punter, J. (Eds), *Capital Cardiff 1975–2020*. Cardiff: University of Wales Press, pp. 293–310.

Morgan, K. and Rees, G. (2000), 'Learning by doing: Devolution and the governance of economic development in Wales', in Chaney, P., Hall, T. and Pitthouse, A. (Eds), *New Governance – New Democracy? Post-devolution Wales*. Cardiff: University of Wales Press, pp. 126–171.

Morphet, J. (2011), 'Delivering infrastructure through spatial planning: the multi-scalar approach in the UK', *Local Economy*, 26(4), 285–293.

National Assembly for Wales (2015), *The Planning (Wales) Act 2015*. Cardiff: National Assembly for Wales.

Needham, B. (2000), 'Making strategic spatial plans: a situational methodology!', in Salet, W. and Faludi, A. (Eds), *Revival of Strategic Planning*. Amsterdam: Royal Netherlands Academy of Arts and Sciences, pp. 79–90.

Powell, K. (2001), 'Devolution, planning guidance and the role of the planning system in Wales', *International Planning Studies*, 6(2), 215–222.

Richardson, T. and Jensen, O. B. (2003), 'Linking discourse and space: Towards a cultural sociology of space in analysing spatial policy discourses', *Urban Studies*, 40(1), 7–22.

Salet, W. and Faludi, A. (2000a), 'Three approaches to strategic spatial planning', in Salet, W. and Faludi, A. (Eds), *The Revival of Strategic Spatial Planning*. Amsterdam: Royal Netherlands Academy of Arts and Sciences, pp. 1–10.

Salet, W. and Faludi, A. (Eds) (2000b), *The Revival of Strategic Spatial Planning*. Amsterdam: Royal Netherlands Academy of Arts and Sciences.

Tewdwr-Jones, M. (2012), *Spatial Planning and Governance: Understanding UK Planning*. Basingstoke: Palgrave Macmillan.

Tewdwr-Jones, M., Bishop, K. and Wilkinson, D. (2000), '"Euroscepticism", political agendas and spatial planning: British national and regional planning policy in uncertain times', *European Planning Studies*, 8(5), 651–668.

Tewdwr-Jones, M. and Williams, R. H. (2001), *The European Dimension of British Planning*. London: Spon.

Tewdwr-Jones, M., Gallent, N. and Morphet, J. (2010), 'An anatomy of spatial planning: Coming to terms with the spatial element in UK planning', *European Planning Studies*, 18(2), 239–257.

Welsh Assembly Government (2002), *A Winning Wales*. Cardiff: Welsh Assembly Government.

Welsh Assembly Government (2003), *Wales: A Better Country*. Cardiff: Welsh Assembly Government.

Welsh Assembly Government (2004), *People, Places, Futures: The Wales Spatial Plan*. Cardiff: Welsh Assembly Government.

Welsh Assembly Government (2006), *Beyond Boundaries: Citizen-centred Local Services for Wales*. Cardiff: Welsh Assembly Government.

Welsh Assembly Government (2007), *One Wales, One Planet*. Cardiff: Welsh Assembly Government.

Welsh Assembly Government (2008), *People, Places, Futures: The Wales Spatial Plan 2008 Update*. Cardiff: Welsh Assembly Government.

Welsh Assembly Government (2012), *Wales Infrastructure Investment Plan for Growth and Jobs*. Cardiff: Welsh Assembly Government.

Regional and local experiences

# 13 Strategic planning for transformation in post-apartheid Johannesburg, South Africa

*Philip Harrison*

## Introduction

Albrechts (2013, 2015) offers the *possibility* of a radical practice of strategic spatial planning that could challenge the existing socio-spatial order, and suggests 'co-production' as the *mode of engagement*. The idea of co-production, which was famously introduced by Elinor Ostrom, describes how incorporating the ideas, resources and practical engagement of actors outside an agency may transform both the actions of the agency and the outcomes of these action (see, for example, Ostrom, 1996). As Watson (2014) indicates, however, the use of the term has evolved and diversified, with Albrechts (2015, p. 515) defining his notion of co-production in planning as:

> a collective endeavour, with citizens as a part of action not its object and as a combination of a needs-based and rights-based approach ... an inclusive and multivocal arena, that is grounded in a deeper understanding of the complex dynamics of urban and regional relations where value systems can be articulated, local and scientific knowledge can be combined on an equal base, shared strategic conviction can grow, and conflicts are reframed in a less antagonistic manner.

Is Albrecht's hope around co-production for strategic spatial planning warranted or naively misplaced? It is, arguably, impossible to answer this question through further speculative theoretical engagement. We may, however, find partial answers as we develop a *corpus* of concretely situated reflections. Have there been actual instances of radical strategic spatial planning – even in a partial form – that would support the aspirations expressed by Albrechts?

The first question is where to look for possible case studies. Albrechts (2015, p. 521) observes that 'the surrounding political regime enhances or inhibits the institutional change needed for the more radical strategic planning to be adopted'. South Africa's transition from racial authoritarianism to non-racial democracy would, at first sight, appear to be precisely the context that would support the emergence of transformative forms of strategic spatial planning. It would surely have offered 'the moments of opportunity when strategic ambitions seem to engage with political structures' (Albrechts, 2015, p. 521). But, have more radical forms of strategic spatial planning actually emerged in this context? If not, what chance is there for them elsewhere? If so, what insight does it provide on the political and institutional conditions that would support this form of practice? Watson (2014) has cautiously identified moments of co-production in community-based planning processes in Cape Town, South Africa, but the possibility of co-production in city-wide planning processes, including strategic spatial planning, remains unexamined.

A further question is whether 'transformative' and 'empowering' forms of strategic planning practice may exist without co-production, and even without significant levels of participation. In other words, could less participatory and more technocratic modes of planning produce outcomes that strengthen the position of the urban poor in both material and political terms?

In South Africa, there is a legislated requirement for strategic spatial planning. The Municipal Systems Act (2000) requires all municipalities to prepare Integrated Development Plans (IDPs) that promote developmental objectives, including greater levels of social and spatial equity. These plans must be prepared through demonstrably participatory process. IDPs have a medium-term time horizon as they are linked to five-year electoral cycles, but they are required to include longer-term Spatial Development Frameworks (SDFs). There are reviews of IDPs which suggest wide variation in performance in terms of both the depth of participation and the extent of the participatory process. As a broad assessment, IDPs have served a transformative purpose by redirecting material resources from areas of wealth to areas of historical deprivation, but their success in changing the underlying inequalities in spatial form is significantly less evident (Harrison, 2006; Todes, 2012).

While IDPs must be prepared by all municipalities, irrespective of size or nature, it is only the larger metropolitan municipalities that have developed longer-term strategic plans. There is no requirement for these longer-term plans, but they have emerged as a strong component of municipal planning in cities, including Johannesburg, the focus of this chapter. The significance of Johannesburg for a study of strategic planning is indeed already acknowledged in an existing literature. There is a highly critical account of the ways in which the strategic plans and policies of the City of Johannesburg (COJ) have been implicated in 'neoliberal agendas' (for example, Bremner, 2004; Murray, 2008; Winkler, 2011), but also accounts that emphasize the messy and frequently inadequate, but complex, actions of the COJ in mediating and balancing the need for economic growth and competitiveness with the imperative to redistribute advantage to the urban poor and historically marginalized communities and individuals (Beall *et al.*, 2000; Parnell and Robinson, 2006; Lipietz, 2008; Robinson, 2008; Todes, 2012).

In exploring the case of Johannesburg I have drawn on these literatures but also on my own experience as a previous official in the COJ.[1] I have complemented this with the insights of two informants who have played a central role in the unfolding narrative. Rashid Seedat was a political activist in the 1980s but was drawn into local government structures in the early 1990s. By 2001, he was the official in charge of strategic planning in the COJ, and from 2011 has worked as the head of the (provincial) Gauteng Planning Commission. Herman Pienaar started his career in the 1980s as a spatial planner in municipal government structures, remaining in municipal government through and beyond the political transition. From the early 2000s, he has worked as the head of strategic spatial planning in the COJ, playing a central role in the construction of new forms of planning. Both informants assisted me greatly with their critical reflections on planning for transitioning and post-apartheid Johannesburg (Pienaar, 2014; Seedat, 2014).

## The context

The turn to strategic spatial planning in Johannesburg must be placed in the context of South Africa's long and turbulent transition from apartheid rule to a non-racial democracy. The bitter conflicts of the 1980s – the final full decade of apartheid rule – compelled both the state and its enemies to become increasingly practised at 'strategizing'. The state manoeuvred frenetically to retain control of the state while the exiled liberation movements, and their internal allies, strategized to defeat the state (Seedat, 2014).

There was a spatial element to this. The apartheid government controlled urbanization to keep black Africans from moving permanently to the cities but in 1986 it dropped these influx controls, replacing them with a still-born policy of 'orderly urbanization' which allowed black people to move to the cities, but which channelled them to the urban peripheries. The civic movement, largely aligned to the African National Congress (ANC), found the gap and mobilized at the grassroots in opposition to the remnants of apartheid spatial controls. There was also an element of forward thinking as the civics – supported by 'progressive planners' in universities and non-governmental agencies – debated the future spatial and governance arrangements of South Africa's towns and cities (Mabin and Smit, 1997; Harrison, Watson and Todes, 2008).

The unbanning of the liberation movements, and the release of political prisoners, including Nelson Mandela, in 1990, dramatically changed the trajectory of South Africa's history. National-level negotiations began formally in December 1991 with the launch of the Convention for a Democratic South Africa (CODESA). The negotiations were protracted and uncertain but did eventually lead to the agreement that resulted in South Africa's first democratic elections in April 1994. A complex institutional compromise emerged from the agreement. The new national constitution makes provision for three 'distinctive, interdependent and interrelated' spheres of government – national, provincial and municipal – required to work together on a cooperative basis (Republic of South Africa, 1996).[2] Although not classically federal, South Africa's system of 'cooperative governance' borrowed heavily from Germany's 'cooperative federalism' and, like Germany, many of the powers and functions of government are held concurrently across the spheres, requiring an extremely complex set of intergovernmental relationships (Klug, 2010).

A new system of local government evolved through the transition process. Fragmented, racially-defined local authorities, covering only urban areas, were consolidated into non-racial democratic municipalities that linked across urban and rural areas to cover all of the country. There was a transitional period from 1996 to 2000 in which local structures were still only partly consolidated. In Johannesburg, a metropolitan council was established but it had to share power with four metropolitan local councils – a costly and unwieldy arrangement that contributed to the near bankruptcy of the city in 1997. At the end of 2000 the transition was formally ended. For Johannesburg, it meant a single-tier metropolitan authority within the Province of Gauteng, which included two other metropolitan authorities, and a number of smaller local authorities. The ANC gained the majority in the provincial and municipal elections in Gauteng but there were, nevertheless, complex relational dynamics across the scale of government relating, at times, to factional politics within the party, but also to the different interests within the entangled system of 'multi-scalar governance' (Allen and Cochrane, 2010).

Strategic planning in the COJ should also be placed in terms of the evolving system of planning across the spheres of post-apartheid governance. Within the *national* sphere there has been a gradual evolution towards greater coherence in strategic planning, with the development of a Medium Term Strategic Framework to guide budgeting decisions, followed by the creation of a Department of Monitoring and Evaluation in the National Presidency and, in 2010, by a National Planning Commission which produced a National Development Plan (Vision 2030). Little progress has, however, been made in creating a coherent and workable national *spatial* framework. The approaches to planning have varied over time, despite the overall continuity of the ANC remaining in power. Immediately after the first democratic elections in 1994, the new government adopted the Reconstruction and Development Programme (RDP), a Keynesian programme of state-led service and infrastructure delivery. Only two years later, in 1996, President Mandela closed the RDP Office, introducing the mainstream macroeconomic stabilization strategy called Growth, Employment and Redistribution (GEAR), which was dismissed by opponents as 'neoliberal' (Bond, 2000) but defended by the government as a necessary response to the destabilizing forces of economic globalization. Under Mbeki's presidency (1999–2008), planning progressed, but mainly as a technocratic instrument to improve the quality of governance, but with the Accelerated and Shared Growth Initiative for South Africa (AsgiSA) of 2006, modifying the harsher elements of GEAR. The twin objectives of the National Development Plan, 2012, were 'eliminating poverty' and 'reducing inequality', although there has been vocal contest over the economic proposals in the plan.

At the provincial scale, planning systems emerged which parallel those of national government, but with considerable variance in effectiveness across the nine provinces. In the Province of Gauteng, strategic planning was relatively weak until the establishment of the Gauteng Planning Commission in 2011, and the election in 2014 of a new Premier with a determined spatial vision. Despite the constitutional requirement for cooperative governance, the linkage across the spheres of government has been difficult, with frequent tensions that were exacerbated by ambiguities in the national constitution over the distribution of planning powers and functions.

The rise of strategic spatial planning in South Africa was framed within these contexts but it also reflected the ideas in circulation globally at the time that South Africa's was making its transition to a non-racial democracy. These included, for example, the rise of strategic planning methodologies; the shift from both master planning and project-based approaches to strategic spatial planning; the 'third way' emphasis on joined-up or integrated planning; the focus on performance management and outcomes; and, the importance attached to participatory governance (Harrison, 2006; Robinson, 2012; Todes, 2012). South Africa's specificity comes from the interplay between a discursive shift in planning globally and the particular demands of a rapidly transitioning society.

## Strategic spatial planning in the city of Johannesburg

### Pre-2000: the seeds of (post-apartheid) strategic spatial planning

The first major thrust towards strategic planning, and the specific sub-form of strategic *spatial* planning, happened in the early 1990s during a period of multiparty dialogue. The apartheid government was outgoing but the ANC was not yet in power. There was little option but to proceed with planning through negotiation and in this period planning in South Africa came closer than at any other time to the ideals of collaborative and deliberative planning. In Cape Town, for example, the Western Cape Development Forum brought together business, labour, civic, political and other interests in a negotiating process to develop a Metropolitan Spatial Development Framework (Watson, 1998).[3] A similar process was happening in Durban where a private sector-led growth coalition known as Operation Jumpstart morphed into a wider multi-stakeholder negotiating process around the preparation of a metropolitan spatial framework (Wyley and Talbot, 1993; Moffett and Freund, 2004).

The most ambitious process happened within the greater Johannesburg region where the Central Witwatersrand Metropolitan Chamber (CWMC) was set up as a sort of mini-CODESA to negotiate metropolitan-level political, institutional and spatial arrangements. The work of the Chamber was suspended in June 1992 in a 'bog of disagreement and recrimination' (Ottaway, 1993, p. 129), but it was formative in seeding new forms of strategic spatial planning. A strategic spatial plan of sorts was finally produced through tough negotiating processes in a technical working group of the CWMC. In this forum, representatives of the civic movements aligned to the ANC demanded spatial equity, while officials of the outgoing administration negotiated to maintain the spatial privileges of the minority under the guise of sustaining the rates base of the city (Seedat, 2014; Pienaar, 2014).

The outcome, hesitantly called the *Interim Strategic Framework for the PWV (Pretoria-Witwatersrand-Vereeniging)*, established many of the principles and

*Figure 13.1* The Metropolitan Municipality of Johannesburg within the Province of Gauteng

Source: Harrison, Gotz, Todes and Wray (2014), Wits University Press

concepts that informed later spatial planning, including, for example, compaction and integration, and the use of integrative corridors and concentrated nodes as key elements of the spatial structure (Harrison *et al.*, 2008; Todes, 2012). At a conceptual level, the framework accommodated most of the demands of the civic movement for spatial equality and integration but it proved difficult to relate its high level of abstraction to the immediate demands for housing and services by an expectant citizenry (Mabin, 1994).

When the interim local governments were set up for Johannesburg in 2006, the opportunities for an effective practice of strategic planning were seemingly in place:

the newly appointed officials had long experience with 'strategizing' through the years of political struggle; there was an interim framework in place; and the demands of creating a transformed city clearly called for effective, long-range strategic spatial planning. The realities of practice, however, were different. The immediate requirements were to set up the new administration and respond to the short-term and pressing demands of a newly enfranchised citizenry. Seedat (2014) recalls 'the rush for capital projects and a certain amount of naiveté on the part of officials'.

It nearly ended in disaster. Within a year, the newly created City of Johannesburg was in deep trouble. The two-tier system of government was too costly to sustain, with the inexperience of new management and the competition between the new metropolitan local governments exacerbating problems. In October 1997 the City of Johannesburg defaulted on its debt, forcing provincial government to intervene. Johannesburg was now in crisis mode, with the focus on an emergency stabilization plan known as *eGoli 2000*, and longer-range strategic planning was even further marginalized (Seedat, 2014).

*eGoli 2000* was an institutional response to crisis involving: institutional consolidation (the single-tier metropolitan authority); the creation of city-owned enterprises to deliver services; and the outsourcing of non-core functions. There was also privatization of a few assets such as a small municipal airport and a gasworks. The plan was resisted by trade unions and a civic breakaway from the ANC, and implemented in the face of concerted opposition. However, as the crisis subsided around 2000, the political leadership of the city acknowledged the need for a longer-term planning horizon. The *eGoli 2010* process commenced with the creation of a Stakeholder Steering Committee (SSC), and proceeded through an ostensibly participatory process. Winkler (2011, p. 264), however, was not convinced, concluding that 'the SSC was designed to disguise rather than resolve conflicts of interest'. In any event, the process was called to a halt shortly before the local government elections of 2000. The political leadership of the COJ's interim administration was uneasy with the direction being taken in the process, and was concerned about the political risk of participation with the continued fall-out over *eGoli 2000* (Parnell and Robinson, 2006).

### 2000–2005: strategy evolves

After the elections of December 2000, the political leadership, now securely confirmed in their positions by a democratic mandate, brought in a 'hard-nosed economist' to produce the long-range strategy, *Jo'burg 2030* (COJ, 2002; Seedat, 2014). The supporting international consultants were Michael Porter's Harvard-based Monitor Group, which was playing a similar role in other South African cities. This time there was little, if any, attempt to consult stakeholders, with new administration no longer needing the legitimation of a participatory process (Parnell and Robinson, 2006; Robinson, 2008; Winkler, 2011). As Winkler (2011, p. 258) put it, the strategy was prepared in a 'closed space'.

The vision statement reveals the orientation of *Jo'burg 2030* which was finally released in 2002:

In 2030 Johannesburg will be a world-class city with service deliverables and efficiencies that meet world best practice. Its economy and labour force will specialise in the service sector and will be strongly outward oriented such that the City economy operates on a global scale. The result of this competitive economic behaviour will be strong economic growth that will drive up City tax revenues, private sector profits and individual disposable income levels such that the standard of living and quality of life of all the City's inhabitants will increase in a sustainable manner. (COJ, 2002)

The strategy was heavily criticized by social movements and academics for its trickle-down economics and neoliberal agendas (Bremner, 2004; Dirsuweit, 2009; Winkler, 2011). It was a plan that provided cover for interventions that had deleterious outcomes for the urban poor, including the eviction and displacement of residents in designated 'bad buildings' in the inner city. It remains debatable why the ANC in Johannesburg, with its largely poor and working-class constituency, adopted *Jo'burg 2030*. The national policy, GEAR, also arguably provided cover for *Jo'burg 2030*, with Seedat (2014) referring to the city strategy as 'a Jo'burg GEAR in some senses ... that would never fly today'. There was also, arguably, the spectre of a return to the financial crisis of the late 1990s, and a fear that the processes of 'spatial disorder' that began in the inner city during the transitional period of the 1990s would lead to city-wide spatial chaos in the future. In any event, there was a biting scholarly critique of *Jo'burg 2030* and concerted opposition by civil society and trade unions which effectively 'de-legitimated' the strategy (Parnell and Robinson, 2006, p. 348). Importantly, there was also discomfort within the city administration over the apparent prioritizing of economic growth over service delivery, including from within the newly established Central Strategy Unit (CSU) in the Office of the Executive Mayor (Parnell and Robinson, 2006; Seedat, 2014).

The political leadership of city was eventually convinced of the need to balance *Jo'burg 2030* with a *Human Development Strategy (HDS)* which was published with the by-line 'Joburg's commitment to the poor' (COJ, 2005). The official position was of two complementary strategies but there clearly were differences between *Jo'burg 2030* (COJ, 2002) and the *HDS* that played to the different orientations within the administration (Seedat, 2014). With the conclusion of the *HDS*, it was possible to argue that the COJ had managed to find a balance of sorts between the concerns for economic growth and competitiveness, and redistributive expenditure and action (Parnell and Robinson, 2006; Robinson, 2008). Houghton (2013) argued, however, in relation to similar processes in Durban, that it was not simply about a 'balance' but rather about a complex 'entanglement' of objectives. The *HDS* was prepared within the COJ as a part response to the criticism of the earlier strategy. It was explicitly pro-poor in its rhetoric, but it was not the outcome of a participatory process, never mind of co-production. The lack of participatory process was indicated by Lipietz (2008), for example, who nevertheless acknowledged that some benefit was brought to the urban poor.

At a technical level certainly, the strategic planning system was evolving. The CSU was playing a growing role in shaping the direction of the administration, and was working with senior officials to ensure that departmental plans were being linked to the long-range strategy, and also to budgeting processes. There was a complementary evolution in strategic *spatial* planning. When the single-tier authority came into being in 2001, it was poorly equipped to manage the rapid spatial transformations in the city. There was the difficult legacy of a historically fragmented spatial form, but also the pressures of a property boom of the early 2000s which was extending the sprawl of the city in ways that were poorly connected to existing infrastructure networks (Todes, 2012; Pienaar, 2014).

In 2001 there was no overarching spatial plan for the city. There were eleven detailed town planning schemes (or zoning plans) which dated back to the apartheid era, and a few, mainly incomplete, local plans from the transitional period. A small office for strategic spatial planning for the metropolitan city was established in 2001 but it was initially comprised of only three spatial planners. There was also no evident political support for spatial planning. Pienaar reports that at a mayoral retreat (referred to locally as a *legotla*) in 2001, 'no one could say anything good about [spatial] planners' (Pienaar, 2014). This had to do with the previous association of spatial planning with the apartheid order, but also with the lack of anything tangible from spatial planning in the 1990s.

In 2001, however, Parks Tau, a young but politically ambitious politician was appointed by Mayor Masondo as the Member of the Mayoral Committee (MMC) for spatial planning. Pienaar (2014) suggests that 'without Tau as MMC, [spatial] planning would have been doomed'. The first step in strategic spatial planning was to prepare a consolidated SDF for the city. This happened under Tau's political cover but still in a 'closed space'. The SDF was approved by the Metropolitan Council in 2002, and elaborated during 2003 into eleven Regional Spatial Development Frameworks (RSDFs) that provided the detail needed for adjudicating development applications. These were also prepared through a technocratic process but participatory processes were included in the biannual reviews of these plans (Pienaar, 2014).

There was a fortuitous moment in 2003 when strategic spatial planning established its leverage over the annual capital budgeting process in the city. Under pressure to show a link between capital budgeting and the strategic priorities of the city, the MMC for Finance accepted a proposal from the planning department to link capital budgets to strategic spatial plans and, within a year, the Capital Investment Management System (CIMS) was designed, developed, implemented, and formally approved by the Metropolitan Council. The CIMS continues to guide budget prioritization in the city and is a critical link in the overall system of strategic planning and budgeting (Todes, 2012; Pienaar, 2014). The relative success of strategic spatial planning in the COJ was recognized by Todes (2012, p. 164): 'In the case of Johannesburg the consolidation of policy and the position of planning have been made possible by a consistent and supportive local political regime that is unusual internationally'.

At the time, cross-scalar coordination in strategic spatial planning was not a major impediment for the COJ. The provincial government released its province-wide SDF in 2000 but it was at a high level of abstraction, representing the entirety of Johannesburg as a 'red blob' of proposed spatial concentration. Provincial and city planners did, however, squabble for nearly a decade over the demarcation of the edge, leading to conflicting positions over a number of new developments (Horn, 2010). The cross-scalar conflicts were more serious at an operational level, with the COJ approaching the High Court to annul the powers of the Provincial Development Tribunal.[4]

### *2006–2010: maturation*

In the period immediately before and after the municipal government elections in March 2006 there was a confluence of events which significantly strengthened strategic planning in Johannesburg, and which shifted strategic planning in a more progressive direction. In 2005, the CSU had decided internally to prepare a new long-range strategy to resolve the tensions between *Jo'burg 2030* and the *Human Development Strategy*, and had employed an academic-consultant, Graeme Gotz, to compile the document. The work was undertaken on-the-sly as political support was uncertain, and so an openly participatory process was not feasible (Seedat, 2014). There was, however, a shift in the orientation of national government which allowed this initiative to come into the open. In July 2005 President Mbeki had launched AsgiSA, which reaffirmed a focus on the econ-omy, setting an ambitious target of 6 per cent annual growth in GDP, but also edged policy away from the hard-nosed orthodoxies of GEAR.

In January 2006 Mbeki called on provincial, metropolitan and district authori-ties to develop long-range strategies and IDPs in support of AsgiSA. As Seedat (2014) put it, 'we went to Mayor Masondo and said we are ready to meet the President's challenge'. The work already undertaken was presented to the Mayoral Committee and, offered Seedat (2014), 'we were able to blow their socks off'. With political support in place, the *Growth and Development Strategy (GDS)* was completed by April 2006, and launched at a public summit. While the *GDS* declared its continuity with *Jo'burg 2030*, its tone and orientation were substantively different. The six key elements of the *GDS* were:

- Proactive absorption of the poor;
- Balanced and shared growth;
- Facilitated social mobility;
- Settlement restructuring;
- Sustainability and environmental justice; and,
- Innovative governance solutions. (COJ, 2006)

The reappointment of Masondo as mayor after the elections provided the political continuity that was required to embed the *GDS* within the city administration. Masondo linked the portfolios of his mayoral committee members, and the structures of the administration, to the strategic priorities of the *GDS*. Tau was appointed political head of finance while his close associate, Ruby Mathang, a trained planner, was appointed as the political head of spatial planning. The institutional and personal connections between the CSU, spatial planning and the city treasury, facilitated the rapid consolidation of a planning-led budgeting in Johannesburg, although there were tensions from time to time between the budget office and the planners (Pienaar, 2014; Seedat, 2014).

From 2006, the CSU worked to strengthen the alignment of departmental plans to the long-term *GDS*, and also to the newly developed medium-term IDP. Through the technical structures led by the CSU, departments were brought together around planning processes. There were, of course, complications. *Jo'burg 2030* was not easily forgotten, and the simple-minded appeal of a 'world class city' continued to shape practice in some sectors of the administration. There was also an enduring tension in the COJ between the finesse of the *GDS* and a crude attempt to impose order on a fluid urban landscape, especially in the inner city. The *GDS* did, however, provide an important point of reference and legitimation for officials within the city who were working towards transformative objectives, including affordable inner-city housing, upgrading of informal settlements, and an extended package of assistance for the urban poor. Clearly, the *GDS* was not an exemplar of co-production, and was not even participatory in its preparation, but it did give an indirect 'voice to the poor' as it was prepared by individuals in the city administration who were empathetically connected with marginalized segments of the population.

The *GDS* boosted strategic spatial planning in the city. It gave explicit recognition to the importance of 'spatial restructuring' in transforming the city and its 'pro-poor emphasis was a better fit with the SDF than with *Jo'burg 2030*' (Pienaar, 2014). The major advance in strategic spatial planning in this period was the introduction of a Growth Management Strategy (GMS) which brought considerations of infrastructure capacity directly into the planning process. The GMS also indicated an early shift to transit-oriented development to increase access across the city as areas of development priority were mainly along the new public transit corridors that were being developed in anticipation of the 2010 FIFA World Cup.

The period 2006 to 2010 was one of relative success in implementing transformative projects. In this period there were significant improvements in public transport, including the introduction of Bus Rapid Transit (BRT); visible improvements in the living environment of the mega township of Soweto; an ambitious greening programme in the barren south of the city; an expansion of free basic services; the partial regeneration of the inner city; new affordable housing, and so forth. This had partly to do with the catalyzing pressure of the upcoming World Cup but also, arguably, was enabled by the policy coherence and direction provided by the *GDS* and related plans.

There are continued debates around the transformative nature of these interventions. There were expanded material benefits – transport, housing, services – for the urban poor and other classes, with an analysis of the capital budget revealing a significant re-orientation of expenditure towards areas of deprivation. However, there was also a continued tension in practice between the deeply embedded desire of many city politicians and officials for orderliness in the urban environment, and the livelihoods of the urban poor, which often depended on 'grey spaces' beyond the regulation of authorities. This was especially apparent in the inner city as 'regeneration' continued to displace the urban poor attracted to the space by livelihood opportunities. Also, apartheid's spatial divides remained resilient, with new divides emerging as the middle class retreated into various forms of enclosed space. The city administration was involved in a complex mediation between its political constituency – the mainly black urban poor and working class – and the white and emergent black middle class on which it depended for its financial sustainability.

### *2011 onwards: re-invigoration*

The long-enduring Masondo administration came to an end with the municipal elections of May 2011. The ANC retained control of the COJ and Parks Tau was appointed as the new mayor. Tau moved quickly to place his stamp on the new administration, instructing the CSU to initiate a major rewrite of the *GDS*.

There was political urgency in this task and so the new *GDS*, known as *Jo'burg 2040* (COJ, 2011), was prepared through an intense eleven-week process. The aspiration of *Jo'burg 2040* is captured in these words:

> Johannesburg – a World Class African City of the Future – a vibrant, equitable African city, strengthened through its diversity; a city that provides real quality of life; a city that provides sustainability for all its citizens; a resilient and adaptive society. (COJ, 2011, p. 3)

Despite the haste, there was a higher level of multi-actor engagement than ever before, with extensive expert and public consultations within the identified thematic areas. A full chapter in the new *GDS* was devoted to explaining the extent of the 'outreach process', which included round-table discussions, ward-based consultation, and the wide use of social media (the first experience of this in the city). The chapter insisted that the *GDS* was prepared through a 'collaborative process' (COJ, 2011, p. 5).

*Jo'burg 2040* sustained the pro-poor priorities of the previous *GDS* but significantly strengthened the focus on resource sustainability, reflecting both the orientation of the new mayor and the changes in the development discourse nationally since 2006. There have been few, if any, criticisms of the substantive and procedural aspects of *Jo'burg 2040*, but there is growing anxiety outside the administration around tardiness in implementation and, more seriously, around the contradiction between the pro-poor policies of the strategy and some of the recent actions of the administration. The COJ was sharply criticized, for example, for *Operation Clean Sweep* in November 2013 which resulted in the large-scale displacement of informal traders in the inner city.[5]

The new *GDS* again emphasized the importance of spatial restructuring in achieving the economic, social and environmental goals of the city. It was, however, the Mayor's announcement of the proposed 'Corridors of Freedom' in the State of the City Address, May 2013, which provided an extraordinary boost for strategic spatial planning in Johannesburg. They built on a nearly decade-long focus on transit-oriented development in the spatial planning in Johannesburg but are significant for the scale of their ambition and the high level of political profile and priority they attract. As Pienaar (2014) explains, with Tau as mayor the planning department came under increasing pressure to show how planning contributes to visible spatial transformation. The department responded by showing how public transit networks could provide the mainstay of spatial transformation and 'then the mayor himself conceptualized and invented the corridors of freedom' (Pienaar, 2014).

With strategic spatial planning now central to the political programme of the city, strategic spatial planning now had the profile and resources never enjoyed before. This was a far cry from 2001 when spatial planners were marginalized, even vilified, in the COJ. The programme is, however, also a major gamble for Mayor Tau and for the city planners. As Pienaar (2014) observed with a degree of anxiety, 'the trick is to get it on the ground'.

The real challenge to the spatial visions of the COJ, however, may come from within government. A new premier, David Makhuru, brought greater degrees of confidence and assertiveness to provincial government. The vaguely stated provincial spatial visions of the past crystallized into a vision of mega projects – even new cities – beyond the boundaries of Johannesburg and the metropolitan cities. This vision of large-scale greenfields development arguably contradicts the city vision of densification around transit corridors.

## Conclusion

Is Albrechts (2015) correct in offering the hope of a transformative and radical practice of strategic spatial planning established through a process of co-production? The Johannesburg case is not promising in terms of co-production, although it does show that forms of co-production may exist under special circumstances. In the transition period in the early 1990s there was indeed a remarkable groundswell of negotiated and deliberative planning processes that were, arguably, exemplars of co-production. However, this happened because participatory democracy had yet to be institutionalized, and so planning required the legitimation of negotiated processes. The turn away from co-production later in the decade also had to do with the demands of setting up a new government administration and the emergency responses that followed on from a near fiscal disaster. There was a tentative turn towards more participatory process near the end of the decade, but new elections provided a secure mandate for the city leadership, and direct participation in planning was no longer needed politically.

It was only in 2011 that a strong element of participation was introduced to the strategic planning processes of the city, although even then the process was too tightly scheduled and closely structured to allow for the uncertainties and fluidity of co-production. Winkler (2011, p. 267) conceded 'the potential of managed participation to generate expectations and participatory skills that might, in the future, lead to more transformative outcomes, since the state is neither monolithic nor omnipotent'. The jury is out on whether the 2011 process was the leading edge of an emergent form of co-production or was a carefully constructed 'post-political project' that reduced potentially contested issues to a carefully managed technical debate. Into the future, the possibilities for more engaging and delibera-tive forms of planning will depend on factors such as the orientation of local political leadership, and the ability of non-state actors to assert their claims in the process. The ANC is no longer as politically secure in Johannesburg as it was, and we may speculate that electoral threats may induce the political leadership to accept some degree of co-production in governance.

While co-production in planning has been limited to short periods of time, this does not mean that the urban poor have failed to benefit from strategic planning processes. The Johannesburg story shows that 'pro-poor' strategies (the *HDS* and *GDS*) emerged through a mainly technical process from the contests within the city administration, although at least in part were responses to sharp opposition from outside the administration. The spatial frameworks were also intended to benefit the urban poor by reducing the costs that poor households pay for transport, and by directing resources to areas of previous marginality through the strong links that planning has within capital budgeting in the city (Todes, 2011, 2012).

State-initiated and controlled strategic planning processes – post-*Jo'burg 2030*, at least – were arguably supportive of poverty alleviation and developmen-tal processes. However, as Todes (2011) observed in relation to spatial planning, they were less successful in addressing inequalities. This may be the heart of the matter. Strategic planning processes that fall short of co-production may be successful in bringing material benefits to the poor but they are unlikely to confront the entrenched relations of power or patterns of inequality that repro-duce existing social and spatial relations.

Strategic planning in the Johannesburg case does indeed indicate 'moments of opportunity', 'innovative practice' and 'adaptation to changing circumstances', but it arguably falls short of being an instrument of 'co-production', and leaves open a debate as to whether it could serve a truly radical purpose in social and spatial transformation.

## Acknowledgements

The author acknowledges the support of South Africa's National Research Foundation through the South African Research Chairs' Initiative.

## Notes

1  As Executive Director, Development Planning and Urban Management, 2006–2009.

2 The constitution was a carefully constructed compromise between the demands of the African National Congress (ANC) for strong central government and of smaller parties, with regional strengths, for decentralized government within a federal structure.
3 From all appearances this was an inclusive and democratic process although Vanessa Watson has revealed a more complex story with unequal power relation and capacities, and multiple conflicting interests (Watson, 1998).
4 The details of the case are contained in the judgments: *City of Johannesburg v Gauteng Development Tribunal (335/08) [2009] ZASCA 106 (22 September 2009).*
5 See, for example, *Financial Mail*, 7 November 2013; *Saturday Star*, 16 November 2013; *Daily Maverick*, 6 December 2013.

# References

Albrechts, L. (2013) Reframing strategic spatial planning by using a coproduction perspective. *Planning Theory*, 12, 46–63.
Albrechts, L. (2015) Ingredients for a more radical strategic spatial planning. *Environment and Planning B: Planning and Design*, 42(3), 510–525.
Allen, J. and Cochrane, A. (2010) Assemblages of state power: Topological shifts in the organization of government and politics, *Antipode*, 42(5), 1071–1089.
Beall, J., Crankshaw, O. and Parnell, S. (2000) Local government, poverty reduction and inequality in Johannesburg. *Environment and Urbanization*, 12(1), 107–121.
Bond, P. (2000) *Elite Transition: Apartheid to Neo-Liberalism in South Africa.* Pluto Press, London.
Bremner, L. (2004) *Johannesburg: One City Colliding Worlds.* STE Publishers, Johannesburg.
COJ – City of Johannesburg (2002) *Jo'burg 2030.* [Online]. Available from: http://www. Jo'burg.org.za/index.php?option=com_content&task=view&id=123&Itemid=58& limitstart=1 [Accessed: 20 July 2015].
COJ – City of Johannesburg (2005) *Human Development Strategy: Joburg's Commitment to the Poor.* [Online]. Available from: http://www.joburg-archive.co.za/city_vision/ hr_strategy-05.pdf [Accessed: 20 July 2015].
COJ – City of Johannesburg (2006) *Growth and Development Strategy.* [Online]. Available from: http://www.Jo'burg-archive.co.za/2006/pdfs/gds_book/chapter1.pdf. [Accessed: 25 July 2015].
COJ – City of Johannesburg (2011) *Jo'burg 2040: Growth and Development Strategy.* [Online]. Available from: http://www.Jo'burg.org.za/gds2040/. [Accessed: 25 July 2015].
Dirsuweit, T. (2009) New urbanism, public space and spatial justice in Johannesburg: The case of 44 Stanley Ave. *Annales de géographie*, 1–2(665–666), 76–93.
Harrison, P. (2006) Integrated development plans and Third Way politics. In U. Pillay, R. Tomlinson and J. du Toit (eds), *Democracy and Delivery: Urban Policy in South Africa.* HSRC Press, Cape Town.
Harrison, P., Watson, V. and Todes, A. (2008) *Planning and Transformation: Learning from the Post-Apartheid experience.* Routledge, London and New York.
Harrison, P., Gotz, G., Todes, A. and Wray, C. (eds) (2014) *Changing Space, Changing City: Johannesburg after Apartheid.* Wits University Press, Johannesburg.
Horn, A. (2010) Telling stories: A history of growth management in Gauteng province. *European Spatial Research and Policy*, 17(2), 41–54.

Houghton, J. (2013). Entanglement: The negotiation of urban development imperatives in Durban's public–private partnerships. *Urban Studies*, 50(13), 2791–2808.

Klug, H. (2010) *The Constitution of South Africa: A Contextual Analysis*. Hart Publishing, Oxford and Portland, OR.

Lipietz, B. (2008) Building a vision for the post-apartheid city: What role for participation in Johannesburg's city development strategy? *International Journal of Urban and Regional Studies*, 32(1), 135–163.

Mabin, A. (1994) 'Forget democracy, build houses': Negotiating the shape of the city tomorrow. Paper for presentation at the History Workshop, July 1994. [Online]. Available from: http://wiredspace.wits.ac.za/bitstream/handle/10539/7901/HWS-255. pdf?sequence-1 [Accessed 20 June 2015].

Mabin, A. and Smit, D. (1997) Reconstructing South Africa's cities? The making of urban planning, 1900–2000. *Planning Perspectives*, 12, 193–223.

Moffett, S. and Freund, B. (2004) Elite formation and elite bonding: Social structure and development in Durban. *Urban Forum*, 15(4), 134–161.

Murray, M. (2008) *Taming the Disorderly City: The Spatial Landscape of Johannesburg after Apartheid*. UCT Press, Cape Town.

Ostrom, E. (1996) Crossing the great divide: Coproduction, synergy, development. *World Development*, 24, 1073–1087.

Ottaway, M. (1993) *South Africa: The Struggle for a New Order*. The Brookings Institution, Washington, DC.

Parnell, S. and Robinson, J. (2006) Development and urban policy: Johannesburg's city development strategy. *Urban Studies*, 43(2), 337–355.

Pienaar, H. (2014) *Interview with H. Pienaar*, 14 October 2014, Johannesburg.

Republic of South Africa (1996) *Constitution of the Republic of South Africa (Act 108 of 1996)*. Government Printers, Pretoria.

Robinson, J. (2008) Developing ordinary cities: City visioning processes in Durban and Johannesburg. *Environment and Planning A*, 40, 74–87.

Robinson, P. (2012) *Future, Change and Choices: Strategic Planning Methods for Built Environment Professionals*. Osborne Porter Literary Services, Durban.

Seedat, R. (2014) *Interview with R. Seedat*, 3 October 2014, Johannesburg.

Todes, A. (2011) Reinventing planning: critical reflections. *Urban Forum*, 22, 115–133.

Todes, A. (2012) Urban growth and strategic spatial planning in Johannesburg, South Africa. *Cities*, 29, 158–165.

Watson, V. (1998) Planning under political transition: Lessons from Cape Town's metropolitan planning forum. *International Planning Studies*, 3(3), 335–350.

Watson, V. (2014) Co-production and collaboration in planning: The difference. *Planning Theory and Practice*, 15(1), 62–76.

Winkler, T. (2011) Retracking Johannesburg: Spaces for participation and policy making. *Journal of Planning Education and Research*, 31(3), 258–271.

Wyley, C. and Talbot, C. (1993) Durban's metropolitan development process. *Urban Forum*, 4(1), 107–115.

# 14 Spatial planning in Flanders and Antwerp 1940–2012

## Movements, clashing values and expertise: drivers for change

*Jef Van den Broeck*

### The roots of strategic planning in Flanders

In Belgium, the modern origins of spatial planning lie in the 1960s. However, spatial planning was strongly influenced by the destruction during the two world wars and by the need for housing due to the growing population, as well as by the planning concepts that were introduced by the German occupiers. Soon after the war households were eligible for substantial subsidies and cheap loans to build a house. These grants were guaranteed by the state. Municipalities and private developers provided the necessary building plots by subdividing agricultural land and green areas owned by large landowners (Figure 14.1). While this process certainly provided an answer to housing needs in the very short term, it also gave rise to sprawl and suburbanisation all over the country and especially in Flanders because a spatial framework was lacking. Sprawl and the fragmentation of space also resulted in ecological problems. The entire river system became polluted because there was no overall sewage network and valuable natural areas and even watery lands were transformed into building areas.

'Road infrastructure' also became a driving force behind all the plans that were made in the 1950s and 1960s as spatial planning became dominated by infrastructural concepts, an evolution that was initiated by the German occupiers during the war (Lombaerde 1997). Equally important was the fact that a whole new generation of young planners had to take over because many of their predecessors had collaborated with the occupier and were relegated to the sidelines after the war. In response to this evolution, the national government enacted a new law (1962) defining a hierarchical set of instruments for spatial planning. A national plan, regional and sub-regional plans and municipal plans should be developed. At the end of the 1970s this led to the development of sub-regional land-use plans for the whole of Belgium on a scale of 1/25000 (Figure 14.2). The design and decision-making process itself, however, took about ten years.

In fact, these plans were a combination of land-use and zoning plans. They defined the possible land use in order to provide legal certainty for landowners. At the same time, the spatial claims of policy sectors and interest groups were localised in specific zones: space for economic development, agriculture, recreation, green and nature, and space for infrastructure. But these plans could not

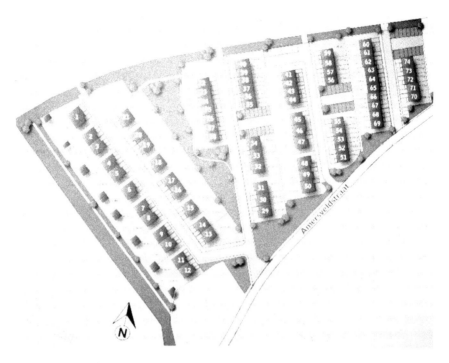

*Figure 14.1* A subdivision plan: a driver for suburbanisation

prevent sprawl as it was already a spatial characteristic at that moment. In fact, these plans have legalised sprawl and stimulated suburbanisation up to the present day (Figure 14.3).

This chapter focuses on the evolution in Flanders as Belgium in the 1970s engaged in a federalisation process, which resulted in completely different planning laws (decrees) and approaches in the three regions (Flanders, Wallonia, Brussels). As a result, the three regions gained full competences in the fields of urban planning, city renewal, monument conservation and environment and nature protection.

The case of the city of Antwerp will be used as an example of what was happening in reality on a local scale and illustrates the long quest towards a more strategic planning. In this chapter, the author attempts to define the roots of strategic planning in Flanders, the use of strategic planning in the city of Antwerp, while also referring to other cities in the 'Reflections' and to deduce the characteristics of the Flemish approach. The author was involved in this process during this period as planner/designer and as an academic. For this article, he relies on several interviews concerning planning history in Antwerp and on existing literature about planning in Flanders and in Antwerp (Van den Broeck *et al*. 2015). In this chapter the author will argue that institutional planning and strategic planning are used for different reasons, namely living 'apart-together' and that real change

one hand, there is an institutional framework with the same two planning instruments on all three policy levels (region, province, municipality), i.e., the 'structure plan' as a policy plan (that is partly binding for governments), which defines a spatial vision and development perspectives and various 'implementation plans' (that are binding for all citizens) to implement this policy. The latter are mainly land-use and zoning plans meant to create legal certainty. On the other hand, there is also a strategic planning tradition in some municipalities and regions, which is seen as a democratic process-based approach, developing a vision, programmes, action plans with specific budgets and means and agreements with stakeholders. In fact, these two different objectives are difficult to integrate in the same planning instrument (Van den Broeck 2013). However, because of the existing legal framework, some municipalities and regions have tried to combine these two objectives in a 'Strategic structure plan', as was the case, for instance, in the city of Antwerp (Secchi andVigano 2009; Van den Broeck, 2009).

Under this new legislation, the city of Antwerp around 2000 started developing such a plan, also because the change in legislation meant that drafting a structure plan had become mandatory. The city has a long planning history. The author will provide a brief overview of this history, identifying possible strategic characteristics in order to explain how the city's approach evolved towards intentional strategic planning. In any event, the present 'Strategic Structure Plan' is the expression of a choice in favour of a strategic approach, combined with the use of the institutional framework.

## Visions, policies and plans in Antwerp 1945–2012

### *1945–1981: from demolition and suburbanisation to modest renewal – growing professionalism*

The destruction that was caused in Antwerp's city centre by the war, the postwar demolition of deteriorated buildings, even of important historic monuments and the policy to orient reconstruction towards the building of offices and car parks instead of dwellings were sufficient reason for people to abandon the city centre and settle in the periphery. As already mentioned, this trend was stimulated by a law which made it financially possible for households to build a house 'somewhere' outside the city. In the 1960s, we can distinguish between two types of reaction. In the larger cities and certainly in Antwerp, civil society, students and artists reacted against these policies, often in a very activist way. They argued in favour of a new kind of city renewal, affordable housing, monument conservation, human public space and better public transport instead of a car-based policy. Influenced by the May '68 movement, they also clamoured for more public involvement in policy-making.

A second reaction in Antwerp came from a group of young politicians who understood the arguments of civil society, which were sustained by young (activist) planners. One of these politicians was a planner, who in 1970 became the vice mayor for urban planning. He established a new city planning organisation and developed 'structure schemes' (spatial visions) for the different neighbourhoods in the city as a framework for urban projects: he focused on social housing in the city, the renewal of public spaces, streets for pedestrians, car-free shopping streets and the protection of monuments. This was a comprehensive approach, based on an integrated analysis, but at the same time, it was a selective process because it was budget- and project-based. The vice mayor also believed in the need for legitimising visions and concepts, using land use and other institutional plans and the 'building permit' as a key instrument to control urban change.

### 1982–1992: social city renewal, lack of means and once again a reaction by civil society

In Antwerp, but also in the rest of Flanders, the 1980s was a decade marked by cutbacks and savings, which also led to the reduction of the city's spatial planning organisation. The only opportunity was the very valuable Flemish social renewal policy, which was supported by the King Boudewijn Foundation, which was established by the then king. This provides support for non-governmental organisations (NGOs), action committees, civil and professional organisations and municipalities that wish to improve people's spatial-social living conditions. The policy wanted to stimulate cities to invest in modest participatory projects, focusing on social housing and the improvement of public space in deteriorated neighbourhoods. In order to obtain subsidies, the Flemish Region required the establishment of neighbourhood committees in order to develop an action programme for the area in cooperation with the city. Social organisations, NGOs, citizens and the administration actively worked together for about ten years, developing a series of programmes. However, the regional subsidies were extremely limited, and so were the number of projects. The overall quality of the projects was low. The lack of quality was also due to the reduced capacity of the planning organisation and the low level of professionalism of planners and designers. In fact, the then generation of young planners and designers lacked a valuable professional education and training, largely due to the war, which they tried to compensate for with their enthusiasm and activism. These factors inspired negative feelings among the population and an atmosphere of distrust in regard to the city's capacity to develop and implement the urban policy that the different neighbourhood committees and civil society clamoured for. It was therefore somewhat strange that the new vice mayor asked civil society to help him design a 'Global Structure plan' for the city. A team consisting of members from the committees, some NGOs, the Antwerp Urban Planning/Design School and the city's planning organisation drafted it in just under a year, based upon extensive analysis and participative visioning. The plan was officially accepted by the town council but lacked the necessary support. In the opinion of the politicians, it was too general and lacked a practical action programme. They also felt that it was not proportionate to the available means: it was a vision without real strategies or an action plan that would remain a dream. Nevertheless, the process brought people together and some of them took different initiatives. 'City and the River', a non-profit organisation that was established in reaction to the city's inactivity, wanted to attract the attention of the population and the politicians to the unique development opportunities provided by abandoned port areas along the quays of the river Scheldt (Van Alsenoy *et al.* 2001). The organisation also reacted against the plans of a neo-liberal minister, who proposed to redevelop the area along the lines of the 'London Docklands' model and other pure real-estate waterfront developments.

The 'City and the River' movement organised events in the field: theatre performances, exhibitions and a competition for new spatial visions for these areas. A neighbourhood development company (BOM) was established by the university and other civil and public organisations. It demanded that the city pay attention to the deteriorated and forgotten poor areas in the nineteenth-century belt. Another organisation, called 'Payoke', reacted in an activist way against the awful working and living circumstances of sex workers in the city. These activities prompted a political response, stimulated by European, Federal and Flemish urban policies and subsidies. The city itself also took action. Its candidacy to be the 'European Cultural Capital Antwerp '93' was accepted and became a turning point, and evidence of a new belief in the values of the city.

### *1993–2012: a new belief in the city and finally the means*

'Antwerp '93' created a new dynamic as well as inspiring pride. Visions that had been developed over a 20-year period became mature and politically acceptable. And there was another influencing factor. In 1991, a nationalist right-wing party won the election, which meant that the traditional parties had no choice but to respond. The 'Cultural Year' was just one answer: it consisted of a very attractive and qualitative programme with cultural events of a different nature, not just 'elitist' events, but also events that targeted the inhabitants of the different neighbourhoods; different urban projects; the renovation of cultural icons such as Antwerp's Central Station and the Bourla Theatre, etc. It is important to note that there also was an 'urban' programme, which focused on the deteriorating nineteenth-century belt. Taking advantage of the European, Federal and Flemish subsidies, various 'socially-inspired integrated' projects were implemented in the nineteenth-century belt (Figures 14.4 and 14.5) and in the 'red light district' (Figure 14.6), which had the support of the BOM and Payoke, both non-profit organisations.

At the end of the 1990s, the city intentionally embarked on the development of a strategic spatial structure plan for the whole city as a result of a new Flemish policy, which introduced new planning instruments. But civil society was also clamouring for a global vision and a clear policy as a framework for the various ongoing projects and actions. The plan designed by Bernardo Secchi, Paola Vigano, Iris Consulting and the Urban Planning Service, under the supervision of the author of this chapter and the planning department, was approved in 2006 (Secchi and Vigano 2009; Van den Broeck 2009). It defined a vision for the city,

*Figure 14.4* The new city library as a social incubator in the neighbourhood

Source and copyright: City of Antwerp

*Figure 14.5* A park bringing people together

Source and copyright: City of Antwerp

*Figure 14.6* A health care centre in the prostitution quarter

Source and copyright: City of Antwerp

a programme and an action plan for the long- and short-term city budget. The process was 'co-productive' to a certain extent. Many stakeholders were involved and information was given in a permanent and structural way. And, most importantly, the vision was based upon existing ideas, opinions and concepts which were mainly developed by the different stakeholders in civil society in the years prior to this. At the same time, the city reorganised the city administration, including the urban planning services, in a very rational and effective way based upon 'better management' principles but also on the need for urban quality. As a result of the planning process, the city established teams dealing with the different tasks of the planning service: the development of a generic policy with spatial frames (partly legal) to steer and control the activities of citizens and authorities, a specific policy focusing at the development of strategic plans for strategic areas and an active policy (Figure 14.7) for the realisation of strategic urban projects. Finally, a 'City Architect' was also appointed to improve the quality of important projects, both public and private.

Today, this approach is also criticised as being too elitist, too city-marketing-driven, too rational, too far removed from the social objectives and approaches of the 1990s (Figure 14.8). However, the results are apparent and qualitative, and the protagonists claim that the city's objectives are clearly efficiency and quality and argue that social objectives by small interventions designed to avoid

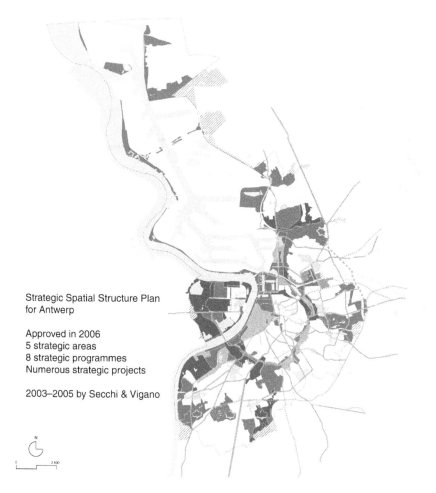

Strategic Spatial Structure Plan
for Antwerp

Approved in 2006
5 strategic areas
8 strategic programmes
Numerous strategic projects

2003–2005 by Secchi & Vigano

*Figure 14.7* A strategic Structure Plan that defined strategic areas

Source: City of Antwerp

aggressive gentrification and focusing on the renewal of public space and deteriorated buildings in 'poor' areas remain the overall goal.

## Learnings from the Flanders and Antwerp case

### *Dealing with the global and local context*

Looking back at the planning history in Flanders and Antwerp between 1940 and
today, 'change and innovation', also on the spatial level, was often strongly influenced by the global social, political and technological context: the war, the

*Figure 14.8* A master plan for an urban project

Source and copyright: City of Antwerp

introduction of Fordism and Modernism, new production techniques and means, the optimism of the 1950s and 1960s, the May '68 revolts, the different economic crises, the growing diversity of the population and the rise of nationalism, neo-liberal visions and policies, new modes of mobility and building techniques, the ecological awakening, the growing importance of religion, etc. For Flanders, more specifically, there is the population's very libertarian character that is supported by laws and subsidies focusing on individual needs and values. This proves the importance of the role of policies, strategies and financial incentives by the 'higher' authorities which aim to influence the context. The Flemish renewal policy in the 1970s and 1980s, the social urban policy and financial incentives by the European, Federal and regional level in the 1990s resulted in very interesting urban and social projects.

The profound understanding of the planning context, which fundamentally influenced the planning capacity, is essential knowledge for planners in order not 'to fight against windmills'. Such knowledge will in a certain sense provide an insight into the boundaries and potential for changing reality and innovating. The context definitely is not a determining factor, especially not when considering local factors (city, region, country). The evolution in Flanders and Antwerp clearly demonstrates that the context can be influenced, which can possibly give rise to structural change.

The knowledge of the factors that define the context and knowing how to work with them is an essential activity in a strategic process. One does not start from a 'blank' page. Like Faludi (1973), we distinguish between factors that can only be influenced in a very limited manner on the one hand, and factors that define the potential for change in a very real manner but which can also be changed if needed. The first category comprises 'norms and values' (such as the importance of property, personal freedom and legal certainty in Flanders), the political culture and government systems, the institutional environment, the technological situation, religion, spatial and physical characteristics, etc. The second category consists of the characteristics and history of an area and of the planning, property situations, existing views, ambitions, interests, clashing values and relationships of power and tensions between stakeholders, their role, their mission and mandate, the policy decisions that have already been made, etc. An analysis of these factors will provide an insight into the key issues, on the one hand, and the problems that might arise during the process. An open debate about these factors will also help clarify the direction for achieving agreement about various elements of the vision, through negotiation, and even about solutions and measures that can be implemented in the short and long term. Such a 'Context and VVIP analysis (Values, Visions, Interests, Power)' also provides an insight into potential partnerships. These factors, especially the second category, are not always stable. Hence the need to permanently monitor them and develop dynamic, flexible processes as well as using research methods and techniques that allow for a swift reaction to change.

The extent to which the context can be influenced depends on the force of the 'movement' that argues in favour of change, the power and persuasion of a vision and strategy and the means developed by its supporters, as well as on the available professionalism of the stakeholders that decide to take action. Throughout the postwar period, such movements had a substantial impact. They often, very purposefully, developed within civil society, in professional organisations and even in political parties. Within such processes, there are often specific moments (momentum) that facilitate change. They are defined by the coinciding of a number of factors of a very diverse nature, which are often political. A momentum can result from the context and specific events but under the right circumstances it can also, to a certain extent, be generated by people, organisations and movements. In Flanders and Antwerp the persistent and sustained activities of a number of citizens' movements, NGOs and professional movements, the electoral victory of an extreme right-wing party, the organisation of the cultural year in 1993, the partnerships between people and organisations all served as drivers for social and spatial change. Charismatic individuals and planners, their knowledge and skill, often played a significant role in this process.

### Need for professionalism: a driving force

Another 'Learning' is the influence of the growing professionalism of a discipline that had suffered as a result of the circumstances during the war. Existing planning schools, which had been integrated in architecture schools, had to reinvent themselves, resulting in new programmes for higher education. Two new planning schools (1961) at the universities of Ghent and Leuven tried to develop a more scientific approach. This took some time. As a result, a young, well-educated generation gradually emerged in the field, from the mid-1990s onwards, also in the public planning organisations on the different policy levels. They introduced new visions, concepts and approaches. In the larger cities, especially, urban planning and development became important issues, sustained by the new professionalism of the administration and by the Flemish government. The latter enacted a new planning law and a Flemish Structure Plan as well as an active spatial sustainable policy (Albrechts 1999). The Flemish 'urban policy', which aimed to realise qualitative urban projects on the city level, focused on training city planning services. Finally, the 'Flemish' architect developed tools to improve the architectural and urban quality of these projects. This new professionalism served to strengthen the discipline, the urban policies and their implementation in space and place. Professional organisations as well as training institutions played a vital role in this evolution. They influenced the new drafting of the new legislation in 1997 and defined the nature of the instruments. They were able to convince the government to enact legislation, whereby each municipality had to include at least one graduated urban planner within the administration, which only improved the quality of the policy and influenced the number of students (the current government unfortunately wishes to repeal this). The content and instruments of the cities' policy, which were described in a 'White Paper', were also defined by academics and people working in the field, with the support of the administration and approved by the government. The collaboration between the various stakeholders, planners, the administration, politicians, civil society and citizens is crucial in this framework. Finally, the good and direct relationship between academics and practitioners, which is under significant pressure today, and the content of the training programmes are prerequisites for the quality of the planning and the power of the discipline. The educational institutions and professional organisations will have to work on achieving this (together) (Scholl 2012).

### A very active and diverse civil society clamouring for participation

What about the relational nature of strategic planning? The debate on 'participation' has been an issue for a long time. Seen in the light of the evolution from 'government to governance' and the population's growing demand, citizens' commitment is steadily growing. This explains why nowadays concepts such as collaboration and co-production are becoming more relevant. Is this possible and realistic? To what extent was the population in Antwerp involved in the planning processes, for instance? Were various population categories approached in various ways? Did groups have a 'relative autonomy and responsibility' as they conceptualised a vision into its realisation? Is power being delegated or do political authorities have the absolute 'priority'? Were new ways of involving specific population groups tested? Is it possible to elaborate a complex political plan in a cooperative manner and discuss it in a rational way? Does the potential exist for a real 'city-wide debate', which extends beyond the discussions on projects, but is directed towards the creation of a 'growing insight'? What is the degree of 'inclusion' and 'exclusion' of the inhabitants in planning and decision-making processes? What is the role of planners in such a relationship?

Such questions are not easily answered but it is obvious that throughout the entire planning history a very diverse civil society and citizens were clamouring for participation and for the increased co-production of policy- and decision-making. A situation that often led to strained relations with the political world: an action-reaction process that often also gave rise to conflicts. The activities of such citizens' groups influenced politicians during the entire period, requiring them to react but also developing visions, concepts and practical proposals, by organising city debates and raising awareness among the population. Antwerp for a long time has been searching for the means and methods to involve the population in rolling out its planning policy. In the 1970s, the city implemented a 'top-down' approach. In the 1980s, the town council tried to strengthen population groups on the community level, trying to understand their needs and expectations during hearings, steering committees, interviews with privileged witnesses, etc. This was all done in a very fragmented manner, without a professional base. Nowadays, Park Spoor Noord and the city's red-light district (Figure 14.9) are interesting experiments in terms of the engagement of various population groups in a complex situation, in order to realise the objectives of spatial and social transformation and innovation.

The preparation of the Park Spoor Noord project (De Wever and Lamberts 2003) gave rise to a different approach, under pressure and thanks to the impetus of the population. The 'Wervend programma' campaign (Geerts *et al.* 2003) involved the neighbourhood in the development of a vision and the definition of the park's nature from the start of the design process, among others, with site visits, day-long workshops, during which the experts and residents committed their ideas to paper and discussed them, and by the organisation of events onsite, which were designed to expose the space's potential. The results of this campaign were passed on to the designers of the park, who were designated in a competition. The park today clearly demonstrates that the design was influenced by the neighbourhood residents and can be considered successful. Was everyone involved? Most certainly not. The immigrant population in the neighbourhood, for instance, did not participate in the process but they do use the park.

*Figure 14.9* Engaging inhabitants in the red-light district

Source and copyright: City of Antwerp

A kind of mature relationship developed during the strategic planning process for the development of the Strategic Structure Plan for the city (2003–2006). It created a 'momentum' (Albrechts and Balducci 2013), a feasible context that was grasped as an opportunity by the city planners and the new mayor and a vice mayor, who wanted to bring about fundamental change and a new and modern image for them and their policies. The mayor, Patrick Janssens, wanted to create a 'new home' for the citizens. Using modern communication strategies, instruments and techniques, he and his collaborators involved the stakeholders and the citizens, who had already been clamouring for an urban vision and a coherent policy for decades, in the process, and organised it in a professional way, relying on a professional administration coached by experts.

During the elaboration of the strategic plan, the team sought to engage the main stakeholders of the various interest and population groups in order to identify their needs, opinions and visions. Intensive discussions were held with the various city services and the majority parties, which resulted in political endorsement. The districts were involved in various stages of the plan's development. Apart from the public hearings, a campaign was organised to show opportunities on the spot, using theatre and art performances. As a result, the local population was able to discover the potential of the loci and the proposed policy. The objective was not to explain the plan to a wide audience, but to 'provide an insight into the possibilities of loci and the proposed policy by means of exploratory planning and design'. Possibly this could lead to a more structural and permanent city debate.

The approach was increasingly dominated by communication techniques aimed at the population as a whole: information, on the one hand, and creating a positive atmosphere, on the other hand, with slogans and campaigns such as 'The City belongs to you' and 'The Wharf of the Century'. The input of the large population of immigrants in the city, however, remained limited.

To date, there has been no 'delegation of power' to the population, nor has there been a structural and political empowerment of the population. In Flanders, the adage continues to be the 'authority of the elected politicians'. Politicians find the growing emancipation of the population, the permanent involvement of civil society in policy and working with citizens' movements increasingly difficult. The active, non-neutral participation of planners in citizens' movements and co-productive processes and the establishment of partnerships with all the stakeholders in Flanders and Antwerp did effectively (strongly) contribute to change and innovation, a third 'Learning'. Therefore the discipline, the training institutions and professional organisations need to permanently develop the required knowledge and skills and be engaged in social debate.

### A strategic plan: the need for a direct relation between visioning and action

For decades, whether having a vision for the future and using frameworks to define a desired future is actually useful has been a point for discussion within the discipline. Counter-arguments point to the impossibility of reaching a consensus about standards and values that constitute the foundation of a vision, the lack of sufficient knowledge to underpin such visions, the uncertainty about future developments, the power of interests and relationships of power, and so on.

The entire period, both in Antwerp planning as well as on the Flemish level, was characterised by the fear, on the one hand, mainly of politicians and part of the business community, that a vision that was too specific and explicit would be too strict. These groups instead argue in favour of the development of specific projects that are not hampered by legal or other frameworks. On the other hand, the population, civil society, the administrations and some experts clamoured for a strong vision, capable of defining a vision for the future. That is why there is a permanent tension between the demand for a vision and a long-term framework and the demand for action. Sometimes visions gave rise to action and projects. Sometimes projects helped define a vision. Both were always implicitly or explicitly present, however, which is a fourth 'Learning'. In Antwerp, the policy for decades focused on the realisation of projects related to an urban vision, that were managed by the city and on their legalisation with different institutional, not only planning, instruments. Until the end of the last century, the vision and the policy that underpinned these projects was fragmented, not comprehensive, not integrated, and incomplete. On the other hand, it was also coherent, focusing on the improvement of the living conditions of the inhabitants and the city's viability. After this, depending on different elements, both global and local, the vision did not fundamentally change but it became mature and explicit, essentially remaining the same vision that was expressed and made legally binding in the strategic structure plan (2006).

The Antwerp strategic structure plan reflects a clear and specific vision, using 'images about a possible future': Antwerp as a water city, Antwerp as a rail city, Antwerp as a port city, Antwerp as a porous city, Antwerp as an eco-city, Antwerp as a city of villages, a metropolis and part of a megacity. These images are explained, detailed and localised in the plan, based on a thorough reading of the area, its space and social context, its weaknesses, strengths and opportunities, its concerns and the power of its population and civil society (Secchi and Vigano 2009).

As well as developing a vision, the Antwerp strategic plan searches for the most appropriate way or strategy to implement this vision by means of a selective – because there never will be plentiful means available – package of oriented strategic actions (projects, frameworks, prescriptions, urban pacts, land-use plans, etc., in the short and middle term and located in specific 'strategic areas', which strengthen the city's overall spatial structure (Figure 14.7).

An important strategic decision refers to the choice made to link the strategic areas with the city's administrative organisation in order to close the gap between planning and implementation. This implementation strategy is based on three pillars: the link of the plan to the city's annual and long-term budget, the reorganisation of the administration based upon the differentiation between a generic and specifically area-oriented and project-oriented active policy and the establishment of municipal action-oriented autonomous legal entities.

A feasible future should always retain enough flexibility to deal with uncertainty and the unexpected. It is not a blueprint for a future. However, it always is an essential factor to achieve collaboration and understanding between the stakeholders concerning specific projects and actions. It can create expectations which can lead to action. Visioning as a collaborative process is a way of developing a movement towards something. However, collaboration concerning the values expressed in a vision will always be limited and selective and agreements will be based on common interests rather than on common (often clashing) values. The degree of specificity depends on the extent to which an agreement can be achieved, on the available knowledge and means for achieving this vision. The legal establishment of visions and long-term frameworks requires prudence, to sufficiently absorb uncertainties and the missing knowledge at the right moment. Visioning, programming, taking action and of course co-production will always be interacting activities within a strategic process, but not in a specific order. Often processes start with a necessary action/project to solve a problem and to build trust, or with an event, or debates, and so on. In the mind of the author, visioning should be a permanent activity because people and society need anchors. They are necessary but not sufficient.

## Conclusion: reflections on strategic planning

### *Change: not without a movement*

When examining the history of some intentional strategic planning processes in Flanders, we can see that the willingness of different cooperating stakeholders to transform reality, an essential objective of strategic planning, the existence or creation of a movement in order to do so, the continuity of the effort and the capacity and skills of the actors are the main success factors. In different cases in Flanders and also in Antwerp, a certain transformation in terms of the vision or/and policy or/and action occurred. But the type of change was completely different and difficult to characterise as 'fundamental or structural'. And in most cases it did not fundamentally influence the relations of power, except possibly in the case of the Ghent Canal Area (Albrechts and Van den Broeck 2004). On the contrary, it often resulted in the strengthening of the existing power structures that took the initiative to start a process. Of course, this often was also a result of former actions by the population and citizens' movements. Different cases have taught us that the richness of a strategic process depends of the type of changes and the degree to which they are realised. The results were mostly related to purely physical transformations concerning an area's viability, the improvement of urban quality, the physical transformation on the level of global issues (energy savings, pollution, etc.) and sometimes in a certain but limited extent to social values (equity, democracy, solidarity, etc.), social innovation and human and political relations. The more these issues are combined and integrated the richer the process. As such a transformation process is not a technocratic 'plan-making' process but a permanent social-political process. Is strategic planning as an intentional organised process the only way to transform reality? Certainly not. However, the creation of a movement is an essential factor for structural change. And such movements can be initiated by everyone. There are ample examples of this, including in Antwerp's and Flanders' planning history. But an intentional and organised process can, at a certain time, reinforce, legitimate and legalise such movements and bring about change. Strategic planning can be a trigger but may not be mystified as the only way for change. Using the planner's creative capacities (Kunzmann 2013), however, it can help bring people together and inspire them, to link political, social and spatial stakeholders and worlds and, most of all, to develop visions, concepts and solutions which are or should be the planner's specific capacities.

### *The nature and organisation of processes: social-political-spatial, flexible yet focused*

Strategic planning as an intentional and organised social-political process can determine this type of development to a certain degree. As a social process it is a 'learning', researching, creative and innovative process aimed at the empowerment of the stakeholders and the development of ideas, visions and concepts. As a political and planning process, it is a 'process of action', focusing on a specific policy and specific selective results that are often related to policy terms, budgets, clashing values, interests, power and human relations. The spatial process searches for spatial and physical characteristics, visions for the future in the short and long term, potential and specific solutions, among others, through 'research by design'. In Antwerp, a team within the planning service was structurally put in charge of this type of research.

The process-architecture deals with the contextual relation between four inter-dependent processes: visioning, acting, collaboration and decision-making (Van den Broeck, 1987, 1995, 2004; Albrechts *et al.* 2000; Albrechts 2002) (Figures 14.10 and 14.11). The process is a 'dynamic trialogue' between these four elements or tracks, a 'trialogue' between the social, the political and the spatial objectives and a 'trialogue' between citizens, authorities and experts. It may possibly result in a vision, an action programme and a plan that is regularly evaluated and adjusted in accordance with budgets and agreements between stakeholders. As such, it is a very complex relational process, which tries to integrate the many influencing factors in a non-linear 'navigating' (Hillier 2013) manner 'surfing on the waves' but always keeping in mind different values. It is not an unambiguous process with a clear sequence of activities. On the other hand, it is necessary to design a process in a certain context, which is clear for people, which is politically and mentally controllable and which leads to a result.

Notwithstanding the fact that these are cyclical, dynamic processes, 'stages/steps' can be distinguished in purposefully organised processes: a 'beginning (there is always a reason or cause), a consequence, a result and the management of the process'. These steps can overlap. That is why a process will always be customised and tailor-made and should never start from the principles and methods of 'management processes' that are propagated by the business community and public administration. In Antwerp the cause for implementing a strategic process was partly due to Flemish legislation, which made the establishment of a spatial structure plan compulsory, in exchange for wider, urban planning competences. Equally important, however, was the demand of the administration, which sought an integrated framework for incremental action and for the many projects

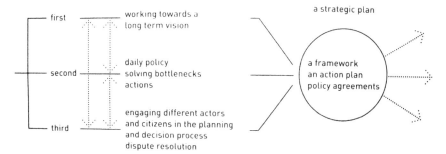

*Figure 14.10* Three-track approach

Source: Van den Broeck 1987

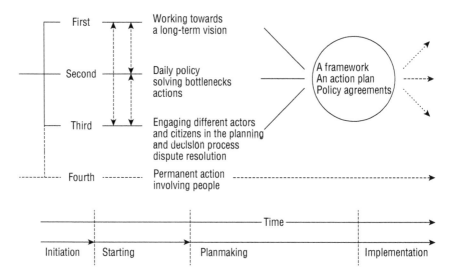

*Figure 14.11* Four-track approach

Source: Van den Broeck 2004

that had been developed *ad hoc*. This demand was endorsed by civil society and the new mayor (2003), who wanted to develop a 'new home' for the city. Hence the option of drawing up a 'strategic spatial structure plan' at this appropriate moment.

### *A planner is not a facilitator*

The perspective of planners and their interests should always be a structural change of the qualitative and living conditions of people within a sustainable environment. Therefore, the role of a planner is definitely not restricted to the management of a process and to act as a facilitator. As an individual, he or she has an own value system and as a planner he or she contributes knowledge and skills. He/she has to make choices that also take into account his/her responsibility for the public interest and the above-mentioned values. Spatial planning is neither a neutral activity nor a discipline. Instead it is strongly linked to interests, ambitions, opinions and values of actors, individuals and groups and with power structures and relationships. Within processes, decisions have to be taken influencing possible 'futures', the use and allocation of means, the involvement of actors, etc. Planners considers decisions that can lead to conflicts and can influence relationships of power relations as well as decisions which can provide a new content, meaning and form for the future. Such a future should be based on solidarity, diversity, equity, social justice, quality and sustainability. A neoliberal context is not a favourable planning 'environment' because it mainly focuses on private interests (Van den Broeck *et al.* 2010; Bajic-Brkovic 2012; Fischler 2012).

### Strategic versus institutional planning

We know that the traditional institutional planning, which in most countries is characterised by land-use and zoning planning, is not an answer to the challenges we should deal with. On the other hand, strategic planning as currently defined is extremely complex and only applicable in a suitable context. The Antwerp case and other cases in Flanders prove that it is possible to combine the different objectives of institutional and strategic planning and to use them in a complementary manner, at least if the institutional legal context and bureaucratic attitudes allows this. The use of an institutional system is important because of the need for the legitimation and legalisation of a spatial policy and because land-use plans sometimes can protect spatial quality.

## References

Albrechts, L., 1974. Strategische factoren in de ruimtelijke stedelijke planning met het parkeren als toepassing (Strategic factors in urban spatial planning, with parking as an application). PhD thesis. Leuven: IISRO.

Albrechts, L., 1999. Planners as Catalysts and Initiators of Change: The New Structure Plan of Flanders. *European Planning Studies*, 7(5).

Albrechts, L., Leroy, P., Van den Broeck, J., van Tatenhove, J. and Verachtert, K., 2000. Gebiedsgerichtbeleid in de steigers (Integrated territorial policy). *Ruimte en Planning*, 20–1.

Albrechts, L., 2001. From Traditional Land Use Planning to Strategic Spatial Planning. In L. Albrechts, J. Alden and A. da Rosa Pires (eds.), *The Changing Institutional Landscape of Planning*. Aldershot: Ashgate.

Albrechts, L., 2002. The Planning Community Reflects on Enhancing Public Involvement: Views from Academics and Reflective Practitioners. *Planning Theory and Practice*, 3(3), 331–347.

Albrechts, L. and Van den Broeck, J., 2004. From Discourse to Facts: The Case of the ROM-project in Ghent/Belgium. *Town Planning Review*, 75(2).

Albrechts, L. and Balducci, A., 2013. Practicing Strategic Planning: In Search of Critical Features to Explain the Strategic Character of Plans. *DisP –The Planning Review*, 194(49.3).

Bajic-Brkovic, M., 2012. Societies in Transition and Planning Education: The Case of the West Balkan Countries. In B. Scholl (ed.), *HESP, Higher Education in Spatial Planning, Positions and Reflections*. Zürich: ETH vdf Hochschulverlag AG.

De Wever, H. and Lamberts, E. (eds.), 2003. *Antwerp, Spoor-Noord: A City Park Off the Beaten Tracks*. Antwerp: Ludion, City of Antwerp.

Faludi, A., 1973. *A Reader in Planning Theory*. Oxford: Pergamon Press.

Fischler, R., 2012. Higher Education for Spatial Planning: What and How? In B. Scholl (ed.), *HESP, Higher Education in Spatial Planning, Positions and Reflections*. Zürich: ETH vdf Hochschulverlag AG.

Geerts, P., De Wever, H. and Lamberts, E., 2003. The Genesis of an Urban Project. In H. De Wever and E. Lamberts (eds.), *Antwerp, Spoor-Noord: A City Park Off the Beaten Tracks*. Antwerp: Ludion, City of Antwerp.

Groep Planning, 1976. *Structuurplan Brugge*. Brugge: Ministry of Public Works.

Hillier, J., 2013. On Relationality and Uncertainty. *DisP – The Planning Review*, 194(49.3).

King Boudewijn Foundation, Municipality of Zoersel (KBS), 1982. *De les van Zoersel. Structuurplanning: een weg naar lokale democratie* (*The Learnings from Zoersel. Structure Planning: A Path to Local Democracy*). Brussels: KBS.

Kunzmann, K. R., 2013. Strategic Planning: A Chance for Spatial Innovation and Creativity. *DisP – The Planning Review*, 194(49.3).

Lombaerde, P., 1997. De verkeersring rond Antwerpen als onderdeel van het Duitse R.A.B.-net (The ring around the city as a part of the German R.A.B.-network). *Interbellum-Cahiers, 9-10, Planning en Contingentie: Aspecten van Stedenbouw, Planologie en Architectuur tijdens de Tweede Wereldoorlog*. Gent: Interbellum/vzw Soma.

Secchi, B. and Vigano, P., 2009. *Antwerp: Territory of New Modernity*. Amsterdam: SUN.

Sholl, B. (ed.), 2012. *HESP, Higher Education in Spatial Planning, Positions and Reflections*. Zürich: ETH vdf Hochschulverlag AG.

Van Alsenoy, J., Van den Broeck, J. and Vanreusel, J., 2001. Antwerpen, Stadt am Fluss. In D. Schubert (ed.), *Hafen- und Uferzonen im Wandel*. Berlin: Leue Verlag.

Van den Broeck, J., 1987. Structuurplanning in praktijk: werken op 3 sporen (Structure planning in practice: a three-track process). *Ruimtelijke Planning*. Antwerpen: Van Loghum-Slaterus.

Van den Broeck, J. *et al.*, 1991. *Structuurplanning: een handleiding voor gemeenten* (*Structureplanning: A Manual for Municipalities*). Brussels: Ministery of the Flemish Community.

Van den Broeck, J., 1995. Sustainable Spatial Planning: A Way to Localize Agenda 21. *Proceedings of the Nakuru Consultative Workshop*. Nakuru, Kenya: KULeuven, UN-Habitat.

Van den Broeck, J., 2004. Strategic Structure Planning. In A. Loeckx, K. Shannon, R. Tuts and H. Verschure (eds.), *Urban Trialogues: Visions, Projects, Co-productions*. Nairobi: UN-Habitat, KULeuven.

Van den Broeck, J., 2009. The Strategic Structure Plan of Antwerp: Traditional Kitchen or Nouvelle Cuisine. In B. Secchi and P. Vigano, *Antwerp: Territory of New Modernity*. Amsterdam: SUN. pp. 233–241.

Van den Broeck, J., Albrechts, L., Segers, R., 2010. *Strategische Ruimtelijke Projecten, Maatschappelijk en ruimtelijk vernieuwend* (*Strategic Spatial Projects: A Social and Spatial Innovation*). Brussels: Politeia.

Van den Broeck, J., 2013. Balancing Strategic and Institutional Planning: The Search for a Pro-active Planning Instrument. *DisP – The Planning Review*, 194(49.3).

Van den Broeck, J., Vermeulen, P., Oosterlynck, S. and Albeda, Y., 2015. *Antwerpen Herwonnen, Maatschappij, Ruimtelijk Plannen en Beleid* (*Winning Back Antwerp: Society, Spatial Planning and Policy Making*). Brugge: Die Keure.

Vermeersch, Ch., 1977. *De structuurplanning als type ruimtelijke planning: een geldig alternatief* (Structure Planning as a Type of Spatial Planning: A Valid Alternative). Brussels: ICASD.

# 15 Regional strategic planning and managing uncertainty in Greater Vancouver

*John Abbott and Christina DeMarco*

## Introduction

The Greater Vancouver area of Canada has a long history of regional planning and governance going back to the 1940s. This chapter explores why and how regional strategic planning emerged and evolved, the governance structures which enabled regional planning, the nature of the plans prepared, and how these plans have continued and changed leading to the current Metro Vancouver 2040 plan, adopted in 2011. Regional planning becomes strategic when it encompasses multiple policy areas, involves key stakeholders, raises possible new futures and provides an effective policy framework for local planning. But broadening policy areas and stakeholder involvement and pushing the bounds of possible new futures raises more unknowns and uncertainties about the future and these uncertainties need to be managed to get agreement about plans (Abbott 2005). These themes are explored and conclusions are drawn about the nature and benefits of regional strategic planning in Greater Vancouver and the lessons for other metropolitan regions.

Greater Vancouver is located on the west coast of Canada in the Province of British Columbia (the Province). The Greater Vancouver Regional District (GVRD) is the legal entity responsible for regional planning and since 2007 it has been known as Metro Vancouver. It includes 23 local authorities as members – 21 municipalities, one electoral area and one treaty First Nation – as shown in Figure 15.1. The population was 2.46 million people in 2014 (Metro Vancouver 2014, p. 31), making it the third largest metropolitan area in Canada, and the population has doubled since 1976. The region has physical and social qualities that help reinforce a sense of regionalism. The north is bounded by the Coastal Mountain range, the United States border is the southern boundary, and the Pacific Ocean is to the west. The Fraser River winds its way from the east and cuts through Greater Vancouver forming a large delta area. Natural assets, including the temperate rain forests and the fertile agricultural land in the Fraser River Valley, are highly valued by the regional community.

Regional planning differs from province to province in Canada. In British Columbia, it is the responsibility of regional tier local governments called Regional Districts and approval of regional plans is not required by the Province.

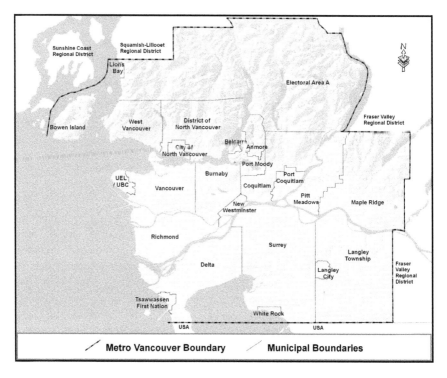

*Figure 15.1* The Greater Vancouver region and municipalities

Source: Metro Vancouver 2011

Regional Districts provide services at a scale that cannot be effectively provided at the local or provincial level. Artibise, Cameron and Seelig (2004, p.195) describe this as 'do it yourself' regional planning. In contrast, in Ontario, the Provincial government is more involved and prepared and implemented the regional plan for the Greater Toronto-Hamilton metropolitan area. Regional planning in Canada is much stronger than in the United States, with most major Canadian metropolitan areas covered by a statutory regional plan.

This chapter is based on a review of relevant literature and plans for Greater Vancouver, interviews with key stakeholders and the involvement of Christina DeMarco as the lead planner for the preparation of Metro Vancouver 2040.

## The emergence and evolution of regional strategic planning in Greater Vancouver

The emergence and evolution of regional strategic planning in Greater Vancouver since 1948 can be considered in terms of four phases and four plans, as follows:

- establishing regional planning: the Official Regional Plan (1966);
- revolutionizing regional planning: the Livable Region Proposals (1975);
- resurrecting regional planning: the Livable Region Strategic Plan (1996); and
- strengthening regional planning: Metro Vancouver 2040 (2011).

The first three phases and plans will be discussed in this section and the fourth phase and current metropolitan plan will be discussed in the following section.

### *Establishing regional planning: the Official Regional Plan (1966)*

Massive flooding occurred across the Fraser River delta in 1948 and revealed a lack of information about flood prone land and development in these areas (Harcourt *et al.* 2007, p.16). The Province reacted to this imperative by establishing a regional planning organization covering the whole delta area in 1949. This was called the Lower Mainland Regional Planning Board (LMRPB) and was a federation of 26 municipalities.

After the Second World War, the population of the Lower Mainland was growing rapidly with an 'immense suburban boom' (Hodge and Robinson 2001, p. 332). The LMRPB thus had to address urban growth as well as flooding issues and it took 14 years before it produced a proposed regional plan in 1963. *Chance and Challenge: A Concept and Plan for the Development of the Lower Mainland Region of British Columbia* (LMRPB 1963) included a vision and showed broad future land-use and infrastructure designations. The regional concept was for the Lower Mainland to 'develop as a series of cities in a sea of green … a valley of separate cities surrounded by productive countryside' (LMRPB 1963, p. 6).

It took a further three years until 1966 before the LMRPB's final plan received the required support of two-thirds of municipalities and could be approved (Hodge and Robinson 2001, p. 333). The *Official Regional Plan for the Lower Mainland Planning Area* (the ORP 1966) (LMRPB 1966) was a statutory land-use plan. It included policies for limiting settlement in areas subject to flooding and for a poly-centric region with 'compact regional towns, each with its own business and civic centre' as the desired pattern for residential and job growth (LMRPB 1966, p. 3). However, the plan's implementation led to conflicts over agricultural land with the Province and the abolition of the LMRPB in 1968.

### *Revolutionizing regional planning: the Livable Region Proposals (1975)*

In 1965 the Province passed legislation allowing the establishment of Regional Districts for service provision and planning at a regional scale. In 1968 the regional planning powers of the LMRPB were transferred to the newly established GVRD and three other Regional Districts. Harry Lash arrived as director of regional planning for the GVRD in 1969 and his approach 'revolutionized the way planning was done in the Greater Vancouver area' (Harcourt *et al.* 2007, p. 80).

GVRD planners and politicians came together in 1970 for a 'landmark semi-nar' which saw the emergence of new planning concepts: 'livability and the livable region would be the goals and the management of growth and change in an ongoing way would be the operational concept' (Lash 1976, p. 21). Under Lash's leadership planners and politicians at the GVRD set out to actively explore what livability meant for the Vancouver community through public engagement, representative committees and interactive meetings. Harcourt *et al.* describe it as 'an open ended exercise in primary democracy' (2007, p. 81). Lash called this interactive process the 'Six Sided Triangle', as shown in Figure 15.2.

For Lash, the ongoing process of public engagement and analysis of planning options leading to agreed actions was more important than producing a formal plan. He summarized it as, 'The Plan is the Process' (Lash 1976, p. 45). This led to tensions between the planners and the politicians, who wanted a 'plan for physical development that could guide municipal decision-making' (Lash 1976, p. 31). The eventual output was a document released by the GVRD in March 1975 called, *The Livable Region 1976/1986: Proposals to Manage the Growth of Greater Vancouver* (the LRP 1975) (GVRD 1975). The LRP 1975 was a non-statutory, strategy and actions document and very different from the ORP 1966 land-use plan. It was based on five spatial strategies for managing growth, as shown in Box 15.1.

Regional town centres were critical and the LRP 1975 noted that little progress had been made. It identified four regional town centres at Burnaby (Metrotown), New Westminster, Coquitlam and North Surrey. It described these as downtowns for new growth areas, serving 100–150,000 people, having a strong pedestrian orientation and a varied mixture of activities. The desired spatial outcome was illustrated graphically in the LRP 1975 in what was called 'The Regional Picture in 1986', as shown in Figure 15.3.

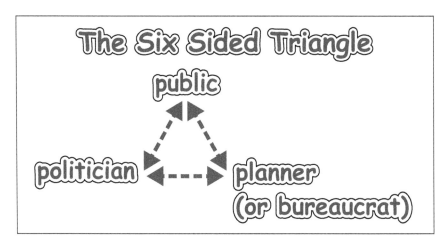

*Figure 15.2* The Six Sided Triangle

Source: Lash 1976, p. 11

---

**Box 15.1 The LRP 1975 strategies for managing growth**

- Achieve residential growth targets in each part of the region
- Promote a balance of jobs to population in each part of the region
- Create regional town centres
- Provide a transit-orientated transportation system linking residential areas, regional town centres and major work areas, and
- Protect and develop regional open space.

Source: GVRD 1975, p. 10

---

The LRP 1975 strategies and focus on managing 'growth and change in jobs, population, housing and transportation' have become the 'dominant themes' in subsequent Vancouver planning (Hodge and Robinson 2001, p. 337). Or as Harcourt *et al.* put it, 'nobody argues any more about whether the Livable Region Strategy, or plan, or process, or whatever you want to call it, worked' (2007, p. 91).

After the release of the LRP 1975, the GVRD and the three other Regional Districts, which had constituted the LMRPB, decided to update their joint Official Regional Plan. This was adopted in 1980 as a statutory, land-use plan called the *Plan for the Lower Mainland of British Columbia* (the ORP 1980) (CFVRD *et al.* 1980). However, the ORP 1980 was short-lived as a newly elected Provincial

*Figure 15.3* 'The Regional Picture in 1986'
Source: GVRD 1975, p. 48

government decided in 1983 to abolish all ORPs and to remove the regional planning powers of Regional Districts – 'the regional planning system … was gutted' (Hodge and Robinson 2001, p. 337).

### Resurrecting regional planning: the Livable Region Strategic Plan (1996)

After 1983, the GVRD continued to provide some regional research and development services to municipalities. However, the challenges of rapid regional population and economic growth led to the re-emergence of a regional planning process in Greater Vancouver in 1989 (Abbott 2012, p. 576). But 'resurrecting' the full legal and policy basis of regional planning would take until 1996 (Harcourt *et al.* 2007, p. 128).

Gordon Campbell was Mayor of the City of Vancouver and Chair of the GVRD planning committee and in 1989 he initiated the Choosing Our Future process. This was an extensive community engagement process about community values leading to an endorsed vision and action program, called *Creating Our Future* (GVRD 1990). But the municipalities wanted more spatial planning guidance. They said 'It's a great vision … but it's not a plan. It doesn't tell us how we can accommodate the next million people on the ground in a way that reflects the vision' (Harcourt *et al.* 2007, p. 128). Although the GVRD had no legislative mandate to prepare a regional plan in 1991, Gordon Campbell, by then the GVRD Chair, directed the GVRD planners to commence this work with member municipalities on a consensus basis.

Transportation planning was also a contested area in Greater Vancouver and in 1983 the transit planning powers of the GVRD had been removed by the Province. However in 1991, following an approach from the Province, the GVRD agreed to work collaboratively on a regional transportation planning project called Transport 2021 (Abbott 2012, p. 580). This work was fully integrated with other GVRD regional planning work on alternative urban growth patterns. The Transport 2021 plan was approved by the GVRD and Province in 1993. After the election of Mike Harcourt as Premier in 1992, there was also active collaboration by the GVRD and the Province about restoration of regional planning powers. The new legislation being developed was closely based on the 'non-hierarchical, consensus-based' process being used by the GVRD to prepare its new regional plan (Harcourt *et al.* 2007, p. 128).

Following the passage of the *Growth Strategies Statutes Amendment Act* 1995 and after extensive negotiations and compromises with municipalities, mainly about population growth targets, the GVRD endorsed the Livable Region Strategic Plan in January 1996 (the LRSP 1996) (GVRD 1996). The LRSP 1996 was a statutory policy and actions document involving a vision and four strategies for managing growth, as shown in Box 15.2. The framing idea of maintaining livability was still central and there was considerable continuity with the spatial strategies of the LRP 1975. A compact metropolitan region strategy was added, four more regional town centres were included, as well as a transportation

---

**Box 15.2  The LRSP 1996 strategies for managing growth**

- Protect the Green Zone
- Build Complete Communities
- Achieve a Compact Metropolitan Region
- Increase Transportation Choice

Source: GVRD 1996, p. 9

---

structure map showing roads and transit corridors. Municipalities needed to take account of the LRSP 1996 in preparing and amending their own local statutory Official Community Plans (OCPs).

The main outcomes of the LRSP 1996 process were the restoration of a statutory regional plan for Greater Vancouver, consistent with previous regional policies about livability, and integrated land-use and transport planning policies agreed between the GVRD and the Province. Although there were disputes about transit project priorities, these policies led to new transit lines linking town centres and the establishment in 1999 of the Greater Vancouver Transportation Authority (GVTA), later called TransLink.

## Strengthening regional planning: Metro Vancouver 2040 (2011)

The GVRD decided in 2006 to proceed with a new regional plan and to review planning instruments that could help create a stronger regional plan. There was agreement that the four strategies of the LRSP 1996 were still relevant (see Box 15.2) but that implementation needed to be reinforced. The LRSP 1996 was an excellent high-level vision but broke down in the specifics of who was going to do what and where. Also some municipalities were not following the intent of strategies and the LRSP 1996 was not specific enough to be able to prevent these inconsistencies.

Managing growth continued to be a major regional issue in Greater Vancouver with an additional one million people and 600,000 jobs expected by 2040. Many other issues also influenced the review (GVRD 2005). TransLink advised that a new plan should provide stronger regional guidance over municipal decisions and thus lead to population and employment growth patterns that were more cost-efficient to serve by transit and the regional road network. Economic development and the location of jobs emerged as issues because previous regional plans did not have explicit economic objectives and also from concerns about the diminishing supply of industrial land. To address climate change, both mitigation and adaption measures were investigated. In response to declining housing affordability, regional housing policy was given more attention. At the time of the regional plan review, the GVRD had adopted a 'sustainable region initiative' for both planning and operations and this helped focus attention on linking social, environmental, and economic elements of the plan (Metro Vancouver 2011, p. 1).

### The nature and focus of Metro Vancouver 2040

Metro Vancouver 2040 was endorsed in July 2011. It is a statutory regional plan under the Provincial *Local Government Act* (Part 25 Regional Growth Strategies) and includes a vision, five strategic goals, as shown in Box 15.3, and specific actions for member municipalities and other partners. The goals and focus of the plan continue the strategies in the LRSP 1996. New elements have been added in relation to: supporting a sustainable economy; adding transit corridors to town centres as the focus of growth; more guidance on affordable housing; and responding to climate change impacts. No new regional town centres were added. However, Surrey regional town centre was designated as a Metro Centre or second regional downtown to serve the rapidly growing southern and eastern parts of the region. An urban containment boundary and land-use designations, defined by land parcel boundaries, were added as shown in Figure 15.4.

The following sub-sections help to further explain the nature and focus of Metro Vancouver 2040 by briefly discussing regional town centres, frequent transit corridors and local statutory planning.

### Regional town centres

An evaluation of the eight regional town centres was carried out as part of the plan review. Progress was generally very good in terms of the location of retail space, the development of higher density housing and the provision of community facilities. High capacity transit linkages were being developed but were behind schedule. However, little progress had been made developing offices in regional town centres and a large proportion of new office space was located in office parks in areas reserved for industrial activity and was poorly served by transit. The location of office jobs in regional town centres was key to achieving jobs/housing balance in each sub-region and essential in helping create vital, attractive centres.

After much discussion with municipalities, it was decided that a regional regulatory tool was needed to help discourage offices from locating on industrial land.

---

**Box 15.3  The five goals in Metro Vancouver 2040**

Goal 1: Create a compact urban area
Goal 2: Support a sustainable economy
Goal 3: Protect the environment and respond to climate change impacts
Goal 4: Develop Complete Communities
Goal 5: Support Sustainable Transportation Choices

Source: Metro Vancouver 2011, p. 7

---

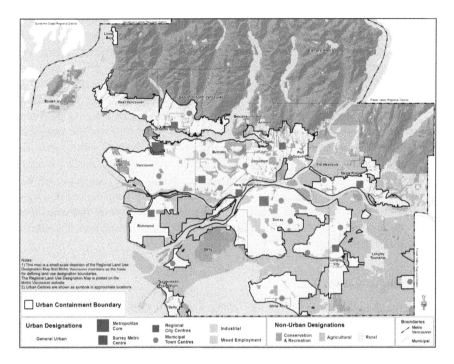

*Figure 15.4* Metro Vancouver 2040 urban containment boundary, centres and regional land use designations

Source: Metro Vancouver 2011, p. 11

This would not only help in the development of regional town centres but also address economic concerns about the diminishing supply of industrial land. This was the most difficult and contentious element of preparing Metro Vancouver 2040. The form of regulation proposed was that industrial areas would be included in a new regional industrial land designation and that municipalities would need to apply for a regional plan amendment if they wished to remove land from the industrial land use designation. This was met with significant opposition from some municipalities and the development sector who wanted ample flexibility to 'up zone' industrial land to other uses, generally office and housing uses. The compromise position that emerged was to establish an 'industrial' regional land use designation but also allow for a separate 'mixed employment' regional land use designation, which included industrial areas that already allowed for office and retail use.

### Frequent transit corridors

Both the LRP 1975 and LRSP 1996 had paid attention to the necessary regional transportation linkages (both transit and roads) to provide access to regional town centres. In 2008 in *Transport 2040*, TransLink introduced the concept of 'frequent transit corridors' and argued that transit-friendly locations were not only in town centres but along transit corridors. This raised questions and uncertainties for the GVRD and municipalities and was much debated. There was concern, particularly for job locations, that identification of all of these corridors as priority locations would result in too much dispersal and reduce the number of jobs in town centre locations. Corridors can also be challenging for building livable residential neighbourhoods, especially if dominated by a busy road. From a market choice point of view, corridors provided more development possibilities, often on land that was trading at a lower price than land in centre locations.

Metro Vancouver 2040 did not designate particular frequent transit corridors but provided a mechanism for municipalities to identify these, subject to GVRD approval. Metro Vancouver 2040 also provided targets for town centres and transit corridor growth, for both dwellings and jobs. So far several municipalities have designated Frequent Transit Development Areas in their OCPs (Metro Vancouver 2014).

### Local statutory planning

Municipalities prepare local statutory plans, known as Official Community Plans (OCPs). A key difference between Metro Vancouver 2040 and the LRSP 1996 is the emphasis in the new regional plan on more effective implementation by clearly specifying what municipalities need to do to support the achievement of regional goals. The plan clarifies the regional interests in land use through parcel-based (cadastral) regional maps and designations. Specific actions are also listed for the GVRD and key partners including TransLink, the Province and Federal agencies. The primary method of implementing the regional plan is for municipalities to prepare or amend their OCPs. The legislation provides for a 'Regional Context Statement' to be included in an OCP to ensure consistency between Metro Vancouver 2040 and the local statutory plan. Each municipality must submit a Regional Context Statement to the Metro Vancouver Board for acceptance. Metro Vancouver 2040 clearly delineates what items municipalities need to include in their Regional Context Statements. Similar direction was not given in the LRSP 1996.

## Multi-level governance in Greater Vancouver

Metropolitan governance refers to the involvement of governments, the private (business) sector and the community sector in the planning and management of metropolitan areas (Phares 2004). In Greater Vancouver, the government sector is multi-level and includes four levels, namely: the Federal Government of Canada; the Province of British Columbia; the GVRD (now called Metro Vancouver); and local municipalities.

The Federal Government has chosen over the last two decades not to be active in regional or city planning in Canada. The Province of British Columbia creates and administers the legislation establishing Regional Districts and local municipalities and the process and products of regional planning. The roles and interests of the Province, the GVRD and municipalities overlap and are interdependent. The Regional Growth Strategies (GVRD) legislation and GVRD meeting processes allow for collaboration and disagreements between the GVRD and member municipalities to be discussed and resolved. No such arrangements or arena exists to collaborate and resolve disagreements between the Province and the GVRD and disputes have led to some unilateral actions by the Province. The ORP 1966 led to 'intergovernmental friction' about policies protecting agricultural land and in 1968 the Province 'dissolved the LMRPB without much warning' (Hodge and Robinson 2001, pp. 333–334). Similarly, after completion of the ORP 1980, there were disputes about urban growth and agricultural land and the Province abolished regional planning in 1983. However, following collaboration between the Province and the GVRD in preparing the LRSP 1996, the Province re-instated regional plan making powers and legislation in 1995.

The Province has a minor direct role in regional planning in Greater Vancouver. They do not approve regional plans nor do they provide services to help implement the plans. They have an impact through three main policy areas:

- The Agricultural Land Reserve (ALR) is administered by the Province and contains 62,000 hectares of protected land. While some boundary amendments have been allowed, it remains as a valuable tool to protect agricultural land and to help provide an urban growth boundary.
- Where the Province chooses to locate education colleges, hospitals, and its offices has an important impact on job/activity distribution in the region.
- The Province remains a direct provider of transportation, even though there is a regional transportation authority (TransLink). TransLink relies on substantial funding from the Province for the provision of Provincial highways and some major transit projects. In some cases, the Province has not agreed with the priorities of TransLink and has funded major projects that may or may not align with regional objectives.

Under these governance arrangements, the Province is not an active player in regional plan-making and implementation. Consequently, regional goals may not align with Provincial goals and budgets and policies may not support the advancement of the regional plan.

The GVRD is governed by a Board of directors made up of elected representatives from all member municipalities. Each municipality decides who should represent them at the Board and the number of directors is determined by population. A weakness is that the Board is not directly elected at the regional level and this can create tensions for directors between local and regional interests and a 'parochial view' (Hodge and Robinson 2001, p. 290). A strength is that regional planning issues are constantly under discussion at the Board and committee meetings. There is also a committee of all municipal planning directors who meet monthly with GVRD planners. These processes generally build an understanding and constituency for regional planning among politicians and staff.

*Governance issues in preparing Metro Vancouver 2040*

In 2006, the LRSP 1996 had been in place for ten years and no amendments had been made to the plan. The consensus process used to prepare the LRSP 1996 and the Regional Growth Strategies legislation had set a very high threshold for both enactment and amendments, requiring all member municipalities to agree. This had the effect of forcing regional growth strategies into a more general and less regulatory format in order to be acceptable to all municipalities.

The GVRD Board made it clear that they were interested in staff exploring the possibility of a stronger (more enforceable) regional plan only if the legislation could be changed to provide a more practical and flexible way to amend the regional plan as needed. The argument had been put forward that the onerous amendment process protected the LRSP 1996 from being weakened in response to short-term crises. On the other hand, it could not be strengthened and it was difficult to keep the plan current. The Province responded by amending the Regional Growth Strategies legislation in 2008. Unanimous acceptance of a new regional plan was still required but the legislation allows for a more flexible plan amendment process.

As plan-making progressed and issues about regional town centres, transit, office location, affordable housing, and industrial land emerged, the conversation with municipalities became more substantial. There was a growing awareness that unilateral actions by individual municipalities would not result in achieving shared regional goals. There was extensive GVRD consultation with municipal councils and the 'hands on' involvement of municipal planning directors was key to acceptance of the plan. Several iterations of draft plans were prepared and debated at both staff and political level.

Active consultation with TransLink was important and was required by legislation. TransLink had prepared its long-range plan, Transport 2040, in 2008 and its policies, particularly those about the frequent transit corridors, influenced land-use policies in Metro Vancouver 2040. However, the collaborative transport and land-use planning process, both at the regional and provincial levels, was not as strong as had occurred in preparing the LRSP 1996.

Wider community and citizen involvement occurred through open houses, town hall meetings in each sub-region and a formal public hearing at the draft plan stage. Community focus groups were also used to check the results of feedback from town hall meetings. Relatively few citizens were actively engaged in the plan review, as generally it did not have an impact at the neighbourhood level. There were some 'anti-growth' voices and groups, but this did not emerge as a significant issue. Interests groups such as land developers and industrial land owners paid a lot of attention to the plan and made several submissions. Some Vancouver academics, such as Tom Hutton, were critical of the continuing 'trade-off' of regional and local municipal interests in the Vancouver governance model which he says 'limits the force of the former . . . to effectively shape regional structure' and to address a more demanding and global twenty-first century economic agenda (2011, pp. 252–254).

Metro Vancouver 2040 was finally enacted in July 2011, almost five years after the GVRD Board had resolved to create a new plan. A regional plan comprising general principles only and less statutory control would have taken much less time to complete and to gain consensus among member municipalities. Time will prove whether it was worth all the effort, but judging from its first three years of implementation, the cadastral-based regional land-use designations and urban containment boundary add valuable clarity and strength to the regional plan.

## Regional strategic planning and managing uncertainty

Regional planning is generally considered by practising planners to be strategic because it deals with a wide range of related planning issues and sets a policy context for local planning. But, as Albrechts and Balducci (2011) ask, what features of regional planning make it strategic? For Friend and Jessop, when decisions on issues such as land use are widened and integrated with related issues such as transportation, then planning becomes 'strategic choice' (1969, p. 97). Van der Heijden says planning opens up a 'strategic conversation' when it involves key stakeholders in discussing scenarios about the future (1996, p. 41). But for Albrechts, strategic spatial planning also needs to be 'selective … strategic implies … making the tough decisions about what is most important for the purpose of producing fair, structural responses to problems' (2004, pp. 751–752). Healey describes strategic spatial planning as 'transformative governance work' that can 'shape the dynamics' through which regions evolve (2009, p. 440). She outlines four phases or dimensions of activity, namely:

- 'mobilising attention';
- 'scoping the situation';
- 'enlarging intelligence'; and
- 'creating frames, selecting actions' (2009, p. 442).

All of the above aspects are important and regional strategic planning is a process of opening up related policy areas, conversations and future options for a region and then closing some of them down by selection and agreement about key framing ideas, strategies and actions.

Another way of looking at strategic planning is as a process of understanding and managing uncertainties and unknowns or rather as plan-making in the context of uncertainty (Friend and Jessop 1969; Abbott 2005, 2009). All planning occurs in 'the shadow of uncertainty' whether planners recognize it or not (Balducci *et al.* 2011, p. 481). Abbott has identified five dimensions of uncertainty affecting planning, as shown in Box 15.4. As discussed above, regional strategic planning is about opening up ideas and future regional options and 'pushing the bounds of possibility' and this will raise uncertainties for those involved in plan-making (Abbott 2005, p. 248). But these uncertainties are also managed, reduced and deferred in the plan-making process by selecting and gaining agreement about key ideas, strategies and actions (Abbott 2012).

---

**Box 15.4  Five dimensions of uncertainty affecting planning**

**Causal uncertainty** relates to imperfect knowledge of the physical, ecological and social environment and of the cause and effect relationships in the processes that link the present to the future;

**Organizational uncertainty** is lack of knowledge about the future intentions, policies and plans, and actions of organizations in the planning environment;

**Value uncertainty** relates to unknown social views and values about a situation or area, about where it is heading, and about its possible futures and includes uncertainties about the views of politicians and of the community;

**External uncertainty** relates to unknowns about external processes and events that cannot be affected directly by planning, but which may affect the planning process and the environment being planned; and

**Chance events** are unpredictable natural and social events that can occur during plan preparation and implementation.

Source: Abbott 2012, p. 573

---

Prior to 1948, the Province and municipalities in the area around Vancouver were not thinking regionally. However, the flooding that occurred that year in the Fraser River delta mobilized attention and raised uncertainties about chance natural events and hazards. It created an imperative for planning to manage flood risks and indicated the required boundaries of the delta planning region. A new Lower Mainland region was identified and a new governance structure, namely the LMRPB, was set up. In scoping the situation, the LMRPB realized that the flooding hazard was interrelated with rapid urban growth and that these two issues should be planned together. There were many causal uncertainties about the new region, including a lack of knowledge about its physical and socio-economic nature and how it was changing. The LMRPB consisted of 26 municipalities that had not worked together before and this raised organizational uncertainties about their views. As plan-making progressed, data collection, mapping and analysis, and municipalities meeting together enlarged intelligence and reduced uncertainties and allowed the LMRPB to select actions and reach agreement about the ORP 1966. Oberlander says this planning and governance work 'began the long process ... of getting the municipalities to talk to each other ... to gestate the regional conscience, the regional ability' (Harcourt *et al.* 2007, pp. 28–29).

Although the LMRPB was replaced by the GVRD in 1968, Greater Vancouver municipalities had learned the importance of working together on regional issues. In 1970, rapid regional growth was the issue mobilizing the attention of GVRD politicians. They adopted the framing idea of 'livability' at the start of plan-making. Under the leadership of planner Harry Lash, the GVRD opened up a proactive dialogue among politicians, planners and the community as shown in the 'Six Sided Triangle' (see Figure 15.2). The scope of the concepts of livability and growth management were explored and widened and intelligence was enlarged. This six-sided dialogue was all about understanding and managing political and community value uncertainties in a time of rapid social and community change.

In preparing the LRP 1975, a critical issue for livability was the balance between population growth and employment growth in different parts of the region and the beneficial role of regional town centres in achieving this balance. This required analysis of urban growth options to address causal uncertainties. Lash was very aware of continual change and the pervasive nature of uncertainties in planning. He says 'the meaning of the planning process is that we will never be certain' (Lash 1976, p. 87). This idea of an ongoing planning process rather than a plan put him at odds with GVRD politicians who wanted an agreed regional plan to guide municipal planning. The resolution of this tension resulted in a transformation of the nature of regional plans in Vancouver. The LRP 1975 was not a fixed, statutory plan but was a non-statutory plan that sought to recognize uncertainties and unprecedented change by focussing on high-level spatial strategies and flexible and adaptable actions (Roberts 1976).

The regional planning powers and statutory plans of Regional Districts were abolished by the Province in 1983. This did not affect the non-statutory LRP 1975, but created many organizational uncertainties about the future planning roles of the GVRD and municipalities (Abbott 2012). The Choosing Our Future program initiated in 1990 was about understanding community values and addressing community value uncertainties. It reaffirmed community support for the framing idea of livability and led to the Creating Our Future vision statement (GVRD 1990). But uncertainties remained about the planning roles of the GVRD and municipalities and the future spatial implications of the GVRD vision. Political leadership by Gordon Campbell, in initiating regional planning on a consensus basis, reduced political value and organizational uncertainties about roles. Early agreement by the GVRD and Province to collaborate on integrated land-use and transportation planning and on new regional planning legislation also reduced organizational uncertainties and greatly widened the scope of regional planning.

As plan-making progressed, exploration of alternative urban growth scenarios enhanced intelligence. But the preferred Compact Metropolitan Area growth option raised causal uncertainties about how this urban pattern could be delivered and organizational uncertainties about the views of municipalities. The Compact Metropolitan Area population growth targets had to be changed from the individual municipal level to the regional level to get agreement of municipalities to the LRSP 1996. There was agreement about the high-level strategies in the LRSP 1996, as shown in Figure 15.3. But agreement about municipal implementation actions was more limited and this created ongoing organizational uncertainties about whether municipalities would include appropriate policies and population growth targets in their OCPs (Abbott 2012, p. 589).

In 2004, Artibise *et al.* wrote about 'dissatisfaction with all this flexibility and adaptability' and suggested 'perhaps it is time for more regional certainty' (2004, p. 208). While the strategies of the LRSP 1996 continued to be supported, there were organizational uncertainties about the implementation intentions of municipalities and this weakened the regional plan. Lack of political leadership meant that mobilizing attention to review the plan was slow. In 2006 the GVRD decided to prepare a new regional plan.

Scoping work for the new plan took into account the Sustainable Region Initiative of the GVRD and broader housing and economic issues, and this raised organizational uncertainties about the role and mandate of the GVRD. The scope of the new plan also focused on better defined implementation and actions. In a sense, the new plan was finishing the job started by the LRSP 1996 by reducing the organizational uncertainties about the actions of municipalities. The Transport 2040 plan prepared by TransLink reduced organizational uncertainties about its views. However, the proposal to allow development along frequent transit corridors increased causal uncertainties about the effects of this development on regional town centres. Intelligence was enlarged through analysis and the strategic conversation with municipalities and TransLink about relationships between centres, offices, and industrial areas and these reduced causal uncertainties. Because the Province was not actively involved, an important ongoing organizational uncertainty was whether their transportation decisions would support the new plan. This uncertainty was a factor that helped gain support for a clearly delineated urban containment boundary.

## Conclusions

The long evolution and current practice of regional planning in Greater Vancouver provides a significant example of regional strategic planning and transformative governance work, in the sense discussed by Healey (2009) and other authors, and lessons for other metropolitan regions. The governance arrangements of the GVRD have provided an arena and forum for member municipalities, TransLink and the regional community to maintain an ongoing strategic conversation about livability and other desired regional outcomes and how the spatial dynamics of regional growth, housing, jobs, town centres, transportation and protecting natural assets relate to these.

In terms of Healey's four dimensions of spatial strategy making (2009, p.442), all of these have played a part in the various plan-making processes in Greater Vancouver. In preparing the ORP 1966, the strategic focus was on scoping and enlarging intelligence by collecting new information about flooding and by municipalities learning to work together. In the LRP 1975, the initial strategic focus was on creating the framing idea of livability and on enlarging intelligence by actively engaging with the regional community to understand what this idea meant for them. In the LRSP 1996, the initial focus was on mobilizing attention and reaffirming the framing idea of livability with the community and on enlarging intelligence by collaborating with the Province on regional transportation planning and on new regional planning legislation. In the latest Metro Vancouver 2040 plan, the strategic focus has been on strengthening and clarifying the regulatory frame and selecting implementation actions to achieve strategic goals.

### Planning in uncertainty

Uncertainties are pervasive in all regional plan-making processes, including those in Greater Vancouver. External uncertainties, such as immigration rates, and chance natural events, such as the risk of large-scale flooding, played a role in making the ORP 1966 and the LRSP 1996. Regional planning in Vancouver also shows that uncertainties are raised by widening the scope and policy areas of planning and by including new stakeholders and the community to develop future visions. These processes occurred particularly with the LRP 1975 and the LRSP 1996 and raised organizational, value and causal uncertainties. These uncertainties were addressed and reduced by analysis and collaboration and by creating frames and selecting actions in order to get agreement of stakeholders to the regional plan. Organizational uncertainties are ever-present in Greater Vancouver planning, and this is related to the governance arrangements of the GVRD with the municipalities, TransLink and the Province. Organizational uncertainties about implementation continued after approval of the LRSP 1996. Addressing these uncertainties and reaching agreement about frames and actions for implementation was the main focus in preparing Metro Vancouver 2040.

The evolution of regional strategic planning in Greater Vancouver also provides insights and lessons about the nature of regional plans in the context of pervasive uncertainty. This is sometimes expressed as a tension between flexibility and adaptability, on the one hand, and certainty and guidance in plans, on the other hand. Harry Lash recognized the difficulty of deciding on a formal plan of actions in the context of ongoing change with his expression 'The Plan is the Process' (Lash 1976, p. 45). However, local politicians wanted an agreed regional plan and actions to guide local municipalities. This resulted in the LRP 1975: a new type of non-statutory plan with broad strategies and flexible actions.

This tension arose again in 1990 with the approval of Creating Our Future by the GVRD. Municipalities said it was a good vision but they wanted more spatial guidance at the local level. This led to the initiation of the LRSP 1996 plan-making process on a consensus basis, because the legislation had been abolished in 1983. When new regional planning legislation was passed in 1995 it also reflected the consensus approach. Because of the high level of consensus (100%) required from municipalities, only broad spatial strategies and actions could be included in the final LRSP 1996. So, ironically, the LRSP 1996 was a statutory regional plan but it provided limited spatial guidance to municipalities and was very difficult to change: it did not improve certainty and was inflexible.

In preparing Metro Vancouver 2040, the challenge was to solve this dilemma by gaining the agreement of the Province to change the legislation and the necessary agreement of municipalities to key regional actions and to the procedures to amend the plan. This led to a stronger and more detailed statutory plan expressing agreed regional interests, but one that was more flexible and adaptable compared to the previous plan.

### Federation of municipalities governance model

The consensus-based, federation of municipalities governance model of Greater Vancouver has strengths and weaknesses. Its major strengths are that it is responsive to community values and it provides an ongoing collaborative framework for municipalities to have conversations about regional growth management and livability and to agree on visions and legally enforceable regional actions. It has endured and evolved in this role for almost 50 years. This governance system necessitates a high degree of consensus because before a plan is adopted, it requires acceptance by municipalities and TransLink. This does result in some compromise and effectively means that for the plan to be acceptable it must contain the minimum amount of regulation possible to achieve regional objectives. The lack of involvement and collaboration by the Province in joint regional planning with the GVRD and TransLink is another weakness. A strong bias in favour of local interests exists in the GVRD because municipalities need the support of others and will often not vote against them.

Regional strategic planning in Greater Vancouver provides a mechanism to address regional opportunities and problems at the scale that is required to resolve them and the planning and governance model has delivered enduring benefits for the region, such as:

- protecting environmental and natural assets;
- creating a livable, high-quality, transit-oriented urban environment that is valued by the regional community and admired internationally;
- integrating regional land use and transportation and creating a regional transportation authority;
- developing regional town centres, bringing jobs and services closer to the population;
- providing more housing choice in all parts of the region;
- reducing both residential and employment sprawl;
- protecting the supply of industrial land; and
- improving local statutory planning by providing regional information and policy guidance.

Regional strategic planning in Greater Vancouver is built on a governance framework that allows strategic conversations to occur primarily among municipalities, the regional transportation authority and the regional community. Formal statutory regional plans are important and are carefully worded to capture agreement about regional values, interests and actions. Regional planning has sought to provide the strategic and statutory guidance and certainty needed in a multi-level system while being aware of and adaptive to regional spatial dynamics and the political and social context of ongoing change and uncertainty.

## Acknowledgements

The assistance of Hugh Kellas, former Manager of Policy and Planning with Metro Vancouver, and Thora Gislason, Corporate Librarian, with Metro Vancouver in preparing this chapter is greatly appreciated.

## References

Abbott, J. 2005. Understanding and Managing the Unknown: The Nature of Uncertainty in Planning. *Journal of Planning Education and Research*, 24(3), 237–251.

Abbott, J. 2009. Planning for Complex Metropolitan Regions: A Better Future or a More Certain One? *Journal of Planning Education and Research*, 28(4), 503–517.

Abbott, J. 2012. Planning as Managing Uncertainty: Making the 1996 Livable Region Strategic Plan for Greater Vancouver. *Planning Practice and Research*, 27(5), 571–593.

Albrechts, L. 2004. Strategic (Spatial) Planning Re-examined. *Environment and Planning B: Planning and Design*, 31, 743–758.

Albrechts, L. and A. Balducci. 2011. Practicing Strategic Planning: In Search for Critical Features to Explain the Strategic Character of Plans. Paper presented at the World Planning Schools Congress, Perth, Australia, 4–8 July 2011.

Artibise, A., K. Cameron and J. Seelig. 2004. Metropolitan Organization in Greater Vancouver: 'Do it Yourself' Regional Government. In Donald Phares (Ed.), *Metropolitan Governance without Metropolitan Government?* Aldershot, UK: Ashgate.

Balducci, A., L. Boelens, J. Hillier, T. Nyseth and C. Wilkinson. 2011. Strategic Spatial Planning in Uncertainty: Theory and Exploratory Practice. *Town Planning Review*, 82(5), 481–501.

CFVRD *et al*. 1980. *Plan for the Lower Mainland of British Columbia*. Vancouver: Central Fraser Valley Regional District *et al*.

Friend, J., and N. Jessop. 1969. *Local Government and Strategic Choice: An Operational Research Approach to the Processes of Public Planning*. London: Tavistock.

GVRD. 1975. *The Livable Region 1976–1986: Proposals to Manage the Growth of Greater Vancouver*. Vancouver: Greater Vancouver Regional District.

GVRD. 1990. *Creating Our Future: Steps to a More Livable Region*. Vancouver: Greater Vancouver Regional District.

GVRD. 1996. *The Livable Region Strategic Plan*. Vancouver: Greater Vancouver Regional District.

GVRD. 2005. *Advancing the Sustainable Region: Issues for the Livable Region Strategic Plan Review*. Vancouver: Greater Vancouver Regional District.

Harcourt, M., K. Cameron and S. Rossiter. 2007. *City Making in Paradise: Nine Decisions That Saved Vancouver*. Vancouver: Douglas and McIntyre.

Healey, P. 2009. In Search of the 'Strategic' in Spatial Strategy Making. *Planning Theory & Practice*, 10(4), 439–457.

Hodge, G. and I. Robinson. 2001. *Planning Canadian Regions*. Vancouver: UBC Press.

Hutton, T. 2011. Thinking Metropolis: From the 'Livable Region' to the 'Sustainable Metropolis' in Vancouver. *International Planning Studies*, 16(3), 237–255.

Lash, H. 1976. *Planning in a Human Way: Personal Reflections on the Regional Planning Experience in Greater Vancouver*. Ottawa: Ministry of State for Urban Affairs.

LMRPB. 1963. *Chance and Challenge: A Concept and Plan for the Development of the Lower Mainland Region of British Columbia*. Vancouver: Lower Mainland Regional Planning Board.

LMRPB. 1966. *The Official Regional Plan for the Lower Mainland Planning Area*. Vancouver: Lower Mainland Regional Planning Board

Metro Vancouver. 2011. *Metro Vancouver 2040: Shaping Our Future*. Vancouver: Metro Vancouver.

Metro Vancouver. 2014. *Progress Toward Shaping Our Future: 2014 Annual Report*. Vancouver: Metro Vancouver.

Phares, D. (ed.) 2004. *Metropolitan Governance without Metropolitan Government?* Aldershot, UK: Ashgate.

Roberts, T. 1976. *PIBC Review of the Livable Region 1976/86*. Vancouver: Planning Institute of British Columbia.

TransLink. 2008. *Transport 2040: A Transportation Strategy for Metro Vancouver, Now and in the Future*. Vancouver: TransLink.

Van der Heijden, K. 1996. *Scenarios: The Art of Strategic Conversation*. Chichester, UK: John Wiley & Sons.

## Website

Copies of regional plans discussed in this chapter can be viewed on the Metro Vancouver library website at http://www.metrovancouver.org/about/library/Pages/Historical-Regional-Planning-Reports-and-Maps.aspx.

# 16 Rio de Janeiro's strategic plan

## The Olympic construction of the corporate town

*Carlos Vainer*

## Introduction

In June and July 2013, some 10 million people went out to protest in over 500 Brazilian cities. The crowds went out into the street to show their disagreement with a inefficient public transportation system and its costs, public services, the enormous expenditure on stadiums and money-guzzling construction projects and forced evictions of poor populations using the FIFA World Cup 2014 and Olympics 2016 (in Rio de Janeiro) as a pretext.[1] President Dilma Roussef, on a national TV and radio speech, on June 21, 2013 acknowledged that:

> Those who went into the streets sent a direct message to the entire society, and, above all, to those in governing positions at all levels. This direct message from the streets is *for a greater voice as citizens*, better schools, better hospitals and health centers, *for the right to participate*. This direct message from the streets is a demand for quality public transportation at a fair price. This direct message from the streets is one for the *right to influence all the decisions of all levels of government, the legislative branch and the judicial branch*.

And, in an unexpectedly self-critical tone, she exclaimed: 'It is the citizenry – and not those with economic power – who should be heard first' (Roussef, 2013).

This speech, due to its unusual courage and frankness, can serve as an inspiration for the effort intended in this chapter to shed light on and analyse what happened in the city of Rio de Janeiro in the three decades after the end of the military dictatorship. Why, after 30 years of democracy, do city dwellers go into the streets to claim for participation, to protest against scarce city services, and in general against conditions of urban development that often reproduce the unequal, unfair cities of 30 years ago?

If what are called the 'June days' were a nation-wide phenomenon, Rio de Janeiro was the city where demonstrations were the largest and protests against mega-sporting events were the most intense. In the end, the city hosted the Pan American Games 2007, the FIFA Confederations Cup 2013, the FIFA World Cup 2014 and will host the Olympic Games 2016.

This sequence of mega-sporting events and, specifically, the holding of the 2016 Olympic Games in Rio de Janeiro constitute the outcome of a trajectory during which a new conception of city and urban planning emerged and became hegemonic. It also expresses the consolidation of a new coalition of local power which was inaugurated and took form under the aegis of the mayor Cesar Maia.[2] The symbolic, if not founding, moment of this conception was surely the drawing up of the Strategic Plan of the City of Rio de Janeiro in 1993 and 1994.

The intention in this chapter is to tell the story of how this Strategic Plan was drawn up and to develop an analysis of how urban dynamics were configured, leading the city of Rio de Janeiro to simultaneously transform itself into an Olympic city and become the centre of major demonstrations, one target of which was these mega-sporting events.

## The birth of Rio de Janeiro's strategic plan

On November 22, 1993, Rio de Janeiro's City Hall, the Business Association (ACRJ) and the Federation of Industries (FIRJAN) signed an agreement for the promotion of the Strategic Plan of the City of Rio de Janeiro (PECRJ). On February 4, 1994, 46 companies and business associations set up the PECRJ's Support Consortium (Consórcio Mantenedor do PECRJ), thereby securing (private) resources for funding its activities, and, specifically, for hiring the services of a Catalan consulting firm[3] as well has those of various professionals to be on the Plan's technical team.

On October 31 of the same year, at a formal event, the City Council (Conselho da Cidade) was put in place. Bringing together those selected by the funders, it was 'the highest level of the Strategic Plan of the City of Rio de Janeiro', according to the invitation sent out by three parties: the presidents of the ACRJ and FIRJAN and the mayor' (Vainer, 2000a: 106).

> The noble scene unfolding in the inner gardens of the Itamaraty Palace,[4] the movement on that sunny, fresh morning must have certainly surprised the iconic swans of the well-kept garden (who had retired after the transfer of the capital to Brasilia). Who are these people, they perhaps asked themselves? They are the 'good men'[5] of the city: elegant businessmen, public figures from Rio high society, politicians and high-ranking civil servants from the state bureaucracy, heads of non-governmental organizations feted in the media, journalists with press passes. [...] The inauguration of the City Council is going to begin. Everyone has been credentialed, they have already signed in and gotten their folders and name tags. The national anthem is sung, and then, a choral group sings Cidade Maravilhosa.[6] Speeches are given by the ACRJ president and the FIRJAN president and applauded. Then comes the Municipal Secretary for Urban Planning and more applause. They speak to us about the city's viability and the importance of citizens taking back their city. They talk about the city being in the vanguard and a pioneer, and that *it would be first city in the Southern Hemisphere to have a strategic*

*plan.* Then, it's the turn of Dr. Jordi Borja, chairman of the consulting firm Tecnologies Urbanas Barcelona S.A.: the erudite rhetoric from a calloused academic, interspersed with praises for the city's potential and the creative spirit of its people – Barcelona is also here. The PECRJ's executive director traced the rise and decline of Rio de Janeiro, finishing up by highlighting its comparative advantages in this era of competition and globalization. Then, the mayor takes the floor to solemnly swear in the members of the City Council. The official speaker then invites all the council members to move to the staircase into the garden where a historic photograph will be taken as the event program stated. (Vainer, 2000a: 108)

In addition to the Support Consortium, the Executive Committee and the City Council, the PECRJ's structure called for a Steering Council to which the Executive Committee was accountable. Among the members of the Steering Committee were individual business people, representatives of business organizations, heads of the city's main universities, the urban development secretary for the city, the state secretary for planning, and some VIPs. On January 20, 1995, the City Council, at the ACRJ's headquarters, approved the Diagnosis of the City of Rio de Janeiro.

Working groups were set up at next stage to define priority projects in various areas of interest. Finally, to top off this process, the 'City Council', approved the Strategic Plan for the City of Rio de Janeiro on September 11, 1995. Out of this came first bid to host the Olympics (1994), with the very same Catalan consultants on board. These were the ones who 'discovered' the 'Olympic mission' of the city. The words below appear in the strategic plan entitled 'Rio Always Rio':

> The sporting tradition in Rio and its natural and human resources make possible its bid as candidate for hosting the 2004 Olympics, with excellent possibilities. And, following the example of other cities, it will take advantage of the games for its own transformation. (Prefeitura da Cidade do Rio de Janeiro, 1996: 52)

Twenty years after, what is the meaning and efficacy of urban planning standard expressed in the Strategic Plan of the City of Rio de Janeiro? What did the Strategic Plan in the recent history of the City of Rio de Janeiro signify? What did this major media operation, headed up by business people and the mayor produce?

## The strategic plan as an instrument for fighting urban planning

In 1992, four years after the end of the military regime and one year before strategic planning kicked off, the Town Council had approved the Ten-Year Master Plan for the city. One of the first in the country,[7] Rio de Janeiro's Ten-Year Master Plan was the outcome of a broad, deep public debate within the context of re-democratization experienced by the country after more than 20 years of dictatorship (Ribeiro and Santos, 1994; Santos, 2013: 2). The plan set up various instruments seen as mechanisms of social interest and control of speculative use of city land, such compulsory building, expropriation with payment in the form of government securities, increasing municipal property tax, adverse possession, special social interest zones, and neighbourhood impact studies (Santos, 2013: 3). These tools would come to be enshrined in the City Statute Law in 2001.

The initiative of the business consortium and City Hall, as would become clear with the passage of time, can be understood as a response to the Master Plan. In contradistinction to the constitutionally established concept of the social function of the city and property, present in the Master Plan and that would be strengthened in 2001 by the Statute of the City law, the business, entrepreneurial (Harvey, 1996) and corporate city was born in Rio de Janeiro.

## Planned production of consensus

The scope of membership of *City Council* could not have been broader, with more than 300 members: individual members (VIPs?), companies, interest-group associations, all of which had been invited by the funding business consortium, the Steering Council or the Executive Committee.

In the end, it would be clear that membership on the City Council was not very important since the City Council did not deliberate or counsel and its function was purely symbolic and propagandistic. The City Council only met to approve documents drawn up by the Executive Committee, approved by the Steering Council. The *councillors* did not interfere in who sat on the Steering Committee or in the orientation or choices of the Executive Committee. The City Council, did not, in fact, constitute a collective body at all because, as the Executive Director clarified during a public debate, it would be 'impossible to administer a debate in such a heterogeneous collective' (interview with the author). This task always remained the duty of the Executive Committee or the Steering Committee.

The process of drawing up and approving the Diagnosis is illustrative in this regard. The Executive Committee structured the Working Groups. Academics, civil servants and business people have been interviewed to establish the Diagnosis, which was supposed to guide the establishment of the *Strategic Guidelines*. A consulting company was also hired, which, on various occasions, sub-contracted individual consultants. All the Working Groups had to work according to a precise methodology following the orientation from the Catalans: evaluate strengths, weaknesses, opportunities and threats. This was the SWOT[8] analysis in action.

The Executive Committee organized what it received from the Working Groups in a strange document, sent onto the members of the *City Council* for suggestions, which brought together no fewer than *268 trends, 180 strong points* and *193 weak points*. The councillors had 20 days to submit their suggested amendments, informed that 'no comment (silence) on any of the items [...] would be interpreted as approval of the proposed text'. Also, they were advised that any suggestion was to be 'referenced to the classification structure of the document' (Plano Estratégico da Cidade do Rio de Janeiro, 1994).

> On January 20, under the protection of its patron saint,[9] the city met in the agora, or better, at the Business Association, to approve its self-diagnosis. Summoned to rubber stamp the document, the Council was not even asked to go through the ritual of voting. The mayor proclaimed, on behalf of the Council, that the city acknowledged the diagnosis. [...] The city is reconstructing itself, united around a consensus of the citizenry [...] and the Business Association. (Vainer, 2000a: 110)

Surely not even 5% of the councillors had even read the long, boring document that strictly adhered to the Catalan strategic planning model: apart from the infinite number of weak points and strong points, the City Council also approved some *Strategic Guidelines*, which, as strange as it might seem, were not in the document previously sent to the councillors for examination. But the fact that the strategic guidelines were not known and were not the object of discussion was no barrier to a rubber-stamping consensus. This was even true, as the PECRJ document states, because consensus is *natural ... and desirable*.

> It was found, nevertheless, that consensual Strategic Guidelines did exist. This is *natural* since urban reality present diversities [sic] but it is also a totality in way people perceive things. At the same time, it is *desirable since the actions to be undertaken will demand, for the most part, the efforts of all social agents*. (Plano Estratégico da Cidade do Rio de Janeiro, cited in Vainer, 2000a)[10]

The PECRJ's next stages followed the same model. After the Diagnostic, working groups were set up to propose, according to the various Strategic Guidelines, projects (*strategic actions*) to be considered on a priority basis. After this, the '*328 strategic actions selected by the 14 Working Groups [...] were grouped into seven Programs, 23 objectives and 94 actions*' (Prefeitura da Cidade do Rio de Janeiro, 1996). The Councillors were asked to grade those they considered a priority on a scale of 1 to 5. And once again, after the counting work done by the Executive Committee, and approval from the Steering Council, the City Council was convened on September 11 to unanimously greenlight what was proudly proclaimed to be the first Strategic Plan of the Southern Hemisphere.

It is essential to understand that this process eliminates any possibility of an effective discussion either on the nature and relevance of various problems, or on the best (strategic? tactical?) ways to analyse and deal with them. The consensus reached at the end was already, in a certain sense, presupposed at the outset. The unity of the business consortium, expressed by the Steering Council, the City Council, consultants and working groups had already banished in an a priori and irreversible manner any risk of dissent.

The executive secretary of the PECRJ explained, in interviews given to this author, that the deadlines on contracts drawn up between consultants in Brazil and abroad and the financial Consortium were an impediment to offering time and opportunities for public debate. When questioned about the legitimacy of a plan created between four walls and guided only by business groups, he argued that he did not understand how there could be diverging opinions on the proposed strategic guidelines.

Political/policy differences, debate and presenting two-sides to an argument come to be threatening for competitive strategies. The two principal consultants for the Strategic Plan of Rio de Janeiro are clear on this point, affirming that it is indispensable to 'generate patriotism in the city that enables its leaders, actors and all the citizenry to assume with pride their past and future, and especially the activity present in all fields' (Borja and Forn, 1996: 46).

External marketing strategies are thus linked to internal ones:

> It is also up to the local government to undertake internal promotion of the city to give its inhabitants a sense of '*civic patriotism*', of belonging, of the collective will to participate and of trust and belief in its future. This internal promotion should also be supported by *visible*[11] construction work and services, that are both monumental and symbolic in nature such as those directed at improving the quality of public spaces and the well-being of the population. (Borja and Castells, 1996: 160 – italics are mine)

The paradox is performed: the strategic plan speaks on behalf of a unified city, the construction of which it intends to engender via the promotion of patriotism.

> The monuments and sculptures (by what they represent and the prestige of their creators), the malleable beauty and originality of infrastructure and equipment design or the care taken in the profiles of public squares and gardens lend dignity to the citizenry, make the city more visible and reinforce identity, including the civic patriotism of its people. (Borja, 1995: 14)

It is no surprise that the multitudes turned out to protest the wasteful use of public resources on money-guzzling construction work and monuments associated with mega-sporting events, the white elephants that constitute veritable abuse in the face of the (infrastructure) shortcomings in a city in which 40% of households do not have treated sewerage, to cite but one example.

## Banish politics to build a pacified, competitive city

Once the methodologies of urban planning are reformed, the concepts of city revolutionized, and the unity and identity of all city dwellers with their city and the new business project restored, what is the meaning of *politics*?

To begin with, it is necessary to express, at the political and institutional level, the social peace introduced into the reconciled urban homeland under the aegis of the entrepreneurialism. After all, the new planning mode is an opportunity for a 'consensual project that somewhat transcends the field of partisan political/ policy affiliations and that can guarantee permanence to investors in terms of certain choices' (Ascher, 1994: 91). The planned depolitization itself is also, as may be seen, part of the guarantees offered to the *private partners*.

In the case of Rio de Janeiro, this was possible thanks to a partisan political structure with little policy or programmatic density, in the context of which various lobbying groups were operating through various political parties in accordance with the vagaries of the moment in electoral politics. Thus, Cesar Maia was elected in 1993 as a candidate for the Brazilian Democratic Movement Party (PMDB), but before his term ended he had moved on to the Liberal Front Party (PFL). His secretary of urban planning, Luis Paulo Conde, at his behest, became a PFL candidate and was elected as a PFL member, but he ended up separating himself from this political mentor for personal reasons. Conde stood and lost the next round of elections for Cesar Maia, who himself returned to government via the Brazilian Labor Party (PTB), then transferred to the Democrats (DEM). He was succeeded by Eduardo Paes, who, after being a member of the Cesar Maia's youth movement (Juventude Cesar Maia) and being the assistant mayor for the Barra de Tijuca district, gave up on his mentor to win the elections for mayor under the banner of the PMDB.

As may be seen, the partisan affiliations and loyalties do not play any role here but stability was ensured for more than 20 years by the (strategic) strength of the business coalition that supported all these governing individuals and funded their electoral campaigns.

## The construction of the Olympic vocation

Twenty years were not needed to reveal the irrelevance of the strategic guidelines of the dozens of programs and projects considered priorities by the PECRJ. At the time, most of the intended 'innovative' proposals rehashed policies and projects that were already underway. The executive secretary justified this based on the necessity of giving the Plan credibility: putting actions into the Plan that were already underway would contribute to people believing that the Plan was viable, that it was 'serious'.

But the citizens of Rio, or Cariocas, even the best informed among them, do not know at all – and have never known – of the existence of this Plan or its proposals and projects. This was, one could say, the price to be paid for the lack of public debate. There is, however, a constant that originated with the Plan and remained on the scene after the Plan itself had fallen into oblivion: the search to host major sporting events.

The first application was made officially in 1996, presented by the 'Rio Barcelona Consultores' (RBC) company, which also counted among its technical team the same Manoel de Forn and Jordi Borja. In close accordance with the vision expressed by these consultants in the Strategic Plan, 'the whole application process for the 2004 Olympic Games was strictly bound to the entrepreneurial role of the city's administration which, in direct coordination with international consulting groups [and added to this should be 'with local business groups'] would promote putting the city on the global market', (Oliveira, 2012: 191). The project called for concentrating Olympic facilities on Island of the University City (*Ilha da Cidade Universitária*). But Mayor Cesar Maia clearly showed his disagreement with this option given the surrounding area: 'The Olympics are, first of all, an economic event related to sports. It has its rationale and requirements. Just imagine the photograph of an athlete on a front page and in the background a shanty town with a squalid man'[12] (cited in Dacosta et al., 2008: 12).

It would be hard to assert, however, that this was the reason why in 1998 Rio de Janeiro was written off since the first round of application assessment. But as a kind of consolation prize, that same year, the Brazilian Olympic Committee would invite the city to represent the country at the competition for the 2007 Pan-American Games. Submitted in 2001 to the Pan-American Sports Organization (PASO), the city's application won out over San Antonio, Texas, at the Xl PASO General Assembly, held in Mexico City on August 24, 2002 (Oliveira, 2012).

In the Rio 2007 plan for the Pan-American Games (Fundação Getúlio Vargas, 2000, 2001) the choice of University City as a site was given up, surely as a way to avoid having 'squalid men' appearing in photographs. The plan called for setting up athletic facilities in the area bordering high-value real estate in the Barra da Tijuca district. In defence of this new geo-political orientation, it was argued that in addition to being a flat area with 'qualified occupancy', easily monitored from the ground and air, the Barra da Tijuca had large, open areas. This choice would consolidate the alliance between City Hall, the major property owners in the area and the major public works' companies.

With the election of Luis Inácio Lula da Silva to the presidency in 2003 and the creation of the Ministry of Sports, the Federal government came to the aid of the city (municipal authority) by taking on almost half of the final costs (Oliveira, 2011). Budgeted initially at 390 million reais, the event ended up costing almost ten times more at 3.7 billion (Oliveira, 2011), even though the promised social legacy was not fulfilled.

In 2003, having secured its bid to host the 2007 Pan-American Games, Rio de Janeiro again put in a bid to the International Olympic Committee (IOC), this time to host the Olympics 2012. The bid, drawn up by MI Associates PTY, also failed and the winner would be London.

In October 2007, in another hosting competition, the Fédération Internationale de Football Association (FIFA) selected Brazil to host the 2014 FIFA World Cup. Hailing this in what was an extraordinary demonstration of confidence about the future and the 'specialists', Minister of Tourism Marta Suplicy, at the National Conference of Architectural and Consulting Engineer Companies declared to the delight of entrepreneurs that: 'According to the specialists we consulted, hosting a World Cup event will foster 50 years of development in the country. We cannot forego this opportunity' (Folha de São Paulo, 2/12/2007, cited in Oliveira, 2012).

The Lula government's complete engagement in the Pan-American Games and in the bid for the World Cup showed that holding sports' mega-events had spilled over the borders of the city of Rio de Janeiro and the local power coalition to become a political priority for the State. No effort, no dime would be spared to bring the games in 2016.

> Orchestrated by specialists such as Mike Lee, a key piece in London being the 2012 winner, Michael Payne, former IOC director of marketing, and Scott Givens, former VP of entertainment at Disney and manager of the opening and closing ceremonies of the 2007 Pan American Games and the 2000 Sydney Olympics, the Brazilian bid used everything it could to achieve its final objective. The speech about the right of South America to host the Olympics for the first time was used as the central argument but not the only one. Other symbolic elements were leveraged in the attempt to convince the first-ever grand electors that represent the International Olympic Committee (IOC) such as emotional images shown in the videos created by the well-known filmmaker Fernando Meirelles; the joy and receptiveness of Cariocas; the need to recapture the city's historical importance that had been vitiated since the federal capital's transfer to Brasilia; or even the new positioning the country would get on the international stage. (Oliveira, 2012: 202)

In the face of first-ever unity of three levels of government (federal, state and local), financial guarantees ensured by the presence of the chairman of the Central Bank of Brazil in Copenhagen, the propagandistic role played by President Lula – then at the pinnacle of his international prestige – should not be disdained. At a press conference, Lula was seeking to seduce and convince: 'I can only guarantee that no country in the world is as certain of its future as Brazil is […]. We want to tell the world that we can. When these words are spoken by an American, they're very pretty, we never say [this]. Because in Brazil, we were used to saying "No, we can't do, we're poor, we can't…" This time we want to look at the world and say "Yes, we can. And we're going to hold these Olympics".'

This time the application to host the Olympics hit gold, winning out over Chicago, Madrid and Tokyo. Everyone celebrated the victory but no one remembered the Strategic Plan of Rio de Janeiro or the TUBSA Catalan consultants who 15 years before had plied their Barcelona experience, landing in the city paid by the Associação Comercial (Business Association), Federação das Indústrias (Federation of Industries) and the consortium of 45 companies, and who were the first to 'invent' the city's Olympic mission, at long last recognized by the outside world … and by the IOC.

## The legacy of strategic planning was the sporting mega-events, and the legacy of sporting mega-events is …

The holding of the Pan-American Games 2007, the FIFA World Cup 2014 and, above all, the Olympics 2016 in Rio de Janeiro express a great victory and complete achievement of the plan spearheaded by the new local-national coalition. And if the transformation of the city into the seat of sports mega-events appears to be the main legacy of strategic planning, this is because it synthesizes and symbolizes the principal characteristics of the neo-liberal city: large-scale urban operations; direct democracy of capital that updates itself through public-private partnerships; and, last but not least, the authoritarianism of repeated *ad hoc* decisions that accommodate the city of exception[13] to market needs.

The adoption of the market-friendly approach, defended by the World Bank since the 1990s (World Bank, 1991, 2000), meant giving up the planning model that came out of the Keynesian Consensus, founded on a comprehensive and rationalist intention as expressed, above all, in master plans and zoning practices. Now, under the Washington Consensus, market-friendly planning accommodates and subjects the city, its structure and dynamics to market forces – enshrined as the most efficient mechanism for the allocation of resources.

If the main legacy of strategic planning in Rio de Janeiro was affirmation of the Olympic city, the city of sports mega-events, only a systematic assessment of the consequences of this series of mega-events on the structure and dynamics of the city would enable an evaluation of the consequences of the process begun in 1993 through the initiative of the PECRJ, funded by a corporate coalition.

From the political-institutional point of view, mega-events accentuate the structure of the city of exception (Vainer, 2015), with *ad hoc* rules and institutions springing up. The World Cup Law (Law Nbr. 12.663 of June 5, 2012), for example, established rules that openly thwart the laws on sports and stadiums as well as the consumer protection laws by authorizing the marketing/sales of alcoholic beverages in stadiums and by creating exclusive commercials for FIFA sponsor companies.[14] FIFA and IOC benefitted from extensive, multiple laws of exception, such as tax benefits, tax exemptions and all types of favours, even regarding control of advertising spaces in the city. On the exceptionality rug were also laid special institutions out of reach of any public control, e.g. the Municipal Olympic Company (Empresa Olímpica Municipal) and the Olympic Public Authority (Autoridade Pública Olímpica) (Vainer, 2015).

Mega-events may not be held liable for the emergence of urban policies that favour large projects, and making legislation and standards flexible to the benefit of public-private partnerships, a configuration that Ascher (2001) has qualified as *ad hoc urban planning*. But it may be affirmed that mega-events deepen and make more widespread mechanisms of exception and the authoritarian tendencies of the entrepreneurial, competitive city. FIFA's Secretary General, in an unexpected show of honesty and frankness, two months before the uprising of June 2013 declared, 'I am going to say something that is crazy, but less democracy sometimes is better for organizing a World Cup. [...] When you have a very strong head of state[15] who can make decisions, maybe like Putin might make in 2018... it's easier for us organizers' (Estadão, 2013).

From the economic and financial point of view, public demonstrations became decisive in denouncing the unbelievable wasting of public resources. It is impossible to know the costs of the 2014 World Cup, and, even less, those of the

Olympics, but it is known that they are very high whereas the promised benefits are more uncertain and incalculable. In the case of the 2014 World Cup, various studies point out losses of gross domestic and local product due to the days off that interrupted the course of business and industry. The São Paulo Business Federation (Federação de Comércio) estimated losses of 30 billion reais in the business sector due to the World Cup (EBC/Agência Brasil, 2014, G1, 2014).[16]

Finally, it would be useful to assess, even if summarily, the consequences of these mega-events on the structure and dynamics of the city. Again, in this regard, it would be a mistake to hold the World Cup and Olympics responsible for urban inequality and the social-spatial segregation that deeply marks the city of Rio de Janeiro. But the FIFA World Cup, and above all the Olympics, intensified if not sparked off, two simultaneous movements that sharpened inequalities and social-spatial segregation. On the one hand, forced evictions reached record levels, leading to true 'social and ethnic cleansing' of the highest value areas where the more affluent reside. More than 100,000 persons were, and are, being evicted on the pretext of making room for Olympic facilities or roadway works undertaken to handle the flows expected during the Olympics.[17] The evicted were sent to distant outskirts of the city, where there is no infrastructure and travel costs are unaffordable.

Concomitantly and synergistically, public expenditure on infrastructure and mobility are concentrated in areas where sports' facilities and the Olympic Park are located, precisely those areas into which real estate capital is moving and out of which the poor are being evicted. Thus, if there is a legacy in terms of urban infrastructure, it is for areas already occupied or to be occupied by the better off since, perversely, public expenditures are made in regions from which the poor are being evicted.

## Final observations

The Strategic Plan of the City of Rio de Janeiro could easily be qualified as a well-orchestrated farce, the goal of which was to legitimize expensive projects and orientations desired by the city's dominant groups. Without any doubt, this assessment considers one dimension of the initiative but is insufficient as to point out what *was* innovative about the PESCRJ. And this was:

- an emphasis on the city's patriotism and the city's unifying rituals around common goals, above political or ideological differences and far removed from political issues;
- association between local economic development and competitive global insertion of the city, through the attraction of mega-events;
- new relationships between the local public sector and private capital shaping a democracy of capital, above all through public-private partnership and large-scale urban operations;
- new cross-scale articulations, linking a local coalition to large domestic corporation in the public works industry and the global industry of major events, a veritable cartel headed up by FIFA and the IOC;

- promotion of the city of exception, a new urban regime marked by the dismantlement of the planning apparatus, discredit of the master plan, making urban regulation flexible and creation of decision-making institutions and mechanisms at the margins of the law and without any social control or transparency.

It would be possible to ask whether the growth in urban inequality and the strengthening of authoritarianism were a consequence of adopting strategic planning or if they were the result of the evolution in the correlation of forces inside the city, or both. To answer this question, it would be necessary to delve into the debate on the principles and procedures proper to this planning methodology (or theory?) (Vainer, 2000b; Novais, 2010). Regardless of the answer, it may be affirmed that the strategic planning in Rio de Janeiro with its corollary the mega-events are part of the history of the increasing of urban inequalities in Rio de Janeiro and contributed to trigger the mass demonstrations in 2013.

## Notes

1 Regarding the urban origins of the June days of 2013, see, for example, Maricato, 2013; Vainer, 2013.
2 To a certain extent Cesar Maia's reign lasted over 20 years as he became mayor the first time in January 1993. Elected by the PDMB, he joined the PFL in 1995. He was mayor for three terms (1993–1996, 2001–2004 and 2005–2008). Luiz Paulo Conde (1997–2000) and Eduardo Paes (2009–2012, re-elected to a new term in 2013) emerged onto the local political stage under the 'custody' and mentorship of Cesar Maia, basically maintaining – and despite some personal differences with him – the same policies, practices and rhetoric.
3 Tecnologías Urbanas Sociedad Anónnima (TUBSA), headed up by Jordi Borja and Manuel de Forn.
4 The fancy palace that was the headquarters of the Foreign Affairs Ministry until the capital was transferred to Brasilia in 1960.
5 During the Colonial Period, the expression 'good men' designated rich men from villages and cities, owners of land and slaves, free from any handwork.
6 The city's anthem.
7 The Federal Constitution, which put an end institutionally to the military dictatorship in 1988, as the result of the struggles and the Movement for Urban Reform, devoted two articles to the urban issue, with an emphasis on the social function of the city and property. It also established that all cities with more than 20,000 inhabitants should have a Master Plan. The Statute of the City (Estatuto da Cidade, Federal Law Nbr. 10.257 of July 10, 2001), which regulated and laid out the constitutional provisions, determined that these plans are ten-year plans. The first Ten-Year Master Plan for Rio de Janeiro in 1992 called for a review of the plan in 2002, but Mayor Cesar Maia, in flagrant violation of the law, deferred it interminably and it was only approved in 2009 with no public debate during Mayor Eduardo Paes's term.
8 This is the acronym for 'Strengths, weaknesses, opportunities and threats', the methodology tool used in strategic planning from its original formulation for corporate planning. All textbooks and MBA coursework teach SWOT analysis as the first step in any kind of strategic planning. See, for example, Porter, 1985 and 1995; Bryson, 1988; Aswortth and Voogd, 1990; Kotler, Haider and Rein, 1994; Mintzberg, 1994; Simbieda, 1994; Bouinot and Bermils, 1995. For a critique of this view, see for example, Arantes *et al.*, 2000 and Vainer, 2000a.

9  The city's patron saint is Saint Sebastian, whose name-day is celebrated on January 20.
10 It is to be noted that at later times, the Executive Committee did not hesitate to change the utterances in the Strategic Guidelines approved by the '*highest level of the Strategic Plan of the City of Rio de Janeiro*'. But, in the end, who cares what the Strategic Guidelines of the Strategic Plan are?
11 This perhaps explains why there is so much expenditure on roadway work and large stadiums, and so few resources put into the sewerage system, with tragic consequences for the city's sanitation and the health of its population.
12 The mayor was certainly referring to the shanty town called Facela da Maré next to the University City.
13 For a discussion on the concept of 'city of exception' and its relationship to strategic planning and mega-events, see Vainer, 2015; Oliveira and Vainer, 2014: 81–118; Stavrides, 2008. For the concept of 'state of exception', see Agamben, 2015; Jessop, 1985, 2009.
14 The Olympic Bill (Law Nbr. 12.035, of October 1, 2009) conferred the same advantages on the IOC.
15 See note 18 for quotations from consultants for the 1995 Strategic Plan of the City of Rio de Janeiro, wich came out in defence of 'strong governments' for cities.
16 'A queda do PIB no segundo trimestre reflete bem a questão da Copa. A economia já não vinha em um bom momento – desde outubro que a indústria está tecnicamente em recessão –, mas a Copa piorou o resultado. Tivemos um período em que o país praticamente parou, e os setores envolvidos no evento não lucraram o esperado' (Carlos Stempniewski, cited in G1, 2014).
17 This figure is the double of the forced evictions at the peak of the military dictatorship, during the last major eviction movement between 1964 and 1975. On the recent evictions, see Azevedo and Faulhaber, 2015.

## Bibliography

Agamben, Giorgio. *The State of Exception*. Chicago, IL, The University Chicago Press, 2015.
Arantes, Otilia, Maricato, Ermínia and Vainer, Carlos. *A Cidade do Pensamento Único: desmanchando consensos*. Petrópolis, Editora Vozes, 2000.
Ascher, François. *Les nouveaux principes de l'urbanisme. La fin des villes n'est pas à l'ordre du jour*. Paris, Éditions de l'Aube, 2001.
Aswortth, G. J. and Voogd, H. *Selling the City: Marketing Approaches in Public Sector and Urban Planning*. London/New York, Belhaven Press, 1990.
Azevedo, Lena and Faulhaber, Lucas. *SMH 2016: remoções no Rio de Janeiro olímpico*. Rio de Janeiro, Mórula, 2015.
Borja, Jordi (ed.). *Barcelona. Un modelo de transformación urbana*. Quito, Programa de Gestión Urbana/Oficina Regional para América Latina y Caribe, 1995.
Borja, Jordi and Castells, Manuel. *Local and Global: The Management of Cities in the Information Age*. London, Earthscan/United Nations Center for Human Settlements (Habitat), 1997. (Based on Habitat Report first presented at the Istanbul Conference, June 1996.)
Borja, Jordi and Forn, Manuel de. Políticas da Europa e dos Estados para as cidades. *Espaço e Debates*, XVI(39), 1996, 32–47.
Bouinot, Jean and Bermils, Bernard. *La gestion stratégique des villes. Entre compétition et cooperation*. Paris, Armand Collin, 1995.
Bryson, John. *Strategic Planning for Public and Nonprofit Organizations*. San Francisco, CA, Jossey-Bass, 1988.

Dacosta, Lamartine *et al.* (eds). *Legados de megaeventos esportivos.* Brasília: Ministério do Esporte, 2008.

EBC/Agência Brasil. *Fecomercio SP estima queda de R$ 30 bi no PIB com feriados da Copa*, 27/02/2014 (http://agenciabrasil.ebc.com.br/FecomercioSP%20estima%20 queda%20de%20R$%2030%20bi%20no%20PIB%20nacional%20com%20feria-dos%20da%20Copa).

Estadão. É mais fácil organizar uma Copa com menos democradia, diz Valcke. *Estadão*, 24/04/2013 (http://esportes.estadao.com.br/noticias/futebol,e-mais-facil-organizar-uma-copa-com-menos-democracia-diz-valcke,1025076).

Faulhaber, Lucas. *Rio Maravilha: práticas, projetos políticos e intervenção no território no início do século XXI.* Niterói, UFF, 2012.

Forn i Foxà, Manuel de. *Barcelona: estrategias de transformación urbana y económica.* S.l, mimeo, 1993.

Fundação Getúlio Vargas. *Realização dos Jogos Pan-Americanos, da Olimpíada e da Para-olimpíada na cidade do Rio de Janeiro: análise de pré- viabilidade e dos impactos sócio-econômicos: proposta técnica e comercial de execução.* Rio de Janeiro: Fundação Getúlio Vargas, 2000.

Fundação Getúlio Vargas. *Jogos Desportivos Pan-Americanos de 2007, candidatura da cidade do Rio de Janeiro: análise de pré-viabilidade técnica e econômica: apresen-tação preliminar para discussão.* Rio de Janeiro: Fundação Getúlio Vargas, 2001.

G1. *Copa e crise na indústria puxaram a queda do PIB, dizem especialistas*, 28/09/2014 (http://g1.globo.com/economia/noticia/2014/08/copa-e-crise-na-industria-puxaram-queda-do-pib-dizem-especialistas.html).

Harvey, David. Do gerenciamento ao empresariamento: a transformação da administração urbana no capitalismo tardio. *Espaço & Debates: Revista de Estudos Regionais e Urbanos*, 39, 1996, 48–64.

International Olympic Committee. *Olympic Agenda 2020 20+20 Recommendations* (approved by the 127th IOC session in Monaco on 8–9 December 2014) (http://www.olympic.org/Documents/Olympic_Agenda_2020/Olympic_Agenda_2020-20-20_Recommendations-ENG.pdf).

Jennings, A., Rolnik, R. and Lassance, A. (eds). *Brasil em Jogo: O que fica da Copa e das Olimpíadas?* São Paulo: Boitempo, 2014, pp. 71–78.

Jennings, Andrew. *Foul! The Secret World of FIFA: Bribes, Vote Rigging and Ticket Scandals.* London, Harper, 2006.

Jennings, Andrew. *The Dirty Game: Uncovering the Scandal at FIFA.* London, Century, 2015.

Jessop, Bob. *Nicos Poulantzas: Marxist Theory and Political Strategy.* London, Macmillan, 1985.

Jessop, Bob. O Estado, o poder, o socialismo de Poulantzas como um clássico moderno. Revista de Sociologia e Política, *Curitiba*, 17(33), 2009, 131–144.

Kotler, P., Haider, D. H. and Rein, I. *Marketing público.* São Paulo, Makron Books, 1994.

Lopes, Rodrigo. O Planejamento Estratégico da Cidade do Rio de Janeiro – Um Processo de Transformação. Instituto de Estudos do Trabalho e Sociedade. *Dez Anos Depois: como vai você Rio? Boletim Rio de Janeiro – Trabalho e Sociedade*, 3(5), março 2003, 48–50 (http://iets.inf.br/biblioteca/O_planejamento_estrategico_da_cidade_do_Rio_de_Janeiro.pdf).

Maricato, Erminia. É a cidade, estúpido. *Cidades Rebeldes: passe livre e as manifestações que tomaram as ruas do Brasil.* São Paulo, Editorial Boitempo, 2013.

Mintzberg, Henri. *The Rise and Fall of Strategic Planning.* Toronto, The Free Press, 1994.

Novais, P. *Uma estratégia chamada 'planejamento estratégico': deslocamentos espaciais e a atribuição de sentidos na teoria do planejamento urbano.* Rio de Janeiro, 7Letras, 2010.

O Globo. *TCU defende fim do acúmulo de cargos de Nuzman no COB e no Comitê*, 30/07/2015.

Oliveira, A. Megaevents, Urban Management, and Macroeconomic Policy: 2007, Pan American Games in Rio de Janeiro. *Journal of Urban Planning and Development*, 137(2), June 2011, 184–192.

Oliveira, Nelma Gusmão de. *O poder dos jogos e os jogos do poder: os interesses em campo na produção de uma cidade para o espetáculo esportivo.* Rio de Janeiro, IPPUR/ UFRJ, 2012.

Oliveira, Nelma Gusmão de and Vainer, C. Megaeventos no Brasil e no Rio de Janeiro: uma articulação transescalar na produção da cidade de exceção. In Sánchez, F. *et al.* (eds), *A Copa do Mundo e as Cidades: Políticas, Projetos e Resistências.* Niterói, Editora UFF, 2014, pp. 81–118.

Plano Estratégico da Cidade do Rio de Janeiro. *Correspondência enviada aos integrantes do Conselho da Cidade*, 1994.

Porter, Michael E. *Competitive Advantage: Creating and Sustaining Superior Performance.* New York/London, The Free Press/Collier Macmillan, 1985.

Porter, Michael E. The Competitive Advantage of the Inner City. *Harvard Business Review*, 3, May–June 1995, pp. 55–71.

Porter, Michael E. What is Strategy? *Harvard Business Review*, 6, November–December 1996, pp. 61–78.

Prefeitura da Cidade do Rio de Janeiro. *Plano estratégico da cidade do Ride Janeiro: Rio Sempre Rio.* Rio de Janeiro: PCRJ/ACRJ/FIRJAN, 1996.

Prefeitura da Cidade do Rio de Janeiro. *Plano estratégico da cidade do Rio de Janeio: as cidades da cidade.* Rio de Janeiro, PCRJ, 2004.

Prefeitura da Cidade do Rio de Janeiro. *Plano Estratégico da Prefeitura do Rio de Janeiro 2009-2012. Pós-2016: O Rio mais integrado e competitivo.* Rio de Janeiro, PCRJ, 2009.

Prefeitura da Cidade do Rio de Janeiro. *Plano estratégico da Prefeitura do Rio de Janeiro 2013–2016. Pós-2016: O Rio mais integrado e competitivo.* Rio de Janeiro, PCRJ, 2013.

Presidência da República. *Sim, o Rio de Janeiro pode e quer organizar os Jogos Olímpicos de 2016*, 1/10/2009 (http://blog.planalto.gov.br/sim-o-rio-de-janeiro-pode-e-quer-organizar-os-jogos-olimpicos-de-2016/).

Ribeiro, Luiz Cesar de Queiroz and Santos, Orlando Alves dos (eds). *Globalização, Fragmentação e Reforma Urbana.* Rio de Janeiro, Civilização Brasileira, 1994.

Roussef, Dilma. *Pronunciamento da Presidenta da República, Dilma Rousseff, em cadeia nacional de rádio e TV*, 2013 (http://www2.planalto.gov.br/acompanhe-o-planalto/ discursos/discursos-da-presidenta/pronunciamento-da-presidenta-da-republica-dilma-rousseff-em-cadeia-nacional-de-radio-e-tv).

Sánchez, F. *et al.* (eds). *A Copa do Mundo e as Cidades: Políticas, Projetos e Resistências.* Niterói, Editora UFF, 2014.

Santos, Rosane Rebeca de Oliveira. Para uma 'nova cidade' um 'novo plano: o processo de revisão do plano diretor do Rio de Janeiro à luz dos preparativos para os megaeventos'. *ANPUR, Anais*, 2013 (http://unuhospedagem.com.br/revista/rbeur/index.php/ anais/article/view/4158/4044).

Siembieda, William. *Adaptation and Application of Strategic Planning in the Public Sector.* 1994, mimeo (Working Paper, Center for Research and Development, School of Architecture and Planning, University of New Mexico).

Stavrides, Stavros. Urban Identities: Beyond the Regional and the Global. The Case of Athens. In Al-Qawasmi, Jamal, Mahmoud, Abdesselem and Djerbi, Ali (eds), *Regional Architecture and Identity in the Age of Globalization: Proceedings of 2nd International Conference of CSAAR*, Tunis, 2008, pp. 577–588.

Swyngedouw, Erik. Post-democratic Cities for Whom and for What? Paper presented in concluding session Regional Studies Association Annual Conference. PeCS, Budapest, 26 May 2010 (http://www.regionalstudies-assoc.ac.uk /events/2010/may-pecs/papers/ Swyngedouw.pdf).

Vainer, Carlos. Pátria, empresa e mercadoria: Notas sobre a estratégia discursiva do planejamento estratégico urbano. In Otília, A., Maricato, E., Vainer, C. (eds), *A Cidade do Pensamento Único: Desmanchando Consensos*. Petrópolis, Editora Vozes, 2000a, pp. 74–104.

Vainer, Carlos. Os Liberais Também Fazem Planejamento Urbano? Glosas ao 'Plano Estratégico da Cidade do Rio de Janeiro'. In Otília, A., Maricato, E., Vainer, C. (eds). *A Cidade do Pensamento Único: Desmanchando Consensos*. Petrópolis, Editora Vozes, 2000b, pp. 105–119.

Vainer, Carlos. Quando a cidade vai às ruas. *Cidades Rebeldes: passe livre e as manifestações que tomaram as ruas do Brasil*. São Paulo, Editorial Boitempo, 2013.

Vainer, Carlos. Como serão nossas cidades após a Copa e as Olimpíadas? In Jennings A., Rolnik, R., Lassance, A. (eds), *Brasil em Jogo: O que fica da Copa e das Olimpíadas?* São Paulo, Boitempo, 2014, pp. 71–78.

Vainer, Carlos. Mega-events and the City of Exception: Theoretical Explorations of Brazilian Experience. In Gruneau, R., Horn, J. (eds), *Mega-events and Globalisation: Capital and Spectacle in a Changing World Order*. New York, Routledge, 2015, pp. 97–112.

World Bank. *World Development Report: Challenges to Development*. Oxford, Oxford University Press, 1991.

World Bank. *Cities in Transition: World Bank Urban and Local Government Strategy*. Washington, DC, World Bank, 2000.

# Part 2

# Conceptual and critical nodes in strategic planning

# 17 Introduction

*Jean Hillier*

Space is provisional. Stabilisations of space, as performed by strategic spatial plans, exemplified by several chapters in Part 1, are inevitably temporary. As Massey (2005, p. 37) writes: 'there are always loose ends'. If we are to consider space, not as a container of activities, 'out-there', but as an 'always-in-process, contingent, unstable, entangled, co-existence of multiple, relational trajectories' (Hillier and Healey, 2008, p. 405), then there is a need for new ways of thinking and doing strategic spatial planning practice which go beyond 'traditional' instrumental rationality (see Sandercock, 2003). If we are really looking for changes in the ways in which strategic spatial planning is conceptualised and practised, then, as Thomas (2007, p. 334) suggests, we need to lose a concern with 'planning systems and institutions for their own sakes' in order to free up possibilities for thinking about transformation.

The various international case studies in Part 1 of this volume critically discuss the intellectual development and implementation of strategic spatial planning in six continents of the world, excluding Antarctica. The authors of the chapters in Part 2 were invited to reflect on the case studies and to present some ontological and epistemological challenges for strategic spatial planning. The contributions by Jean Hillier and Willem Salet, which frame this Part, offer broad theoretically-informed discussions of what strategic spatial planning is and what it might become in the future. The chapters by Glen Searle and Loris Servillo address practice-related issues concerning what Servillo, following Janin Rivolin (2012), terms a 'culture of performative planning', while the chapters by Raine Mäntysalo and Kristi Grišakov and Alessandro Balducci focus on process-related issues.

The authors aim to open up critical debates, such as the ways in which 'knowledge' is framed, developed and applied and how ways of controlling conflict reduce, or evacuate, political impulses in the search for practical, technical outcomes. Analyses of strategic spatial planning practices, therefore, should pay attention not only to descriptions of organisations, actors and their practices, but to the cultures which contextualise such practices. Transformative agendas may involve engaging strategic planning practitioners in confronting neo-liberal models of urban and regional development which 'reduce(s) human life to materially-self-interested individuals' (Healey, 2010, p. 47) and also politics centred on a singular model of a 'good society' (Healey, ibid.). This would inevitably involve planners in problematising and understanding the power dynamics of the contexts which frame the ways they plan and in reflecting on their own positions as practitioners, as the chapter by Willem Salet illustrates.

The specific contributions to knowledge of the material in Part 2 of this volume include emphasising both that planning theories need to engage in greater empirical depth with practice experiences and that planning practices could benefit from greater conceptual depth. The chapter authors offer critiques of strategic spatial planning and suggest ideas which could be developed as a basis for alternative approaches (see Part 3). As such, most of the arguments are fairly generalised, rather than addressing specific societal challenges in detail. Nevertheless, several challenges of mutual concern stand out: these relate to issues of uncertainty, knowledge, conflict and culture change.

Strategic spatial planners 'are always thinking about and making plans for possible futures while continually being dragged back to the messiness of "going on in the world"' (Patsy Healey, in Hillier, 2010, p. 13). As a means of coping, many planners choose not to reflexively question either the nature of space, of time, or of planning practice, a suggestion echoed by Monno's (2010, p. 161) claim that planning scholars and practitioners demonstrate a 'failure of imagination'. As Hillier (2010, p. 13) comments, 'planning is ... always incomplete'.

Monno (2010) argues for the need for alternative approaches to the 'business as usual' which several of the authors in Part 1 of this volume describe. She laments the relatively limited visions of strategic planners and their inability to imagine radically different processes and outcomes from the current status quo, a sentiment which Salet's chapter fully supports. In fact, all the authors in this Part deal in some form or other with Monno's 'failure of imagination', suggesting innovative, experimental ways in which the academic and practice lacunae may be addressed.

Experiments recognise the uncertainties of the worlds in which planners plan and the uncertainties of planning practices and plans themselves. Jean Hillier's chapter helps set the theoretical scene for Part 2 by discussing how concepts of certainty and uncertainty have been framed in strategic spatial planning literature. She suggests that planning considerations are typically indeterminate in the longer term, and calls for development of methodologies of strategic spatial planning which offer both short-term investment confidence or 'certainty', and longer-term flexibility in the face of indeterminacy.

Loris Servillo acknowledges the limited power and effectiveness of planners and strategic spatial plans in times of rising complexity and uncertainty. He argues for development and adoption of more flexible measures according to 'changing spatial configurations and dimensions of phenomena'. Servillo identifies a need for innovation in thinking and practice, but is clear that successful institutionalisation of new modes of thinking and acting will require institutional transformation. Regarding strategic spatial planning as performing in an institutional arena in which different cultural/technical imaginaries encounter each other, Servillo engages the metaphor of water in karst landscapes to reflect on the dynamics that can prompt strategic planning episodes with the capacity to generate changes in planning cultures, or, on the contrary, let them disappear into seemingly bottomless sinkholes.

Raine Mäntysalo and Kristi Grišakov also discuss the issue of coping with uncertainty in practice. The authors concentrate on the question of 'what is "evidence"?' in strategic spatial planning and whether planners can be certain about their knowledge. They challenge the hegemony of evidence-based knowledge as inherently problematic: 'planning is largely about coping with the yet unknown future, that of which we cannot have evidence'. Arguing that strategic planning practice is an art as well as a science, Mäntysalo and Grišakov advocate that practitioners engage the three Aristotelian intellectual virtues of episteme, techne and phronesis. The authors suggest that scenario-based (rather than forecast-based) strategic plan and strategy preparation engages all three virtues together with the critical judgement skills crucial for good strategic practice.

The framing, development and application of knowledge is further problematised in the chapters by Loris Servillo and by Alessandro Balducci. Servillo engages Friedmann's (1987) concern of how to make technical knowledge effective in practice, to which Balducci's discussion of Trading Zones offers a potential response. Trading Zones are those in which expert and lay knowledges, their multiple values and perspectives, come together in an open process of 'trading' or negotiation which can be capable of dealing with uncertainty. Establishing and working with Trading Zones would be an innovative, experimental process for strategic spatial planning practitioners. It would require a culture change in that planners would need to shift 'from the conviction of being right, having the right solutions' to search for strategies which 'can meet the different interests, the objectives and the values of the various actors, without seeking to convince them all'.

Such Trading Zones will inevitably involve the expression and performance of conflict and power games. In his chapter, Glen Searle focuses on the particular issue of relationships between strategic and statutory planning. He argues that strategic–statutory boundaries are not as fixed as current conceptualisations frequently imagine and demonstrates how boundary blurring is often the product of particular institutional and political contexts and power games between municipal councils. Searle suggests that the involvement of statutory planning agencies in the preparation of strategic spatial plans is more likely to result in production of strategic goals which are adopted by the statutory bodies. He adds that if the goals allow discretion or 'reasonable freedom for implementation in statutory plans and development approvals', in order to deal with uncertainties and local circumstances, they are more likely to be implemented. On the other hand, highly directive and restrictive strategic legislation, regulation and control appears to lead to conflict between authorities which is non-conducive to implementation of strategic plans.

Many of the 'new ideas' discussed in this Part will necessitate culture changes in strategic spatial planning which will take it outside its usual boundaries. Planning culture may be defined as 'the collective ethos and dominant attitudes of planners regarding the appropriate role of the state, market forces, and civil society in influencing social outcomes' (Sanyal, 2005, p. xxi). As such, planning cultures will differ significantly around the world, between and within states, as the case studies in Part 1 illustrate.

Willem Salet, for instance, claims that strategic spatial planning often tends to be introverted or 'inside-out', planner-centric, engaged in instrumental specified end-means juridification, prioritising physical design. He argues that the path-dependent pragmatic 'wisdom' of retaining the practical status quo needs to be challenged by outward-looking and outward-seeking visionaries and visions: 'outside-in'. Salet suggests that the planning profession needs to 're-invent itself' if it is to achieve 'more plausible legitimacy and effectiveness'. Understanding the deep-seated cultural embeddedness of strategic spatial planning practices is important, as Servillo points out in his chapter, if changes to practice are to be effective. However, even though cultures may appear stable and path-dependent, they are actually dynamic, affected by issues such as political change, technological innovation, economic crises, and so on.

In the early twenty-first century, old planning 'certainties' and cultures are breaking down and new theories, projects and practices are attempting to gain hegemonic status. But they themselves are underpinned by contradictions which, in turn, create opportunities for challenge, disjunction and ruptures in which alternative strategies may emerge. As Healey (2010, p. 52) suggests: 'planning practices need to be appreciated as important empirical sites where struggles are being played out over what and whose material conditions and which governance mentalities/cultures will get privileged in emerging urban futures'.

The chapters in this Part problematise, debate and challenge both the theoretical underpinnings of strategic spatial planning practices and also the processes of practices themselves. They present epistemological and ontological challenges to issues of knowledge, power and conflict. The precarious assemblages of theories and practices highlighted in Part 1 may be challenged by ideas in Part 2, to lead on to Part 3 which develops some 'ingredients' for revisiting strategic spatial planning.

## References

Friedmann, J. (1987) *Planning in the Public Domain: From Knowledge to Action.* Princeton, NJ: Princeton University Press.

Healey, P. (2010) Introduction to Part 1. In J. Hillier and P. Healey (Eds.), *The Ashgate Research Companion to Planning Theory: Conceptual Challenges for Spatial Planning.* Farnham: Ashgate, pp. 37–55.

Hillier, J. (2010) Introduction. In J. Hillier and P. Healey (Eds.), *The Ashgate Research Companion to Planning Theory: Conceptual Challenges for Spatial Planning.* Farnham: Ashgate, pp. 1–34.

Hillier, J. and Healey, P. (2008) Introduction to Part III. In J. Hillier and P. Healey (Eds.), *Critical Essays in Planning Theory*, Vol. 3. Aldershot: Ashgate, pp. 405–412.

Janin Rivolin, U. (2012). Planning systems as institutional technologies: A proposed conceptualization and the implications for comparison. *Planning Practice and Research*, 27(1), 63–85.

Massey, D. (2005) *For Space*. London: Sage.

Monno, V. (2010) When strategy meets democracy: Exploring the limits of the 'possible' and the value of the 'impossible'. In M. Cerreta, G. Concilio and V. Monno (Eds.), *Making Strategies in Spatial Planning*. Dordrecht: Springer, pp. 161–183.

Sandercock, L. (2003) *Cosmopolis II: Mongrel Cities of the 21st Century*. New York: Continuum.

Sanyal, B. (2005) Preface. In B. Sanyal (Ed.), *Comparative Planning Cultures*. New York: Routledge, pp. xix–xxiv.

Thomas, H. (2007) From radicalism to reformism. *Planning Theory*, 6(3), 332–335.

# 18 Strategic spatial planning in uncertainty or planning indeterminate futures?

## A critical review

*Jean Hillier*

## Introduction

> where the future is unpredictable and surprise is likely
>
> (Folke, 2006, p. 254)

Faced with issues such as climate change, financial crises, social upheaval and political ruptures, individual practitioners would likely agree in theory with Louis Albrechts (2010, p. 4) that 'places are faced by problems and challenges that cannot be tackled and managed adequately with the old intellectual apparatus and mindset'. Nevertheless, it would appear in practice, in Australia at least (Searle, this volume; Maginn *et al.*, this volume), that moves towards rethinking spatial planning as a dynamic and complex set of processes often revert towards stand-ardisation and predictability. This may be due as much to ontological conditions of cultural doxa and inertia – with planners clinging to clichés such as 'certainty' – as to the power of entrenched economically-oriented interests demanding guaran-teed private property rights and returns on their investments (see also Abbott and DeMarco, this volume).

One of the tensions at the core of strategic spatial planning practice is that between an often-specified aim to 'deliver certainty' and the seemingly inherent uncertainty of the world that planners seek to plan. Steele and Ruming (2012, pp. 155–156) refer to the pursuit of both certainty and flexibility as 'the holy grail of planning'. I suggest that there is another tension, between uncertainty and indeterminacy. In quantum physics, the concept of uncertainty concerns probabil-ities of determinate events relating to measurable entities, whereas indeterminate states involve complex, unpredictable emergent assemblages. Spatial planning practitioners tend to regard the indeterminate as uncertain, imposing artificial intellectual boundaries round entities and events. Certainty is an ideological construct, which serves to reduce practitioners' understandings of the worlds they seek to plan and the options available to them.

In this chapter I critically review how concepts of certainty and uncertainty have been treated in spatial planning literature.[1] I then clarify several key differ-ences between uncertainty and indeterminacy. I demonstrate how uncertainty is unlikely to relate to spatial planning considerations, unless in micro (small-scale, short-term) conditions, if at all, and that strategic spatial planning theories and practices need to understand and incorporate the concept of indeterminacy if they are to be appropriate and useful.

I accept that planning practitioners need to offer 'stakeholders' some degree of what might be termed 'certainty'. The question is whether they are able to build uncertainty and indeterminacy, or, in Luzzi's (2001, p. 11) terms, 'the discomfort of ambivalence', into strategic spatial planning praxes and still offer stakeholders a 'necessary level of certainty'. I adopt a poststructuralist perspective, inspired by the work of Deleuze and Guattari, which permits an openness to indeterminacy. Deleuze and Guattari's ideas are concerned with continual creation. This means that questions, such as 'what might the city be like?', should not be answered by reference to models, rules, prescriptions and so on, but through appropriate experimentation: critical thinking about situations, relations between elements and being open to what might happen if...; what might emerge. In this vein, I suggest that working creatively with longer-term strategic visions, infrastructure plans and short-term, local area plans may offer flexibility over the 15+ year lifetime of a strategic plan, yet some reduction of 'uncertainty' in the shorter term. I conclude that while there can be no universal answer to the question raised above, strategic spatial planners should take courage to work with uncertainty and indeterminacy rather than against them.

## Strategic spatial planning in uncertainty

Those who aren't sure are weak ... Faithless

(Moore, 2011, p. 24)

Until the later years of the twentieth century in the Western world, conceptions were dominant of 'the planner' as 'trusted technocrat above and apart from the messy bustle of the world' (Healey and Hillier, 2008, p. xv), implementing plans to control and order market processes in line with predetermined goals and standards. As several of the case studies in Part 1 of this volume demonstrate, the task of strategic planning is often regarded as that of articulating future development goals and targets. Plans may be characterised by the assumption of a definable public interest in a determinable 'good city' and reliance on rational-based approaches grounded in evidence-bases and forecasting. 'Solutions' to 'problems' may be scientifically identified through processes of systematic, deductive logic. The unexpected was discounted in a quest for order and certainty: 'perfect certainty is what man [sic] wants' (Dewey, 1929, p. 21).

As Albrechts and Balducci explain in the Introduction to this volume, and Albrechts (2015) describes, strategic spatial planning is a somewhat slippery concept. In this chapter I regard strategic spatial plans as policy-documents outlining future-oriented, speculative trajectories for a spatial area (see Hillier, 2007). Many strategic plans (see, for example, chapters in Part 1 by Van den

Broeck, Maginn *et al.*, Bryson and Slotterback, Cao and Zheng) were character-ised by a rational approach (Balducci, this volume) which assumes that applica-tion of forecasting and analytical techniques should lead to predictable, and therefore controllable, outcomes. However, as McLoughlin (1992) and Healey have demonstrated, cities keep 'running away from the planners' plans' (Healey, 2010, p. 167) as 'small p' (and sometimes 'big P') politics intervene in questions of the where, when and how of physical development and property rights (see Healey, 2007, p. 182).

The chapter by Searle (this Part) emphasises the difference between plans as specific statements of regulatory norms and standards for detailed land-use change (e.g. zoning plans, statutory plans, local plans) and spatial strategies which give statutory plans orientation frameworks and integrated various policy programmes (see also Healey, 2007, 2010). Albrechts and Balducci (2012, p. 2) suggest that 'in many cities, in the last 20 years, some kind of strategic spatial planning [is replacing] statutory planning'. In some instances (see, for example, Fedeli, this volume) strategic planning is becoming rather 'a set of concepts, procedures and tools' (Albrechts and Balducci, 2012, p. 8) – a field of practices (Balducci, 2011) – which contribute to a dynamic, creative process of strategy-making by 'creating synergies and potentials' (Healey, 2010, p. 165).

Within such definitions, however, lie actors' widely differing expectations of strategic planning, including 'stabilising or lending certainty to developers and investors, setting priorities, co-ordinating actions and justifying choices' (Healey, 2010, p. 166). These expectations reflect not only the specific histories or trajectories of planning in a place, but also underlying assumptions about issues of control and stability, of 'space and place, economy and society, politics and administration, law and regulation, rights, obligations and citizenship, the individual and the collective' (Huxley, 2011, p. 23).

What do actors mean by 'certainty'? It often involves notions of inevitability, predictability, removal of doubt that something is or will be true, is happening or will happen. For Mack, it is 'the gap between what is known and what needs to be known to make *correct* decisions' (1971, p. 1, cited in Abbott, 2012, p. 572, emphasis added), though the construct of correct decisions is an ideological construct as subjective as that of certainty. Uncertainty refers to an incomplete knowledge of either how systems – such as urban systems, ecological systems and so on – work, or/and of the impacts of planning decisions on such systems, particularly as impacts are often incremental and cumulative. Scientists and prac-titioners often attempt to predict impacts (such as of climate change) through calculating risks using probability algorithms. The belief that 'better' data, 'better' models and so on can substantively reduce, if not eliminate causal, organisational and value uncertainties (Abbott, 2005, 2009) is largely unfounded and may actually raise additional questions and uncertainties (Abbott, 2012).

As Rosenhead commented in 1980, 'planners and planning theorists may pay lip-service to the need for flexibility. But very practical needs of planning organi-sations are served by its reverse' (1980a, p. 210). Strategic spatial plans affect financial investment (e.g. of property developers, home-owners, infrastructure providers) and management practices (e.g. of water catchments) even though it is now generally accepted that the time taken to produce a strategic spatial plan often results in it being incongruent with the plan area before its official adoption (Friedmann, 2004, p. 54). The worlds which planners attempt to plan can and do change rapidly, with uncertainties (especially economic uncertainties) produced by the behaviour of the actors themselves (Esposito, 2013). As such, outdated theoretical doxa and 'best practices' may turn into 'lethal pitfalls' (Lagadec, 2009). As Lagadec (2009, p. 473) emphasises, the challenge is not to 'open additional boxes fitting the same models', but to rethink the models: to cultivate disconcertment (Law and Lin, 2009).

The models which have traditionally underpinned spatial planning are practical realist models which assume that 'most of our experience consists of statements that can be objectivated' (Murphy, 1998, p. 211). This tends to assume the presence of some pre-given entity – such as sustainability and/or housing markets (Van den Broeck; Abbott and DeMarco; Demazière and Serrano; Maginn *et al.*; Searle; Bryson) or a planned economy (Cao and Zheng, all this volume) – as the condition of knowledge, or what Deleuze and Guattari (1994) term a plane of reference. However, as quantum physicists Werner Heisenberg and Niels Bohr demonstrated in the early twentieth century, and as John Law (2004) has emphasised more recently, 'knowledge' or 'evidence' cannot be separated from the devices that measure it. Planning academics and practitioners inevitably participate in the actualisation of the world through their representations of it. This means that what is actualised is never fully actual – there are always elements excluded – and the set of relations which emerges in planning knowledge is never fully determinate. A strategy, therefore, is always in relation to its outside.[2]

As the world in its entirety is effectively objectively unmeasurable and unknowable, I argue that planners need to ask different questions from those they have typically asked; to regard uncertainty and indeterminacy as a resource rather than as a threat (Esposito, 2013); to plan for uncertainty and indeterminacy rather than certainty; to think in terms of relations – especially power relations – between elements rather than seeing each element either in isolation, or as merely 'integrated'; and to move beyond the linear of trend analysis and forecasts, to open up the spectrum of potentiality. The notions of uncertainty and indeterminacy do not imply a lack of reason, or randomness, but they do imply the impossibility of strategically planned control. A major question for Esposito (2013, p. 120) is thus 'how can we abandon randomness without giving up structures, describing a world that is unpredictable without being random, which is … always surprising?'

There is a demand for strategic planning theory and practices that embrace uncertainty and indeterminacy, multiple possible alternative futures, which recognise that people's desires are likely to change over the life of a strategic spatial plan, and that many decisions need to be flexible, exploratory and experimental (Balducci *et al.*, 2011, p. 485). Yet there is also a need for shorter-term 'commitment' (Thomas, Minett *et al.*, 1983). Hence the question of what to try to fix (albeit temporarily), what to leave to emerge and how (Healey, 2013, personal communication).

## Uncertainty and indeterminacy

A 'task of theory is to describe the preparation and management of surprises'
(Esposito, 2013, p. 105)

'We have moved slowly from the era of the blueprint or the master plan into the phase of continuous review – a period when flexibility and adaptability are emphasised. What is happening is that we are coming round to recognising that uncertainty is the future, that no matter how glossy we make our plans, we cannot be sure what will happen. More and more, the perhaps unpalatable truth is dawning that one of the greatest certainties is that our plans will be wrong. It is good that this is now being recognised and that our preoccupation should be to devise new approaches and techniques for coping with uncertainty' (Centre for Environmental Studies (CES), 1970, np, cited in Rosenhead, 1980b, pp. 331–332). This statement was written in 1970. However, as illustrated by case studies in Part 1 by Abdelwahab and Serag, Van den Broeck and Abbott and DeMarco, far from emphasising flexibility and adaptability and devising new ways to cope with uncertainty, planning theorists and practitioners appear to have relegated coping with uncertainty to the proverbial 'too hard basket'. Perhaps the 'unpalatable truth' is too unpalatable, even in theory?

Nonetheless, as Gert de Roo reminds me (2013, personal communication), it may be possible to be more confident (or 'certain') about some issues than others. He distinguishes between issues that are likely to be (fairly) straightforward, those that are more complex and those that are highly complex and suggests that if planners can differentiate between such issues, they may be able to select more appropriate processes and techniques for dealing with them. Similarly, Giezen (2013) refers to three 'categories' of uncertainty: risk, structural uncertainty and unknown uncertainty. Both categorisations of complexity and uncertainty, however, will inevitably be subjective, based on bounded representations and interpretations of the terms involved and may further assume that issues do not change over time.

On the other hand, Wynne (1992) claims that there is a 'key distinction' between uncertainty and indeterminacy. He argues that indeterminacy, rather than uncertainty, 'underlies the construction of scientific knowledge, as well as the wider social world' (1992, p. 112). Systems are often less determined by controlling forces than analysts and practitioners have recognised, especially with regard to issues such as climate change, pollution effects and so on. Social and environmental systems are not technological artefacts and, as such, 'cannot be designed, manipulated and reduced to within the bounds of existing analytical knowledge' (Wynne, 1992, p. 113). In attempting to construct models of such systems, or even strategic spatial plans, it is often that externally-defined goals or outcomes, or pragmatic considerations of what can be measured as 'evidence', dictate the resulting 'knowledge'. (See Mäntysalo and Grišakov on evidence, and Bryson and Slotterback on indicators, both this volume). While such practices may reduce the 'unknowns' in play, they do impose an artificial intellectual closure around what is, in reality, open-ended (see Wynne, 1992). Nevertheless, it is possible to make a distinction between uncertainty, in which the main parameters are known and there is some idea of probabilities, and indeterminacy, where networks/assemblages are open and contingent, events are unpredictable and there are unknown unknowns.

This is one of the fundamental tenets of a key debate in quantum physics. From about the 1920s, physicists increasingly recognised that the objects and events that they were trying to understand could not be subject to a reductionist approach. The work of Werner Heisenberg and Niels Bohr, in particular, changed the way that many scholars think about the limits of reductionism and determinism.

The notion of uncertainty is epitomised by the famous anthropocentric[3] thought experiment of Schrödinger's Cat (1980 [1935]) which locks a hypothetical cat into a sealed steel box together with a Geiger counter, a radioactive atom, a hammer, and a flask of hydrocyanic acid. These are all pre-existing, known entities with a linear cause and effect. The key to the experiment is probability. We know the 'measured' states of the cat (alive), the substance and the acid at the beginning of the experiment (t = 0). Using Schrödinger's equation, it is possible to calculate the probability that, in a given time period (t = m), the radioactive atom will decay, the Geiger counter tube discharge and release the hammer to smash the flask of hydrocyanic acid, which poisons and kills the cat. Schrödinger gave the experiment a 50:50 probability that the atom will decay in one hour. The fate of the cat is, therefore, uncertain. It is entangled with the fate of the atom. If the atom decays, the cat dies. If the atom does not decay, the cat lives. Schrödinger's equation actually predicts that after one hour, the entangled state of the system will be that of superposition – a non-decayed atom with a live cat *and* a decayed atom with a dead cat – with either being equally probable. Until we open the box to check, the cat is both dead and alive. What will happen to the cat is essentially unpredictable with any degree of certainty. Uncertainty relations can thus be considered as spreads of the probability distributions of several determinate physical quantities (Heisenberg, 1958, 1983 [1927]).

For Niels Bohr (1987), the issue is that of indeterminacy rather than uncertainty. He argues that entities do not exist in fully determinate states. Schrödinger's cat, for instance, would be entangled with the radioactive atom both epistemically and ontically. As Barad (2007, p. 170) explains, 'the cat and the atom do not have separately determinate states of existence, and, indeed, there is no determinately bounded and propertied entity that we normally identify with the word "cat", independently of some measurement that resolves the indeterminacy and specifies the appropriate referents for the concepts of "cat" and "life state"'. Therefore, as Barad continues, the life state of the cat (alive or dead) cannot exist independently of it being measured or defined in some way. Quantum physics deconstructs the belief that 'things' are units with inherently determinate boundaries, properties and meanings (Barad, 2007).

Since measurement not only gives meaning to a physical quantity, but creates a particular value for it, the meaningfulness of the entity is equivalent to the existence of what purports to measure it. If what we measure or define only describes the effects of the interaction between the 'measuring instruments' and the 'things' measured, then representing and/or modelling urban social and/or environmental systems accurately is impossible. Methods and practices thus produce the reality that they understand (Latour and Woolgar, 1986; Law, 2004). So definitions and measurements can only be applied 'provisionally' (Bohr, 1987:1, pp. 56–57). Bohr's epistemology offers a 'rational version of the ... irreducibly unknowable' (Plotnitsky, 2002, p. 234). As Bohr himself stated, his ideas offer a generalisation which 'permits the inclusion of regularities decisive for the account of fundamental properties of matter, but which transcends the scope of deterministic description' (1987:2, p. 74).

Bohr also developed the principle of complementarity – a dichotomic relation between two types of description – from mathematician Bernhard Riemann's work on geometry. The relevance of Riemann for our understanding of spatiality and planning has been explored by Cao and Zhang (2013), while the complementarity of different meanings and interpretations of places, events, plan objectives and so on, is widely discussed in planning case study literature (see, for example, Van den Broeck, Maginn *et al.*, this volume).

Complementarity entails both mutual exclusivity and mutual necessity (Barad, 2011). What Law (2004) terms 'absence', for instance, is the necessary excluded Other to presence. It is enacted along with presence and helps to constitute it. Law distinguished between manifest absence as 'that which is absent, but recognised as relevant to, or represented in, presence' (2004, p. 157), such as the manifest absence of ancestors for Australian Indigenous peoples. Absence as otherness, in contrast, is 'that which is absent because it is enacted by presence as irrelevant, impossible, or repressed' (2004, p. 157); the nineteenth-century bodies which were once interred under what is now a Melbourne CBD car park disappear in current planning practice. Both forms of absence are necessary to presence. They are complementary.

For Deleuze, for instance, there is always an 'out-of-field'; that which is beyond or excluded from the framed image. The out-of-field 'refers to what is neither seen nor understood, but is nevertheless perfectly present' (Deleuze, 1986, p. 17). A strategy may 'out-of-field' politics or global financial markets, yet they are always 'present' in their absence.

If a problem, according to Riemannian non-linear mathematics, is divorced from both the conditions of its intuition and from those of its solution (Smith, 2012, p. 300), then problems may be regarded as chaotic multiplicities of directional vectors or singularities. Deleuze and Guattari (1987) introduce the idea of a refrain as a rhythmic regularity which brings some form of order to potentially chaotic situations. 'The refrain is a prism, a crystal of space–time. It ... has a catalytic function: not only to increase the speed of the exchanges and reactions in that which surrounds it, but also to assure indirect interactions between elements devoid of so-called natural affinity, and thereby to form organised masses' (Deleuze and Guattari, 1987, p. 348).

Every refrain has three basic aspects (Deleuze and Guattari, 1987, pp. 311–312): a point of order or space of familiarity or safety which keeps the forces of chaos temporarily at bay (Grosz, 2008, p. 52); a circle of control which defines a territory (territorialisation); and a 'line of flight', an unstable aspect which serves both as constituent of the territory and source of its potential dissolution or deterritorialisation (Bogue, 2007, p. 28). A refrain, such as certainty in strategic planning, is thus a territorial motif which relationally organises internal impulses and responds to external circumstances (Bogue, 2003, p. 21). The territorialising process comes through the plan in a refrain which expresses 'the patterning of the ensemble of territorial components' (Bogue, 2003, p. 22). Yet by juxtaposing uncertain and indeterminate elements in the plan, the potential exists to deterritorialise the plan, making its constituent elements resonate differently, 'liberating' (Grosz, 2008, p. 54) or reconfiguring the plan with elements not conceived on the original plane of reference, such as social and environmental justice.

Ideas (such as planning strategies) thus give determinacy to the chaos of the virtual, but without rendering it fully determined (Deleuze, 1983, 1985). A problem does not have a single, simple once-and-for-all solution, but rather offers a set of different and often conflicting challenges which transform the problem, throwing up new challenges (Williams, 2003). If we 'solve' a problem of traffic congestion by constructing an urban toll motorway from A to B, then some people will be able to drive from A to B more quickly. But others will refuse to pay the toll and will find rat-runs through residential streets. In addition, the local community through which the new tollway has been built may be severed by the road and also have to endure massively increased levels of noise and pollution. Loss of property value is also inevitable. Wildlife and pets will be affected too as they will be forced to change their movement patterns or risk being run over. Stormwater runoff will contain toxic pollutants from vehicles, etc.

Deleuze problematises the traditional problem-solution relation, turning it on its head. When spatial planners think about 'problems', they tend to think in terms of 'solutions'. (See Balducci's discussion of the garbage can model of decision-making and chapters by Servillo and Cao and Zheng, this volume.) 'It is though a problem were merely a particular lack or fault that a solution will fill or rectify' (May, 2005, p. 83). A solution makes problems disappear! Practitioners and politicians may fall into the trap of allowing a solution to define a problem, as Fedeli's chapter illustrates in Part 1. For instance, we can control farmers burning stubble near motorways on days when hot air presses down on cooler air nearer the ground (a temperature inversion), but we cannot – or do not want to – control car usage. Motorway smog thus becomes a problem of farming rather than of driving. Or, if there is lottery money available to build a sports arena but not a medical clinic, the problem may well become a shortage of sports facilities.

As Deleuze notes, 'far from disappearing in this overlay, however, [the problem] insists and persists in these solutions' (1994, p. 163). Perhaps instead of regarding problems as something to be definitively 'solved', planners could regard them as opening up areas for discussion and negotiation of different possibilities, recognising that every possibility will capture something, but not everything, of the problem, and thinking through what it renders present and absent.

We must be careful not to allow the solution to define the problem (what we think that politicians or the public want; what there is lottery funding for; what 'best practice' tells us to do, and so on). Solutions are actual – real, stable identities, whereas problems are virtual – inexhaustible 'open fields' (May, 2005). We thus tend to see solutions in terms of their actuality rather than their virtuality. In other words, we let the solution determine how we see or frame the problem. We may, therefore, ignore many potentialities, opting for a particular version which is already constrained by an overdetermined structure that we have imposed.

It is more important to Deleuze to explore the specific and unique development or 'becoming' of each individual element or issue than to categorise them. The trajectory (or genealogy) of an individual, element or issue, therefore, is not based in its commonality with others, but rather 'in a process of individuation determined by actual and specific differences, multitudinous influences and chance interactions' (Stagoll, 2010, p. 75). Becoming is thus based on dynamic, undetermined relations between entities which are themselves not entirely determinable. 'The closest thing there is to determinacy is the relative containment of chance' (Massumi, 1992, p. 58) – or uncertainty.

## Dealing with uncertainty and indeterminacy in planning

> Dealing with uncertainty is a duty of planning (Silva, 2002, p. 336)
> A sort of control box for indeterminacy (Joseph, 2009, p. 236)

Communicative planning theory and practice methodologies could be argued as attempting to cope with uncertainty. However, it should be noted that in several instances, communicative planning is attached or 'bolted on' to a methodology of rational comprehensive planning to add 'public legitimacy' to goals or options which are often pre-selected. (See, for example, Stoeglehner, 2010; Stoeglehner and Neugebauer, 2012; Demazière and Serrano, this volume.) Further, communicative planning[4] is only 'uncertain' as far as the goals are to be negotiated. Once negotiated, they become 'certain' (De Roo, 2012, p. 143). Communicative planning allows for different actors' framing of situations and is ethical in its democratic inclusiveness (theoretically), but still essentially regards time as t = 0, with decisions about the future made based on interpretations of the present.

Recent collaborative/communicative theories increasingly reference complexity. Innes and Booher (2010; Booher and Innes, 2010), for instance, cite Axelrod and Cohen's (1999) *Harnessing Complexity* as a key influence on their thinking with regard to adaptive governance. Innes and Booher suggest that the purpose of governance shifts from questions of '"where do we want to be and how do we get there?" to "how do we move in a desirable direction in the face of uncertainty?"' (Innes and Booher, 2010, p. 207).

While some scholars following complexity criteria seek to measure the seemingly contradictory 'uncertainty precision', aiming to reduce the error boundaries of outputs in probabilistic forecasting models (see Rasouli and Timmermans, 2012), others seek to model how elements of urban systems interact and can emerge spontaneously (see Batty and Longley, 1994; Batty, 2005). Batty (2012) concludes that with increasing complexity, models become more difficult, if not impossible, to validate. It appears that we are not yet able 'to build models whose predictions we might have confidence in, and models that are designed to inform processes that no longer have any sense of the quest for an optimum' (Batty and Marshall (2012, p. 43). As Wardekker *et al.* (2010, p. 996) comment, 'the potential for coping with surprises is very limited'.

The question remains, how might strategic spatial planners design interventions in a complex world where existing strategic planning systems are too rigid to respond to both uncertainties of rapid change and the indeterminate unexpected. Portugali (2012) suggests that theorists and practitioners should treat both cities and planning processes as complex systems. (See also chapters by Balducci and Fedeli in this volume.) Complex systems are those which are 'incomplete in that we have no certainty that we have identified all the key components that are necessary for an acceptable understanding' (Batty and Marshall, 2012, p. 43). Crucially, the authors continue that, 'if we know that the system is incomplete, then we cannot make predictions of its future state'. By definition, complex systems are open, interactive, non-linear, chaotic, far-from-equilibrium, emergent and unpredictable (Cilliers, 2005; Hillier, 2010; Portugali, 2012): i.e. indeterminate. They tend to adapt as circumstances change in what are known as complex adaptive systems (CAS). The key characteristics of CAS are matters of often intense debate. Characteristics typically include: self-organising (autopoietic) agent behaviour, pervasive interconnectivity of elements, emergent behavioural patterns with limited predictability and that observers affect the systems observed (Hillier, 2010, p. 384).

Dutch scholars (for example, de Roo and Porter, 2007; de Roo, 2010, 2012; de Roo and Rauws, 2012; Rauws, Cook and van Dijk, 2014) are increasingly attempting to locate strategic spatial planning with regard to complex environments. De Roo and Rauws (2012, p. 219), for instance, seek adaptive capacity 'based on flexibility on the one hand and robustness on the other', which Rauws *et al.* (2014) translate into proposals for Dutch area development plans. The authors present four useful principles: an overarching development plan should have multiple independent smaller scale plans; apply incremental development strategies; install requisite 'carrying structures'/infrastructures; and define loose rules rather than detailed regulations (2014, pp. 143–146).

Luuk Boelens (2013; Boelens and de Roo, 2016) develops a form of planning 'beyond the plan' in 'undefined becoming'. Building on insights of quantum-related theories, such as those described above, Boelens and de Roo argue that 'planning processes unfold in time, without a clear beginning or at least without a clear and definite end' (2016, p. 48). Planning practice may thus adapt as 'part of possible co-evolutionary assemblages of becoming' (ibid) with other human and non-human actants.

Adaptability in strategic spatial planning practice depends on resolving fundamental tensions between institutional stability (organisational conservation) and flexibility, which would place differentiation,[5] or the creative new, as the horizon for change. If we are to actualise strategies as 'revisable, fluid conceptions continually interacting with unfolding experiences and understandings, but yet holding in attention some orienting sensibility' (Healey, 2007, p. 267), I suggest that there is a need to develop a different, more diachronic, emergent, ethical approach to strategic spatial planning which embraces uncertainty and indeterminacy and which allows for contingencies of 'would-be-worlds' (Thrift, 1999, p. 58) and non-linear temporalities.

For me, as for those mentioned above, this demands a poststructuralist approach to strategic spatial planning theory and practice. This would be an open methodology designed to stimulate strategic planners to think and plan – perhaps to envision the impossible (Monno, 2010) – in what is predominantly an indeterminate, rather than an uncertain, world where 'strategic planning does not claim to eliminate uncertainty [and I would add indeterminacy] through the making of predictions, [but] seeks to work as well as possible within the context of uncertainty, and to enable the actors to open up the spectrum of possibilities' (Albrechts and Balducci, 2012, p. 11).

I appreciate that actors desire some form of investment 'certainty', at least in the short term (3–5 years may be the limit given the fluidity of global markets), couched within some indicative, yet flexible, longer-term broad vision as an 'orienting sensibility' (see also Albrechts, 2004; Albrechts and Balducci, 2012; Rauws *et al.*, 2014). I find resonance here with the ontological conceptualisation of multiple planes or plans used by Deleuze and Guattari (1987). The authors typically use the plane for a type of thinking which mediates between 'the chaos of chance happenings … on the one hand, and structured, orderly thinking on the other' (Stagoll, 2005, p. 204). As such, I find their ideas to be extremely relevant to the praxis of strategic spatial planning.

My conceptualisation of a multiplanar practice of planning is inspired by Deleuze and Guattari's (1987, 1994) planes of immanence and organisation (Hillier, 2007). It resonates strongly with Rauws *et al.*'s (2014) and Boelens and De Roo's (2016) recent thinking. The plane of immanence is a temporarily coded, disorganised flux of forces open to 'new connections, creative and novel becomings that will give it new patterns and triggers of behaviour' (Bonta and Protevi, 2004, pp. 62–63). It is a 'virtual realm of potentials' which leaves the ends of each line of knowledge open to extension, rather than being closed or the end of a process. Such a plane could be a long-term strategic plan or trajectory (of, perhaps, 15 years); of foresight, creative transformation; of what might be. It 'is at once the act of charting out a pathway and the opening of that pathway to the event of the chance encounter' (Kaufman, 1998, p. 6) of credit crises, increases in fuel prices, and so on. The plane 'functions like a sieve over chaos' (Boundas,

2005, p. 273), implying a sort of 'groping experimentation' (Deleuze and Guattari, 1994, p. 41) towards the future.

Shorter-term plans (of 3–5 years duration) or project briefs resonate with Deleuze and Guattari's planes of organisation which support day-to-day elements of life. These planes contain hierarchical power relations which regulate or stratify our worlds (into land-use zones, for example) and fix identities (such as land-use type). This is a teleological plane concerned with the development of forms and the formation of subjects supported by stability of judgement and identity. The plane of organisation could be a master plan or blueprint with defined goals for development. These goals are predetermined standards (such as land-use regulations or a design guide) to which things are submitted in judgement and ordered by the forms of representation (whether applications meet the standard criteria, etc.). Local area action plans, design briefs, project masterplans are typical planes of organisation. They tend to be relatively local or micro-scale, short-term and content-specific. They facilitate small movements or changes along the dynamic, open trajectories of planes of immanence.

Multiplanar planning thus comprises broad visions or trajectories – such as sustainability, liveability, and so on, which have been inclusively and democratically negotiated – as frames of reference which provide justification and navigational context for shorter-term, location-specific substantive acts – such as area action plans or major projects – which mark small movements and changes. I suggest that a multiplanar conceptualisation of strategic spatial planning addresses the concerns of how to incorporate flexibility for practitioners to cope with emerging socio-economic issues and objectives and also coordination for shorter-term investor 'certainty'.

Patsy Healey (2013, personal communication) asks the all-important question of why it seems so difficult to translate a combination of shorter-term investor certainty and longer-term flexibility/adaptability into planning practice. A response to this question would include the roles of politics (as played by politicians, interest groups, local and non-local residents, investors in land and property, and so on) as actors formally and informally argue and lobby for policies that reflect their desires, usually in the shorter-term of political cycles, rather than longer-term trajectories of environmental sustainability, etc. It could also suggest that the conceptualisations with which practitioners frame their strategies (perhaps unconsciously?) are inappropriate for coping with longer-term uncertainties: that they should ask different questions.

In attempting to translate these ideas, questions and responses into a methodology for strategic spatial planning practice which could deal with uncertainty and indeterminacy, I have outlined an approach (Hillier, 2011, 2015) which develops what Deleuze and Guattari (1987) term pragmatics or cartography, Foucault's (1984) genealogy and Hames' (2007) organisational management concept of strategic navigation. This approach emphasises the relational dynamics of forces, such that analysis entails both tracing in detail the conditions of possibility of how things/places/problems came to be constituted, as products of particular contingencies through unfolding power-laden relations between elements, and also mapping them into the future. As such, there is a need to identify the determinants or drivers of change, the interdependencies or power relations between these drivers and between them and human and non-human actors.

The methodology above is one of diachronic emergence or the creative production of new patterns in a complex assemblage. It is a process concerned with experimentation and asking questions about 'what might happen if …?' A lack of certainty means that detailed prediction is impossible: there is no 'truth' as such. The methodology attempts to think time as past-present-future (time = m). However, even with the aid of prospectives, this will be difficult in practice. The aim, for Deleuze, is to accept that the future is outside one's control, conceptually and behaviourally. Practitioners should thus attempt to embrace 'a future that is not characterised by the continuity of the present, nor by the repetition of its actions, but by a difference that can never be brought fully into one's grasp' (May, 2005, p. 62). There is nothing transcendent which guides the present, determining the future in a particular direction. Even though actualisation of what might happen is inevitably constrained to some extent by structures – including capitalism, institutional norms, and so on – and some degree of path-dependence, actors immersed in the play of events can and will also affect the future. If strategic spatial planners can begin to comprehend the power or force relations between human and non-human actors and structures, they might be able to derive some responses to 'what might happen if …?' But we can never be certain of the future. We must respect the unexpected.

I suggest that strategic spatial planners could usefully shift perspective from attempting to control change to enhancing their capacity to live with and tweak change in more democratically and inclusionary, negotiated, desirable directions (hopefully towards social and environmental justice). Albrechts and Balducci (2012, p. 12) envisage a methodology for strategic spatial planning which can create a long-term vision or frame of reference – 'a geography of the unknown' – which can point direction and justification for actions in processes of planning with change. As indicated above, several scholars have taken up this challenge and are actively working on such methodologies.

## Conclusions: speculative overkill or useful distinction?

> The future of a city is … intrinsically undetermined: novelty and surprise are fundamental aspects of the urban process
>
> (Alexander *et al.*, 2012, p. 47)

There will always be elements beyond both certainty and uncertainty; beyond calculation, measurement and control. As Massey (2005, p. 111) states, the spatial is produced by 'that – sometimes happenstance, sometimes not – arrangement-in-relation-to-each-other that is the result of there being a multiplicity of trajectories' which come together or move apart. Strategic spatial planning as a process cannot succeed if it seeks to manage uncertainties and indeterminacies through their attempted control, reduction or elimination. Any 'certainty' thereby created is inevitably illusory.

As I have attempted to demonstrate, spatial planning academics and practitioners have often conflated notions of uncertainty and indeterminacy. Is making a distinction between these notions merely speculative overkill, as Bonta and Protevi (2004, p. 201, n. 49) suggest, or it is a useful distinction which may potentially help planners to recognise the inherent undecidability of strategic decisions and to develop suggestions and strategies for ways of operating with dynamic thresholds and trajectories.

I have suggested that the philosophy of Gilles Deleuze can help us to breach the wall of certainty (Luzzi, 2001, p. 11) and can take us from the notion of uncertainty to a much more complex and sophisticated engagement with indeterminacy. Strategic spatial plans could become 'contingent, working notebooks' (Luzzi, 2001, p. 13) of strategic navigation, rather than rapidly out-dated documents of inappropriate targets and standards.

Features of quantum physics, such as uncertainty, indeterminacy and complementarity, are always-already 'intra-actively entangled with questions of politics and power' (Barad, 2011, p. 451). While I disagree with Steele and Ruming's (2012, p. 173) comment that debate around planning certainty versus flexibility is 'impotent', 'overemphasis[ed]' and a 'straw man [sic]', I do agree with the fundamental importance of questions of for whom, and for what, with what values and purposes, do and could our planning systems and practices perform. I conclude with the words of Nobel Laureate, Ilya Prigogine (1999, np): 'we come to the end of certainty, but the end of certainty means the possibility of novelty, of evolution'.

## Acknowledgements

My thanks to Jonathan Metzger for stimulating comments on a draft of this paper and, in particular, for making me recognise the inherent anthropocentrism of Schrödinger's Cat.

## Notes

1 Lack of space prohibits consideration of planning practices and plans.
2 For Deleuze (1988) the outside comprises contextually non-organised, often imperceptible, entities not included in, for example, a society or a planning strategy. The outside is not fixed, however, but affects and is affected by the foldings together of elements which make up the 'inside'. 'What conditions a society is precisely what remains outside of it, [while] the inside [i]s something that is continually in motion to adapt itself to what threatens its stability' (Symons, 2006, np). As Deleuze and Guattari (1987, p. 360) write: 'the State itself has always been in a relation with an outside and is inconceivable independent of that relationship'. The outside might include, for instance, multinational enterprises, international religious formations, local minority groups and so on (Deleuze and Guattari, 1987, p. 360).
3 The Schrödinger's Cat experiment is inherently anthropocentric, presented from the standpoint of a human observer using human-defined instruments of measurement.

Presented from the standpoint of other agents, such as the cat, the atom, the hammer, potential airborne micro-organisms in the box, fleas on the cat and so on, the cat cannot be represented as 'alive' or 'dead'. What the thought experiment illustrates, however, is the human-centric representation of uncertainty.
4 Here I refer to communicative planning as consensus-building as distinguished from Healey's later work on collaborative planning which is concerned with planning as a relational process that emphasises interaction rather than consensus.
5 Deleuzean differenciation refers to actualisation of the virtual (Deleuze, 1994, pp. 208–214).

# References

Abbott, J. (2005). Understanding and managing the unknown. *Journal of Planning Education and Research*, 24(3), 237–251.
Abbott, J. (2009). Planning for complex metropolitan regions: a better future or a more certain one? *Journal of Planning Education and Research*, 28, 503–517.
Abbott, J. (2012). Planning as managing uncertainty: making the 1996 Livable Region Strategic Plan for Greater Vancouver. *Planning Practice and Research*, 27(5), 571–593.
Albrechts, L. (2004). Strategic (spatial) planning re-examined. *Environment and Planning B, Planning and Design*, 31, 743–758.
Albrechts, L. (2010). How to enhance creativity, diversity and sustainability in spatial planning: strategic planning revisited. In M. Cerrera, C. Concilio and V. Monno (Eds.), *Making Strategies in Spatial Planning* (pp. 3–25). Dordrecht: Springer.
Albrechts, L. (2015). Ingredients for a more radical strategic spatial planning. *Environment and Planning B, Planning and Design*, 42, 510–525.
Albrechts, L. and Balducci, A. (2012). Practising strategic planning: in search for critical features to explain the strategic character of plans. Paper presented at WPSC, Perth, 4–7 July.
Alexander, E. R., Mazza, L. and Moroni, S. (2012). Planning without plans? Nomocracy or teleocracy for socio-spatial ordering. *Progress in Planning*, 77, 37–87.
Axelrod, R. and Cohen, M. (1999). *Harnessing Complexity*. New York: The Free Press.
Balducci, A. (2011). Strategic planning as exploration. *Town Planning Review*, 82(5), 529–546.
Balducci, A., Boelens, L., Hillier, J., Nyseth, T. and Wilkinson, C. (2011). Strategic spatial planning in uncertainty: theory and exploratory practice, *Town Planning Review*, 82(5), 481–501.
Barad, K. (2007). *Meeting the Universe Halfway*. Durham, NC: Duke University Press.
Barad, K. (2011). Erasers and erasures: Pinch's unfortunate 'uncertainty' principle. *Social Studies of Science*, 41(3), 443–454.
Batty M. (2005). *Cities and Complexity: Understanding Cities with Cellular Automata, Agent-based Models and Fractals*. Cambridge, MA: MIT Press.
Batty, M. (2012). A generic framework for computational spatial modelling. In A. Heppenstall, A. Crooks, L. See and M. Batty (Eds.), *Agent-Based Models of Geographical Systems* (pp. 19–51). Dordrecht: Springer.
Batty, M. and Longley, P. (1994). *Fractal Cities: A Geometry of Form and Function*. Oxford: Academic Press.
Batty, M. and Marshall, S. (2012). The origins of complexity theory in cities and planning. In J. Portugali, H. Meyer, E. Stolk and E. Tan (Eds.), *Complexity Theories of Cities Have Come of Age* (pp. 21–45). Heidelberg: Springer.

Boelens, L. (2013). De ontspannen versus de jachtige metropool; pleidooi voor een horizontale ruimtelijke planning. Inaugural lecture, University Ghent, 18 April 2013. In I. Coninx, J. Ast and H. Bruyninckx (Eds.), *Ruimte & Maatschappij: Vlaams-Nederlands tijdschrift voor ruimtelijke vraagstukken*, (pp. 46–71). Gent: Garant.

Boelens, L. and de Roo, G. (2016). Planning of undefined becoming: first encounters of planners beyond the plan. *Planning Theory*, 15(1), 42–67.

Bogue, R. (2003). *Deleuze on Music, Painting and the Arts*. New York: Routledge.

Bogue, R. (2007). *Deleuze's Way: Essays in Transverse Ethics and Aesthetics*. Aldershot: Ashgate.

Bohr, N. (1987). *The Philosophical Writings of Niels Bohr* (3 vols). Woodbridge, CT: Ox Bow Press.

Bonta, M. and Protevi, J. (2004). *Deleuze and Geophilosophy: A Guide and Glossary*. Edinburgh: Edinburgh University Press.

Booher, D. and Innes, J. (2010). Governance for resilience: CALFED as a Complex Adaptive Network for resilience management. *Ecology and Society*, 15(3), 35. Retrieved from http://www.ecologyandsociety.org/vol15/iss3/art35/ [accessed 26/11/2010].

Boundas, C. (2005). The art of begetting monsters: the unnatural nuptials of Deleuze and Kant. In S. Daniel (Ed.), *Current Continental Theory and Modern Philosophy* (pp. 254–279). Evanston, IL: Northwestern University Press.

Cao, K. and Zhang, Y. (2013). Urban planning in generalized non-Euclidean space. *Planning Theory*, 12(4), 335–350.

Centre for Environmental Studies (CES) (1970). *The LOGIMP Experiment*. Information Paper IP25, London: CES.

Cilliers, P. (2005). Complexity, deconstruction and relativism. *Theory, Culture and Society*, 22(5), 255–267.

De Roo, G. (2010). Being or becoming? That is the question! Confronting complexity with contemporary planning theory. In G. De Roo and E. Silva (Eds.), *A Planner's Encounter with Complexity* (pp. 29–38). Farnham: Ashgate.

De Roo, G. (2012). Spatial planning, complexity and a world 'out of equilibrium': outline of a non-linear approach to planning. In G. De Roo, J. Hillier and J. Van Wezemael (Eds.), *Complexity and Planning* (pp. 141–175). Farnham: Ashgate.

De Roo, G. and Porter, G. (2007). *Fuzzy Planning: The Role of Actors in a Fuzzy Governance Environment*. Farnham: Ashgate.

De Roo, G. and Rauws, W. (2012). Positioning planning in the world of order and chaos. In J. Portugali, H. Meyer, E. Stolk and E. Tan (Eds.), *Complexity Theories of Cities Have Come of Age* (pp. 207–220). Heidelberg: Springer.

Deleuze, G. (1983). Cinema – Vérité et temps. Cours 49 du 13/12/1983. Partie 1. La voix de Gilles Deleuze en ligne. Retrieved from http://www2.univ-paris8.fr/deleuze/article.php3?id_article=271 [accessed 13/05/2014].

Deleuze, G. (1985). Foucault – les formations historiques. Cours 6 du 26/11/1985. Partie 4. La voix de Gilles Deleuze en ligne. Retrieved from http://www2.univ-paris8.fr/deleuze/article.php3?id_article=426 [accessed 13/05/2014].

Deleuze, G. (1986) [1983]. *Cinema 1: The Movement-Image* (Trans. H. Tomlinson). Minneapolis, MN: University of Minnesota Press.

Deleuze, G. (1988) [1986] *Foucault* (Trans. S. Hand). Minneapolis, MN: University of Minnesota Press.

Deleuze, G. (1994) [1968]. *Difference and Repetition* (Trans. P. Patton). London: Athlone.

Deleuze, G. and Guattari, F. (1987) [1980]. *A Thousand Plateaus: Capitalism and Schizophrenia* (Trans. B. Massumi). London: Athlone Press.

Deleuze, G. and Guattari, F. (1994) [1991]. *What is Philosophy?* (Trans. H. Tomlinson and G. Burchill). London: Verso.

Dewey, J. (1929). *The Quest for Certainty: A Study of the Relation of Knowledge and Action.* New York: Minton, Balch and Co.

Esposito, E. (2013). The structures of uncertainty: performativity and unpredictability in economic operations. *Economy and Society*, 42(1), 101–129.

Folke, C. (2006). Resilience: the emergence of a perspective for social-ecological systems analyses. *Global Environmental Change*, 16, 253–267.

Foucault, M. (1984). Polemics, politics and problematizations, interview with Paul Rabinow, (Trans. L. Davis). Retrieved from http://foucault.info/foucault/interview.html [accessed 02/02/2007].

Friedmann, J. (2004). Hong Kong, Vancouver and beyond: strategic spatial planning and the longer range. *Planning Theory and Practice*, 5(1), 50–56.

Giezen, M. (2013). Adaptive and strategic capacity: navigating metaprojects through uncertainty and complexity. *Environment and Planning B, Planning and Design*, 40, 723–741.

Grosz, E. (2008). *Chaos, Territory, Art: Deleuze and the Framing of the Eart.* New York: Columbia University Press.

Hames, R. (2007). *The Five Literacies of Global Leadership.* San Francisco, CA: Jossey-Bass.

Healey, P. (2007). *Urban Complexity and Spatial Strategies: Towards a New Relational Planning for Our Times.* Basingstoke: Routledge.

Healey, P. (2010). *Making Better Places.* Basingstoke: Palgrave Macmillan.

Healey, P. and Hillier, J. (2008). Introduction. In J. Hillier and P. Healey (Eds.), *Critical Essays in Planning Theory*, Vol. 1 (pp. ix–xxvii ). Farnham: Ashgate.

Heisenberg, W. (1958). *Physics and Philosophy: The Revolution in Modern Science* New York: Harper & Row.

Heisenberg, W. (1983) [1927]. The physical content of quantum kinematics and mechanics. *Zeitschrift fur Physik*, 43, 172–198. In J. Wheeler and W. Zurek (Eds.), *Quantum Theory and Measurement.* Princeton, NJ: Princeton University Press.

Hillier, J. (2007). *Stretching beyond the Horizon: A Multiplanar Theory of Spatial Planning and Governance.* Aldershot: Ashgate.

Hillier, J. (2010). Introduction to Part 3. In J. Hillier and P. Healey (Eds.), *The Ashgate Research Companion to Planning Theory* (pp. 367–398). Farnham: Ashgate.

Hillier, J. (2011). Strategic Navigation across Multiple Planes: towards a Deleuzean-inspired methodology for strategic spatial planning. *Town Planning Review*, 82(5), 503–527.

Hillier, J. (2015) Strategic Navigation. *EspacesTemps.net*, Traverses, 23.02.2015. Retrieved from http://www.espacestemps.net/articles/strategic-navigation/ [accessed 11/03/2015].

Huxley, M. (2011). The specific and the general: the designation of planning problems. *CRIOS*, 2, 21–30.

Innes, J. and Booher, D. (2010). *Planning with Complexity.* New York: Routledge.

Joseph, B. (2009). Chance, indeterminacy, multiplicity. In J. Robinson (Ed.), *The Anarchy of Silence* (pp. 210–238). MACBA: Barcelona. Retrieved from www.macba.cat/uploads/publicacions/Cage/branden-eng.pdf [accessed 13/05/2014].

Kaufman, E. (1998). Introduction. In E. Kaufman and K. J. Heller (Eds.), *Deleuze and Guattari: New Mappings in Politics, Philosophy and Culture* (pp. 3–19). Minneapolis, MN: University of Minnesota Press.

Lagadec, P. (2009). A new cosmology of risks and crises: time for a radical shift in paradigm and practice. *Review of Policy Research*, 26(4), 473–486.

Latour, B. and Woolgar, S. (1986). *Laboratory Life: The Construction of Scientific Facts* (2nd edn). Princeton, NJ: Princeton University Press.

Law, J. (2004). *After Method*. London: Sage.

Law, J. and Lin, W.-Y. (2009). Cultivating disconcertment. Retrieved from http://www. heterogeneities.net/publications/LawLin2009CultivatingDisconcertment.pdf [accessed 16/11/2010].

Luzzi, N. (2001). *The Rational Planning Model in Forest Planning: Planning in the Light of Ambivalence*. EWP Working Paper 3, Ecosystem Workforce Program. Eugene, OR: University of Oregon.

Mack, R. (1971). *Planning on Uncertainty: Decision Making in Business and Administration*. New York: Wiley.

Massey, D. (2005). *For Space*. London: Sage.

Massumi, B. (1992). *A User's Guide to Capitalism and Schizophrenia: Deviations from Deleuze and Guattari*. Cambridge, MA: MIT Press.

May, T. (2005). *Gilles Deleuze: An Introduction*. Cambridge: Cambridge University Press.

McLoughlin, J. B. (1992). *Shaping Melbourne's Future?* Cambridge: Cambridge University Press.

Monno, V. (2010). When strategy meets democracy: exploring the limits of the 'possible' and the value of the 'impossible'. In M. Cerreta, G. Concilio and V. Monno (Eds.), *Making Strategies in Spatial Planning: Knowledge and Values* (pp. 161–183). Dordrecht: Springer.

Moore, S. (2011, December 30). I'm sure that I'm unsure. *The Guardian Weekly*, p. 24.

Murphy, T. (1998). Quantum ontology: a virtual mechanics of becoming. In E. Kaufman and J.J. Heller (Eds.), *Deleuze and Guattari: New Mappings in Politics, Philosophy and Culture* (pp. 211–229). Minneapolis, MN: University of Minnesota Press.

Plotnitsky, A. (2002). *The Knowable and the Unknowable*. Ann Arbor, MI: University of Michigan Press.

Portugali, J. (2012). Complexity theories of cities: First, Second or Third Culture of Planning. In G. De Roo, J. Hillier and J. Van Wezemael (Eds.), *Complexity and Planning* (pp. 117–140). Farnham: Ashgate.

Prigogine, I. (1999). The arrow of time, inaugural lecture. The Chaotic Universe workshop, International Center for Relativistic Astrophysics, Pescara. Retrieved from www. icra.it/publications/books/prigogine/motivation.htm [accessed 13/05/2014].

Rasouli, S. and Timmermans, H. (2012). Commentary: uncertainty, uncertainty, uncertainty: revisiting the study of dynamic complex spatial systems. *Environment and Planning A*, 44, 1781–1784.

Rauws, W., Cook, M. and van Dijk, T. (2014). How to make development plans suitable for volatile contexts. *Planning Practice and Research*, 29(2), 133–151.

Rosenhead, J. (1980a). Planning under uncertainty: 1. The inflexibility of methodologies. *The Journal of the Operational Research Society*, 31(3), 209–216.

Rosenhead, J. (1980b). Planning under uncertainty: II. A methodology for robustness analysis. *The Journal of the Operational Research Society*, 31(4), 331–341.

Schrödinger, E. (1980) [1935]. The present situation in quantum mechanics (Trans. J. D. Trimmer). *Proceedings of the American Philosophical Society*, 124, 323–338.

Silva, E. (2002). Indecision factors when planning for land use change. *European Planning Studies*, 10(3), 353–358.

Smith, D. W. (2012). *Essays on Deleuze*. Edinburgh: Edinburgh University Press.

Stagoll, C. (2005). Plane. In A. Parr (Ed.), *The Deleuze Dictionary* (pp. 87–89). Edinburgh: Edinburgh University Press.

Stagoll, C. (2010). Difference. In A. Parr (Ed.), *The Deleuze Dictionary*, revised edition (pp. 74–76). Edinburgh: Edinburgh University Press.

Steele, W. and Ruming, K. (2012). Flexibility v certainty: unsettling the land use planning shibboleth in Australia. *Planning Practice and Research*, 27(2), 155–176.

Stoeglehner, G. (2010). Enhancing SEA effectiveness: lessons learnt from Australian experiences in spatial planning. *Impact Assessment and Project Appraisal*, 28(3), 217–231.

Stoeglehner, G. and Neugebauer, G. (2012). Integrating sustainability assessment into planning: benefits and challenges. In A. Bond, A. Morrison-Saunders and R. Howitt (Eds.), *Sustainability Assessment: pluralism, practice and progress* (pp. 245–262). London: Routledge.

Symons, S. (2006). Deleuze and the various faces of the outside, *Theory and Event*, 9(3). Retrieved from https://muse.jhu.edu/journals/theory_and_event/ [accessed 27/07/2015].

Thomas, D., Minett, J., Hopkins, S., Hamnett, S., Faludi, A. and Barrett, D. (1983). *Flexibility and Commitment in Planning: A Comparative Study of Local Planning and Development in The Netherlands and England.* The Hague: Martinus Nijhoff.

Thrift, N. (1999). The place of complexity. *Theory, Culture and Society*, 16(3), 31–69.

Wardekker, J. A., de Jong, A., Knoop, J., and van der Sluijs, J. (2010). Operationalising a resilience approach to adapting an urban delta to uncertain climate changes. *Technological Forecasting and Social Change*, 77, 987–998.

Williams, J. (2003). *Gilles Deleuze's 'Difference and Repetition': A Critical Introduction and Guide.* Edinburgh: Edinburgh University Press.

Wynne, B. (1992). Uncertainty and environmental learning: reconceiving science and policy in the preventive paradigm. *Global Environmental Change*, June, 111–127.

# 19 Strategic planning and land use planning conflicts

## The role of statutory authority

*Glen Searle*

## Introduction

This chapter focuses on the particular issue of the relationship between strategic planning and statutory planning, and sets this within wider consideration of the nature of strategic planning and how strategic planning deals with uncertainty in a multi-level governance situation. It uses two case studies from Australia to develop several propositions about the relationship between spatial strategic planning and statutory authority. While strategic planning is conceptually distinct from statutory planning (see Chapter 1, this volume), in practice the two can overlap, as in one of the case studies here. Comparison of that case study with another involving a more typical non-statutory strategic plan allows for a more nuanced analysis of the statutory–strategic planning relationship.

The chapter challenges current conceptions of spatial strategic planning on several fronts. It shows that the strategic–statutory boundary is not as fixed as current conceptualisations imagine it. The role of statutory planning in attempting to provide greater certainty can be shifted to an extent onto that of strategic planning, for example through housing targets in strategic plans. Strategic plans themselves may also be statutory. The extent to which the strategic–statutory boundary is fluid is a function of contextual factors such as the relative size and power of the strategic and statutory planning agencies, interaction between the two in the process of strategic plan development, and the extent to which there is a tradition of statutory subordination to strategic planning.

This leads to the possibility of re-thinking strategic planning processes. For example, the analysis below suggests that achieving the aims of strategic planning – to the extent that these are intended to shape statutory plans – might be improved by greater involvement of larger statutory planning agencies in the preparation of strategic plans. Conversely, the analysis also suggests that the looser the strategic plan constraints on statutory plans within its remit, the more likely it will be that the strategic plan aims are incorporated into statutory planning because this will give statutory planning agencies a wider range of locally suitable ways to implement relevant strategic plan elements.

The chapter also shows how analysing the relationship between statutory and strategic planning can illuminate understanding of whether attempts to reduce uncertainty in strategic planning can be successful. In particular, the case studies focus on quantitative target-setting in strategic plans, and the processes through which targets were or were not achieved. In this, the extent to which conflict with the statutory level was generated by the targets is analysed. It is shown that the contextual factors listed above were fundamental in determining the level of conflict, in addition to whether the strategic plan itself was statutory.

In order to situate the case study discussion within the general concerns of this book, the chapter briefly overviews some theoretical and practical aspects of these concerns with an emphasis on the issues raised by the particular planning context of Australia. The next section considers questions relating to the focus and content of strategic planning, the issues being covered and what kinds of outputs there might be. Then, the focus of this chapter – the tension between strategic plans and statutory authority – is considered. That section incorporates consideration of the role of uncertainty and the related issue of relationality in contributing to this tension.

These sections provide a frame for the case studies, from Sydney and South East Queensland (the Brisbane region). The role of statutory authority is illuminated by the selection of the case studies, with one strategic plan having a statutory status and the other one not being a statutory plan. The case studies illustrate various ways in which this difference influences the effectiveness with which strategic planning directs local statutory plans.

## The content of strategic planning

The content of strategic planning will obviously vary according to the purpose of the planning, but it is also true that this content has undergone significant change over the last half century. In Australia, the early metropolitan strategic plans in the middle of the last century, starting with the 1948 Sydney plan, were city-wide land use plans in the manner of earlier American city plans (see also Maginn *et al.*, this volume, for further discussion of Australian strategic spatial planning). This reflected emerging town planning systems, in which land use and development control functions to be carried out by local government were being defined and legislated. The mid-century metropolitan plans set out desired city-wide spatial structures that statutorily delimited future land use. This set a framework for the land use and development decisions that local government would make under their new town planning powers (the exception being Brisbane, where the City Council, which contained nearly all of the metropolitan area population unlike the fragmented local government areas of the other cities, made its own statutory plan in 1965 under the City of Brisbane Act 1924 (Minnery and Low Choy, 2010)). Thereafter, Australian metropolitan spatial strategies moved away from detailed land use prescription to setting out a broad framework for statutory local planning via designation of future growth areas, preferred activity centres, major transport routes, and the like. This set the scene for potential tension between the non-statutory strategic metropolitan plans and the statutory local plans. Again, the exception was Brisbane/South East Queensland, where the first regional plan was a statutory one that was not published until 2005. This statutory contrast between Queensland and the other states is the starting point for the case study below.

Comprehensive strategic spatial plans encompassing principal new or intensified activity locations and major transport infrastructure initiatives, such as those in Australian cities and other cities such as London and Vancouver, are the most common type of strategic plan. The other principal type of strategic plan is a transport strategy. In US cities, these are required to be produced for Federal Highway Administration funding to cities. In Australia, strategic highway plans date back to Sydney's roads plan of 1944. In the late 1960s and early 1970s, American consultants produced motorway strategies for several of the largest cities (Sydney, Brisbane, Adelaide) that served as an input into subsequent government highway strategies in Brisbane and Sydney. By the 1990s, the need for integrated transport strategies embracing public transport as well as roads was being recognised, with public transport becoming a more prominent concern as the emphasis on environmental sustainability increased from the 1980s. In Sydney and Brisbane, integrated transport strategies were produced in parallel with, and largely incorporated into, the comprehensive metropolitan strategies. Thus the picture of ongoing evolutionary change in strategic planning has been very evident in Australia since the first metropolitan strategic plans.

## Strategic planning and statutory authority

The extent to which there is tension between strategic planning and statutory authority is a function of several factors. The most important factor can be argued to be the extent to which a strategic plan can legally oblige key stakeholders to follow the plan's remit, i.e. its statutory status. In the typical situation in which a metropolitan strategy is intended to serve as the framework for planning and development control by local government, the degree to which local planning follows the strategy will depend in the first place on whether this is legally required by act of parliament or regulation, i.e. whether the strategy has statutory authority. Within a legal requirement, there might be very different degrees of required adherence to the strategy, for example depending on whether a local plan has to merely 'consider' the strategy in its formulation, or whether it is required to completely conform to the strategy. Local, cadastral-based land use plans themselves invariably have a statutory authority, and are the principal basis for assessing development applications.

Overall, however, statutory status for strategic plans appears to reduce conflict with local land use planning controls and decision-making, although not necessarily the extent to which statutory strategic directives are opposed at the local level. In many parts of the US, the Standard State Zoning and Enabling Act or similar state legislation provides that local zoning ordinances should be in accordance with the comprehensive or strategic plan (Stein, 2012). One court decision, *Udell v. Haas* (21 N.Y.2d 463, 470 (1968)), has stated that a key factor to be used by courts in deciding whether zoning accords with the comprehensive plan is whether forethought has been given to the community's land use problems. The effect, as Stein notes, is that all policies and long-range planning are in the comprehensive plan, restricting planning schemes to whatever is necessary to enforce the comprehensive plan policy (Stein, 2012, p. 16). This system is also adopted in Germany and Scandinavia, where comprehensive plans set out spatial goals and policies that dictate the development plans (Stein, 2012, p. 16) (see also Olesen and Metzger, this volume, for a discussion of strategic spatial planning in Denmark and Sweden, including the example of the statutory Copenhagen Region spatial plan that controls municipal plans). Similarly, a primary method of implementing Vancouver's statutory regional plan is via preparation or amendment of municipal (local) plans (Abbott and DeMarco, this volume). Stein sees that one advantage of this system is to reduce the emphasis on *ad hoc* decisions. Nevertheless, it should be noted that such strategic plans in the US in particular usually cover only one local council area, and need to be integrated into wider metropolitan strategic plans where they exist, although Bryson and Slotterback (this volume) also describe US cases of strategic spatial planning at state and regional levels.

The scope given to local authorities in formulating land use plans in statutory accordance with a regional strategy can be considerable, which reduces the potential for conflict but increases the potential for deviation from strategy goals. For example, the Metro Vancouver Regional Growth Strategy of 2011 requires municipalities to prepare housing projections and action plans, but there are no targets or related regional guidance (see Hutton, 2011). This raises, within the wider question of whether statutory strategy status reduces conflict with local land use planning, the issue of the extent to which local freedom to determine local futures should disregard regional strategic objectives. This is exemplified by recent planning policy in the UK. The Localism Act of 2011 provided for the abolition of regional spatial strategies outside London, based in part on their lack of democratic accountability and the 'thousands of objections' to the local housing targets they imposed (Bowie, 2012). Nevertheless, the strategic London Plan, with its housing targets for each borough, was retained.

The very possibility of rigid strategic planning targets is challenged by the new relational planning paradigm. This abhors precision and locational fixity, and instead focuses on flows across space and fluid outcomes that accept that the future is essentially highly uncertain (Healey, 2007; Hillier, 2007; see also Chapter 1, this volume). In turn, this questions whether it is possible to give a quintessentially relational strategy a statutory status that will control lower level plans and development decisions. It could be argued that the vaguer the strategic planning parameters, the less precise will be their control over subordinate plans and policies, and the more they will merely guide such plans, making statutory status rather moot. However, in the case of systems based on discretionary decision-making, notably that of England, it could also be argued that the tightness of strategic planning parameters is not central in adjudicating development. Rather, in the English system it would be only one of a range of relevant 'material considerations' required to be considered, in conjunction with undefined 'amenity', while common law based on precedent would also be central (see Booth, 2007). Indeed, the extent to which strategic planning in general can control development is called into question in such a system. This issue is not confined to England, as even in an essentially rule-based planning system such as Australia's, there may be considerable scope for discretionary decisions because of similar 'material provisions' clauses in planning legislation (as is the case for Sydney and South East Queensland) or because the rules do not fully specify property rights (Searle, 2016).

A major factor in the turn to relational strategies has been the emergence of a new governance landscape involving a range of actor/actant networks at various scales (Healey, 2007). In this, strategic planning is regarded as an activity involving large institutional networks at multiple scales of governance (Neuman, 2007). This wider range of players in the strategy process potentially makes it more difficult for a (higher) level of government to impose statutory controls in strategies. But this can depend on the extent to which the various actors have the power to negotiate acceptable controls with the government concerned. Powerful local councils, for example, might be willing to accept statutory controls that they have helped determine, as found in the case study reported below. The converse of this, where a local council makes a strategic plan that requires resources and various approvals from higher levels of government, is likely to result in a strategy that is more relational and suggestive, without statutory status, as in the case of the recent City of Sydney strategic plan (Searle, 2013). Where governance is more circumscribed and centralised, the need for relational planning is reduced, and thus the possibilities for statutory strategies are increased. In Australia, the strong control of planning and infrastructure provision by the state governments has allowed them to prepare metropolitan strategies akin to old-style blueprint plans that eschew relational elements (Searle and Bunker, 2010). Despite this, however, all except one of these strategies are basically non-statutory, although there is a trend for individual key components such as growth boundaries to be given statutory status. In this, with overtones of the UK Localism Act, it appears that the need for state governments to retain popular legitimacy has required them to allow local governments to retain some freedom in determining their development futures.

The chapter now develops these themes via a case study that compares strategic–land use planning conflicts in the South East Queensland and Sydney metro regions, located in different state planning systems. The strategic plans for the two cities differ in their statutory authority, with greater such authority being found to be associated with greater control and less conflict over local government regulation of land use. This is exemplified by strategic housing targets, which are used in this chapter as the basis for analysing strategic–land use conflicts in the two regions.

## Strategic and local planning in Sydney and South East Queensland

### Sydney

Sydney's first strategic plan, the County of Cumberland Planning Scheme of 1948, was prepared under the auspices of the Cumberland County Council, a joint state and local government planning authority. This was a statutory plan that prescribed zoning for every site in the region. Since then, strategic plans for the Sydney region have been non-statutory but have been prepared by the state government with little local government or public consultation. Comprehensive plan-making powers were given to local government in 1979 under the Environmental Planning and Assessment Act (EPA Act). Strategies since 1995 have set dwelling targets for each sub-region. The government has required local councils to adopt planning strategies to meet these targets.

Under the EPA Act, local plans are required to be consistent with the metropolitan strategy, though there is no positive obligation to align planning controls to be consistent with the strategy (Simington, 2013). The strategy does not prevail over development controls set by councils in their local plans. At best, it might be a matter for consideration for assessment of the public interest under the EPA Act.

### South East Queensland

Queensland's first planning act, the Integrated Planning Act, was not enacted until 1997. It was replaced by the Sustainable Planning Act in 2009, which retained the main features of the previous act. From 2004 these acts provide(d) for regional plans that would have statutory authority over local plans. From 1990 to 2003, a cooperative non-statutory approach to regional planning in South East Queensland (SEQ) was in place, in which regional planning issues – notably environmental and infrastructure costs generated by SEQ's rapid growth – were addressed jointly by local and state governments (Abbott, 2012). This cooperation produced a framework for local planning, the *SEQ Regional Framework for Growth Management*. Despite the constitutional powers of the state government, the emergence of a cooperative approach owed much to the relative strength of Brisbane City Council, by far the largest council in Australia, with a population approaching one million and controlling its own major infrastructure authorities.

Nevertheless, the cooperative framework failed to significantly ameliorate unplanned urban sprawl. In 2004 the planning act was amended to provide a statutory basis for regional planning (Heywood, 2008). Work had already started on a statutory regional plan, which was released in 2005 as the *South East Queensland Regional Plan 2005–2026*. It was replaced by a revised regional plan in 2009. The state government's 2005 regional plan was prepared in cooperation with the SEQ local government mayors' group. Brisbane City Council supported the plan's statutory status as a way of controlling urban development in surrounding council areas, where leapfrog development beyond the City boundaries had generated long journeys to work through city roads and public transport routes (Papageorgiou, 2014). Dwelling and employment targets in the regional plan for each council area were agreed with local government. The regional plan did not specify how the dwelling and job targets were to be achieved.

## The Sydney experience

The state government's policy of urban consolidation (densification) for Sydney, which started in the early 1980s, was reflected in the 1988 strategy *Sydney into its Third Century*. This strategy did not set out specific targets or actions for each local government area. However, it heralded a range of government actions that used state powers (in particular, State Environmental Planning Policies that over-rode local council planning powers) under the Environmental Planning and Assessment Act to require local councils to allow residential development at densities above those prevailing at that time (Searle, 2007). Local resistance meant that the government had to negotiate for, and accept, only small increases in zoning for consolidation in areas such as the high amenity professional and managerial upper North Shore area.

The slow progress in achieving higher densities led the government to speed up consolidation by focusing on inner areas with obsolete industrial land where results would not be so dependent on the reactions of local residents. So it promulgated a state planning policy which allowed the government to make regional plans requiring local government to re-zone obsolete industrial areas for urban consolidation. The main target of this policy was the old harbourside suburb of Balmain, where the local council had refused government and developer pressure to re-zone five old industrial sites on the harbour. Council resistance arose from the predominantly upper middle-class community's concerns about their property values, traffic impacts, and lack of open space (Bonyhady, 1995). Government interventions to effect re-zoning were countered by court actions started by residents and the council. These delayed re-zoning until the 1995 state elections (Searle, 2005).

In the face of such local opposition to intensification in older suburbs, the government moved to take full control of redevelopment of disused state-owned waterfront land and adjacent old industrial sites at Pyrmont and Ultimo on the harbour just west of the Central Business District (CBD). A regional plan for the area was made by the government in 1992, which re-zoned the area for high-density residential and commercial development. The government followed this in 1993 with Urban Development Plans that set out development controls for the precinct. The regional plan also provided for Master Plans on key sites around the waterfront. The Master Plans could be provided by the owners or lessees of sites and gave the Minister for Planning, not the council, authority to approve developments in those areas (Searle, 2007). Thus re-zoning, development control specification, and development approval for redevelopment involving a projected population of 15–17,000 and employment of up to 50,000 was taken from local government by the state. In this case, community opposition was ineffective, with a local population of less than 5,000 that was not unified against redevelopment (Searle, 2007).

Despite this initiative, there was growing opinion that urban consolidation policy was not working (Public Accounts Committee, 1993, pp. 23–24). This generated momentum for the Department of Planning to produce a new metropolitan strategy in 1995 (Caulfield and Painter, 1995, p. 239). The new strategy introduced dwelling targets for each sub-region (Department of Planning, 1995), leaving it to individual local councils within each sub-region to negotiate how the target was to be split between them and how to achieve the target their area. Subsequent regional strategies have kept dwelling targets for each sub-region to achieve increased densification, although the Department of Planning now uses a separate sub-regional planning model to allocate dwelling targets to individual council areas in an optimal manner (Bunker, 2008, p. 12).

In 1996 the new state government gave more freedom to local councils to achieve urban consolidation, but this freedom was tempered by the new requirement, albeit a non-statutory one, to achieve specific targets. State planning policies allowing certain types of consolidation in all residential zones, were repealed. Then councils were requested to prepare (by September 1996) residential development strategies which would achieve the urban consolidation targets. Councils that did not produce endorsed strategies would be subject to a state planning policy, enabling the Minister to re-zone sites and areas for residential redevelopment.

The largest of the old industrial precincts identified in the 1995 metropolitan strategy as the focus for urban consolidation was the Central Industrial Area around Green Square, with a target of 30,000 new residents. To facilitate its redevelopment, the state set up a development corporation as one element of a partnership with local and state government. The local council retained basic development control powers but referred all larger development applications to the corporation for review, which could in turn refer the application to the Minister for final determination. The council and the community both had representatives on the corporation, reflecting the local strength of the Labor Party, which was now also the ruling state government party (Searle, 2005). However, in remaining significant old industrial sites, along the harbour and Parramatta River, the government reverted to unilateral direction with a new state environmental planning policy in 1998. This policy allowed land owners to prepare master plans that set development parameters for their sites. The master plans could be approved by the Minister if the local council failed to do so. Council opposition to proposed densities at Rhodes, the largest of these remaining old sites, caused the state government to promulgate a regional environmental plan that gave consent authority to the Minister (*Sydney Morning Herald*, 20 November 1999).

Elsewhere the government's requirement for councils to prepare strategies to meet dwelling targets under the 1995 metro strategy was resisted, or else adopted despite strong local opposition. By September 1997, thirteen councils – including some of the wealthiest – had failed to produce strategies (*Australian Financial Review*, 26 September 1997, p. 65). The strongest opposition was in northern Ku-ring-gai, where expensive detached houses predominated. By 2002 the council had still not produced a strategy, so the government took planning control of six precincts around rail stations and re-zoned them for medium density housing (*Australian Financial Review*, 14 May 2003) to help effect its goal of 10,000 new dwellings in Ku-ring-gai from 2004 to 2030 as part of metro strategy targets. However, by 2008 the government considered that the council was taking too long to assess development applications in the new zones and was delaying in creating plans for higher densities in town centres to achieve dwelling targets. So it stripped the council of its planning powers (*Sydney Morning Herald*, 7 May 2010). The government then appointed a planning panel which produced a town centre plan with high densities that was deemed unlawful on appeal to the court by a community group (*Sydney Morning Herald*, 3 August 2012, p. 2). The council was given back its powers by the new state government.

Elsewhere there had also been fierce resistance by residents to council plans to re-zone residential areas to higher densities to meet the 1995 metro strategy targets (Searle, 2007, pp. 10–11). An anti-consolidation backlash across higher-income suburbs in southern Sydney in the local, council elections of 1999 gave control of councils to candidates who had campaigned on a platform of 'grass-roots representation, controlled development, and the preservation of neighbour-hood amenity' (Morris, 1999). Sub-regional dwelling targets have continued to be specified in metro strategies since 1995 and continued to generate local oppo-sition, as the Ku-ring-gai case above indicates. The shift from state-mandated regulations about the permissible type and location of consolidation to pursuing consolidation by giving councils greater discretion via local targets has been associated with a significant shift towards higher-density dwelling development across Sydney (although other factors have also been significant in this trend). It seems that communities would rather decide for themselves how strategic goals that might be locally unpopular will be implemented.

### The South East Queensland experience

The most significant element of the 2005 SEQ regional plan and its 2009 succes-sor has been that of the compact city, involving an urban footprint and half of new dwellings to be constructed in the existing urban areas. This required Brisbane City Council to ensure that 115,000 of its overall target of 145,000 new dwellings by 2026 were met by infill and urban renewal under the 2005 plan. The City Plan of 2001 did not anticipate these targets. The council started its Neighbourhood Planning program in 2005 – the year of the first regional plan – under which Neighbourhood Plans were introduced as overlays allowing extra development beyond City Plan provisions in selected areas (principally the central and inner areas and the activity centres). These neighbourhood plans short-circuited resident resistance to new development with the reference to the mandatory regional plan targets. In the early public meetings, the planning chal-lenge was presented as 'which areas are best suited to absorb increased density' and not whether there should be any increase for Brisbane as a whole. Brisbane's dwelling target was presented as a planning 'given' for the various reasons included in the SEQ regional plan, which had been well received at the time and was almost universally acknowledged as a 'good thing'. It was hard for local action groups to oppose directly: their arguments tended to use the regional plan objectives to point out why the development should go elsewhere in Brisbane (Papageorgiou, 2013).

Many development applications from 2005 quoted the new regional plan's dwelling targets and made a pitch to provide more density and/or greater heights to 'assist' the city meet its statutory targets (Papageorgiou, 2013). But Brisbane City Council was keen to ensure that residents' expectations and concerns could be managed and that there should be a strategic approach to where increased densities could occur. Nevertheless, there was a general feeling in those boom times before 2008 that planning scheme changes were too slow in bringing in provisions to allow increased development potential. So the City Council was disposed to approve increased height and density ahead of the changes, especially where current planning work was underway and could be seen as giving 'weight' to the departure from the existing controls (Papageorgiou, 2013). Local resident opposition was focused on securing increased amenity and infrastructure (more parks, public transport improvements and car parking) rather than challenging overall planning objectives of the SEQ plan (Papageorgiou, 2013).

Nevertheless, resident action groups have achieved only sporadic success in preventing the high-density development intended by the regional plan. In inner city West End, a Neighbourhood Plan introduced significant density increases to a maximum of 30 storeys across the precinct. The community association claimed that 96 per cent of 5,487 submissions made to the council about the draft neighbourhood plan rejected the 30-storey limit, but supported medium rise (6 to 8 storeys) development (Calligeros, 2011). The City Council rejected these submissions, and the draft plan was adopted. This leads to consideration of the way in which an extremely large council, such as Brisbane City, can largely ignore NIMBY-style opposition to its city planning goals, including the implementation of the regional plan. Each single-member council ward has about 23,000 voters, so that local opposition to council planning policies has to be very significant to have potential impact. In the West End case, this significant opposition was offset because the local councillor was not a member of the City Council's ruling party.

## Synthesis

Findings from the two case studies support the expectation that a regional spatial strategy that has statutory status causes local plans to control development outcomes to more closely conform with its objectives than does a strategy without statutory status. The statutory status of the SEQ Regional Plan underpinned Brisbane City Council's implementation of controls that would produce regional plan dwelling targets despite local opposition. The non-statutory status of Sydney region strategies meant that the government had to use a range of special planning policies to get local councils to produce plans that would meet regional strategy dwelling targets, and these were able to be circumvented in some instances.

We might observe that the effectiveness of the statutory strategy in directing local planning in this instance rests to a large extent on a counter-intuitive perspective. In Sydney, the use of special state planning policies and state-imposed plans was resisted in part because they told councils exactly how urban densification should be achieved, or else took away the powers of councils to do anything. In SE Queensland, on the other hand, the regional plan dwelling targets were not accompanied by prescribed dwelling controls or zonings. This gave councils such as Brisbane City freedom to achieve the targets in ways that most suited their local geographical and political contexts. Thus local-strategic planning relationships depend in part on the amount of control that strategic planning leaves local planning to achieve strategic objectives.

Nevertheless, the case studies reported here also show that the effectiveness of strategic-local planning relationships depends on several factors besides the statutory status of the strategic plan. The first of these concerns the size and influence of the local planning authority compared with those of the regional planning area/authority. In SE Queensland, the very large size and power of Brisbane City Council meant that it had a traditionally significant independence from the state government, with its own regional infrastructure networks and major planning capacity. This meant that it was given considerable planning freedom when the regional plan was eventually produced. Hence relatively little spatial detail was imposed within Brisbane City in the plan (Bunker and Searle, 2009). The major state-sponsored regeneration precinct at Bowen Hills, for instance, is not shown in the 2009 SEQ regional strategy (Searle, 2010). In Sydney, the plethora of councils, none exceeding one quarter of the population of Brisbane City, meant they had little power to control the structure of regional strategies. In contrast with a relative lack of spatial detail in the SEQ regional plan, the 2005 Sydney metropolitan strategy's supporting documents prescribe the structures of the major greenfield areas (the NW and SW Growth Centres) in great detail, for example.

Related to this is the issue of the way in which local government size relative to regional strategy boundaries might produce communalities in planning issues and goals. The larger the local planning agency, the more the local becomes the regional, and the more the local plan's concerns become represented by those of the regional strategic plan. This will tend, as in SEQ, to allow the regional strategy to give more freedom to local plans to achieve what are more likely to be common goals.

A further significant factor is the extent to which local planning authorities are involved in the making of the regional strategy. In SEQ, the first regional plan (2005) emerged at the end of a number of years of joint regional planning between state and local governments. The regional plan continued this tradition, and was prepared by the state government in close consultation with, and input from, local government. Thus local councils accepted the premises of the plan, and introduced local plans and assessed development applications in conformity with the regional plan.

Lastly, the case studies suggest that the influence of long-standing versus recently developed regional strategic contexts can be influential. In SEQ, a comprehensive planning system has been introduced relatively recently by the government. This resulted in the 2001 City Plan being produced within a joint local-state regional growth framework and not a statutory regional plan context. The early introduction (1948) of regional planning in Sydney established a long-standing framework of state control over the direction of local planning. A comprehensive local planning system emerged within an existing context of state-initiated regional plan guidance, unlike SEQ.

The case studies in this chapter indicate that the statutory status of a regional strategy is significant in determining the extent of conflict with local plans, with a statutory strategy allowing or requiring less conflict. But the case studies also show the importance of contextual factors in influencing the level of strategic–local plan conflicts. Thus the size and power of local planning authorities relative to the strategic planning authority, and their involvement in the formulation of the strategy, both appear to be significant. In this, the chapter confirms the importance of wider planning themes around power and participation in understanding strategic–local planning conflicts.

## Conclusions

This chapter has drawn on two case studies to address key elements that are the focus of Part 2 of this book. First, the chapter raises ontological issues about the nature of strategic planning. In particular, the boundary between strategic and statutory planning is not necessarily clear-cut. Statutory planning authorities may co-produce their own statutory plan parameters/targets with strategic planning agencies, for example. Thus the burden of statutory plans to attempt to provide certainty can be shifted somewhat to the strategic level. Strategic plans themselves may have statutory status. However, such blurring is the product of particular institutional and political contexts.

Secondly, the chapter points to types of strategic planning process that might be more successful in achieving strategic goals. The case studies suggest that the equal involvement of lower-level statutory planning agencies in the production of strategic plans can produce strategic goals that are more likely to be positively embraced and adopted by the statutory bodies. Further, the desirability of municipalities in the production of regional strategies is increased where the strategy is going to have statutory status, since in theory this will reduce discretion in making plans and deciding on development proposals. Equal involvement seems less likely where local institutional evolution has produced smaller, weaker local statutory agencies or where there is a long tradition of local statutory planning being subordinate to higher-level strategic planning: these are issues that will need time to change, if desired. If the goals allow reasonable freedom for implementation in statutory plans and development approvals, adoption is even more likely because this will allow a range of locally suitable and acceptable responses to be considered. To this extent, more relational forms of strategic planning should be more easily accommodated at the statutory level. Conversely, attempted implementation of the strategic plan via highly directive legislation, regulations and controls, which by-pass local statutory bodies or compel them to follow, seem less conducive to the implementation of strategic goals by lower-level statutory authorities. The case studies point to a history of local resistance when such state instruments were imposed on local (statutory) councils in Sydney. In the context of the two case studies, it could be concluded that the need for such prescriptive legislation and controls was increased because the strategic plan had no statutory force.

A third element of Part 2 of this book includes the role of themes such as uncertainty and conflict in strategic planning. The previous paragraph drew attention to circumstances where the strategic planning process can produce more, or less, conflict. The role of uncertainty has several facets. For example, strategic plans that allow more possibilities at the (lower) statutory level – more uncertainty – might, paradoxically, have a greater chance of being successfully implemented at the local statutory level. On the other hand, attempts by the strategic authority to impose greater certainty on strategic goal implementation at the local statutory level via detailed regulations may be strongly resisted and delayed, especially where local communities have power because of their size or economic and social capital.

A wider consideration relating to the role of uncertainty concerns planning discretion. Few planning systems lack any power to apply discretion in the application of rules and controls over development. In some cases, as already noted, this may enhance the achievement of strategic targets by allowing municipal authorities to choose implementation mechanisms that best suit local circumstances. But the existence of planning discretion may also mean that strategic planning goals – even if mandated with statutory status – become just one of several considerations in determining development applications, if not in preparing local plans. In countries such as England and Australia, planning discretion is legislated via clauses that require additional consideration of matters outside formal planning documents, while rules and codes themselves may require discretion in their application because they incompletely define property rights.

## References

Abbott, J., 2012. Collaborative governance and metropolitan planning in South East Queensland, 1990 to 2010: from a voluntary to a statutory model. Australian Centre of Excellence for Local Government, University of Technology Sydney.

Bonyhady, T., 1995. The battle for Balmain. In P. Troy, ed., *Australian cities: issues, strategies and policies for urban Australia in the 1990s*. Cambridge: Cambridge University Press, pp. 112–141.

Booth, P., 2007. The control of discretion: planning and the common law tradition. *Planning Theory*, 6(2), 127–145.

Bowie, D., 2012. The impact of the localism agenda on strategic planning in London. Paper for RSA Research Network conference: Governing metropolitan regions within a localist agenda, 21 September.

Bunker, R., 2008. Metropolitan strategies in Australia. City Futures Research Centre Research Paper No. 9. University of New South Wales, Sydney.

Bunker, R. and Searle, G., 2009. Theory and practice in metropolitan strategy: situating recent Australian planning. *Urban Policy and Research*, 27(2), 101–116.

Calligeros, M., 2011. Tensions rise over tower plan for West End. *Brisbane Times*, 22 July (www.brisbanetimes.com.au).

Caulfield, J. and Painter, M., 1995. Urban policy and management in Sydney. In M. Laffin and M. Painter, eds., *Reform and reversal*. South Melbourne: Macmillan Education Australia, pp. 237–255.

Department of Planning, 1995. *Cities for the 21st century*. Sydney: Department of Planning.

Healey, P., 2007. *Urban complexity and spatial strategies: towards a relational planning for our times*. Abingdon and New York: Routledge.

Heywood, P., 2008. Regional planning for the whole of Queensland. Paper presented to the Planning Institute of Australia Queensland State Conference, 17–19 September, Longreach.

Hillier, J., 2007. *Stretching beyond the horizon: a multiplanar theory of spatial planning and governance*. Aldershot: Ashgate.

Hutton, T., 2011. Thinking metropolis: from the 'livable region' to the 'sustainable metropolis' in Vancouver. *International Planning Studies*, 16(3), 237–255.

Mees, P., 2009. *Transport for suburbia: beyond the automobile age*. London: Earthscan.

Minnery, J. and Low Choy, D., 2010. Early innovations and false starts. In B. Gleeson and W. Steele, eds., *A climate for growth: planning South-East Queensland*. St Lucia, Qld: University of Queensland Press, pp. 23–38.

Morris, L., 1999. Crowded houses. *Sydney Morning Herald*, 5 October.

Neuman, M., 2007. Multi-scalar large institutional networks in regional planning. *Planning Theory and Practice*, 8, 319–344.

Papageorgiou, M., 2013. Personal communication (email), 23 May.

Papageorgiou, M., 2014. Personal communication, 3 June.

Public Accounts Committee, 1993. Infrastructure management and financing in New South Wales, Volume 1, Report no. 73. Sydney: Parliament of NSW.

Searle, G., 2005. Power and planning consent in Sydney's urban consolidation program. In D. Cryle and J. Hillier, eds., *Consent and consensus: politics, media and governance in twentieth century Australia*. Perth: API Network, pp. 297–317.

Searle, G., 2007. Sydney's urban consolidation experience: power, politics and community. Urban Research Program Research Paper 12, Griffith University.

Searle, G., 2010. Too concentrated? The planned distribution of residential density in SEQ. *Australian Planner*, 47(3), 135–141.

Searle, G., 2013. 'Relational' planning and recent Sydney metropolitan and city strategies. *Urban Policy and Research*, 31(3), 367–378.

Searle, G., 2016. Towards equitable intensification: restricting developer gain and compensating planning costs. In R. Leshinsky and C. Legacy, eds., *Instruments of planning*. London: Routledge, pp. 19–30.

Searle, G. and Bunker, R., 2010. Metropolitan strategic planning: an Australian paradigm? *Planning Theory*, 9(3), 163–180.

Simington, S., 2013. The new planning system for NSW and draft Metropolitan Strategy to 2031 – some observations. Sydney: Lindsay Taylor Lawyers (www.lindsaytaylorlawyers. com.au/.../the-new-planning-system-for-nsw-.../) *[accessed 21 May 2013]*.

Stein, L., 2012. A review of international best practice in planning law. Paper prepared for the New South Wales Department of Planning.

# 20 Strategic planning and institutional change

## A karst river phenomenon

*Loris Antonio Servillo*

## Introduction

The chapter focuses on the (potential) institutional changes introduced by strategic spatial planning (SSP) episodes and different forms of innovation and effectiveness in planning. It reflects on the procedural and institutional dynamics that occur in different planning systems in the long run, while this book offers a great opportunity to overview episodes and practices of SSP in different world-wide contexts (see chapters in Part 1). As Friedmann stated, 'All planning must confront the meta-theoretical problem of how to make technical knowledge in planning effective in informing public actions' (1987, p. 36). In this perspective, the debate about planning systems and planning theory encompasses an umbrella of different theoretical reflections that have conceptualized ways to achieve effectiveness (intended in its broader meaning) in a constantly changing environment (Hillier, 2011). Within this domain, SSP became one of the most powerful answers to the request for effectiveness of planning processes.

SSP and its specific normative body (Newman, 2008) encompasses capacities of prompting structural innovation (Albrechts, 2006, 2010a), offering a strong ethical stance (Moulaert, 2010; Albrechts, 2013), and depicting governance arrangements to combine flexibility and effectiveness (Friedmann, 2004; Healey, 2006a, 2006b). In a way, it is a product of a 'culture of performative planning' (Janin Rivolin, 2010) associate to the aim of pursuing collective interests.

Nevertheless, there is disaffection towards these long-term normative stances, in particular concerning their evolution in practice, and some further reflections could be made about the breaking through capacity of SSP approach(es) to provoke changes in planning culture. Provocatively, it would be possible to question the extent to which SSP has managed to provoke a shift in mainstream practices, or whether its co-existence with traditional planning is a latent struggle embedded in every context. At the same time, the ethical dimension and the power of innovation that some authors advocate in the SSP approach seem to lose momentum when SSP is mainstreamed, unless, for example, the threat of being a vehicle for neo-liberal interests (taking for granted, for the context of this chapter, that neo-liberalism as such is unethical) is the tribute required to be paid in order to achieve effectiveness and result-oriented planning practices.

Hence, the procedural and institutional dynamics that are induced by SSP practices and the capacity of normative stances to generate long-term changes and innovation in different contexts are worth investigation. At the same time, however, the complexity of addressing this interest requires a different perspective in the analysis. So far, most of the time SSP initiatives and its innovation capacity are circumscribed to specific episodes with a starting frame, an independent development, and a conclusion due to a series of specific circumstances. Later in time and in space, other initiatives might take place, partially building on existing knowledge, partially due to key actors that are carrying certain technical expertise, or due to specific socio economic issues that generate a new quest of effectiveness and prompt specific forms of SSP.

Therefore, the observation of SSP practices seems to depict a phenomenon that looks somehow similar to the one of water in karst areas. A karst area, due to the specific porosity of the soil and rock (such as limestone, dolomite and gypsum), is characterized by sinkholes, in which water is collected and disappears underground, and springs, out of which water comes back to the surface. At the same time, streams of water can disappear underground and reappear miles away a number of times, often with different names (e.g. the river Ljubljanica in Slovenia, known as the river of seven names). If this phenomenon is not seen in a wider scale, it would look like a heterogeneous system of different streams of water that come out and die due to some irrational logic, and not as a continuity of flows which alternately passage under-ground and above-ground.

This karst metaphor allows a reflection on the dynamics that prompt SSP episodes and the capacity to generate changes in planning culture, or, on the contrary, to let episodes disappear in sinkholes. Even if not completely matching the dynamics at stake, it is useful to introduce a different conceptual way of reading SSP and its innovative practices in planning, and their consequences.

For this purpose, SSP, including its normative apparatus, is proposed in this chapter as a cultural/technical imaginary. At the same time, an institutionalist perspective allows consideration of planning systems as socially constructed (Servillo and Van den Broeck, 2012), based on an hegemonic socio-cultural and technical imaginary supported and replicated by actors in their practices. Hence, the technical and procedural knowledge (using Friedmann's expression in the above quote) of SSP imaginaries is confronted in its capacity to interact and modify hegemonic imaginaries in planning systems (practices and governance processes). In order to conceive how SSP encounters interact with institutional contexts and produce change in the long run, a conceptual model is proposed to read these dynamics, as generated by confrontation of different socio-technical imaginaries that determine the under-ground or the above-ground of streams of knowledge and practices.

The challenge for this chapter is to reflect on the position of SSP as a driver for innovation in technique(s), discourse(s), and as cognitive dimension(s) of local planning styles, hence generating micro-attempts of applying specific knowledge and recommendations to daily practices, intertwining with what would be called 'traditional' planning practices. The assumption is that SSP generates dynamics that affect not only the mere technical dimension of SSP (the planning tools), but also a wider socio-institutional imaginary, in relation to the discourses mobilized and the cognitive aspects in support of them. For this, the actors involved are crucial because they are the agents that determine continuity and rupture in the process of evolution of the planning systems.

## SSP as a normative socio-technical imaginary seeking innovation

Since the 1990s, strategic approaches to spatial planning are discussed in theory and in practice, reflecting on its innovative characters. It has been described (and circumscribed) as a 'public-sector led socio-spatial process through which a vision, actions, and means for implementation are produced that shape and frame what a place is and may become' (Albrechts, 2004, p. 747). This quote, a part of the technical dimension of SSP (vision, actions, means), emphasizes the procedural dimension and the public realm, addressing space as policy domain, which is distinguished from other types of strategic planning, e.g. in private market, in advertisement, etc. Moreover, at least two differences can be highlighted in literature about SSP's normative approach in relation to traditional spatial planning: a limited rationality instead of a comprehensive approach, and also the search for transformative practices with new forms of governance and wider arena of actors (Healey, 2009) instead of relying (only) on technical expertise and narrower decision-making processes.

First, SSP approaches acknowledge the 'bounded rationality' in decision-making processes and the limited power of planners in times of rising complexity and uncertainty (Innes and Booher, 2010; Hillier, 2011). SSP is selective, focusing on specific spatial issues and procedural ways in order to tackle wicked problems. Second, SSP insists on the procedural dimension in planning practices, in which the necessity of being as inclusive as possible is advocated. The involvement of actors from the public-sector as well as actors belonging to the economic and civil society sectors allows processes to go beyond simple collaborative approaches and to aim at structural changes through social innovative practices (Moulaert *et al.*, 2013) and co-production of space (Albrechts, 2013).

This normative dimension constitutes an innovative imaginary that acts as a reference for a community of experts, scholars, actors involved in field activities. It is a sort of system of values that embeds all the innovative stances represented by the SSP approach, which is confronted in each planning context. In each planning context, the role of 'transformative practices', enabled by SSP imaginary and related practices, becomes relevant. Such practices are meant to 'refuse to accept that the current way of doing things is necessarily the best way; they break free from concepts, structures and ideas that only persist because of the process of continuity' (Albrechts, 2010b, p. 1117). SSP, therefore, aims at introducing new governance arrangements which help to take 'decision makers, planners, institutions, and citizens out of their comfort zones and compels them to confront their key beliefs, to challenge conventional wisdom, and to examine the prospects of "breaking out of the box" (Albrechts, 2010b, p. 1115).

Innovation is here intended as a capacity to change routinized ways of doing, using new practices for 'thinking out of the box'. It is a struggle between different cultural imaginaries. The interruption of traditional processes of continuity through practices and innovative ideas leads to innovative ways of doing. These transformative capacities are embedded in governance strategic planning episodes, which address contemporary and contextualized socio-spatial challenges (Walsh and Allin, 2012). They are based on rationalities that have the power to break through a system of well-established practices that constitute hegemonic imaginaries. At the same time, different value, strategic, communicative and instrumental rationalities are mobilized in SSP practices (Albrechts, 2004), together with new ways of conceiving space. Part 1 of this volume widely indicates how this process has taken place in different contexts.

The elements that characterize the SSP repertoire are conceived as forms of innovation that can be identified in the wider domain of planning practices and cultures. As such, they are not a priori better than others. They are attempts to implement planning initiatives, making them more effective. They can be found in various plans and programmes, which may vary from regional or metropolitan governance plans (Healey, 2006b; Balducci *et al.*, 2011) to local development initiatives (Moulaert *et al.*, 2010). In this volume, Maginn *et al.*'s discussion of Australian cases, Esho and Obudho's discussion of African cases, Demazière and Serrano on France, Fedeli on Italy and Abbott on Vancouver bring a world-wide overview of forms of innovation. Building a SSP normative, imaginary, international literature – as well as the cases in this volume – highlight as a main innovation, a more or less pronounced capacity to define a new and shared vision that is able to coordinate different actions addressing contemporary spatial dynamics through inter-sectorial and inter-scalar actions (Wilson and Piper, 2010); the overcoming of silos-mentality and bounded-territory traps (Stead and Meijers, 2009); and the achievement of social innovative processes based on the search for mutual consensus among different interests with inclusive decision-making processes (Albrechts, 2004, 2006) that pay attention to unexpressed voices in society (Moulaert *et al.*, 2013).

These elements are an expression of different values and innovative practices that can affect a variety of fields in the public domain, in particular those that are more in proximity with spatial planning as an act of practices. It does not belong only to specific instruments that can be labelled as 'strategic spatial plan', but rather to a way of conceiving planning and approaching socio-spatial challenges based on 'new ideas' and 'out of the box' approaches that interrupt the 'process of continuity'. They are forms of innovation that can affect planning practices and cultures.

Following this line of argumentation, it is interesting to reflect on the possible hybrid outcomes of dynamics between existing institutional settings of spatial planning and innovation brought by different episodes having specific theoretical and/or methodological novelty.

The role of evolution in planning and innovation in practices has been the focus of different approaches, in particular those which addressed SSP as 'transformative episode'. Healey's scheme (2006b), in which she articulates the differences between governance episodes/practice/culture, is inspirational. Using an actor-structure approach she states that 'to have transformative effects, governance innovations (such as new discourses, new allocatory or regulatory practices, the formation of new arenas or networks) must move from explicit formation episodes to arenas of investment and regulatory practice. To endure, they have to become institutionalized in the routines of governance practices' (Healey, 2006b, p. 305). There is a temporal passage between these bottom-up phases of innovation in governance, in which change is first seeded in episodes, then becomes embedded in practices and afterward is mainstreamed in planning culture.

However, the institutionalization of change is everything but a linear process, and looks rather as a stream of water in a karst area, with specific aspects disappearing from the surface and reappearing again miles away (see Olesen and Metzger in Part 1 on the ups and downs of strategic planning in the Øresund Region). First, changes are not always bottom-up. They can be brought by topdown dynamics, which do not have an origin in localized experimental episodes but rather in mainstream agency, as, for instance, indicated by Gunn and Hillier (2012) in relation to UK reform, or in the Chinese cases by Xu and Yeh and by Cao and Zheng in Part 1 of this volume. Second, not all episodes and elements of innovation are successful. On the contrary, there are unavoidable dynamics that lead to either the dispersion of innovative aspects of experimental practices, which lose momentum and have no follow-up, or 'mainstreaming' processes that blur innovative characters (Janin Rivolin, 2010; Reimer, 2013), leaving simplified concepts as buzzwords for business-as-usual or even exploitative practices, as, for instance, the case of Rio de Janeiro (Vainer in Part 1 of this volume). Third, however, in spite of some failures, those different sets of values, localized knowledges, socio and cultural capitals, which disappear from current practices, might get hidden in space and society and ready to be re-mobilized, as, for instance, in the case of Antwerp (Van den Broeck in Part 1 of this volume).

In these dynamics, SSP has two potential innovative dimensions. First, it is itself a socio-technical imaginary that attempts to break through existing 'ways of doing'. Transformative practices produce new frames for action and create innovative environments for experimentation within existing planning settings. They gather different ways of approaching socio-spatial transformation, constituting bundles of discourses that create an 'alter' planning imaginary in rupture with its continuity. Still, the innovation that 'springs up' is the outcome of silent processes and flows of knowledge that belong to various contextualized actors and are embedded in localized capital.

Second, it embeds the capacity to mobilize new sets of values because of its openness (in principle) to wider arenas. The normative dimension of SSP about its governance dynamics indicates the opening of the decision-making arena to a larger groups of stakeholders that might bring in different cultural imaginaries as a connotative feature. Reflections about co-production (Albrechts, 2013) and the necessity to reach silent voices in order to generate social innovation dynamics for providing answers to unexpressed needs (Moulaert *et al.*, 2013) imply that SSP episodes have the potentiality to generate the momentum to release hidden and un-expressed values.

These sets of innovative approaches interact with the planning conditions of a local context, generating hybrid processes and new place-bounded approaches, as is well indicated in Part 1 of this volume by the various national cases, in which a socio-technical imaginary struggles with national planning cultures. However, as these cases can show, forms of innovations are far from being granted in practices. In some cases they are only partially achieved, or even seem to fail in providing new way of 'producing' space. Achievement depends on several factors and the 'accumulation' process in planning cultures is relatively unpredictable. The passage through episode, practice and culture presents underground dynamics, devious paths and high chances of failure in the short term that might turn out subsequently to be useful capital for new episodes further in time and space. The capacity to maintain new rationalities 'on the surface', and the direction of the original path that is generated are at stake.

## Planning system as hegemonic institutional frame

The interpretation of SSP as governance episodes and transformative practices brings the debate about SSP to a crossing path with that of thoughts on planning cultures and socio-institutional characteristics of planning systems. References to new planning cultures across Europe and elsewhere emphasize the fact that planning practices are deeply embedded in cultural contexts and, therefore, vary greatly (Sanyal, 2005; Getimis, 2012; Othengrafen, 2012; Othengrafen and Reimer, 2013). It thus becomes interesting to reflect on the capacity of SSP to destabilize the institutional settings in which spatial planning operates.

Following an institutionalist perspective (Gonzales and Healey, 2005; Reimer and Blotevogel, 2012; Servillo and van den Broeck, 2012), we can distinguish two broad perspectives when talking about the institutional 'embedded-ness' of spatial planning activities. The first one concerns the 'institutional technologies' (Janin Rivolin, 2012), which prescribe legal and administrative structures for spatial order and structure, for securing land uses and for development within a specific, defined area, and which are articulated in different competences along different administrative tiers. They constitute a framework or formal institutional setting in which spatial planning operates (Albrechts *et al.*, 2001). In this case, innovation brought by the SSP debate can be measured in terms of factual elements: adaptation of formal rules and laws, introduction of specific plans, etc.

However, the growing discontent with these formal descriptions and the subliminal feeling that 'it remains a matter of dispute whether planning reality is in fact fundamentally determined by its basis in law' (Reimer and Blotevogel, 2012, p. 10), as well as the evidence of a large variety of outcomes in the application of the same concepts/methods/tools in different places (Healey and Upton, 2010; Othengrafen and Reimer, 2013) has led to a second perspective that points to the more 'hidden' institutional aspects in which specific planning systems are embedded (Knieling and Othengrafen, 2009). The formal institutional framework for spatial planning activities is subject to the interpretation and appliance of actors in different spatio-temporal settings (Servillo and van den Broeck 2012). Informal institutions, i.e. the perception of spatial challenges, actors' ideas, values and norms as well as rites and routines can have great influence on spatial planning practices (see Harrison on South Africa and Abdelwahab and Serag on Egypt in Part 1 of this volume).

Both debates on planning culture and socio-institutionalism in planning have pointed at (a) the importance of a wider institutional framework that goes beyond mere technical elements (tools, instruments and defining laws); and (b) the role of social dynamics, and actor-driven processes, which make the planning dynamics socially-embedded and a non-neutral setting. The context-related and context-bounded characteristics of the planning system can be seen as a bundle of techniques, and allocative mechanisms and rules embedded in an institutional frame and produced by groups of actors. These are hegemonic imaginaries of planning systems supported by coalitions of actors that maintain them in and through practices.

Therefore, it becomes interesting to reflect on how innovation in planning induced by SSP as cultural imaginary is comprised of different socio-institutional dimensions. To explain these issues further I will use strategic-relational approach (SRA) (Jessop, 2001, 2008) and its application to planning system interpretation (Servillo and Van den Broeck, 2012), associated with the role of imaginaries in a cultural political economy approach (Sum and Jessop, 2013).

In this interpretation, a planning system can be seen as a system of rules and practices embedded in a wider institutional frame. Relevant actors support and replicate the system through practices and acts. Going further, Jessop's strategic-relational perspective points at how institutions' and actors' interaction is based on two processes: 'structurally inscribed strategic selectivities' and 'structurally oriented strategic calculation' (Jessop, 2001, 2008). SRA means that there is a reflexively–recursively dialectal form of interaction between actors and institutions. Particular institutions may privilege (but not determine) some actors, some actions, some techniques, etc. over others ('structurally inscribed strategic selectivities'). At the same time, actors orient their actions in function of their institutional frame ('structurally oriented strategic calculation').

SRA is useful because it indicates that actors in planning not only 'support' the consolidated way of doing, but also that the planning system itself steers the actors' behaviour and selects implicitly who and what can be involved and the types of practices that can be performed (see Sartorio about practices in Wales in Part 1). Hence, the institutional construction and sets of values/practices are an expression of the supportive coalition of actors, which, at the same time, selects and frames their course of action. It is as a sort of magnetic field, which Foucault (1980) discussed in terms of *dispositif* (Pløger, 2008). It maintains together the institutional setting and its strategic selectiveness and actors with their strategic orientation. At the same time, it explains how, in the presence of structural change, some prominent actors remain, but with different main-streamed attitudes.

These hegemonic cultural imaginaries support the formal institutional setting (i.e. the technical dimension of planning) and its allocative and authoritative power, being functional for its reproduction. 'Agency has both material and discursive bases and, although economic power is grounded in control over economic resources and state power is grounded in coercion, struggles among competing forces and interests in these domains are normally waged as much through the battle for ideas as through the mobilization of primarily material resources and capacities' (Sum, 2008, p. 1).

Therefore, SSP innovation and 'thinking out of the box' practices imply forms of interference, with the alteration of sets of values and reorientation of actors' behaviours. As mentioned before, SSP is first of all an alternative set of technical knowledge advocated by experts and practitioners (a different way of conceiving planning practice), thus a socio-technical imaginary. Moreover, it is methodologically prone to mobilize different sets of values due to its openness (in principle) towards different voices. Hence, it potentially enables new sets of values in planning practices. In both cases, the interaction with the dominant frame (Pløger, 2004) remains the challenge for innovation.

Following this interpretation, and on the base of a previous version of this interpretative scheme (Servillo and Van den Broeck, 2012), Figure 20.1 illustrates the dynamics between a hegemonic institutional frame and the role of actors in planning systems.

The scheme indicates a spatial planning system as a set of technical devices inscribed in a socially-constructed institutional frame, which is based on imaginaries 'produced' from a supportive group formed by certain dominant actors. Governance dynamics are planning practices that are the material reproduction of a planning system and of the reflexively–recursively dialectal interaction between

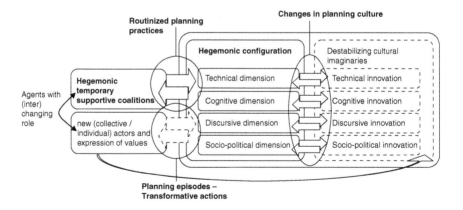

*Figure 20.1* Changes in planning systems through planning episodes

Source: Re-adaptation of the original scheme in Servillo and Van den Broeck (2012)

actors and institutions. Through these processes, these actors – showing different degrees of intentionality and most probably different interests – come to share the same cognitive, cultural, political, structural frame, covering the role of a temporarily supportive coalition of the hegemonic institutional frame (Servillo and Van den Broeck, 2012).

The introduction of SSP innovation calls for the role of different individual and collective actors that (re)produce ways of conceiving practices. The arrival of new actors and their concomitant imaginaries corresponds to the internal evolution of existing institutions, due to some shift in dominant values, and are the primary factors of institutional change. Potentially transformative episodes that take place within the hegemonic institutional frame might generate change in some of its components.

Being SSP primarily characterized by a governance dimension, the scheme shows how the passage between episodes, practices and culture, which is the ultimate stage of embedded-ness of different cognitive dimensions, is not a linear dynamic. The role of actors in supporting the passage between phases is crucial. The positioning of actors involved in strategic planning episodes, the strife of imaginaries (Pløger, 2004), their relationship with supportive coalitions of the hegemonic institutional frame of planning and the sets of values brought in will determine the evolution of SSP insights in planning cultures. At the same time, it redefines the composition of the hegemonic supportive actors, as is well indicated in the Rio de Janeiro cases (Vainer in Part 1), in which SSP became the conceptual, methodological and rhetorical platform for a new hegemonic coalition ruling the city.

The different composition of actors and related cultural imaginaries in practices determines the above- or under-ground presence of certain sets of values and technical expertise. At the same time, the affirmation of certain values in the hegemonic frame occurs through a structurally inert process and also implies an unavoidable process of simplification, or of redistribution, of power.

The affirmation of new technical devices (e.g. types of strategic plan) and/or related legislation, the affirmation of new forms of knowledge (e.g. programmes in schools), allocative and normative mechanisms (e.g. in relation with EU structural funds expenditure), public and private interaction (e.g. contractual forms, investment opportunities) or the affirmation of discourses (e.g. interpretation of discourses on sustainable development, territorial cohesion, resilience, etc.) are forms of changes in the institutional frame that can be mobilized by SSP cultural imaginaries. They can be generated through SSP episodes and experimental practices in which different sets of values are brought in by new actors or by dynamics that generate different collective/dominant imaginaries.

SSP transformative (governance) episodes may challenge the dominant institutional frame if they carry a different set of rationalities, which may introduce changes in practices and eventually in planning culture (Lowndes, 2005). The mobilization of different cultural imaginaries can be done by excluded actors – unexpressed voices in society – or actors in the supportive coalitions who change rationalities (e.g. changes of discourses and of cognitive dimension), for instance influenced by new discourses and a shift of cognitive domain (e.g. the rise of the collaborative planning turn).

## SSP and changes in institutional frames

The scheme in Figure 20.1 can be used to describe the dimensions of a contextualized institutional frame of spatial planning: technical, cognitive, discursive and socio-economic dimensions. At the same time, these dimensions can be used to break down changes inducted by SSP. It is assumed that changes occurring in planning systems are spread over these domains, albeit being mutually related categories in the institutional frame of the planning system in specific contexts.

### a. Institutional technique

The first dimension concerns the legal and administrative structure for spatial planning, which is conceived as an institutional technique. Here, the forms of innovation brought by SSP are the most evident and have been long discussed in the literature (Mintzberg, 1994). They include the various types of instruments, tools, and rules, and also the legislative changes in the frame that draws the boundary of spatial planning practices. The most evident innovation is the constituency of the strategic spatial plan as a well-defined instrument (Healey, 1997).

Since the 1980s, there has been a world-wide proliferation of strategic plans, which vary in terms of scale (from region to neighbourhood interventions) and technical setting (role of vision and actions, type of decision-making, etc.). Methodological indications have been elaborated, such as the four-track approach (Albrechts, 2004, 2010b), which appears to be one of the most comprehensive ways of conceiving the components of a strategic planning approach, comprising: (1) an integrating vision that can steer different policies and interventions in an integrated fashion; (2) coherent and pragmatic sets of means and actions to implement the vision; (3) the inclusion of a wider arena in the decision-making process; and (4) a specific communicative strategy for the larger public audience in order to have a larger awareness of the process going on. These are the characteristics of some of the most successful episodes in the recent history of planning both in Europe and world-wide (Albrechts, 2006, 2010a).

Strategic plans can have different legislative formats and constituencies, and in some cases even be without formal legislative legitimacy, which induces interesting institutional struggles and forms of innovation (e.g. in Italy – for an overview, Sartorio, 2005; Servillo and Lingua, 2014; and see Fedeli in Part 1 of this volume).

Moreover, the legislative dimension can also refer to the spatial pertinence of the plans. SSP cases have induced governance arrangements for metropolitan and urban regions in which the tailoring of policy measures for aggregated areas that go beyond traditional administrative boundaries remains one of the biggest challenges in planning (Kunzmann, 2004; Allmendinger and Haughton, 2009; Balducci *et al.*, 2011), as well illustrated in the Øresund cross-border Region

(Metzger and Olesen in Part 1 of this volume), in the metropolitan plans in Australia (Maginn *et al.*, this volume) in the French way of dealing with city-regions (Demazière and Serrano, this volume), in the Italian metropolitan experimentation (Fedeli, this volume), and in the Greater Vancouver plan (Abbott and DeMarco, this volume). Also in these cases, the formal institutional setting of inter-municipal cooperation and enabling different tools varies substantially according to the context (Gualini, 2006; Healey 2006b). Nevertheless, the discussion about strategic plans should not be confused with a wider interpretation of SSP and its influence in the planning domain. Innovations can be found in sectorial approaches or in new ways of conceiving traditional planning dynamics, as well as in regional/local development strategies (e.g. some case of EU structural funds programmes and as also indicated in the chapter about the North American experiences by Bryson and Schiverly Slotterback in Part 1 of this volume).

### b. Cognitive dimension

The frame of innovations induced by SSP can, therefore, be extended to the cognitive dimension – a second dimension that depicts the planning domain as a heuristic area. SSP represents an agent of innovation because it is conceived as a cultural construction within the planning debate. The challenged cognitive dimension is characterized by the implicit and explicit knowledge that is produced in planning practices and research.

It is possible to recognize in this dimension both the normative concepts of the SSP debate and the variety of approaches that have been experimented and fine-tuned in different contexts – and this volume represents an extraordinary collection of contextualized productions of knowledge which address the debate internationally. Challenges for the planning domain include, on the one hand, the plea for a more result-oriented attitude and, on the other hand, a social innovative agenda in which the aim is not only a technical structuring of the process but also the opening to unexpressed voices of decision-making arenas in order to be more 'efficient' (from a wider socio-spatial perspective). Practices and theoretical reflections are attempts at responses to these challenges in each contextual cognitive dimension of planning.

Part of the issue is also the cognitive construction of spatial imaginaries and wider general ethical principles that lead the professional actors in planning and the public realm. First, it is the way space is conceived (e.g. the social-relational interpretation of space) and how it is embedded in practices, such as the ways in which urban areas are imagined and how they are rooted in collective and 'expert' imaginaries. Second, it is what Albrechts addresses as value rationality (2004), in which concepts such as sustainability, equity and spatial justice, and cohesion are conceived.

Within this framework, SSP generates opportunities for challenges to re-utilize practices and well-established systems of value. SSP as a cultural construction based on existing but unexpressed and latent values interacts with the contextualized cognitive dimension of planning, which has a strong national and regional bias. At the same time, this dimension is challenged not only internally, but also by international flows of knowledge, 'ways of doing' and best practices (Peck and Theodore, 2010; Stead, 2012). Relevant actors which mobilize different cognitive dimensions and their involvement (or not) in episodes determine changes to existing imaginaries and the rise of different imaginaries.

### c. Discursive dimension

The cognitive dimension in planning systems has a mutual interaction with discourse production (the third dimension), which becomes the vehicle for knowledge and ideas transfer. Discourses, discursive chains and key- (or buzz-) words (Müller, 2008; Sum, 2008; Servillo, 2010) are crucial to understanding the policy agenda in planning and socio-economic dynamics, because they represent the translation of the cognitive dimension into communicative practices (MacCallum, 2009). An evident example is the way in which policy agenda swings between the recurrent use of discourses on integration and social inclusion on one side and growth and development on the other side, and how values are mobilized (Servillo, 2010). At the same time, and as an additional example, the now-dominant theme of 'smartness' shows how some discourses become hegemonic topics in specialized, political and generalist debates, steering policy agendas and practices (see Metzger and Olesen in Part 1).

Groups of discourses and ideas constitute cultural imaginaries (Sum, 2008) that at the same time inform the cognitive dimension and steer the construction of policy-agendas in the public domain as well as in spatial planning (see, for instance, the African case, as indicated by Esho and Obudho in Part 1). In this perspective, SSP is both a self-standing discourse in planning (as a method in planning) and a fundamental carrier of planning-related themes (an enabler of un-expressed needs). First, the role of SSP in addressing changes in the planning domain is itself a heuristic field that generates instrumental discourses, in which methodological and technical insights constitute its normative dimension (e.g. in Italy, as Fedeli indicates in Part 1). Second, the debate on SSP is able to bring in other rationalities, as, for instance, ways of conceiving specific spatial entities, such as cross-border or metropolitan areas.

Therefore, methodological discourses on SSP convey both changes in a planning system, working on the instrumental knowledge and on the policy agenda. Methodological and procedural dimensions are combined with contents of policy approaches, which are mutually supportive for the affirmation of a group of actors' policy agenda. As an example, critiques of SSP as enabler or opponent of neo-liberal dynamics (Olesen, 2013) show how themes are blended in integrated discursive chains. If seen from this perspective, the various rationalities that compose the SSP imaginary become shaped by the dominant discourses in the context in which SSP took place as an act of practice. The African and Rio de Janeiro cases (see Part 1 in this volume) typify this regard.

### d. Socio-economic characteristics

The final dimension concerns the socio-economic characteristics in which the planning system is embedded. This is a wider dimension, and it does not only refer to the political regime in a specific area (a conservative versus progressive, or a nationalist versus federalist political coalition in power), but also to the socio-economic regime that characterizes the place, which includes the welfare system, its redistributive capacity, the health of its economy, the cohesiveness of its society, and so on.

This dimension influences the capacity to address SSP in specific places, and at the same time the role of innovation brought by SSP practices. For instance, the way in which private sector and corporations are considered in socio-economic contexts has repercussions on different forms of interaction between public and private spheres and consequent implications for public-private partnerships and the role of private actors that can be advocated in planning practices (see the national cases in Part 1 of this volume). At the same time, SSP episodes and discourses related to SSP may interfere, producing ruptures and questions for change. Inequality, forms of discrimination, socio-spatial injustices, but also specific interests, can become sources of opposition and a strong lobby in SSP dynamics that may generate structural change (see Van den Broeck in Part 1 of this volume).

All in all, as shown by the chapters in Part 1, transformative practices of SSP activate a kaleidoscope of effects along different dimensions of planning culture and the institutional frame of planning systems. These transformations are socially and spatially bounded in contextualized planning systems. At the same time, international agreements and regulations, foreign planning approaches spread through 'best practice', together with global political turns, internal debates and quests for change, enrich the debate and encourage reforms in national and regional contexts which interfere with the contextualized frames in these domains.

Changes are activated in sets of values and norms by relevant actors and make unpredictable the shape of innovation that will be determined, as they are blended with a large variety of local and supra-local socio-spatial dynamics. At the same time, struggles among imaginaries are caused by new episodes and new actors that reproduce planning through practices. Transformative episodes, together with changes in technical, cognitive, discursive and socio-economic values, encourage changes of perspectives that combine trans-national similarities and context-based specificities.

The effects can be a combination of short- and long-term elements of innovation, of which it is not possible to predict the persistence. Paradoxically, even controversial applications of SSP normative stances can make a breakthrough in consolidated practices in the long run, while 'best practices' can lose momentum and reach a dead end rather quickly.

## Conclusive thoughts: SSP for institutional resilience

Returning to Friedmann (1987, p. 36) and his meta-theoretical question of 'how to make technical knowledge in planning effective in informing public actions', we can sum up that SSP is a vehicle of innovation that determines a shift in consolidated practices and related planning culture because of two meta dimensions. First, it is a technical imaginary (made of normative stances). Second, it is conceived as a governance process through which new imaginaries and a different set of values can be mobilized. SSP has a technical component, which leads to innovation in practices, but it has a wider reverberation effect given by the possibility of introducing new cultural imaginaries. It is the plea for thinking 'out of the box' and bringing actors 'out of their comfort zone', as indicated by Albrechts (2010b).

Changes in planning do not happen through linear accumulative processes, but depend on several factors. In order to challenge the hegemonic imaginary, a new cultural imaginary and set of values need to be mobilized. These are generated through the opening of arenas to a variety of actors and struggles between different sets of values. The capacity to transform episodes in governance culture depends on the breakthrough of innovative elements in the dominant institutional frame. In this sense, the role of discourses and the effects on the cognitive dimension in planning are the key dimensions to challenge current ways of doing and up-scaling insights from innovative governance episodes.

This approach provides support for a thorough investigation of how creative practices of actors and relevant social groups may give rise to a search for new solutions to perceived problems, resulting in new planning instruments and systems. When investigating the effects of SSP in the long run, the level of investigation that refers to the adopted policies is generally insufficient. The imaginaries that are confronted, the hidden and unexpressed ones that could be mobilized, and the efforts to open up the arena to these 'alter' imaginaries are crucial factors in determining the emergence of innovative elements in governance processes. Otherwise, like rivers in the karst areas, these imaginaries and sets of values will continue to run hidden below the surface in social groups that do not enter the fora of public decision-making.

The above also allows further reflections on the conceptualization of the 'institutional resilience' of a planning system. It extends the discussion about resilience capacity (Klein *et al.*, 2003; Folke, 2010; Davoudi *et al.*, 2013) to the capacity of the planning system being structurally able to cope with spatial challenges and the 'disturbances' they might represent. Hence, it concerns the capacity of the planning system to address these challenges in a strategic and integrated way, in order to pursue resistance and adaptation (to mention some of the different interpretations that resilience debate might raise).

Nevertheless, despite its interpretative approach, a crucial aspect of a resilient planning system becomes the institutional capacity to set meaningful and feasible strategies in a selective manner and to adopt flexible measures according to changing spatial configurations and dimensions of the phenomena. It implies a socio-spatial context with high learning capacity and adaptability (Davoudi *et al.*, 2013). It represents the ultimate scope of effectiveness in planning brought via innovative SSP, which can generate an accumulation of knowledge in order to properly address oncoming socio-spatial challenges.

Institutionalization of practices that are able to cope with them is the challenge for the long run, for which SSP can be a domain of social learning and experimentation. Socio-spatial challenges related to macro dynamics (e.g. world-wide demographic flows and changes, climate-generated dynamics, etc.) require new ways of conceiving public actions in planning (Friedmann, 2004). Therefore, the achievement of a modern understanding of the public realm and its governance dimension, which should facilitate resilience to macro and micro socio-spatial dynamics, is the long-term challenge.

# References

Albrechts, L., 2004. Strategic (spatial) planning re-examined. *Environment and Planning B: Planning and Design*, 31(5), 743–758.

Albrechts, L., 2006. Shifts in strategic spatial planning? Some evidence from Europe and Australia. *Environment and Planning A*, 38(6), 1149–1170.

Albrechts, L., 2010a. In pursuit of new approaches to strategic spatial planning: a European perspective. *International Planning Studies*, 6(3), 293–310.

Albrechts, L., 2010b. More of the same is not enough! How could strategic spatial planning be instrumental in dealing with the challenges ahead? *Environment and Planning B*, 37(6), 1115–1127.

Albrechts, L., 2013. Reframing strategic spatial planning by using a coproduction perspective. *Planning Theory*, 12(1), 46–63.

Albrechts, L., Alden, J. and da Rosa Pires, A., Eds., 2001. *The changing institutional landscape of planning*. Aldershot: Ashgate.

Allmendinger, P. and Haughton, G., 2009. Soft spaces, fuzzy boundaries, and metagovernance: the new spatial planning in the Thames Gateway. *Environment and Planning A*, 41(3), 617–633.

Balducci, A., Fedeli, V. and Pasqui, G., Eds., 2011. *Strategic planning for contemporary urban regions: City of cities: A project for Milan*. Aldershot: Ashgate.

Davoudi, S., Brooks, E. and Mehmood A., 2013. Evolutionary resilience and strategies for climate adaptation. *Planning Practice & Research*, 28(3), 307–322.

Folke, C., Carpenter, S., Walker, B., Scheffer, M., Chapin, T. and Rockstrom J., 2010. Resilience thinking: Integrating resilience, adaptability and transformability, *Ecology and Society*, 15(4), 20–28.

Foucault, M., 1980. *Power/knowledge: Selected interviews and other writings by Michel Foucault, 1972–77*. Ed. C. Gordon. Brighton: Harvester.

Friedmann, J., 1987. *Planning in the public domain: From knowledge to action*. Princeton, NJ: Princeton University Press.

Friedmann, J., 2004. Strategic spatial planning and the longer range. *Planning Theory & Practice*, 5(1), 49–67.

Getimis, P., 2012. Comparing spatial planning systems and planning cultures in Europe: The need for a multi-scalar approach. *Planning Practice and Research*, 27(1), 25–40.

Gonzales, S. and Healey, P., 2005. A sociological institutionalist approach to the study of innovation in governance capacity. *Urban Studies*, 42(11), 2055–2069.

Gualini, E., 2004. Regionalization as 'experimental regionalism': The rescaling of territorial policy-making in Germany. *International Journal of Urban and Regional Research*, 28(2), 329–353.

Gunn, S. and Hillier, J., 2012. Processes of innovation: Reformation of the English strategic spatial planning system. *Planning Theory and Practice*, 13(3), 359–381.

Healey, P. Ed., 1997. *Making strategic spatial plans: Innovation in Europe*. London: Psychology Press.

Healey, P., 2006a. Transforming governance: Challenges of institutional adaptation and a new politics of space. *European Planning Studies*, 14(3), 299–320.

Healey, P., 2006b. *Urban complexity and spatial strategies: Towards a relational planning for our times*. London and New York: Routledge.

Healey, P., 2009. In search of the 'strategic' in spatial strategy making. *Planning Theory & Practice*, 10(4), 439–457.

Healey, P. and Upton, R., Eds., 2010. *Crossing Borders: International exchange and planning practices*. London and New York: Routledge.

Hillier, J., 2011. Strategic navigation across multiple planes. Towards a Deleuzean-inspired methodology for strategic spatial planning. *Town Planning Review*, 82(5), 503–527.

Innes, J. E. and Booher, D. E., 2010. *Planning with complexity: An introduction to collaborative rationality for public policy*. London: Routledge.

Janin Rivolin, U., 2010. EU territorial governance: Learning from institutional progress. *European Journal of Spatial Development*, 38, 1–28.

Janin Rivolin, U., 2012. Planning systems as institutional technologies: A proposed conceptualization and the implications for comparison. *Planning Practice and Research*, 27(1), 63–85.

Jessop, B., 2001. Institutional (re)turns and the strategic-relational approach. *Environment and planning A*, 33(7), 1213–1235.

Jessop, B., 2008. *State power: A strategic-relational approach*. Cambridge: Polity Press.

Klein, R. J., Nicholls, R. J. and Thomalla, F., 2003. Resilience to natural hazards: How useful is this concept? *Global Environmental Change Part B: Environmental Hazards*, 5(1), 35–45.

Knieling, J. and Othengrafen, F., Eds., 2009. *Planning cultures in Europe: Decoding cultural phenomena in urban and regional planning*. Farnham: Ashgate.

Kunzmann, K. R., 2004. An agenda for creative governance in city regions. *DisP*, 40(158), 5–10.

Lowndes, V., 2005. Something new, something old, something borrowed: How institutions change (and stay the same) in local governance. *Policy Studies*, 26(3/4), 291–309.

MacCallum, D., 2009. *Discourse Dynamics in Participatory Planning*. Farnham: Ashgate

Mintzberg, H., 1994. The fall and rise of strategic planning. *Harvard Business Review*, 72(1), 107–114.

Moulaert, F., 2010. Commentary on part I: When solidarity boosts strategic planning. In S. Oosterlynck, J. Van den Broeck, L. Albrechts, F. Moulaert, A. Verhetsel, Eds., *Strategic spatial projects: Catalysts for change*. London: Routledge, pp. 79–84.

Moulaert, F., Swyngedouw, E., Martinelli, F. and Gonzales, S., 2010. *Can neighbourhoods save the city?: Community development and social innovation*. London: Routledge.

Moulaert, F., MacCallum, D., Mehmood, A. and Hamdouch, A., 2013. General introduction: The return of social innovation as a scientific concept and a social practice. In F. Moulaert et al., *The international handbook on social innovation: Collective action, social learning and transdisciplinary research*. London: Edward Elgar.

Müller, M., 2008. Reconsidering the concept of discourse for the field of critical geopolitics: Towards discourse as language *and* practice. *Political Geography*, 27(3), 322–338.

Newman, P., 2008. Strategic spatial planning: Collective action and moments of opportunity. *European Planning Studies*, 16(10), 1371–1383.

Olesen, K., 2013. The neoliberalisation of strategic spatial planning. *Planning Theory*, 13(3), 288–303.

Othengrafen, F., 2012. *Uncovering the unconscious dimensions of planning: Using culture as a tool to analyse spatial planning practices*. Farnham: Ashgate.

Othengrafen, F., and Reimer, M., 2013. The embeddedness of planning in cultural contexts: Theoretical foundations for the analysis of dynamic planning cultures. *Environment and Planning A*, 45(6), 1269–1284.

Peck, J. and Theodore, N., 2010. Mobilizing policy: Models, methods and mutations. *Geoforum*, 41, 169–174.

Pløger, J., 2004. Strife: Urban planning and agonism. *Planning Theory*, 3(1), 71–92.

Pløger, J., 2008. Foucault's dispositif and the city. *Planning Theory*, 7(1), 51–70.

Reimer, M., 2013. Planning cultures in transition: Sustainability management and institutional change in spatial planning. *Sustainability*, 5(11), 4653–4673.

Reimer, M., Getimis, P. and Blotevogel, H., Eds., 2014. *Spatial planning systems and practices in Europe: A comparative perspective on continuity and changes*. London: Routledge.

Sanyal, B., Ed., 2005. *Comparative planning cultures*. New York and London: Routledge.

Sartorio, F. S., 2005. Strategic spatial planning: A historical review of approaches, its recent revival, and an overview of the state of the art in Italy. *DisP – The Planning Review*, 41(162), 26–40.

Servillo, L. A., 2010. Territorial cohesion discourses: Hegemonic strategic concepts in European spatial planning. *Planning Theory & Practice*, 11(3), 397–416.

Servillo, L. A. and Van den Broeck, P., 2012. The social construction of planning systems: A strategic-relational institutionalist approach. *Planning Practice and Research*, 27(1), 41–61.

Servillo, L. A. and Lingua, V., 2014. The innovation of the Italian planning system: Actors, path dependencies, cultural contradictions and a missing epilogue. *European Planning Studies*, 22(2), 400–417.

Stead, D., 2012. Best practices and policy transfer in spatial planning. *Planning Practice and Research*, 27(1), 103–116.

Stead, D. and Meijers, E., 2009. Spatial planning and policy integration: Concepts, facilitators and inhibitors. *Planning Theory & Practice*, 10(3), 317–332.

Sum N. L., 2008. *Toward a cultural political economy: Discourses, material power and (counter-)hegemony*. DEMOLOGOS spot paper.

Sum, N. L. and Jessop, B., 2013. *Towards a cultural political economy: Putting culture in its place in political economy*. London: Edward Elgar.

Walsh, C. and Allin, S., 2012. Strategic spatial planning: Responding to diverse territorial development challenges: Towards an inductive comparative approach. *International Planning Studies*, 17(4), 377–395.

Wilson, E. and Piper, J., 2010. *Spatial planning and climate change*. London: Routledge.

# 21 Framing 'evidence' and scenario stories in strategic spatial planning

*Raine Mäntysalo and Kristi Grišakov*

## Introduction

Recently, the so-called evidence-based knowledge has had an increasingly dominating role in societal decision-making. With the sustainability and climate
change debates, and the related demands on impact assessments, its role has been
heightened in spatial planning,[1] too (e.g. Davoudi, 2012; Krizek *et al.*, 2010).
However, in planning, the hegemony of evidence-based knowledge is problematic, as planning is largely about coping with the yet unknown future; that of
which we cannot have evidence. This is especially true for strategic spatial planning that incorporates the methods of scenario planning (Albrechts, 2005; Zegras
and Rayle, 2012). The evidence-based approach addresses the future as a continuation of the existing and known development paths. While, in scenario planning,
there is indeed a need to project the future implications of the present development paths, we also need an ability to imagine such development trajectories, of
which we do not have evidence yet, but which might emerge in the future.

In scenario planning, the evidence-based approach is thus not sufficient. The
'knowledge' produced in scenario planning is rather based on stories that are able
to integrate convincingly the future extensions of known development trends
with imagined future possibilities. According to Peter Schwartz (1991), scenario
planning is not a science but an art. It aims to identify relevant societal and environmental driving forces that push development forward to certain directions.
Further, it aims to anticipate the not yet existing and hidden driving forces that
may emerge in the future and interact with the known and existing driving forces.
Based on such an analysis, alternative scenario stories are made, stemming from
the organization's activity horizon.

Patsy Healey (2009) also recognizes the art dimension in strategic spatial planning, in the form of design thinking. However, she claims that additional sensitivity is required that would surpass the limitations of both scientific analysis and
design thinking. According to Healey, the generation of spatial strategies
demands skills to perceive how people and places interrelate in time, drawing
from an understanding that builds on history, an anthropological view and
geographic imagination. A degree of comprehension of the material and cultural
history of the place or region is needed to enable one to perceive the potentiality

and desirability of different development trajectories. According to Healey, this kind of understanding builds critical judgement skills in assessing how and to what extent positive resonance and transformative capacity can be gained among the actors to strategic initiatives. This entails experiential probing, as well as targeted analysis, imaginative learning as well as reliance on hard evidence. Following John Dewey, Healey perceives such strategy work to generate around itself a 'community of inquiry' which nurtures the collective intelligence of those brought within. This is what Healey calls 'strategic framing' (Healey, 2009; see also Abbott and DeMarco and Bryson and Schively Slotterback in this book).

In Healey's vein, it is thus a matter of critical judgement in strategic framing how scientific evidence and artistic creativity should be combined to gain wisdom and joint momentum towards a desired future. While alternative scenario stories would probe possible futures, building imaginatively and creatively on the evidence of existing development paths and local potentialities, critical judgement is about selecting the scenario that we value as desirable, and deciding on actions that are needed in striving for it.

So, with Healey's account on strategic framing, we arrive at three distinct capabilities that are essential in strategic spatial planning:

- the capability to provide scientific evidence on that which exists;
- the capability to create scenario stories, stretching towards the possible future from that which exists;
- the capability to critically judge which future scenario we value as desirable, and to decide on the actions to be taken in striving for it.

In this chapter, our intention is to elaborate on these capabilities by drawing on Bent Flyvbjerg's (1992, 2004) reading on Aristotle's three 'intellectual virtues': episteme, techne and phronesis. We will start our account by first recalling the development of scenario planning. Then we will study scenario planning as part of strategic spatial planning in the sense of strategic framing. Finally, we will discuss how Aristotle's three intellectual virtues can be distinguished as essential constituents of strategic spatial planning.

## Scenario planning

Scenario planning emerged during the Cold War as a method by which to contemplate the 'unthinkable', namely nuclear warfare. Herman Kahn, a military strategist, developed scenario planning to analyze the likely consequences of nuclear war and the techniques that would be needed to survive them. He presented those strategies as stories, which he called scenarios, hence giving the name to the method (Kahn, 1962).

However, the method of scenario planning did not become widely known until it was adapted to business use at Royal Dutch Shell (Wack, 1985). In 1971, Pierre Wack started developing a more practical use of scenario planning, as a forecast method to guide strategies for Royal Dutch Shell. After the Oil Shock in 1973, scenario planning was welcomed in the commercial world as a tool to include a spectrum of forecasts, 'unwanted' ones as well as desired ones, in a business strategy. Today, the scenario planning method still thrives in the corporate world as a tool for looking into the future, being more popular than SWOT analysis[2] or the Delphi method[3] (Konno *et al*., 2014).

The method of scenario planning was not clearly defined until the 1980s. Until then, it was dependent on the capabilities and imagination of the 'scenario gurus' of the time (e.g. Kahn and Wack) (Ogilvy, 2006). A clear step-by-step process for novices was only published in Schwartz's 1991 book *The Art of the Long View*, the key textbook for scenario planners, and still relevant today. New practices, trends and links to strategy development are discussed in several academic journals, most notably in *Futures* and *World Futures*.

In the context of spatial planning, urban planning and architecture, scenario planning as a method has most commonly extended to the fields of land use and transportation planning. Urban planning as a field has been slow to incorporate all aspects of scenario planning (Chakraborty *et al*., 2011). In the US, the Department of Housing and Urban Development has even awarded grants for scenario planning at regional and metropolitan scales that would further promote this practice. Scenario planning is typically used by various public and private agencies to identify common regional issues and formulate decisions that serve multiple jurisdictions. The general goal of many such 'vision documents' seems to be to develop large-scale regional or metropolitan visions and concurrent strategy directions. However, the practice is often still too focused on developing a single preferred scenario and fails to adequately consider multiple uncertain futures (Chakraborty *et al*., 2011).

## Making scenarios

The scenario planning method is about finding new opportunities, storytelling, questioning assumptions and pinning down the critical uncertainties. It includes a thorough analytical part, for which an extensive amount of data is needed. These data include recognizing global/local trends and drivers (social, technological, economic, environmental, political, values), identifying actors and their agendas (niches) and uncertainties. The actors can range from individuals to businesses, organizations, public officials, etc. It is equally as important to recognize the role of global forces as it is to determine the local forces that are expected, or desired, to have a key role in making every scenario come true.

As a starting point, a central question for the object area, a focal issue, is formulated. This can have quite a general form, such as lack of vision, need of new functions, bad connectivity, etc. Additionally, a timespan is decided, ranging usually from five to 50 years. A shorter timespan would make the outcome too predictable and a longer one usually makes the results too unpredictable. In terms of analysis, the scenario method assumes that there is never enough information on which to base a decision that would require certainty about the future (Garreau, 1994; Ogilvy, 2006). Moreover, it assumes that the future is not predictable. If it were predictable, there would be no need for planners. It further assumes that if the future were predictable, there would be no need for alternative scenarios. Thus it emphasizes the necessity to prepare for multiple futures, not relying on deterministic predictability, because, as history has shown, we can rarely count on predictions.

> The fantasy of deterministic predictability lives on and lurks among the assumptions of those who regard scenario planning as insufficiently scientific. Connect these points together in any of several combinations and you will see that judging scenario planning against the standard of deterministic science is non-sensical, paradoxical, and ultimately absurd. (Ogilvy, 2006: 337)

The strength of scenario planning lies also in its ability to talk about undesirable futures – in the end, this motivated the whole origin of the method. It concentrates on the 'unthinkable' and searches for critical uncertainties that influence the outcome of the problem that is being tackled. A critical uncertainty is something that exists in every plan and it is very much related to all the elements we think are predetermined. We can find these aspects of uncertainty by questioning our assumptions about the predetermined elements or facts. For example, we know that the population is aging, the oil reserves will be exhausted, global warming will accelerate, new technologies such as 3D printing and augmented reality are emerging, but what we do not know is the willingness of people to change their habits in the face of these developments – and if so, how. It forces us to imagine the extreme situations, to find coping mechanisms we would not be able to conceive in safe and comfortable contexts. It can also make us understand better the outcomes of our actions, or even illustrate what would happen if no action were to be taken at all.

The other key aspect of the scenario planning method is that it enables us to tell each other stories about how the world might work (Garreau, 1994). A key element of a great scenario is its capacity to captivate you as if you were a great character in a novel. The character of a good scenario might be a villain or a hero, but nevertheless it has a familiarity and credibility to it. A scenario is not a linear, mechanistic, number-driven process; it is rather about the story and the assumptions, perceptions and imaginations that underpin it (Garreau, 1994). Like a good history lesson, it concentrates on explaining the forces that influence the outcome of events, rather than plain numbers and names. In this way, it is easier for people to react to the scenarios, choose a desirable future and start discussing how to make it happen.

The identified development trends and the imagined future possibilities are fused together into alternative scenario storylines. At the same time, the emerging scenario storylines are mapped in relation to each other by the use of bipolar conceptual axes. A few characterizing distinctions are identified to map the scenarios in relation to other, such as hetero-/homogeneous area character, innovative/conservative policy, local/global focus, etc. The bipolar axes of such distinctions may further be combined into four-fields, and other arrangements, to provide a mapping framework for the alternative scenarios (Konno *et al.*, 2014).

Besides the more known scenario planning method utilized in the field of economics, there are also other methods, especially those developed by the French future thinkers in the end of the 1950s, e.g. Gaston Berger and Bertrand de Jouvenel. These methods are motivated by humanist and societal concerns. As always, the methods diverge, but the overarching title is Prospective or Foresight, sometimes also Prospective Through Scenarios. In the latter case, the scenario building process is not too different from the scenario planning method described above. However, here the scenarios themselves are not interrelated in terms of bipolar axes, but variables. With this method, the number of resulting scenarios is very high, and only a small number of scenarios are selected on the basis that they illustrate a good spectrum of possible futures. The link between the two branches of scenario thinking, on both sides of the Atlantic, developed in the 1960s, giving rise to a large number of organizations dedicated to futures research in the 1970s. Over the last decades the main areas of research have changed along with the methods and main protagonists (de Jouvenel, 2004).

However, regarding Prospective Through Scenarios, it is important to notice some key problems associated with such a scenario planning method that is not based on foresight but rather on forecasting. First, forecasting relies of precedent, analogy and extrapolation. It is based on the assumption that we live in a stable world where the same things always change in the same way at the same rate according to immutable laws. Foresight thinking, in turn, derives from the idea that there are phenomena of discontinuity and abrupt changes that surprise us, among them also those that we bring upon ourselves. One should not extrapolate on the basis of past trends (see de Jouvenel, 1999, 2004). This is also the problem of poor scenario planning. Often, those which are called 'alternative scenarios' are just median projections of economic growth, transportation flows, even collaboration opportunities. Indeed, they are not alternative scenarios but simply projections of the 'same old system' operated optimally or otherwise (de Jouvenel, 2004). A proper alternative scenario should be capable of creating a completely new story that is built on structural and qualitative changes to the system, not merely calculated derivations.

Second, the Prospective Through Scenarios method seems not to have an emphasis on strategic planning or a strategic outcome, but rather on exploration. Nonetheless, de Jouvenel (1999) emphasizes that the future thinkers within both scenario planning and prospective schools generally share the attitude of the navigator: 'The navigator makes an effort to anticipate in what way the wind blows and asks, at the same time, what actions shall he take to arrive to a good port. He uses tools of vigilance and instruments of piloting' (Jouvenel, 2004; compare to Hillier, 2011). Albrechts, however, argues that strategic planners 'must be more than navigators keeping the ship on course and they are necessarily involved in formulating that course' (Albrechts, 2015: 514).

## Scenario planning as part of strategic spatial planning

In strategic spatial planning, the main focus is not on the long-term spatial plan to be produced, in the sense of blueprint. The focus is actually on the here and now: how can we gain broad and long-term insights to make strategically wise decisions in our immediate activity horizon (see Bryson and Schively Slotterback in this volume)? As John Friedmann notes, in strategic spatial planning, the object 'is not to produce "plans" (not even strategic plans), but insights into prospective change to encourage and promote public debates about them. [...] It is a way of probing the future in order to make more intelligent and informed decisions in the present' (Friedmann *et al.*, 2004: 56). Healey emphasizes a similar view: 'While strategic thinking may shape planning documents, strategies do not "live" inside them. They have to be continually "given life" as people call them up in justifications in the flow of practices' (Healey, 2013: 49). What is needed is strategic wisdom in planning practices. The objective, then, is not to produce strategic plans *per se*, but to produce (and reproduce) such strategic plans that can be used as tools in strategically wise planning practices.

This is where the scenario planning method shows its relevance. As argued above, proper scenarios are not made to serve as forecasts of the future but to offer foresight into plausible futures in order to inform our decision-making today (Schwartz, 1991; Zegras and Rayle, 2012). Planning projects, such as redevelopment of former industrial sites and urban densification or completely new neighborhoods, are contingent processes that can take some 20 years only to be planned. Scenario planning can be a useful tool, not only to manage the vision-making process and participatory planning of any planning project, but also to help to monitor and guide the process until it is finished. According to Louis Albrechts (2005: 256), '[s]cenarios help us to think about how places/institutions will operate under a variety of future possibilities and they enable decision-makers/civil society to detect and explore all or as many as possible alternative futures in order to clarify present actions and subsequent consequences'. As further noted by Albrechts (2005: 255), being stories, the scenarios can be integrated with the tradition of stories in planning (Albrechts, 2005; see also Throgmorton, 1996; Forester, 1999).

However, there is a lot of work to be done to fully utilize scenario planning as part of strategic spatial planning. While there are quite a lot of step-by-step guides for scenario planners to start from, there are only a few modified guides for spatial planners (see Petrov *et al.*, 2011). Today, the scenario planning method is often linked with spatial planning in the cases of big regional and cross-border projects, through background analysis compiled by experts with a background in economic geography or public administration, in some cases also think tanks. In such cases, scenario planning is usually used to create background documents for visions and strategies. A good example is the planning process around the connection of the capitals of Finland and Estonia, which has a multitude of scenario documents of varying quality linked to it (Uusimaa Regional Council, 2004; Demos Helsinki, 2009; Terk, 2012). Such documents often concentrate on various processes, most notably on investments, business climate, transportation and governance, but they rarely have spatial implications or a spatial dimension to the scenarios. This means that the scenario storylines of possible future developments are seldom played out on a map or a physical plan. If they were, it would offer a very different understanding and illustration of the impact of each of the scenarios. As noted by Petrov *et al.* (2011: 245): 'Many stakeholders/policy-makers are familiar with scenarios work, but less with spatial modeling'.

Scenario work has also been mentioned as a typical method of strategic planning in Europe, the USA, Canada and China (see the chapters by Abbott and DeMarco, Bryson and Schively Slotterback, Xu and Yeh, Cao and Zheng, Fedeli, and Olesen and Metzger in this volume). However, a methodological description of how it is actually carried out is often missing. A likely deduction, then, is that 'scenarios' are used to describe a variety of approaches, starting from the actual scenario planning method described in this chapter, to mentioning transportation scenarios or spatial scenarios to denote various models, plans and visions. Scenario work is also mentioned as a method of participation for various interest groups involved in the strategic planning process. In the Canadian (Abbott and DeMarco) and Italian (Fedeli) cases presented in this volume, the need for scenario planning was rather linked to the need to deal with uncertainties in general. Even if scenario planning is carried out fully, the related documents are presented only as an appendix of the actual planning document, thus further reducing its value and further use (Myers and Kitsuse, 2000).

Both vision and scenario planning belong to the family of futures approach and are both used as techniques in spatial planning alongside the Prospective Through Scenarios approach. These futures exercises, undertaken by towns, cities and regions, vary in regard to their aims, structures, budgets, timescales and methodologies (Krawczyk, 2007). The outcome and quality of any futures approach depends on who is involved in the process, especially the capabilities of experts behind the futures methodology (Myers and Kitsuse, 2000; Gaffikin and Sterrett, 2006).

Scenarios and visions are thus often mentioned in literature as parts of the wider strategic planning process, but the actual method or meaning behind the terms 'vision' and 'scenario' remains vague, and the terms can be used to mean almost anything. A vision is not a fantasy, but an 'optimistic picture of what might be achieved in a municipality or region given available capacities and resources' (Myers and Kitsuse, 2000). The visioning movement has generally emphasized process and goal-setting over the means of accomplishing the goals. However, it has been criticized for not meaningfully informing future-oriented action and for remaining merely a version of future, disconnected from the present. Similar vagueness is also associated with the use of urban modelling or models, which is rather regarded as one of the tools for illustrating scenario work. 'It assumes a concept of the city, rather than a creation of a conception' (Healey, 2007). As modelling works on fixed assumptions about the cause–effect relations, the extensive use of modelling can rather limit the imaginative scope necessary to perceive urban qualities and dynamics (Healey, 2007).

## Strategic momentum as a second-order effect of scenario planning

In adapting the scenario planning method to strategic spatial planning, we also have to address the issue of organizational complexity. The business world, where the method has been developed, provides organizational contexts of private enterprises and corporations that are considerably simpler in their goal-setting and distribution of duties than the world of spatial planning, where the relationships between the public and private sectors and the civil society are complicated. Whose strategic practice are we talking about? The local or regional government that is in charge of making the strategic plans, or also the stakeholders (e.g. developers, investors, citizens, non-governmental organizations) who are needed in implementing the strategic decisions and in giving legitimacy to the decision processes themselves, but who also have strategic practices, and related motivations, of their own? Whereas in the business world the organizational boundaries are relatively clearly defined, spatial planning has fuzzy boundaries involving multiple organizations, thus making it difficult to determine who and what is inside and outside. As noted by Christopher Zegras and Lisa Rayle (2012: 314), 'given heterogeneous participants with different realms of influence, factors clearly external to one organization might be within the influence of another, making it difficult to separate scenarios that represent uncertainties from scenarios that represent possible strategies'.

On the other hand, Zegras and Rayle (2012) emphasize the potentiality of scenario planning to overcome the difficulties of organizational complexity in strategic spatial planning. At best, scenario planning becomes an educational and transformative exercise that may 'persuade participants to dislodge pre-existing views, improve understanding of the organizational context, provide a common instrument of communication among disparate actors, and encourage relationships among participants. In particular, the scenario planning process may be a means of building networks and initiating collaboration' (Zegras and Rayle, 2012: 303). Scenario planning can thus also be a capacity-building exercise, widening narrow perspectives, revealing the stakeholders' mutual interdependencies and inviting joint momentum towards an envisioned future. Zegras and Rayle regard such collaboration-inducing properties of scenario planning as its 'second-order effects' (Zegras and Rayle, 2012: 305).

With her concept of strategic framing, Healey has such second-order effects in mind. In Healey's view, strategic framing brings together local resources and imaginative visioning into a setting that invites the actors to change their thought and action schemes and their approaches to each other (Healey, 2009: 451).

> Spatial strategies get to 'work' by providing an orientation, or reference frame, which gets shared by many stakeholders in urban development processes. [...] Spatial strategies which get to have transformative effects accumulate the power to frame discourses and shape action through their resonance with issues and problems which are causing concern within a political community, or 'polity', and through the persuasive power of their core arguments and metaphors. (Healey, 2009: 441)

In attempting such joint momentum towards strategic action, Healey stresses the role of critical judgement:

[W]hat is the momentum for an explicit spatial strategy-making initiative? What forces and actors are driving this? […] How strong is the momentum? Can it be strengthened and what might weaken it? […] How are the initiators situated in relation to this momentum, and how am 'I' as an actor in such a process situated, in terms of role, skills, potential to exert influence and legitimacy? (Healey, 2009: 443)

Most importantly: 'What seems to be at stake and around which issues will critical judgements have to be made?' (Healey, 2009: 443).

Healey regards critical judgement in strategic framing as a 'practical art' (Healey, 2009: 440), but here her notion of 'art' is different from Schwartz's notion of the 'art' of scenario planning. Healey's 'practical art' addresses the 'second-order' level of scenario planning, while Schwartz's 'art' remains at the 'first-order' level. Schwartz sees scenario planning as an art in the sense of being able to create coherent narratives of alternative futures, integrating existing and imagined driving forces in a given activity horizon. Healey, in turn, deals with the 'practical art' of framing the produced palette of alternative scenarios, in the sense of identifying a desired scenario and probing on the initiatives, arrangements and decisions to be made, in order to gain consent and joint momentum behind this scenario. For Healey, this is less an art of creative production and more an art of dealing with people in politically contentious contexts.

However, Ogilvy (2006) additionally stresses the role of desire in critical judgement. Desire often misreads facts, meaning that our values, hopes and biases can cause us to misread evidence. Alternative scenarios are the medium to represent the age-old dialectic of the creative art of what we want and the science of what must be. For Ogilvy, scenario planning should strive towards articulating shared hopes in order to move towards futures we truly desire not towards futures that must be.

Next, we will elaborate on these different types of capacity, which are necessary in strategic spatial planning utilizing scenario planning. For this purpose, we will draw on the three 'intellectual virtues' that Aristotle identified in his *Nicomachean Ethics*.

## Aristotle's three intellectual virtues in strategic spatial planning

The first of Aristotle's intellectual virtues, 'episteme', is familiar today as the etymological origin for the word 'epistemic'. Episteme concerns knowledge that is universal and invariable in time and space and achieved with the aid of analytical rationality. It corresponds to the modern scientific ideal, as expressed in natural science. With the Enlightenment tradition, this scientific ideal has become dominant. According to Flyvbjerg (2004: 285), '[t]he ideal has come close to being the only legitimate view of what constitutes genuine science, such that even intellectual activities like planning research and other social sciences, which are not and probably never can be scientific in the epistemic sense, have found themselves compelled to strive for and justify themselves in terms of this Enlightenment ideal'. Accordingly, in the beginning of this chapter we noticed the hegemony of the evidence-based approach in the production of knowledge in planning. In scenario planning, the episteme type of inquiry would concentrate on knowledge regarding existing conditions and development paths and their projections to the future.

Aristotle's second virtue, 'techne', can be translated into English as 'art' in the sense of 'craft' (Flyvbjerg, 2004: 286). Unlike episteme, techne does not deal with the universal truths of existence; instead, it has to do with the goal-oriented production of new things. According to Flyvbjerg (2004: 286), '[p]lanning research practiced as techne would be a type of consulting aimed at arriving at better planning by means of instrumental rationality, where "better" is defined in terms of the values and goals of those who employ the consultants, sometimes in negotiation with the latter'. Regarding scenario planning, we associate the 'craft' of techne with the ability to produce imaginative, yet convincing, scenarios that are not mere projections of existing trends. However, we do not see them as instrumental in the sense of producing a scenario for a given goal, but rather as explorative in their effort to generate plausible scenarios that can be deemed both desirable and undesirable.

Aristotle's third intellectual virtue, 'phronesis', concerns practical wisdom and ethics. It has to do with deliberation on how things ought to be done for the purpose of doing well, of making ethical choices. It does not deal with the invariables of episteme, as you cannot deliberate and make ethical judgements on the eternal truths. Thus its concern is on the context-dependent variability of production – yet, itself, phronesis is not production in the sense of techne, but action. As Aristotle says, 'production aims at an end other than itself; but this is impossible in the case of action, because the end is merely doing well' (*Nicomachean Ethics*, cited in Flyvbjerg, 2004: 287). Phronesis is closely associated with political action, which, according to Hannah Arendt (1958), was treated in ancient Greek political philosophy as an art among other arts. Contrary to the 'productive arts', such as painting and sculpture, it was likened to such activities as healing or navigation, where, as well as in a dancer's or play-actor's performance, the 'product' is identical with the performing act itself (Arendt, 1958: 207). As in dancing, where the dance is brought to existence and maintained by the very activity of dancing, the political community is created and maintained by people acting politically. Political action is an end in itself, and it is not instrumental to any external purpose. Regarding strategic spatial planning, we associate Healey's notion of critical judgement with phronesis. It is a practical art of political action that aims to develop a 'community of inquiry' of strategic planning.

Thus, we can link Aristotle's three intellectual virtues to the three capacities of strategic spatial planning, suggested in our Introduction, as follows:

- episteme – the capability to provide scientific evidence on the local-historical developments and trends that exist;
- techne – the capability to create scenario stories, stretching towards the possible future from that which exists;

- phronesis – the capability to critically judge which future scenario we value as desirable, and to decide on the actions to be taken in striving for it.

For Aristotle, phronesis was superior to the other two virtues. Using Max Weber's distinction between instrumental and value rationality, Flyvbjerg reformulates Aristotle's argument by stating that '[p]hronesis is most important because it is that activity by which instrumental rationality is balanced by value-rationality' (Flyvbjerg, 2004: 285). Concerning strategic spatial planning, we also regard phronesis as superior to episteme and techne, in the sense of the 'second-order' framing of plausible scenarios and judging critically which scenario to hold as desirable and how political consensus and momentum can be gained behind it. Accordingly, in scenario planning, as a constituent of strategic spatial planning, techne can be seen as superior to episteme. Through creating scenario stories, it frames the relevance of evidence on existing local properties and resources, and development trends, integrating it narratively with imagined future development directions and possibilities. Conversely, episteme can be seen as a knowledge resource for the techne of imaginative scenario stories, which, in turn, can be seen as a resource of providing alternative future development paths for the phronesis of choosing a desirable path.

   Hence, all of Aristotle's intellectual virtues are essential for strategic spatial planning utilizing scenario planning. Flyvbjerg's claim is that the phronetic approach is most appropriate in planning research, which in his interpretation would focus especially on detailed case analysis and normative reflection of power in planning (Flyvbjerg, 2004). We, however, emphasize that for understanding and learning strategic spatial planning, whether as researchers or practitioners, we need to grasp the interplay of all of Aristotle's three intellectual virtues: how phronesis frames techne, and how, in turn, techne frames episteme.

## Conclusion

For strategic spatial planning, scenario work is a valuable tool, in its attempt to identify critical uncertainties and opportunities for longer-term development, and to base its strategically wise choices here and now. However, there is much room for methodological development to fully utilize the potential of scenario work.

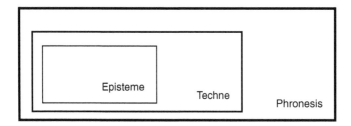

*Figure 21.1* The nested hierarchy of Aristotle's three intellectual virtues in strategic spatial planning utilizing scenario planning

While there is a lot to learn from the elaborate scenario planning methods developed in the world of business management, they tend to neglect the spatial implications and resources related to scenario work. On the other hand, strategic leadership in business management is less complicated than in strategic spatial planning, where the stakeholders are more diverse, new networked governance forms are ambiguous in their relationship to existing institutional governance structures, and thereby the political legitimacy of strategic governance is often contested. The strategic leadership ideas are thus not straightforwardly applicable in the context of strategic spatial planning. What is perhaps most valuable to learn from the corporate world, though, is its readiness to explore also those plausible scenarios that go against the normative visions. Such readiness can be much more difficult to achieve in the political world of public governance.

Indeed, the capability to explore various scenarios without prior judgement makes scenario work a most useful planning instrument. It utilizes our imaginative powers to frame the scope of possibilities, and thereby shapes the agenda for critical judgements on what to choose as the normative scenario and what decisions need to be made in striving for it. In the format of rhetorically strong stories (both verbally and visually), the scenarios, as a medium, can be easily accessible beyond disciplinary and cultural boundaries, inviting broad political dialogue. Thus, they have potential for widening perspectives, revealing mutual interdependencies and generating joint momentum towards an envisioned future. These second-order effects of scenario planning are instrumental for establishing such strategic framing capacities that Healey recognizes to be at the core of strategic spatial planning.

In our view, planning, especially strategic spatial planning, requires the full utilization of all of Aristotle's three intellectual virtues. This is emphasized when strategic spatial planning utilizes the foresight of scenario planning. In turn, if reduced only to forecasting, often based solely on precedent and analogy, scenario work loses much of its intellectual and transformative potential. In Aristotle's terms, it overlooks our intellectual virtues of phronesis and techne, relying only on episteme. As such, scenario work may perform as a tool of analysis, but not as a proper planning instrument.

## Notes

1 With the concept 'spatial planning' we refer to a view (or set of views) on planning, recently emerged in continental Europe, that Haughton *et al.* (2010: 5) identify to have four key dimensions: (1) long-term strategic thinking that draws on visions agreeable by the stakeholders; (2) a policy mechanism for bringing together and building coherence between the different policy braches of governance; (3) a central tool for bringing society to a more sustainable development path; and (4) an emphasis on openness and inclusivity of planning to wider groups of society. With the notion of 'strategic spatial planning' we, in turn, refer especially to those approaches to spatial planning that emphasize the first dimension.
2 The SWOT analysis is a structured planning method used to evaluate the strengths, weaknesses, opportunities and threats involved in a project or in a business venture.

3  The Delphi method is a structured communication technique, originally developed as a systematic, interactive *forecasting* method, which relies on a panel of experts. The experts answer questionnaires in two or more rounds. After each round, a *facilitator* or change-agent provides an anonymous summary of the experts' forecasts from the previous round as well as the reasons they provided for their judgements.

# References

Albrechts, L. (2005). Creativity as a drive for change. *Planning Theory* 4(2), 247–269.

Albrechts, L. (2015). Ingredients for a more radical strategic spatial planning. *Environment and Planning B: Planning and Design*, 42, 510–525.

Arendt, H. (1958). *The human condition*. Chicago, IL: The University of Chicago Press.

Chakraborty, A., Kaza, N., Knaap, G.-J. and Deal, B. (2011). Robust plans and contingent plans. *Journal of the American Planning Association*, 77 (3), 251–266.

Davoudi, S. (2012). The legacy of positivism and the emergence of interpretive tradition in spatial planning. *Regional Studies*, 46 (4), 429–441.

Demos Helsinki (2009). *Talsingi/Hellinn*. [pdf] Tallinn: Helsingi-Tallinn Euregio and Helsinki city. [pdf] Available at: http://www.demoshelsinki.fi/wp-content/uploads/2012/11/TalsinkiHellinna_EST.pdf [accessed 9 July 2015].

Flyvbjerg, B. (1992). Aristotle, Foucault and progressive *phronesis*: Outline of an applied ethics for sustainable development. *Planning Theory*, 7–8 (Summer–Winter), 65–83.

Flyvbjerg, B. (2004). Phronetic planning research: Theoretical and methodological reflections. *Planning Theory and Practice*, 5(3), 283–306.

Forester, J. (1999). *The deliberative practitioner: Encouraging participatory planning processes*. Cambridge, MA: MIT Press.

Friedmann, J. *et al.* (2004). Strategic spatial planning and the longer range. *Planning Theory and Practice*, 5(1), 49–67.

Gaffikin, F. and Sterrett, K. (2006). New visions for old cities: The role of visioning in planning. *Planning Theory and Practice*, 7(2), 159–178.

Garreau, J. (1994). The Global Business Network. *Wired* 2(11), 98.

Haughton, G., Allmendinger, P., Counsell, D. and Vigar, G. (2010). *The new spatial planning: Territorial management with soft spaces and fuzzy boundaries*. Abingdon: Routledge.

Healey, P. (2007). *Urban complexity and spatial strategies: Towards a relational planning for our times*. London: Routledge.

Healey, P. (2009). In search of the 'strategic' in spatial strategy making. *Planning Theory and Practice*, 10(4), 439-457.

Healey, P. (2013). Comment on Albrechts and Balducci 'Practicing Strategic Planning'. *DisP*, 49(3), 48–50.

Hillier, J. (2011). Strategic navigation across multiple planes: Towards a Deleuzean-inspired methodology for strategic spatial planning. *Town Planning Review*, 82(5), 503–527.

de Jouvenel, H. (1999). 'You must discover trends not to be caught unprepared', interview with J. Rodrigues [online]. Available at: http://gurus.janelanaweb.com/uk/conteudos/jouvenel2.html [accessed 22 June 2015].

de Jouvenel, H. (2004). *An invitation to foresight*. Trans. H. Fish. Paris: Futuribles.

Kahn, H. (1962). *Thinking about the unthinkable*. New York: Horizon Press.

Konno, N., Nonaka, I. and Ogilvy, J. (2014). Scenario planning: The basics, world futures. *The Journal of New Paradigm Research*, 70(1), 28–43.

Krawczyk, E. (2007). Geography, planning and the future. In P. van der Duin, ed., *Knowing tomorrow? How science deals with the future*. Delft: Eburon, Chapter 7.

Krizek, K., Forsyth, A. and Slotterback, C. A. (2010). Is there a role for evidence-based practice in urban planning and policy? *Planning Theory and Practice*, 10(4), 459–478.

Myers, D. and Kitsuse, A. (2000) Constructing the future in planning: A survey of theories and tools. *Journal of Planning Education and Research*, 19, 221–231.

Ogilvy, J. (2006). Scenario planning, art or science? *World Futures: The Journal of New Paradigm Research*, 61(5), 331–346.

Petrov, L. O., Shahumyan, H., Williams, B. and Convery, S. (2011). Scenarios and indicators supporting urban and regional planning, *Procedia- Social and Behavioral Sciences*, 21, 243–252.

Schwartz, P. (1991). *The art of the long view*. New York: Doubleday.

Terk, E. ed. (2012). *Twin city in making: Integration scenarios for Tallinn and Helsinki capital regions*. [pdf] Tallinn: Tallinn University Estonian Institute for Future Studies. Available at: https://www.tlu.ee/UserFiles/Eesti%20Tuleviku-uuringute%20Instituut/twin_city_veebi.pdf [accessed 9 July 2015].

Throgmorton, J. A. (1996). *Planning as persuasive storytelling: The rhetorical construction of Chicago's electric future*. Chicago, IL: The University of Chicago Press.

Uusimaa Regional council (2004). *UTU35: A future for you too? Uusimaa 2035: Scenario project*. [pdf] Helsinki: Uusimaa Regional council. Available at: http://www.uudenmaanliitto.fi/files/6168/UTU35_A_future_for_you_too. [accessed 9 July 2015].

Wack, P. (1985). Scenarios: Uncharted waters ahead. *Harvard Business Review*, 63(5), 73–89.

Zegras, C. and Rayle, L. (2012). Testing the rhetoric: An approach to assess scenario planning's role as a catalyst for urban policy integration, *Futures*, 44, 303–318.

# 22 Strategic planning and 'trading zones'[1]

*Alessandro Balducci*

> The third task (of planning theory) is to translate concepts and knowledge generated in other fields into our own domain and to render them accessible and useful for planning and its practice. I call this the task of *translation*.
>
> (John Friedmann, *The uses of planning theory*, 2008)

This chapter is an attempt to use the concept of the 'trading zone', as elaborated by Peter Galison (1999) in the field of the history of science, to indicate new opportunities for fostering innovation in planning, beyond the illusion of conquering a general consensus about values and objectives among the different actors involved in strategic planning. To do this, I will first illustrate how, in the field of planning, there has been for a long period a kind of mirroring between the debate about rationality, rooted in political science, and the development of the theory of planning (Webber, 1969; Faludi, 1973), a process of mirroring that was somehow suspended when the most complex decision-making model was proposed by Cohen, March and Olsen in 1972, the so-called 'garbage can model': a provocative theory that emphasized the extreme complexity of collective decision-making processes. My point is that we have to re-start today from that kind of complexity to elaborate a vision of strategic planning which is adequate to the emerging problems of the contemporary city. The 'trading zone' concept is a promising tool to move us in that direction.

## Planning and the technical rationality

Planning is a young discipline. Only five years ago, in 2009, we celebrated the centenary of the institution of the first chair in urban planning in Europe, at the University of Liverpool. In other countries, this happened even later. In Italy the first chair in urban planning was established in 1930 at the School of Architecture in Rome (Balducci, 2001). Since the Second World War the development has been rapid and pervasive across Europe and North America. Planners who have occupied the scene in this exciting period were mainly trained as architects, geographers or social scientists. Pushed by their passion, they have struggled to obtain the recognition of planning as an independent discipline in the educational field, as well as in the professional field.

What did happen really: the Association of Collegiate Schools of Planning (ACSP) was created in 1969 in the USA, and the European sister association, the Association of the European Schools of Planning (AESOP), was founded in 1982. It is interesting to notice that the period between these two dates has been one of extraordinary growth and institutionalization of the discipline. Shortly after, in 1993, the Asian Planning Schools Association (APSA) was created, and in 1994 the Australia and New Zealand Association of Planning Schools (ANZAPS). There was indeed the belief that it was possible to change society through planning activity, to provide the opportunity of an equitable and rational use of space, to be able to attack spatial injustice, and to solve emerging urban problems through a rational and democratic process of design. It was nothing to do with the world of architecture being confined to the single artefact, nothing to do with geography or social science being limited to the description of phenomena.

What kind of foundation was at the basis of this endeavour? On the one hand, the extension of the architectural design or engineering approach to the urban environment seemed quite natural; on the other hand, planning appeared to be the ideal field for the application of a reformist ideology, according to which it would have been possible to correct the malfunctions produced by market forces through a process of accurate design and programming.

In that same period, an entire process of development had been completed in the field of political science. In the attempt to provide an explanation of the failures in public policies, the rational reformist approach had been under attack since the 1940s. It had been through this critical discussion that it had been possible to characterize the 'rational approach' to decision-making as the implicit, predominant foundation of the reformist movement and of early planning thought.

In fact, the rational model proposes an approach that is guided by well-defined problems, clearly understandable preferences, describable and enumerable alternatives, and an ability to calculate the best choices capable of maximizing the benefits and minimizing costs. The critical reflection developed by Herbert Simon (1955) and Charles Lindblom (1959) emphasized the impossibility of following this model unless there were conditions of complete information and unitary, single-minded, collective actors could be identified.

However, since the period between the two World Wars, but also immediately after the Second World War, the rational model has long been the basis of the planning project: it has been the basis of many planning laws, of the idea of the Soviet, but also of the French, planning ideology, in the USA as well as in Italy. It has been the basis of the paradigm of the so-called 'technical rationality', as described by Donald Schön (1983), and of the idea of the supremacy of professional-scientific knowledge to solve social and urban problems. It is possible to recall here the roots of the traditional paradigm of planning, and particularly of land-use planning, with a sharp division between those who plan and those who are planned. This is a quite simplistic and straightforward translation from an individual to a collective decision-making process, with the aspiration of streamlining the city and the society.

In Italy and elsewhere, this form of rationality has formed a very strong foundation of the heroic era of planning, until the early 1970s, and was perfectly compatible with the architectural roots of urban planning. Luigi Piccinato, one of the founding fathers of Italian urban planning, claimed that it was possible to define a typology of cities – radial, grid, port-cities, etc. –which corresponded with a repertory of possible plans (Piccinato, 1988); Giovanni Astengo promoted a scientific approach to land-use planning in a direct dialogue with the Athens' Charter of the Modern Movement (Astengo, 1991). It was an approach that, immediately after the Second World War, was opposed by figures like Giancarlo De Carlo, who as early as in 1948 gave a lecture at the Architectural Association, and who argued against the narrowness of the scientific technical approach and the need to open up towards the participation of citizens in the design of the city (De Carlo, 1973; Hall, 1988).

## Towards bounded political rationality

The work of Herbert Simon and Charles Lindblom attacked the two conditions of impracticability of the rational approach. Simon dealt with the first: the incompleteness of information, with the idea of a rationality which is limited by uncertainty, to which actors respond by producing frames and routines and limiting their explorations to alternatives and solutions considered 'good enough' according to what their problem definition allows (Simon, 1955). Lindblom released the second condition: the decision-maker is not unitary or a composite organization; rather, it is made by a set of different actors who are formally in very different positions (Lindblom, 1965). Those who have an interest or stake are actors of the decision-making process, even if they do not have any formal role in the institutional process. Not only is there incomplete information, but also conflicts about goals among decision-makers.

In addition, it is impossible to distinguish between means and ends. All the actors are in a situation of mutual partisan interdependence. All the actors, in pursuing their goals, are forced to interact with others and to adjust to others' goals. All have partisan interests, even if they claim to act in the public interest. All adopt an incremental approach, considering only a few alternatives that are not very different among them and not very different from the current situation/policy producing an incremental change.

But the 'disjointed incrementalism' is not only the best way to describe the processes; it is also the approach which allows the most 'rational' results. In fact, Lindblom asks: when do we define that a decision is good or rational? When it minimizes adverse consequences. How do we attain it in the best way? The plurality of actors is the source of rationality, because all of them defend and promote their own interests and the decision is the outcome of this mutual adaptation. This is, according to Lindblom, the expression of 'the intelligence of democracy' (Lindblom, 1965).

These reflections have been very important in offering a different perspective to the evolution of the planning project.

A number of very important contributions to the 'translation' were those offered by Melvin Webber in the second half of 1960s. He is an author who has been extremely influential, also in Italy, even though he never wrote a book, but a number of thoughtful essays. Of special interest are the two papers published in *Town Planning Review* entitled 'Planning in an environment of change. Part I: Beyond the industrial age' (Webber, 1968) and 'Planning in an environment of change. Part II 'Permissive planning' (Webber, 1969), and a paper, written with Horst Rittel in 1973, published in *Policy Science*, entitled 'Dilemmas in a general theory of planning'. In an open dialogue with the work of Lindblom and Simon, Webber introduced the idea of planning as a process which is intrinsically inter-active and conflictual, emphasizing the partisan role of experts, the value of the ordinary knowledge, and the 'wicked' character of planning problems compared with the 'tamed' problems of science. In a very direct way the article states that the wicked planning problems are characterized by a number of features that force the abandonment of technical rationality: they tend to be unique and it is impossible to categorize them; their formulation is uncertain; they are never solved but are only attacked; the tempted solutions are not true-or-false, but good-or-bad according to the positions of different actors; there is no opportunity to learn by trial and error, every attempt counts significantly, etc.

After this process of translation, there was a growing recognition of the politi-cal nature of the planning process. The work of Webber, and others, opened up the first recognition of the impossibility to divide in a clear way planners and planned, decision-makers and decision-takers. The consequences have been the very idea of 'advocacy planning' (Davidoff, 1965), but they have also led to the rise of participatory approaches. These became very popular in a period when planning started to appear less effective, after the fall of the initial rationalistic illusion: if the rationality of a planning process comes from interaction and mutual adjustment, why not organize this, enlarging the opportunity to expose planning decisions to the formal participation of a plurality of actors? Participation and communicative planning, based upon the Habermasian principle of non-distorted communication, have been important developments.

After the heroic phase, there was a long period in which planning was under attack, on the one hand, for ideological reasons, but, on the other hand, for the scarcity of results by which the movement could justify its role, both as a rational discipline and as part of an open process of decision-making. This period started at the beginning of the 1980s under Ronald Reagan in the USA and Margaret Thatcher in the UK, and continued throughout the last decade of the twentieth and the first decade of the twenty-first century.

A period of deep social, economic and spatial change, characterized by grow-ing globalization, an increased fragmentation of society, the emergence of new media, and the acceleration of the urbanization process, which transformed the very notion of city, blurred the administrative boundaries, and challenged the traditional idea of planning based upon a linear relation between territory and authority (Sassen, 2006). At the end of this period, we find ourselves in a situation of cognitive dissonance: the generation who made the strongest effort for the affirmation of planning is now retiring, the tools which have been elaborated to plan urban and metropolitan development are losing their capacity, spatial relations are redefined by the immaterial flows of information, and the process of fragmentation produces a multiplication of actors, languages and spaces that are different from the traditional ones. The very idea of planning that is based upon rational analysis, participation and persuasion seems to be less effective. In this same period there has been a growing attention towards forms of strategic spatial planning which have tried to react to some of the shortcomings of land-use planning, not substituting but complementing it (Bryson and Roering, 1987; Albrechts, 2004).

## No Translations for the 'Garbage Can' Model

Returning to the debate in political science, there was a fourth decision-making model which had always been treated as an extreme model. It was something like a radical view of the irreducible complexity of the reality of decision-making processes: the so-called 'garbage can' model, proposed by March, Olsen and Cohen (1972), according to whom we face 'a collection of choices looking for problems, issues and feelings looking for decision situations in which they might be aired, solutions looking for issues to which they might be the answer, and decision makers looking for work' (Cohen, March, and Olsen 1972, p. 2).

March, Olsen and Cohen (1972) highlighted four ambiguities regarding decisions:

1.  Actors' goals are unstable, they change over time, they are discovered in the process and therefore it is difficult to attribute to them steady positions.
2.  Actors' participation to decision-making processes is fluid and inconstant, therefore decisions cannot be taken as the product of a stable set of actors because they tend to distribute their attention in an unpredictable way.
3.  The context of a decision is formed by limited opportunities to decide and many problems compete to enter into the agenda, some of which never reach the opportunity to be treated.
4.  There is not a search for solutions to be found for well-defined problems, but the decision-making arena is rather made of many problems and solutions that are mixed up, as in the metaphor of the 'garbage can'. Providers of solutions may search for problems rather than solutions being sought for problems; the structure of the decision-making process is governed by casual combination.

The garbage can model was describing a situation of extreme complexity, in which conflicts were not resolvable because of the many ambiguities of the context of interaction and because of their wicked nature. But even with this apparently de-structured approach, the 'garbage can' model was not only descriptive; a number of prescriptive implications could be derived from it: work on problem redefinition; attempts to try to bring in new actors, and to establish new connections between problem-holders and solution-providers; and renounce to any comprehensive treatment.

This model did not have a significant impact on planning theory. There has not been a 'translation' until quite recently, when a number of reflections resonated with the theoretical contribution of Cohen, March and Olsen (1972): the work of Hillier (2007), De Roo, Hillier and Van Wezemael (2012) and all those who have been working upon the relationship between planning and complexity.

## Strategic planning 'boundary objects' and 'trading zone'

Somehow, in the same attempt to produce an approach to (strategic) planning that is appropriate to the level of complexity of contemporary urban regions, I have been exploring and searching for theories in other fields that could help in defining a new theoretical framework to go beyond the limits of participatory, communicative approaches that I have practised extensively. Together with Raine Mäntysalo, we started from a re-interpretation of Lindblom, not only as the proponent of a rationality based upon partisan mutual adjustment and agreement, but rather of a rationality based upon conflict and antagonism (Mäntysalo, Balducci and Kangasoja, 2011). For Lindblom, in fact, it is not relevant whether or not you share, in general terms, the values of your counterpart, as long as you are able to bargain on a concrete (planning) decision. What matters is whether your counterpart agrees with a concrete proposal, not why s/he agrees. If you move in this direction, you can make sense of many failures in mutual understanding and of unexpected case-specific opportunities, even among actors in a situation of radical conflict. From this perspective, the issue is how to deal with the situations of ambiguity proposed by the garbage can model: the instability of the actors, their fluid participation, the complex game of entering into the agenda of public decisions, the casual combination between problems-holders and solutions-providers.

In the translation of Lindblom's thought into the planning debate, which opened up to the participatory approach, these dimensions were generally ignored. The implicit assumption of a steady 'set of actors' – all those who have a stake in the decision-making process – to be brought to the table in order to include them in an open dialogue, is the reason of many failures, due to the difficulty of holding together a 'process' with a beginning, a development and an end. It was in following this line of reflection that Raine Mäntysalo suggested to me that we explore the use of the concept of 'boundary objects', formulated by Star and Griesemer (1989), to explain the positive results of interaction between groups either in conflict or with opposing objectives in unstable environments. The hypothesis put forward is that in order to succeed in carrying out projects of any nature in complex contexts, it is necessary for these to belong to or intercept different strategies contingently without requiring them to converge.

> Boundary objects are objects which are both plastic enough to adapt to local needs and the constraints of the several parties employing them, yet robust

enough to maintain a common identity across sites. [...] They have different meanings in different social worlds but their structure is common enough to more than one world to make them recognisable, a means of translation. (Star and Griesemer, 1989, p. 393)

Star and Griesemer claim that the creation and management of boundary objects is a crucial process in the development and maintenance of coherence between different worlds, which intersect around a specific decision event. It is not the capacity to make the right choices, from the viewpoint of the contents and the working method, which leads to the successful initiatives. In this context, it is the ability to co-design the infrastructure of boundary objects (Star and Griesemer, 1989), or an action that is *per se* a boundary object between the different strategies of the actors involved.

In the field of planning, this is a recurrent type of problem. Even when you do succeed in organizing a fair process around a specific decision or plan, the different intensity of preferences, the degree of involvement, and the meaning of the 'object' vary greatly among planners, municipalities, different department officials, associations, citizen groups, and other institutional or non-institutional actors. It was through this access point that we arrived at the wider concept of 'trading zone' proposed by Peter Galison (Balducci and Mäntysalo, 2013).

Galison has defined 'trading zones' as those infrastructures and those concepts which function as 'exchangers' for dialogues between different sub-cultures. He shows, through empirical observation, how innovations in science occurred historically – ranging from physics to nanotechnologies – how these give rise to concrete spaces or conceptual spaces where scientists belonging to different disciplinary fields are obliged to find simplified and intermediate languages to be able to work together. It is from this essential communication, which requires partial agreements, that innovations are born. A trading zone is a platform where highly elaborate and complex questions can be transformed into 'thin descriptions' (as opposed to 'thick descriptions'), with the objective of exchanging information in a specific local context. This explains the ability to build coordinated forms of mutual interaction, despite a limited capacity on the part of each group to understand the conceptions, the methodologies and the objectives of the others.

> Over a very broad range of battles – from power generating stations to fisheries, we have scientists and practitioners struggling to find a common, but restricted, language. It would be powerful if we could understand more systematically, why some disputes can be productively advanced through the formation of delimited trading zones, while other such attempts fail. If we could do that, our understanding might lead us to strategies to encourage positive outcomes. Here, it seems to me, is a theoretical problem that bears on the most practical side of trading zone work today. (Galison, 2010, p. 51)

There is a connection here to Lindblom's partisan mutual adjustment. There is a relation with the idea of searching for boundary objects in a situation of conflicts and turbulence. There is also a possible relation with the principles of the garbage can model. The added value is the idea of a 'zone' rather than of a 'process'. A zone can be a physical space and/or a contingent conceptual space of interaction.

From this viewpoint, the strategic action is the action that enters a zone of out-talk and trade. A zone is not necessarily an arena but is rather a recognized practice which aims at the production of the exchange. The concept of trading zone suggests that instead of seeking to organize a process aiming at the creation of a general agreement, we must try to seek those solutions, which can belong to different life-worlds and to the different strategic viewpoints of the actors involved, while at the same time assuming that these actors are and remain in conflict.

We may wonder, at this point, if strategic spatial planning, which, in the most interesting definitions, we describe as an open process, capable of dealing with the multiple values and perspective of actors, capable of dealing with uncertainty and dynamic, exploration, and capable of changing the sense of direction (Albrechts, 2004; Albrechts and Balducci, 2013), cannot be conceived as 'the intentional creation of a trading zone', which requires an effort to translate expert knowledge, which has not to be hidden, entering into a dialogue to produce partial agreements and solutions.

It is usually recognized that strategic planning is working on visions and on the involvement of stakeholders in a reflection about the future in order to produce a change in the immediate action and in partial choices (Albrechts and Van den Broek, 2004). It is also recognized that strategy-making is the process that helps specific episodes of innovation to be transformed into institutionalized practices which, if they are successful and 'travel', can in the end transform the governance culture (Healey, 2007). There is a parallelism here with the description that Peter Galison gives of anthropological linguists who show that Pidgin English is a simplified form of language, which is essential for allowing communication and exchange between local populations in the colonies and their colonizers. Over time, this simplified form can evolve eventually into the full language of Creole. But without the original pidgin, no language can exist.

The idea of strategic planning is the intentional attempt to create a trading zone that opens towards a perspective of an explicit recognition of the kind of social work that must happen in the process of strategy-making: not the progressive persuasion of the actors about common goals to produce the right choices, but the creation of a coordination structure (Kellogg, Orlikowski and Yates, 2006, p. 39), an area of understanding, exchange and translation between actors to produce partial agreements and innovations. An area 'always on the making', contingent and dynamic, which cannot be simply 'planned or prescribed, but is highly dependent on the situated activities of the various communities' (Kellogg *et al.*, 2006, p. 39).

Intentionality is rooted into the planning tradition, but this time it is emptied of any technocratic dimension. It is the frame with which a specific actor enters into a world of complex, unstable and conflicting relations to try to produce partial assemblages (Beauregard, 2012).

## To conclude

We have discovered in the last 30 years that planning cannot change society. This notion created disillusionment, particularly in the generation that was the protagonist of the early stages of planning movement. We have discovered that both planning based upon technical rationality and on political rationality have important limits. In a period of instability and complexity, globalization and dispersed urbanization, we know that we still have to probe and explore how to plan working with democracy (Lindblom, 1990). We still have to work on visions, strategies and the long term, with a politics which is forced more and more to live in the short term, but we also know that this has to be done in a different way, to be well-equipped to start a process of 'navigation', as Jean Hillier puts it, rather than to follow precise 'road maps' (Hillier, 2011; also Balducci *et al.*, 2011). We know that we have to move from the conviction of being right, having the right solutions, to an experimental approach which is in search of 'boundary strategies' where we can meet the different interests, the objectives and the values of the various actors, without seeking to convince them all.

Having the privilege of working with the physical space, which is the only shared object in a rapidly changing and liquid society, we need to develop the ability to translate our jargon, to create an inter-language accessible to all, a 'trading zone' as Peter Galison puts it: an area in which we can mobilize our expertise in a creative way, and be able to intermix with other expert and lay knowledge.

We know that working in this way is not the solution of fundamental issues like social injustice, climate change, environmental unsustainability, demographic decay. We also are aware that similar coordination practices are not able to avoid conflicts, misunderstanding, ambiguity and uncertainty in heterarchical conditions like those in which we currently live (Kellogg *et al.*, 2006). At the same time, we should be aware that adopting the trading zones perspective is not simplifying our work: how (if) can they be created or nurtured? In other words, as Gorman reminds us, 'they require a considerable work on the part of at least some participants if their potential is to be realized', and interactional expertise is central in this respect (Collins, Evans and Gorman, 2007, p. 21). But it is probably the only way we have to attack these problems and try to make some progress, and planning can find a new role towards contemporary society challenges. Of course, urban planning cannot be assimilated to the scientific communities' contexts, in relation to which the concept of trading zones was originally formulated (Healey, 2013). Nevertheless, we believe that its role as interactional expertise can be better focused through the eyes of trading zone theory and, in particular, the concept of boundary objects can be particularly inspiring in order to reflect and design planning processes. This can also be central in developing a research agenda on strategic spatial planning, in so far as it offers elements to interpret the potential of innovations contained in some of the approaches described in the chapters of this book, and also some warnings against the limits of some interpretations, especially those who risk to reproduce or do not deal with the limits of the rational approach to planning.

# Note

1 A preliminary version of this text has been published in the online journal *CTA City Territory and Architecture*, Springer, 2:7, 2015.

# References

Albrechts, L., 2004. Strategic (spatial) planning re-examined. *Environment and Planning B: Planning and Design*, 31, 743–754.

Albrechts, L. and Van den Broeck, J., 2004. From discourse to facts: The case of the ROM project in Ghent, Belgium. *Town Planning Review*, 75(2), 127–150.

Albrechts, L. and Balducci, A., 2013. Setting the scene (a special issue on strategic planning). *DisP*, 194(49.3).

Astengo, G., 1991. La ricerca di un metodo scientifico. In F. Indovina, ed., *La ragione del piano. Giovanni Astengo e l'urbanistica italiana*. Milano: Franco Angeli, pp. 343–349.

Balducci, A., 2001. L'istituzionalizzazione dell'urbanistica tra professione e formazione. *Territorio*, 18, 127–136.

Balducci, A., 2011. Strategic planning as exploration. *Town Planning Review*, 82(5), 529–546.

Balducci, A., Fedeli, V. and Pasqui, G., 2011. *Strategic planning for contemporary urban regions*. Farnham: Ashgate.

Balducci, A. and Mäntysalo, R., eds., 2013. *Urban planning as a trading zone*. Dordrecht: Springer.

Beauregard, R., 2012. In search of assemblages. *CRIOS, Critica degli Ordinament Spaziali*, 4, 9–16.

Bryson, J. M. and Roering, W. D., 1987. Applying private-sector strategic planning in the public sector. *Journal of the American Planning Association*, 53(1), 9–22.

Cohen, M. D., March, J. G. and Olsen, J. P., 1972. A garbage can model of organizational choice. *Administrative Science Quarterly*, 17(1), 1–25.

Collins, H., Evans, R. and Gorman, M., 2007. Trading zones and interactional expertise. *History and Philosophy of Science Part A*, 38(4), 657–666.

Davidoff, P., 1965. Advocacy and pluralism in planning. *Journal of the American Institute of Planners*, 31(4), 331–338.

De Carlo, G., 1973. *L'architettura della partecipazione*. Milano: Saggiatore.

De Roo, G., Hillier, J. and Van Wezemael, J., eds., 2012. *Planning and complexity: Systems, assemblages and simulations*. Farnham: Ashgate.

Faludi, A., 1973. *A reader in planning theory*. Oxford: Pergamon Press.

Friedmann, J., 2008. The uses of planning theory: A bibliographic essay. *Journal of Planning Education and Research*, 28(2), 247–257.

Galison, P., 1999. Trading zone: Coordinating action and belief. In M. Biagioli, ed., *The science studies reader*. New York/London: Routledge, pp. 137–160.

Galison, P., 2010. Trading with the enemy. In M. E. Gorman, ed., *Trading zones and interactional expertise: Creating new kinds of collaboration*. Cambridge, MA: MIT Press, pp. 25–52.

Hall, P., 1988. *Cities of tomorrow*. New York: Blackwell.

Healey, P., 2007. *Urban complexity and spatial strategies: Towards a relational planning for our times*. London: Routledge.

Healey, P., 2013. Urban planning as a trading zone. In A. Balducci and R. Mäntysalo, eds., *Urban planning as a trading zone*. Dordrecht: Springer.

Hillier, J., 2007. *Stretching beyond the horizon: A multiplanar theory of spatial planning and governance*. Aldershot: Ashgate.

Hillier, J. 2011. Strategic navigation across multiple planes: Towards a Deleuzean-inspired methodology for strategic spatial planning. *Town Planning Review*, 82(5), 503–527.

Kellogg, K. C., Orlikowski, W. J. and Yates, J., 2006. Life in the trading zone: Structuring coordination across boundaries in postbureaucratic organizations. *Organization Science*, 17(1), 22–44.

Lindblom, C., 1959. The science of muddling through. *Public Administration Review*, 19(2), 79–88.

Lindblom, C., 1965. *The intelligence of democracy*. New York: Free Press.

Lindblom, C., 1990. *Inquiry and change: The troubled attempt to understand and shape society*. New Haven, CT: Yale University Press.

Mäntysalo, R., Balducci, A. and Kangasoja, J., 2011. Planning as agonistic communication in a trading zone: Re-examining Lindblom's partisan mutual adjustment. *Planning Theory*, 10(3), 257–272.

Piccinato, L., 1988. *La Progettazione Urbanistica-La città come organismo*. Venice: Marsilio.

Rittel, H. and Webber, M. M., 1973. Dilemmas in a general theory of planning. *Policy Science*, 4, 155–169.

Sassen, S., 2006. *Territory, authority rights: From medieval to global assemblages*. Princeton, NJ: Princeton University Press.

Schön, D. A., 1983. *The reflective practitioner*. New York: Basic Books.

Simon, H., 1955. A behavioral model of rational choice. *Quarterly Journal of Economics*, 69, 99–118.

Star, S. L. and Griesemer, J. R., 1989. Institutional ecology, 'translations' and boundary objects: Amateurs and professionals in Berkeley's Museum of Vertebrate Zoology. *Social Studies of Science*, 19, 387–420.

Webber, M. K., 1968. Planning in an environment of change. Part I: Beyond the industrial age. *Town Planning Review*, 39(3), 179–195.

Webber, M. K., 1969. Planning in an environment of change. Part II: Permissive planning. *Town Planning Review*, 39(4), 277–295.

# 23 Reinventing strategic spatial planning

## A critical act of reconstruction

*Willem Salet*

## Introduction

The downgrading of strategic spatial planning is observed and reported in a wide number of states, not only in Europe, which used to take an advanced position, internationally, but also in a number of states and regions overseas. The withdrawal of strategic spatial plans is taking place in the first instance at the national and the regional level of scales, with retreating movements recently reported in the UK, France, the Netherlands and Denmark (Lord and Tewdwr-Jones, 2014; Geppert, 2015; Zonneveld and Evers, 2014), but also in metropolitan regions, for instance, as reported earlier in this book, in Rio de Janeiro and Øresund (Vainer and Olesen and Metzger, both this volume). Some observers are more confident of strategic spatial planning in metropolitan regions, such as the contributions in this book by Van den Broeck about Antwerp and Fedeli about metropolitan regions in Italy, but both call for the need of changing the contemporary approach. In all cases, one might have expected a more visible role of strategic planning in an epoch of economic and social turmoil and in times of dramatic climate change – providing ways to a better future – but strategic spatial planning has suffered a serious setback, being perceived by successive political coalitions as an expression of opaque administration and as another bureaucratic obstacle to social and economic progress, rather than embodying strategic guidance to a better future (Vainer and Olesen and Metzger, both this volume).

Often, the political climate of opportunism is blamed by practitioners and scholars in the field, compromising in particular the prevailing ideology 'neo-liberalism' (Peck and Tickell, 2002; Sager, 2011; Campbell et al., 2013; Lord and Tewdwr-Jones, 2014). Whatever might be true of this, the claim of this chapter is different. I will not express sentiments of planning nostalgia, neither will I take a position of political repudiation. The planning profession needs a more critical self-diagnosis in order to re-invent itself with more plausible legitimacy and effectiveness. The problems at stake reflect the more structural shortcomings and vulnerabilities of the modernist and supply-led planning systems and the profession is in need of a more critical self-reflection. One should wonder whether the planning domain did not turn too much inside-out in an expansive period of material growth. The roots of the current crisis of planning are nested deeper and go back further in time than the temporary social and economic stagnation and the political fluctuation. The claim in this chapter is that an endemic propensity to planning subjectivism has been the structural vein of strategic spatial planning in times of modernism, which has been covered in the stages of construction of the postwar welfare states but has become completely out of place in the current stages of pluralism, social complexity and permanent dynamics of macro- and micro-level processes of sociological rescaling. The strategic spatial planning approaches tend to be introverted, planner-centric, and engaged in trajectories of specified end-means juridification; they clearly should be adapted to cope with the challenges of the new sociology.

In this chapter, I will first explore the general nature of planning subjectivism and several of its utterances in planning voluntarism, planning instrumentalism and the 'providence bias' of modernist strategic spatial planning. I will briefly illustrate these abiding traps with some cases of strategic planning in the Netherlands that may exemplify the dramatic shifts of time. The Dutch strategic spatial planning was renowned internationally for its advanced position both at the national and at the lower levels of the scale. Its comprehensive fabrication was even promoted as a product to be exported to other nation states (Faludi and van der Valk, 1994). But in the most recent decade it has been torn down almost completely. It was also the prototype of inside-out 'planning subjectivism'. I will analyze some of the traps that are inherent to this approach in order to find realistic keys for a more social-entrepreneurial style of planning. In the final part of the chapter, I will elucidate some new and promising experiences of planning, in which planning is perceived as an act of reconstruction in social settings of action, instead of inside-out initiatives of planning authorities. This type of planning is not preoccupied with a comprehensive spatial design of society, but with the actual changes of spatial use that are actually occurring in society (initiated by private sector investment or by functional policy decisions in goal-specific policy sectors). Here, the practitioners of spatial planning have to envisage how to add in a social-entrepreneurial way a higher and integrative quality of space to these functional initiatives. The uses of space are no longer perceived as the outcomes of a planning design but the design of planning is trying to reconstruct the real unfolding uses of space in specific contexts of action. Obviously, these outside-in strategies of planning would need the legal conditions and facilitation of higher tiers of the planning system, but the core mechanism of strategic spatial planning have turned upside down.

## Planning subjectivism

The first and utmost planning fallacy is the inherent propensity towards planning subjectivism. Taking a planner-centric position in the thought and action perspectives of strategic spatial planning is an evergreen in the history of planning practices and planning thought. Also, the criticizing of this planning subjectivism and its problems is all but new, not in planning practices and not in scholar thoughts of planning. The phenomenon is thoroughly known and has been frequently analyzed since the beginning of the modernist planning era in the early twentieth century (and even sublimated in the world of literature, such as in Robert Musils' luminous dialogues of Arnheim and Ulrich in the prewar epoch of Vienna, hailing the dauntless rational and constructive planning subject which is facing the complexity of a pluralist and individualizing civic world (Musil, 1953–1960)), but the endemic propensity to centre the planning process around the core planning subject has never disappeared from the stage. The underlying structure is simple: there are aspirations to be achieved and problems to be solved in spatial interdependence, thus the planning subject is prompted to the organization of comprehensive spatial strategies of action. In the case of Dutch strategic planning, this was the prevailing attitude from the early 1960s until the 1990s. All strategic plans, instigated by public-led planning authorities, aimed to integrate the actions of other agents over space, not just in the here-and-now but over a range of years, and not just with a focus on spatial destination of activities but comprehending all public and private sector aspirations on the use of space, including the spatially relevant sector domains. The planning subject is considered as the centrepiece of all this activity. The problem is not the existence of a planning authority or the making of plans by this authority, the problem is in the positional fallacy of its subjectivism. The vulnerability of this sociological mechanism has been hidden for many years behind the veil of economic and social growth enduring in the arranging of the welfare state, but it was deemed to denude itself at an earlier or later date. The lack of credibility and supportive basis make this strategic planning subjectivism very fragile in times of urgency, as Vainer has elucidated in the case of Rio de Janeiro, where technocratic task-forces easily replaced the strategic plan with a focused commercial project development (Vainer, this volume).

Planning subjectivism is not similar to the centralization of planning competences and resources in the hands of one core planning subject (even in the wide reach of the Dutch case, the equipment of planning resources and capabilities at the central level is rather modest). Its expression is more subtle and more difficult to eradicate in the thought and action perspectives of spatial planning. The meaning of planning subjectivism can be better defined as the tendency to consider the planning subject as the centre of all action; it refers to the attitude of planner-centrism rather than being based on the centralization of capacities (Den Hoed et al., 1983). The planning subject thinks of being the centre of all action while in reality the world turns on its own. The persistence of this phenomenon might be explained by the continuous appeal of planning subjects to deal with urgent (future) problems and to design strategies for solutions. The progressive agenda of spatial planning is nurtured and triggered time after time by aspirations and by social needs and problems and not by a critical institutional reflection on the real position of the planning subject.

In most cases it is the governmental planning authority that takes the central position of planning subjectivism and starts proactively arranging and mobilizing social action (Faludi, 1995; Alexander, 1998; Albrechts, 2004), although in more mitigated practices the empirical appearance of the 'planning subject' is gradually enlarged in networks of agency, including stakeholders (also from private sector), and also endowed with strategies of participation. However, the mitigation of the pure model of planning subjectivism does not overcome the endemic subject-object structuration of the designing and mobilizing planning subject that is pursuing its constructions on an object: the world to be planned.

## Planning voluntarism

The second trap of planning modernism – closely related to the problem of planning subjectivism – is labelled 'planning voluntarism'. It is a style of planning led by the drive of politicians and/or planners to achieve certain aspirations of spatial coherence or spatial quality in a future situation. The normative drive to achieve a better future, obviously, is the quintessence of all spatial planning, although centring the full planning process around the ideals expressed by the planning subject is the Achilles' heel of this endeavour. The vulnerability of this voluntarism is not just in relying on ideals that reach further than planners' reach but, more specifically, in taking the sole normative point of view of the planning subject as the input of the process. The planning subject (be it the responsible politicians, the planning agency or a cooperative leading network representing selected agencies in the public and the private sector in a joint perspective of action) is taken for granted to perform a proactive role in the mobilization of political will by establishing the objectives, setting the frames and even the discourses of the process. A voluntarist planning subject is not activated by dynamic forces in society but departs from its own potential of activation and mobilization, using the tools of framing, persuasion and symbolic communication to seduce social actors to becoming involved. The space for manoeuvring in a 'voluntarist' way is relatively large in strategic spatial planning – in particular in the preparatory stage of open strategic planning – because the objectives are set on the scale of the long term and usually surpass the organized interests and power of particular actors. But the optimism of 'making plans work' in an overt setting of planning voluntarism and relying on its strategies of seduction (often promoted in communicative planning approaches) is often belied (Dembski and Salet, 2010).

Examples of planning voluntarism can be found not just at the level of the central state. There are plenty of examples of planning voluntarism in urban arenas dreaming of building the ultimate metropolis. Several contributions in this book demonstrated the fragile condition of national and metropolitan planning in a voluntarist style: it is simply neglected in the real decision-making processes of public and private sector actors (Vainer, Fedeli and Van den Broeck, all this volume; see also Balducci et al., 2011). The most vulnerable show the glamour projects parachuted in with the superb persuasive power of visualization (in an explosive combination of political and designer visualization of desired future states directing their mobilizing vector immediately to the senses of the masses). A recent example in metropolitan Amsterdam is the superb landscaping of a new 30-kilometre connection between Amsterdam and Almere, launched by the politicians responsible for the spatial planning of both cities in close cooperation with some of the most high-profile architects and landscapers in the country. While dimensioning a 5 billion euro bridge connection, which (as it turned out later in the mandatory cost–benefit analysis) would not even give structural added value to the network of public transportation, the designers addressed the claims of the estimated costs to the national Ministry of Infrastructure. One does not need prophetic insights to imagine the outcome of such an outspoken voluntarist project. However, the real impact of voluntarism is not in being too greedy and in reaching too far (visualizing a potential future state might give positive inspiration), but first of all in promoting and selecting the sole planning subject view and – even worse – in the consequent tunnelling of the full planning process towards the desired state, constraining in this way a serious consideration of alternative options (Salet et al., 2013). This style of planning and policy-making runs the risk of trapping the complete planning process in a voluntarist gaze. In the above mentioned case, this indeed became a crucial problem.

Having emphasized the bias and negative impact of planning voluntarism, one may also learn from successful experiences of proactive spatial planning, where agencies take a profiled stance but carefully consider their institutional position. Both Fedeli and Van den Broeck (both in this volume) demonstrated not just the failure of planning voluntarism, but also gave successful examples of normative strategic planning where the plans are carefully embedded in social and political contexts of continuing debate and are carried forward by active local configurations of civic groups and business circles. Fedeli mentioned the differentiation of metropolitan contexts, the one profiled by overwhelming economic interests and the other by social and civic groups. The strategic plans did not initiate these processes of planning but were brought forward (sometimes even as an antidote to statutory planning) from without these metropolitan contexts. However, even within this embeddedness, it appeared to be difficult to effectuate the strategic missions. Their function is sometimes more in visualizing perspectives than in guiding implementation (Fedeli, this volume). Also, Jef Van den Broeck emphasized the complexity of social context underlying successful strategic planning. In the case of Antwerp, it took 40 years of struggling until, at the end of 1990s, the strategic plan embodied the yeast of change that matched the moods of the time, enabling the urban processes to catalyze. Van den Broeck ascribes the success of this strategic plan to 'the taking of the momentum', in which all energies of a local society are in concordance (Van den Broeck, this volume).

Also, the Dutch case of strategic spatial planning (although often overstating their position) may elucidate some cases where the institutional position of strategic planning was carefully considered. Dutch spatial planning is institutionalized as a separate field in the intergovernmental and underlying societal relationships. Spatial planning is closely interconnected with other disciplines, such as infrastructure, housing, environmental policies, or agriculture, but the domains are organized separately. As such, spatial planning is lightly institutionalized, it is not equipped with strong financial resources and most of its legal powers only work via local spatial interventions. Also, with regards to the social embeddedness, the organization of interest and social power is more articulated in the provision of specific services, such as infrastructure, agriculture or real estate, than in the coordinating qualities of spatial planning. As a consequence, the positioning and the potential impact of spatial planning rest on being successfully linked with more activated and equipped societal and governmental powers. Information, coordination and persuasion do matter in this particular context. This goes in particular for the fragile strategic dimension of spatial planning. Here is a very thin and sensible demarcation between successful positioning and being simply neglected in the heavier-dimensioned surrounding domains.

There are some impressive examples of strategic connection with successful experience. The Greenheart planning strategy was successful at least for a number of years in keeping the landscapes within this dynamic part of the Randstad relatively open. National spatial strategies were relatively successful in spatially distributing social housing to peri-urban areas. The national spatial strategy was also successful in promoting the intercontinental main port development (the seaport, the airport and the green port). In all cases, the power of strategic persuasion and coordination needed the underlying support of more powerful interests to become effective. This is a very delicate specification. This is no longer planning subjectivism and also not planning voluntarism *per se*; it is a matter of meticulous conditioning founded on a very precise insight in the underlying principia media (the structuring principles) of society (which is expressed in manifold social practices, such as the investment in land use, social and political discourses, etc.). The case of the 'green heart' needed the combined power of major cities, which were promoting urban compactness and opposing the urbanization in their competitive outside areas, and agricultural interests to curb the urban expansion in their rural areas. The case of spatially distributing social housing was endorsed by the major cities and the expansive housing associations. The case of promoting main ports was a perfect fit at the beginning of the new liberal epoch in the early 1990s, stressing the international competitiveness of regional economic systems in a globalizing economy. While the infrastructure department was bounded to heavy sector interests and lacked the manoeuvring space to jump to a new level of international infrastructure policy, strategic spatial planning conquered the vacancy. Once accepted on the national agenda, the infrastructure powers took over control again. At the time of writing this chapter, one might have hoped that the need of structural social and economic transitions on behalf of a climate-proof development would endorse a revitalization of strategic planning. However, it should be carried forward by an active society; it never can rest on its own shoulders.

## Planning instrumentalism

The next trap is the inherent propensity towards increasing planning instrumentalism. This refers to the tendency to get more and more entangled in the claws of a closed end-means rationality without reflecting on the rules of social order in which the *métier* of spatial planning is embedded (Albrechts, 2010). Enduring the epochs of planning expansion in the 1970s and 1980s, the subtleties of the lightly institutionalized strategic spatial planning made room for increasing instrumentalism. In the contributions by Van den Broeck and Fedeli in this volume, it is highlighted how informal strategies of planning emerged in some metropolitan areas as an 'antidote' to statutory planning, but also strategic planning might be instrumentalized in states of advanced spatial planning. In the Netherlands, for instance, initially, the principle of subsidiarity was underlying the spatial planning law, enabling national strategic plans only a 'global' and 'indicative' status that needed the endorsement of social driving forces to subtly guide lower tiers of government and social action with perspectives, information and relatively soft indirect control. In practice, however, this subtle fabric of strategic guidance was gradually replaced by increasing central planning capacities and fixed policy instruments of direct control. The indicative guidelines in the national White Papers were amended by hundreds of detailed instruction and methods of implementation: the indicative programmes were implemented with intergovernmental and private law contracts précising the terms and time paths of agreement. Although still being lightly positioned in the wider societal order of social and intergovernmental relations, the quest for certainty of the prevailing ends-means rationality resulted in a cocoon type of bureaucratized spatial planning, radically at odds with the wider social order. The underlying principle of subsidiarity transfigured in fixated, contractualized, top-down trajectories of planning, and the indicative plans were elaborated in instrumental programmes. It is the dubious triumph of teleocratic articulation of spatial planning practice that is imprisoned in its lore of ends-means rationality and because of this, utilitarian fixation is not even aware of its displacement of the more complex underlying nomocratic order of a society (Rijswick and Salet, 2012; Moroni, 2015).

The negative implications of this lack of deliberation on institutional meaning are not immediately apparent. On the contrary, policy-makers and lobby groups usually insist on the progressive fixation of policy views and pathways of implementation in order to create more certainty about the realization of the aimed policy outcomes. However, circumstances change and political agreements are changeable over time: the ends-means fixations turn easily into obstacles of policy-making processes. The negative implications of planning instrumentalism have been demonstrated widely. In the Netherlands, the opaqueness of planning bureaucracy was one of the major reasons for recent governments to devolve the operations of spatial planning. Instrumental fixation, a lack of adaptability and increasing opaqueness of operations are not good recipes for survival. This also goes for the more heavily equipped fields of sector policies that have been devolved as well. But spatial planning suffered from the additional vulnerability that showing its instrumental muscle was highly at odds with its institutional position, not only within the governmental fabric but even more in society.

## The providence bias of spatial planning

The fourth structural flaw in planning modernism is its propensity to connect the governmental planning strategies with the public sector providence of what

Castells has labelled the 'collective consumption goods' (Castells, 1977). On the European continent, the postwar expansion of strategic spatial planning was highly correlated with the national establishment of the providing state. An example is the Dutch case of making this state a collaboration of the nationally organized non-profit producers of services and the national government ministries. The government agencies were deeply involved in the financial arrangements of the provision and, by impact, also in the detailing of the quantities, qualities and accessibilities of the collective consumption goods. National spatial planning expanded in the shadow of the mighty provision agreements made in the sector domains. It even pretended at a certain time to integrate the spatial distribution of services that were provided in the policy sectors. The crux of this strategy was the set of coordinating links with the providing arrangements of government agencies, which was supported by an integral coordinating spatial policy council, where the representatives of several departments prepared joint decisions.

Relying on this policy integration strategy of 'coupled interests', spatial planning indeed managed to amplify its organizational position for a certain time. Housing, infrastructure, and agriculture were powerful spending departments, and by underwriting the coupled interests with these interests, spatial planning became a part of the national powerhouse. However, the spatial planning strategies overstated their position in several ways. In the first place, they were too audacious in expecting the mighty sectors to comply with the spatial planning lines of policy integration. The sectors did not always consider the spatial aspects as the most important of their considerations, to put it mildly. In the second place, spatial planning became 'addicted' to the power of the coupling interests of the providing policies but neglected its relations with the underlying societal fields of space users and producers in an increasingly dynamic society. It had become a part of the technocratic providing state. This lack was revenged when, in the liberalizing 1990s, one sector after another was urged to liberalize the provision of collective consumption goods. The role of governmental providence changed into a role of (more or less) conditioning of the provision of these goods by the market. The spatial planners complained about the loss of 'coupling interests' while not realizing that they themselves had neglected to link with the real games of space users and producers in society. Spatial planning had lost contact on the ground. In the course of the 1990s the national spatial planners persisted in perceptions of the compact city while, on the ground, the market was already producing its own conditions of emerging urban decentralization and policentricity in urban peripheries. The national spatial reports were persisting with new compact urban regions and development axes between Schiphol Amsterdam and Almere, while the market already avoided Almere and sprawled its own spatial patterns around the airport and eastwards. The new spatial challenges of the in-between city are overt – also in the Netherlands of the last two decades – but they have never reached the national spatial planning agenda (Wouden, 2015).

## The turn into a new entrepreneurial style of planning

The crisis sealed the 'deconfiture' of spatial planning modernism in the Netherlands, but the analysis above has revealed that the roots of disarray are deeper and more far-reaching than the actual fluctuation of crisis and recent post-crisis. The withdrawal of modernist spatial planning opens ways for new and more (social-) entrepreneurial styles of planning and this is exactly the spirit that may be felt in the upcoming generation of young planners that are now leaving the planning schools. Spatial planning is reinventing itself in new inventive and entrepreneurial ways. Many initiatives are popping up, in particular at the local and regional levels of scale, in the decentralized climate of bottom-up initiatives, outside-in relationships and the grassroots of self-organization. What I consider as promising in the actual revival of entrepreneurial planning, however, is not the upcoming sociocracy as a replacement of the experiences of technocracy, not the abrupt fluctuation from regulation to initiatives of self-regulation, not the topical shift of 'moods of planning' that are moving from the one to the other side under fluctuating economic and political conditions, because spatial planning strategies will always have to navigate between aspects of both sides of the regulation and self-regulation dilemmas (Savini et al., 2015). What I consider as promising in the actual climate of spatial planning is the beginning of a change of attitudes with regards to the underlying principles that I have attempted to identify above. There are hopeful signs indeed of reinventing spatial planning as an act of reconstruction instead of modernist construction, endorsed by institutional reflection on the assumptions of the act of planning and its position in society. New entrepreneurial styles of planning that are no longer conditioned by the underlying structuration of 'subject–object relationships', planning practices that are no longer imprisoned in a 'voluntarist gaze' of fixated aims, and that no longer persevere in the 'propensity of instrumentalism' and no longer isolate the planning thought and action in the teleocratic 'provisional layer' of interventions.

The first and most important condition of this style of planning is the institutional awareness that the spatial planning subject is not the centrepiece of action. Obviously, the spatial planner – governmental or not – has a normative stake in processes of action, an engaged planner does not hold a neutral position. He or she cares for the legacy of spatial quality which is context-bounded and integrative. At the same time, however, the spatial planning subject is not the agent of change. There are many initiators of change within the society and within the governmental fabric and the spatial planning subject is not in a position to arrange or to mobilize the occurrences of change. Rather, he might be mobilized himself by powerful forces in society, at least in cases where he is taken seriously. Not being the mobilizer of change, the planning subject must take care first of all to give act of presence in all spatial relevant situations where major initiatives of action in space are taken or are under preparation. Already, this anticipating condition is a dramatic change compared to the prevailing state of postwar planning modernism. Going where the action is instead of following the envisioned plans of action is a more fundamental change than usually is realized. The contribution by Olesen and Metzger in this volume gave an impression of this type of change. Also, the case of strategic planning in the Netherlands may elucidate the fundamental differences. As indicated above, the Dutch spatial planners and designers since the early 1990s are following the envisioned lines of urbanization of the last spatial plans (following, for instance, the developments on the axis Schiphol–Almere) while being absent in the real processes of urbanization in the in-between city dynamics of market development. The real processes of urbanization and the new crucial challenges entailed herein with regards to a sustainable development and mobility in fragmentary peripheral spaces, are simply neglected. 'Going where the action is' would imply following where the dynamic investments in built-up areas are going: the investments by the private sector or the investments and conditions shaped by policy sectors. These are not investments in spatial planning objectives but functional investments with large unplanned spatial implications, such as changing investment in economic technology, real estate, water safety, energy transition, infrastructures, horticulture, food, health.

Functional investment in space is following its own autonomous logic and often is not even interested in possible implications for the aimed spatial order. The recent national agreement on energy transition in the Netherlands (with huge implications for the uses of space) does not once mention spatial implications; the recent water plans aiming at water safety and water quality (a long-term project of some 30 billion euro) mentions only marginally the meaning of space; private investments in real estate or technology usually do not consider spatial implications; infrastructure investment (for instance, highways) is highly mono-functional. The act of spatial reconstruction starts here: being present on the spot first, jumping on the bandwagon of initiatives next, and only then starts the struggle of spatial integration with making visible the spatial implications of different trajectories of investment. In the search of integrative trajectories, real spatial qualities are invented *in situ*, in the specificity of context, while being related to more general norms of spatial quality. The search has to be focused on the invention of contextual qualities of space in relation to general conditions and rules of spatial order. The latter requires a set of general conditions established by central and regional governments which is not always adequately available because of the focus of the modernist planning tradition on the making of its own plans and instruments instead of conditioning the action of others. Finally, the most challenging step of the entrepreneurial style of spatial reconstruction is the legitimation and effectuation in action. Effective realization of this planning is all but evident, the spatial planning subject has to prove the added value of its spatial reconstruction in order to be taken on board. Spatial interventions have specific capacities and other auxiliaries at their disposal, but if the added value of the aimed spatial reconstruction is not convincing, its effectuation will be very unlikely. The legitimation and effectuation of new spatial planning have to be conquered in action (Salet et al., 2015).

It is fascinating to observe that the turn to planning as reconstruction is inducing the start of planning thought and action precisely in those actions and investments that were most disliked in the modernist tradition of planning (Woltjer, 2008). Indeed, the elevation of dykes, the expansion of seaport areas in the sea, the settlements of windmills, the enlargement of infrastructure such as highways, the expansion of green houses in urbanized regions, and the peripheral investment of housing and real estate are not much liked in the postwar spatial envisioning of future plans in the Netherlands. The new entrepreneurial style of planning, however, has discovered these real investments as the new frontlines of planning where the struggle for spatial quality is situated. The functional initiatives are no longer the impediments of the envisioning plans but the opportunities to prove added qualities of spatial integration.

The landscapers took the lead in the practical experiments of the new planning strategies. Being eradicated in the national planning of the modernist dream of idealized landscapes, such as the perspective for 'the main national structure of ecological landscape' (the national agency of nature development is now radically devolved), the landscape planners jumped on the bandwagon of the huge initiatives for water adaptation as a result of the changing climate. The Sachzwänge of water safety and water quality as a result of the raising levels of water in the rivers, the sea, and the inner lake of the Netherlands has urged huge investments in strengthening the dykes and flood defences. Local and regional landscaping planners jumped on this bandwagon and very successfully managed to integrate the functional initiatives with objectives of nature, recreation, agriculture, and increasingly urban functions. As a result, the highly contested abrupt flooding defences, such as high and steep dykes, have been avoided and a high differentiation of locally contextualized solutions have been reinvented along the rivers, the coast and in the Ijsselmeer (such as in the successful 'space for the river' programmes, the sand supplements and multi-functional flood defences along the coast). As a result, the spatial and landscaping quality of these spaces has improved dramatically. The recent water landscape planning is widely considered as one of the most convincing successes of Dutch spatial planning.

Similar strategies of planning are starting in different fields where economic or social investment is unfolding but are yet embryonic. Energy saving and energy transition are considered as a huge challenge which is already going on in market de-investment and new investment and in sector policies. The same goes for changing investments in food or health, and for infrastructure and real estate (Salet et al., 2015). In the current planning debate, one of the questions is whether planning should withdraw to this 'back hand' position of re-acting on initiatives in society instead of a proactive anticipation and design of envisioned spatial future plans. Undoubtedly, spatial planning should not withdraw from the national level; it has a 'system responsibility'. This responsibility should be translated in general legal conditions and indeed (why not) in a revival of occasional indicative national planning perspectives. However, before thinking of taking proactive spatial planning roles at the national level, spatial planners must understand first that planning as re-construction is not a back hand strategy but the real forehand that enables legitimation and effectiveness in real perspectives of action.

# References

Albrechts, L., 2004. Strategic (spatial) planning reexamined. *Environment and Planning B: Planning and Design*, 31(5), 743–758.

Albrechts, L., 2010. More of the same is not enough. *Environment and Planning B*, 37(6), 1115–1127.

Alexander, E. R., 1998. Planning and implementation: Coordinative planning in practice. *International Planning Studies* 3(3), 303–320.

Balducci, A., Fedeli, V. and Pasqui, G., 2011. *Strategic planning for contemporary urban regions. City of cities: A project for Milan*. Aldershot: Ashgate.

Campbell, H. J., Tait, M. A. and Watkins, C. A , 2013. Is there space for better planning in a neo-liberal world? Implications for planning practice and theory. *Journal of Planning Education and Research*, 34(1), 45–59.

Castells, M., 1977. *The urban question*. London: Arnold.

Dembski, S. and Salet, W., 2010. The transformative potential of institutions: How symbolic markers can institute new social meaning in changing cities. *Environmental Planning A*, 42(3), 611–625.

Faludi, A., 1995. Framing with images. *Environment and Planning B*, 23, 93–108.

Faludi, A. and van der Valk, A., 1994. *Rule and order: Dutch planning doctrine in the twentieth century*. Dordrecht: Kluwer.

Geppert, A., 2015. Planning without a spatial development perspective? The French case. In Knaap, G. J., Nedovic-Budic, Z. and Carbonell, A. (Eds), *Planning for states and nation-states in the US and Europe*. Cambridge, MA: Lincoln Institute of Land Policy, pp. 381–410.

Hoed, P. den, Salet, W. and van der Sluijs, H., 1983. *Planning als onderneming*. V33 WRR. The Hague: Staatsuitgeverij.

Jones, M. and Ward, K., 2002. Excavating the logic of British urban policy: Neoliberalism and the 'crisis of crisismanagement'. *Antipode*, 34(3), 473–494.

Lord, A. and Tewdwr-Jones, M., 2014. Is planning 'under attack'? Chronicling the deregulation of urban and environmental planning in England. *European Planning Studies*, 22(2), 345–361.

Moroni, S., 2015. Complexity and the inherent limits of explanation and prediction: Urban codes for self-organising cities. *Planning Theory*, 14(3), 248–267.

Musil, R., 1953–1960. *The man without qualities*. London: Secker & Warburg.

Peck, J. and Tickell, A., 2002. Neo-liberalizing space. *Antipode*, 34(3), 380–404.

Sager, T., 2011. Neoliberal urban planning policies: A literature survey 1990–2010. *Progress in Planning*, 76(4), 380–404.

Rijswick, M. van and Salet, W., 2012. Enabling the contextualization of legal rules in responsive strategies to climate change. *Ecology and Society*, 17(2), nr. 18.

Salet, W., Bertolini, L. and Giezen, M., 2013. Complexity and uncertainty: Problem or asset in decision-making of mega infrastructure projects. *International Journal of Urban and Regional Research*, 37(6), 1984–2000.

Salet, W., Vermeulen, R. and van der Wouden, R., 2015. *Toevoegen van Ruimtelijke Kwaliteit*. Amsterdam: Advies Ruimtelijke Onderzoeksinstituten in het Jaar van de Ruimte.

Savini, F., Salet, W. and Majoor, S., 2015. Dilemmas of planning: Intervention, regulation, and investment. *Planning Theory*, 14(3), 333–348.

Woltjer, J., 2008. Strategic spatial planning and planning evaluation: Developing an entrepreneurial urbanization strategy in South-Holland. In Hull, A., Khakee, D. and Woltjer, J. (Eds), *New principles in planning and evaluation*. Aldershot: Ashgate, pp. 201–219.

Wouden, R. van der, 2015. *De ruimtelijke metamorfose van Nederland 1988–2015*. Rotterdam: Publicatie Planbureau voor de Leefomgeving. Nai010/ PBL.

Zonneveld, W. and Evers, D., 2014. Dutch national spatial planning at the end of an era. In Reimer, M., Getimis, P. and Blotevogel, H. H. (Eds), *Spatial planning systems and practices in Europe: A comparative perspective on continuity and changes*. New York/ Abingdon: Routlegde, pp. 61–82.

# Part 3

# Epilogue

# 24 Some ingredients for revisiting strategic spatial planning

## *Louis Albrechts*

Our book explores the circulation of strategic planning ideas and practices. The cases, in their diversity, mirror the various ways of thinking about strategic planning to be found in world-wide practices. Many ideas, although often formed in response to very particular problems in specific contexts, have spread beyond national borders through networks created by academics, professionals and by political and economic relationships (see Healey and Upton, 2010; Gonzáles, 2011). Almost all of the chapters in this book illustrate that it is often unclear where ideas, concepts, approaches, techniques have come from, and yet they get to be used in particular contexts that remain unique in their specific configuration.

The purposes for embarking on strategic planning are diverse: economic development (most cases), controlling urban sprawl (France), planning reform (Italy), flooding (Vancouver), political integration geared at macro-economic issues (East Africa), economic restructuring and institutional reform (China), change in the political landscape (France, Italy, South Africa), industrial decline (Øresund), legal obligation (Antwerp), availability of funding bodies – the European Union, international aid agencies, higher tier government funding programmes – (Italy, France, Øresund), competition, branding of cities (China, Øresund), addressing the transcalar dimension of problems and transformation processes with the rising relevance of metropolitan governance (Australia, Pearl River Delta, Johannesburg, France), nation building (Wales), rapid urban development, managing growth (Vancouver), coordination of strategies/issues/policies between territories that are institutionally distinct but interdependent in functional terms (Øresund, metropolitan planning in Australia, city-regions in France, experimentation with the metropolitan level in Italy and Vancouver – all covered in this volume).

It is also clear that strategic planning does not work on its own. It needs change agents – what Kingdon (2003) has described as 'policy entrepreneurs' (a champion in the terminology of Bryson, 1995) – to take the approach and deploy it, as exemplified by strong mayors in Italy, Johannesburg, party officials in China, a minister and a chief planning officer in Wales, and a planning director in Vancouver. Ideas allow policy-makers to construct frames with which to legitimize their policy proposals. Ideas also facilitate policy-making action, not just by serving as road maps but also by providing concepts (see the framing idea of livability in Vancouver and balancing economic growth with redistribution in Johannesburg), symbols (see Wales) and other discursive schema that actors can use (Sevillo, this volume; see also Sorensen, 2010: 120).

Most strategic planning processes react against perceived shortcomings of statutory planning. In China, for example, statutory planning carries the legacy from the planned economy. For other cases it is a lack of political, economic and environmental consideration, rigidity of planning methods, incapability to deal with uncertainty, to tackle flexibility, the view of space as a container that holds objects inside with distinctive physical and administrative boundaries (Egypt, in this volume), the fact that statutory plans serve only (mainly) as binding documents to obtain building permits. So in other words, statutory plans serve the purpose of both generating a conception of a place and the locales within it and of defining the legal and spatial parameters within which rights to develop sites and properties are developed (see also Vigar *et al.*, 2005: 1408). The chapters by Searle and Abdelwahab and Serag (in this volume) illustrates that the boundary between strategic and statutory planning may not be clear-cut (see also Mäntysalo, 2013). The most important factor in the tensions between strategic planning and statutory planning is the extent to which strategic planning has statutory status. The critical question in this respect is whether the content of a strategic plan is binding for actors (public and private) (see Searle, this volume). In some places (see China, Italy, Egypt, Antwerp, in this volume) strategic planning has been able to interact with statutory planning in different ways (in China, as an input for master planning preparation; in Antwerp, as a frame for implementation plans). As the LRSP 1996 in Vancouver proved to be very difficult to change, Vancouver 2040 became a stronger and more detailed statutory plan on agreed regional interests but more flexible and adaptable compared to the previous plan (Abbott and DeMarco, this volume). The statutory South East Queensland Regional Plan 2005/2009 sets dwelling targets that offer some flexibility for local plans. The Welsh Infrastructure Plan was prepared in order to cater for those actors in search of more certainty to justify their investments (Sartorio, this volume).

The influence of strategic planning works through multiple processes in which the relevant actors can see an opportunity to use strategic planning to push forward a policy change (see Sorensen, 2010: 133). For instance, dominant models are reimagined as smoke screens behind which agendas of privatization can be implemented (see Rio de Janeiro) and recommendations from international consultants are often de-contextualized (Wu, 2007: 390). For Vainer (this volume; see also Vainer, 2000) and Leal de Oliveira (2000), the Barcelona model has opened up a door in Rio for a discriminatory use of strategic planning, with a focus on more corporate-friendly techniques and mega urban projects (see also Gonzáles, 2011: 1412). In this sense, it can be considered as an interesting counter-case. Contracting strategic plans to external consultants is a means to enhance publicity for prestigious projects and to market the city (Wu, 2007). All the cases make it clear that actors interpret strategic planning differently and will adopt those aspects of the approach which they perceive as best fitting their own situation. This may be a choice of elements that increase the credibility of government intentions that promise to solve some problems and can be implemented or reinterpreted within the frameworks of existing planning tools (see Wu, 2007; Healey and Upton, 2010).

All the cases demonstrate that every situation in which strategic planning is carried out needs some understanding of the contextual factors (political, institutional, legal), some grasp of who the key actors are, the size and power of the strategic and statutory planning agencies (see Searle, this volume), and what networks are in play and how these relate to local social, economic and political dynamics (see Healey, 2010: 14).

The consensus process in Vancouver forced regional growth strategies into a more general and less regulatory format in order to be acceptable to all municipalities. Wider community and citizens involvement occurs through open houses, focus groups (Vancouver), formal public hearings (Vancouver, Antwerp, the UK), and theatre and art performances (Antwerp). Many strategic plans become elitist as they promote certain rationalities and logics which resonate very little with the experiences of most ordinary citizens (China, Øresund, Rio, East Africa; see also Salet in this volume). Many cases indicate that strategic planning evolves in phases (waves), from enhancing competitiveness to transformation in China; new and mainstream innovation in Italy; from detailed land use to broad frameworks for statutory planning in Australia; and incubation, maturation and re-invigoration in Johannesburg. Plans are considered strategic in the sense of enlarging intelligence by actors (municipalities, sectors, private actors, etc.), learning to work together, to think at different scale levels (metropolitan, regional, municipal, community) (Vancouver, Antwerp, China, the USA), enlarging the scope and policy boundaries of planning. Strategic planning processes introduce new planning concepts (livability, Vancouver, Milan). Given the tight deadline of Strategic planning (see China), there is a danger that Strategic planning introduces new concepts without rigorous research (Wu, 2007: 390).

In several cases a tension emerges between flexibility (favoured by planners) and certainty (favoured by politicians and developers) (Searle, Mäntysalo and Grišakov, and Hillier in this volume; see also Friend and Jessop (1969)).

As mentioned in the Introduction to Part 1 of this book, the critiques in general, and more specifically in this volume, focus on very different registers of the strategic spatial planning approach. Economic-political ideological critiques draw a link between the rise of strategic spatial planning and a strengthened neo-liberal political climate (for most cases in the book; see also Cerreta *et al.*, 2010; Olesen, 2011, 2012; Olesen and Richardson, 2012). They reflect the fear that the ideal of strategic spatial planning could be easily used to favour highly aggressive neo-liberal models of urban and regional development (Vainer, this volume; see also Vainer, 2000; Leal de Oliveira, 2000; Cerreta *et al.*, 2010: x; Olesen, 2011; Sager, 2013). The South African case is interesting in this respect. It shows positive results but concludes that it is not (yet?) fully in line with the more radical strategic planning. Salet (this volume) observes a downgrading of strategic planning (mainly at the national and regional level) in a number of states and regions (the UK, France, the Netherlands, Denmark). In other places strategic planning is on the rise (China, Italy, France, the USA, Australia, Flanders).This may (in part) be explained by its usefulness to political decision-making (the USA, China, Italy), or simply because it seems to work (Bryson and Schively Slotterback in this volume; see some Italian cities).

## In search for the added value of strategic planning and for ingredients to revisit strategic planning

A growing literature on strategic planning and a critical dissection of strategic planning processes and their normative stance reveal key elements which may underpin 'successful' strategic planning. I translate these key elements in a more abstract way into a composite set of criteria that may make it possible to revive strategic planning. These critical features (see also Healey, 2009; Albrechts and Balducci, 2013; Albrechts, 2013, 2015; Bryson and Schively Slotterback, this volume) should be seen as conditions, or ingredients, to be aimed for, although I realize they can never be fully achieved. I organize them into five relevant dimensions: (1) context, (2) becoming, (3) space–time geographies, (4) content, and (5) legitimacy.

### Context: sensitive to the political, economic and institutional environment

#### Political and institutional context

The cases illustrate that the context forms the setting of the strategic planning process but also takes form and undergoes changes in the process (see also Dyrberg, 1997). For some, strategic planning needs a specific political and institutional context (Johannesburg, this volume; see also UN-Habitat, 2009; Olesen and Richardson, 2012: 1690; and Needham, 2000 for success factors) and is sensitive to specific intellectual traditions. Therefore, the capacity of a strategic spatial planning system to deliver the desired outcomes is dependent not only on the legal-political system itself, but also on the conditions underlying it. This demands a contextual understanding of power dynamics (see Salet, this volume) and material interests, of (leading) discourses and the constraints of a more-of-the-same, business-as-usual attitude (Mäntysalo and Grišakov, and Servillo, both in this volume; and see also proposition 4 by Huxley and Yiftachel, 2000: 339). In most cases one can witness neo-liberal attempts to create competitive cities and regions by generating investments (see also Marshall, 2000; Swyngedouw *et al.*, 2002; Monclús, 2003; Gonzáles, 2011; Olesen and Richardson, 2012: 1692). Such investments (projects) have become a key component of a neo-liberal shift from distributive policies, welfare considerations and direct service provision towards more market-oriented and market-dependent approaches aimed at pursuing economic promotion and competitive restructuring (Vainer, this volume; see also Leal de Oliveira, 2000; Swyngedouw *et al.*, 2002: 572).

A major challenge in strategic planning consists of the dialectic between movements that seek democratization, collective decision-making and empowerment of citizens on the one hand and the established institutions and structures that seek to reabsorb such demands into a distributive framework on the other (see also Young, 1990: 90). A crucial element in this respect is the way in which people are excluded or included in strategic planning processes and the way the relationship between people – technologies of government, norms of self-rule (Roy, 2009) – are organized. The question concerning who is to be considered an actor in a particular context or situation is not only an epistemological challenge, but also a fundamentally ontological issue (Metzger, 2012: 782). In all cases one finds a very wide variety of actors engaged in strategic planning practices (see all the cases in this volume; see also Leal de Oliveira, 2000; Vainer, 2000; Albrechts, 2006): city, regional, and national governments, sector departments, agencies, banks, universities, chambers of commerce, trade unions, associations of entre-preneurs, cultural organizations, civic associations, consumer organizations, in addition to individual citizens. Searle (this volume) stresses the benefits of involving statutory planning agencies in strategic planning processes. It is impor-tant that strategic planning connects with the dynamic of society. The involve-ment of citizens is often regarded as an attack on the legitimacy of political institutions as it reverses and upsets the relationship between the state and its citizens. It is clear that the representative government articulates merely political and not all values. If we accept that representative democracy is not a single completed thing but that it is capable of 'becoming' in a new context and in rela-tion to new issues at hand, then we may conclude that a more major direct involvement of citizens (see Albrechts, 2013, 2015 on coproduction) does not reject representative democracy but complements it. It adds to the fullness of concrete human content, to the genuineness of community links (see Zizek, 1992: 163 about the very notion of democracy). The narrative of a more radical strategic planning is a narrative of emancipation: it fulfils a legitimating function, and it legitimates social and political institutions and practices, forms of legislation, ethics, modes of thought and symbolism. It grounds this legitimacy not in an original founding act but in a future to be brought about, that is, an idea to realize. This idea (of equity, fairness, social justice) has legitimating value because it is universal (see Lyotard, 1992: 50).

## From visioning as an extended present towards visioning as becoming

### Envisioning

Envisioning does not claim to eliminate uncertainty through the making of predictions; rather, it seeks to work as well as possible within the context of uncertainty (with scenarios like China, this volume), and to enable the actors to open up the spectrum of possibilities – to push the bounds of possibility (Abbott and DeMarco, this volume), and to frame the scope of possibilities (Mäntysalo and Grišakov, this volume). This will raise uncertainties for those involved in the process (see Abbott, 2005: 481). Envisioning is, above all, a state of mind (imagination and anticipation) that leads to behaviour (hope and will) (see Godet, 2001: 8). In the final analysis, it must come back to what 'is' if it wants to present ideas and concepts that are solid, workable and of testable value. To get to these ideas, it needs both the solidity of the analysis and the creativity of the design of alternative futures. In a similar way, Mäntysalo and Grišakov (this volume) argue that 'the knowledge produced in scenario planning is rather based on *stories* that are able to integrate convincingly the future extensions of known development trends with imagined future possibilities'. Since envisioning is also the journey and not just the destination – the Plan is the Process (Abbott and DeMarco, this volume) – and as visions are so central to transformation and so all-invasive, it cannot be confined to a single actor or institution in the process. The values and images of what a society wants to achieve are not generated in isolation, but rather are socially constructed and are given meaning and validated by the traditions of belief and practice; they are reviewed, reconstructed, and invented through collective experience (see Ozbekhan, 1969; but also Foucault, 1980: 11; Hillier, 1999; Elchardus et al., 2000: 24). Ideas and concepts need to be able to travel into different contexts to change the dominant culture. Envisioning is linked to values, to choices, and therefore it is far from neutral. This highlights the ideological role that envisioning may play, and the danger of manipulation that is inherent in the process. The danger of manipulation should decrease if envisioning is accessible to everyone, i.e. if all those concerned can participate, and not only the planners and the leadership (see Godet, 2001).

*Becoming*

Becoming is the ability to cope with action, movement, emergence, relationship, and creative experimentation. Based on dynamic, undetermined relations between entities which are themselves not entirely determinable (Hillier in this volume), becoming produces, in a non-linear way, visions and frames of reference. It provokes a shift from an ontology of being, which privileges the outcome and end state, towards an ontology of becoming, in which actions, movement, relationships, process, and emergence are emphasized (Chia, 1995: 601, 1999: 215; Hillier 2011). Strategic planning thus becomes an activity whereby (taking structural constraints into account) that which might become is envisioned or mapped, for the purpose of assisting the transformation of what is into what it might become. This requires a change to the status quo of planning culture. The world of planning and planners will inevitably become more complicated and messy. However, it is in making planning issues and approaches messy – equity, social justice versus the daily decisions of individual actors – that transformative practices can take place (see also Campbell, 2002: 351). The cases in this volume illustrate that the surrounding political regime and the social and cultural context enhance or inhibit the cultural institutional changes needed for transformative change (see also Inch's work in the UK (Inch, 2010)).

*Building uncertainty and indeterminacy into the strategic planning process*

Unlike land-use planning, strategic planning does not claim to eliminate uncertainty through making predictions; rather, it seeks to work as well as possible with uncertainty, and to enable the actors to open up the spectrum of possibilities. Planning practitioners, politicians and citizens need to think beyond the customary job descriptions, conventional knowledge, and traditional government structures in order to address the problems in new ways and to accept that the past is not a blueprint for how to go forward. Arenas create formal places where new approaches, new concepts, ways of acting and ways of valuing are introduced, discussed, understood and transformed. Actors in a strategic process need a mindset that is willing to explore new concepts and new ideas and to look for alternatives. Indeterminacy underlies the construction of scientific knowledge (see Mäntysalo and Grišakov, this volume) as well as the wider social world (Wynne, 1992, cited by Hillier, this volume). The main distinction/difference between uncertainty and indeterminacy is that with uncertainty the main parameters are known and there is some idea of probabilities, while with indeterminacy networks/assemblages are open and contingent, events are unpredictable and there are unknown unknowns (Hillier, this volume). In this way, indeterminacy is more in line with our concept of future(s) that transcends mere feasibility and that results from judgements and choices formed, in the first place, with reference to the idea of 'desirability', to the idea of 'betterment' and to the practice of the good society (Friedmann, 1982) but not on a singular model of the latter (Healey, 2010: 47). In strategic planning, these concepts have a 'generative capacity', allowing them to be (re)created in different ways to work within existing and emerging policy frameworks (see Faludi, 2001; Abrahams, 2013). Several cases indicate that creating particular future states is an act of choice involving valuation, judgement and the making of decisions that relate to the selection of perceived appropriate means for going forward.

## Space–time geographies: from stable entities towards many space–time geographies

### Relational in nature

Most of the cases in this book illustrate that it is impossible to understand material places and social nodes such as 'the city', 'the city-region' and 'the region' in terms of a one-dimensional hierarchy of scales (see also Healey, 2007: 267). Strategic spatial planning focuses on place-specific qualities and assets (social, cultural, and intellectual, including physical and social qualities of the urban or regional tissue) in a global context – see the process of exchange and the local endogenous development of narratives in Wales (Sartorio, this volume). In a strategic planning process it is important to think in terms of relations between issues/actors/scales rather than seeing each actor/issue/scale level either in isolation or as merely integrated (Hillier, this volume). In this way, the objects/issues with which society engages are not 'things' *per se*, but are rather an interconnecting set of shifting relations in which action is undertaken not only based on the identification and engagement with materialities, but also on an awareness of divergent understandings, such as, say, different professional codes or local norms (Chia and Holt, 2006: 649).

The term 'spatial' brings into focus the 'where' of things, whether static or dynamic; the creation and management of special 'places' and sites; the inter-relations between different activities and networks; and significant intersections and nodes that may be physically co-located (Healey, 2004: 46). A focus on spatial territorial relations allows for a more effective way of integrating differ ent agendas (economic, environmental, cultural, social, and policy agendas). As these agendas have a variable reach, they also carry a potential for a 'rescaling' of issue agendas down from the global, continental, national, or regional, and up from the municipal scale (see France, Italy, Vancouver, and China in this volume). Places become both the text and context of new debates about fundamental socio-spatial relations, about *thinking without frontiers* (Friedmann, 2011: 69), providing new kinds of practices and narratives about belonging to and being involved in the construction of a place and in society at large (see also Holston, 1995; Yiftachel, 2006; Watson, 2011). The search for new multi-scales of policy articulation and new policy concepts is also linked to attempts to widen the range of actors involved in policy processes, with new alliances, actor partnerships, and consultative processes (Albrechts *et al.*, 2001, 2003; Healey *et al.*, 1997).

In the different cases in this book actors discover layers of stakes (see also Healey, 1997: 69, 91–92; Healey, 2006: 542) that consist of existing, but perhaps as-yet unconscious interests, in the fate of their city, their region. Hence the need for strategies that treat the territory of the urban not just as a container in which things happen, but as a complex mixture of nodes and networks, places and flows, in which multiple relations, activities and values co-exist, interact, combine, conflict, oppress and generate creative synergy (see also Healey, 2007: 1).

### Content: selective and action/project-oriented

The strategic planning processes in the cases in this book aim for different products: visions, frames, policies, plans and concrete actions that accept the full complexity of a place while focusing on local assets and networks in a global context. Few cases (see Johannesburg, Wales, Portland, Vancouver) aim for social justice, spatial quality, and a fair distribution of the joys and burdens. In some places, the process of 'discourse structuralization' and its subsequent 'institutionalization' becomes perhaps more important than the plan as such (Hajer, 1995; Albrechts, 1999, 2003; Albrechts and Van den Broeck, 2004; Balducci *et al.*, 2011). In this way, new discourses may become institutionalized, i.e. embedded in the norms, attitudes and practices, thus providing a basis for challenging current ways of doing and for structural change (see Servillo, this volume).

*Selectivity*

Much of the process, which is inherently political in nature, lies in making tough decisions about what is most important for the purpose of producing just, structural responses to problems, challenges, aspirations, and potential (see Wales, Portland, Johannesburg in this volume). Thus, strategic planning involves choice, valuation, judgement, and decisions that relate to envisioned agreed-upon ends (Vancouver) and to the selection of the most appropriate means, not in a purely instrumental sense, for coping with and implementing such ends. In strategic planning, the overall picture that inspires choices is not given by a comprehensive analysis, but rather by a synthetic long-term vision (see Mäntysalo and Grišakov, this volume). Futures must symbolize some perceived and desired 'good', some qualities, and some virtues (diversity, sustainability, equity, livability, inclusiveness, accountability – see Portland, Vancouver, Wales, Johannesburg) that the present lacks. Speaking of sustainability, spatial quality, virtues, and values are a way of describing the type of place people want to live in, or think they should live in. Where statutory planning ends up – as a result of its legal status – in a closed system, the political potential of strategic planning lies in its dimension to broaden the scope of the possible and imagine the impossible. This implies the development of relational, more-than-human perspectives as a way to broaden the concepts used (see Metzger, 2014).

*Strategic planning is action- or project-oriented*

Traditional spatial planning is concerned with the production of plans as a reaction to problems, challenges or just as a reaction to something people want to achieve. Strategic spatial planning relates to the pattern of purposes, policy statements, frames, plans, programmes, actions (short-, medium- and long-term), decisions and resource allocation (see Abbott and DeMarco, Sartorio, Searle and Maginn *et al.* in this volume) that define what a policy is in practice, what it does, and why it does it – from the point of view of the various affected publics (Bryson and Crosby, 1992: 296). This stresses the need to find effective connections between political authorities and implementation actors (planning officers, individual citizens, community organizations, private corporations, developers and public departments) (Hillier, 2002; Albrechts, 2003). Most actors will not go on the long march unless they see compelling evidence, within a reasonable period of time, that the process is producing acceptable results. Therefore, short-term results are needed to build the credibility needed to sustain efforts over the long haul and to help test visions against concrete conditions (Kotter, 1996; Kotter and Rathgeber, 2005). But a strategic planning process should not maximize short-term results at the expense of the future. It means that strategic planning implies moving from episodic to continuous change (Chia and Tsoukas, 2003; Kotter, 2008: 17; Chia, 2011).

**Output**

In most statutory plans (the UK is an exception), the relationship between policy and control is expected to be determined through a binding detailed land-use plan. In strategic planning the focus on becoming produces quite a different picture from traditional planning in terms of:

- *Products*: strategic plans/policies, frames, strategies versus master plans or land-use plans. Land-use planning is basically concerned – in an integrated and qualitative way – with the location, intensity, form, amount, and harmonization of land development required for the various space-using functions: housing, industry, recreation, transport, education, nature, agriculture, cultural activities. Strategic planning produces visions to frame problems, challenges, and short-term actions within a revised democratic tradition (Albrechts, 2004).
- *Type of planning*: providing frameworks and justification for specific actions (a geography of the unknown; see Albrechts, 2006) versus technical or legal regulation geared at promising legal certainty for landowners, investors and developers (see the cases in this volume).
- *Type of governance*: government-led versus a government-led but co-productive forms of governance (see Harrison, Sartorio, Bryson and Schively Slotterback in this volume). Co-production is constructed as an inclusive and multi-vocal arena, that is grounded in a deeper understanding of the complex dynamics of urban and regional relations (see Healey, 2006: 541) where value systems can be articulated, local and scientific knowledge (see Mäntysalo and Grišakov on the dominating role of evidence-based knowledge; see also Servillo and Balducci, all this volume) can be combined on an equal base, shared strategic conviction can grow, and conflicts are reframed in a less antagonistic manner (see Albrechts, 2015: 515).

## Legitimacy

In some cases (China, in particular, this volume), strategic planning is inside the planning system but outside the legal system. Owing to their (mainly) non-statutory status (see cases in this volume), questions are raised about the kind of legitimacy of strategic planning processes (see Mazza, 2013: 40). Legitimacy is not only a procedural problem (who decides), but also a substantive problem (the link between strategic planning and statutory planning; see Searle, this volume). For Mazza (2011, 2013) and Mäntysalo (2013), the possible detachment of strategic spatial planning from the statutory planning system into an informal parallel system would pose a serious legitimacy problem. Rather than detaching strategic from statutory planning, Mäntysalo (2013: 51) identifies strategic planning as a planning framing the statutory-strategic planning relationship. In line with Friedmann (2004: 56), he argues that, as a consequence, the object of strategic planning should not be on the production of plans themselves (not even strategic ones) but on the production of insights of prospective change and in encouraging public debates on them. It is a way of probing the future in order to make more intelligent and informed decisions in the present (Friedmann, 2004: 56; Mäntysalo and Grišakov, this volume). The strategic probing of future uncertainties frames the fixing of 'certainties' in the present. The non-statutory nature of most strategic planning experiences makes them more flexible and less constrained by existing planning regulations and seems, for some commentators, to act as a structural antidote against marked standardization (see Sartorio, 2005; Balducci, 2008). For others, the product may consist of a critical analysis of the main processes and structural constraints shaping our places, which amounts to realistic, dynamic, integrated, and indicative long-term visions (frames), plans for short-term and long-term actions, a budget, and flexible strategies for implementation. It constitutes a commitment or (partial) (dis)agreement between the key actors. Apart from legitimacy stemming from a representative mandate, for protagonists of a more radical strategic planning (Albrechts, 2013, 2015) legitimacy may come from performance of strategic planning as a creative and innovative force and its capacity to deliver positive outcomes and actually gaining benefits.

## To conclude

The theory and practices of strategic planning, as examined in this book, demonstrate that strategic planning involves content and process, statics and dynamics, constraints and aspirations, the cognitive and the collective, the planned and the learned, the socio-economic and the political, the public and the private, the vision and the action, the local and the global, legitimacy and a revised democratic tradition, values and facts, selectivity and integrativity, equality and power, the long term and the short term.

Strategic spatial planning, both in the short term and the long term, focuses on results and implementation by framing decisions, actions and projects, and it incorporates monitoring, evaluation, feedback, adjustment and revision (see Bryson and Schively Slotterback, this volume). It invents or creates policies and practices in relation to the context and to the social and cultural values to which a particular place or society is historically committed as something new rather than as a solution arrived at as a result of existing trends.

The cases examined in this volume illustrate that in some places actors are receptive, finding real value in a new planning idea and a political opportunity to deploy it, whereas elsewhere the idea falls on barren ground, is actively resisted, is transformed into something quite different or is simply misunderstood. The spread of ideas occurs in varied ways depending on the context (see also Sorensen, 2010: 134). Crucial in this respect (see all the cases) is the (in)tolerance of the context for real shifts in power relations and the danger that weakly theorized models are adopted elsewhere in equally under-theorized or invisible power contexts (see also Marshall, 2000: 315).

The more radical strategic planning reacts to a type of planning that shifted to become normatively aligned with advancing neo-liberal forms of democracy, managing change and growth as a technical rather than political exercise (see also Oosterlynck and Swyngedouw, 2010). It argues for a move away from the trend to depoliticize planning by translating (potential) political issues into questions of technical knowledge, skills and expertise. Its purpose is to broaden the scope of possibilities as a clear reaction against post-politics. As a post-political project, strategic planning may turn out to be the leading edge of evolving transformative practices (see Johannesburg, this volume). As in Wales, Johannesburg and Portland, equality is seen as the premise of democracy that needs to be verified over and over again (see Rancière, 1992). A good example is the call in Portland (this volume) to use an equity lens when making infrastructure decisions. Therefore, strategic planning needs an arena – a space of deliberative opportunities in Forester's (2010) terms – an open dialogue in which a plurality of interests and demands, opinions, images, conflicts, different values and power relationships are addressed (see Balducci on trading zones, and Searle on the performative logics of control and power, both in this volume). In these arenas, actors may reflect on who they are and what they want, and, in this way, articulate their identities, their traditions, their values. The focus on context can be partly understood as a critique of uniformity and repetition of strategic planning models and procedures exerted by global processes in cities (see Rio de Janeiro, this volume) and regions, and partly as a way to acknowledge the irreducible nature of living space as a social product historically and culturally determined but also geared at broadening the scope of the possible and imagining the impossible.

The cases make it clear that strategic practices cannot simply be extracted from the context where they emerged, to be uprooted and 'planted' somewhere else (see also Healey, 2012: 190). The cases or ideas-in-practice presented in this volume must be looked upon as occasions for planners to challenge their own knowledge and values and critically engage with their activity as a praxis (Salet, this volume; see also Lieto, 2015: 125).

Some ideas discussed in this chapter take strategic planning beyond its usual boundaries and traditions (see also Servillo, this volume). Therefore, it is stressed that strategic planning needs an ongoing critical self-diagnosis in order to re-invent itself (see Salet, this volume). The ingredients presented in this chapter can be seen as a first step in this direction.

## References

Abbott, J. 2005. Understanding and managing the unknown: The nature of uncertainty in planning. *Journal of Planning Education and Research*, 24(3): 237–251.

Abrahams, G. 2013. What 'is' territorial cohesion? What does it 'do'? Essentialist versus pragmatic approaches to using concepts. *European Planning Studies*, (22)10: 2134–2155.

Albrechts, L. 1999. Planners as catalysts and initiators of change: The new Structure Plan for Flanders. *European Planning Studies*, 7: 587–603.

Albrechts, L. 2003. Public involvement: The challenges of difference. *DisP*, 155(4): 18–27.

Albrechts, L. 2004. Strategic (spatial) planning reexamined. *Environment and Planning B: Planning and Design*, 31: 743–758.

Albrechts L, 2006. Shifts in strategic spatial planning? Some evidence from Europe and Australia *Environment and Planning A*, 38: 1149–1170.

Albrechts, L. 2013. Reframing strategic spatial planning by using a coproduction perspective. *Planning Theory*, 12(1): 46–63.

Albrechts, L. 2015. Ingredients for a more radical strategic spatial planning. *Environment and Planning B: Planning and Design*, 42(3): 510–525.

Albrechts, L., Alden, J. and da Rosa Pires, A. (Eds) 2001. *The Changing Institutional Landscape of Planning*. Ashgate, Aldershot.

Albrechts, L., Healey, P. and Kunzmann, K. 2003. Strategic spatial planning and regional governance. *JAPA*, 69(2): 113–129.

Albrechts, L. and Van den Broeck, J. 2004. From discourse to facts: The case of the ROM-project in

Ghent, Belgium. *Town Planning Review*, 75: 127–150.

Albrechts, L. and Balducci, A. 2013. Practicing strategic planning: In search of critical features to explain the strategic character of plans. *DisP*, 194(49.3): 16–27.

Balducci, A. 2008. Constructing (spatial) strategies in complex environments. In Van den Broeck, J., Moulaert, F. and Oosterlynck, S. (Eds), *Empowering the Planning Fields: Ethics, Creativity and Action*. Acco, Leuven, pp. 79–99.

Balducci, A., Fedeli, V. and Pasqui, G. (Eds) 2011. *Strategic Planning for Contemporary Urban Regions*. Ashgate, Farnham.

Bryson, J. 1995. *Strategic Planning for Public and Nonprofit Organizations*. Jossey-Bass, San Francisco, CA.

Bryson, J. and Crosby, B. 1992. *Leadership for the Common Good: Tackling Public Problems in a Shared-Power World*. Jossey-Bass, San Francisco, CA.

Campbell, H. 2002. Thinking about discourses: Theory is practical? *Planning Theory and Practice*, 3(3): 351–352.

Cerreta, M., Concilio, G. and Monno, V. (Eds) 2010. *Making Strategies in Spatial Planning: Knowledge and Values*. Springer, Dordrecht.

Chia, R. 1995. From modern to postmodern organizational analysis. *Organization Studies*, 16(4): 579–604.

Chia, R. 1999. A 'rhizomic' model of organizational change and transformation: Perspective from a metaphysics of change. *British Journal of Management*, 10: 209–227.

Chia, R. 2011. Complex thinking: Towards an oblique strategy for dealing with the complex. Allen, P., Maguire, S. and McKelvey, B. (Eds), *Sage Handbook of Complexity and Management*. Sage, London, pp. 182–198.

Chia, R. and Tsoukas, H. 2003. Everything flows and nothing abides: Towards a 'rhizomic' model of organisational change, transformation and action. *Process Studies*, 32(2): 196–224.

Chia, R. and Holt, R. 2006. Strategy as practical coping: A Heideggerian perspective. *Organization Studies*, 27: 635–655.

Dyrberg, T. B. 1997. *The Circular Structure of Power*. Verso, London.

Elchardus, M., Hooghe, M. and Smits, W. 2000. De vormen van middenveld participatie. In Elchardus, M., Huyse, L. and Hooghe, M. (Eds), *Het maatschappelijk middenveld in Vlaanderen*. VUB Press, Brussels, pp. 15–46.

Faludi, A. 2001. The application of the ESDP: Evidence from the North West Metropolitan area. *European Planning Studies*, 9(5): 663–676.

Forester, J. 2010. Foreword. In Cerreta, M., Concilio, G. and Monno, V. (Eds), *Making Strategies in Spatial Planning*. Springer, Dordrecht, pp. v–vii.

Foucault, M. 1980. *The History of Sexuality*. Vintage, New York.

Friedmann, J. 1982. *The Good Society*. MIT Press, Cambridge, MA.

Friedmann, J. 2004. Strategic spatial planning and the longer range. *Planning Theory and Practice*, 5(1): 49–67.

Friedmann, J. 2011. *Insurgencies: Essays in Planning Theory*. Routledge, London and New York.

Friend, J. K. and Jessop, W. N. 1969. *Local Government and Strategic Choice*. Tavistock, London.

Godet, M. 2001. *Creating Futures*. Economica, London.

Gonzáles, S. 2011. Bilbao and Barcelona 'in motion': How urban regeneration 'models' travel and mutate in the global flows of policy tourism. *Urban Studies*, 48(7): 1397–1418.

Hajer, M. 1995. *The Politics of Environmental Discourse*. Oxford University Press, Oxford.

Healey, P. 1997. *Collaborative Planning; Shaping Places in Fragmented Societies*. Palgrave Macmillan, Basingstoke.

Healey, P. 2004. The treatment of space and place in the new strategic spatial planning in Europe. *International Journal of Urban and Regional Research*, 28: 45–67.

Healey, P. 2006. Relational complexity and the imaginative power of strategic spatial planning. *European Planning Studies*, 14(4): 525–546.

Healey, P. 2007. *Urban Complexity and Spatial Strategies: Towards a Relational Planning for Our Times*. Routledge, London.

Healey, P. 2009. In search of the 'strategic' in spatial strategy making. *Planning Theory and Practice*, 10(4): 439–457.

Healey, P. 2010. *Making Better Places: The Planning Project for the Twenty-first Century*. Palgrave Macmillan, Basingstoke.

Healey, P. 2012. The universal and the contingent: Some reflections on the transnational flow of planning ideas and practices. *Planning Theory*, 11(2): 188–207.

Healey, P., Khakee, A., Motte, A. and Needham, B. (Eds) 1997. *Making Strategic Spatial Plans: Innovation in Europe*. UCL Press, London.

Healey, P. and Upton, R. 2010 *Crossing Borders: International Exchange and Planning Practices*. Routledge, Abingdon, pp. 1–25.

Hillier, J. 1999. What values? Whose values? *Ethics, Place and Environment*, 2(2): 179–199.

Hillier, J. 2002. *Shadows of Power*. Routledge, London.

Hillier, J. 2011. Navigation across multiple planes: Towards a Deleuzean-inspired methodology for strategic spatial planning. *Town Planning Review*, 82(5): 503–527.

Holston, J. 1995. Spaces of insurgent citizenship. *Planning Theory*, 13: 35–51.

Huxley, M. and Yftachel, O. 2000. New paradigm or old myopia? Unsettling the communicative turn in planning theory. *Journal of Planning Education and Research*, 19: 331–342.

Inch, A. 2010. Culture change as identity regulation: The micro-politics of producing spatial planners in England. *Planning Theory and Practice*, 11(3), 359–374.

Kingdon, J. W. 2003. *Agendas, Alternatives and Public Policies*. Longman, New York.

Kotter, P. 1996. *Leading Change*. Harvard Business School Press, Boston, MA.

Kotter, P. 2008. *A Sense of Urgency*. Harvard Business School Press, Boston, MA.

Kotter, P. and Rathgeber, H. 2005. *Our Iceberg is Melting*. St Martin's Press, New York.

Leal de Oliveira, F. 2000. Strategic planning and urban competition. *Planners Network*, 143(September/October): 11–13.

Lieto, L. 2015. Cross-border mythologies: The problem with traveling planning ideas. *Planning Theory*, 14(2): 115–129.

Lyotard, J. F. 1992. *The Postmodern Explained*. University of Minnesota Press, Minneapolis, MN.

Mäntysalo, R. 2013. Coping with the paradox of strategic spatial planning. *DisP*, 194(49.3): 51–52.

Marshall, T. 2000. Urban planning and governance: Is there a Barcelona model? *International Planning Studies*, 5(3): 299–319.

Mazza, L. 2011. Personal Communication by email, 24 August.

Mazza, L. 2013. If strategic 'planning is everything maybe it's nothing'. *DisP*, 94(49.3): 40–42.

Metzger, J. 2012. Placing the stakes: The enactment of territorial stakeholders in planning processes. *Environment and Planning A*, 45: 781–796.

Metzger, J. 2014. The moose are protesting: The more-than human politics of transport infrastructure development. In Metzger, J., Allmendinger, P. and Oosterlynck, S. (Eds), *Planning against the Political*. Routledge, New York, pp. 191–213.

Monclús, F.-J. 2003. The Barcelona model: An original formula? From reconstruction to strategic urban projects (1979–2004). *Planning Perspectives*, 18: 399–421.

Needham, B. 2000. Making strategic spatial plans: A situational methodology! In Salet, W. and Faludi, A. (Eds), *Revival of Strategic Planning*. Royal Netherlands Academy of Arts and Sciences, Amsterdam, pp. 79–90.

Olesen, K. 2011. Strategic spatial planning in transition: Case study of Denmark. PhD thesis, Department of Development and Planning, Aalborg University.

Olesen, K. 2012. The neoliberalisation of strategic planning. Paper presented at the AESOP 26th Annual Congress, Ankara, 11–15 July.

Olesen, K. and Richardson, T. 2012. Strategic spatial planning in transition: Contested rationalities and spatial logics in 21st century Danish spatial planning. *European Planning Studies*, 20(10): 1689–1706.

Oosterlynck, S. and Swyngedouw, E. 2010. Noise reduction: The postpolitical quandary of night flights at Brussels airport. *Environment and Planning A*, 42: 1577–1594.

Ozbekhan, H. 1969. Towards a general theory of planning. In Jantsch, E. (Ed.), *Perspectives of Planning*, OECD, Paris.

Rancière, J. 1992. Politics, identification and subjectivization. *The Identity in Question*, 61: 58–64.

Roy, A. 2009. Civic governmentality: The politics of inclusion in Beirut and Mumbai. *Antipode*, 41(1): 159–179.

Sager, T. 2013. *Reviving Critical Planning Theory*. Routledge, New York and London.

Sartorio, F. 2005. Strategic spatial planning: A historical review of approaches, its recent revival, and an overview of the state of the art in Italy. *DisP*, 162: 26–40.

Sorensen, A. 2010. Urban sustainability and compact cities ideas in Japan: The diffusion, transformation and deployment of planning concepts. In Healey, P. and Upton, R. (Eds), *Crossing Borders: International Exchange and Planning Practices*. Routledge, Abingdon, pp. 117–140.

Swyngedouw, E., Moulaert, F. and Rodriguez, A. 2002. Neoliberal urbanization in Europe: Large-scale urban development projects and the new urban policy. *Antipode*, 34(3): 542–577.

UN-Habitat, 2009. *Global Report on Human Settlements 2009:Planning Sustainable Cities*. Earthscan, London.

Vainer, C. 2000. Light and shadow in the strategies of consultants on strategies. *Progressive Planning Magazine*, 18 September.

Vigar, G., Graham, S. and Healey, P. 2005. In search of the city is spatial strategies: Past legacies future imaginings. *Urban Studies*, 42(8): 1391–1410.

Watson, V. 2011. Planning and conflict – moving on. Paper, World Planning School Congress, Perth.

Wu, F. 2007. Reorientation of the city plan: Strategic planning and design competition in China. *Geoforum*, 38: 379–392.

Wynne, B. 1992. Uncertainty and environmental learning: Reconceiving science and policy in the preventive paradigm. *Global Environmental Change*, June: 111–127.

Yiftachel, O. 2006. Re-engaging planning theory? Towards 'south-eastern' perspectives. *Planning Theory*, 5(3): 211–222.

Young, I. 1990. *Justice and the Politics of Difference*. Princeton University Press, Princeton, NJ.

Zizek, S. 1992. *Looking Awry: An Introduction to Jacques Lacan through Popular Culture* (paperback edition). MIT Press, Cambridge, MA.

# Index

For Product Safety Concerns and Information please contact our EU
representative  GPSR@taylorandfrancis.com
Taylor & Francis Verlag GmbH, Kaufingerstraße 24, 80331 München, Germany

www.ingramcontent.com/pod-product-compliance
Ingram Content Group UK Ltd.
Pitfield, Milton Keynes, MK11 3LW, UK
UKHW021023180425
457613UK00020B/1034